PENGUIN B

THE TWO-STATE

Padraig O'Malley is the John Joseph Moakley Distinguished Professor of Peace and Reconciliation at the McCormick Graduate School of Policy and Global Studies, University of Massachusetts Boston. He has spent his career helping to resolve conflicts around the world and has written extensively on the subject, including the books *Shades of Difference: Mac Maharaj and the Struggle for South Africa* and *Biting at the Grave: The Irish Hunger Strikes and the Politics of Despair*, one of the *New York Times*'s ten best books of 1990. He also created the online resource *Heart of Hope: South Africa's Transition from Apartheid to Democracy.* O'Malley is the founder of the Forum for Cities in Transition, an international network of divided cities that work together to promote reconciliation, civic participation, and economic development.

> > < <

Praise for *The Two-State Delusion*

"Impressive . . . [O'Malley] has done a tremendous amount of research about the Israeli-Palestinian conflict. . . . The result is a book so packed with information that it will reward even the reader so dedicated that she consumes the Israel-Palestine stories buried on Page A17 of *The Times*. . . . O'Malley is not only knowledgeable; he's also honest."

—*The New York Times Book Review* (Editors' Choice)

"*The Two-State Delusion* provides an impartial, empathic, but relentlessly objective look at our reality . . . [and] a refreshing departure from the blame game in which Israelis and Palestinians and their respective international champions try to make the other side responsible for the peace process's failure. And it diverges from the tendency to find the trick that will do the job and comes to a conclusion as intellectually compelling as it is dismaying."

—*Haaretz* (Israel)

"On the basis of a meticulous research effort . . . O'Malley argues very persuasively that the two-state solution is dead. . . . This volume provides valuable and very timely explanations for the persistence of the Israeli-Palestinian conflict. One can only hope that Israeli, Palestinian, and American decision makers will absorb the major lessons taught so very convincingly by O'Malley."

—*Middle East Policy*

"An honest assessment of where the Israelis and Palestinians are right now."
—*The Cleveland Plain-Dealer*

"A thoughtful autopsy of the failed two-state paradigm . . . [O'Malley] carefully sifts through the intractable coexistence between the Palestinians and Israelis and finds both sides so traumatized by the 'narrative' of their respective struggle that they are unable to view the other with respect or humanity—the beginning of true reconciliation. . . . Evenhanded, diplomatic, mutually respectful, and enormously useful." —*Kirkus Reviews* (starred review)

"Exhaustively researched . . . There are no heroes in O'Malley's account, and no clear villains either." —*Publishers Weekly*

Praise for *Shades of Difference*

"A striking success." —*The New York Times Book Review*

"An original and important work . . . An entry for the reader into a wider understanding of the elements of the Struggle, the contradictions that had to be overcome to bring us freedom."
—Nadine Gordimer, winner of the Nobel Prize in Literature

"[O'Malley] is knowledgeable and sure-footed as he recounts this story . . . making a complex narrative on the whole quite clear." —*San Francisco Chronicle*

"Meticulous and unflinchingly honest." —*The New York Sun*

"Brilliantly written." —*Library Journal* (starred review)

"A groundbreaking biography of a central figure in the fight to end South African apartheid." —*Publishers Weekly*

"An extraordinarily well-researched work . . . O'Malley has a deep understanding . . . and is perhaps one of the few outsiders who could readily understand the South African struggle." —*The Independent* (South Africa)

Padraig O'Malley

The Two-State Delusion

Israel and Palestine—
A Tale of
Two Narratives

PENGUIN BOOKS

PENGUIN BOOKS
An imprint of Penguin Random House LLC
375 Hudson Street
New York, New York 10014
penguin.com

First published in the United States of America by Viking Penguin,
a member of Penguin Group (USA) LLC, 2015
Published in Penguin Books 2016

THE LIBRARY OF CONGRESS HAS CATALOGED THE
HARDCOVER EDITION AS FOLLOWS:
O'Malley, Padraig, author.
The two-state delusion : Israel and Palestine :
a tale of two narratives / Padraig O'Malley.
pages cm
Includes bibliographical references and index.
ISBN 9780670025053 (hc.)
ISBN 9780143129172 (pbk.)
1. Arab-Israeli conflict—Causes. 2. Arab-Israeli conflict—1993—Peace. 3. Arab-Israeli conflict—Political aspects. 4. Palestinian Arabs—Politics and government—21st century. 5. Israel—Politics and government—21st century. 6. Palestinian Arabs—Ethnic identity. 7. Jews—Identity. 8. Israel—History—21st century.
9. Palestinian Arabs—History—21st century. I. Title.
DS119.76.O45 2015
956.9405'4—dc23
2014038545

Printed in the United States of America

Set in Minion Pro
Map Illustrations by Daniel Lagin

For Ntombikayise Gladwin Gilman:
a Mandela child, who will turn the promises of his vision
into living realities

Any fool can make things bigger, more complex, and more violent. It takes a touch of genius—and a lot of courage—to move in the opposite direction.

—ALBERT EINSTEIN

Contents

Chronology

1516–1918 Ottoman rule over Palestine

1882–1902 First aliyah: 25,000–35,000 Jews immigrate to Palestine

1897 Theodor Herzl convenes First Zionist Congress in Basel, Switzerland; World Zionist Organization (WZO) is founded and announces goal of establishing a home for the Jewish people in Palestine

1901 Jewish National Fund is established

1904–14 Second aliyah: 40,000 Jews immigrate to Palestine, account for 12 percent of Palestine's population; HaShomer (the first Jewish "defense organization" in Palestine) is founded

1908 Palestine Office is founded in Jaffa

1914 World War I begins

1915–16 Husayn ibn Ali–McMahon correspondence between Britain and the ruler of Hijaz

1916 Sykes-Picot Agreement between Britain and France

1917 Balfour Declaration

1919–23 Third aliyah: 40,000 Jews immigrate to Palestine

1920 San Remo conference assigns mandate for Palestine to Great Britain

1920–21 Arab attacks on Jewish areas of Jerusalem and Jaffa; the Haganah is formed (and in 1948 is absorbed into the Israeli Defense Forces, IDF); Histadrut is founded

1922 British White Paper reaffirms Balfour Declaration and limits Jewish immigration to absorptive capacity of Palestine; British Mandate ratified by League of Nations includes Balfour Declaration

1923 Paulet-Newcombe Agreement, or Paulet-Newcombe Line, defines boundaries of Palestine

1924–29 Fourth aliyah: more than 80,000 Jews immigrate to Palestine

1925 Hebrew University of Jerusalem opens

1929–39 Fifth aliyah: more than a quarter of a million Jews immigrate to Palestine

1929 Palestine Office, renamed the Jewish Agency, is designated to represent the Jewish people provided for in the League of Nations Mandate for Palestine; riots at Western Wall, Jerusalem, Safed, and Hebron

1930 Shaw Commission investigates causes of riots and produces Hope Simpson Report to address immigration, land-settlement, and development issues; report recommends *limiting* Jewish immigration based on economic absorptive capacity of Palestine; Passfield White Paper halts Jewish immigration and land sales

1931 British prime minister Ramsay MacDonald letter negates the Passfield White Paper

1933–45 Holocaust

1936 Arab Higher Committee is formed

1936–39 Arab revolt: seven years after Hope Simpson Report, Jewish population has risen by more than 150 percent, an additional sixty-two settlements have been created, and Arab and Jewish clashes in Jaffa trigger uprising

1937 Peel Commission recommends partition

1939 British White Paper rejects Peel recommendations, proposes unitary state and majority rule; Jewish immigration is restricted; World War II begins

1942 Zionist conference is held in New York City; Biltmore Declaration calls for Jewish state throughout Palestine

1945 Arab League is formed in Cairo; Germany surrenders; World War II ends; United Nations is created

1946 Menachem Begin's Stern Gang bombs British headquarters at King David Hotel, Jerusalem, aiming to evict British authorities from Palestine; U.S. president Harry Truman announces support for partition of Palestine into Jewish and Arab states

1947 British cabinet decides to refer question of Palestine to UN General Assembly; UN establishes special committee on Palestine (UNSCOP); UNSCOP recommends partition of Palestine; UN General Assembly votes to partition Palestine into a Jewish state and a Palestinian state and to internationalize city of Jerusalem; Jewish Agency welcomes report; Palestinians reject it

1947 Israeli-Palestinian intercommunal war; *Nakba* catastrophe begins, creating Palestinian refugees

1948 British Mandate in Palestine ends; Chaim Weizmann meets with Truman; United States proposes UN trusteeship in Palestine; Jewish attack on Deir Yassin; Arab attack on bus convoy to Mt. Scopus; Haganah captures Haifa; Israel declares independence; United States extends de facto recognition; Arab armies invade; UN Resolution 194 calls for repatriation of 750,000 refugees who were expelled or fled from Palestine (the *Nakba*) and the internationalization of Jerusalem

1949 Israel signs armistice agreements with Jordan, Lebanon, Syria, and Egypt; conflict ends

1950 West Bank and East Jerusalem annexed by Transjordan; Israel becomes member state of UN

1956 Suez Crisis

1959 Fatah, Palestinian nationalist organization, is founded

1964 Palestine Liberation Organization (PLO) is founded in Cairo by Arab League Palestinian National Council (PNC); legislative body of PLO is formed

1965 Fatah undertakes first guerrilla attack on Israel

1967 Six-Day War: Israel defeats Egypt, Syria, and Jordan, annexes East Jerusalem, and occupies West Bank, Gaza, Sinai, and Golan Heights; Khartoum Conference reaffirms Arab efforts to eliminate effects of Israeli aggression on grounds that lands occupied are Arab lands and the task of regaining these lands is on Arab states; United Nations Security Council (UNSC) passes Resolution 242, calling for withdrawal of Israeli armed forces from territories occupied in Six-Day War and for states in region to recognize one another's sovereignty; Fatah joins PLO

1968 First PLO plane hijacking

1969 Fatah founder Yasser Arafat is recognized as head of PLO

1970 Throughout the '70s and '80s, the CIA conducts secret dialogue with the PLO

1972 Nine Israeli Olympic athletes are murdered by Black September, a Palestinian terrorist group; four members of group are also killed

1973 Egypt and Syria attack Israel in Yom Kippur War/Ramadan War; UNSC Resolution 338 calls for direct negotiations based on Resolution 242

1974 Arab League summit in Rabat recognizes PLO as sole legitimate representative of Palestinian people; Arafat addresses UN General Assembly; Gush Emunim, settlement movement in Occupied Palestinian Territories (OPT), is founded

1975 UN allows PLO to participate in debate on Israeli-Palestinian relations

1977 Menachem Begin and Likud coalition win Israeli general election

1978 Israel calls for new settlements in OPT; Camp David Accords: peace treaty between Egypt and Israel signed in Washington DC by Egyptian president Anwar el-Sadat and Israeli president Menachem Begin, who jointly receive Nobel Peace Prize

1985 Agreement between PLO and Jordan allows Jordan to represent Palestinians in negotiations

1987 First Intifada begins in OPT; Hamas (the Islamic Resistance Movement), an offshoot of the Muslim Brotherhood, is formed

1988 PLO Declaration of Independence, adopted in Tangiers, recognizes existence of Israel in 78 percent of Palestine it occupies; King Hussein renounces Jordan's claim to the West Bank; Arafat addresses UN in Geneva, says PLO accepts Resolutions 242 and 338

1991 First Intifada ends; U.S. president George H. W. Bush convenes peace conference in Madrid: multilateral and bilateral talks involving Israel, Egypt, Lebanon, and a joint Jordan/Palestinian delegation; Washington talks begin (and will total twelve rounds between December 1991 and September 1993); Hamas denounces peace initiative and announces armed wing: *Izz ad-Din al-Qassam* Brigades

1992 Yitzhak Rabin elected prime minister of Israel

1993 Secret Oslo talks occur January–August between Israel and PLO; Oslo I Accord: Arafat and Rabin sign letters of mutual recognition (Israel recognizes the PLO as the sole representative of the Palestinian People) and the Declaration of Principles (DOP) on Palestinian interim self-government; Hamas rejects Oslo Accords

1994 Jordan and Israel sign peace agreement; Jewish settler massacres twenty-nine Palestinians praying at Ibrahim Mosque in Hebron; first Hamas suicide bombing kills eight Israelis; Gaza-Jericho agreement signed in Cairo: Israel cedes Jericho and Gaza to PLO; Arafat arrives in Gaza; Nobel Peace Prize awarded to Arafat, Shimon Peres, and Yitzhak Rabin

1995 Oslo II Accord, agreement on Palestinian interim self-rule, reached at Taba, establishes Palestinian Authority (PA) and divides West Bank into three zones, provides for a final settlement agreement (FSA) within five years and schedule of Israeli troop redeployments; Israel withdraws from Jenin; Rabin is assassinated by a Jewish extremist

1996 Elections are held for president of the Palestinian Authority and for the Palestinian Legislative Council (PLC); Arafat is elected president; Hamas boycotts elections; Benjamin Netanyahu is elected prime minister of Israel

1997 Hebron Agreement: Israel agrees to redeploy troops; United States adds Hamas to list of terrorist organizations after suicide bombings in Jerusalem

1998 Wye River Memorandum signed in Washington DC after negotiations over further Israeli redeployments and territorial transfers; UN upgrades status of PLO delegation to represent Palestinian Authority; PNC, in a letter to U.S. president Bill Clinton, renounces clauses in PLO charter offensive to Israel

1999 Ehud Barak elected prime minister of Israel; Sharm el-Sheikh Memorandum signed between Israel and PLO, setting February 2000 as target date for declaration of principles on outstanding issues and September 2000 as date to reach an FSA; final status talks begin in September; twenty-one rounds of talks are held; redeployment talks begin in December for Israel to withdraw from 6.1 percent of West Bank

2000 Secret talks are held in Stockholm to prepare way for Camp David summit; Camp David summit is convened in July 2000 by President Clinton for purpose of PLO and Israel finalizing and agreeing to an FSA and "end of claims agreement"; both Barak and Arafat attend; talks fail; talks resume in August; in September Ariel Sharon visits Temple Mount/Haram al-Sharif; Second Intifada begins in October; meeting held in October in Paris among U.S. secretary of state Madeleine Albright, Arafat, and Barak, to curb violence, stalls; Sharm el-Sheikh "summit" of Clinton, Kofi Annan, Barak, Arafat, Javier, and Albright is held in late October to restart stalled talks and halt violence; Barak resigns; new elections are set for February 2001; in December Clinton Parameters are unveiled

2001 George W. Bush is sworn in as U.S. president; a number of delegates from Camp David convene an unofficial conference in Taba in January; Ariel Sharon is elected prime minister of Israel; EU adds Hamas to list of terrorist organizations

2002 Arab Peace Initiative (Saudi peace plan) is proposed; Bush calls for a Palestinian state; Israel begins construction of security wall/separation barrier; Middle East Quartet is formed, comprising UN, U.S., EU, and Russia and headed by former British prime minister Tony Blair

2003 Quartet's Road Map for Peace is proposed; Geneva Accord announced as a result of a series of unofficial talks between senior-level Palestinian and Israeli negotiators

2004 Yasser Arafat dies

2005 Sharon unilaterally disengages from Gaza; Mahmoud Abbas is elected to succeed Arafat as president of Palestinian Authority; Abbas and Sharon meet in Sharm el-Sheikh to declare a mutual ceasefire; Second Intifada ends

2006 Hamas wins overall majority in first PLC elections since 1996, attempts to form unity government with Fatah; Israeli corporal Gilad Shalit kidnapped and held in Gaza

2007 In Mecca, Hamas and Fatah agree to a power-sharing government; new government is sworn in, but unity does not last; Hamas seizes control of Gaza after five days fighting Fatah; Fatah personnel and security flee Gaza; Israelis blockade Gaza; U.S.-sponsored peace talks between Israel and Palestinians begin in Annapolis; Israeli prime minister Ehud Olmert and PLO president Abbas play prominent roles

2008 Annapolis talks end inconclusively in November with no FSA reached; in December 2008 and January 2009 Israel invades Gaza (Operation Cast Lead)

2009 Barack Obama is inaugurated president of the United States and appoints Senator George Mitchell as Special Envoy for Middle East Peace; Netanyahu is elected prime minister of Israel; Obama's Cairo speech calls for a halt to settlements as a precursor to resumption of talks; PLO quickly follows suit; Netanyahu agrees to a ten-month settlement freeze; peace talks fail to get off the ground

2010 Moratorium on settlement construction expires and attempts to resuscitate it fail; construction of new settlements in West Bank and East Jerusalem resumes

2011 Arab Spring erupts; reconciliation talks between Fatah and Hamas in Cairo lead to Doha Agreement; Doha falls apart, as did other reconciliation attempts that preceded it; Gilad Shalit is released; PLO's bid for state membership at the UN fails; Obama calls for a Palestinian state based on the 1967 borders; Obama's proposal is rejected by Netanyahu

2012 UN votes overwhelmingly to award Palestine non-member-state observer status; Palestinians become member of UNESCO; Muslim Brotherhood's Mohamed Morsi is elected president of Egypt in country's first free and fair democratic elections; rocket fire and air strikes are exchanged by Gaza and Israel in November War (Operation Pillar of Defense); Israel does not invade; cease-fire is brokered by Morsi and United States

2013 Obama is inaugurated for second term and appoints John Kerry secretary of state; Netanyahu is reelected; in August John Kerry announces talks between Israel and PLO to reach a framework agreement; talks will last nine months; Netanyahu agrees to release 104 Palestinian prisoners in return for Abbas putting PLO's applications to international agencies on hold; final batch of prisoners is to be released in April 2014; Morsi is ousted from power in Egypt; Egyptian military headed by General Abdel Fattah el-Sisi, seals some 1,400 tunnels between Gaza and Egypt; Egyptian military declares Hamas a terrorist organization

2014 Settlement construction in West Bank reaches unprecedented levels; FSA talks collapse; Reconciliation Pact between Hamas and Fatah is signed in April; Abbas signs on to fifteen international treaties; Abbas swears in Palestinian Authority's technocratic "unity" government on June 2, 2014; the kidnapping and murder of three Israeli teens in June, the killing of a Palestinian youth in Jerusalem that followed, and economic distress in Gaza lead to new Gaza war; Israel invades Gaza in Operation Protective Edge on July 8

August 26, 2014 After 51 days a cease-fire is agreed

December 30, 2014 Jordan, on behalf of the Palestinian Authority, submits to the UNSC a draft resolution on Palestinian statehood calling for a peace deal with Israel within a year on the basis of pre 1967 borders and an Israeli withdrawal from Palestinian land within three years

December 31, 2014 The UNSC rejects the Jordanian resolution. Abbas signs the Treaty of Rome, the founding treaty of the International Criminal Court (ICC), and seeks membership of the court

January 1, 2015 The ICC says the PA has formally submitted papers accepting the court's jurisdiction to investigate alleged war crimes committed during the Gaza war

January 4, 2015 Israel withholds $127 million in tax revenues from the PA

January 6, 2015 UN Secretary General Ban Ki-moon says the PA will become a member of the ICC on April 1, 2015

Key Abbreviations

AIPAC American Israel Public Affairs Committee
API Arab Peace Initiative
CA Civil Administration
CBM confidence-building measures
DOP Declaration of Principles
EOC ethos of conflict
FSA final settlement agreement
ICC International Criminal Court
ICG International Crisis Group
IDF Israeli Defense Forces
IRA Irish Republican Army
ISIS Islamic State of Iraq and Syria
NGO nongovernmental organization
OCHA Office for the Coordination of Humanitarian Affairs (UN)
PA Palestinian Authority
PASF Palestinian Authority Security Forces
PLC Palestinian Legislative Council
PLO Palestine Liberation Organization
PNC Palestinian National Council
UNISPAL United Nations Information System on the Question of Palestine
UNRWA United Nations Relief and Works Agency for Palestine Refugees in the Near East
WBG West Bank and Gaza
WZO World Zionist Organization

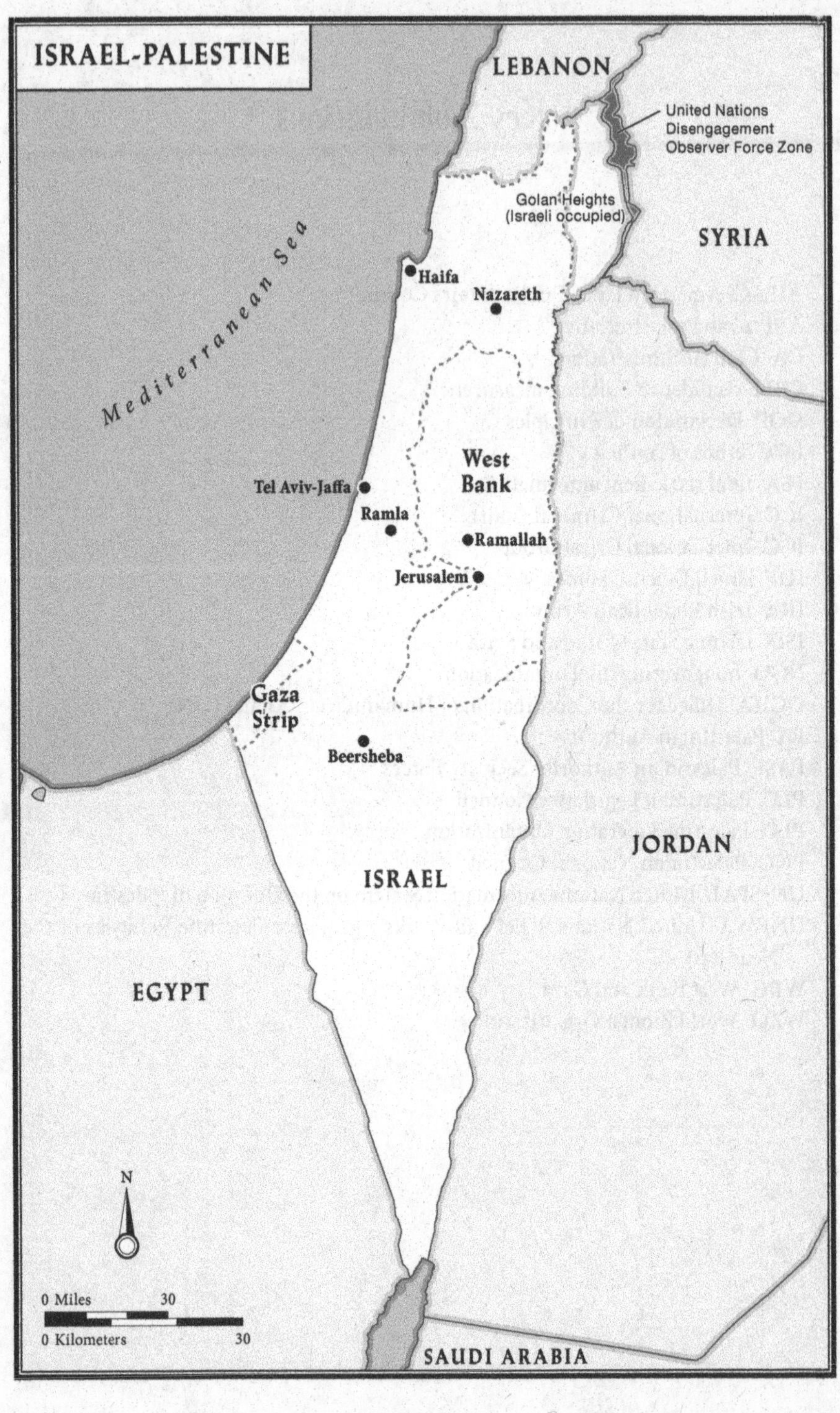

ISRAEL-PALESTINE
LEBANON
United Nations
Disengagement
Observer Force Zone
Golan Heights
(Israeli occupied)
SYRIA
Mediterranean Sea
Haifa
Nazareth
West
Bank
Tel Aviv-Jaffa
Ramla
Ramallah
Jerusalem
Gaza
Strip
Beersheba
JORDAN
ISRAEL
EGYPT
N
0 Miles 30
0 Kilometers 30
SAUDI ARABIA

Introduction

Within forty-eight hours of taking the oath of office in January 2009, President Barack Obama appointed Senator George Mitchell as his Special Envoy for Middle East Peace. Obama's Joint Chiefs were already telling him the anti-Americanism among Muslims that U.S. soldiers encountered in Afghanistan, in Iraq, and elsewhere in the region posed a danger to their mission and lives. While much of this sentiment could be attributed to post-9/11 sensitivities, Muslims' perception of America's lack of evenhandedness during the long Israeli-Palestinian conflict and their perception that the United States always sides with Israel no matter the circumstances served as ongoing sources of resentment. Settling the conflict in the Middle East could no longer be left to the protagonists. Now American national-security interests superseded their parochial concerns. For decades the two peoples, Israelis and Palestinians, had fought one calamitous engagement after another, dithered from one fruitless negotiation to another, always managing to end up further from peace than ever. A resolution of this conflict was required.

Obama agreed with the Joint Chiefs' assessment. Finding a settlement to the Israeli-Palestinian conflict became one of the new administration's foreign-policy priorities. Getting Israelis and Palestinians to the negotiation table, with the United States "running interference" and prepared to play "tough love" if necessary, could lead the two sides to agree to some kind of two-state solution—perhaps one that neither side was entirely satisfied with but one that met their needs, if not necessarily sufficiently meeting their interests. Perhaps the new borders for the two states would be even more complicated than gerrymandered congressional districts and the map-making creatively accommodating. But no matter: A two-state resolution was the only feasible option. All of the "experts" agreed—and on this alluring subject there are hundreds, if not thousands, of experts.

"It's not rocket science," said Robert Malley, then director of the Middle East program at the International Crisis Group (ICG), now a senior director of Obama's National Security Council. "And a lot of people who have looked at this have reached the conclusion that the parties won't reach there on their own. If the U.S. wants it done, it will have to do it."[1]

Wanting it done, yes; putting its own proposals on the table, a very different matter.

Special Envoy Mitchell hit the road, shuttling throughout the Middle East, with numerous stops in Tel Aviv and Jerusalem to visit Israel's newly elected prime minister, Benjamin Netanyahu; in Ramallah to visit Mahmoud Abbas, president of the Palestinian Authority (PA) and president, too, of the Palestine Liberation Organization (PLO); and in the capitals of Arab countries in the region.

"The most relevant question to the two sides," Mitchell told me in 2012, "is how they cannot see that their interests would best be served by getting into a serious negotiation in which they could reach an agreement that would then allow them to achieve what they say they want to achieve. That the longer it goes without that kind of negotiation and without that kind of agreement, the less likely they are going to be able to achieve it."[2]

> > < <

Act I opened in Cairo.

On June 4, 2009, at Cairo University, President Obama delivered a speech that reverberated throughout the Muslim world.[3] He promised "a new beginning" to undo the damage to the relationship between the United States and its Muslim counterparts, which had deteriorated badly following 9/11. Addressing the Palestinian-Israeli conflict, he reiterated that the United States did not accept the legitimacy of continued Israeli settlements and cautioned that further construction should stop.

Days later, during a speech at Bar-Ilan University, Netanyahu reluctantly embraced a two-state solution for the first time, albeit postulating a Palestinian state in terms that fell well short of what hitherto had been discussed in negotiations.[4] Netanyahu's coalition was one of the most right-wing governments in Israel's sixty-year history, and his policies on the Palestinian issue were dictated by the need to hold his coalition together. Any proposal that would further arouse the ire of parties in the Likud, the party he headed, or any to the right of it, of which there were several in his governing coalition, would almost certainly be rejected out of hand if it threatened their time-worn shibboleths.

The Israelis were deeply insulted that Obama did not follow up his Cairo speech with a trip to Israel and furious that he would admonish Israel on settlements before an Arab audience. Israel interprets anything less than overt displays of unwavering support on the part of every American administration as signaling some kind of policy shift, now signified, it believed, by Obama's calls for halting settlements. Meanwhile, the PLO seized upon Obama's repeated insistence on a halt to settlement construction and made it a condition for resuming talks. After much cajoling—and some pressure from his allies in Europe—Netanyahu offered a ten-month freeze, which would not include construction already in the works or in East Jerusalem. He made the formal announcement in Tel Aviv on November 25, 2009.[5] Weeks earlier, during a visit to Israel, U.S. secretary of state Hillary Clinton had praised Israel for making "unprecedented" concessions on West Bank settlement construction and urged both sides to renew stalled peace talks.[6] The Palestinians insisted that the freeze had to include East Jerusalem.[7] Haggling over the issue ate into the ten-month moratorium.

In May 2011, Netanyahu visited the White House, following a March 2010 visit that had gone badly.[8] By all accounts the May meeting wasn't much better,[9] further acerbating the already strained relations between the two men going back to Obama's Cairo speech. In the joint press debriefing that followed, Obama was unequivocal: Settlements had to stop. In response, Netanyahu ignored the issue and focused on their discussion of the threat Iran's continued enrichment of uranium posed.

In September, the freeze lapsed with the Israelis and Palestinians still hunkered down in their bunkers. The Palestinians were adamant: no freeze on settlements, no talks. The Israelis met obstinacy with obstinacy: no preconditions, no talks.

The curtains closed on act 1.

> > < <

Meanwhile, events across North Africa, hitherto unimaginable but with far-ranging and unforeseeable repercussions, moved to the fore. Spontaneous mass demonstrations of "people power," beginning in Tunisia in December 2010, toppled long-entrenched dictators.[10] Demonstrations in Cairo's Tahrir Square, where hundreds of thousands of Egyptians from all walks of life demanded the ouster of Hosni Mubarak, who had ruled Egypt with an iron fist for thirty years, were a riveting spectacle and ushered in the Arab Spring. The Middle East was being remade.

When Syria's president, Bashar al-Assad, ordered his troops to kill unarmed Sunni Muslim demonstrators in March 2011, what had begun as a peaceful protest escalated into a revolt by Sunni Muslims against the ruling minority Alawites, a Shia offshoot.[11] The scale and brutality of Assad's attempts to quell the revolt led to massive opposition to his regime; the revolt drew increasingly large numbers of the population to its side. Assad's response: "Kill my citizens." Although the ranks of rebel groups swelled, they lacked the weapons to withstand Assad's savagery. Their appeals for arms from the West were met with silence, with the usual excuses of weapons falling into the "wrong" hands, but jihadists from across the Muslim world heard the call and made their way to Syria to wage jihad and help the rebels.[12] When Assad's regime appeared on the verge of collapse, Hezbollah, the Shia "resistance" movement from southern Lebanon, sent its elite units to fight on his behalf; they stopped the hemorrhaging and Iran, of course, remained the regime's staunchest ally, ensuring Assad had the weapons he needed and on occasion sending units of its elite Revolutionary Guard to give additional weight to his counteroffensive. The Israeli air force struck Syrian convoys whenever it believed they were being used to transport sophisticated missiles to Hezbollah in southern Lebanon. Hundreds of thousands of refugees poured into Kurdistan in Northern Iraq, Lebanon, Jordan, and Turkey.

The war, in its fourth year in 2015, still threatens to drag neighboring countries into the conflict or lead to internal instability, always regime threatening—Jordan stretched to cope with more than 627,000 refugees; 1.2 million refugees fled to Lebanon (which means that one of every four of Lebanon's population is a refugee, unbalancing the country's tenuous confessional equilibrium); close to 1.7 million fled to Turkey; and roughly a quarter of a million into Kurdistan. None of the countries is being given the financial humanitarian aid required to accommodate such huge deluges. The war in Syria has already and will continue to reconfigure the geopolitics of the Middle East, a proxy war between the Sunni Saudis and Shia Iran for regional hegemony, with Egypt's president, Abdel Fattah el-Sisi, itching to reassert Egypt's once-preeminent status in the region, and Turkey maneuvering to establish its own political space. Meanwhile, the self-proclaimed Islamic State of Iraq and Syria (ISIS), which now calls itself simply the Islamic State, cut an arc across much of Anbar Province in Iraq and northern Syria, intent on establishing a Caliphate in the region, sweeping all in its path with a brutality that defied understanding.[13]

For Palestinians, the Arab Spring provided a dollop of much-needed hope: They had no doubt that once democratically elected Islamists had secured their governments they would take up the Palestinian cause. They are still waiting as the Arab Spring countries flounder, submerged in chaotic transitions.[14] Israel reacted warily to the unfolding drama but with disbelief that Obama could call for the deposing of Mubarak, a U.S. ally but an ally, too, for Israel because he ensured the Camp David Accords (1978) were rigidly adhered to. Obama, Israel concluded, was very definitely not a reliable friend, although he provided it with more military aid than any of his predecessors.*

Speaking at the State Department, Obama briefly revisited the Palestinian-Israeli conflict in May 2011 when he called for a two-state settlement along the lines of the 1967 borders.[15] His speech elicited little response from jaded publics in both communities who had become immune to repetition. Besides, it was overshadowed by the regional turmoil. That same month, Senator Mitchell, who had persevered in his increasingly futile mission of employing his impeccable diplomatic skills to push and prod for the leverage that might break the deadlock, called it a day after twenty-eight months.†

> > < <

Act 2.

Once Obama was reelected to a second term, he instructed John Kerry, his new secretary of state, to take up the cudgels. After six trips to Israel and the West Bank between March and July 2013[16] and with an indefatigable resourcefulness that earned him the admiration of Israelis and Palestinians alike, he coaxed the two sides to agree to talks for nine months. Talks resumed on July 28 in Washington DC. The naysayers had a field day. The news was met with skepticism and scoffing between intermittent yawns. The best of the pundits and the cream of Middle East experts were left flat-footed

*"President Obama fought for and obtained an additional $650 million over the last four years to support the Arrow, David's Sling, and Iron Dome defense systems. On February 13, 2012, he released his fiscal year 2013 budget, which provided the largest aid package to Israel in U.S. history: $3.1 billion, a $25 million increase from 2012, which fulfills the commitment made in the ten-year Memorandum of Understanding." See "President Obama and Israel—September 2012," Joint Action Committee for Political Affairs, https://www.jacpac.org/index.php/component/content/article?id=224:president-obama-and-israel-february-2012, and Jeremy M. Sharp, *U.S. Foreign Aid to Israel*, Congressional Research Service Report RL33222, April 11, 2014 (Washington DC: Library of Congress, Congressional Research Service), http://www.fas.org/sgp/crs/mideast/RL33222.pdf.

†In his article "Israel & the US: The Delusions of Our Diplomacy," *New York Review of Books*, October 9, 2014, Nathan Thrall asserts that Mitchell resigned because he lost the struggle with Dennis Ross over control of Middle East policy, which came to a head "when Obama sided with Ross and refused to call for the division of Jerusalem in an important policy speech in May 2011."

and flabbergasted that Kerry had actually gotten the two sides to the table. So much for punditry and its predilections. Few of the "experts" expected much to come of the talks; most expected them to collapse at some point; none saw them as paving the way to a two-state solution. And on this score they were right.

In an extensive interview with David Remnick in the *New Yorker* in January 2014 on whether an agreement could be reached between Israel and Palestine, Obama, toughened by the vicissitudes of five years in office that had quenched much of his idealism and tempered his pragmatism, expressed what would be difficult to interpret as other than an assessment loosely laced with pessimism. Obama told Remnick that each of his three major foreign policy issues—the Israeli-Palestinian conflict, the Iranian nuclear issue, and the civil war in Syria—had a "less than fifty-fifty" chance of success. "[I]n all three circumstances," he said, "we may be able to push the boulder partway up the hill and maybe stabilize it so it doesn't roll back on us. . . . the region is going through rapid change and inexorable change. Some of it is demographics; some of it is technology; some of it is economics. And the old order, the old equilibrium, is no longer tenable. The question then becomes, What's next?"As it turned out, Ukraine was, and then ISIS.[17]

> > < <

In an op-ed in the *New York Times* on September 14, 2013, the scholar Ian Lustick, professor of political science at the University of Pennsylvania and a longtime advocate of two states, drew attention to the fact that for more than thirty years all sides had been "wedded to the notion that there must be two states, one Palestinian and one Israeli," while also for three decades "experts and politicians have warned of 'a point of no return.'" John Kerry, he said, was merely "the latest in a long line of well-meaning American diplomats wedded to an idea whose time is now past."

What irked him most, perhaps, was that the "true believers" in a two-state solution couldn't see beyond the position they so dearly clung to. They had no alternatives to propose, were not open to rethinking their basic assumptions, and as a result were "forced to defend a notion whose success they can no longer sincerely portray as plausible or even possible."[18]

Critics descended on Lustick like locusts. His peers severely rebuked him, questioning his logic and bemoaning his loss of "faith."

But what if Lustick is right? What if a two-state solution is now more remote than ever? And what if repeated attempts to negotiate one are actually damaging, rather than enhancing, the peace process?

The obstacles to implementing a sustainable and enduring two-state-solution agreement have exponentially multiplied over the past twenty-five years. The idea that a settlement will emerge from the labyrinth of intricacies, conceits, disparagements, unfathomable misunderstandings, endemic fears, and competing claims layered with hate is becoming ever more remote. Negotiating a two-state solution requires a degree of trust on both sides that even the miraculous cannot conjure. And even if an agreement between them were reached, it would not necessarily be sufficient to secure a lasting peace. What's more, the tectonic plates of history are always shifting and over time different sets of dynamics—demographics, the detritus of the Arab Spring, the civil war in Syria, the developing global war on ISIS and other transformative changes in the region—will change the contours of the conflict. The protagonists themselves may have less of a say in what the eventual outcome will be than they themselves believe.

A resolution to the Israeli-Palestinian conflict calls for a lot more than rocket science, as the current administration has now seen.

By every yardstick the conflict qualifies as intractable. Violence perpetuates violence and further entrenches each side in its "narrative," the prism through which each views the other and themselves. A half century's repression in the West Bank, settlements, settler violence ignored by the IDF, "armed resistance," political parties and other movements avowedly dedicated to "liberating" all of Palestine, the Second Intifada, and the political reconfigurations following the 2014 showdown between Hamas and the IDF in Gaza have compounded distrust at accelerating rates over the years. Not only has distrust hardened and deepened, but it has increasingly become a source of hatred and paranoia. Posttraumatic stress disorder (PTSD) is rife in both societies and with it the socio-psychological convulsions it generates. Both sides see the conflict as existential, zero-sum, and therefore seemingly irresolvable. It is psychologically embedded in their DNA. Both Palestinians and Israelis "double down" on their respective historical narratives of the roots of the conflict, take refuge in their collective memories, disparage the other party's narrative, and luxuriate in the righteousness of their respective cause, creating what experts in conflict resolution label an "ethos of conflict"—an ethos that entraps both sides.[19] The conflict becomes a compelling, in some ways psychologically fulfilling, way of life. The moral clarity of blaming the other entirely is intoxicating. They have become addicted to it.

This existential dynamic makes reaching an agreement on any number of more concrete political issues and "facts on the ground" even more insurmountable and becoming more so every day. The Israeli settlements in the occupied West Bank and East Jerusalem continue to proliferate at an accelerating rate, complicating any eventual resolution. The hundreds of thousands of disenfranchised Palestinian refugees and their descendants living in the abysmal camps in neighboring Jordan, a dismembered Syria, and Lebanon continue to grow in number, as do the refugees still living in camps in the West Bank and the Gaza Strip. As these populations swell, so does the difficulty (and, ultimately, expense) of addressing their eventual status in any agreement.

What's more, the internal politics of both Israelis and Palestinians are virtually defined by the overarching conflict, and nothing in these politics drives the leaders to a resolution. Just the opposite: The most powerful political tides, often driven by extremists, undermine any spirit of compromise and reconciliation. There are groups on both sides that would move tomorrow, and in all sincerity, to resolve the conflict—the basic elements for such a rational agreement are well established—but these doves are a small minority.

Given the facts on the ground and, just as important, the "facts in the mind," giving a final settlement agreement (FSA) a "less than fifty-fifty" chance is more wishful than realistic. Skepticism, like Lustick's, regarding any initiative that seeks an enduring two-state solution is more than justified. After two and a half decades of failure and more than five decades of bitter animosity, which both sides continue to stoke, it is time to recognize the impossibility of reaching a two-state solution as it has been articulated and start engaging in a new process no longer hamstrung by false assumptions.

> > < <

I began work on this book in 2010, with the aim of uncovering why the seventeen attempts[20] to reach a fair and just peace had failed and understanding how these lessons might be applied to ensure a more positive outcome for further rounds of negotiations. I wanted to know whether prospects for the two-state solution were any better now than they had been two and a half decades earlier.

Since 1972, I have been involved in the conflict and post-conflict situation in Northern Ireland. I have written about it extensively, including three books; brought the warring protagonists together on a number of occasions; and conducted hundreds of interviews in Catholic and Protestant communities throughout the 1970s, 1980s, and 1990s. Since the Good Friday/Belfast

Agreement in 1998, which finally brought the conflict to an end, I have continued my involvement in a reconciliation process that will be ongoing for decades while healing slowly evolves into a full recovery. In 1989 I began my research in South Africa, documenting the transition from apartheid to freedom. I ended up spending the better part of twenty years there, interviewing all the prime players on an annual basis. Many of these interviews took place while negotiations were still being conducted.[21] I eventually wrote a book about South Africa, which President Mandela graced with a fifteen-thousand-word introduction.

Feeling I had a solid grasp on the dynamics of these two conflicts and how they had been resolved, I decided to turn my attention to the third of the world's most intractable conflicts: Israel and Palestine.

> > < <

How could a people, I asked myself, themselves the victims of the most heinous human atrocity in recorded history, subject another people to life under occupation? How could two peoples living cheek to jowl not find a way to resolve their differences after close to fifty years of conflict?

Between 2010 and 2012, tape recorder in hand, I interviewed numerous Israeli Jews and West Bank Palestinians, most of whom had been involved in some senior capacity in every peace initiative since Madrid 1991. I also spoke with individuals who held senior positions in Hamas, a number of prominent Palestinian Israelis, civic society leaders, academics, an assortment of other leaders in both societies, and solicited the opinions of "the street" whenever the opportunity arose. The sum of these conversations forms the core of this book. Most of the interviewees are quoted in the text, many more than once; in some cases their responses are aggregated. All of them have been the bedrock of my understanding of the conflict, past, present, and future.

Not one of my interviewees in Israel, the West Bank, or Gaza disagreed with Lustick's conclusion. Most acknowledged that the "tipping point" for finding a two-state solution had been or was on the verge of being passed. They might not have described it as a "delusion," but they were no longer optimistic that such a resolution could be reached. Neither is a single political leader in the conflict. Neither are their constituents. Poll after poll confirms as much. Nevertheless, both sides cling tenaciously to the belief that somehow, someday, the necessary leadership will emerge, throw off the yoke of the political mire their societies are sunk in, and rescue them. Given the increasing mistrust between both parties, the increasing complexity of the facts on the ground, and the political instinct for self-preservation, this seems extremely unlikely.

In the end, many years down the long and winding road, many of the issues so contentiously and bitterly disputed today will simply become irrelevant as ineluctable political, economic, social, and natural forces over which the warring parties have little or no control shatter cherished dreams and long-held myths; erode the power of national narratives; redraw geopolitical maps to take account of the inexorable; compel human beings to reconfigure the ways in which they make choices; and realign the relationship between Israel and its allies and the Palestinians and their allies. In short, the facts on the ground will make the two-state solution not just delusional but simply irrelevant, and the only *lasting* solution to this conflict will slowly but surely begin to reveal itself once the two sides, in concert, agree that they must first *heal* themselves.

Chapter 1

Early History: The Two Narratives

Narratives are stories. Historical narratives tell us about our past, from whence we emerged centuries ago, our trials and travails as we weathered all kinds of natural disasters, wars with other people, territories conquered and relinquished, whether we were part of empires at one time or another, how we emerged in our own right, how we came to be where we live, how our culture developed, and how our values formed. Our histories include enemies who attacked us and were repulsed, wars won and lost, the many different forms of government we lived under, whether we were colonized by another people, and how we fought colonization and found independence and self-determination. The evolution of our arts and literature, heroes we revere and our sense of moral being, how we became distinct and, ultimately, as we progressed through the vicissitudes of history, how we became a country or whether we are still aspiring to become one.

Narratives are subjective and selective. They frame and filter concepts, images, and information according to desirable beliefs, values, symbols, traditions, and preferences. They are motivational tools that reinforce existing social identities and uniqueness. They arouse deep passions and allegiance.

For the most part historical narratives can be verified, although facts are sometimes intertwined with mythologies, which, repeated often enough, become in themselves "facts." Historical narratives tell us who we are. Compressed, they provide the building blocks for our distinctive identities. They place us in time, endow us with meaning. We thwart attempts to disrupt our narratives or have them questioned. In the modern era, historical narratives were the linchpins for emerging nationalism and the world's various and multitudinous nationalities. Narratives can evoke a strong and complex array of emotions. They bind us to their rhythms.

The Two-State Delusion is the tale of two historical narratives that clashed due to a unique set of circumstances and the consequences that followed; and of the efforts to somehow reconcile two irreconcilables, which unfortunately have made the conflict more intractable, adding to the tragedy.

> > < <

The Israelis and the Palestinians: two peoples with two histories that traverse and transcend millennia. These histories intersected in the late 1880s and clashed because both claimed the same land—Palestine—as theirs by immutable right: the Palestinians by virtue of historical presence, the Jews by divine ordinance, which they asserted took precedence, and because Great Britain, one of the great powers before World War I, lent support to their claim. The two claims were irreconcilable and ultimately led to conflict between the two claimants, a conflict that has persisted in one form or another for the better part of a century and has no immediate end in sight.

The Jewish Israeli narrative begins with the expulsion of the Jews from their "homeland" (a concept that didn't exist at the time) in Judea circa 70 CE.* After that, they spread across the earth—often involuntarily, throughout much of what is now Europe, Russia, and North Africa. Outcasts, despised as Christ killers, discriminated against, ghettoized, persecuted, and subjected to frequent pogroms, they nevertheless clung to the belief—for two millennia—that one day they would return to the land from which they had been expelled.

By the 1870s, Jewish emancipation in most Western countries allowed Jews to enjoy the same rights, for the most part, as their fellow citizens. In Eastern Europe, especially Russia, where anti-Semitism was pervasive, the situation was very different. Under the rule of Alexander III (1881–94) hatred for the Jews reached its zenith. According to Conor Cruise O'Brien, author of *The Seige: The Saga of Israel and Zionism*, "By the end of 1881, pograms had hit 215 communities in southern and southwestern Russia, where most Jews lived." The scale and frequency of pogroms increased; from 1882 onward the implementation of anti-Semitic measures was official policy;[1] the worsening conditions and the rise of Zionism,† which evolved among Russian Jews from

*Many authorities refer to the era 66–73 CE. According to the Israel Science and Technology Homepage, 70 CE marks the date when the Jewish people were exiled by the Romans following the destruction of the Second Temple. See Israel Science and Technology Homepage, "Brief History of Israel and the Jewish People," http://www.science.co.il/Israel-history.php.

†Zionism, as both a modern political movement and an organization, was founded by Theodor Herzl in 1897. Zionism aimed to establish "a legally assured home in *Eretz Yisrael*." See World Zionist Organization, "Mission Statement" and "About the World Zionist Organization," http://www.wzo.org.il/index.php?dir=site&page=pages&op=category&cs=3018&language=eng. See also a select group of statements made by Theodor Herzl and hosted on the Knesset Web site: Knesset, "World Zionist Organization (Since Its Establishment in 1897 Until the Balfour Declaration, 1917)," https://www.knesset.gov.il/vip/herzl/eng/Herz_Zion_eng.html.

the mid-1850s and precipitated waves of Jewish immigration—aliyahs—into Palestine. This migration, along with a complex web of other events and the relentless politicking of Zionist leader Chaim Weizmann, culminated in the Balfour Declaration of 1917, giving a green light to the creation of a national "homeland" for Jews in Palestine under the protective umbrella of Great Britain.*[2]

The Palestinian narrative is more straightforward: The Palestinians were the indigenous population in Palestine without interruption for 1,500 years. For over 600 of those years, from 1516 to 1923, Palestine was part of the Ottoman Empire. Jews from Europe and Russia began coming, sporadically and in small numbers, for much of the nineteenth century. Palestinian natives welcomed these Jews, but beginning in 1882 they came in larger numbers: some 25,000–35,000 in the first aliyah (1882–1902) and then thousands more in the aliyahs prior to the beginning of World War I in 1914. When the Balfour Declaration was promulgated near the end of the war, the 66,000 Jews in Palestine totaled close to 9 percent of the population. The Palestinian population was not consulted. More aliyahs followed the end of World War I. Palestinians and Jews lived on the land in relative harmony until August 1929.

In the years before 1929, Jews in Palestine slowly began to cohere around a concept of *nationhood* in the ancestral homeland that augmented, if indeed it did not replace, the glue of a shared religious tradition.[3] Distinctions between Zionist Jews and Arab Jews became blurred as this growing nationalism became the most common source of Jewish unity. Any spirit of communal amity with the Palestinians, any sense of shared endeavor in a harsh land, began to give way to a dream not just of a homeland but of an internationally recognized state; not just a state that included Jews but a *Jewish state* with every Jew around the globe eligible for citizenship.†

*The Balfour Declaration (dated November 2, 1917) was a letter from the United Kingdom's Foreign Secretary Arthur James Balfour to Baron Rothschild (Walter Rothschild), a leader of the British Jewish community, to the Zionist Federation of Great Britain and Ireland: "His Majesty's government view with favour the establishment in Palestine of a national home for the Jewish people, and will use their best endeavours to facilitate the achievement of this object, it being clearly understood that nothing shall be done which may prejudice the civil and religious rights of existing non-Jewish communities in Palestine, or the rights and political status enjoyed by Jews in any other country." http://avalon.law.yale.edu/20th_century/balfour.asp.

†The idea of Jewish immigration to Israel has historic roots in the Talmudic reference to seeking the Land of Israel. In the modern era, the Knesset passed the "Law of Return" in July 1950, which authorized Jews from anywhere in the world to immigrate to Israel. According to the Jewish Virtual Library, the Law of Return (Right of Aliyah) was "published in Sefer HaChukkim (Book of Laws) No. 51, p.159. Two amendments were later added on to the Law of Return—one passed August 23, 1954, and the other passed March 10, 1970." For more on the Law of Return and

The Palestinians understood the implications of this vision for their own communities. In August 1929 a simmering dispute between Muslims and Jews over access to the Wailing Wall in Jerusalem, one of the holiest sites in both the Jewish and Muslim faiths, turned deadly.[4] "On the 15th August, 1929, some hundreds of young Jews organised a demonstration at the Wailing Wall, in the course of which the Zionist flag was raised and the Zionist anthem sung. Incensed by this, Moslems held a counter-demonstration at the same spot on the following day, when written prayers placed in the crevices of the wall by Jewish worshippers were taken out and burned."[5] Over the following week, 133 Jews and 110 Arabs were killed, 339 Jews and 232 Arabs injured in Hebron, Jerusalem, and Safed.[6] Then, on August 29, an Arab riot in Hebron killed 67 Jews, among them women and children. Jewish businesses were pillaged and synagogues desecrated. This violence transmogrified Jewish-Arab relations almost overnight.[7] Harmony was now ancient history, and the ethnic animosity in Hebron became the template for future relations between the two communities. The Jewish "beliefs were clearly counterpoised to the aspirations of the Arabs," Hillel Cohen, author of *1929: Year Zero of the Jewish-Arab Conflict*, writes, and "[those beliefs] turned all the Jews who subscribed to those principles into a single amorphous mass. And therefore, during the 1929 murderous riots, the Arabs in their own view were not killing their Jewish neighbors, but their Zionist foes who were trying to take over their country."[8]

In one sense, it was no different from neighbors suddenly turning on each other for no reason other than ethnic identity or religious persuasion.

In the lead-up to World War II, the numbers of Jewish immigrants increased dramatically, in large measure because of increasing Nazi oppression in Germany, but a still larger number were prevented from immigrating because of British restraints limiting Jewish immigration. Resentment among the Palestinians simmered until 1936, when Palestinian Arabs revolted against the British colonial presence that permitted Jewish immigration on such a large scale. The insurrection lasted three years before the Palestinians surrendered. Nothing had changed. The number of Jews in Palestine had increased from 84,000 in 1922 when the first official census was taken to 450,000* on the eve of World War II.[9] Eight years later, in 1947, the

---

its amendments, see Jewish Virtual Library, "Israel's Basic Laws: The Law of Return (July 5, 1950)," https://www.jewishvirtuallibrary.org/jsource/Politics/Other_Law_Law_of_Return.html.

*The White Paper of 1939 was a British government policy paper abandoning the idea of partitioning Palestine. It provided, as an alternative to partition, for the creation of an

nascent United Nations made the Palestinian fear of an Israeli state more threatening when the General Assembly passed Resolution 181,* which would have partitioned Mandatory Palestine into two states, one an official homeland for the Jewish people and the other an official homeland for the Palestinian people. The Jews, who would be given 55 percent of the land but be saddled with a large Palestinian minority, accepted, albeit reluctantly. The Palestinians just as swiftly rejected it.[10]

Two wars followed. The first, known by the Israelis as the war of independence and by the Palestinians as *al-Nakba*, or "The Catastrophe," lasted less than a year, from December 1947† to March 1948, and was an intercommunal conflict between the Palestinians and Jews that triggered the exodus of Palestinians. The Haganah, the Jewish paramilitary organization founded in 1920,[11] routed the depleted Palestinian army, which had never recovered from its defeat by the British the previous decade.[12]

On May 14, David Ben-Gurion proclaimed the foundation of the state of Israel, and eleven minutes after midnight on the fifteenth, the day before the British Mandate was to expire, the United States extended de facto recognition. The second war—which lasted from May 15, 1948, to March 1949—followed immediately. On May 15 armies from Jordan, Syria, and Egypt invaded, intent on destroying the new state of Israel and returning the land to its rightful Palestinian owners. However, their actions were not entirely altruistic; they were also motivated by their own territorial ambitions. To repulse the advancing Arab armies in 1948, the Haganah, now the Israel

---

independent Palestine by 1949 to be governed by Palestinian Arabs and Jews in proportion to their numbers in the population. See "British White Paper of 1939," http://avalon.law.yale.edu/20th_century/brwh1939.asp.

*United Nations Resolution 181 was passed by the (UN) General Assembly in 1947. It called for the partition of Palestine into Arab and Jewish states, with the city of Jerusalem as a *corpus separatum* ("separate entity") to be governed by a special international regime. See G. A. Resolution 181 (II), Future Government of Palestine, UN Doc. A/ RES/ 181(II) (29 November 1947), http://unispal.un.org/unispal.nsf/0/7F0AF2BD897689B785256C330061D253.

†The UN General Assembly vote of November 29, 1947, supporting Palestine's partition, kicked off violent protests. In December 1947, as hostilities mounted, Arabs began to flee areas slated for Jewish statehood and areas adjacent to them. Many refugees were from the country's upper- and middle-class families. By February and March 1948, an exodus of 75,000 Arabs from cities—particularly Haifa, Jaffa, and Jerusalem—and the countryside had occurred. Some of that flight was due to direct Jewish expulsion orders, along with psychological intimidation. All of this was against the backdrop of the May 15, 1948, British withdrawal deadline from Palestine. "The Arab evacuees from the towns and villages left largely because of Jewish—Haganah, IZL or LHI—attacks, or fear of impending attack, and from a sense of vulnerability," says Benny Morris, an Israeli professor and historian. This period is detailed in Morris's book *Birth of the Palestinian Refugee Problem* (paperback, 1998), 29–60. Chapter 6 discusses in more depth the ongoing debate of whether the exodus of the Palestinians was a calculated, officially sanctioned expulsion.

Defense Forces (IDF), enlisted 2.0 percent of the total Yishuv (the Jewish population of Israel) for the national defense.[13] (The equivalent in the United States today would be a standing army of 7 million instead of the 1.5 million currently serving in the U.S. military.)

The invaders were easily repulsed by the Haganah. Armistice agreements signed in 1949 awarded Israel an additional 23 percent of Palestine and part of the Sinai desert. The Israeli state now comprised 78 percent of Mandatory Palestine. The West Bank, including East Jerusalem, was annexed by Transjordan. When the fighting finally stopped, some 750,000 Palestinians had fled their homes and communities between December 1947 and March 1949, either voluntarily or involuntarily as a result of expulsion; they waited to return to their homes, as was mandated by UN Resolution 194.* They and their descendants are still waiting.

>> <<

Israel barred Palestinians from returning to their homes, violating the Geneva Conventions† and leaving them a stateless people—what the Jews *had* been—dispersed throughout refugee camps in Lebanon, Syria, Jordan, and Iraq. In 1948, about 80 percent of Palestinians had become refugees.[14]

For Palestinians redressing this mass flight today, the *Nakba* and the Right of Return‡ elicit as much hopelessness and passion as ever. Palestinians insist

In article 11 of UN Resolution 194, "Progress Report of the United Nations Mediator," the General Assembly "[r]esolves* that the refugees wishing to return to their homes and live at peace with their neighbours should be permitted to do so at the earliest practicable date, and that compensation should be paid for the property of those choosing not to return and for loss of or damage to property which, under principles of international law or in equity, should be made good by the Governments or authorities responsible." See United Nations General Assembly, "Resolution 194 (III): Palestine—Progress Report of the United Nations Mediator," December 11, 1948, UN Doc. A/RES/194 (III), http://domino.un.org/unispal.nsf/0/c758572b78d1cd0085256bcf0077e51a?OpenDocument.

†"Article 49 states that 'individual or mass forcible transfers, as well as deportations of protected persons from occupied territory to the territory of the Occupying power or to that of any other country, occupied or not, are prohibited, regardless of their motive.' Since Israel has actually carried out such mass population transfers of Palestinian refugees by means of force and psychological warfare, it stands in violation of the Fourth Geneva Convention. While there is no explicit language in the Convention regarding its retroactive application, the expulsion of the Palestinian refugees from their homeland represents a violation of the spirit and letter of international law articulated repeatedly prior, during, and after the war of 1948. Article 49 of the Convention embodies the opinion of the international community regarding persons displaced during war, and further buttresses international opinion on the right of return of the Palestinian refugees as enunciated by UN Resolution 194." http://www.thejerusalemfund.org/ht/d/ContentDetails/i/2152.

‡See UN Resolution 194, article 11, footnote p. 16.

that this core issue must be resolved in negotiations according to the letter of international law. Israel, however, is adamantly insistent that it will never accede to the demand—to do so would threaten the very Jewishness of Israel. Moreover, Israel did *not* recognize the Palestinian population as "indigenous" to Palestine in the first place, arguing the land has always been theirs by divine right. The 13 percent to 15 percent of the Palestinian population who remained in their homes during the 1947–49 wars lived under military rule until 1966,[15] and although they were given citizenship, they were not given equal rights.* They and their descendants are classified as Arab Israelis; the designation "Arab" perpetuates the belief that they came originally from *one* of many Arab countries and *could have returned* to one of many countries.† Israel itself has been "redesigned" since 1948, with every vestige of a Palestinian presence erased: street names, neighborhoods, artifacts all scrubbed clean of any Arab association and replaced with Hebrew nomenclatures.[16] History is perceived as one of continuity.[17] Jews were forced out of Palestine and after two thousand years they returned. The space between is a blank.

To this day, Israeli Jews and Palestinians claim to be the legitimate owners of the same land. For over a hundred years they have faced off. Israeli Jews live in a country that is prosperous and democratic, a highly developed homeland for Jews from every corner of the earth; Palestinians have never accepted the logic that declares that *their* homeland must be sacrificed to that purpose. Agreement to *share* the land seems impossible. The respective historical narratives that justify each side's ownership of the same land are *competing* narratives and irreconcilable,[18] hence the interminable political struggle for a resolution that will somehow accommodate both narratives, and hence the intractable conflict. The human toll of dead and injured has had profound effects on the psyches of both Israeli Jews and Palestinians.[19]

*Over the years, Palestinian Israelis' rights to self-determination and freedom have been limited and/or denied in a number of areas, prompting a number of inquiries, reports, and offers of assistance from NGOs, coalitions, and legal experts, many of them Israeli. Be it political representation, access to water and sanitation, a decent education, employment, housing, or even the powers to plan and build, Palestinian Israelis have faced numerous restrictions. A comprehensive picture of efforts to secure civil and political rights; criminal justice; economic, social and cultural rights; and land and planning rights can be obtained by visiting Adalah: The Legal Center for Arab and Minority Rights in Israel at http://adalah.org/eng/.

†The argument that they were not a people, but simply Arabs who occupied Palestine for 1,500 years before Jews began their migration at the end of the nineteenth century, was widely perpetuated in Israel. In 1969 then–prime minister Golda Meir's infamous remark that "There is no such thing as a Palestinian people" encapsulated this reading of history. Quoted in *Washington Post*, June 16, 1969.

From the First Intifada in 1987 until April 2014,* nearly 10,000 Palestinians and 1,636 Israelis were killed—a six-to-one ratio; as regards injuries, between 2000 and 2014, 8,549 Israelis were injured while between 2000 and 2009—a time frame five years shorter—approximately 35,000 Palestinians were injured. There were 16,626 Palestinians injured in 2014 alone, double the number of injuries to Israelis from 2000 to 2014. Interpret as you will.†

Since 1962, with massive U.S. assistance, Israel has amassed the most formidable military in the Middle East. The Six-Day War in 1967 was an embarrassingly one-sided confrontation. Israel overwhelmed a coordinated attack by Egypt, Jordan, and Syria and found itself in military control of *all* of Palestine, including the West Bank and the Gaza Strip (together referred to as WBG). Israel subsequently annexed East Jerusalem and refused to withdraw to the armistice lines of 1949, in violation of the Fourth Geneva Convention and in defiance of UN Resolution 242, which called for "withdrawal of Israeli armed forces from territories occupied in the recent conflict."‡ Consequently, Israel has occupied the West Bank and Gaza for close to half

*During the First Intifada, in 1987, until the beginning of the Second, September 2000, a total of 1,551 Palestinians were killed, of whom approximately 304 were minors (B'Tselem, "Statistics: Fatalities," http:// www.btselem.org/statistics [accessed on April 14, 2015]); 29,000 children were in need of medical treatment for injuries from beatings, and between 6,500 and 8,500 for injuries from gunfire (http://imeu.org/article/25th-anniversary-of-the-first-intifada). During the Second Intifada, 2000–2005, some 6,650 Palestinians were killed; 17,358 were injured in Gaza and 13,650 in the West Bank (http://www.pchrgaza.org/portal/en/index.php/index.php?option=com_content&view=article&id=3044:statistics-related-to-the-al-aqsa-second-intifada-&catid=55:statistics&Itemid=29). In Operation Cast Lead, December 2008–January 2009, 1,391 Palestinians in Gaza were killed; in Operation Pillar of Defense, 167 were killed and 1,202 injured (http://www.btselem.org/download/201305_pillar_of_defense_operation_eng.pdf). Between January 2009 and April 2014, 630 Palestinians were killed. See B'Tselem, "Statistics: Fatalities," http://www.btselem.org/statistics (accessed on April 14, 2015).

†During the First Intifada, 1987–93, 179 Israelis were killed, 114 civilians and 65 IDF soldiers. The first Hamas suicide attack in Israel killed eight people in April 1994 in the center of Afula. Between 1994 and September 2000, the beginning of the Second Intifada, 151 Israelis were killed in suicide and bombing attacks. Altogether since the start of the Second Intifada in 2000 until the end of 2013, 1,127 Israelis were killed and 8,549 were wounded. See B'Tselem, "Statistics: Fatalities," http://www.btselem.org/statistics (accessed on April 14, 2015—not including fatalities in Operation Protective Edge) and Israel Ministry of Foreign Affairs, "Victims of Palestinian Violence and Terrorism Since September 2000." http://www.mfa.gov.il/mfa/foreignpolicy/terrorism/palestinian/pages/victims%20of%20palestinian%20violence%20and%20terrorism%20sinc.aspx (accessed on April 14, 2015).

‡The operative clause is paragraph 1, which "affirms that the fulfillment of Charter principles requires the establishment of a just and lasting peace in the Middle East which should include the application of both the following principles: (i) Withdrawal of Israel armed forces from territories occupied in the recent conflict [and] (ii) termination of all claims or states of belligerency and respect for and acknowledgment of the sovereignty, territorial integrity and political independence of every State in the area and their right to live in peace within secure and recognized boundaries free from threats or acts of force." See United Nations Security Council,

a century and the Palestinians, an occupied people under its military rule, have lived in subjugation.*

Our meta narratives define our values and norms and provide the underpinnings of our identity.[20] When they clash with the meta narratives of another community that makes competing claims, the narratives develop a stranglehold on the political and cultural life in both communities and ensure, for better or, more often, for worse, that the past virtually dictates the future. In the Palestinian-Israeli conflict this makes it almost impossible to find common ground; and in its absence a peace process is hamstrung from the outset.

It is impossible to understand the failures of the negotiations since those in Madrid in 1991† without understanding the protagonists' respective narratives. And perhaps, just perhaps, their respective *willingness* to acknowledge the right of the other to its narrative and accord it *due respect* might provide a key to unlocking the prison to which they confine themselves, and thereby tentatively begin to chart the way to finding a *different* future.

In my conversations with West Bank interviewees, the refrain is just that—the refrain. Every Palestinian interviewee wants the outside world to understand the historical injustice: the deviousness and hypocrisy of the great powers that endorsed the Jewish colonization of Palestine just as these powers were beginning to divest themselves of their own colonies. Israel, in their view, is a colonial creation imposed on the basis of an insupportable logic, the result of the deliberate expulsion of Palestinians from their homeland in 1947–48 and the expropriation of everything they owned except what could

---

Resolution 242 (1967), November 22, 1967, UN Doc. S/RES/242 (1967), http://unispal.un.org/unispal.nsf/0/7D35E1F729DF491C85256EE700686136.

*Israel argues that it is not in violation of international law and draws on a number of legal arguments to support its position. For example, "As the West Bank and Gaza Strip were not under the legitimate and recognized sovereignty of any state prior to the Six Day War, they should not be considered occupied territories." Therefore to Israel, the second paragraph of article 2 of the Fourth Geneva Convention applies only to "occupation of the territory of a High Contracting Party." According to the Israel Ministry of Foreign Affairs, "UN Security Council Resolution 242, which was adopted following the Six Day War, places *obligations on both sides* (as does Resolution 338, adopted following the 1973 Yom Kippur War). *242 does not call for unilateral withdrawal from the territories. . . . Resolution 242 does not require Israel to withdraw from all the territories* [emphasis added] gained as a result of the 1967 war. . . . Instead, the resolution deliberately restricts itself to calling for Israel's withdrawal 'from territories' while recognizing the right to live within secure and recognized boundaries." See Israeli Ministry of Foreign Affairs, "Disputed Territories: Forgotten Facts About the West Bank and Gaza Strip," February 1, 2003, http://mfa.gov.il/MFA/MFA-Archive/2003/Pages/DISPUTED%20TERRITORIES-%20Forgotten%20Facts%20About%20the%20We.aspx.

†For a timeline of major summits and conferences aimed at Israeli-Palestinian peace, October 1991–July 2013, see http://www.reuters.com/article/2013/07/29/us-palestinians-israel-timeline-idUSBRE96S13220130729.

be carried away on a cart. Israel was consequently responsible for the suffering in the diaspora, especially Lebanon, and now for the day-to-day misery of living under occupation, subject to the whims of a capricious overseer.

Because their experiences dictate their behaviors, they view their world through the prism of seemingly permanent *humiliation*, indignity, dispossession, and disrespect. The word "humiliation" suffused my conversations with West Bank Palestinians, leaving little room for other issues to become part of the dialogue. So while the Palestinian national narrative is invariably cast in terms of the *Nakba* and the occupation, a subnarrative is daily life in occupied territory. The protagonist is not an enemy on a battlefield in an ongoing war—that would have a certain clarity—but something much more insidious: the near-impotent life of the occupied at the hands of the occupying power.

The proliferation of checkpoints, long queues at those checkpoints, routine inconveniences, bureaucratic pettiness, ill treatment and abuse by soldiers, roads reserved solely for Israeli settlers' use, settler violence that is not checked by the IDF, arbitrary detainment with no recourse to due process all coalesce into the humiliation that is the real psychic cost of their being trapped in circumstances over which they have no control.

Every Palestinian has a story about the arbitrariness of administrative detention: some neighbor or friend picked up in the dead of night, the lengths to which the family had to go simply to find out where the detainee was being held. And of course there is closure,[21] which the IDF uses to restrict imports to and exports from the West Bank, stunting economic growth and levels of employment, threatening Palestinians' livelihoods, creating uncertainty, and hence inhibiting investment.[22] In addition, there is the separation barrier that cuts into the West Bank and encircles the settlements built around Jerusalem. The barrier sometimes cuts through fields and villages, separating Palestinian families, stranding neighbors on opposite sides, preventing farmers' access to their farmland and other workers from reaching their jobs, restricting freedom of movement, and isolating Palestinians from the world beyond the walls.*

*When complete, the barrier will run 725 kilometers, more than double the length of the demarcation (Green Line) set out by the 1949 armistice agreements, with 85 percent located inside the West Bank (including East Jerusalem). The barrier will isolate approximately 9.4 percent of West Bank territory, including East Jerusalem and No-Man's Land. Approximately 385,000 settlers in eighty settlements will be located between the barrier and the Green Line. Approximately 25,000 West Bank Palestinians will be located between the barrier and the Green Line, in addition to the majority of the approximately 250,000 residents of East Jerusalem. Approximately 125,000 Palestinians in twenty-eight communities will be surrounded on three sides by the barrier. Approximately 26,000 Palestinians in eight communities will be surrounded on four sides by the barrier, with a tunnel or road connection to the rest of the West Bank. See

Ironically, perhaps one of the more powerful evocations of the occupation dynamic comes from a young Israeli soldier, Oded Na'aman, who served two of his three years of compulsory military service at a checkpoint. In his essay, "The Checkpoint," Na'aman captures the moment:

> Since the military occupies the land on which the enemy resides, it cannot conquer the enemy's land any more than it already has. And insofar as the enemy has no land, it has no political independence, no real capacity for civic life. It is therefore impossible for Israel—logically impossible—to "go to war" with the Palestinians in the West Bank: Palestinian individuals may suffer to a greater or lesser degree, but the Palestinian people, as a people, cannot be further defeated. . . . But the checkpoints' primary mission is to demonstrate presence, to exhibit the army's constant surveillance and its overwhelming force. . . . [Y]ou cannot hide and you cannot fight; Israel is both omnipresent and omnipotent.[23]

Akram Hanieh, whose connection with the peace process goes back to the Madrid conference and who is founding editor of the newspaper *Al-Ayyam*, recalled the shame he felt after a particular incident with his daughter:

> I remember that I was going with my child ten years ago, she was three. There were Israelis inside Ramallah. We were stopped by an Israeli Jeep and [the soldier] said, "Where are you going?" My child began to look queer at this guy who was asking her daddy these questions. After he allowed us to leave, she said, "Who is he, Dad? Why did he stop us? What is his uniform?" I didn't say anything. How can you tell a three-year-old that it's our country but there is an Israeli occupation?[24]

A similar story with identical import is told by Issa Kassissieh, then deputy head of the PLO's negotiations unit, for whom the humiliation had become unbearable: "It's all about my dignity," he said.

> When I go from Jerusalem to Bethlehem with my children, to go to Nativity Church, and then the troops will get me out and get their dog to sniff me, and see how my daughter and my son see me humiliated, this is bad. You don't want to be in our shoes. And what we are struggling for? Justice and

---

UN Office for the Coordination of Humanitarian Affairs, Occupied Palestinian Territory, *Special Focus: Barrier Update* (East Jerusalem, UN OCHA, July 2011), http://www.ochaopt.org/documents/ocha_opt_barrier_update_july_2011_english.pdf.

dignity. Keep it in your mind. That's it. I care less about a national state. I care about my dignity.[25]

And the same refrain is reiterated, yet again, by veteran negotiator Abu Ala:

> There are no good occupations in history. Occupiers are enemies to the people who are under occupation and rob them of their dignity. Protecting their dignity is the first thing people under occupation look out for. Why does this foreigner take away my dignity? Anybody who goes from one city to another will pass through an Israeli checkpoint. "Stop! Stop! Your ID? Your card?"[26]

Jabril Rajoub is a Fatah party "heavy," a member of the Central Committee, and often touted as possible successor to Abbas. At the time of our interview, he was president of the Palestinian Women's National Soccer League, forced to spend large amounts of his time trying to navigate through interminable dealings with Israeli authorities on permits and visas for women playing soccer either at the club level or for the Palestinian national team or for foreigners, mostly FIFA or IOC members that want to come to the West Bank to assist in building the national teams. Permits are slow in coming, problematic at best, sometimes one-way only. "The problem," he said, "is that the Israelis sometimes don't give permits, or they exert pressure on countries from outside not to come to play in Palestine, or they do not let some Palestinian players leave to play, and sometimes they give the permit to leave, but they do not give the permit to come back. Once it happened with the goalkeeper; he waited ninety days in Jordan till they let him come back. Once, also, the captain of the national team had to wait sixteen months in Amman till the Israelis let him come back."*[27]

In March 2010 Saeb Erekat, the PLO's chief negotiator, accompanied U.S. secretary of state Hillary Clinton and special envoy Senator George Mitchell to Benjamin Netanyahu's home to discuss where things stood. One can feel the reverberations of Erekat's anger when he describes the rude, dismissive way he believes Netanyahu treated him. First he had to wait outside the office while the Israeli prime minister talked with Clinton and Mitchell. Finally summoned into the inner sanctum, when he tried to present Netanyahu with the sheaf of papers the PLO had prepared, setting out

*"FIFA President Urges Israel to Ease Travel Rules for Palestine Footballers," Voice of America, June 11, 2014, http://www.voanews.com/content/reu-fifa-president-urges-israel-to-ease-travel-rules-for-palestine-footballers/1934904.html.

the recent understandings reached by Mahmoud Abbas in his capacity as PLO chairman and former Israeli Prime minister Ehud Olmert on border and security issues, Netanyahu brusquely waved the papers aside with a flick of his wrist and informed Erekat that this was not the way he negotiated. Through the rest of the meeting, Erekat sat silently, an irrelevant appendage in the discussion.[28]

At least once in every interview with me, Saeb Erekat rhetorically asked: "Who said life is about justness and fairness?" I had no answer for him.

For every Palestinian, the humiliation and dispossession meted out by the omnipresent accoutrements of the occupation trigger both individual and collective memory. Different questions in different interviews with the same individual often elicited virtually the same verbatim answer. The response might have been laced with frustration, simmering resentment, barely concealed anger, derogatory remarks, accusations of duplicity, and/or claims of moral superiority, but it was mainly a recitation of the history and the humiliation of occupation, a demand for dignity and justice.

Palestinians are singularly self-centered and absorbed with their loss. In my interviews, the Palestinian leadership in the West Bank, as well as men and women on the street, rarely acknowledged conflicts and travail other than their own. Egypt and Syria are next-door neighbors, the Arab Spring and its ensuing tumult were at their doorsteps, but their reactions to questions about those conflicts were tepid almost to the point of disinterest. Although they had been witnesses to two Gaza wars[29] between Israel and Hamas, Gaza was rarely mentioned in the interviews, and then only in passing. Some interviewees did opine that the Arab Spring uprisings simply didn't measure up to the standards set by the Palestinians' intifadas and that, of course, once democratically elected Islamic governments had their own houses in order, they would turn their attention to the Palestinians' cause. Many emphasized that the Second Intifada was the wellspring for the Arab Spring: They were not averse to claiming some ownership of other peoples' revolutions.

Many West Bank interviewees appeared to be intellectually depleted, unable to engage in an exchange of ideas, cynical about further talks with the Israelis, and less than hopeful that a two-state solution would somehow be achieved anytime in the near future. Why should they want to explore issues they deemed irrelevant?

Specifically, they had little interest in discussing the implications of the changing character of the Israeli state; how the Arab Spring and the general chaos in the region might impact Israeli security concerns; or how the regional balance of power, which is in a state of flux, was bound to change and might affect Palestinian aspirations and hence require a recalibration in the ways they pursue those aspirations. They politely answered questions about these subjects, but they rarely raised them as key concerns. They'd rather dwell on the narrative. They wanted an end to the divisions between Fatah and Hamas, but accounts of reconciliation between the two being imminent have proved false on so many occasions that new renditions are shrugged off. Perhaps the latest on April 23, 2014, that the two sides had agreed on a reconciliation pact will be taken more seriously if the stages of implementation it calls for begin to materialize.[30] No one is holding his breath.

In the West Bank, interviewees passed over the implications of Iran's advancing nuclear capability (though the weight of opinion, unsurprisingly, came down in Iran's favor). In Gaza the Iranians are cheered on. Questions about the efficacy of negotiating tactics and strategies were treated as sideshows of little importance, given the dismal record of the past and endemic distrust that has become more corrosive with every passing year, irrelevant in the context of the occupation.

Over 50 percent of Palestinians in the West Bank and more than 70 percent of Gazans are classified as refugees. Some 70 percent were born into powerlessness; about half are under seventeen years of age.* The occupation is part of the normalcy of life; even the youngest succumb to its psychological conditioning. It is impossible not to empathize with their dismal predicament. However, it is also clear that Palestinian leaders share at least *some* responsibility for their situation. They are not as powerless as they appear to be. Internal Palestinian politics, especially factionalism in Fatah and the inability or unwillingness of Fatah and Hamas to reconcile their differences have had debilitating and divisive impacts on the Palestinian polity. The fractious fighting in Fatah itself may yet be the party's undoing,[31] as different factions jostle contentiously, trying to ensure that their preferred candidate succeeds Abbas.[32]

Palestinian interviewees invoked the sanctity of human rights at every

*According to the UN's Relief and Works Agency for Palestinian Refugees in the Near East (UNRWA), of the total 1.5 million people who are refugees in Gaza, 1.2 million are "registered" refugees. UNRWA, "Where We Work: Gaza Strip," last modified January 1, 2014, http://www.unrwa.org/where-we-work/gaza-strip. Among the West Bank population of 2.4 million, 754,441 are "registered" refugees. UNRWA, "Where We Work: West Bank," last modified January 1, 2014, http://www.unrwa.org/where-we-work/west-bank. See also UNRWA, "Gaza in 2020: UNRWA Operational Response," May 2013, http://unispal.un.org/UNISPAL.nsf/361eea1cc08301c485256cf600606959/aa1b7b90f79c031e85257b9d004de092?OpenDocument.

opportunity, but the PA's adherence to democratic norms in the West Bank is dubious at best. Human rights are routinely violated—the rule of law is capriciously applied, arbitrary arrests, detention without trial of potential political adversaries, occasional torture, press censorship, repression of union activity, suppression of dissent and restrictions on assembly for most forms of opposition.[33] Nongovernmental organizations (NGOs), once the backbone of local development, routinely come under the surveillance of branches of the Palestinian Authority Security Forces (PASF) and, of course, of the Israelis. The PASF itself, once praised for achieving a high degree of professionalism, is increasingly problematic.[34] Low-intensity authoritarianism corrodes pluralism; new economic and political elites emerge, and their agendas take precedence over the best interests and the needs of their people.

Such criticisms remain largely unmentioned and definitely unaddressed by the Palestinians themselves. Interviewees just didn't want to go there. It didn't serve the narrative. An intifada? Always unpredictable, but at the time of my interviews, unlikely. Every allusion to an intifada, however, comes with the invariable caveat: "You never know." "Today," said Hiba Husseini, a PLO negotiator during the Stockholm track,* "there's a sense of deep fatigue, deep exhaustion, and disillusionment as to whether the occupation will ever end. Israel has managed to break our spirit in terms of violence, because the price has always been very, very, very high."[35]

Indeed, given the way in which the IDF, the undisputed overlord, has doled out death over years short of half a century, always using disproportionate force to remind Palestinians of the price they must pay for every "transgression," resistance fatigue is understandable. But in a struggle that Palestinians perceive as a war against colonialism, epic resistance comes in waves, after which the tide recedes before powerful currents again propel them shoreward.

> > < <

Palestinians never forget—because they are not allowed to forget—the asymmetry of power *on the ground* in the West Bank that permeates their daily lives. Israel sees to that. Nor do they forget the asymmetry of power at the negotiating table and on the world stage. The word "asymmetry" is part of their lexicon. It has many uses, sometimes to cover up self-inflicted

*The Stockholm track consisted of fifteen substantive sessions, culminating in three long weekends, two in Sweden and one in Israel. See Sher, *Israeli-Palestinian Peace Negotiations*, 21–39; Ben Ami, *Scars of War*, 282–83; and Qurei (Abu Ala), *Beyond Oslo*, 230–44.

derelictions in their behaviors that undermine their cause. But there is little questioning of the fact that Palestinian negotiators are disadvantaged at the negotiating table because the dynamic is not of one free people negotiating with another free people. Instead, it is of one free, powerful people (Israel) negotiating with a people it oppresses (Palestine), with the third-party mediator—the United States—irredeemably biased in favor of Israel. "Washington will never be in a position to put pressure on Israel," says Hanan Ashrawi, a member of the PLO Executive Committee. "It is Israel who puts pressure on Washington."[36] The sentiment encapsulates the complaints of pro-Israel bias expressed by all Palestinian interviewees. Much as the United States and Israel might protest, the United States is psychologically predisposed to being biased, even unknowingly.* Akram Hanieh recalled a singular incident when the United States showed a conspicuous lack of empathy with the Palestinians' circumstances, noting how distressed President Mahmoud Abbas was at President Obama's address at the United Nations in September 2011, when he called on the General Assembly to reject the PLO's application for membership as an officially recognized state on a par with Israel.[37] "There was something very shameful about Obama's speech," Hanieh said. "He only adopted the Israeli narrative. He didn't say a word about our suffering. I remember President Abbas in New York asking me something like seventeen times over two days, 'Why didn't he talk about our suffering?' I believe this affront was something killing to us. I don't care about the daily politics. I care about the narrative."

This asymmetry of power in the Mideast is *guaranteed by America*. Indeed, there is no gainsaying the fact that the Palestinian-Israeli conflict has entered its sixth decade in large measure because Israel enjoys the

*Despite the lengths the United States goes to insist on its impartiality, the findings of neuropsychology show we are by nature biased in favor of any group with whom we can identify, regardless of how flimsy the connection may be. In *Subliminal*, 161–175, Mlodinow cites numerous studies that show the affinities between us and our in-groups: "[R]esearch suggests that, whether with regard to religion, race, nationality, computer use, or our operating unit at work, we generally have a built-in tendency to prefer those in our in-group. . . . [W]e also tend to favor in-group members in our social and business dealings, and we *evaluate their work and products more favorably than we might otherwise, even if we think we are treating everyone equally* [emphasis added]. . . . It is not necessary for you to share any attitudes or traits with your fellow members, or even for you to have met the other group members. It is a simple act of knowing that you belong to a group that triggers your in-group affinity. . . . People unambiguously choose to discriminate in favor of the in-group, rather than acting for the greatest good."

In my October 26, 2011, interview with Gilead Sher, he insisted that Israel had been "hit by the stick" on more than a few occasions (with threats) but admitted that aid/support had never been cut.

absolute protection of the United States; Congress provides unquestioning protection and unprecedented levels of foreign aid to enhance Israel's already formidable military capacity.[38]

The impact of the American Israel Public Affairs Committee (AIPAC) is indisputably unsurpassable.[39] According to the Congressional Research Service (CRS), "Israel is the largest cumulative recipient of U.S. foreign assistance since World War II. To date, the United States has provided Israel $121 billion (current, or non-inflation-adjusted, dollars) in bilateral assistance. Almost all U.S. bilateral aid to Israel is in the form of military assistance, although in the past Israel also received significant economic assistance." That assistance is manifested in other ways. The CRS says:

> Strong congressional support for Israel has resulted in Israel receiving benefits not available to any other countries; for example, Israel can use some U.S. military assistance both for research and development in the United States and for military purchases from Israeli manufacturers. In addition, U.S. assistance earmarked for Israel is generally delivered in the first 30 days of the fiscal year, while most other recipients normally receive aid in installments.... In addition to receiving U.S. State Department-administered foreign assistance, Israel also receives funds from annual defense appropriations bills for rocket and missile defense programs. Israel pursues some of those programs jointly with the United States.[40]

When sequestration slashed federal spending at all levels in 2013, with no exceptions, the trade journal *Defense News* noted, "Despite sequestration and protracted fiscal constraints, Israel can expect an additional decade of sustained and possibly increased levels of security assistance once its current $30 billion, 10-year military aid package expires in 2018."[41]

Stuart Eizenstat, a former official who negotiated an earlier aid package on behalf of the administration of then-president Bill Clinton, says simply, "Support for Israel in the United States is astonishing."* While every U.S. administration is adamant in pronouncing that peace in the Middle East is a matter of U.S. national security and every administration calls further construction of Israeli settlements detrimental to peace, Israel continues

*Opall-Rome, "US Experts Forecast Military Aid." See also Chris Carlson, "US Senate Approves More Aid to Israel Despite Deficit," International Middle East Media Center, August 1, 2014, http://www.imemc.org/article/68704. In August 2014, in the middle of the war between Israel and Hamas, before adjourning for a month with most Congressional business undone, Congress approved $225 million for the Israeli military's Iron Dome defense system.

building new settlements and expanding older ones. The weak-kneed U.S. admonitions are meaningless. So are UN General Assembly resolutions calling the settlements illegal, because the resolutions are vetoed by the United States if they reach the Security Council.* Yes, there are differences between the United States and Israel, but they are within the family and will result in, at worst, a temporary and functionally inconsequential estrangement. They will never be allowed to do real damage.

In contrast, since the establishment of the Palestinian Authority (PA) in the mid-1990s, "the U.S. government has committed approximately $5 billion in bilateral assistance to the Palestinians," which puts them "among the world's largest per-capita recipients of international foreign aid."[42] The aid, however, is allocated according to U.S. priorities: "Preventing terrorism against Israel from Hamas and other militant organizations. Fostering stability, prosperity, and self-governance in the West Bank . . . with . . . a 'two-state solution'" in mind. "Meeting humanitarian needs."[43] Aid to Israel, on the other hand, is allocated according to the priorities Israel sets. With fiscal year 2014–15 as a baseline, Israel received $3.1 billion annually and the Palestinian Authority $400 million.†

Consider Secretary of State John Kerry's telltale choice of Martin Indyk as his point man in the last round of negotiations (2013–14). Indyk is an "insider" on the Middle East peace process, America's first Jewish ambassador to Israel, and an important player at Camp David but one who is not

*When the moratorium on settlement construction ran out in September 2010, a UN resolution supported by 141 countries calling settlements illegal reached the Security Council, and the United States vetoed it. The official U.S. position is that the settlements are illegitimate, not illegal. See United Nations Security Council, "Security Council Fails to Adopt Text Demanding That Israel Halt Settlement Activity as Permanent Member Casts Negative Vote," February 18, 2011, http://www.un.org/News/Press/docs/2011/sc10178.doc.htm.

†Appropriations for Israel fiscal year 2014–15 are now set at $3.1 billion. In addition, the United States "provides another $504 million in funding for research, development, and production of Israel's Iron Dome antirocket system ($235 million) and of the joint U.S.–Israel missile defense system's David's Sling ($149.7 million), the Arrow improvement program (or Arrow II, $44.3 million), and Arrow III ($74.7 million)." See Sharp, U.S. Foreign Aid to Israel, 2. From fiscal year "2008 to the present, the [U.S.] annual Economic Support Fund (ESF) assistance to the West Bank and Gaza Strip has averaged around $400 million, with that amount divided between U.S. Agency for International Development (USAID)-administered project assistance, (through grants to contracting organizations) and direct budgetary assistance to the Palestinian Authority (PA). . . .

"Annual International Narcotics Control and Law Enforcement (INCLE) nonlethal assistance for PA security forces and the criminal justice sector in the West Bank has averaged around $100 million. In line with Obama administration requests, funding levels declined slightly in [fiscal year] 2013, with a new baseline of overall annual ESF assistance of $370 million. . . ." See Zanotti, U.S. Foreign Aid to the Palestinians, 2.

trusted by the Palestinians. (Nabil Sha'ath, also an important player at Camp David, described Indyk as "partial, biased, pro-Israel" and said he "defended Israeli settlements more than Israelis did.")

Indyk is a fine writer and his accounts of both Camp David and the Oslo process in *Innocent Abroad* are vivid, fascinating in detail, and riveting reading, but his portraits of the two principals—Barak and Arafat—reveal not-too-nuanced admiration for the one and near disdain for the other.

We learn that Barak was not just "Israel's most decorated soldier," but that he had also "gained these accolades as a commando involved in daring operations behind enemy lines"; had developed the IDF's "Sayeret Matkal, the army's elite commando unit"; had planned meticulously; and "insisted that an exit strategy always had to be built into the plan, so that if an operation went awry, the unit would be able to extricate itself before dawn." Barak was prepared to make "tangible, far-reaching concessions to end the conflict once and for all." Indyk says of Arafat, on the other hand, that he "inhabited a self-made, mythical world in which he claimed to be the only undefeated Arab general"; that "over many decades he had managed to blackmail his stronger partners by threatening collapse"; that he "understood that he was now the only game in town"; that "standing up to Barak and Clinton . . . was a surer way to survive than risking concessions that might risk him being devoured." He claimed that "Arafat resorted to one of his tactics when finding himself in a tight corner: he lied"; that "Arafat was narcissistic enough to imagine himself following in the footsteps of these two great heroes of Muslim history" (Caliph Umar Bin al-Khattab and Saladin al-Ayyubi); that "Arafat had been seeking an escape route from the moment he arrived at Camp David."[44]

The overall impression he leaves you with is that Barak was prepared to make far-reaching and daring concessions to put the future of his country above personal considerations of power, that he had come to broker an end to the conflict. On the other hand, Arafat was conniving, dishonest, apt to change his mind, manipulative, not to be trusted, and he invariably put personal survival above what might be best for his people.

His book reveals throughout an implicit pro-Israel bias, however, much as he may wish to be seen unbiased.* Considering his background as a Washington establishment insider, this particular "asymmetry" is perhaps a given. The Palestinians certainly believe so. Interestingly, when I interviewed Indyk in August 2011 in Washington DC, he was quite forthcoming:

*See the footnote on page 26 regarding the dynamics of relationships among in-groups.

"I'm not at all confident that an American-led effort can resolve the conflict anymore. Whereas previously I would have said that we were indispensable to the resolution to the conflict."[45] However, such ruminations did not stand in the way of his immediately accepting the role Kerry assigned him.

> > < <

Palestinians are a gracious and generous people. They are smart and enterprising and intersperse accounts of their tribulations with mordant humor. The occupation has not robbed them of their humanity, but after almost fifty years their hope for the future is ambivalent. Their bitterness and resentments are palpable when they talk about Netanyahu and perhaps best encapsulated by Saeb Erekat's cutting remark that

> If Thomas Jefferson was the president of Palestine, Montesquieu the speaker of our parliament, and Mother Teresa the prime minister of the Palestinians, and they insisted on two states 1967, Netanyahu would brand them as relatives of bin Laden. He is not a partner for peace. He was elected to undermine and destroy the two-state solution, and he's done a good job, under protection of the American Congress. He doesn't believe in two states. He wants to create a third state for the settlers in the West Bank.[46]

Their fading faith that the future can and will bring change exacerbates their sense of powerlessness.[47] After decades of occupation and loss of dignity, their behaviors have adapted to the humiliation of subjugation: Palestinians have developed defense mechanisms to shield the psyche from the intolerable. Perhaps the behaviors of decades under total domination have become subconsciously ingrained. Perhaps rebelliousness has given way to accommodation and lethargy. Certainly their responses to my questions were reflexive. The constancy of conformity has sapped the energy to engage. Instead, they tighten their grip on victimhood. Israel or the United States or other powerful interests in the West are to blame for all their grievances. "Never in the history of mankind," they will tell you, "have any people endured oppression as harsh as ours." To some extent, this has become a self-fulfilling prophecy.

Without exception the subtext is always the same one: Humiliation and indignity are the staples of life.

What the Palestinians want and what takes precedence over all else is restorative justice and an end to the occupation. They want their dignity back. It is often said—by Israelis, by the unaffiliated, but also by the

Palestinians themselves—that they come to negotiations not so much to address the issues they must resolve to secure a future state but to redress the injustices of the past—specifically, the refugee question following the wars of 1947–49 and the right of return. Tal Becker, an insightful Israeli negotiator, said: "Statehood is not why they're in the room. What drives the Palestinian ethos is a sense of dispossession and humiliation, and if statehood is part of rectifying that, and it is only a relatively small part—then it's relevant to discuss it. If it's a way of avoiding those issues, then it's not on the table. If you're offering them statehood so as not to talk about the issues of dispossession and humiliation in history, and their connection to Jerusalem, and so on, they're not interested in statehood."[48]

In Tangiers in November 1988, Yasser Arafat's PLO recognized the existence of the state of Israel on the 78 percent of Palestine that it then occupied. In return for forfeiting what it believed was the Palestinians' legitimate claim to their birthright, the PLO would settle for a Palestinian state on the remaining 22 percent.[49] It was a historic concession the Palestinians cried over, a break with their own history and narrative, all in the hope of peace. Yet Israel was dismissive. Why? Because no matter what, it could not be dislodged from the 78 percent of the land it occupied and besides, all the land, it believed, was theirs in the first place. Rather than seeing the PLO position as a major Palestinian concession, Israel saw it as the PLO's acknowledgment of reality. The PLO believes it made a preeminent concession of unprecedented proportions forfeiting much of their birthright, and to have it disparaged by Israel as little more than a gesture to reality, coupled with Israel's unwillingness to concede the remaining 22 percent for the creation of a Palestinian state,* created a chasm between Jewish Israelis and Palestinians that negotiations have failed to narrow, much less bridge. In most of my

*"The most controversial clause in Resolution 242 is the call for the 'Withdrawal of Israeli armed forces from territories occupied in the recent conflict.' This is linked to the second unambiguous clause calling for 'termination of all claims or states of belligerency' and the recognition that 'every State in the area' has the 'right to live in peace within secure and recognized boundaries free from threats or acts of force.'

"The resolution does not make Israeli withdrawal a prerequisite for Arab action. Moreover, it does not specify how much territory Israel is required to give up. The Security Council did not say Israel must withdraw from 'all the' territories occupied after the Six-Day war. This was quite deliberate. The Soviet delegate wanted the inclusion of those words and said that their exclusion meant 'that part of these territories can remain in Israeli hands.' The Arab states pushed for the word 'all' to be included, but this was rejected. They nevertheless asserted that they would read the resolution as if it included the word 'all.' The British ambassador who drafted the approved resolution, Lord Caradon, declared after the vote: 'It is only the resolution that will bind us, and we regard its wording as clear.'

interviews with Palestinians the fact that the PLO's groundbreaking, unilateral action was hardly acknowledged by Israel, and then only in a negative way, came up time and time and time again.

"When I am sitting with an Israeli at the table, I know they are powerful; I know they are stronger than me," says Akram Hanieh, "but I feel that I have the moral high ground and that I am stronger morally, so I am proud of myself, my people, of my struggle, and sometimes you feel that you have nothing to lose, you know, and at the same time you know that they know that, and they find it disconcerting, because, oddly enough, it empowers us at their expense."[50]

Such is the psychological power of righteousness and false solace, but "victories" on this battlefield of moral absolutes have yielded almost *nothing* of concrete benefit for the Palestinian people, after more than sixty years. Shlomo Ben-Ami, Israel's chief negotiator at Camp David, acknowledged that the Palestinian insistence on hewing to the idealistic, impractical high road is difficult for the Israeli mind to "decode." Palestinians, he inferred, prefer to fight on the grounds of moral absolutes, a field where, they believe, they hold the high ground.[51] Unfortunately for the Palestinians, considerations of morality play no role in hardball negotiations. History is littered with injustices. History moves on.[52]

> > < <

Israel exists—in fact, it thrives—in spite of what seems like a determined propensity to tear itself apart. It is riddled with schisms—political, religious, economic, cultural—some potentially profoundly grave, some sufficiently pervasive to threaten its social cohesion.[53] Yet Israel is held together, despite the multitudinous differences among its multilayered ethnic components, by this one primal fact: While the West looked the other way and found pious excuses for inaction, only a whisper of fate saved the Jewish people from total annihilation. Such knowledge—and the belief that it could happen again—is the key component of the ethos of the extraordinary bonds of a shared vicarious experience ensconced in a transcendent collective memory.

The Israeli center holds, and it does so because the Holocaust, an evil of

---

"This literal interpretation was repeatedly declared to be the correct one by those involved in drafting the resolution. On October 29, 1969, for example, the British Foreign Secretary told the House of Commons the withdrawal envisaged by the resolution would not be from 'all the territories.' [Emphasis added by author.] *When asked to explain the British position later, Lord Caradon said: 'It would have been wrong to demand that Israel return to its positions of June 4, 1967, because those positions were undesirable and artificial.'*" Jewish Virtual Library, "U.N. Security Council: The Meaning of Resolution 242."

unimaginable dimensions and the bonding, primal element of Jewish identity,[54] is enveloped in the national narrative of the return of Jews to Judea and Samaria (which is how Israeli Jews refer to the West Bank) after expulsion more than two thousand years ago. Jewish Israeli interviewees rarely mentioned the "Final Solution"; indeed, they did so only when I specifically addressed it. Why not? The Holocaust is a *given*.

In a 2009 survey of Jewish Israelis, 98 percent stated that "remembering the Holocaust" is a "guiding principle" of their life, more so than feeling part of the Jewish people, feeling part of Israeli society, or even living in Israel.[55] The Holocaust rewired the brain of the Israeli Jews—indeed, of Jews everywhere. The Holocaust is omnipresent, the core of their identity as an acquired living memory.[56] "Every day," says Anat Hoffman, executive director of the Israel Religious Action Center, "everyone experiences a 'Holocaust moment.'"[57] Second- and third-generation carriers of the Holocaust legacy and memory contribute to maintaining the Holocaust as an integral part of Israeli life.* There are constant references to the Holocaust in the media, books, art, and cinema; it is a mandatory part of school curricula. Of high school students, 76 percent say that the Holocaust affects their worldview, and 94 percent say they are committed to preserving the memory of the Holocaust.[58]

None of this should come as a surprise. Since the 1960s, Yom Ha'Shoah has been an official holiday dedicated to remembrance. For two minutes, sirens sound throughout the country. All activity comes to a complete halt. The entire population stands at silent attention. "For many decades," the highly respected rabbi Michael Lerner writes in *Embracing Israel/Palestine*, "one of the rituals of induction to the IDF, had been to climb the steep hills leading to Masada, the ancient fortress where the Jewish revolutionary extremists who rebelled against Rome in 67–70 CE found refuge and later launched new attacks on the occupying forces. When the Romans finally

*No matter what reparations have been made, mea culpas profusely offered ad nauseam, forgiveness sought, memorials built, tears belatedly wept on their behalf, Jews *cannot* forget—and cannot be expected to forget. The world did close its eyes to the Holocaust. Even today, additional information of the breadth of its far-reaching tentacles continues to be unearthed. The latest research has catalogued that between 1933 and 1945 there were some 42,500 Nazi camps—ghettos, slave labor, and "killing camps"—spread throughout Europe, with an estimate of between 15 and 20 million people either imprisoned or murdered. "The Holocaust Just Got More Shocking," *New York Times*, March 1, 2013, http://www.nytimes.com/2013/03/03/sunday-review/the-holocaust-just-got-more-shocking.html?pagewanted=all&_r=0. The sole purpose of these camps was the eradication of all Jews, a genocide so thorough that there could be no recovery.

breached the fortress . . . , in 73 CE, they found close to one thousand bodies—the scene of a mass suicide."[59]

Here, he says, is an implicit message central to the Zionist theology of Israel: "Unlike those diaspora Jews who failed to resist and were marched into the gas chambers of Europe singing pious religious songs about the coming of the messiah, we, the new breed of Jews, will never again give up our state. If necessary, we will follow the example of the Masada Jews, who killed themselves rather than let others kill them." Unless you understand "how deeply this message is embedded in the collective unconscious," he says, "you cannot understand Israel." There are still plenty of Jews, he explains, "who have absorbed the Masada complex into their deepest beings—such that if faced with a perceived return to the vulnerability of statelessness, they might choose the path of Masada rather than surrender . . ." And although "most Israelis would not follow a destructive path, they'd find it difficult to constrain a militant minority who articulated the fear of the majority that the Jewish people were about to once again face a dangerous period of total powerlessness."[60]

Moreover, every year the IDF organizes trips for thousands of officers, accompanied by a Holocaust survivor, to Auschwitz-Birkenau or other death camps in Poland.[61] "The danger," Lerner concludes, "is that we are unwittingly strengthening a kind of narcissistic entitlement. This gets Jews and Israelis off the hook for confronting their own aggression and developing a self-awareness that they split off and project onto Palestinians, Arabs, or all non-Jews in order to see themselves as the eternal victim."[62] Hence the sense of hereditary victimhood and the mantle of exceptionalism that accompanies it.

The Jews, Lerner maintains, were never afforded the space in which they could properly grieve the Holocaust and the losses that emanated from it.[63] When Israel was founded, he contends, Jews were not in a position to acknowledge to themselves the extent of the pain and trauma they had suffered, and the added trauma of having to fight for survival in Palestine. With the Holocaust such an omniferous presence, they do not believe the rest of the world can ever understand how a concatenation of factors can trigger automatic, perhaps even unconscious, fearful associations with it, and hence the proliferation of possible existential threats.[64] For Jews, it is not possible to put the trauma of the Holocaust "behind us."

Every challenge to the narrative only reinforces the collective memory. Therefore an ethos of permanent alertness to perceived threat is seen as a prerequisite for national survival and is an integral part of the political environment that permeates every aspect of Israeli society. This sense of having to protect against threats, real or otherwise, has bred a sense of exceptionalism. It is a self-validating belief that there are few red lines Israel cannot cross in the name of defending itself. Therefore, Israel's actions, according to the Israeli perspective, cannot be judged in conformity with universal norms but must be understood in the context of the driving imperatives of its need to survive and the belief that in the end Jewish Israelis are on their own, all alone, in a small country surrounded by over 100 million people in hostile Arab states that would wipe it off the face of the earth, given the opportunity.

This sense of omnipresent threat and the need to defend aggressively against perceived threat make it impossible for Israelis to view themselves as victimizing others. When the UN appointed the Goldstone Commission to investigate possible war crimes following Israel's invasion of Gaza (initiated in December 2008), the conclusion that *both* Israel and Hamas had committed war crimes and that Israel may have been guilty of committing crimes against humanity ignited a firestorm of fury across Israel.* The very suggestion that a people who had been the victims of what was perhaps the most reprehensible crime against humanity in history—one that had almost resulted in the extinction of the Jewish people—might have committed war crimes themselves was incomprehensible. Any insinuation that Israeli actions may have victimized another people is inimical to Israelis' understanding of themselves. The government, which had refused all cooperation during the commission's investigation, condemned the report in the harshest language,[65] and with U.S. connivance the report never reached the Security Council—it was buried among the rubble of thousands of UN reports on one thing or another and became fodder for academic studies.

Many Jewish Israeli interviewees justified Israel's exempting itself from compliance with UN resolutions, injunctions of the Geneva Conventions, the

*The commission's frame of reference was to investigate possible war crimes following Israel's two-month invasion of Gaza (December 2008/January 2009). Surrendering to relentless pressure, Goldstone withdrew his concurrence with the finding that the Jewish Israelis had been guilty of crimes against humanity, saying more information had come to light that caused him to drop the charge; but his fellow commissioners stuck with their findings. The Goldstone Commission Report can be found at http://www2.ohchr.org/english/bodies/hrcouncil/specialsession/9/FactFindingMission.html. For a brief bio of Richard Goldstone and the commissions he headed, see http://www.law.stanford.edu/profile/richard-goldstone. Richard Goldstone, "Reconsidering the Goldstone Report on Israel and War Crimes," Washington Post, April 1, 2011, http://www.washingtonpost.com/opinions/reconsidering-the-goldstone-report-on-israel-and-war-crimes/2011/04/01/AFg111JC_story.html. Goldstone later retracted, although the other two members of the commission stood by their findings. See Ethan Bronner and Isabel Kershner, "Head of U.N. Panel Regrets Saying Israel Intentionally Killed Gazans," *New York Times*, April 2, 2011, http://www.nytimes.com/2011/04/03/world/middleeast/03goldstone.html.

human-rights yardsticks of both Amnesty International and Human Rights Watch, and its own human-rights organizations because these reports and resolutions are not contextualized in an understanding that Israel's overriding imperative is for Israel *itself* to guarantee its existence. Like the Goldstone Commission, reports of investigative international commissions end up in the trash can.[66]

And likewise, too, they assert that in the Arab world the acknowledgment that the Holocaust had occurred is invariably coupled with caveats that it had not occurred on the scale documented in the West: perhaps one or two million killed, but not the six million claimed by Jews.* Israel dismisses UN resolutions as either anti-Semitic or attempts to delegitimize the state of Israel. As they see it, the many countries that came into existence when they secured self-determination after World War II had no knowledge of Jewish history. Most had emerged after bitter conflicts with their occupying colonial powers; all could identify with the Palestinians and their "struggle" against another colonial power; few, if any, would ever give the benefit of doubt to the Jewish state. Many nations that routinely voted in the UN to condemn Israel for violating the human rights of Palestinians were dictatorships where human rights were squashed and opposition suppressed. Israel simply dismisses them as inconsequential hypocrites. Israelis are well aware of comparisons between their presence in Palestine and South Africa–style apartheid.[67] They dismiss them as ludicrous slurs that smack of latent anti-Semitism. How easily the world forgets the nearly two *millennia* of persecution the Jews have endured. Thus, the word "apartheid" serves only to harden the resolve that Israel will forever be the Jewish state, home of the Jewish people.† Besides, they cannot be "occupiers" in the West

*See: Achcar, *Arabs and the Holocaust.* I have interviewed many Muslims/Arabs during the last several years, and I always ask them about the Holocaust. Most answers have been dismissive, but none have denied it. Very few would concur with a figure of six million; a million or two perhaps, but nothing more. The Holocaust is a Western concern. They had nothing to do with the Holocaust yet they had to pay the price for it. (A 2014 Anti-Defamation League report stated that about a quarter of the world's population, or one in four adults, were anti-Semitic; only 54 percent had heard of the Holocaust, and two out of three had not heard of the Holocaust or thought the historical account was inaccurate. See Naftali Bendavid, "Poll Says Anti-Semitism Is Global Matter," *Wall Street Journal*, May 13, 2014, http://online.wsj.com/news/articles/SB100014240527 02304655304579551974194329920, and Saban Center for Middle East Policy, "2010 Israeli Arab/ Palestinian Public Israeli Arab/Palestinian Public Opinion Survey," http://www.brookings .edu/~/media/research/files/reports/2010/12/09%20israel%20public%20opinion%20telhami/ israeli_arab_powerpoint.

†Alon Liel, former Israeli ambassador to South Africa, interview with the author, June 2011. "So people in the extreme left say, okay, we better live in a democratic state than in an apartheid

Bank, because their stay is temporary, pending a peace settlement. (After half a century, many have a convoluted definition of "temporary.")[68]

In 2012, 138 countries voted to approve the Palestinian application for observer status at the UN (only the United States, Canada, Israel, and six minor states opposed the resolution).[69] A petulant Netanyahu responded to the Palestinians' successful bid by authorizing plans for settlements in the E1 corridor abutting Ma'ale Adumim,* the disposition of which in future negotiations will determine whether the Palestinians have a contiguous state with direct access to East Jerusalem. The governments of major Western powers, among Israel's closest allies, called in Israel's ambassadors—a first—for a rebuke, but Netanyahu responded to his domestic and international critics by defiantly approving a further round of settlement construction.[70] In the end, German chancellor Angela Merkel met with Netanyahu in Berlin and administered the obligatory slap on the wrist. But her government subsequently announced several new measures to strengthen the economic ties between the two nations.[71]

Israel, if it can, will never let Western Europe off its guilt-ridden hook, and for its part Western Europe is still sensitive to the fact that it abetted the anti-Semitism that facilitated the Final Solution and is reluctant to offer more than mild criticism of Israel's actions, let alone turn off the spigots of aid.[72] As for the United States, Israel rests comfortably. It knows it can count on U.S. support in just about all circumstances. But on occasion the relationship becomes frayed. Israel has not forgotten that President George H. W. Bush, prodded by James Baker, his secretary of state, pulled the plug on $10 billion in loan guarantees when Israeli prime minister Yitzhak Shamir refused to accept the condition that the money would not be spent on settlements.[73] Nor was the Obama administration's announcement that it would work with the technocratic government, Hamas and Fatah agreed to, that would govern the PA between August 2014 and promised elections in November 2014 well received.[74] The already damaged relationship between Obama and Netanyahu would further deteriorate.

> > < <

The bottom line for Israeli Jews is that the West, even America, cannot be *completely* trusted in every conceivable situation. In fact, when the issue of Iran's nuclear capability came to the forefront and the international talks in

---

state. But because the left will not come to power and the right will stay in power they will not be given their rights. They will not be given their full rights and this apartheid scenario is frightening, very frightening."

*See chapter 7, page 208.

Geneva got under way in November 2013 to resolve the threat, what the United States and nations in the West saw as "breakthroughs" were scathingly rubbished by Netanyahu.[75] Obama's visit to Cairo but not Tel Aviv or Jerusalem shortly after taking office in 2009 deeply alienated Netanyahu, and the accusation that Obama was not pro-Israel stuck.

The deeply held convictions of "never again" and "we are alone" combine to create a powerful juggernaut of self-justification of whatever measures are taken to safeguard Israel's national interests and eliminate perceived threats.* Judgment is distorted because the consequences of embarking on a particular course of action are not subject to a cost-benefit analysis in terms of the possible repercussions in the international community. If the threat is "existential"—the definition of which is very different to America or Europe than to Israel—to employ Netanyahu's word regarding Iran's nuclear capability, the repercussions simply do not matter.

A poll by the Anti-Defamation League in the United States found that 82 percent of Jewish Israeli youngsters between the ages of fifteen and eighteen believe that Israel faces a significant threat of extermination; 77 percent of adults agree.[76] Certainly many of the Jewish Israelis I interviewed cling to the belief that the real agenda of the Palestinians is to drive the Jewish people out of Palestine and into the proverbial sea, and that no peace agreement in the world would deter them if they could find an opportune way.

The results of longitudinal studies of Israeli adolescents and young adults do not suggest that the power of this narrative is on the wane. Just the opposite. They suggest a coming Israel that will be more anti-Palestinian Israeli, with a disturbing propensity to expressions of hatred (25 percent); more ultra nationalistic; more suspicious of the Arab world, more right wing; less committed to democratic values; less tolerant and will have little trust in most institutions other than the defense forces.†[77] Young people put far less emphasis on peace as the primary goal of the state and far more on its Jewishness.

*Prime Minister Netanyahu told President Obama to stop second guessing him on Hamas during the 2014 Gaza war. Similarly Secretary of State John Kerry was criticized for his peace initiative that brought in Qatar and Turkey. See "Netanyahu to US: 'Don't Ever Second-Guess Me Again,'" YNetNews.com, August 2, 2014, http://www.ynetnews.com/articles/0,7340,L-4553575,00.html; Matthew Lee, "Netanyahu Tells U.S. 'Not to Ever Second Guess Me Again' on Hamas," *Huffington Post*, August 2, 2014, http://www.huffingtonpost.com/2014/08/02/netanyahu-hamas_n_5643852.html; and Ron Kampeas, "Israel's Spat with Kerry Fueled by Turkey, Qatar," *Haaretz*, July 29, 2014, http://www.haaretz.com/news/diplomacy-defense/1.607755.

†According to the Third Youth Study, carried out in 2010, when Jewish youth were asked what feelings arise when they think about Arabs, most responded neutrally: 54 percent chose "neither positive nor negative," but the second most frequent answer, at 25 percent, was "hatred."

> > < <

On the operational level—the tactical and strategic level—the Israeli narrative can be condensed into just one word: *security*. It trumps every other consideration.

"What has changed since the Holocaust is our determination and ability to defend ourselves by ourselves," Netanyahu said at the Holocaust Memorial in 2013. Then he vowed: "We won't leave our fate in the hands of others, not even the best of our friends."

Moreover, he left little doubt as to what Israel would do if it decides Iran has reached the ultimate point of nuclear capability, paraphrasing the Passover Haggadah: "In every generation there are those who rise up against us to destroy us. In every generation, every one of us must think of himself as though he has survived the Holocaust and established the state [of Israel]. In every generation, we must ensure that there will not be another Holocaust."[78]

As a direct result of Palestinian suicide bombers and militants, intent on committing acts of violence, crossing into Israel from the West Bank, work began on the separation barrier in 2002, making it virtually impossible for Palestinians to enter Israel, unless they have permits to do so. The barrier has had the desired impact: Between 2007 and 2012 militants carried out seven suicide attacks, killing 24 and wounding 201.[79] If the barrier is ever finished, it will encircle most of the West Bank but leave 10 percent, including the major settlements, on the Israeli side—a maneuver, Palestinians believe, to predetermine the borders of a future Palestinian state. In any event, there have been no PLO militant attacks, thanks to both the barrier and Mahmoud Abbas's 2005 directive that the PLO abandon armed resistance, forgoing violence and henceforth seeking self-determination for Palestine through peaceful means only.

In Gaza, between 1967 and 2005, when Israel unilaterally withdrew, 87 Israeli civilians and 179 members of the IDF were killed, and 1,074 civilians and 3,777 members of the IDF were wounded.[80] In 2007, after Hamas crushed Fatah and took control of the Strip, Israel fortified the wall that seals Gaza from Israel, detaining all Gazans within the Gaza Strip and prohibiting travel from Gaza to the West Bank and vice versa—an important subject for future discussion. The walls have afforded Israelis an unprecedented sense of freedom from terrorism. Would they settle for any negotiated agreement that would lower that sense of security? It's hard to imagine.

Among the recent developments that have altered the matrix of Israel's security concerns: the cataclysmic ruptures in Egypt; the relentlessly brutal and dehumanizing civil war in Syria, where jihadists from foreign countries and Hezbollah do much of the fighting; porous borders between Turkey and Syria; the possibly destabilizing impact of the flow of refugees from Syria into Lebanon and Jordan; the self-described Islamic State (ISIS);[81] possible jihadist threats to Jordan; the hand of Iran everywhere; its dissatisfaction with the talks of the P5+1* with Iran over denuclearization; and, of course, the aftermath of the 2014 Gaza war. No land-for-peace swap or other offer will ever take precedence over these security concerns. No agreement will ever negate the Israelis' prerogative to engage in military incursions in a demilitarized Palestine in pursuit of terrorists. And under no circumstances whatsoever will there be an FSA, unless Hamas and Islamic Jihad and other militant groups decommission their weaponry and destroy their inventories. Wishful thinking.

Every Jewish Israeli interviewee homed in on the Israeli withdrawal from Gaza in 2005, which was framed as a unilateral act of goodwill. Here, they said, Palestinians were given the opportunity to create their Singapore; but rather than build for their people, Hamas used it to attack Israel, launching hundreds of rockets into southern Israel, often in numbers sufficient enough to result in war.†

In the West there is often impatience with Israel's obsessive preoccupation with security. Palestinians are particularly puzzled, since Israel possesses the sixth most powerful military machine in the world and enjoys total dominance over the capabilities of any army in the Arab world. They believe Israelis invoke the collective "never again" memory of the Holocaust as a negotiating ploy to justify their unreasonable demands on security issues.

In this assessment they are mistaken. Israeli security concerns are not a ploy. Some aspects of what Israel sees as a threat to delegitimize it in the global community are real; some are imagined. It doesn't matter. Many of Israel's specific tactical and strategic fears are grounded in circumstances on the ground; others are not. It doesn't matter.

The fact that a fear is based on an imagined reality and is therefore "baseless" doesn't make the experience of that fear any less real. Illusionary

*"P5+1: France, Germany, and the United Kingdom (the EU3); China, Russia, and the United States joined the three European countries in 2006 as part of a format known as the "P5+1"—in reference to the permanent five members of the UN Security Council plus Germany." See: http://www.armscontrol.org/factsheets/Iran_Nuclear_Proposals.

†The Gaza wars of 2008–09, 2012, and 2014.

forebodings are no less real—to individuals or to cultures—than more grounded ones. Memories of the Holocaust do trigger Israel's perceptions of existential threat. So do memories of the intifadas. So does Iran's nuclear capability. The enemy is always out there, and so is its ultimate goal. Only the enemy is real.[82]

The Israelis' collective memory of near annihilation and the actual circumstances of a hostile region are conditions that have no cure. With appropriate defense antidotes, they can be arrested and go into remission for a period of time, but they cannot be eliminated. Even if, by some miracle, the Palestinians should accede to every single security demand, the Israelis would still fear that a Palestinian government in the future would be unable to meet its obligations, not out of malevolence but simply because it is not psychologically equipped to do so. Of course, who knows what new threats and fears the future may bring? One could say that the fears are self-fulfilling and self-perpetuating, since preemptive actions can provoke a response or may result in a cycle of violence. Impregnable security measures will remain the Israelis' sine qua non in negotiations.

> > < <

Jewish Israeli interviewees proved as adept as the Palestinians at not directly addressing uncomfortable questions. Like their Palestinian counterparts, they have internalized the rationales for their situation. Their responses suggest that the Israelis believe that the Palestinians are not as deeply wedded to their nationalism as Israeli Jews are to their own. They see the Palestinians' aspirations as essentially negative—that is, *not* wanting a Jewish presence on the land of Palestine, rather than passionately wanting a Palestinian state per se. While most would not agree with Golda Meir's widely debunked remark that "there is no such thing as a Palestinian people," many continue to harbor suspicions, perhaps at some subconscious level, that Palestinian nationalism is only a collage of events and materials hastily patched together to justify territorial claims. Shlomo Ben-Ami, head of the Israeli negotiation team at Camp David, puts it this way: "The Palestinians related to the emergence of the Zionist onslaught by negating the right of the Zionists to establish themselves in this part of the land, and at no moment did they believe that they should present a political alternative. They only wanted the Zionist penetration stopped."

Accordingly, he argues, "Palestinian nationalism did not conform to the rise of nationalisms in Europe in the nineteenth century."[83]

The implication is that if an emerging nationalism does not neatly fit into the European paradigm, something is amiss. It must be a flawed and inferior and illegitimate nationalism.

The Israelis see themselves as having assiduously invested their labor and their capital into building the institutions of a modern nation-state even prior to the official establishment of the Israeli state in 1948. A decimated people, they turned victimhood into vibrant nationalism. Meanwhile, from their perspective, the Palestinians invest little of themselves in state building, accomplish little, and instead sit back and wait for history to vindicate them. Ben-Ami is far from alone in comparing the Jews, who worked their butts off to advance their position even if the returns were incremental, to the Palestinians, who are passive, luxuriating in the "poor me" posture, more disposed to globe-trotting to sell their victimhood than to getting down to the nitty-gritty of what will undoubtedly be tough negotiations to resolve the problem.

Governing institutions such as the Palestinian Authority are not the result of collective collaboration of the Palestinian people but are reliant on foreign subsidies that ward off financial meltdown; if the subsidies were withdrawn, the PA would collapse, with disastrous consequences.[84] "The Palestinians did not know how to create state institutions," Ben-Ami asserts. "The entire international community had to come here and put pressure on Arafat, appoint a prime minister, a parliament, elections, because to him none of these things were imperatives. This is what they define as their homeland, and they never thought of it in terms of a modern state."[85] But why should the Palestinians have to think in "statehood" terms when the concept is a European import and alien to the way they had been governed for centuries? Why should conformity, with the architecture of nation-states and concepts of nationalism that emerged in Europe in the mid–nineteenth century and provided the paradigm for a Jewish state and Jewish nationalism, become the defining criterion for the Palestinian right to self-determination? The questions don't compute for the Israelis.

Jewish Israeli interviewees were unanimous in blaming the Palestinians for missed opportunities and failure. They believe Abba Eban had it exactly right when he famously said that "the Arabs [Palestinians] never miss an opportunity to miss an opportunity,"[86] a remark frequently quoted, usually with an air of condescension. Israelis are very comfortable discussing the Palestinian leadership's shortcomings and what they should do instead.

The Israeli interviewees rarely referred to the Palestinians as "occupied" people, with Israel the occupier. The preferred nomenclature is "disputed" territories.[87] They had little to say about the restrictions placed on Palestinians.

They know that Palestinians are poorer, yes (much poorer, in fact: the per-capita income disparity is thirty to one), but Israelis have little knowledge of Palestinians' daily circumstances. The separation barrier cuts them off from any interaction with Palestinians, who have been psychologically erased from their consciousness. A cultivated ignorance protects Israelis from comprehending the impact of hundreds of checkpoints, arbitrary detention without trial, the military presence in the West Bank that "rules" as it sees fit and acts without being answerable to any authority.

Not a single Jewish Israeli interviewee raised the matter of settler violence, despite its thorough documentation and the frequent references to "price tag wars" in the media.* No one questioned the injustice of the special roads for settlers' exclusive use, speeding their journeys to Tel Aviv and Jerusalem while Palestinians have to navigate winding, circuitous routes and bypass roads, with checkpoints, to get from Ramallah to Nablus.

The Palestinians' obsessive invocation of their "humiliation" does not resonate with Israelis. Given their own history of humiliation, they cannot imagine themselves as being the cause of the humiliation of others. Denial scrapes it off the mind. Recall the vehement reaction to the Goldstone Commission. Although Israel says that the occupation is temporary, after almost fifty years the temporary and the normal have become coterminous. Indeed, almost 80 percent of Jewish Israelis age fifty or younger were born into an Israel in which the West Bank is regarded as an extension of Israel proper. They were raised to see it as part of the normalcy of life and to see all Palestinians, with whom they have little or no contact, as a potential existential threat—"terrorists" who must be kept on a tight leash.

Just as Palestinians do not want to sully their narrative by acknowledging the deficiencies in their own culture and institutions that have contributed to their current precarious status so, too, were Jewish Israeli interviewees disinclined to consider how the drastic asymmetry of economic and military power might have a corrupting influence on *both* cultures. Palestinians are mired in poverty? Palestinians are Arabs. As such, they have a different value system from the West, different attitudes toward time and work. Beyond that charged stereotype, the economic disparity is not something the Israelis spend much time thinking about.

They definitely do not want to consider that decades of humiliation and

*"In recent years, settlers have carried out violent acts under the slogan 'price tag.' These are acts of violence aimed at the Palestinian population and Israeli security forces." "Settler Violence: Lack of Accountability," B'Tselem, last updated June 3, 2012, http://www.btselem.org/settler_violence.

dispossession may have so mutilated the Palestinian psyche that the people have, in order to survive psychologically, internalized the humiliations and passively accept subordination until, of course, it erupts into outbursts of violence. The IDF arrests fifteen-year-olds for throwing stones.[88] Is it disturbing that the ordinary Israeli believes that the arrests are justified, that the kids need to be taught a lesson, that they are probably budding terrorists? My interviewees are appalled only that the Palestinians' behavior elicits sympathy in the West, which theoretically shares Israeli values.

Jewish Israelis I spoke to rejected out of hand the idea that Israel is the impediment to the peace process. On the contrary, they asserted that Israel has actively promoted a final resolution to the conflict for over two decades. In negotiations, according to their perspective, it is Israel that always puts "bold" proposals on the table while the Palestinians endlessly prevaricate. "The Palestinians," Ben-Ami said, "think there is no need to be urgent. There will always be another opportunity. I sometimes feel that another UN resolution condemning Israel has become the elixir of life for Palestinian nationalism, whereas the elixir of life should be the resolution [of the conflict]. Having Israel isolated and in the dock of the tribunal of the international community has become substitute for the real thing. This is a clash of mentalities." Jewish Israeli interviewees did not see any contradiction between Israel's avowed efforts to promote the peace process and the construction of settlements for up to 500,000 in the West Bank, or the Judaization of East Jerusalem, or the acceleration of both initiatives during Netanyahu's first term and a massive acceleration during his second term.[89] They were almost dismissive of the idea that the settlements are a barrier to peace: Once negotiations determine final borders, they assert, all settlements outside the borders would be dismantled and if necessary up to 100,000 settlers evacuated. This is a rational, clinical analysis that misses the point: Jewish Israelis do not take into account the humiliation Palestinians feel as they *hear* Israelis talk peace but *see* Israelis gobble up their land.

At a conference examining what went wrong at Camp David, Yossi Ginossar, a member of the Israeli delegation and former senior official in Shin Bet,* brought the humiliation of Palestinians to the forefront of the discussion. He said:

*Shin Bet is Israel's internal intelligence service.

> I have believed that until Israelis humanize Palestinians as a society and as individuals, and thus also rationalize the Israeli–Palestinian conflict, the conflict will not be ripe for the conclusion of any peace agreement. [Our governments have] failed to humanize Palestinian society in the eyes of the Israeli public and make Israelis see Palestinians as a normal society. . . . As a society we must learn to treat Palestinians as human beings who have the same authenticity that we ascribe to ourselves. . . . I believe we are not yet ready to do so.[90]

His Israeli colleagues took little heed.

But on this account they cannot be faulted; Palestinians do not listen either. The constancy of the clamor of both to assert their rights to which their narratives entitle them leaves little room for listening on either side. The deafness is self-imposed and predetermines that negotiations on a two-state solution will always find barren ground.

Chapter 2

Dueling Narratives and Addiction to Narrative

The Palestinian perspective is anchored in the Great Catastrophe, the *Nakba*, and the ensuing occupation of their homeland. The Israeli perspective is anchored in the belated return to their homeland and the Holocaust. Both claim the same land. The people who lost their homeland—the Palestinians—feel humiliation and demand restorative justice. The people who won theirs—the Israelis—feel historic vindication and an obsession with security to protect themselves from the losers. The twain will never meet.

For seven years (2002–2009), three highly respected academics, Sami Adwan, professor of education, Bethlehem University; Dan Bar-On, PhD., department of behavioral sciences, Ben Gurion University (deceased Sept 4, 2008), and Eyal Naveh, professor of history, Tel Aviv University, supervised a group of Israeli and Palestinian teachers working under the auspices of the Peace Research Institute in the Middle East (PRIME) to develop a history text drawing on the two narratives with a view to creating a single "bridging" narrative.[1]

The teachers were unable to craft the document. "After the renewal of widespread violence—after the breakout of the Al Aqsa Intifada," Adwan et al. write in their book, *Side by Side*, the teachers reached "the painful conclusion that no such bridging narrative appears likely to be viable among our people at the grassroots level for some time, perhaps not for generations to come. The mutual suspicion, hatred, and poisoning of the minds among both peoples in relation to the 'other' have become so intense that sustaining a common bond has become impossible, except within very small and exclusive elite groups on each side."[2]

In place of the common narrative, the teachers developed two *parallel* narratives. In the book the authors examined the two sides' understandings of the same events side by side. They found little overlap of understanding. The authors note that "in our teachers' seminars we observed that there was a constant tension between the fact that the two narratives were regarded equally, whereas outside the seminar room there was a continuous power of asymmetry between the parties to the conflict; Israel's dominance and occupation of the Palestinians in the occupied territories and the domination of the Palestinian minority by the Jewish majority within the State of Israel."[3] Israeli Jews, on the other hand, "tend to perceive themselves as a minority in a hostile Muslim Middle East and thereby construct an opposite asymmetry of feeling inferior."[4]

Animosity is rife, outright hatred not uncommon. Distrust of the other's motives and ultimate aspirations is almost total. Each believes the other wants to get rid of it; each wishes the other did not exist. Polarization is virtually absolute. The other has become "the other." Over sixty years of repression under the boot of an occupying force (the Palestinian perspective) and in fear of retaliatory terror attacks (the Israeli perspective) attitudes have hardened. Each sees itself as the real victim, and their respective behaviors reflect their perceptions of themselves as such. Studies with Jewish Israeli and Palestinian participants have found that individuals who are perceived (and perceive themselves) as victims become socially "exempt" from recognizing and taking responsibility for the pain they cause the "other." They become exempt from accusations of having perpetrated aggressive acts against the other.[5] Jewish Israelis are comfortable with their rationale for having to police Palestinians as they do, and the Palestinians are comfortable with their rationale for acts of terrorism that justly counter the inhumane way they are policed. Because each conceives of itself as the victim, neither views its actions as those of an aggressor.

In the last round of talks (August 2013–April 2014),* even though the matter was outside the agreed parameters, Prime Minister Netanyahu threw a wrench in the works when he insisted that the Palestinians must publicly recognize Israel as "the Jewish homeland" *before* the talks could get down to the really serious business of negotiating a peace.[6] Such recognition, he said repeatedly, "is the real key to peace," "the minimal requirement," and "an essential condition."[7] On another occasion he said, "The core of this conflict has never been borders and settlements—it's about one thing: the persistent refusal to accept the Jewish state in any border."[8] It is his drumbeat. Talks are dross unless this demand is addressed a priori. Addressing the AIPAC conference in Washington in March 2014, he hammered the point home: "It's time for the Palestinians to stop denying history," he declared. "Just as Israel is prepared to recognize a Palestinian state, the Palestinians must be prepared to recognize a Jewish state." He called explicitly for President

*Direct negotiations between Israel and the Palestinians began on July 29, 2013. Talks collapsed within days of the deadline on April 29, 2014.

Abbas to "recognize the Jewish state." In doing so, he told Abbas, "you would be telling your people, the Palestinians, that while we might have a territorial dispute, the right of the Jewish people to a state of their own is beyond dispute. [Y]ou would finally [make it] clear that you are truly prepared to end the conflict."[9]

The PLO rejected his demand out of hand.

To anyone who is not an Israeli or a Palestinian, the term "Jewish state"—for a country whose population is already about one quarter non-Jewish—is an ambiguous misnomer. But for Palestinians and Israeli Jews it brings into sharp relief the Gordian knot of their opposing narratives. It is an abbreviated code for articulating two crucial components of Israel's a priori, nonnegotiable demands that challenge three main tenets of the Palestinian narrative.

First, to recognize "the Jewish state" would require Palestinians to accept that Israel is the exclusive homeland of the Jewish people. Second, it would explicitly concede Palestinian acquiescence that the refugees have no right of return and implicitly concede that Israel bears no responsibility for their exodus. Third, it would undermine the prospects of a Palestinian state with East Jerusalem as its capital.

Conceding the right of return would abnegate the *Nakba*. The *Nakba* is one of the building blocks that concretized a cohesive Palestinian national identity post-1949; such a concession would undermine the very foundation of what it means to be a Palestinian. In other words, it's a concession no Palestinian leader could make.[10] Finally, if Israel is the homeland for the Jews, the future of Palestinian Israelis becomes problematic—up to 1.6 million could have their citizenship revoked.

"The core of the Palestinian conflict is the refugee problem," says Muhammad Shtayyeh, a senior Palestinian negotiator, "and it's the most complicated one. For us, the cause of the refugees launched the Palestinian revolution in 1965, two years before the occupation of the West Bank. Therefore, the issue of refugees is the crucial issue. Without solving it, you will not have resolved the whole problem."[11] The responses of both Palestinian and Jewish Israeli interviewees were invariably contextualized in their respective narratives. Likewise, twenty-five years of putative peacemaking is littered with evidence that often enough the two sides cannot even agree on what was the *substance* of the conversations they had conducted on core issues. These are not just "two ships passing in the night." Nor does the metaphor of "parallel worlds" suffice. Israelis and Palestinians live in parallel universes, and the radical asymmetry of power—with the Palestinians' behavior shaped by weakness, the Israelis' by strength—only reinforces the *dueling* narratives.

"Parity of esteem," in the parlance of negotiation experts, is a simple concept but requires a fundamental reorientation of behavior on both sides. Each says to the other: "I know your narrative and I *reject* it in its entirety, yet I *accept* your right to define your own narrative as you wish, and I will *respect* that right and its aspirations." The important component is *respect*; respect is more embracive than trust. Until each side reaches a level of understanding of the other's narrative that facilitates a *willingness* to accord parity of esteem, peace agreements will likely falter, perhaps not immediately but in a corrosive ambience that slowly emerges and is conducive to disregarding some of their provisions. Peace agreements are pieces of paper. The task of translating them into *sustainable* reconciliation is a long and difficult process; former protagonists are in "recovery." Unless they nurture that recovery, their peace agreement will fall apart or lapse into "frozen" pacts.

In Israel and Palestine there is no parity of esteem for the respective narratives and therefore no trust. This is why the onset of *any* negotiation is often *not* welcomed by either the leadership or the constituencies of either side. Instead, the prospect brings latent fears to the foreground, and the leaderships play to these fears, feeding their constituencies the same stale and divisive pronouncements about "the other" that have been repeated ad nauseam over decades. They engage in debilitating tit-for-tat exchanges, talk only about what the other side has to do, what the other side needs to tell its people, never about what they themselves have to do, what their own people need to understand. All this prepares the way, should the talks collapse, for one more repetition of the blame game and violence, which becomes self-fulfilling and self-motivating.

The Palestinian and Israeli leaderships, over twenty-five years of negotiations in one form or another, have made no effort to *prepare* their respective constituencies for change, to spell out unambiguously the scope and nature of the compromises and sacrifices they would be called on to accept if they truly want to resolve the conflict. For example: that for the Palestinians there will be no right of return; and for the Israelis there will be no undivided Jerusalem. Instead, the leaderships offer meaningless recitations that both sides will have to make "painful" compromises. Instead of concentrating on understanding and coming to terms with what a negotiated settlement will cost their side, they focus on the costs the other side is being asked to incur and convince themselves that the other side either cannot or will not live up to such obligations. But if one side takes no responsibility for its own part in a conflict, neither will the other side acknowledge responsibility for its part. Hence the standoff.

For the Palestinians it's simple: Israel is fully responsible for all problems stemming from 1948 and must take responsibility in order to fix them. For the Israelis it's equally simple: The Palestinians and their Arab sponsors started the 1948 war (*all* the wars, in fact) and are therefore responsible for the consequences. Both sides know that neither narrative is fully correct, but rather than explore that narrow ground where the self-justifying constructions cross, they stick adamantly to their positions. The rare attempt at a compromise is rejected. For example, Olmert in 2008 offered the following wording to Mahmoud Abbas: "Israel is sensitive and is not indifferent to the suffering of Palestinians who live in what became Israel and were forced out of their homes as a result of the conflict and then lived in misery for years."* For Olmert this was as far as Israel would go to acknowledge that it had had a significant role in creating the refugee problem. However, when I read Olmert's words to Akram Hanieh, he said they were an insufficient acknowledgment and therefore unacceptable. When the price a settlement will exact is high (and it certainly will be for both sides in this particular conflict), when different segments of each society are confused about or unsure of the direction their society should take, when there's no ultimate trust (or no trust at all) between the two parties in the conflict—add it all up and the natural inclination is to balk, back off, procrastinate, retreat into the comforts of the narrative, and blame the other for the failure.

Under these challenging circumstances, what chance is there for peace? In each community a substantial majority believes that this conflict that has immersed them in a loathing for the humanity of the other may never end. Given all the UN resolutions; years of studying maps and haggling over miniscule percentages and square meters of ground; Palestinian humiliation and passivity; Israeli exceptionalism and paranoia about existential

*Bernard Avishai, "A Plan for Peace That Still Could Be," *New York Times*, February 7, 2011, http://www.nytimes.com/2011/02/13/magazine/13Israel-t.html?pagewanted=all\. When I read Avishai's statement to Akram Hanieh that Olmert and Abbas had met on thirty-six occasions, he dismissed it. As one of Abbas's key advisers and an insider, he insisted, he would have known about these meetings; Abbas would have discussed such talks with those close to him. From Akram Hanieh, interview with the author, October 22, 2011. All quotes from Hanieh in this chapter are from this interview unless otherwise noted.

threats—given all this, it's hard to hope that resurrecting peace talks on a two-state solution that rehash the rehashed will lead to breakthroughs.

> > < <

After sixty-seven years violence persists, which only perpetuates the killing, further entrenching the two sides in their respective narratives that are the roots of the conflict and providing each with justification for its killing. Violence, actual or impending, and the fear of violence assume pivotal roles in the lives of both societies, according to Daniel Bar-Tal, Branco Weiss Professor of Research in Child Development and Education at the School of Education, Tel Aviv University, and an acclaimed Jewish Israeli scholar who studies the socio-psychological foundations of intractable conflicts and peacemaking.[12] Both sides perceive the stakes as zero-sum, winner take all.

In *Embracing Israel/Palestine*, Rabbi Michael Lerner argues that both cultures also suffer from a social form of PTSD[13] that can consume an entire culture when it is unable to return to "normal" after a grave threat or actual act of violence or abuse has triggered a hyper-alert, "fight-or-flight survival response." "The person remains in a somewhat decreased but nevertheless heightened state of attention to danger and mobilization of body and mind," he writes. "The person perceives the dangers as still being present when they are not, or interprets present dangers through the lens of past dangers that were far greater . . . may perceive her or himself to be in the same situation as the original trauma or may feel as if the current situation is so close to the original trauma as to be indistinguishable."[14] As a result, "the person may unconsciously participate in recreating dynamics that do in fact resemble the original trauma."[15]

More recently, researchers have described "continuous traumatic stress" (CTS), building on the insights associated with PTSD. CTS emerges from ongoing trauma exposure within situations of protracted conflict and violence. According to psychologists Garth Stevens and Gillian Eagle, Debra Kaminer, and Craig Higson-Smith, CTS trauma exposure is both current and to be realistically anticipated in the future, rather than being past or "post."[16]

One of the contexts in which CTS has immediate relevancy, Eagle and Kaminer, write in their seminal article "Continuous Traumatic Stress: Expanding the Lexicon of Traumatic Stress," are situations where "danger and threat are largely faceless and unpredictable, yet pervasive and substantive," that is, "low intensity warfare, in which there are frequent terrorist attacks, including upon civilian targets, or in which repressive state forces operate with impunity"—criteria the Palestinian/Israeli conflict seamlessly meets. CTS "becomes a permanent emergency, something constant and internal that colors the whole web of relations across the society and the daily calculations of its citizens." Moreover, "when the primary focus of traumatic awareness is upon anticipated danger," thinking tends to be "dominated by fantasies of what might occur and ways of avoiding this." Thus, "the mental life of the person experiencing CTS is characterized by preoccupation with thoughts about potential, future traumatic events . . . rather than with the details of a previous unprocessed event."[17]

A further significant dimension of CTS is that "the *absence* of protections from threat and danger is perhaps of equal significance as actual risk of exposure." Such situations arise where there is no "normally functional system" of law and order, especially when "the perpetrators of violence and atrocity [are] precisely those who would usually be charged with the regulation of violence and the protection of communities." Ruptures in the social order associated with the collapse of those responsible for upholding it instill "desperation and rage . . . when there is no recourse to protection and justice." In a world perceived as inherently unjust and with no means of rectification, "passivity and hopelessness," may become manifestations of "a sense of impotence or 'learned helplessness,'" and ultimately nihilism. Or members of the community may assume "control . . . in violent and threatening ways." In short, CTS may be expressed "as unbearable and unmanageable as a consequence of the rupture of the social fabric."[18]

> CTS involves exposure to a highly unpredictable environment in which it becomes useful to map out areas, sites, or even likely time periods of safety and danger. Flexible employment of defensive adaptation is required, allowing for continued engagement with the world at the same time as being able to draw upon whatever limited protections may be available at short notice, where and when required. This may translate into a high level of vigilance that becomes subliminal and habitual.[19]

The noted late Jesuit psychologist Ignacio Martín-Baró, who was among the Jesuits massacred by the Salvadoran army in 1989, summarized the responses of people living under conditions of extreme fear as revealing "a sensation of vulnerability; exacerbated alertness; a sense of impotence or loss of control over one's own life; and an altered sense of reality, making it impossible to objectively validate one's own experiences and knowledge."[20] He cites the work of the psychologist J. Samayoa who studied the behavioral changes that occur as a result of people having to adapt to war that results in dehumanization. Samayoa categorized the changes: "selective inattention and a clinging to prejudices; absolutism, idealization, and ideological rigidity; evasive skepticism; paranoid defensiveness; and hatred and desire for revenge." Moreover, "the anticipatory anxiety" that comes from "worrying if a threatening situation will occur, whether that fear is realistic or not, can permanently transform how people respond to threats." A distinguishing characteristic of CTS is the complexity of distinguishing between real and perceived or imagined threat. The lense of the imagined is more fear driven than the lense of the real. Both PTSD and CTS feed voraciously on a sense of victimization. Studies show that when a group is convinced that its culture is being persecuted, the ongoing threats link past and present.[21] Individuals categorized as enemies today are perceived as reincarnations of former adversaries, whether they belong to the same group or not.[22]

PTSD and CTS, along with perceived victimization and righteousness, distort the ways in which each group perceives its own narrative. Narratives can foster insidious and repetitive cycles of stimulus, response, and impact—patterns that resemble addictive behavior. They are elements within the functional "societal psychological (i.e., sociopsychological) infrastructure" that help societies cope with living under harsh conditions, generating "severe negative experiences, such as threat, stress, pain, exhaustion, grief, trauma, misery, and hardship, and cost, both in human and material terms."[23]

Bar-Tal refers to them as narratives of "collective memory" and the "ethos of conflict." The two have overlapping characteristics that are carefully nurtured and maintained by social institutions and political processes. They are sustained in public discourse, rituals, ceremonies, and offer mind-sets that preserve the existing order, however horrific—because an uncertain future is too terrifying.[24]

The narrative of collective memory is partial, selective, and distorted; it serves to foster group cohesion by appealing to existential threats. One's own group is both hero and victim; the history of suffering and losses gives weight to the righteousness of the cause. In contrast, the opposing group is viewed as wicked, illegitimate, and responsible for both the outbreak and the continuation of the conflict. "In other words," Bar-Tal and his colleagues write, "focusing on the injustice, harm, evil and atrocities associated with the adversary, while emphasizing one's own society as being just, moral, and human, leads society members to present themselves as victims. Beliefs about victimhood imply that the conflict was imposed by an adversary who not only fights for unjust goals, but also uses violent and immoral means to achieve them."[25]

The narrative of the present, write Bar-Tal and Gauriel Salomon, is an "ethos." An "ethos of conflict" emerges as central shared beliefs in societies undergoing long periods of intractable conflict. "The narrative of the ethos indicates to society members that their behavior is not just random but represents a coherent and systematic pattern of knowledge. This narrative implies that the decisions of society's leaders, the coordinated behavior of the members of society, and the structure and functioning of the society, are all based on coherent and comprehensive beliefs that justify and motivate members of society to accept the system and to act in a coordinated manner."[26]

The degree to which each side nurtures and adheres to its ethos of conflict determines its ability to motivate and mobilize the masses to continue the conflict, even in the face of adversity and, on occasion, defeat. It provides the rationale for the pain, suffering, stress, hardship, and dislocation. Each side's ethos is all-encompassing and all-powerful. They are complementary. They require each other.

An ethos of conflict refracts a community's shared experience through the prism of a remembered past. It also provides focal points that contribute to the continuation of the conflict.[27] Bar-Tal identified eight interrelated themes of societal beliefs that are the hallmark characteristics of intractable conflict: societal beliefs about the justness of the in-group's goals; beliefs about security; beliefs about positive collective self-image; beliefs about in-group victimization; beliefs that delegitimize the opponent; beliefs of patriotism; beliefs of unity; and beliefs about peace.[28]

Conflict narratives also serve several other functions. They shape the political process by providing meaning, clarification, and direction into highly stressful and threatening circumstances. They promote victim/persecutor dichotomies and breed in-group self-righteousness and superiority. In turn, they justify collective action—however violent it might be—by attributing it to circumstances caused by a violent, immoral, subhuman "enemy." As a result, conflict narratives inspire mobilization and action. They arouse a form of patriotism and willingness to sacrifice, both to defend and to avenge past grievances and prevent future harm, even obliteration, by the enemy. Along the way, one's own standing and collective identity is solidified, with beliefs and practices institutionalized throughout the cultural and political system.[29]

> > < <

This brings us to the key concept in this discussion: the *habits* of attitude and behavior* assiduously cultivated by both Israelis and Palestinians over the past decades that permeate their societies and have evolved into *addictions*.† As humans, our brains are wired to react reflexively; our addictions, specifically, are rooted in unconscious, or at least involuntary, reactions. They have a dysfunctional internal logic that elicits little understanding from non-addicts. The two cultures are addicted to an inextricable, intertwined nexus of factors: PTSD, victimization, fear, and demonization—the status quo, that is, because this status quo bestows, literally if perversely, the comfort of the known.

In a scathing report in 2012, the International Crisis Group (ICG) called the peace process "an addiction." It said:

> [T]he reason most often cited for maintaining the existing peace process is the conviction that halting it risks creating a vacuum that would be filled

*In *The Power of Habit: Why We Do What We Do in Life and Business* (New York: Random House, 2012), Charles Duhigg examines in depth the pioneering work of MIT researchers who began in the 1990s to explore how habits are formed and broken. "They were curious about a nub of neurological tissue known as the basal ganglia," one of the primitive structures of the brain that "control our automatic behavior, such as breathing." The basal ganglia, they found, is "central to recalling patterns and acting on them. . . ." It stores habits, even as the rest of the brain sleeps.

"Habits, scientists say, emerge because the brain is constantly looking for ways to save effort. Left to its own devices, the brain will try to make almost any routine a habit, because habits allow our minds to ramp up more often. This effort-saving instinct is a huge advantage."

†Duhigg notes: "The line separating habits and addictions is often difficult to measure. The American Society of Addiction Medicine defines addiction as 'a primary, chronic disease of brain reward, motivation, memory and related circuitry. . . .' Addiction is characterized by impairment in behavioral control, craving, inability to consistently abstain, and diminished relationships. . . . cravings are what drive habits." See Duhigg, *Power of Habit*, 59.

"In general, say many researchers, while addiction is complicated and poorly understood, many of the behaviors that we associate with it are often driven by habit. . . . A physical addiction to nicotine, for instance, lasts only as long as the chemical is in the smoker's bloodstream. . . . Many of the lingering urges that we think of as nicotine's addictive twinges are really behavioral habits asserting themselves—we crave a cigarette at breakfast a month later not because we physically need it but because we remember so fondly the rush it once provided each morning. Attacking the behaviors we think of as addictions by modifying the habits surrounding them has been shown, in clinical studies, to be one of the most effective modes of treatment. . . . [S]ome studies show that a small group of people seem predisposed to seek out addictive chemicals regardless of behavioral interventions." See Duhigg, *Power of Habit*, 69, 203.

Alcoholism is classified as an addiction and a disorder by the *Diagnostic and Statistical Manual of Mental Disorders* (*DSM-5*). Alcoholics Anonymous (AA) is widely regarded as perhaps the most effective program for treating the addiction. Writing about it, Lee Ann Kaskutas, a senior scientist at the Alcohol Research Group, writes that one part of the AA program indirectly "provides a method for attacking the habits that surround alcohol use." See Duhigg, *Power of Habit*, 306.

> with despair and chaos. The end result is that the peace process, for all its acknowledged shortcomings, over time has become a collective addiction that serves all manner of needs, reaching an agreement no longer being the main one. And so the illusion continues, for that largely is what it is. . . .
>
> The inescapable truth, almost two decades into the peace process, is that all actors are now engaged in a game of make-believe: that a resumption of talks in the current context can lead to success; that an agreement can be reached within a short timeframe; that the Quartet is an effective mediator; that the Palestinian leadership is serious about reconciliation, or the UN, or popular resistance, or disbanding the PA. This is not to say that the process itself has run its course. *Continued meetings and even partial agreements—invariably welcomed as breakthroughs—are possible precisely because so many have an interest in its perpetuation.* [Emphasis added.] But it will not bring about a durable and lasting peace. The first step in breaking what has become an injurious addiction to a futile process is to recognise that it is so—to acknowledge, at long last, that the emperor has no clothes.[30]

So how do we put the Palestinian-Israeli conflict in a "habit/addiction" context? What are the routines that became habits and what are the cues and reward systems that make these habits impervious to change? The last hundred years are strewn with them. A history of repetitions: nothing learned; habits of interaction unchanged; process unchanged; accusatory fingers unchanged; incitement unchanged; hatred unchanged. The Israelis and Palestinians are, one could say, addicted to their conflict.[31]

In *The Power of Habit*, Charles Duhigg writes that neurological researchers have found that "the process within our brain is a three-step loop. First there is a cue, a trigger that tells your brain to go into automatic mode and which habit to use. Then there is the routine, which can be physical or mental or emotional. Finally, there is a reward, which helps your brain figure out if this particular loop is worth remembering for the future. Over time this loop—cue, routine, reward—becomes more and more automatic. The cue and reward become intertwined until a powerful sense of anticipation and craving emerges. Eventually . . . a habit is born."[32]

A Palestinian-Israeli "habit/addiction" context can be illustrated using Duhigg's cue-routine-reward addiction loop. Some examples of Palestinian "cues" include persistent humiliation, victimization (*Nakba*/right-of-return narrative), powerlessness, and imposed peace-process attempts. For Israelis "cues" include persistent fear, victimization (Holocaust/anti-Semitism narrative), exceptionalism, and imposed peace-process attempts. "Routines" for Palestinians include armed and civil resistance, provocation (rockets fired from

Gaza), and unilateral actions outside of previous agreements (such as seeking UN status before reaching an agreement on borders). "Routines" for Israelis include pervasive securitization of territory and population, the overwhelming use of force and collective punishment, and unilateral actions outside of previous agreements (such as the expansion of settlements). The "reward" responses gained in both cases are placated feelings of self-righteousness, vindication, maintaining the status quo, and sustaining global attention on the conflict regardless of the negative consequences of these behaviors. The danger of addiction is that appeased feelings are temporary and routines have to be repeated in order to maintain levels of satisfaction/reward.

Among some of the habit loops that become self-perpetuating and thus addictive are (1) *cue*: U.S. intervention, *routine*: a negotiations process that repeats itself, ensuring failure, *reward*: blaming the other side for failure and attribution of actions on its part that ensure failure, reassertion of the righteousness of one's positions (narrative based); (2) *cue*: the *Nakba*, *routine*: insistence on the implementation of the right of return, knowing it is not going to happen, *reward*: end of negotiations, but an affirmation by the Palestinians to the public that this is one demand they will not yield on, coupled with a reiteration, again, of Israeli intransigence, righteousness, adherence to historical narrative; (3) *cue*: Holocaust/*Nakba*, *routine*: obsessive compulsion to remember, *reward*: solidification of identity; (4) *cue*: conflict; *routine*: ethos of conflict; *reward*: reinforcement and reaffirmation of ethos of conflict and the righteousness of one's cause; (5) *cue*: conflict, *routine*: use of disproportionate force, *reward*: threat reduced or eliminated. (The Israeli response to threat of war is to use disproportionate force, in the belief that this will eliminate the perceived threat, but the same perceived threat always reappears in a few years; Israel resorts again to the use of disproportionate force, again believing deterrence has been achieved, but the same threat appears, yet again, a few years later. Addiction literature draws on Albert Einstein's definition of insanity: the propensity to do the same thing over and over again, believing the result will be different if you just repeat it one more time. The Gaza wars of 2008–9, 2012, and 2014 are illuminating examples of this phenomenon and the unquestioning logic that sustains it.)

In *Soldiering Under Occupation*, Erella Grassiani, a lecturer in anthropology at the University of Amsterdam, identified addictive behavior among soldiers in the IDF. Her research led her to conclude that in most cases soldiers realized that their activities in the West Bank and Gaza caused harm to Palestinians. However, the majority of the soldiers did not act on this knowledge and did not try to change the situation.[33] *Routines*—whether policing at checkpoints or patrolling, which contributes to a *numbing* process, normalizing harassment and aggression in the soldier's mind—had metamorphosed into *habits*. Young soldiers internalized the feelings of dominance and power. "Corrective punishment" was often used to show who is in charge. They became *addicted* to controlling people. Sometimes soldiers arrested Palestinians for no reason other than to break the monotony. Those who experience war, she concludes, may find it exhilarating and addictive.[34] In *War Is a Force That Gives Us Meaning*, Pulitzer Prize–winning journalist Chris Hedges, drawing on his experience as a war correspondent, writes:

> The rush of battle is a potent and often lethal addiction.... It dominates culture, distorts memory, corrupts language, and infects everything around it.... The communal march against an enemy generates a warm, unfamiliar bond with our neighbors, our community, our nation, wiping out unsettling undercurrents of alienation and dislocation. War, in times of malaise and desperation, is a potent distraction.... Once we sign on for war's crusade... once we embrace a theological or ideological belief system that defines itself as the embodiment of goodness and light, it is only a matter of how we will carry out murder.... The myth of war sells and legitimizes the drug of war. Once we begin to take war's heady narcotic, it creates an addiction that slowly lowers us to the moral depravity of all addicts.[35]

As I have already pointed out—and will again—central to the Palestinian narrative is humiliation, the profound sense of loss the collective memory of the *Nakba* engenders, the loss of dignity and pride at the hands of the occupying power. At every opportunity the Palestinian ethos of conflict emphasizes the *humiliation*, the asymmetry of power, the learned helplessness, the devastating damage to the culture. In her research, Evelin Lindner found that *humiliation is addictive*.[36] When a group is sucked into such an addiction, it loses all sense of self-definition; it succumbs to a collective lack of self-esteem. There is a compulsive need on the part of victims to have their humiliation acknowledged and a propensity, if the acknowledgment is insufficient, to create situations to fill the deficit, to manipulate the perpetrator into inflicting further humiliation and hence perpetuate the cycle of retribution and conflict. Or sometimes, as Lindner has observed: "People... compensate for early experiences of humiliation in rigid ways. They are not interested in changing their predicament; the satisfaction is already entirely theirs.... They are obsessed with provoking others into giving them the opportunity to appear as heroic victims of humiliation."[37]

Nearly 80 percent of Palestinians in the West Bank and Gaza were born after the occupation started. They have absorbed the norms and values of the degradation that followed. It's not their new normal. It's their *only* normal. Powerlessness is the Palestinian's birthright. The litanies of woe are lifted by their separate waves, some more tumultuous than others, but ultimately washing onto the same shore of identity. By this point, the Palestinians *have* no other identity. The Israeli Jews are to blame for everything—no equivocations. The rewards of letting go of this conviction would have to be great indeed to overcome the loss.[38]

"We are a very ego-centered people," says Sari Nusseibeh, former president of Al Quds University. "We look at the world through our own lens, and we don't see anything else. We think this is the worst human tragedy that could ever happen to anyone. . . . Imagine all the people that are suffering in the world! We don't think of them. We think only of ourselves. Occupation has created a state of self-centeredness. We are a mirror image of the Jews."*[39]

Narcissism has dispelled doubt; victimhood makes self-reflection unnecessary; dependency is a comfort zone that paralyzes thought, a license for self-excuse and for holding the "other" responsible for one's own behavior. The world of the addict shrinks to obsessive preoccupation with one's own victimhood.

In "Checkpoint Jitters," an essay Raja Shehadeh wrote for the *New York Times*:

> Every day, at hundreds of checkpoints throughout the West Bank, Palestinians are stopped and made to wait, often for a long while, before they are let through. Last week I was halted at the Jabaa checkpoint on my way from my home in Ramallah to dinner at a friend's house in Bethlehem. . . . I looked around. The drivers were silent and seemed to be taking all this meekly, without any visible manifestation of anger. How docile people have become, I thought.

In short, *the people had accepted the status quo.*

Shehadeh continues:

> Before the Oslo Accords we would challenge the Israelis, all of us would, each in our own way. We were not submissive then. Today we are subdued. No one in the cars around me was pounding on the steering wheel or even cursing.

*Shlomo Ben Ami, interview with the author, March 9, 2012. Shlomo Ben Ami says, "I think that we are in many ways the mirror image of each other."

> These are new times. It seems that as soon as those accords were signed in 1993, as soon as our leaders shook hands with the enemy on that White House lawn, the struggle was called off. That illusory peace has achieved little except to dampen people's appetite for struggle. Now we endure our ordeal at checkpoints, as docile as too-well-mannered children.[40]

But why do people become addicted to the range of *negative* emotions evoked by humiliation? Jennifer Goldman and Peter Coleman try to provide some answers with their study "How Humiliation Fuels Intractable Conflict."[41] They look at the "benefits" conferred upon the humiliated and the victimized. The powerlessness under the occupation has become transmuted into that bitter but also sweet resentment of the Israelis. As mentioned in the discussion of dueling narratives, the humiliation also grants the victims a social exemption: they don't need to look at the pain caused by their own aggressions against "the other."[42]

> > < <

The Jewish Israeli addiction is different, although all addictions share similar attributes. Theirs pivots on the collective memory of the Holocaust, existential fear, and the "never again" syndrome. Its corollaries are numerous. The problem is that such obsessive remembrance interferes with the stages that cultures as well as individuals must go through to deal effectively with loss. Pounding the Holocaust into the collective memory stunts the society.[43] It arrests "healing" at an unnatural developmental stage and traps the culture into interpreting the present through a prism that has been shaped by fear and reasons to fear. The Holocaust is the "host" to multiple fears, and these fears are amplified by the dangers inherent in Israel's neighborhood. Still, the addiction to these fears and trauma, tapping into the subconscious, encouraging every threat to evoke some aspect of the Holocaust, only ensures that Israeli culture will be imprisoned by the past—held hostage, with fear generating fear.[44] Moreover, as a number of scholars have observed, fear "can become a socially conditioned habit, which in turn increases the grip of the culture of fear"; reactions to fear are also a habit.[45] In such a world, there is no such thing as "too much security." No matter what, more is called for. Like all addictions, this leads to a dead end, with no way out.

Israel's addiction is fed by an enabling America providing Israel with ever more aid, more weapons with no one of serious influence questioning how these munitions advance the peace process. The same holds for Hamas, which is always seeking more sophisticated rockets and more secure launching pads. Better Iron Domes are met with better rockets. One is always chasing the other. The perfect missile is *surely* just a matter of time. Likewise, Israel's perfection of the Iron Dome missile defense system is *surely* just a matter of time. It's an interminable arms race, and both parties and their more powerful sponsors are addicted to the insanity—doing the same thing over and over again, expecting a different outcome.

Israelis remain in thrall to *fear*: hence weapons and disproportionate military responses to actual or perceived threats of violence out of *habit*.[46] The separation barrier has done an excellent job of thwarting suicide bombers and other attacks. Nevertheless, after sixty-seven years of independence, this habit—this addiction—to military solutions has done little to alleviate Israel's fear that the visceral intent of the Palestinians—the real endgame they have in mind—is to use a peace agreement to take over all of Palestine and expel the Jews. Compulsive military behavior can never alleviate that fear. Repetition of failure is a kind of insanity. The need for the next fix supersedes every other consideration.

Breaking addictions requires behavioral reorientation. So, too, do addictions' subset, deeply embedded habits. On cue, our defense of "two states" becomes routine. "When a habit emerges," Duhigg explains, "the brain stops fully participating in decision making."[47]

While both sides have engaged in positive steps toward peace, their collective addiction overrides these measures and reasserts itself as an overpowering will of each side to declare retaliatory control over its respective narrative, circumstances, and survival at the expense of the other, feeding addictive cycles of violence and hate that are passed on generation after generation. Addictions, if left unaddressed, will make it virtually impossible to bring an end to the conflict.

Breaking their habits/addictions will require that Palestinians and Israelis adapt to new sets of *behaviors*, something that is incredibly difficult, that indeed may be beyond the ability of either side. The behavior patterns we repeat are literally etched into our neural pathways. Duhigg points to the growing body of research showing that we can "learn and make unconscious choices without remembering anything about the lesson or decision making. . . . [H]abits, as much as memory and reason, are at the root of how we behave."[48]

Of course, all Palestinian interviewees called for an end to the occupation and all supported a Palestinian state, but in terms of their own interests, not

Israel's. "The status quo," Hulda Thórisdóttir, and John Jost* write, "no matter how aversive, is a known condition and is therefore easier to predict and imagine than a potentially different state of affairs that could be either better or worse."[49] Hence the Israelis' propensity to prevaricate on negotiations; Palestinians face their own barriers. Humiliation, as we have described, is a constant in their lives, and so, too, is the addiction it gives rise to.[50] The *Nakba*, which is at the core of the humiliation, is also the core of Palestinian identity. Letting go involves a loss.[51] Letting go of collective memories of the Holocaust, the core part of Israel's identity, involves a loss. All losses are mourned. The genuine "dissolution" of the Palestinian-Israeli conflict would also be fraught with difficulty. That's how it works with addictions. Compulsion to stay put smothers the desire to change. *Overcoming an addiction also involves a loss.*

If peace is actually the goal, neither the Palestinians' addiction to the comforts of humiliation and resentment nor the Israelis' addiction to the comforts of fear and security has worked very well. Both have been counterproductive. Both always will be. Another fix is not the answer.

*Hulda Thórisdóttir is a professor of political science at the University of Iceland, and John Jost is a professor of psychology at New York University.

Chapter 3

Two-State Paradigm, Decades of Failure, and Addiction to Process

The Oslo Accords—Oslo I (September 1993)* and Oslo II (July 1995)—laid the foundations for a two-state solution, although they were not designed specifically to meet this end. The accords did not define the endgame; as a direct result, many of the problems that subsequently complicated their implementation can be traced to the ambiguities that suffuse the agreements. They did not explicitly call for establishing an independent Palestinian state, nor did they call for a halt in settlement construction.

In the Declaration of Principles (DOP), agreed upon at Oslo in 1993, Israel recognized the PLO as the sole representative of the Palestinian people and its partner in peace talks and agreed to Palestinian autonomy in the West Bank and Gaza Strip, beginning with Israeli withdrawal from the cities of Gaza and Jericho—an exchange of land for peace. The PLO in turn recognized Israel's right to exist and renounced the use of terrorism and their calls for Israel's destruction. The declaration was accompanied by letters: from Yasser Arafat, promising to change the PLO Charter, which called for destruction of Israel, and from Yitzhak Rabin, proclaiming Israel's intent to allow normalization of life in the occupied territories.

Oslo II in 1995 provided for the creation of the Palestinian Authority (PA), the governing body for the autonomous regions of the West Bank that would fall under its jurisdiction during the interim period before a final settlement agreement (FSA). The occupied West Bank was divided into three parcels—Areas A, B, and C.† In Area A, which comprised 18 percent of the

*The architects of the secret talks were Uri Savir on the Israeli side and Ahmed Qurei (Abu Ala) on the Palestinian side. For the accounts of both on how they reached the accord, see Savir, *Process*, and Qurei, *Beyond Oslo* and *From Oslo to Jerusalem*. Officially Oslo I was called "Declaration of Principles on Interim Self-Government Arrangements"; in abbreviated form Declaration of Principles (DOP).

†For a description of Areas A, B, and C, see Article XI Land, concerning areas A, B, and C in "Israeli-Palestinian Interim Agreement on the West Bank and the Gaza Strip" ("Oslo II or Taba"), September 28, 1995, signed September 24, 1995, in Taba, Egypt, and countersigned four days later in Washington DC, http://www.usip.org/sites/default/files/file/resources/collections/peace_agreements/interim_agreement_09282005.pdf.

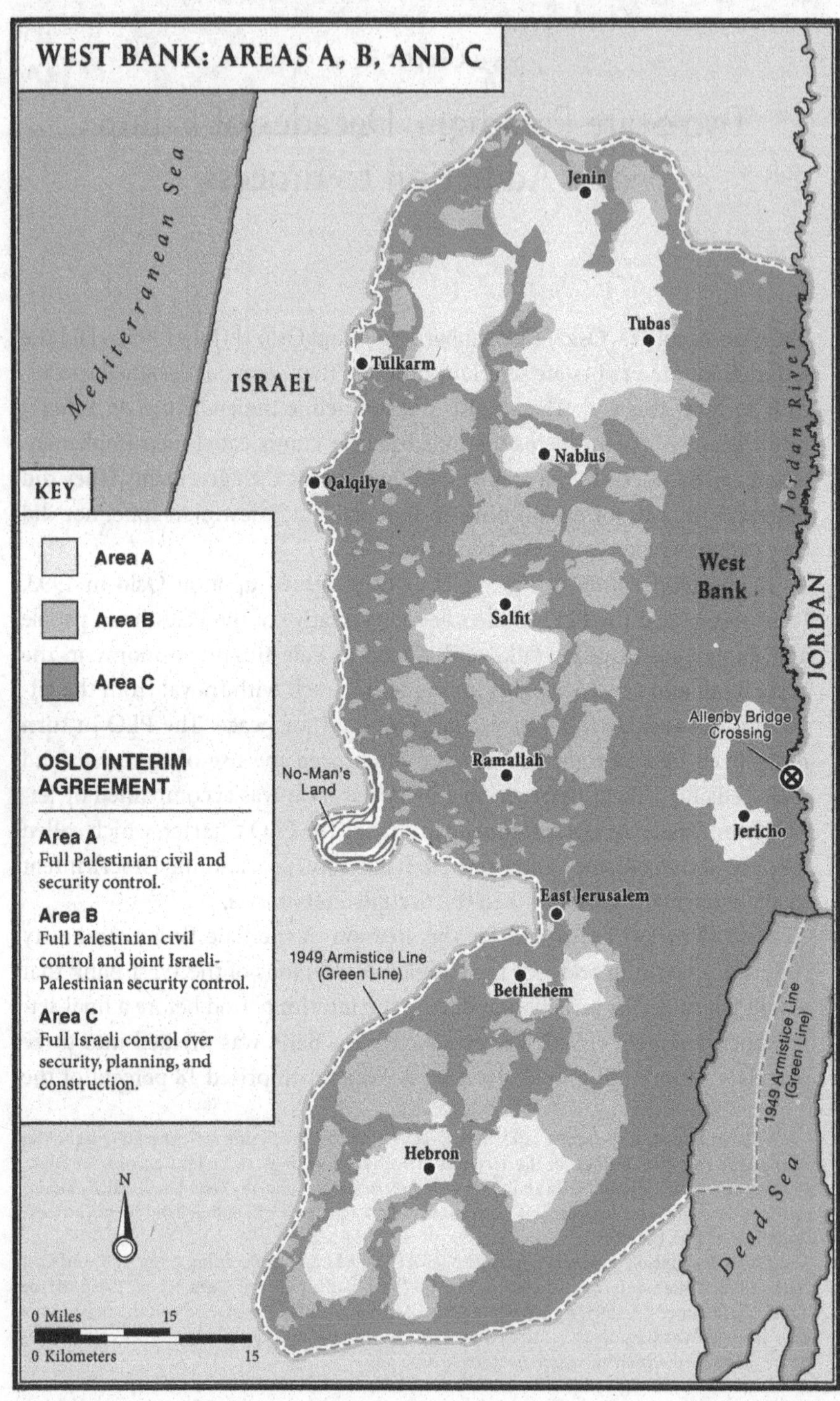
WEST BANK: AREAS A, B, AND C
Mediterranean Sea
ISRAEL
Jenin
Tubas
Tulkarm
Nablus
Qalqilya
Salfit
West Bank
JORDAN
Jordan River
Allenby Bridge Crossing
Ramallah
No-Man's Land
Jericho
East Jerusalem
1949 Armistice Line (Green Line)
Bethlehem
Hebron
Dead Sea
N
KEY
Area A
Area B
Area C
OSLO INTERIM AGREEMENT
Area A
Full Palestinian civil and security control.
Area B
Full Palestinian civil control and joint Israeli-Palestinian security control.
Area C
Full Israeli control over security, planning, and construction.
0 Miles 15
0 Kilometers 15

total area, the PA would have full remit, exercising administrative and security control, with the caveat that the IDF could still make forays into the area if convinced that "security" considerations were at stake (a practice that occurs frequently). In Area B, 21 percent of the territories, the PA would exercise full administrative control but share security with the IDF. In Area C, comprising 61 percent of the demarcated whole and encompassing the bulk of Palestinian resources and the agricultural abundance of the Jordan Valley, the IDF would exercise total control.* Area B and some of Area C would be handed over to the PA in a series of Israeli redeployments. After five years, negotiations for a final settlement agreement would get under way. The FSA would address the "core" outstanding issues—settlements, borders, security, right of return, and Jerusalem. In addition, both parties would sign an "end of claims agreement," which would bring finality to any claims one side harbored against the other and end the conflict. The accords called for each side to implement a number of steps—confidence-building measures (CBMs) designed to build trust in the lead-up to the final round of negotiations. Over the five years that followed, the CBMs were repeatedly and egregiously violated by both sides: Israeli redeployments were not carried out according to agreed schedules and the PA failed to rein in violence. Rather than enhancing trust, these circumstances created *more* distrust. Since 1995 that distrust has hardened, and no final settlement agreement is in sight.

Although a majority of Israelis and Palestinians are committed to a two-state solution, support has been a little tenuous in recent years and likely to ebb and flow on occasion, and none see it in the immediate future.[1] Moreover, when the compromises each side would be required to make for two states to become a reality are spelled out to both,[2] support on each side rapidly falls.[3] In fact, the phrase itself—"two-state solution"—has been bandied about with scant attention to what it means to different people and how its meaning has evolved over the years. For the most part, each protagonist conceives of it quite differently. The West Bank Palestinian interviewees I spoke with envisage a state along the lines of the 1967 borders, with East Jerusalem as its capital. It would be a modern nation-state, a full-fledged member of the international community enjoying full sovereignty, control of its borders, and the ability to defend itself. It would have an integrated economic and social system and be territorially contiguous, with geographic

*It is important to keep in mind that these percentages are percentages of the 22 percent of Palestine.

mobility ensuring the free movement of people and goods between the West Bank and Gaza. It would be demilitarized (although a growing number of voices are questioning why), have a commercial airport and a harbor, and be free to enter into trade arrangements with other states. It would control its airspace and electromagnetic spectrum but be open to making arrangements with Israel for their use on mutually acceptable terms. Interviewees did not envision or want a state that is a mere appendage of the Israeli economy, although they understood that a high degree of dependency would exist for some time, necessary not only because of the interrelationships that already exist and the fact that Israel would be by far the most important market open to them, but also to lay the foundations of a more diverse economy that could in time open exports to other markets.

The Jewish Israelis I spoke with envisage a different Palestine. It would not be geographically contiguous. Underground tunnels and the like would connect East Jerusalem and the West Bank (WB). Some borders would still remain under the control of Israel, at least for some specified period of time, and there would be an IDF presence in the Jordan Valley, also for some period of time. There would be an Israeli settler city, Ariel,* at its heart, connected by special transport facilities to Tel Aviv and Jerusalem. The larger settler bloc of Ma'ale Adumim would not fall within Palestine's territorial boundaries. Palestinians would *not* have a direct connection to East Jerusalem, nor even perhaps have East Jerusalem as their capital. And even if East Jerusalem were its capital, this Palestine would have to settle for an indirect access route, underscoring its lack of contiguity. It would have to bow to Israel's will and share control of its airspace (on terms largely determined by Israel), and it would not be in full control of its electromagnetic spectrum. In short, it would be an incomplete state, one that lacked full sovereignty and would be subject to many restrictions with regard to how it could exercise control of its territorial domain.

Of course, Palestinians would not agree to a two-state solution in which one state exercises full sovereignty and the other starts out with perhaps 80 percent sovereignty and can only hope that the remaining 20 percent will be doled out over a number of years as certain benchmarks are reached. These dueling visions of Palestine don't even touch on some of the most recalcitrant

*Ariel is a Jewish settlement of 18,000 residents and another 10,000 students that forms part of the Ariel-Elkana "bloc." The bloc has a population of at least 50,000 in the heart of the West Bank. Shalom Yerushalmi, "Israeli Settlements Are Irreversible," *Al-Monitor*, January 14, 2013, http://www.al-monitor.com/pulse/politics/2013/01/the-situation-in-the-territories.html# and Ariel Municipality, http://www.ariel.muni.il/?CategoryID=457.

core issues: the relocation of up to 100,000 settlers, the repatriation of refugees, the right of return, compensations, water, and an array of separate issues relating to the Old City in Jerusalem.

> > < <

Since Oslo I, there have been numerous attempts to find an accommodation to reach an FSA and an end of claims agreement.[4] Since the Clinton Parameters in 2000 through 2010, seventeen plans were proposed in attempts to secure a permanent agreement. All came to nought, despite the indefatigable efforts of negotiators on both sides and innumerable think tanks using every method of analysis, homing in on every possible permutation that might breach the fire wall on both sides. Indeed, the study of this conflict and its broader ramifications in the Middle East is an industry unto itself.

Every pundit has his or her explanations for how negotiations have gone wrong and why key players continue being intransigent. Each has suggestions for what *should* be done to give talks a better chance in the future. My interviewees were no exception, freely expressing their opinions, albeit with a jaundiced perspective and a rather alarming absence of introspection. Nevertheless, a pattern of responses emerged that contributes to an understanding of the repetitious impasses.

Not only are there two very different visions for what a Palestinian state would look like, but there are two different ideas of how the *process* of negotiation itself should be handled. Negotiations to date have been carried out under the rubric that "nothing is agreed until everything is agreed." Most Jewish Israeli interviewees believe that this formula ensures permanent paralysis. Better, they argue, to reach agreement on a particular issue, lock it down, and implement it. This would assuage some of the distrust in both communities as their respective publics saw some real progress being made. The more both Israelis and Palestinians became accustomed to seeing real change, they argue, incremental and slow though it may be, the better the prospects for completing the process to the endgame. Palestinians are implacably opposed to this incremental, halting approach. First, such a process would be a concession to the Israeli way of negotiating, adding still more asymmetry to the relationship. Second, it would send negative signals to the Palestinian street that once again Palestinians are capitulating to Israeli pressure. Third, as they experienced with the Oslo Accords, the provisional becomes the permanent. Fourth, implementation of provisional agreements could have unforeseen consequences: They could change the context in which other issues are addressed; assume a different importance if developments in the region take a different turn[5]; make it less likely that the Israelis will make the more far-reaching concessions the Palestinians are pushing for; severely diminish the Palestinian space to bargain; and require the Palestinians to afford Israel a level of trust that is simply absent.

Jewish Israeli interviewees understood that such an instrumentalist approach for returning territory is a nonstarter for the Palestinians. Nevertheless, Israel persists in coming up with variations of this mode. The more the Israelis press for gradualism, the more truculent Palestinian opposition becomes. Such pressure to adopt this negotiating mode adds to distrust: Obviously, in the Palestinian perspective, the Israelis would not be so insistent if they did not see it as beneficial to themselves.

Palestinians favor "nothing is agreed until everything is agreed," aka the "all-or-nothing model." This process poses serious problems for any negotiation. It encourages actors at different levels, as has been the case since Camp David, to advance their own agendas. Negotiators have to navigate their way through and find a successful accommodation among the proposals of the different interests on their own side *before or while* negotiating with the other party, which is undergoing a similar process. The back-and-forths *within* each party and *between* the two sides are intertwined; the process is tedious and an excuse for prevarication, and perhaps, even in the best of circumstances, it would be impossible to find an agreed congruence in the absence of cold-blooded pragmatism, which, had it existed, would have seen this conflict settled twenty-five years ago. If accommodation *within* the ranks of either side falters, the talks collapse. If accommodation with the *other* side falters, the talks collapse. In the Palestinian-Israeli dispute, a "nothing is agreed until everything is agreed" negotiating formula is a recipe for a stalemate. Hence the interminable deadlocks.

Interviewees identified several deficiencies in the process used at Camp David (2000) that has varied little since. The first category of problems could be labeled "procedural." How was the negotiation organized and managed? Was the preparation sufficient? What were the mechanisms for presenting, considering, and resolving proposals? The process, they said, did not have in place the basic structures, preparations, and procedures germane to complex negotiations. Interviewees referred to the absence of detailed agendas laying out not only time schedules and locations of negotiating sessions but also the specific issues to be addressed; a structure with specific tasks assigned to specific committees; feedback mechanisms to identify potential obstacles and deal with them before they reached the negotiating table; agreement on whether sufficient preparatory work (pre-talks) had been laid as groundwork; definition of redlines and discussion of what mechanisms might be put in place to obviate them; detailed documentation of each day's proceedings so that interlocutors were able to confirm the proceedings of the previous day, flag misunderstandings and misrepresentations, and prepare their next moves; a road map indicating the linkages between issues or suggesting where linkages might be found; contingency planning and fall-back strategies to preclude paralyzing deadlocks; and teams of highly skilled mediators to deal with the delegations without their leaders having to face each other across the table (at Jimmy Carter's Camp David, Israel's Menachem Begin and Egypt's Anwar Sadat never went head to head and met only once the agreement was sealed).

Among the Israeli negotiators, Tal Becker is as forthcoming and even-handed as any regarding the litany of flawed negotiations. "There is a widespread assumption that there is a coherent presentation of the position by one side to the other side," he said.

> But unfortunately this is not the case. There is a lot is posturing, of gamesmanship, and a lot depends on who you speak to and the politics within their own side as to what they're saying and why they're saying it at that moment. So to be able to state what the Palestinian position is on an issue, or what the real Israeli position is, sometimes is quite hard to nail down because it depends who you were talking to, at what time in the negotiations, and what the perspective of each is at that time. What is the goal each has in mind? Sometimes an Israeli side might want to be harsh on a certain issue because it wants to achieve something somewhere else, so if you take that as its position on that issue, you'd be misled. Approaches are tactical. Sometimes, for the most trivial of reasons a person will all of a sudden come out and say certain things, which they didn't say before. So you don't know what their position is, that their motivations may be somewhat different.[6]

Akram Hanieh talked at length of similar difficulties dealing with Israeli negotiating teams representing different interests:

> You feel that there are three delegations all the time when you talk to the Israelis, so you should know to whom are you talking and which one represents the real position. Does that mean that the prime minister is the one who gives order? Or when the foreign minister speaks, it doesn't mean this is the Israeli position as it is. You can see that whenever one of them talks, he is

> looking right and left. He was talking to *his* delegation more than talking to *our* delegation. You should focus—to whom should I be talking with?[7]

The list is long and could be even longer. Postmortems after Clinton's Camp David and after Annapolis were numerous, and although crucial lessons about how to proceed in future negotiations were discussed, there is little evidence that they were ever implemented.[8] Another even more alarming component too often missing in Israeli-Palestinian negotiations is a map of the "big picture": the precise purpose of specific talks; terms of reference for each issue, setting out each side's opening gambits and a detailed description of the obstacles to resolution, sequentially ordered and with relative importance attached to each obstacle; assurances that no proposal is put on the table without careful groundwork, details fully fleshed out, ramifications explored, possible unforeseen consequences examined, and possible responses and rejoinders played out in "mock trial." Also missing are feedback mechanisms to ensure that the veracity of assumptions be put to test; mechanisms for differentiating between "engineered" breakdowns (those due to factional infighting within the ranks) and breakdowns resulting from genuinely irreconcilable differences; unambiguous understanding as to what precisely the endgame is; and agreement that these negotiations are part of a more comprehensive process. A final component is the acknowledgment that failure to reach agreement does *not* mean the end of negotiations, period, but is in fact an inevitable feature of negotiations, which often stumble from one difficulty to the next because they are not dispassionate clinical exercises but a process where human beings try to grapple with problems over which they have profoundly different beliefs and to which they have almost insurmountable attachments.

"In the negotiations, there are too many people on both sides inside the room and also too many people outside the room. All think they have a role to play—they certainly want a role to play—and they may be trying to help or hurt. I would say," Tal Becker said, and not in jest, "that as difficult as negotiating with my Palestinian interlocutors was the way I had to work with the Israeli side. I have no doubt that many of the Palestinians would say the same thing. The problem is that it is very hard to move people away from their respective modus operandi. [Addictive behavior.] The model of negotiating we use actually increases the chances of failure because it increases animosity and distrust on both sides. It's very hard to shake people out of adhering to that model. [Addictive behavior.] As a result, a good number of the people on both sides, either deliberately or not deliberately, sabotage the process." Becker did not venture to say what negotiation model should replace it.

The oversupply of principal players, adjunct negotiators, and layers of staff creates an ambience in which the principals are often unsure of who is speaking on behalf of whom, who is expressing the other side's position, and what is the *real* position. Uncertainty and suspicion follow. Factional infighting is a given in complex negotiation, and the Israeli-Palestinian conflict is second to none in this regard. The negotiating forum is an arena in which to maneuver for advantage, play out internecine rivalries, and settle scores—especially in the case of the Palestinians and specifically in the matter of Fatah versus Hamas. Tal Becker explained:

> One of the big differences between Camp David and Annapolis is that at Annapolis the negotiations with Israel were first and foremost a weapon for Fatah in their fight with Hamas. The actual dealing with us was a secondary issue. The nature of our conversation was so focused on what they needed to defeat Hamas, what political achievements they could reach to prove that they were the best representatives of the Palestinian cause. They'd say, "Listen, you need to help me here. I've got to come out of this showing that I have delivered." The agreement becomes a tool. Abu Mazen [Mahmoud Abbas] is able to say, "I'm the guy who can deal with the world. I'm the guy who can deal with Israel. And what do these guys offer you?" And so these agreements are part of the fight that's going on between Hamas and Fatah, and we are pawns in that discussion.

All in all, given the addictions of each side, it is not surprising that despite formal negotiations and countless rounds of Track II endeavors and innumerable meetings, the two sides have not advanced much beyond point scoring. One side's accusing finger always points to the other side as the villain; self-criticism is something only the "other" needs to practice.

Becker adds another important dimension that, he says, should be taken into account. "It can never be forgotten," he emphasizes, "that these negotiations are between two traumatized and therefore distrustful people. As a result, you're taught that the way to negotiate is in the manner of a Middle East bazaar. That means that you stake out an extreme position because you don't trust the other side, and they stake out an extreme position because they don't trust you. And then you engage in this elaborate theatrical dance, where you concede a little bit, they concede a little bit." Suspicions about the other side "can only be broken down by the relationships that are created in the room." But how is that accomplished? Difficult? Yes, because, as Becker says, "*The people who are involved in resolving the conflict are rarely people who know anything about how to solve conflict.* [Emphasis added.]" By any yardstick, this is quite a remarkable admission, and of course I should stress that it is Becker's only. But it is corroborated in some measure when one consults the many books written by interviewees who were involved in the peace processes under discussion. And if what Becker says is indeed true, then one can hardly look to the future with much optimism.

Also corroborating Becker's observation is the fact that leadership itself is an obstacle to success. Since Camp David, indeed in some cases Madrid, why are the same old hands—Abu Mazen, Abu Ala, Saeb Erekat, Nabil Sha'ath, Yasser Abed Rabbo, and others—still at the negotiating helm? What more have they to say, given their almost exclusive immersion in the peace process for twenty-five years, thrashing out every possible variation on the same issues in both formal and informal settings (innumerable conferences, workshops, seminars, and media interviews), adhering rigidly in formal negotiations to positions they carved in stone more than two decades ago but flexible when it doesn't count? They've had their opportunities. They've rejected every conceivable permutation of the two-state solution, and their decisions are made in the context of their narrative of occupation, humiliation, and restorative justice. They repeat the same palliatives ad nauseam. Their minds are fossilized—addicted to habits of thought whose shelf lives have long expired. At least four—Saeb Erekat,[9] Abu Ala,[10] Hanan Ashrawi,[11] and Yasser Abed Rabbo[12]—have publicly announced the "death" of the two-state solution on one occasion or another yet blithely pursue it.

On the other hand, complicating matters for the Palestinians is the fact that, in most cases, the average life span of an Israeli government is less than two years.[13] Every incoming government selects its own peace team; there is no continuity among the players, and no Israeli government feels bound to accept the understandings that had been reached during its predecessor's negotiations as its own starting points. So starting points are constantly being revisited, and every time there are new players unfamiliar with the process. Hanieh says: "I was talking to [then–foreign minister] Tzipi Livni about the DOP and she asked, 'What does DOP mean?'"

Israeli and Palestinian protagonists are, of course, caught in dueling narratives. The "procedural" ineptness and breakdowns sketched above may reflect the fact that negotiators on the two sides, in their deepest hearts, either do not *unequivocally* believe in what they are doing or do not believe they can succeed. Or, under the addiction model, they may not actually want to succeed,[14] they may not even be conscious of either but may act out in a way that reaffirms what lies in the recesses of their subconscious.* They believe they are trying their best—and most of them *are* genuinely trying their best—but these subconscious intangibles get in the way, with different neural pathways always running parallel, sabotaging their efforts.

Interviewees on both sides displayed recurring patterns of response to different questions, obviating the need to understand each other. Their responses were invariably contextualized to suggest that *their* side is more open to making far-reaching compromise. In fact, neither side is, as negotiations prove.

Consider just one issue rooted in the narratives: Whose land is it, anyway? Specifically, who rightfully owns the West Bank, which the Israelis have occupied since 1967? The operative legal framework for the debate is United Nations Resolution 242, which declares the "inadmissibility of the acquisition of territory by war" and calls for the "withdrawal of Israel armed forces from territories occupied in the recent conflict." But who exactly did the Israelis take territory from? It is not as though they annexed territory "legally" belonging to another sovereign nation. The West Bank was absorbed by Transjordan in the aftermath of the Arab-Israeli war in 1948, a claim relinquished by King Abdullah Hussein in 1988 to the PLO, but this did not confer sovereignty; neither does UN 242 require Israel to return all the territory. Nor does it specify to whom the land should be returned.†

Until the 1960s, the liberation of the Palestinian homeland was primarily

*With breakthroughs in neurology in recent years, the relationship between the conscious and the subconscious has produced a large body of research, which Leonard Mlodinow summarizes in his book *Subliminal*. Among the findings: "Human behavior is the product of an endless stream of perceptions, feelings, and thoughts, at both the conscious and unconscious levels. The idea that we are not aware of the cause of our behavior can be difficult to accept. . . . [T]o ensure our smooth functioning in both the physical and the social world, nature has dictated that many processes of perception, memory, attention, learning, and judgment are delegated to brain structures outside conscious awareness" (16–18).

†The Israeli Jews interpret Resolution 242 as follows: "The Palestinians are not mentioned anywhere in Resolution 242. They are only alluded to in the second clause of the second article of 242, which calls for 'a just settlement of the refugee problem.' *Nowhere does it require that Palestinians be given any political rights or territory.* [Emphasis is mine.] In fact, the use of the generic term 'refugee' was a deliberate acknowledgment that two refugee problems were products of the conflict—one Arab and another Jewish. In the case of the latter, almost as many Jews fled Arab countries as Palestinians left Israel. The Jews, however, were never compensated by the Arab states, nor were any UN organizations ever established to help them." See Jewish Virtual Library, "U.N. Security Council: The Meaning of Resolution 242," http://www.jewishvirtuallibrary.org/jsource/UN/meaning_of_242.html.

a pan-Arab cause, with Palestinians playing a secondary role, but at the second Arab League summit, held in Alexandria in September 1964, those states shifted responsibility to the Palestinians themselves and approved establishing the PLO for that purpose.[15]

Fatah, founded by Yasser Arafat and Khalil Ibrahim al-Wazir in 1959, was by far the most significant resistance/terrorist/liberation movement to try to wrest Palestine from the control of Israel by engaging in low-intensity guerrilla warfare. The tenacity of Fatah's resistance against the military might of the IDF, especially after the Arab humiliation in the Six-Day War (1967), reverberated to its political advantage in the diaspora community. By the end of the decade, Fatah had taken over effective control of the PLO, with Yasser Arafat at its head.[16] Henceforth the PLO evolved into the main Palestinian player on the local and world stage, the acknowledged advocate for Palestinian self-determination, the de facto "government" of a Palestinian state that did not exist.[17]

In the 1970s and 1980s, the PLO engaged in widespread terror campaigns, including plane hijackings and forays into Israel, where Israeli civilians were sometimes the victims, all in the name of drawing the world's attention to the plight of the Palestinians, all condemned in uncompromising terms by the West.

From exile in Tangiers, the PLO watched from the sidelines as the First Intifada (1987) convulsed Palestine. The intifada was homegrown. In the beginning it was all body, no head: a children's war, youngsters throwing stones at IDF troops at checkpoints. Resistance broadened as action and reaction fed on each other and increased public support. Orders from Yitzhak Rabin, who was minister of defense at the time, that the IDF should break the knuckles of children and young people throwing stones, inflamed the situation but were indicative of the harsh measures he was prepared to take to break the intifada. Rabin was first and foremost a military man, "Bone Breaker Rabin" to the locals. "I was engaged in it," says Hanan Ashrawi. "It was something that we Palestinians felt very deeply, because it was a way for people to express themselves, refusing to bow to the power structures of the Israeli occupation. It was really a battle of wills. The local Palestinian civic leadership, which emerged after 1967, created its own institutions in defiance of the Israeli-imposed institutions; the intifada generated a democratic system of elections and governance from the ground up, neighborhood committees and popular committees. It was true democracy, driven by a very active civil society and became a source of empowerment." But as it progressed it led the local leadership, in the sense the PLO's "on the ground" presence, to the realization that violence would not end the occupation. Hence its outreach to the PLO: "We wrote initiatives to the PLO," she says, "but the most important stressed that we have the confidence and the strength that we can let the world know that even though Israel may be confiscating our land, it will not break our will or our voice. As victims, we can reach out to our oppressors and say, 'We want to make peace.'"[18]

In short, violence would not end the occupation. Nor was any Arab state about to invade Israel in a vain attempt to "free" the Palestinians. Israel was a powerful military force in its own right, and it also had the support of the United States and the major European powers. The Palestinians would have to deal with it as a reality that could not be dislodged.

All of these factors reinforced what Arafat and the PLO had come to believe. Reflecting on what armed resistance had achieved, they acknowledged—first to themselves, and then to the world—the futility of pursuing a policy of armed struggle to reclaim *all* of Palestine; hence the Tangiers proclamation in November 1988.

The experience of the intifada also had a profound effect on Rabin—his coming to the realization that Israel's occupation of the captured territories could not be sustained *indefinitely*. One intifada crushed left another in the making. Some political arrangement was required. Two new perspectives, driven by different motivations, led to a congruence of interests and ultimately opened the way to Oslo.

The Palestinian Declaration of Independence in Tangiers in November 1988 was a paradigm shift, a heartbreaking reckoning with the past, abandonment of an old dream for a new and uncertain one, but not an explicit relinquishment of the aspiration to one day reclaim the land.

The 1988 concession also implicitly acknowledged that the Palestinian leadership had erred in 1937 by not accepting the recommendation of the Peel Commission, which called for a partition that would have left 80 percent of the territory in Palestinian hands; that the Arab rebellion (1936–39) had been ill conceived and poorly executed; and that the leadership had erred again when it rejected the United Nations' 1947 partition plan, which would have yielded a Palestinian state on 43 percent of the land (the area of Jerusalem and Bethlehem was to become an international zone), twice the size the PLO had just accepted in Tangiers. In 2011 a rueful Mahmoud Abbas, president of the Palestinian Authority, admitted on Israeli television that the UN's 1947 partition plan was the "best offer" the Palestinians had ever received.[19] (Former special envoy George Mitchell concurs: "The problem with the Palestinians," he told me, "is that they keep coming back looking for more and they are not going to get it. The best offer was in forty-seven and they turned it down."[20])

Dozens of polls over the years confirm that "the Israeli public is fully aware of the Arab (Palestinian) desire to settle the conflict on the basis of the 1967 borders, leaving Israel with 78 percent of historical Palestine." Even this allotment, however, is rejected by a large Israeli majority, "which wants much more," including maintaining "the occupation of the Syrian Golan Heights" and annexing "as much as possible of the occupied West Bank."[21]

But Palestinians see no need for counterproposals to Israeli proposals because these would involve acquiescing to Israel's interpretation of Resolution 242. They believe that they are being asked to *compromise their compromise.* On this score, the Palestinian interviewees were unanimous: They will not budge from their position. They do not understand why Israel does not sufficiently acknowledge the extent of the Palestinian 1988 concession: whittling down their claim to a mere 22 percent of the land they believed was rightfully theirs, land their forefathers had tilled without interruption for 1,500 years. "For the Palestinians, the 1967 borders are the compromise that cannot be further compromised," says Ghassan Khatib, former head of the PA's communications department, "and I think that this is a very important point. This is a very problematic defect in the peace process. The Israelis keep coming back and saying, 'Why don't you put a counterproposal forward?' And we are saying, 'Well, you see, there's no need for us. We don't have a counterproposal because we don't basically accept where you're coming from."[22] Of course, to reverse the context, Jewish Israelis don't see the land as something the Palestinians have a right to. On the contrary, *all* the land is theirs.

The fact that Palestinians talk about "occupied" territories and the Israelis about "disputed" territories means that this fundamental, narrative-driven disagreement has undermined every negotiation since 1991. Their respective initial starting points on the matter of the West Bank territory have never been integrated into a mutually agreed understanding. If they are unable to agree to a starting point, how are the negotiators supposed to make real progress on other outstanding issues? Such poorly defined frames of reference were the pivotal reasons why both the 2000 Camp David and the 2007 Annapolis talks unraveled.

Another obstacle is the need for each side to be perceived by its public as the victor, having protected their core interests. "One of the misconceptions about the Israeli-Palestinian conflict that many people have is that it's about trade-offs," Tal Becker says.

> They believe it's a "we give up a bit of this and you give up a bit of that" process. In essence, however, when you think about . . . a dynamic that works, you are actually trying to create a plausible case about why you achieved your interests on *every* single issue, not that you gave up one to gain another. It doesn't work for an Israeli leader to say, "Well, I had to give up some of Jerusalem, but I got what I wanted on refugees." Or for a Palestinian leader to say, "I had to give up some of refugees in order to get something of what we wanted in Jerusalem." In a way . . . maybe that's true, but that's *not* the way you talk about it because what you're actually trying to achieve is *a success story* for both people. These negotiations are *not* about convincing the other side that you're right. It's just what package of things can plausibly be created that cross a threshold for both sides so that each has a success story on every issue. It has to be win-win on every single issue.

Hence, announcements of progress being made during negotiations are usually damaging. The word begs the question: Progress toward what? Politicians in both Israel and Palestine, because of domestic political considerations, will, not unsurprisingly, interpret the word either to assuage or to exacerbate the fears of their respective constituencies, and both sides will be quick to exploit the implications associated with the word. Moreover, for negotiations to succeed, they must be managed so that neither side feels under threat—and they must be seen as nonthreatening by their respective publics. Nevertheless, the two publics have to be *prepared* in advance for the truth, for what's possible, for the compromises needed. Interviewees on both sides agreed unanimously with this but also unanimously added a caveat: There is no real leadership; if leadership were to emerge, it still would require the kind of trust in the other side that does not exist in this conflict.

"Netanyahu," Tamar Hermann, director of the Israel Democracy Institute, wrote in 2010, "who was immersed in Jewish history from the cradle, subscribes to a version of Jewish nationalism that is in significant ways different from that of his (immediate) predecessors, who were profoundly secular and, in a way, detached from Jewish tradition. The extreme threat perception that he derives from Jewish history apparently accounts for his urge to ensure very wide margins of security for the nation. Netanyahu opposed the peace plans negotiated by his predecessors on the grounds that they entailed territorial compromises that severely jeopardized Israel's security."[23] His actions in the subsequent years confirm the accuracy of her observations.

In *Leadership*, the seminal book on the subject, the late James MacGregor Burns distinguished between "transactional" leaders—those who take a more short-term approach to achieving goals through negotiation and compromise—and "transformational" ones, who seek to create change by helping followers become better versions of themselves. "Truly great and creative leaders do something more," he wrote in an essay in 1978. "They arouse peoples' hopes and aspirations and expectations, convert social needs into political demands, and rise to higher levels of leadership as they respond to those demands."[24]

Neither Mahmoud Abbas nor Benjamin Netanyahu falls into the "transformational" characterization, and surveying the leadership in Israel's political parties and Fatah for would-be successors to both, there is little reason to believe that one is about to emerge.

Moreover, the Israeli and Palestinian people themselves are losing faith: Both constituencies support a two-state solution *in theory*, but they do not see one in the cards in the foreseeable future. The Israelis fall back on the mantra drummed into their consciousness since the failure of Camp David that they do not have a Palestinian partner for peace. Palestinians' pessimism stems from their overall frustration and loss of hope that Israelis are really interested in a solution.

"The Israelis don't want to make peace with us," says Samih Al-Abed, the PLO's mapping expert. "They want the process to continue, because they benefit from that. We are dragging this process on forever. We are implementing everything the Israelis want on the ground. We are doing everything to police our society in the way they want. They have firm control over everything. So the process can live for another fifteen years and after fifteen years the Palestinians wake up, nothing left for them. That's [the Israelis'] strategy. They were never serious about making a deal, except dragging us with a process that makes the international community feel good about it. And the international community pays everything for us to live and to continue this peace process."[25]

Few of the other Palestinian interviewees disagreed. The lesson Palestinians have learned is that they have been duped not once or twice but many times by a powerful protagonist that can rely on an even more powerful ally, the United States, and they have to fall into line, although without much enthusiasm.

Over time, positions have hardened. Since neither public believes that a sustainable two-state solution will happen, they're not motivated to fight for it. Meanwhile, those who oppose a two-state solution (Hamas and far-right Israelis, including settlers) are willing to fight *against* it—although throughout the seven years prior to the Hamas-Fatah reconciliation-pact process Hamas equivocated on the issue. West Bank Palestinians I spoke with *want* to create a new paradigm. The old ways of doing things are moribund. Israelis are by and large satisfied with the status quo, although aware enough that it can't last forever. The Palestinians would like to move the whole peace process from U.S. to UN sponsorship, make it multilateral, and conduct it according to the principles of international law. However, given the UN's propensity for indefinite delays and weak responses to crises, perhaps the Palestinians should entertain second thoughts about this option.

> > < <

At meetings since Camp David, the negotiators repeat their positions "of principle"; spread out the same maps; mark yet again the contours of the Green Line and the separation barrier; identify which acres might be swapped for which acres; identify Israeli settlement blocs and haggle over the fate of each, even as the window for dismantling *any of them* gets smaller and smaller; revisit one more time the question of the contiguity of the Palestinian state, or lack thereof; squabble over the fate of Ma'ale Adumim and Ariel; argue borders and security and the Jordan Valley; mouth the same platitudes over the right of return of the refugees; rehash the innumerable but increasingly implausible ways of dividing Jerusalem; and now, as demographics and climate begin to exact their toll, debate who "owns" the water and how it should be allocated (something that has climbed the ladder of core issues).*

Then, at the end of the proverbial day (usually measured in months), they gravely stand and proclaim with regret either "We were close" or "If only we had a little more time" or "We do not have a partner for peace," invoked most recently when the 2013–14 talks collapsed and Fatah signed a reconciliation pact with Hamas. Palestinian interviewees blamed the Americans for doing Israel's bidding and vowed in 2011–12 that they were finished with this process—bilaterals, that is, head-to-head negotiations. "The mechanisms of

*Israel's per-capita consumption of water is twice that of Palestinians, who have to purchase their water from the Israelis at higher prices than Israelis pay. See B'Tselem, "Water Crisis."

negotiation in the past are no longer suitable to be used the same way as they previously have been," Abu Ala concludes. "If we go to bilateral negotiations again, close the door, talk together, and then come back, nothing will be achieved."[26] Which is precisely what happened in the 2013–14 talks.

It's not that West Bank Palestinian interviewees want to freeze the United States out of the multilateral process it has become accustomed to alluding to, but they believe U.S. involvement should be tempered by the presence of others. The Palestinians also know who butters their bread and snap to when the United States calls. Or they can talk the talk of a new process while they wait for the old process to be dusted off and resuscitated with a tweak here and there—then again embrace it or damn it with faint praise which, of course, is the route they chose when they became a party to the 2013–14 talks. Reengagement on these grounds is a *habit* and an attribute of their addiction. Jewish Israelis march to the same drummer, although the beats are slightly different. They will comply with an American peace initiative, not because they agree with it or even want it to succeed but because they risk a great deal if Israel is identified as impeding peace talks.[27] Invariably, during the months both sides do engage in negotiations, their leaderships lambast each other and debase the process they are supposedly promoting. American initiatives are *triggers* to which both sides respond positively on *cue* and engage in the same *routine*—a process that repeatedly fails because negotiations are framed within the same context every time—and when talks collapse each side *rewards* itself with the subsequent blame game, confirming to its constituency yet again its justification for saying that progress is impossible because of the other side's intransigence. But should another opening to reengage with the Netanyahu (or any other Israeli) government emerge, the Palestinians will grasp it. The "street" would expect as much, even given the widespread skepticism. Both constituents and leaders would be true to their addiction and seize the ephemeral opportunity.

> > < <

After the ten-month moratorium on settlement construction ran out in November 2010, I was told repeatedly by some interviewees on the PLO Executive Committee that it was coming up with a new approach. "When?" I asked, as time went by. "Soon" was the invariable response. But when asked whether these remarks were shots across the bow, gestures of exasperation rather than statements that reflected *actual* positions they held and, if so, whether they had raised the matter at meetings of the Executive Committee and, if so, whether they had drawn up a menu of alternatives, they demurred. A new paradigm was being worked on, and when it became public the whole world would have the answers. The outlines are in focus: the PLO's applications for UN statehood, its application or pending application for membership in *all* agencies and institutions, attempts to internationalize the conflict, mass non-violent demonstrations,[28] moving negotiations under the aegis of the UN, and the long-awaited, now fragile, reconciliation between Fatah and Hamas. Should this last attempt fail, Palestinians will have expected as much. No leader of substance has seriously addressed the Palestinian people on whether a two-state solution is beyond reach, despite a survey in December 2013 indicating that just over a majority (53 percent) of all Palestinians and less than a majority (48 percent) of young people thought it was[29] and a June 2014 survey indicating that at least two thirds of Palestinians no longer supported a two-state solution.[30] These sentiments reflected the diminishing commitment to a two-state solution expressed by the Palestinians I spoke with. A surprising number had concluded that the depth of Israeli penetration into the West Bank had become too much of an obstacle to achieving a viable Palestinian state within the two-state structure. But there was no aura of desperation; the winds of history are blowing in the Palestinians' direction.

And the new paradigm? For the most part it is amorphous.

Chapter 4

Specific Failures

The Oslo Accords were hailed in 1993 as a stepping-stone to peace. Twenty years later we are still tiptoeing on the same stone. Few of the Oslo principles were implemented, many were trampled on (some were conceivable only on paper), and the "facts on the ground" are now very different in several important respects. Bill Clinton's parameters, George W. Bush (and the Quartet's) road map, the Arab League's initiative—all have been egregiously violated if calling for specific actions or ignored otherwise. Uri Savir describes in *The Process* how he and Abu Ala during their first meeting in Oslo exchanged their respective narratives, and then he says, "Never again would we argue about the past."[1] At that first meeting they had acknowledged the disconnect between their respective historical narratives and endowed each with "parity of esteem." In the years following, in subsequent negotiations of Oslo II, Wye, Camp David, Bolling Air Force Base (AFB) and Annapolis, the spirit of Savir and Abu Ala did not prevail. In part, the missing parity of esteem is the underlying source of all the failure. For without it there can be no sustainable compromises. Photographs taken on the White House lawn in 1993 of a sprightly Yasser Arafat and a reluctant Yitzhak Rabin, after they had signed Oslo I,[2] became instantly famous the world over. The Oslo process was hailed at the time for its farsightedness, for offering hope that a conflict long thought intractable would be resolved by negotiations, not violence. Why, more than twenty years later, has that goal not been achieved?

No signed document in the Oslo DOP or subsequent agreements contains the word "occupation" or acknowledges Israel as an occupying power, because Israel regards itself as the rightful proprietor of all the territories in Palestine, by divine right and/or as the spoils of a war started and lost by the Palestinians and their Arab sponsors. The land is merely "in dispute" and under its control until final disposition is settled. "In the interim agreement implementation," Nabil Sha'ath wryly recalls, "they were very careful not to trespass anything that would affect the permanent negotiations; for example words such as 'state' or 'national' or 'Palestine' were taboo because they indicated something permanent. We were to the Israelis in an interim stage, and therefore we had a provisional government. Therefore, what you have is not a state and you don't have the authority or the sovereignty of a state. You have jurisdiction. You have authority, but no sovereignty."[3]

Oslo, rather than bringing deliverance to the Palestinians, as at least some believed it would at the time, actually *cemented and sealed* Israel's presence in the West Bank and Gaza. The PLO's agreement to negotiate the future of these territories bilaterally with Israel conveyed a degree of legitimacy to the Israeli presence that it had heretofore lacked. Nevertheless, when Oslo I went to the Knesset for ratification, Likud leader Benjamin Netanyahu lambasted it: "It is not just autonomy and it is not just a Palestinian State in the territories but the start of the destruction of Israel in line with the PLO plan."[4]

> > < <

The Oslo process was flawed from its inception due to the asymmetry of the negotiations between a state with power and a non-state actor, between the occupier and the occupied, between one protagonist holding a straight flush and the other with a pair of deuces. Throughout, the opposing historical narratives hovered over the proceedings—the baselines—humiliation for the Palestinians, exceptionalism for the Israelis. The failure to bridge the gap between them exacerbated the differences, contributing to undercurrents of anger among the Palestinian interlocutors about Israel's refusal to treat seriously their demands for procedural, transitional, and compensatory justice throughout the process.[5]

The Palestinians argued that a new balance between the two sides, based on equality of status of the two parties, was indispensable to a sustainable agreement. "They could not accept an agreement that exploits Israel's greater relative power, which would prevent their realizing their own demands and just and fair rights and would impinge upon their honor."[6] "We derived our power from the justice of our case," Abu Ala wrote in *From Oslo to Jerusalem*, "as opposed to the Israelis, who sought to define what was just on the basis of their power."[7]

Contrary to the Palestinians' requests for equal status, the Israelis set the agenda and rejected out of hand Palestinian demands for transitional and compensatory justice.[8] They would not entertain the Palestinian demand that Israel accept responsibility for the injustices perpetrated in the 1947–49 war and for the *Nakba* or the concomitant demand for the right of return. The Israelis said they were there to negotiate the future, not to rehash the past with accusation and counteraccusation. Indeed, as a condition of the negotiations, they insisted that the Palestinians drop all such demands.[9]

Although the Israelis certainly knew that reaching any agreement would require some negotiating symmetry, they found it difficult to treat the Palestinians as equal partners.[10] In the end the Israelis thought they were making a great concession by allocating *much* of the West Bank and Gaza Strip as the territorial domain of the newly created Palestinian Authority.

The accord signed on the White House lawn in 1993 punted for five years the search for common ground on other core issues (settlements, Jerusalem, borders, right of return). "The agreement was open ended in too many different ways," says Ghassan Khatib. "It allowed the two sides to have different understandings of it. At that time they were encouraging us to go for what they used to call constructive ambiguity in order to reach compromises, but then these ambiguous clauses in the agreement allowed each of the two sides to have their own version and consequently allowed conflicting understanding and practices and behavior between the two sides. The agreement did not allow an improvement in the economic situations of the Palestinian people."[11]

However, the acrimonious circumstances prevailing in further negotiations to implement the DOP,* especially the IDF redeployments called for—Gaza-Jericho (1994), Oslo II (1995), Hebron (1997), and Wye River (1998)[12]—extinguished the spirit, and Oslo slowly collapsed because of the inbuilt internal contradictions. Rather than violence abating, it increased; rather than taking place in line with the agreed time lines, the redeployments lapsed; rather than circumstances in the occupied territories improving, IDF presence increased, with closures an increasingly common practice, disrupting commerce between the West Bank and Jerusalem; checkpoints proliferated and severely curtailed mobility; settlements increased. Rather than sunshine, more rain.

> > < <

Often it appeared that few PLO leaders had thought through the implications of the DOP. Some say that Arafat didn't give the accord more than a passing glance once he got what he sought most: getting his foot on the ground in

*"In the Declaration of Principles and in subsequent agreements signed in 1994, Israel and the PLO committed to a series of steps to advance the cause of peace. For Israel, this meant a phased withdrawal from designated areas of the West Bank and Gaza to the PLO, a transfer of governing powers to the PLO (in the fields of education and culture, health, social welfare, direct taxation, and tourism), and allowing for the creation of a Palestinian police force. For its part, the PLO was required to recognize Israel's right to exist, renounce terrorism against Israel, crack down on Palestinian terror groups, and hold free elections for the establishment of Palestinian self-government—in addition to assuming a range of governing powers." See http://www.cija.ca/resource/milestones-in-the-quest-for-peace/1993-oslo-peace-process/.

Palestine and Israel's recognition of the PLO as the sole representative of the Palestinian people.[13] The Oslo agreement, says Hanan Ashrawi, "was the way of getting the PLO back to Palestine as quickly as possible because in the wake of the intifada it was afraid of losing control of the internal movement."[14] In *The Much Too Promised Land*, David Aaron Miller writes: "For Arafat, Oslo was a trade-off: in exchange for recognizing him as the only Palestinian partner for Israel and America, he agreed to an interim process that deferred big issues like Jerusalem and refugees, and focused on mundane matters, such as actually governing what would become the Palestinian Authority."[15]

In July 1994 Arafat was back from Tunisia and at home in Gaza, his native soil, as the undisputed leader of the Palestinian people and soon-to-be president of the putative PA.[16]

One prominent PLO leader who *did* read the text, Dr. Hanan Ashrawi, immediately went to Arafat and asked whether it could be renegotiated, such was the level of her alarm.* She had noticed a little something missing from the document: the assurance that after five years, with the final settlement agreement (FSA) negotiated and signed and with the PA having proved its peacekeeping and governance mettle, the reward would be a Palestinian state in the West Bank and the Gaza Strip. Palestinians expected a sovereign, independent state within a two-state solution, but this resolution is precisely what the Oslo Accords did *not* include. Palestinians were supposed to pass a number of "tests" and qualifications and prove their fitness, as it were, before the FSA could be concluded. The failure to define an endgame all but ensured that the process would fail. "[That] the agreement left the Palestinian side captive to Israel and with no leverages at all was another problem and mistake," says Ghassan Khatib.

Uri Savir recalls Abu Ala telling him: "You may try to force your approach on Arafat. And if you use your strength to push him into a corner, he may have no choice but to accept your approach. But remember: if you do that, you will isolate him. A one-sided agreement will not stand."[17]

Not only was the agreement one-sided and ambiguous but its implementation presented innumerable problems, with animosity quickly apparent on

*"What you've done," she told the PLO negotiators, "is you've kept Israel in control of everything, you're at the mercy of Israel and you're bringing the PLO to live under occupation."

"I told Arafat," she said, "'You should sign if you want to recognize Israel and then have them recognize our right to self-determination as Palestinians.' He said, 'Well, the PLO embodies the national identity and our right to self-determination. It's embodied in the PLO.' So while we recognize the state, they recognized an organization, a system of political governance."

both sides, partly because of the flaws in the agreement itself and partly because the teams who negotiated Oslo had *nothing to do with its implementation.*

"It took the Palestinians a long time to appoint new negotiation teams, military defense staff, et cetera," says Savir. "I think there was an intention to implement, but the Palestinian clock was very slow, and on the Israeli side too much authority was given to the army in the implementation process."[18] Nabil Sha'ath sees it a little differently. "Once Oslo was signed, which was done in secret," he recalls, "we went into intensive negotiations for what was called the Gaza Jericho Agreement, which was the first implementation agreement that brought us into Palestine. These negotiations sometimes were really tough. I would wonder many times whether the Israelis were serious. We were talking about an interim agreement, not a permanent agreement." The recently deceased Ron Pundak, who was intimately involved with the Oslo process, ruefully recalled that "Oslo was conceived as a dialogue based as much as possible on fairness, equality, and common objectives. These values were to be reflected both in the character of the negotiations, including the personal relationships between the negotiators, and in the covered solutions and implementation. Unfortunately it didn't achieve that."[19] Not even close.

Curbing violence was one of the obligations Arafat had committed himself to. However, he had not foreseen the ascendency of Hamas, the militant, Islamic party that had emerged out of Gaza during the First Intifada. Hamas opposed the Oslo Accords because it was committed to eliminating the Israeli state and returning Palestine to the Palestinians.[20] In the wake of Oslo, it stepped up its attacks on Jewish Israelis, especially in Jerusalem, and intensified its armed struggle against the IDF. The newly created Palestinian Authority Security Forces (PASF) crushed dissent, but not sufficiently to convince the Israelis that Arafat was really serious about his commitment. Paradoxically, by creating the Palestinian Authority and pitting Fatah against Hamas, Oslo mangled Palestinian nationalism.

After the first elections for the PA's Legislative Council and president in 1996, the Palestinian Authority was ruled by Fatah as its majority party for the next thirteen years. The PLO was little more than an appendage. With an ironclad grip on the levers of power, Fatah disenfranchised political competition, entrenching itself as the embodiment of the Palestinian right to self-determination. With no governance experience, little familiarity with democracy, a history of trampling on human rights, and no regard for due process, it failed on almost every count. It was a bloated bureaucracy whose inefficiency, incompetence, and endemic corruption were the hallmarks of its performance. Government appointees were vetted not for their technical and professional skills but for their affiliation with Fatah. Patronage and paranoia ruled the day. The PASF silenced anyone who posed a challenge to Fatah. Maintaining order took precedence over democracy and human rights, with the rationale that order and stability were Israeli prerequisites for conceding more territory. Political and civic life, which Palestinians in the West Bank and Gaza had cultivated in the first two decades of occupation, underwent a destructive turnabout. Political activism and civic virtue (for decades essential to the way Palestinians lived) were vitiated. Nongovernmental organizations (NGOs), once the backbone of local development, were disempowered and subject to surveillance. Pluralism was co-opted by authoritarianism. New economic elites emerged. Press censorship, repression of union activity, suppression of dissent and most forms of opposition, and restrictions on assembly became the new norms. Israel had given Arafat a statelet he could call his own. There was no equality before the law and no pretense otherwise. Human rights were routinely violated. Arbitrary arrests, detention without trial, and torture were not uncommon.

There were deep and contentious divides between the local Palestinians and the cohorts Arafat brought with him from Tangiers, strangers who knew nothing about the local culture, the people's relationships with the IDF, or the manner in which resistance was practiced. In a scathing indictment, Sara Roy, a noted Harvard scholar on Palestine, wrote, "Those excluded are the majority poor who arguably have no more access to the system's resources than they did before Oslo. . . . It is not only an alternative source of power that the leadership feared, but an alternative source of thought. . . ." The PA's behavior "increasingly is regarded not only as a form of betrayal but of complicity with the Israeli occupation and its policies of separation and isolation." The peace process was emasculated not just because of Israeli actions but because Palestinians were betrayed by their own leaders. "Palestinians know that a state will come, but many increasingly fear the kind of state it will be."[21]

Public support for the new government inevitably dissipated. This disillusionment, coupled with what were perceived as egregious violations of the accords by the Israelis, caused the Palestinian public's faith in the efficacy of future negotiations to dwindle.[22] The Palestinians were angered by the ongoing construction of settlements in the West Bank, IDF incursions, and non-implementation of scheduled redeployments. Although the accords did not call for settlements to be frozen, the Palestinians felt creating new facts on the ground that could be used to eke out further concessions during negotiations violated "the spirit of Oslo." If Israel were serious about the creation of an independent Palestinian state, why would it expropriate and assist new settlements on the land destined to comprise the territory of that new state? Meanwhile, Israelis were also losing faith, justifying closure on security grounds. They felt that Arafat had not rejected terrorism, was in serious dereliction of his commitment to weed out and imprison terrorists, and still encouraged hatred of Israel among his people.

The widespread belief that Rabin envisioned a sovereign state of Palestine sharing peaceful borders with the sovereign state of Israel certainly does *not* reflect what he had in mind when Oslo I was negotiated. Rabin was a realist, not an idealist. All he had in mind at that point was some form of autonomy, a governance structure that would devolve substantial powers to the Palestinians but leave Israel's ultimate authority unchallenged—a benign, unobtrusive, but also pervasive presence that would be prepared to reassert itself on a moment's notice with whatever force was deemed necessary. With time his thinking evolved and although he may have been Hamlet-like on various details, at the time of his assassination in 1995 he was closer to accepting that an independent Palestinian state was the only route to take.* The notion was still a work in progress.

Moreover, it is often conveniently forgotten that despite his post assassination sanctification, Rabin instigated closure to control the movement of Palestinian militants from the West Bank and Gaza into Israel, bringing hardship to ordinary people, whose movements were also curtailed, and playing havoc with the economy. And although Rabin despised the settlers, especially the Gush, Oslo did not provide for a halt to construction and Rabin abided by the letter of the agreement.†

To this day, it remains unclear how the assassin broke through the security

*No one was able to say that Rabin had declared himself *unequivocally* in favor of a Palestinian state at the time of his assassination, only that his thinking was moving in that direction. Uri Savir says, "I spent a lot of time with Rabin along with Peres; *everybody who was in their right mind in this knew when we started on this that this would end up as a state, and that was also Rabin's view* [emphasis added]." (Savir, interview with the author, February 14, 2014.) If this is true, it was certainly never an outcome spelled out with any specificity and never one conveyed to the Palestinians. The late Ron Pundak, one of the architects of Oslo II, said, "Regarding a Palestinian state I would call it 'mixed feelings,' meaning that objectively, and rationally, Rabin understood that there was no other option but two states, but he was not completely sure that either this is what he wanted, or that this was good for Israel, or that the Palestinians were sincere." (Pundak, interview with the author, November 6, 2011.)

†For more on Rabin's plans to build settlements abutting Tel Aviv and concerns in general about settlement expansion, see Clyde Haberman, "Israel Weighs Expanding West Bank Settlements Near Tel Aviv," *New York Times*, September 29, 1994, http://www.nytimes.com/1994/09/29/world/israel-weighs-expanding-west-bank-settlements-near-tel-aviv.html.

cordon so easily. The fact that there are many on both sides who hold tenaciously to the belief that had Rabin lived an FSA would have been reached and a two-state solution successfully implemented is a reflection of their belief that neither side has leaders capable of taking—or willing to take—the political risks that would be required.

In some Israeli circles, many doubted whether Arafat actually wanted peace on Oslo's terms. General Jacob Perry, who acted as the intermediary between Rabin and Arafat, says, "After meeting with Arafat three or four times after Oslo, I told Rabin that Arafat would never sign a final status agreement. He wanted to somehow be seen as above it all, a Palestinian symbol, the personality who raised the Palestinians' problem and brought it to the attention of the world, the personification of Palestine. He was not ready to come to a final settlement. There was a huge gap between what he would say and his real fear of signing an agreement with the Zionist enemy."[23]

Arafat did not want to be remembered as the Palestinian leader who promised to liberate all of Palestine but settled instead for a meager 22 percent. He knew he could never bring himself to make the compromises required on some of the core issues because they would compromise his sense of self. Whether or not any of this is true, it allows Israelis to shift the blame onto Arafat's bad leadership. The conviction that Rabin, had he lived, could have persevered and triumphed allows Palestinians to shift the failures of the last twenty years onto the Israelis' inability to produce leaders of sufficient caliber. This sleight of hand gets everyone off the hook for their own shortcomings.

> > < <

In August 1999 the Egyptians took the lead and initiated a series of talks aimed at getting the Oslo agreement preparations back on track. Many of these meetings took place at the residence of Muhammad Bassiouni, Egypt's ambassador to Israel, between small teams of negotiators, including Saeb Erekat and Mohammad Dahlan on the Palestinian side and Gilead Sher, Michael Herzog, and Daniel Reisner on the Israeli side, leading to the signing of the Sharm el-Sheikh Memorandum on Implementation Timeline of Outstanding Commitments of Agreements Signed and the Resumption of Permanent Status Negotiations. The agreement provided for a number of IDF redeployments between September 1999 and January 2000.* It also provided

*The memorandum was signed on September 4, 1999, by Barak and Arafat in the presence of Madeleine Albright and cosigned by Hosni Mubarak and King Abdullah of Jordan. Among its provisions, the memorandum provided for redeployments of 7 percent from Area C to Area B on

for the release of 350 prisoners, a safe passageway between Gaza and the West Bank, and the building of a seaport in Gaza.[24] An FSA would be wrapped up by September 2000. On September 5, 1999, the day after the memorandum was signed, talks on final status negotiations began.

In the run-up to Oslo's final status negotiations, a small group of Palestinian and Israeli negotiators[25] were authorized to hold clandestine preliminary talks in May 2000 in Stockholm.[26] Depending on whose account you read, these were either querulous and contentious and exposed the depth of the sides' differences on the core issues, leaving interlocutors unable to reach even the outlines of a framework agreement, or had the makings of breakthroughs. For Hiba Husseini, a member of Abu Ala's team, the talks were exhilarating. "Stockholm was intense," she recalls. "Serious progress was made. Jerusalem was discussed for the first time, even though Barak had given his negotiators specific instructions not to discuss Jerusalem."[27] Shlomo Ben-Ami talks of the optimism the exchanges during the talks engendered. "The surroundings were tranquil," Ben-Ami wrote in his diary. "[T]he atmosphere was right, the approach was pragmatic. So much so that we constructed a written framework for an agreement, and we even entered into consultations with experts in international law on the correct legal construction of the agreement. Our assessment was that we were truly on the way to an Israeli-Palestinian peace agreement."[28] However, that was not to be. "The Palestinians," he writes, "grasped that the Israelis were making far-reaching proposals and concessions, but they were unable to endorse them precisely because of their internal disputes."[29] Gilead Sher, Barak's Chief of staff, simply concludes, "[T]he Swedish channel, like its predecessors, fell victim to Palestinian infighting, thus undermining once again any attempt to move toward an agreement."[30] Abu Ala, on the other hand, provides a bleak analysis: He wanted agreement on borders and then a discussion of Israeli security needs; Ben-Ami wanted the reverse. "We had approached Stockholm with high hopes," he writes, "but these were not to be realised.... I warned him that there had to be progress on major issues if the [Camp David] summit was to have any chance of success."[31] But when he discusses the reasons for the failure of the Camp David summit, he appears to contradict himself when he says, "I hold Ehud Barak and the U.S. administration responsible for failure. I believed the 'Swedish Track'... had achieved a

September 5, 1999; 2 percent from Area B to Area A, and 3 percent from Area C to Area B on November 15, 1999; 1 percent from Area C to Area A; and 5.1 percent from Area B to Area A, on January 20, 2000.

breakthrough of sorts. In Stockholm I had agreed with Shlomo Ben-Ami on the issues that needed to be discussed regarding the permanent solution framework. I was therefore taken by surprise when Ben-Ami told me in May 1999 that Barak wanted to hold a summit meeting. . . . [T]he Americans, who saw themselves as facilitators, failed to do enough ground work to see if it was possible to reconcile the two opposing positions and to build something on the basis of the few understandings that had already been achieved."[32]

One thing is clear. Whatever Ben-Ami's so-called great strides, nothing of substance would carry over to the Camp David talks in 2000.

What is striking, however, is the sheer scale of the talks, involving countless meetings between both the same interlocutors on both sides and different teams, during the eighteen months that preceded Camp David—and the lack of progress on virtually every front. According to Nabil Sha'ath, there was no need for this frenzied rush before the looming 2000 deadline for final status talks. "We could have started permanent negotiations in parallel with the interim negotiations," he says, "but the Israelis refused and delayed the permanent negotiations for seven years until we went to Camp David in July 2000 for our first real negotiating arena." Given the way events were unfolding on the ground, the absence of strategic guidance from the principals, the lack of preparation on the part of the United States,* Barak's tenuous hold on his coalition government,[33] the warning by Israeli intelligence of an imminent outbreak of violence, the prospect of elections in Israel,[34] Arafat's reluctance, and Clinton's own impending departure from office, there was little reason to believe that any summit would be successful, but Clinton nevertheless convened everyone at Camp David on July 5, 2000.

Whether there had been sufficient advance preparatory work remains contentious.[35] Barak had talked of having a "grand plan, convinced that he could reach a historic settlement."[36] Arafat insisted, vociferously at times, that sufficient groundwork had *not* been done and that the time "was not ripe" to embark on final status negotiations.[37] Nor did the Palestinians trust Barak, who had reneged on the third redeployment in the West Bank called for by the Oslo Accords.[38] Barak argued that a "grand bargain" at Camp David would more than compensate. Arafat finally agreed to come, but only after wringing a promise from Clinton that he would not blame the Palestinian leader should the talks collapse.[39]

"We went to Camp David," U.S. secretary of state Madeleine Albright told

*Miller, *Much Too Promised Land*, 298. "We didn't run the summit; the summit ran us."

Aaron David Miller, "on his [Barak's] word."[40] But Barak did not have a grand plan, although the one proposal he put on the table regarding one of Israel's core-protected issues had the potential to be a game changer. He violated an Israeli taboo and offered the Palestinians some sovereignty (and a degree of security oversight) over the Temple Mount (Haram al-Sharif). Arafat demurred, pointing out (correctly, as it turned out) that neither he nor the Palestinians alone could possibly make any agreement concerning Jerusalem without getting the approval of the Arab states.[41] Jerusalem is revered as the third-holiest city in Islam, in particular the Haram al-Sharif, where Prophet Muhammed is said to have ascended to heaven to receive the first revelations of the Quran* and which is considered *waqf* land.† If Arafat had returned to Ramallah after agreeing on his own to Barak's proposals, or to alternative Jerusalem proposals from Clinton, he would have paid for the transgression with his life.[42]

Before the conference, Arafat's overall concerns had been brushed aside. Now this specific concern was also trashed, almost derisively, by both American and Israeli interlocutors. It was just another of the excuses in his bag of tricks, they said. Through the prism of the Western technocratic value system, he was simply being intransigent or irrational. No one, apparently, including Clinton, had any inkling of the importance to the Muslim world of Jerusalem and the Haram al-Sharif in particular. The Israelis and Americans at Camp David believed that Barak's offer was daring and courageous and that it would be seen in the same way by close to a billion Muslims around the world, especially by Arabs. It appeared that they, in their impatience, believed that all Arafat had to do was get on the phone with a few Arab leaders and get their consent, as if a matter of such religious import

*See United Nations General Assembly and Security Council, "Letter Dated 23 February 1968 from the Permanent Representative of Jordan Addressed to the Secretary-General: Addendum," February 23, 1968, UN Doc. A/7057/Add.1–S/8427/Add.1, Part IV: The Respective Claims of the Two Parties, sections (d) and (e), http://unispal.un.org/UNISPAL.NSF/0/59A92104ED00DC468525625B00527FEA.

"In the seventeenth Sura of the Qoran, reference is made to the Prophet's celestial journey, during which he visited Jerusalem" (remembered every year during Ramadan). "Laylat al-Qadr is a night awaited by all Muslims due to its significance to Islam, marking the night when Prophet Muhammed received the revelation from the angel Jibril (Gabriel). Laylat al-Qadr represents the first phase when the first verses of the Quran were passed on." See http://www.dailynewsegypt.com/2013/07/13/ramadan-a-spiritual-journey/). "Jerusalem and especially the Temple area, for a certain period, became the first Kibla (the direction) [turned to in five daily prayers]) for Muslims, . . . and it was not till later on that Mecca became definitely the Kibla." See also for Islamic *waqf*: http://unispal.un.org/UNISPAL.NSF/0/59A92104ED00DC468525625B00527FEA.

†*Waqf* land is land held in trust for Muslim religious and charitable purposes. For more on how this relates to Israel/Palestine, see Suleiman and Home, "'God Is an Absentee, Too,'" 49–65.

could be summarily disposed of with a few calls followed by a decision made on the spot. Even though the substance of what Barak proposed had merit, Arafat had to show the Arab world that he wasn't a pushover, ready to accept almost unhesitatingly what Israel proposed.

As it happened—as it had to happen—the key Arab and Muslim leaders sided with Arafat in turning down the offer,[43] a fact not too often publicized because it does not fit the narrative of how the negotiations were conducted. Then, Egyptian president Hosni Mubarak went on television the day after Barak's proposal to make the situation clear "that Arafat did not have the authority to divide Jerusalem and the Old City. This was an all-Arab and all-Muslim matter, and that whoever agrees to the partition would be considered a traitor to Arab and Muslim history."[44] Gilead Sher, who had been one of those dismissive of Arafat's qualms about making a peremptory decision on the Haram al-Sharif, was *still* dismissive eleven years later. "Jerusalem," Sher told me in 2011, "is the capital of Israel since the days of King David, three thousand years and more from now. Jerusalem is mentioned in the Bible, in the Old Testament, eight hundred times. It's not mentioned in the Quran even once. The Palestinians, or should I say Arafat, played a very skillful game here. By putting Jerusalem as the nonflexible issue on the table, he didn't have to deal with any of the other core issues, right?" However, by elevating Jerusalem's importance to Jews, Sher was, relatively speaking, diminishing its importance to Muslims. His implication: Even though it is of greater importance to us, we were prepared to sacrifice some for the sake of peace. Why can't you do the same? That said, there is no excusing the Palestinian's lack of understanding of the importance of Jerusalem to Jews. In the event, Arafat's handling of the talks was approved by 68 percent of Palestinians, Barak's by only 25 percent of Israeli Jews.[45] Moreover, "both publics felt there was no further room for compromise." In fact, each public believed its leaders had already gone too far in accommodating the other.[46]

Like the United States, Israel has an unparalleled diplomatic/media/public-relations/academic cluster of experts that kicks into operation should things start to go awry, and this public-relations blitz invariably leaves the Palestinians at the starting blocks. This explains why, with the exception of Abu Ala's book, the innumerable volumes written about the 2000 Camp David summit by negotiators themselves, aides, and observers reflect Israel's and the West's spin on the proceedings: Barak and Clinton made an unprecedented offer and Arafat walked.[47] This invention became the accepted truth: Arafat was vainglorious, famished for approval and hero worship, manipulative, double-dealing, endemically suspicious and distrustful of everyone, even paranoid, and a serial liar more interested in his legacy than in the interests of his people. He was a leader who threw peace into the dustbin of history for his own self-centered sense of grandiosity.[48]

Though this is a gross mischaracterization, Arafat did grave injury, almost irreparable, to his cause at Camp David when he displayed his own breathtaking and inexcusable ignorance of the importance of Jerusalem to Jews. He opined at one point that Jews have no historical connection to Jerusalem because the Second Temple was built in Nablus, not in Jerusalem, as Jews claim. No members of his negotiating team corrected him or were inclined to question their boss's ignorance, much less to apologize to the Israelis.

Along with the disagreement over the core issues, this dueling ignorance of religious iconography helped sabotage Camp David. Barak, according to Ben-Ami, "was too slow to grasp the centrality of the issue of Jerusalem at this conference and was therefore unprepared for the far-reaching concessions that were required."[49] In addition, for the Israelis any compromise on the right of return of refugees to the homes in Palestine from which they had been expelled, and Israel's acknowledgment of its responsibility for the *Nakba*, were out of the question. Negotiations were conducted on parallel tracks that had little relation to each other. The cultural divide could not be crossed. "When Israeli leaders say that they have changed their positions and come up with far-reaching proposals," Ben-Ami said:

> we come with bold ideas. They are bold in relations with the internal Israeli political discourse, but they are not bold enough to meet the minimal requirements of the Palestinians. That is something that it is extremely difficult for the Israeli mind to decode. Zionism, historically, used to accept whatever was put on the table, and there were two reasons for that. One is that it was driven by a positive ethos. Ben-Gurion believed that it doesn't matter what territorial space we get. We put our foot on the ground and will unleash the Jewish genius in this part of the world and make wonders.[50]

In short, either the Israelis are prepared to make all the concessions or the Palestinians do not possess the necessary "genius" to make something out of nothing. Or Ben-Ami is unwittingly being condescending.

After two weeks, the Camp David leaders and negotiators dispersed empty-handed. Arafat and Barak did not have a single one-on-one substantive conversation during the summit. The late general Amnon Lipkin-Shahak, former chief of staff of the IDF and a key member of the Israeli security delegation, says security demands weren't even touched.[51] Nor was the question of refugees addressed in any substantive way.[52] Clinton broke his promise to Arafat. His support of Barak's assertion that Arafat had sabotaged the talks was a breach of diplomatic protocol, inexcusable for a statesman of his caliber. He publicly seconded Barak's repeated insistence that Israel "did not have a partner for peace," which became a convenient Israeli mantra and stymied negotiations until Annapolis in 2007.[53] It is virtually impossible to imagine Clinton making similar damning statements about Israel if he believed, perchance, that Barak was the culpable party.

And again, from Ben-Ami: "We can say in all honesty that we tried everything and that we found, to our regret and sorrow, that the Palestinian leadership rejected the boldest possible proposals—including, in fact, the return of the territories—while trapped in a myth of return, exile, return, and Islam, and that it is not capable of a compromise that would recognize Israel as a Jewish state's moral right to its legitimacy as a Jewish state." For Palestinians, in Ben-Ami's view, the peace process is "a political journey to justice and to the sanctity of Islam, which—if it fails—becomes a violent journey intended to compel the Israelis to recognize and acknowledge the justness of the Palestinian cause and the Islamic claims of ownership of Jerusalem."

The Palestinian reading of events is, not unsurprisingly, quite different. Sari Nusseibeh wrote: "[C]onsider situations—and the conflict we are dealing with is sadly a paradigm of such situations—in which one or both sides view life itself as expendable. . . . they . . . deem some value so essential that without it life ceases to be worth living. When such a value is on the line, negotiations, however rationally pursued, are futile. At the Camp David meetings in 2000, the value in question from Arafat's standpoint was Jerusalem, or its place in the collective Muslim, and therefore political, psyche. With regard to that value, Clinton's proposal did not fit into political coordinates Arafat could accept."[54]

Among those who have tried to provide balance of perspective is UN special coordinator for the Middle East peace process Terje Roed-Larsen. "It is a terrible myth that Arafat and only Arafat caused this catastrophic failure. All three parties made mistakes, and in such complex negotiations everyone is bound to," he told the *New York Times*, concluding that "no one is solely to blame."[55] During our interview in 2011, Gilead Sher opined that the "no partner for peace" spin was effective in Israel, but said that he had come to understand the damage it did to the peace process: "It was a very short-term victory, because the notion of having no partner made even the most confident, supportive audiences in Israel to the peace process, to the two-state solution . . . turn their back. . . . The notion of having no partner, which was the caption of all the public discourse of the Israeli diplomatic and governmental bodies, actually destroyed the internal Israeli peace camp for a decade or more."[56]

Though many have attempted to explain why it failed, few ever addressed the question of why Camp David should have been expected to succeed when Arafat was practically coerced into being there, because at the time he had made it abundantly clear that he opposed the proposed summit because he did not believe that sufficient preparations had been made.*

Nevertheless, Arafat met with President Clinton, U.S. secretary of state Madeleine Albright, UN secretary-general Kofi Annan, EU representative Javier Solana, and Barak at Sharm el-Sheikh, and on October 17, 2000, they renewed their commitment to resolve their differences by peaceful means.[57] However, these talks stalled, and Clinton, in the twilight days of his presidency and looking to broker a historic breakthrough that would seal his legacy, called everyone back to Bolling AFB in Washington DC the week before Christmas in 2000. He provided the parties with a set of guidelines that he believed created a viable framework for peace. He stipulated that the proposals he would outline would be a "take it or leave it" offer on the table. Neither side could make changes. They became known as the "Clinton Parameters."[58]

In his autobiography, *My Life*, Clinton writes that he read his "parameters" to the parties "slowly, so that both sides could take careful notes."† It was not

*For a blunt account of the Palestinian leadership's opposition to the Camp David summit, see Ginossar, *Camp David*, 54. In Shamir and Maddy-Weitzman's *The Camp David Summit: What Went Wrong?*, Zeev Maoz, a professor of political science at Tel Aviv University, provided a summation: "The main lesson to be learned from the Camp David Summit, is that in the future [the procedural aspects of the summit] should be done in an entirely different way. . . . The notion to which former prime minister Barak subscribes, that the other side was entirely to blame while his moves were unimpeachable and that there is therefore no need to revisit them, is unproductive and not useful; it will not help Israel to find a way out of a stalemate." Maoz, "The Pitfalls of Summit Diplomacy," in Shamir and Maddy-Weitzman, *Camp David Summit*, 208. In *The Myth of Camp David or the Distortion of the Palestinian Narrative*, Birzeit professor Helga Baumgarten provides an insightful analysis of how the Israeli "spin machine" succeeded in placing full blame for the failure of Camp David and hence the Second Intifada, which erupted just two months later, on Arafat's shoulders and how the absence of a Palestinian response allowed the myth to take an unshakable hold. (It was left, according to her, Deborah Sontag, that Hussein Agha, an Arab-American academic, and Robert Malley tried to set the record straight.)

†Bill Clinton, *My Life* (New York: Alfred A. Knopf, 2004), 936–38, 943–45. According to Dennis Ross, in September he drew up Clinton's proposals in discussions himself, along with the other members of Clinton's team—Aaron David Miller, Gamal Helal, Jon Schwartz, and Robert Malley. President Clinton, Ross says, was not consulted. See Ross, *Missing Peace* (paperback 2005), 725.

submitted as a written document. He laid out a set of once-only schematic propositions. The most important element related to an exchange formula: "refugees for Jerusalem." The Palestinians would relinquish the right of return—the bedrock of both their narrative and their negotiating stance from the beginning—in exchange for Israel's relinquishing sovereignty over the Temple Mount. (Israel would maintain some symbolic control in the area.) "On Jerusalem," he wrote, "I recommended that the Arab neighborhoods be in Palestine and the Jewish neighborhoods in Israel, and that the Palestinians should have sovereignty over the Temple Mount/Haram Al-Sharif and the Israelis sovereignty over the Western Wall and the 'holy space' of which it is a part with no excavation around the wall or under the Mount at least without mutual consent."[59]

The division of land would leave the Palestinian state with almost 97 percent of the West Bank. While 80 percent of Israeli settlers would remain under Israeli sovereignty, in compensation Israel would relinquish a certain unspecified area within the Green Line (the 1949 armistice line). Israel would relinquish sovereignty over the Jordan Valley. However, the IDF would maintain a presence for six years—half of the time under Israeli sovereignty, half under Palestinian authority—in order to be able to respond to threats from the east. Israel would be permitted to deploy forces along the Jordan River during times of emergency when there was a demonstrable and imminent threat to its security. It would be allotted three warning stations (with the presence of Palestinian liaison officers) for a period of ten years. An international force deployed along the Jordan would control the external checkpoints of the Palestinian state.

The Palestinian state would be nonmilitarized. "Mutual use" was the term Clinton used regarding airspace: Sovereignty went to the Palestinians, but they would acknowledge Israel's right to use the airways for training and operational purposes. Finally, and most important, the agreement would mark the end of the mutual claims of both sides, that is, the end of the conflict, period.

The Knesset accepted the parameters *with reservations* as the basis for a settlement. The PLO did, a little later, also *with reservations* but without fanfare, reinforcing the impression that Israel was prepared to do all the giving while the recalcitrant Palestinians had nothing to offer.[60] In his memoirs Clinton later wrote that the Israeli reservations were within the parameters and that the Palestinians' were outside.[61]

According to most analysts, the main contribution of Clinton's parameters was to establish reasonable principles for a possible overall agreement. On the two most sensitive issues, Jerusalem and refugees, he proposed an exchange formula—refugees for Jerusalem—that marked the first time in the peace process that each side was called on to trade a core-protected value for one on the other side. Clinton's formula for the division of East Jerusalem is still invoked. The ideas received broad support within the Israeli cabinet, which was, at that point, in its death throes. In January 2001 Clinton's tenure as president of the United States ended, and ended, too, the formal negotiating process between Israelis and Palestinians that had begun at Camp David in July 2000. Both Ariel Sharon, Barak's successor, and George W. Bush, Clinton's successor, rejected the parameters as no longer valid.[62]

Many observers believe that the Clinton Parameters will serve, at some point, as the basis for the conceptual framework for an overall agreement. This belief persists in spite of the fact that the two sides had arrived at Camp David and then Bolling AFB with opposing strategic objectives. The Palestinians continued to insist that the two sides could not deal with the issues of the present until they resolved the injustices of the past. The Israelis turned that on its head: You started the wars, remember, and are responsible for the consequences that followed. We'll deal with the facts on the ground and the future. The Palestinians thought they were negotiating a state for the 22 percent of the land the PLO had not conceded to Israel in the Tangiers declaration in 1988. The Israelis did not acknowledge any requirement to return to those 1967 borders. Today, moreover, the neighborhoods of East Jerusalem have changed in complex ways due to successive Israeli governments' policies of Judaization that make the application of the Clinton Parameters problematic.[63]

Says Danny Yatom, Barak's former chief of staff:

> When you talk with senior Palestinians today, like Nabil Sha'ath and Saeb Erekat, they would say that they regret the fact that they did not seize the opportunity in Camp David, which was followed by a continuation of talks at Bolling, because at the end, the Israeli suggestion—or the American suggestion that was accepted in principle by Israel—was that there would be a Palestinian state, that the Palestinian state would have the entire area of the Gaza Strip and between 94 and 95 percent of Judea and Samaria, there would be swap of lands at the scale of one-to-one, that in Jerusalem what is Jewish will be Israeli, what is Arab would be Palestinian, a special regime in the Old City, special regime in the Temple Mount, demilitarize the Palestinian state.... We rejected totally—as everybody before and everybody

> afterwards—to accept any refugees on the basis of right of return to Israel, but Barak was ready to accept ten thousand people, refugees or others, on a humanitarian basis.[64]

Ben-Ami later wrote: "The Israelis arrived [at Camp David] ready to seek a compromise solution to the problems of 1967 and found themselves crashing into the wall of 1948 problems . . . with the Israelis speaking of a dream come true through a process of reasonable compromise during which they relinquish some of their dearly-held myths about Jerusalem and the Land of Israel, while the Palestinians are refusing to abandon their perception of Israel as a state born in sin that needs to admit as much and pay the price. The apparently weaker side, the Palestinians, strove for Israel's moral defeat, to the point of dealing a fatal blow to her legitimacy as a Jewish state."[65]

> > < <

On September 28, 2000, just two months after the collapse of the Camp David talks, Ariel Sharon, the Likud party leader and front-runner to become prime minister after the elections scheduled for March 2001, entered the Temple Mount surrounded by an enormous security contingent and said, "The Temple Mount is in our hands and will remain in our hands. It is the holiest site in Judaism and it is the right of every Jew to visit the Temple Mount."[66] Barak was aware of the impending visit but refused to interfere, believing he was not in a position to tell the leader of the opposition what he should do or not do.[67] The Muslim and Palestinian reaction was almost instantaneous. The day marked the beginning of the *Al Aqsa*, or the Second Intifada. For Palestinian Muslims, Sharon's visit was a carefully arranged, arrogant insult to their faith and to any hopes for peace. For Israeli leaders the visit only jump-started a premeditated insurrection Arafat had already planned.[68]

Whether planned or unplanned, the Second Intifada, like the first, began in slow motion, first with stoning, rioting, and a disproportionate police response leaving some unarmed young people dead. Then it developed a life of its own and mutated into a genuine Palestinian uprising. The Palestinians were sick of the degradations that defined their lives, the economic deterioration, the failure of Oslo, the relentless growth in settlements: In sum, the grievances and resentments of the past converged with the dissolution of hope for the future, and the toxic brew exploded. The gunning down of Muhammad al-Durrah, a twelve-year-old boy, who along with his father was caught in crossfire between the IDF and Palestinian militants outraged Palestinians. The image of a frightened little boy crouching by his father, who was screaming at the shooters to stop, had been caught on video and circulated worldwide. It became the enduring symbol of the intifada. To this day, Akram Hanieh told me, he frequently watches the video of the killing.

The initial IDF response was ferocious.[69] According to the published account of Idith Zartel and Akiva Eldar, the Israeli army, headed by Chief of Staff Shaul Mofaz and his deputy Moshe Ya'alon, engaged in "an unprecedented and disproportionate military reaction with the help of tanks, anti-tank missiles, helicopters, and Air Force jets. The use of massive fire-power exacted a price in victims on the Palestinians beyond anything that had been known in the past, as compared to nearly zero losses on the Israeli side."[70] Ben-Ami notes that "Israel's disproportionate [addictive behavior] response to what had started as a popular uprising with young unarmed men confronting Israeli soldiers armed with lethal weapons fuelled the Intifada beyond control and turned it into an all-out war. This was one more case in Israel's history where the overreaction of the military ended up defining the national agenda in terms that the politicians never planned."[71]

In turn, Hamas and the military wings of Fatah, especially the Tanzim Brigades, headed by Marwan Barghouti, ferociously and indiscriminately attacked Israeli targets. Some students of the intifada believe that if the punch and counterpunch escalation had not been so ferocious, Arafat might have had some leeway to lower the temperature on his side. As it happened, he didn't, and matters quickly got out of control. During the first two weeks of the uprising, Palestinian casualties outnumbered Israelis by twenty to one. Barak instructed General Ephraim Sneh to investigate reports that the IDF had more or less taken matters into its own hands, disregarding orders from its top commanders—and his own orders. Sneh did and reported, "from the chief of staff to the last of the sergeants at the roadblocks, no one is implementing your policy."[72] When I asked Sneh a dozen years later whether that published account was accurate, Sneh replied, "Verbatim, word by word, that's what I wrote to him."[73] Asked why Barak didn't take action, Sneh demurred. Subsequently, I raised the question frequently with interviewees—both Palestinian and Israeli Jews—I thought might have been in a position to throw some light on the matter. The consensus, but not the unanimous opinion, was that Barak didn't genuinely care about Palestinians and that his attitude filtered down to his field commanders—a view Barak's interview with Benny Morris in the *New York Review of Books* would go a long way to confirming.[74]

General Lipkin-Shahak also tried to give clarity to the situation:

> First, there were no clear orders by the government. I was a minister at the time and the government said, "Stop the Palestinian violence." The government never gave instructions like "Shoot here and shoot there," but I will say that the IDF was almost free to decide how it should be done, technically. . . . The IDF did nothing without the approval of the minister of defense. Barak was fully aware, and if Barak ordered the IDF to do it in a different way, the IDF would do it as it was told. I can say that the frustration within the IDF made them act in certain areas in a way in order to punish Palestinians. I believe that if the number of casualties on the Palestinian side were much lower, or if there had been only a few casualties, perhaps the reaction of the Palestinians would have been different. The aggressiveness of the IDF in the beginning . . . contributed fuel to the fire. There was a feeling that the IDF was reacting in a very tough way and being very aggressive and that Barak was not really controlling the IDF either, because he didn't want to, or because—I don't know.[75]

Ironic that in those first few weeks when the Israelis believed Arafat could control the violence, perhaps even end it, the IDF was doing everything it could to fuel the violence.

The failure of the Camp David talks put the finishing touches to Barak's already unlikely prospects of retaining the premiership in the March 2001 elections. His (and Clinton's) "no partner for peace" mantra stuck in the minds of Israelis and was the kiss of a lingering death for the peace movement. Such was Barak's bitterness and disappointment at the outcome, and then at his subsequent electoral defeat, that he became obsessed with demonizing Arafat. In a 2002 interview he resorted to an extraordinarily vitriolic impugning of the Palestinian leader *and his people*:

> They [come from] a culture in which to tell a lie . . . creates no dissonance. They don't suffer from the problem of telling lies that exists in Judeo-Christian culture. Truth is seen as an irrelevant category. There is only that which serves your purpose and that which doesn't. They see themselves as emissaries of a national movement for whom everything is permissible. There is no such thing as "the truth."[76]

This, then, is his assessment of the people he was so desperate to live in peace and neighborly harmony with, hardly one in consonance with "the man of vision" his admirers enthused about.

Of course, if indeed these sentiments reflected what Barak really believed, no progress could have been made, much less an agreement reached, at Camp David or Bolling AFB or anywhere else. Lack of trust between the two principals has been a problem from the start in this conflict, and over decades it has become more pervasive.[77] Arafat distrusted Barak because of issues arising from the IDF redeployment, but Barak's lack of respect for Arafat betrayed sentiments that were nothing less than a racist indictment of Arafat and the people he represented, a people who were under the boot of Barak's own government.

After the first months of extreme violence, the Second Intifada simmered for five long years, but with the usual contours of Israeli dominance quite clear: the Palestinian Authority on its knees, resistance in the West Bank smashed, the IDF controlling the whole of the West Bank, with much of the infrastructure reduced to rubble and incessant closures and checkpoints throttling the economy and setting back living standards ten years. Israel also severely curtailed the number of Palestinian workers allowed to work in Israel. During the intifada there were numerous suicide bombings, most carried out by Hamas, in Israel itself. The random suicide bombings that killed ordinary citizens in Jerusalem and Tel Aviv had a profound impact on the collective perception among Israelis of the Palestinians as a people.[78] The late general Lipkin-Shahak believed that suicide bombings in the 1990s of buses, shopping centers, and restaurants were one of the reasons that more and more Israelis lost trust in the Palestinians as a potential partner for peace. "And I think that until today, memories of the Second Intifada are the main reason why fewer Israelis believe that we have a partner."

It is almost impossible not to come to the conclusion that both sides were highly dysfunctional in their dealings with each other. Despite the fact that many of the opposing interlocutors had known each other for years and were quite friendly, the aggregate of their remarks, observations, and viewpoints shows that theirs was a surface understanding. They were unable to penetrate each other's psyches and more especially unable to *empathize* with each other. Preoccupied as they were with their own suffering, there was no room to consider the suffering of the other.

> > < <

In January 2001, one month after Clinton dictated his parameters, a number of the Camp David negotiators renewed discussions at Taba, an Egyptian resort at the northern tip of the Gulf of Aqaba and a busy border crossing into Israel. The Taba talks were conducted while the Second Intifada raged. The main

Israeli interlocutors were, as Ben-Ami put it, "the four most emblematic doves in Israeli politics . . . [including] Yossi Beilin—people laugh at him and say his name is Mohammed Beilin—Amnon Lipkin-Shahak, chief of the army some years ago and one of the most dovish people here, and myself."[79] The Palestinians were led by Abu Ala and included Saeb Erekat, Nabil Sha'ath, Yasser Rabbo, and Mohammad Dahlan.

Taba was unofficial; Barak did not authorize it.[80] Not even a Taba breakthrough would have saved his electoral skin. Besides, he said in advance that he would reject everything that came out of the conference.[81] In that sense, Taba was a "make believe" exercise to see how far the most dovish interlocutors could go in compromising their core issues. Freed of the constraints imposed by formal negotiations, they could negotiate in an environment that allowed more latitude to engage in give-and-take. But though there were indications of flexibility on many of the core issues on both sides, no concrete arrangements on any of them were reached. On the question of Israeli security, there was a sharp difference of opinion about Palestinian sovereignty, which would entail, inter alia, there being no deployment of Israeli soldiers in the Jordan Valley, permanently or during emergencies. The Palestinian side was unwilling to cede overriding control of its air space to Israel. And, as for Israeli military operations and training in Palestinian air space, the Palestinian side rejected this request.[82] On the issue of refugees, according to Yossi Beilin, the Israeli negotiator who ran that track, "the menu of solutions" was finalized during discussions with his counterpart, Nabil Sha'ath. They agreed that details such as the composition of the international organization that would handle compensation and rehabilitation of refugees, as well as formulate certain alternatives on the "right of return" question, would be decided by their leaders. Beilin believed these issues could be solved.[83]

The question of Jerusalem was also sidelined: Only one meeting on this issue was convened, and it came to no agreement. The Israelis presented their view that the Holy City, including the Old City, should be governed under a special regime and that special issues relating to the impact on the daily lives of the residents of that area should be agreed upon in advance. Only then would sovereignty be discussed. The Palestinians wanted to reverse the order of the agenda.[84]

At meeting's end, the heads of the respective delegations, Ben-Ami and Abu Ala, issued a joint declaration: "The sides declare that they have never been closer to reaching an agreement and it is thus our shared belief that the remaining gaps could be bridged with the resumption of negotiations following the Israeli elections. However in light of the significant progress in narrowing the differences between the sides, the two sides are convinced that in a short period of time and given an intensive effort and the acknowledgment of the essential and urgent nature of reaching an agreement, it should be possible to bridge the differences remaining and attain a permanent settlement of peace between them."*

"I didn't notice in my Palestinian interlocutors the sense of a lost opportunity," Ben Ami told me. "They were blasé about it. This would have never happened with Zionism." (Two other interviewees in different contexts made the same point: The Zionists were *always* prepared.) Of course, this attitude is virtually part of the Israeli narrative.[85]

Ben-Ami is putting Taba in a context that did not exist at the time. Everything may have been on the table, but nothing was agreed, and nothing would have come of any agreements anyway. Conducting "negotiations" in a situation where participants know that the talks are not "real world" simply does not work; any "agreement" reached will be nothing more than an exercise without consequences to follow. Moreover, in the absence of the actual decision makers, the negotiators cannot drill their way into those people's subconscious and fathom how they would weigh different factors, including the prevailing and extremely complex political environment. (Any simulation, no matter how skillfully modeled, has the same limitations.) The negotiators *cannot* reproduce the element of "trust" that permeates formal negotiations, cannot conjure the conflicting emotions underlying decisions when the decisions have real and very far-reaching consequences, when the decisions might cost you your life; when psyches are as important as substance.

This conflict is replete with *hate*—not a quantifiable variable.

Amnon Lipkin-Shahak called Taba a "bluff." As expected, even though no "formal" agreement came out of it, Barak did not accept the mutual understandings that were achieved between Ben-Ami and Abu Ala, and on assuming office in March 2001, Ariel Sharon peremptorily dumped them in the dustbin.

*See "Special Document File, The Taba Negotiations (January 2001)," *Journal of Palestine Studies* 31, no. 3 (Spring 2002): 80. This document is based on the proceedings of the Taba conference kept by Miguel Ángel Moratinos, the EU's special envoy to the Middle East, the only outsider who sat in on the conference. Moratinos cross-checked his documentation with all parties and they vouched for its accuracy. The document subsequently has been referred to as "The Moratinos 'nonpaper.'"

The communiqué that Ben-Ami and Abu Ala issued when the proceedings were wrapped up (and after Israeli voters had ejected Barak from office), claiming that the two sides were on the verge of an agreement and that "if only they had a few more days . . . ," was a piece of political chicanery, perhaps what some might label theater of the absurd, providing the public at least with the illusion that both sides were still trying to bridge the unbridgeable. Everyone could walk away with a feeling of "well done," where the "well done" related to agreements that had precious little to do with the actual positions of their respective governments. Indeed, Taba, like the Geneva exercise in 2003, was in a sense more *threatening* to the peace process than helpful. Since both resulted in "outcomes" with semblances of success, they fostered the illusion that all the elements of a fair and just FSA were in place, waiting for the propitious moment when the leaders would initial it. The inference, of course, was that the leaders were at fault, belying the intractability of the conflict itself.

But the crucial lesson of Taba is that although both sides fielded their most dovish teams, which worked in an environment that allowed the players more give-and-take latitude, free of the many constraints imposed by formal negotiations, the Taba negotiators still could not come up with an FSA.

> > < <

A little more than a year after Taba, the Arab Peace Initiative (API) was unfolded and adopted at the Arab states' summit in Beirut in March 2002.[86] The sponsor was then Crown Prince Abdullah of Saudi Arabia. The API proposed a resumption of normal relations with Israel in return for an Israeli withdrawal from the Golan Heights, the Gaza Strip, and the West Bank, including East Jerusalem, based upon UN Resolutions 242 and 338, which establish the principles of territories for peace. Israel would be required to take steps resulting in an independent Palestinian state and would also "agree to a just solution to the problem of Palestinian refugees in accordance with Resolution 194."*

This was a sufficiently nuanced formulation on the right of return to provide room for interpretation in the future. With all of this accomplished, the Arab-Israeli conflict would be considered resolved. The initiative was directly addressed to Israel, which failed to grasp the sea of change it represented in the Arab position—no negotiations with Israel under any

*See chapter 1, first footnote, on page 16.

circumstances—and rejected it out of hand. Ariel Sharon had no interest in a two-state solution, as was abundantly apparent from the large-scale expansion of settlements under way in the West Bank. Besides, the idea of an Israeli withdrawal from East Jerusalem was anathema. In the West, the initiative was received with reserved ambivalence—not embraced but not dismissed; the reaction was lukewarm—perhaps reflecting the U.S. disposition during George W. Bush's presidency not to appear to be at odds with Israel on any issue. The PLO endorsed the plan, which was important because it indicated in a public way that any right of return of the refugees would have to take account of the realities on the ground and show some flexibility. The PLO continues to believe that the API provides the best platform for mapping the way forward.[87] Nevertheless, the initiative atrophied, but not to the point of extinction. It is a point of reference, along with the UN resolutions, to the international community in relation to matters pertaining to the Palestinian-Israeli conflict, and although it still lies in abeyance, it is nevertheless a possible point of departure for Israel to start negotiating with its neighboring countries.

Another year on, in October 2003, at the height of the Second Intifada, a small number of informal negotiators of substantive standing, led by the indefatigable Yossi Beilin and the tenacious Yasser Abed Rabbo, drafted a document that they envisaged as a replacement for the Oslo Accords.[88] A ceremony to mark its signing was held in Geneva in early 2004, hence the appellation "the Geneva Accord." The accord was presented to both the PLO and the Israeli government as an alternative to Oslo. In this document the Palestinians essentially conceded the refugees' right of return in exchange for having ultimate control over Haram al-Sharif. Israel would relinquish its claim of sovereignty over the same site, which Jews call the Temple Mount. Israel would keep full control of the Western (or Wailing) Wall, the Jewish place of prayer that borders the compound. Some refugees would remain in the countries where they now lived, others would be absorbed into the new Palestinian state, and some would be absorbed by willing host countries. All would receive compensation. Refugees could not return to their old land inside Israel *without Israeli consent*.*

*For a summary of the various peace proposals over the years 1967–2003, see "History of Failed Peace Talks," BBC News, November 26, 2007, http://news.bbc.co.uk/2/hi/world/middle_east/6666393.stm. The summary of the Geneva Accord says:

"The agreement provides for the permanent and complete resolution of the Palestinian refugee problem, under which refugees will be entitled to compensation for their refugee status and

The Geneva Accord found no takers either in Tel Aviv or Ramallah. Nevertheless, the accord, intended as an FSA, broke new ground: Palestinian negotiators were willing to break a taboo and compromise on the core-protected "right of return,"[89] sacrosanct to the PLO leadership. Yes, the negotiations were unofficial, another exercise in "make believe," as they had been at Taba, but the Palestinians' acquiescence on the issue in exchange for Palestinian sovereignty over the Haram al-Sharif indicates that among a high-level tier of Palestinian negotiators—and not just prominent doves—the most sacrosanct value was tradable. Similarly, the Israelis were prepared to compromise on the Temple Mount, it, too, a sacrosanct value. However, given the ascendency of the right wing in Israel, the Geneva Accord (Initiative) has little relevance in the current state of play.

While teams of Palestinian and Israeli negotiators were hammering out the details of the Geneva Accord, "The Road Map," an initiative of President George W. Bush, was intended to lead the way within two years to final status negotiations in three "stages," in accordance with a detailed timetable for implementation.[90] The Road Map (2003) established the Quartet—the U.S., UN, EU, and Russia—with former British prime minister Tony Blair appointed as the ringmaster. Two years were deemed sufficient to reach a framework for negotiations, but suffice it to say that the Road Map was merely a repeat performance of the Oslo initiative. Neither side in the conflict complied fully with the stipulated steps; each challenged the other's violations while ignoring its own. The Palestinians challenged the Israelis' failure to freeze settlements, which the Road Map called for. The staged implementations designed as confidence-building measures instead generated increasing levels of mutual mistrust.

> > < <

In November 2007, the Bush administration called just about everyone to Annapolis, Maryland: Israelis, Palestinians, the Quartet entities, Arab and Muslim countries—including Egypt, Jordan, Syria, Saudi Arabia, Malaysia,

---

for loss of property, and will have the right to return to the State of Palestine. The refugees could also elect to remain in their present host countries, or relocate to third countries, among them Israel, at the sovereign discretion of third countries." For more on the Geneva Accord principles and provisions, go to the Geneva Initiative homepage at http://www.geneva-accord.org/mainmenu/summary. See also "The Geneva Initiative," *YNetNews*, March 23, 2009, http://www.ynetnews.com/articles/0,7340,L-3691154,00.html; and Amram Mitzna, "Israel-Palestine: An Exit Strategy via Geneva," *Global Policy Forum*, December 2003, http://www.globalpolicy.org/component/content/article/189/38199.html.

Sudan, and Lebanon—and various global powers, including China. The goal was to restart the peace process, stalled since Taba but reenvisioned in the Road Map. Three days of speechifying and grand exhortations were held, intending to provide the stimulus for the Israelis and Palestinians to reach a resolution. Mahmoud Abbas, the new chief of the PLO after Arafat's death in 2004,[91] and Ehud Olmert, who had assumed the Israeli premiership when Ariel Sharon was felled by a stroke, committed themselves to reaching an agreement before the end of 2008—an ambitious proposition given the soured relationships between the Israelis and Palestinians since the Second Intifada.

The talks following the ceremonies at Annapolis proceeded on three tracks—one between Abbas and Olmert, who would be the final arbiters of whether an FSA had been reached; a second between teams headed by Tzipi Livni and Abu Ala, which would conduct the negotiations to reach a package acceptable to all—a track in which Udi Dekel, head of the Israeli negotiation team, and Saeb Erekat also played pivotal roles; the third track was composed of teams, mostly drawn from professional ranks, that researched issues pertaining to the negotiations. The talks were conducted on the principle that "nothing is agreed until everything is agreed," and therefore proposals that emerged from one strand of the talks were *only* proposals until woven into the other proposals emerging from the other strands, when the grand tapestry would be complete. In the most bizarre reported episode from the talks, Olmert tried to pressure Abbas to initial an agreement on the borders designated on a map, but he would not provide a copy of that map. The PLO leader had to trace the lines of Olmert's map onto a small piece of paper, which he showed his colleagues, one of whom, the PLO mapmaker Samih Al-Abed, reconfigured it onto an actual map. The Israelis say they never heard another word from Abbas after he left that meeting—the Palestinians had simply walked out. Nonsense, say the Palestinians, adding that they sent the Israelis a long list of questions to clarify Al-Abed's replication of the lines Abbas had sketched, and they never received a response. Whom to believe? There are also accounts that Livni signaled Abu Ala that Olmert, who was aware of a number of corruption charges he might be indicted for, was making offers to Abbas that had no cabinet approval. Once again—as at Taba—the clock ran out on Annapolis. Or, rather, the talks seem to have simply petered out.

In retrospect, the failure of the Annapolis initiative is perplexing. The Palestinians say the Israelis simply walked out when the moment of truth was at hand; the Israelis insist exactly the opposite. Accounts wildly vary. In recent years Abbas has never lost an opportunity—in public forums, television interviews, or newspaper accounts—to reiterate how close to an agreement they came at Annapolis. Gidi Grinstein, founder and president of the Reut Institute, is not surprised that Annapolis crashed. "Since January 2006," he says, "with the election of Hamas and the breakdown of the Palestinian political system and constitutional structure—which means that the carrying capacity of the Palestinian system for a comprehensive agreement with Israel has declined dramatically—that to me has become a mission impossible. Therefore, all the attempts to negotiate a comprehensive agreement since 2006 have been exercises in futility. I wasn't a bit surprised that they failed, that the Palestinians did not take Olmert's offer. I can tell you that we [the Reut Institute] said to the Olmert government, when they started in July 2007, that this is futile and it cannot lead to an agreement no matter what Israel puts on the table, unless Israel signs on to all the Palestinian demands as they are." Udi Dekel concurs. "During the negotiations," he says, "I spent many hours with Saeb Erekat and I told him, 'Saeb, you can now achieve something like 95 to 97 percent of your ambitions. You are speaking about '67 ambitions. We can give you immediately 97 percent. Why don't you respond positively for those ideas?' And his answer always was 'All or nothing. We prefer to stay in the current situation, if we don't achieve all of our goals, and all of our rights.'"[92]

In 2010, the Palestinian minutes of the Annapolis meetings, including the various committees addressing different issues, were leaked to the *Guardian* and Al Jazeera. Sixteen hundred pages in all, *The Palestine Papers* provide a rare insight into the behavior of both Palestinian and Israeli negotiators during this period.[93] Palestinian commentary on the papers excoriated their negotiators for their apparent willingness to make concessions. A comprehensive account of thirty-six meetings between Olmert and Abbas, which both verified took place during the talks, was published by the highly regarded author and blogger Bernard Avishai in February 2011.[94] Both confirmed what Avishai wrote. On the security issue, Avishai says the two leaders had reached agreement; on land swaps and settlements they had not, although they were close to getting there; the refugees' right of return was the real stumbling block. Avishai revealed that Olmert had agreed to allow five thousand refugees to return to Israel proper, one thousand a year for five years, each applicant to be reviewed by Israel, each accepted "for humanitarian reasons." As an "integral part" of this offer, Olmert had said, a signing statement would strongly emphasize how repatriation of any refugees would be carried out "in the spirit of the Arab League peace initiative of 2002." Olmert's colleague Livni had been opposed to any return, even on the grounds of family reunification.[95]

Of course, any proposal that would limit right of return to a mere one thousand refugees per year over a period of five years is totally unacceptable to every Palestinian of any influence who has ever commented on the issue, including every Palestinian interviewee in this book. Such a clause would never have been approved in a referendum and certainly would not have received the sanction of Hamas.

From the beginning, Palestinian leadership has encouraged refugees to believe that, yes indeed, their right of return, enshrined in international law and UN resolutions, will be upheld. Of course, any Israeli prime minister who deviates from the iron wall of "no right of return" or simply agrees to a larger number on humanitarian grounds than what Olmert put on the table would soon be turned out of office. Annapolis, close to success before the Palestinians walked and Ehud Olmert had to resign as prime minister, was just another peace-process jeremiad. Despite what Saeb Erekat professes, other interviewees who were intimately involved with Annapolis emphasized that many barriers to a final status agreement had not been dismantled and no FSA was in the offing.[96] George Mitchell listened to both sides' accounts of the talks and bluntly says that "the Annapolis negotiators were *not* close at all. *Understandings* are not *agreements*."[97]

> > < <

The shelf life of the Road Map has expired, but Blair continues to act as an interlocutor and representatives of the Quartet still meet to assess the situation and trot out the usual exhortations for the resumption of negotiations. But the overriding problem with the Quartet is its domination by the United States. In the end, the United States believes it "owns" the Israeli-Palestinian conflict. The 2013–14 talks were the result of a U.S. initiative, and it played a prominent role in the proceedings with the same dismal results. It covets the global domain; allowing others to have a say in this conflict would undermine that control. Put the conflict under the UN umbrella—highly unlikely—and the outcome will be much the same. The United States is not about to let any country or institution butt in. Former Palestinian prime minister Salam Fayyad points out that the Quartet has never made a reference to the 1967 borders as the starting point for negotiations because the

United States does not want it to (because Israel does not want it to). Fayyad, who met with every American official who counts during his years as prime minister, is highly critical of the Quartet's performance:

> There is not adequate involvement on the part of all members of the Quartet. It is passive, not proactive. It does not investigate, act, and report on incidences clearly within its purview, like settler violence, for example. The Quartet should be saying loud and clear, "This is not acceptable." The political process and the manner it is handled by the Quartet over recent years are out of focus. It is a toothless overseer.[98]

Since 1967, no Israeli political party has clearly laid out its positions on the core interests that would be the basis of its negotiations with the Palestinians. The conventional wisdom says that the public debate would tear the country apart, that its fragile social and political institutions could not withstand the huge differences among the multilayered constituencies that would emerge. (In the 2013 national elections for the Knesset, party platforms omitted *any position* on Palestine but concentrated on bread-and-butter issues.) The Palestinian problem is left to "the leadership" in Israel, which might conceivably negotiate a proposed agreement and put it before the people in a national referendum. But if a pre-election debate would tear the country apart, why wouldn't the referendum debate? (A referendum is required if it involves *annexed* territory—Golan Heights or East Jerusalem and any sovereign land involved in a swap. The referendum requirement does not apply to the West Bank or Gaza.[99])

In 2013, Tzipi Livni's party, Hatnuah, was the first to join Netanyahu's coalition, and Livni was rewarded with the justice portfolio and the promise that she would handle talks with the Palestinians. Other parties followed: Jewish Home (led by Naftali Bennett) and Yesh Atid (led by Yair Lapid), and Netanyahu was reelected prime minister—chastened, it was mistakenly assumed, by his near fall from grace. During the feverish haggling that preceded the outcome, what mattered most was not differences on major policy issues or political ideology or the platform the parties had campaigned on, but self-serving aggrandizement as party heads bartered over which should occupy the most prestigious ministries and the number of ministries their parties should be allotted.

The new government, which at first glance appeared to have moved somewhat from the right, was in fact as far right as the previous one, although for the first time since 1992, the orthodox and the religious parties were not part of the ruling coalition. The Likud party, which merged with Avigdor Lieberman's Yisrael Beytenu party, whose electoral base is immigrants from the former Soviet Union, is dominated by settlers or their supporters. Although they constitute a little over 4 percent of Jewish Israelis, settlers account for 9 percent of Knesset members.[100] About half of the new members joining Likud in the last few years have been settlers. Jewish Home is committed to annexing 60 percent of the West Bank.[101] Netanyahu and his right-wing allies dispersed right-wing ministers, chairpersons of key Knesset committees, departmental director generals, and the most important state agencies, creating a checkerboard with pieces distributed that could thwart political opponents who were calling for a freeze on settlement construction, a re-conceptualization of the Zionist project, and talks with the Palestinians to reach a two-state solution.[102]

In these circumstances, it is difficult to see how Netanyahu (or any center-right prime minister) could reconcile the Palestinians' minimum demands with those of his coalition, key parts of which would virulently oppose him and probably ensure the governing coalition's demise. In July 2013, as part of a package negotiated by Secretary of State John Kerry to induce everyone to come to the table for a new round of talks, Abbas agreed to postpone for nine months application to fifteen UN agencies in return for Netanyahu's agreement to release 104 Palestinians serving long sentences in Israeli jails. For Israelis, the prisoners were "terrorists"; for Palestinians, "freedom fighters."[103] Naftali Bennett said, "Terrorists must be killed, not released. In every one of my previous positions, I fought against releasing terrorists, and I have no intention of acting any differently when I'm in the cabinet. Let my hand be cut off should I vote in favour of releasing terrorists. We support the peace process, but no country in the world would agree to release murderers as a gift."[104] Netanyahu was not caught flat-footed. In an "open letter" to his constituents, he wrote that "prime ministers from time to time make decisions that go against public opinion, when it is important for the country to do so."[105] To appease the Right he also announced a flurry of construction tenders.[106]

> > < <

Indeed, even during the talks, Netanyahu moved to reassure elements in his coalition who opposed them and *any* talk of land swaps or restrictions on settlements or evacuations from settlements with a blistering speech at

Bar-Ilan University. Summarizing the speech, the Jerusalem Post wrote: "The root of the conflict is that the Palestinians don't want Jews to be in Israel. The Palestinian Authority says it recognizes Israel, but that isn't enough. They need to recognize Israel as the *Jewish state* and homeland of the Jewish people; and until that happens, there cannot be peace."[107] After four months, Saeb Erekat, Abbas's chief negotiator, resigned because he believed the talks were just another charade; a few months later Muhammad Shtayyeh followed suit. Abbas persuaded Erekat to return, but not Shtayyeh. Disillusioned, Shtayyeh called upon the Palestinian Authority to turn to "resistance."[108] Even Yasser Abed Rabbo said the talks were going nowhere. "I don't expect any progress at all," he said, "unless there is huge and powerful American pressure."[109]

Slowly the goalposts shifted, away from negotiations on the core issues to recognition of Israel as a Jewish state, and then to the release of prisoners. First Netanyahu made the continuation of talks after their expiration date in April 2014 contingent on Palestinian recognition of Israel as a Jewish state. With that acknowledgment, peace, he said, would surely follow.[110] But unless that acknowledgment was incorporated in some form in Kerry's framework—now downgraded from "agreement" to "outline"—Israel would walk.[111] Of course, the "Jewish state" demand was a nonstarter for the Palestinians.

As the March 29 deadline for the release of the final batch of prisoners approached, a second problem emerged. Kerry had allowed the Palestinians to believe that Palestinian Israeli prisoners would be among those freed, although he had not secured Netanyahu's agreement.* Netanyahu balked; Palestinian Israelis were Israeli *citizens*, and he was adamant he would not release *citizens* who had tried to overthrow the state. In addition, he added a rider: no release of prisoners unless the Palestinians agreed to extend the talks. There was great scurrying about while all sides tried to find an acceptable formula that would enable the talks to continue.[112] The first nail in the coffin, however, came on April 1, 2014, when Housing Minister Uri Ariel republished an old tender for 807 apartments in East Jerusalem's Gilo. The Palestinians, who had watched with dismay as settlement construction

*In *Matter*, Nathan Thrall writes, "The Palestinians provided Kerry with a list of all 104 pre-Oslo prisoners, including 14 Palestinian citizens of Israel, and Kerry assured them that Israel had accepted. Israel had not. Netanyahu never agreed to release the 14 Palestinian citizens of Israel, which the Israeli cabinet decided would require a separate vote. *But the Palestinian negotiators say they were led to believe the opposite* [emphasis added]." Thrall, "Faith-Based Diplomacy."

proceeded at a furious rate—about 13,000 new units—during the nine-month negotiations period could no longer stomach the blatant and insulting provocation.[113] Abbas on television signed the documents to join the international conventions. And then, on April 23, came the second nail: To the consternation of all (Israelis, Americans, and Europeans), Fatah and Hamas announced they had reached a reconciliation agreement. The Israelis pulled out. The Americans were taken completely by surprise.[114] When the talks were over, the blame game began in earnest.

> > < <

Even as the failures pile up, only a few voices have queried whether the two-state paradigm and the framework that calls for the staged implementation of "confidence-building measures" (which inevitably become confidence-*destroying* measures) might be the real miscalculation. Perhaps another paradigm and another framework might, in the end, become a more effective route to accommodation.

Count the thousands of hours that various interlocutors have toiled at the behest of their governments or in the informal gatherings between 1993 and 2014, including the nine months of the talks. Then throw in the countless hours of discussion neither officially nor unofficially acknowledged, where every permutation on a core issue has been put on the table. Then consider that the issues under discussion are always the same—security, borders, settlements, Jerusalem, refugees, and the right of return—and that progress has been made on none of them. Only addictions to their narratives, to fear, to the ethos of conflict, to the conflict itself explain the two sides' willingness to return again and again to the same failed process.

Is it time, perhaps, to consider other options? Face reality?

Chapter 5

Hamas: Spinning Wheels

In the last four chapters, the arguments advanced were that since 1991—taking Madrid as the starting point of the peace process—addictive habits associated with historical narrative, collective memories, ethos of conflict, and the process itself are a nexus of factors sufficiently formidable to make reaching a two-state solution next to impossible.

However, there is a hard-to-fathom omission in this saga of peacemaking that makes it even more illusory. Although the endgame supposedly is an FSA that would culminate in a Palestinian state in the West Bank and the Gaza Strip, Gaza was rarely part of the negotiating conversations. The tangible issues—settlements, security, and borders (and to a lesser extent East Jerusalem)—were all matters that were regarded as pertinent only to the West Bank; Palestinian negotiators were all West Bank based, were secularists, and came with secularist perspectives, and many had been exposed to Western norms and culture, many having studied at either U.S. or UK universities. The countless thousands of hours spent inside and outside negotiating chambers since Madrid 1991 have been focused on issues almost exclusively with the West Bank. Even Jerusalem became a West Bank issue insofar as a Palestinian state with East Jerusalem as its capital would have to have geographical continuity with the West Bank. Of course, the question of linking the West Bank and the Gaza Strip did arise, but it posed no serious differences since it was assumed that contiguity between the two would be ensured by either an underground tunnel or a protected overpass, and there was some talk of an airport and a harbor for trading purposes.

Little attention was given to the fact that the Gaza-based Hamas did its best to undo Oslo with violence—and to a large measure was successful—or that it opposed Camp David, Annapolis, the 2013–14 talks, and made it unequivocally known that it would oppose any agreement that might result and that it had been a self-governing entity since 2007. Even as circumstances within the Palestinian Authority changed dramatically, negotiators pressed ahead, seemingly oblivious to the fact that they were dealing with an illusion, ignoring the fact that the PLO did not represent all Palestinians (after 2007 Abbas's authority extended no further than the West Bank) and

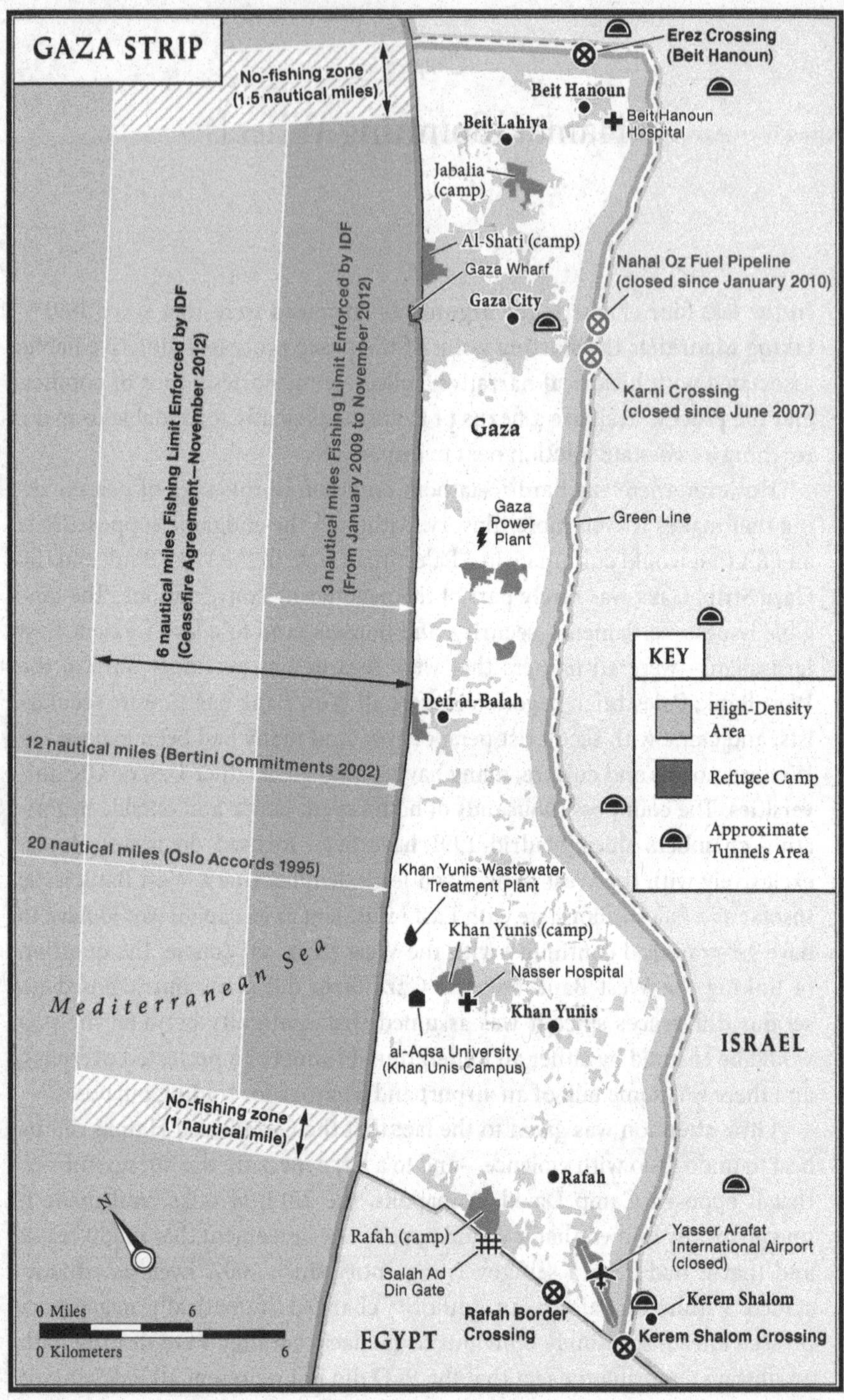
GAZA STRIP
No-fishing zone
(1.5 nautical miles)
Erez Crossing
(Beit Hanoun)
Beit Hanoun
Beit Hanoun
Hospital
Beit Lahiya
Jabalia
(camp)
Al-Shati (camp)
Gaza Wharf
Gaza City
Nahal Oz Fuel Pipeline
(closed since January 2010)
Karni Crossing
(closed since June 2007)
6 nautical miles Fishing Limit Enforced by IDF
(Ceasefire Agreement—November 2012)
3 nautical miles Fishing Limit Enforced by IDF
(From January 2009 to November 2012)
Gaza
Gaza
Power
Plant
Green Line
KEY
High-Density
Area
Refugee Camp
Approximate
Tunnels Area
Deir al-Balah
12 nautical miles (Bertini Commitments 2002)
20 nautical miles (Oslo Accords 1995)
Khan Yunis Wastewater
Treatment Plant
Khan Yunis (camp)
Nasser Hospital
Khan Yunis
Mediterranean Sea
al-Aqsa University
(Khan Unis Campus)
ISRAEL
No-fishing zone
(1 nautical mile)
Rafah
N
Rafah (camp)
Salah Ad
Din Gate
Yasser Arafat
International Airport
(closed)
Kerem Shalom
Rafah Border
Crossing
Kerem Shalom Crossing
0 Miles 6
0 Kilometers 6
EGYPT

assuming that an FSA that both the Israeli prime minister and the president of the Palestinian Authority signed off on would be ratified by most Palestinians in both the West Bank and the Gaza Strip and that thereafter everything would fall into place.

One small measure of the scant attention paid to Gaza and Hamas: in June 2014, shortly after the kidnapping of three Jewish Israeli teenage settlers in the West Bank, *Harper's* magazine published the proceedings of a forum it had hosted in Jerusalem where Bernard Avishai brought together a panel of experts for a conversation about the prospects for a lasting resolution to the Israeli-Palestinian conflict.* The published proceedings ran for thirteen pages.[1] The word "Hamas" was mentioned once, "Islamists" nine times, and "Gaza" twenty-one times, but within very specific contexts that had little to do with the conflict.

It is difficult to understand why so little attention was paid to Hamas, because it is understood by all that without it on board, the prospects for a sustainable two-state solution are next to zero. In fact, many Jewish Israelis have already concluded that even with Hamas on board one may not be sustainable. So what is this elephant in the room? And why is it likely that it makes a two-state solution highly problematic?

> > < <

In the 1970s, despite the objections of moderate Palestinians, the Israeli government allowed Sheikh Ahmed Yassin, the leader of the Muslim Brotherhood in the Gaza Strip, to register an Islamist group called Mujama al-Islamiya,† first as a charity and then in 1979 as an association. In its early years the group focused on building libraries, clinics, schools, and other social amenities. Although Mujama al-Islamiya refrained from violence, it sometimes clashed with the PLO, which saw it as a potential rival. However, when the First Intifada broke out in 1987, Sheikh Yassin and some of his

*The participants were Bernard Avishai, author of *The Hebrew Republic* and *The Tragedy of Zionism*, who teaches at the Hebrew University and Dartmouth College; Dani Dayan, former chairman of the YESHA Communities of Judea and Samaria and now its foreign envoy; Forsan Hussein, CEO of the Jerusalem YMCA; Eva Illouz, professor of sociology at the Hebrew University and president of the Bezalel Academy of Arts and Design; Bassim Khoury, a pharmacist and industrial entrepreneur who has served as president of the Palestinian Federation of Industries and as an economic minister for the Palestinian Authority; Erel Margalit, a venture capitalist and a member of the Knesset from the Labor Party; Danny Rubinstein, a journalist who has covered Palestinian affairs for over forty years and now teaches at Ben Gurion University; and Khalil Shikaki, director of the Palestinian Center for Policy and Survey Research in Ramallah.

†For more on Mujama al-Islamiya, see American Foreign Policy Council, *World Almanac of Islamism*.

colleagues founded the militant Hamas movement.* Its charter committed it to waging an armed struggle to destroy the state of Israel.[2] In 1992, it formed an autonomous military wing, the Izz ad-Din al-Qassam Brigades,† and mounted a deadly campaign of violence opposing the Oslo Accords. Between 1994 and 2005 Hamas carried out a series of suicide bombings in Israel. In Israel, Hamas and suicide bombers have been indelibly synonymous ever since. Israel, the United States, and the EU countries have designated Hamas a "terrorist" group.[3] Hamas sees itself not only in terms of its Islamic roots, however, but also as a liberation movement at the vanguard of Palestinian nationalism, with the goal of liberating Palestine from those it sees as colonial settlers à la the Front de Libération Nationale in Algeria in the 1960s and other liberation (or "terrorist," depending on one's viewpoint) movements that emerged after World War II.

Ariel Sharon unwittingly helped it solidify its identity as such when he unilaterally pulled out of Gaza and "evicted" the 7,500 Israeli settlers living there in September 2005. From the perspective of Israel's cost-benefit analysis, Gaza had become a liability. Israel's real interests were in the West Bank. The withdrawal was the first step of what amounted to a bait-and-switch operation: return Gaza to the Palestinians but hold on to the West Bank, easing the demographic threat for decades. Sharon did so, according to West Bank interviewees, without coordinating with the Palestinian Authority and Fatah. Interviewees repeatedly returned to this refrain: All would have been different if only Sharon had worked with the PA, thus enhancing the status of Fatah. The PA, they said, had argued in vain that setting up the Israeli withdrawal as a *joint* endeavor would show its constituency that Fatah could be effective in furthering the Palestinian cause. Otherwise, Hamas would reap the credit. Sharon and other Israeli policy makers, they say, were uninterested.

Documents disclosed in January 2014, however, cast doubt on this version of events.[4] The "Sharon documents" suggest that the prime minister had

*"Hamas" is an acronym for "Harakat al-Muqawama al-Islamiya" ("Islamic Resistance Movement").

†According to the Terrorism Research and Analysis Consortium (TRAC): "The *Izz ad-Din al-Qassam* Brigades is the military wing of Hamas whose roots go back to 1986. The primary objective of the group was to build a coherent military organization to support the goals of Hamas, which was at the time concerned with blocking the Oslo Accords negotiations. From 1994 to 2000, the *Izz ad-Din al-Qassam* Brigades carried out a number of attacks against both Israeli soldiers and civilians. The Brigades were the first Palestinian group to carry out a suicide attack against an Israeli target the following year and deadly suicide and rocket attacks continued throughout the 1990s and 2000s." See http://www.trackingterrorism.org/group/izz-ad-din-al-qassam-brigades.

tried to find a way to involve the PA but that, for a number of reasons, things didn't work out.[5] They imply that Sharon had further unilateral withdrawals from the West Bank in mind but would not go through with them because he remained unconvinced that the PA was serious about curbing violence.[6] In any event, Sharon's unilateral withdrawal from Gaza gave Hamas the opportunity to boast that "the Palestinian resistance, with its military wings and qualitative martyrdom operations, and with the significant impact of our people's second uprising [the intifada], was able to force the Zionist enemy to leave the Gaza Strip and dismantle its settlements for the first time in the history of the Zionist entity."[7]

In January 2005, national elections, the first in a decade, were held in the West Bank and Gaza for the presidency. Abbas was elected president. In January 2006, elections for the Palestinian Legislative Council (PLC) followed, and Hamas rode the Gaza narrative to victory, winning 76 seats out of 132; Fatah, the former ruling party, won 43 seats.[8] The election results stunned everyone, including Hamas itself. In fact, Hamas would have preferred not to win, because winning would mean having to deal with Israel. While the Israeli withdrawal from Gaza had strengthened Hamas's hand, victory was in large measure due to voters' revulsion at Fatah's corruption, which had begun the day Arafat had first set foot in Gaza after Oslo in 1994.

The election results appalled Israel and the West, which goes to show how out of touch both were with the realities on the ground in the WBG. The United States and the rest of the West immediately cut all financial assistance to the PA because a Hamas-led government would not meet their conditions: denouncing terror and recognizing Israel. Fatah, the dominant power since the 1960s, had difficulties, both political and psychological, handing over the keys of government to Hamas, especially surrendering its control of the security forces. The new PLC, now dominated by Hamas, did meet but was more of a squabbling arena than a legislative one.[9] While a unity government was formed, with Ismail Haniyeh as prime minister, it quickly floundered amid recrimination and a growing hostility between the two parties, and efforts to resuscitate it failed despite intense negotiations in Mecca, arranged by the Saudis, between Abbas and Mohammad Dahlan, speaking for Fatah, and Ismail Haniyeh and Khaled Meshaal for Hamas.[10]

After Hamas's election success, it faced a new set of problems—significant differences between the political wing (the pragmatists led by prime minister Ismail Haniyeh and Khaled Meshaal, head of the Political Bureau, who wanted to establish a government along more established lines) and Ahmed al-Jabari, commander of the Izz ad-Din al-Qassam Brigades, who wanted to pursue a confrontational engagement with Israel. The differences between the competing visions took an explosive turn in June 2006 when the Army of Islam, a small militia controlled by Gaza's powerful Dormush clan,* and the Popular Resistance Committees, a fringe militia founded in 2000 by Abu Samhadana (a member of another powerful Gaza family),† orchestrated the kidnapping of the Israeli soldier Gilad Shalit, with the charismatic Jabari playing a key role behind the scenes.‡ This one event reverberated through the power hierarchies of Hamas and reconfigured the balance of political and military power in Gaza. In what can only be described as a silent putsch, Jabari used the kidnapping to catapult himself to the top: the most powerful leader in Gaza. His leadership of the Tanfithiya Army was pivotal in Hamas military operations in Gaza. He was a hard-liner: He opposed reconciliation (none came) and any unity government with Fatah. Instead he advocated for a strong, independent government in which the military wing of Hamas would set the course for the entire movement. Jabari's aim was to transform the movement from a communal and welfare organization that happened to have a military wing into a military organization that happened to have a government.

Jabari and his fellow kidnappers were freelancing without the knowledge of either Haniyeh or Meshaal. Both men were furious. Jabari's actions belied Hamas's self-perpetuated myth of discipline: Members do not act unilaterally. Shalit's kidnapping dented that belief. Haniyeh believed that Israel

*The Dormush clan had its own small militia: "The Army of Islam is one of the Salafist jihadi terrorist organizations operating in the Gaza Strip. It is considered a dominant organization, having the highest operational capabilities of all the global jihad networks in the Gaza Strip. The Army of Islam splintered off from the Popular Resistance Committees at the beginning of 2006, and is headed by Mumtaz [Dormush] Dughmush, who comes from a powerful clan centered in the Sabra neighborhood of Gaza City. The Army of Islam has close ties to Hamas, which allows it to operate in both the Gazan and Egyptian arenas, despite its Salafist jihadi identity." "Profile of The Army of Islam, a Salafist Organization Affiliated with the Global Jihad Operating in the Gaza Strip," http://www.terrorism-info.org.il/en/article/20385.

†Sami Abu Samhadana (head of the Fatah Tanfithiya) was one of the Fatah leaders from powerful families who fled Gaza during the 2007 Hamas takeover. See "Inside Gaza: The Challenge of Clans and Families Crisis Group, Middle East Report N°71—December 20, 2007," International Crisis Group, http://www.crisisgroup.org/~/media/Files/Middle%20East%20North%20Africa/Israel%20Palestine/71_inside_gaza_the_challenge_of_clans_and_families.ashx.

‡I am indebted to Shlomi Eldar for the account in this section of Shalit's kidnapping, its repercussions, Meshaal's approach to Shin Bet, and the Coexistence document, all of which he deals with definitively in his award-winning book *Lehakir et Hamas* ("To Know Hamas"), for giving me access to the English-translated chapter 8, and for an extensive interview in Washington DC in December 2013.

would retaliate on a massive scale. Aides rushed him from his home to a safe house. The Israeli government soon knew that the kidnapping had been unauthorized, but pinning the blame on the terrorist group sworn to destroy it made strategic sense because the more it demonized Hamas, the more it heightened public awareness to the omnipresent threat it posed. A massive retaliation followed. Hamas ministers and members of the PLC were arrested in the West Bank, and Gaza was subjected to a land, sea, and air blockade. Hamas was desperate to offload Shalit. He was a liability. On the other hand, Hamas couldn't just surrender him. It asked for a prisoner exchange as a face-saving maneuver to get out of the jam Jabari had created. Israeli prime minister Ehud Olmert, however, was adamant: He refused to consider a prisoner exchange despite advice that he could strike a quick deal with Hamas for a small number of prisoners and that the longer the matter dragged on, the more expensive the exchange price would become. Shalit was held captive until October 2011, when he was freed in return for the release of one thousand–plus prisoners in Israeli jails.[11]

The kidnapping sabotaged a peace initiative Meshaal had undertaken.

Months before the kidnapping, he had used the help of a foreign envoy to open lines of communication with Yuval Diskin, the head of Shin Bet, Israel's internal security service. At Diskin's request, Meshaal submitted a document titled "Coexistence and Peace," outlining how Israel and Hamas might develop a strategic relationship. Diskin was impressed enough that he brought Olmert into the loop, although at arm's length.

After the kidnapping, with Olmert's approval, Diskin asked the foreign envoy to return to Israel for a meeting with him to streamline the channels through which messages were conveyed between Meshaal and the prime minister. Meshaal also updated his document with a clause outlining how Gilad Shalit's release might be secured. On this occasion, however, the foreign envoy received no response. Olmert had concluded that Meshaal could not deliver. The channel via the envoy went cold.

Today Olmert vehemently denies receiving any document in which Meshaal proposed how Hamas might conduct any dialogue with Israel. However, Shlomi Eldar, author of the award-winning *Lehakir et Hamas* ("To Know Hamas"), the seminal book on Hamas, meticulously verifies the authenticity of the document itself, as amended after Shalit was kidnapped. There's no point in guessing how Meshaal's initiative might have developed had it not been derailed by the Shalit kidnapping. For the record, though, the document begins with a discussion of a cease-fire and the building of long-term trust. It ends with a coexistence agreement to last twenty-five years and the establishment of a Palestinian state within the 1967 borders. It does not mention recognition of Israel or a peace agreement per se. It does, however, stipulate not only a *tahadiyeh* (cease-fire) but also cooperation on the civilian front, such as the opening of border crossings and a renewal by Israel of tax-money transfers to the Palestinians (see the appendix).

Most important, Eldar, who was given full access to these documents by Hamas and confirmation from Diskin that verified the connection, demonstrates that while the official Hamas position put formidable barriers in the way of dialogue with Israel, the political principles that guided the organization on a day-to-day basis are another matter. Despite all official proclamations to the contrary, Hamas and the Israeli government were holding ongoing secret talks, at the highest level, at the time of the Shalit crisis. Pragmatism trumped ideology, always, of course, in the service of the ideology.

Meanwhile, relations between Fatah and Hamas continued to deteriorate. In June 2007, fighting between Fatah and Hamas broke out in Gaza and quickly escalated with a ferocity that matched the best efforts of each party against the Israelis during the Second Intifada. Hamas shot Fatah militants "in the back and in the kneecaps . . . and threw them off the roofs of the city's tallest buildings," and paraded those it captured on the streets of Gaza to humiliate them.[12] Hamas won easily, and Fatah officials[13] either fled Gaza or were expelled. Hamas purged the security forces, civil service, and municipalities of all Fatah-aligned employees and established its own statelet. In the West Bank, the Palestinian Authority remained under Fatah control. Hamas members of the PLC boycotted it.[14] In Gaza, Hamas members of the PLC established themselves as members of a new legislative chamber.

Israel tightened the blockade. It became siegelike.

> > < <

There is one pedestrian crossing into and out of Gaza, at Eretz; two cargo crossings—at Karem Shalom and Karni,[15] where Israel determines what commodities enter and leave the Strip and in what quantities. Israel controls when the crossings are open.[*16] Gazans are prohibited from leaving without

*In the 1994 Interim Agreement on the West Bank and the Gaza Strip, it was stated that "the security fence erected by Israel around the Gaza Strip shall remain in place and that the line demarcated by the fence, as shown on [the map], shall be authoritative only for the purpose of the Agreement" (i.e., the barrier does not necessarily constitute the border). The barrier was completed in 1996. "Draft Agreement on the Gaza Strip and Jericho Area (archived copy)," *Palestine Israel*

a temporary pass and then only for a specified time and purpose. Obtaining this pass is a humiliating experience, and in leaving one runs the risk of never being allowed to return. The waiting period for requests to leave is long (sometimes indefinite), and of course there are quotas on the number allowed out on any given day. No one from the West Bank can enter Gaza without being subjected to a similar set of restrictions. Gazans are also subjected to around-the-clock surveillance.* The narrow confines of the Strip—41 kilometers (25 miles) long, and from 6 to 12 kilometers (3.7 to 7.5 miles) wide, with a total area of 365 square kilometers (141 square miles)—define the limits of travel for Gazans; these are the boundaries of their world, making Gaza the largest open-air prison in the world.

The bifurcation of the two Palestinian territories altered the status quo, perhaps in a fundamental way. One people is increasingly becoming two separate political entities.† With political and psychological distance between the two growing wider every year, Gaza is a (relatively) distant and different "place," an Islamic statelet, remote from the political center of gravity in secular Ramallah. Fatah did not allow Hamas to distribute its newspapers in the West Bank, and likewise, Hamas banned Fatah-aligned newspapers—a practice that ended with the April 2014 reconciliation pact. Keeping Gaza and the West Bank as two separate political entities is part of Israel's strategic design.[17]

Journal of Politics, Economics and Culture, April 26, 1994; Doron Almog (Major General, res.), "Lessons of the Gaza Security Fence for the West Bank," Jerusalem Issue Brief 4, no. 12 (December 12, 2004), Jerusalem Center for Public Affairs, http://www.jcpa.org/brief/brief004-12.htm.

*"[O]n September 12 a group of forty-three officers and soldiers from Unit 8200," second only to "combat squadrons of the air force, published a letter" to Netanyahu and Benny Ganz, IDF chief of staff "in which they state[d] that they [would] no longer serve in their former capacity. They wrote:

'The Palestinian population under military rule is completely exposed to espionage and surveillance by Israeli intelligence. . . . There's no distinction between Palestinians who are, and are not, involved in violence. Information that is collected and stored harms innocent people. It is used for political persecution and to create divisions within Palestinian society by recruiting collaborators and driving parts of Palestinian society against itself. In many cases, intelligence prevents defendants from receiving a fair trial in military courts, as the evidence against them is not revealed. Intelligence allows for the continued control over millions of people through thorough and intrusive supervision and invasion of most areas of life.'"

David Shulman, "Gaza: The Murderous Melodrama." *New York Review of Books,* November 20, 2014. http://www.nybooks.com/articles/archives/2014/nov/20/gaza-murderous-melodrama/.

†After reunification, the East Germans and West Germans experienced considerable trouble integrating and becoming one people. Fred Edmund Jandt wrote: "The irony of unification is that it has produced an Eastern identity that decades of Communist propaganda failed to achieve. Products made in the East sector are experiencing a revival as a way to assert a separate identity. . . . The invisible wall that now exists will take generations to fall because the redevelopment of a homogeneous society takes time." Quoted in Evelin Lindner, *Making Enemies: Humiliation and International Conflict* (Westport, CT: Praeger, 2006), 73.

The longer it can enforce the separation between them, the deeper the sense of alienation, the higher the mental barriers, and the less they feel like one people—the less they *are* one people; thus the goal of one united Palestinian state becomes less paramount. (Nevertheless, all Palestinian interviewees were adamant that a Palestinian state would have to include both the West Bank and Gaza.) Hence, too, Israel's vociferous objections to the Hamas-Fatah reconciliation pact announced in April 2014: It was one small step toward alleviating that sense of separateness.[18]

On the matter of governance, as the steward of the 1.8 million Palestinians living in Gaza,[19] Hamas has been a total failure. It never made the delivery of services to the people, beyond the most rudimentary, a priority, was too adept at stifling dissent, and kept an iron grip on all levers of power, shutting down NGOs that promote ideas that challenged its hegemony. What it did deliver, but not too overtly, was repression and injustice. While it claims to be the Palestinian liberation movement committed to individual and human rights and routinely charges Israel with violating the human rights of all Gazans—which Israel does—Hamas itself ruled with no respect for human rights.[20]

The difficulties facing the Palestinian economy will be more fully addressed in chapter 8, but the key factor here is that the blockade Israel imposed in 2007, illegal under international law,[21] and the devastating impact of the 2014 war left the economy in tatters, to a point that would require billions of dollars to breathe life into it—some estimates say it will take twenty years to get it back to where it was before the war started.[22] Without the United Nations Relief and Works Agency (UNRWA), its second-largest employer, what is left of the economy would collapse. In my conversation with a senior UNWRA official (who wanted to remain anonymous) in November 2011, he characterized his agency as "a state within the state, resented because we are a constant reminder to Hamas of its inability to provide for the needs of its population." In 2012 the UN reported that unless immediate measures were taken to address a plethora of problems, Gaza would be unlivable by 2020.[23] After the 2014 war, it was close to having reached that benchmark.

One factor that made the intolerable slightly less intolerable was the massive tunnel project into Egypt that Hamas spearheaded. Between 2007 and 2013, at least 1,400 increasingly sophisticated tunnels were dug, some able to bear the tonnage of heavy durable goods and cement. They were used to smuggle just about everything, from cars to iPhones to candy bars. The irony was rich: Israel's hopes of crippling Hamas with the blockade only enriched it because Hamas taxed all of the commerce coming through the tunnels. By 2013 such taxes accounted for two thirds of government revenue (about $460 million). The head of a relief agency (who also wished to remain anonymous) told me that "the blockade is effectively a blockade on the international agencies and the UN and the ordinary people of Gaza, but it is not a blockade on Hamas."

Ali Abu Shahla, a Gazan businessman and a member of one of the Fatah-Hamas reconciliation committees, described the tunnels as a gold mine for Hamas: "They had a monopoly on trade. Trade is with Egypt through tunnels, instead of trading with Israel. Now they were trading all over the world and impose taxes on such items as fuel, cars, about every commodity except for foodstuffs. Before the coup all of our trade was with Israel. Imports came to about $3 billion a year for both Gaza and the West Bank. Gaza's share was about $1.2 billion. Our [combined] exports to Israel and abroad amounted to about $400 million to $500 million. So the deficit was always on our side. The smuggling tunnels brought goods to Gaza worth $1 billion a year, according to an estimation made by the Egyptian ambassador to Ramallah. . . . Who is losing? Israel is losing and Hamas is getting more powerful."[24] Egypt also benefited. And the tunnel "merchants" became rich, increasing inequality. (On one visit I lost my $10 reading glasses and went looking for a pharmacy to buy a replacement. All I could find was a few stores selling $200 designer glasses.) Robert Danin, closely involved with Clinton's peace team as a political analyst in the State Department and today a member of the Council on Foreign Relations, explains: "The traditional economic powerhouses [in Gaza], the ruling families, largely secular, [were] largely eclipsed by a burgeoning nouveau riche that is basically mafioso and using their vast capital to buy up property. They are Gaza's Russian oligarchs. Many in high positions benefited enormously from the tunnel economy. You did not hear them calling for further loosening of Israeli restrictions on goods coming into and out of Gaza."[25]

For the moment a Palestinian state along the lines of the 1967 borders, with East Jerusalem as its capital, and the right of return for the refugees inviolate would be tolerable to Hamas as *an interim solution* to the problem. However, when Hamas speaks of the right of return, it means *literally*—not a Fatah-negotiated right to compensation, not the right to move from a refugee camp to some other country, but the right of refugees to return to their homes, regardless of whether they are still standing. Of all the issues that must be resolved, Hamas interviewees fixated on this right. . . . But the ultimate goal is to liberate "all of Palestine," which means reclaiming the Palestinian homeland from "the colonial settlers" who were given a slice of the land as *their* national home by the imperial powers following World War II. Hamas holds that just as the Western colonial presence around the world was erased in the twentieth century by national wars and liberation movements (invariably labeled "terrorist" at the time) and the land restored to its rightful original owners, Palestinians have an analogous right to erase the colonial presence in their country. Hamas will *never* recognize the existence of the state of Israel; to do so would negate the reason for Hamas's existence.[26]

> > < <

Every Hamas member I spoke to emphasized that the fact that the "colonists" are Jews is immaterial: It's not about the Jews—it's about the liberation of the homeland from an occupier who happens to be Jewish.[27] However, the textbooks children use in Hamas-run schools and the constancy of anti-Jewish diatribes that fill the media suggest otherwise.[28]

Israel incessantly invokes provisions of Hamas's charter that call for the elimination of Jews and the destruction of Israel, and its refusal to recognize the state of Israel.* This recognition, Hamas argues, must come from the state of Palestine, not from political parties. Hamas may continue to adhere to its non-recognition position; what the state of Palestine might choose to do is a different matter. Parties or individuals do not have to agree with the positions their governments take. Hamas also calls attention to clauses in the Likud charter that explicitly denounce a two-state solution.[29] A double standard, says Hamas.

Most West Bank interviewees agreed that Hamas should become part of the PLO, the authorized organ for conducting negotiations with Israel, and that developing one vision that unites Fatah and Hamas was a matter of utmost priority. Hamas interviewees also agreed that unity was a priority but made distinctions among unity in governance, unity in aspirations, and unity on their positions on armed resistance. The two sides worked out assorted agreements on paper addressing these points over seven years, and all were either abrogated or stored in the deep freeze shortly thereafter.

There are many factions within Hamas, which often complicates decision making. The Izz ad-Din al-Qassam Brigades, the Hamas military arm on

*For a translated text of the Hamas charter see endnote 2.

the ground in Gaza, and the Political Bureau (headquartered in Damascus before the Syrian civil war and now relocated to Qatar) each have points of view, and within each there are also different strands.[30] Specifically, there are nuanced disagreements about the efficacy of the armed struggle. Ordinary Gazans have paid an enormous price, and the costs have to be carefully calibrated against the outcomes.* Some Hamas interviewees fear that the movement, confined to Gaza, waging a war it cannot win, hemmed in on one side by Israel and on the other by a hostile Egypt, unable to negotiate with an enemy it did not recognize—not that Israel would ever be receptive to any form of negotiations, other than indirectly for cease-fires mediated by Egypt—with Gaza always on the brink of economic catastrophe,[31] might be heading toward a *political* dead end.[32] But for the Qassam Brigades, it's not the politics that counts.[33] Armed resistance always takes precedence.

There are also differences within Hamas regarding the imposition of Sharia law; ideological conflicts between Hamas's roots in the Muslim Brotherhood (founded as a religious charitable organization) and its role as a political resistance movement; the depth of the divisions between Fatah and Hamas as a factor threatening national cohesiveness; and whether to submit its control of Gaza to the Palestinian Authority and face the hazards of elections.

One of the most fundamental divides is between Islamists who are far more rigidly ideological regarding the Palestinian *waqf* and a more

*Before the Gaza war of 2014, estimated damage in 2008–09: "An indication of the scale of the destruction of Gaza's industry and business and its financial implications is the amount of aid—US$4,481 million [4.4 billion]—pledged by international donors for the Early Recovery and Reconstruction Plan for Gaza at the International Conference in Support of the Palestinian Economy for the Reconstruction of Gaza, held in March 2009." Amnesty International, "Israel/Gaza: Operation 'Cast Lead': 22 Days of Death and Destruction," 2009, 61, http://www.amnesty.org/en/library/asset/MDE15/015/2009/en/8f299083-9a74-4853-860f-0563725e633a/mde150152009en.pdf.

For statistical analysis of the damages, see also "'Operation Cast Lead': A Statistical Analysis August 2009 by Al-Haq—the West Bank affiliate of the International Commission of Jurists—Geneva," http://www.icawc.net/fonds/Gaza-operation-Cast-Lead_statistical-analysis%20by%20Al%20Haq_August%202009.pdf.

For the 2014 Gaza war, see "Assessing the Damage and Destruction in Gaza," *New York Times*, August 15, 2014, http://www.nytimes.com/interactive/2014/08/03/world/middleeast/assessing-the-damage-and-destruction-in-gaza.html; "Israel Caused $5 Billion in Damage to Gaza, 40,000 Homes Destroyed or Damaged," *Informed Comment*, August 6, 2014, http://www.juancole.com/2014/08/billion-destroyed-damaged.html; Reuters, "Cost Of Gaza Truce 'Almost Too Much to Bear'—UN Chief," *Gulf Business*, August 7, 2014, http://gulfbusiness.com/2014/08/cost-gaza-truce-almost-much-bear-un-chief/#.U-UmPPldVCg; "Before and After: Satellite Photos Reveal Extent of Gaza Destruction," *Haaretz*, August 7, 2014, http://www.haaretz.com/news/diplomacy-defense/.premium-1.609296.

pragmatic faction searching for ways to accomplish Hamas's goals with strategies that honor the *waqf* but are elastic enough to push the ultimate fulfillment of liberation well into the future.

In the West Bank, Hamas has a strong base of support; in Gaza, support fluctuates. It will always have the allegiance of a core of dedicated Islamists who see a huge difference between *not being able to win a war* and *not allowing your enemy to win either.* Regardless, for the more pragmatic Hamas leaders, any accommodation with Israel would be labeled "temporary," with the definition of temporary also elastic. Resistance is a means, not an end.

Regarding the acceptability of a state with pre-1967 borders, East Jerusalem as its capital, and the right of return acknowledged, Hamas interviewees' responses tended to be convoluted and featured subtle differences, some straddling the ideological/pragmatic divide. They agreed almost unanimously that if such an agreement were endorsed in a referendum by a majority of Palestinians in all three constituencies—West Bank, Gaza, and the diaspora—Hamas would not oppose the will of the majority, but neither would such an agreement constitute an "end of claims." But then again, because Palestine is a *waqf*, hard-line Islamists say Gazans, indeed West Bankers, too, are prohibited from voting in a referendum that would cede part of Palestine to Israel. The land is not theirs to give. Sovereignty is with God. No matter what, the pursuit of national liberation would continue; nonviolent popular resistance would have its place, but armed struggle is *always* justified. All interviewees, surprisingly, also concurred that no agreement would emerge unless the United States was prepared to be far more forceful with Israel and act as an honest broker.[34]

Ghazi Hamad, the then–deputy secretary of foreign affairs in the Hamas government in Gaza, told me that "Hamas is not looking for an Islamic state. Our goal is to liberate our homeland. After that, the people will choose. If they choose secular or Islamist or communist, we will accept the choice of the people. We want to establish a democratic state."[35] An October 2012 Human Rights Watch (HRW) report documents how Hamas security services in Gaza routinely conduct arrests without presenting warrants, refuse to promptly inform families of detainees' whereabouts, deny detainees access to a lawyer, and torture detainees in custody. The intra-Palestinian political rivalries among the various militant jihadists are the root cause of many abuses against detainees, but reports have been increasing of custodial abuse against detainees accused of nonpolitical crimes, including collaborating with Israel or the Palestinian Authority in the West Bank, drug offenses, and fraud. Human-rights lawyers in Gaza report that they continue to receive the same kinds of allegations.* This hypocrisy reinforces the belief that the constant invocation of commitment to "human rights" and representative democratization is just pabulum for Western consumption. (This holds, too, for Fatah in the West Bank.)

> > < <

In December 2010, the self-immolation of the Tunisian street vendor Mohammed Bouazizi in protest of the oppressive corruption in his country catapulted the Middle East and North Africa into tumultuous political upheavals. Within months the Arab Spring had ousted dictators, including Egypt's Hosni Mubarak, who had oppressed their citizens for decades. After democratic elections in Egypt for a national assembly, the Muslim Brotherhood, subjugated for decades by Mubarak, became the governing party and Mohamed Morsi, Egypt's first freely elected president. Across the region similar revolts were under way and dictatorial regimes were forced from office. Preparations for democratic elections followed and in some countries democratically elected Islamic governments were poised to assume power. Bitter disputes, however, between secularists who wanted pluralistic constitutions and Islamists who wanted Sharia law enshrined, shattered the illusion of collective harmony and moved political Islam center stage, creating an ongoing region-wide conflict that continues to convulse many Arab states. The Arab world underwent seismic change; it was rife with turbulence, and social upheaval that moved unpredictably. Shaken by the implications for their respective fiefdoms, both Hamas and Fatah moved quickly, banning spontaneous gatherings in Gaza and Ramallah to celebrate Egypt's Tahrir Square uprising—but to judge by the utter absence of any apparent activist impulse,

*"The abusive practices of the security services in Gaza," HRW said, "flout human rights norms that Hamas has pledged to uphold, and also violate Palestinian laws. . . . Members of the Internal Security agency apparently continue to enjoy absolute impunity despite consistent allegations of severe abuse. Former detainees who alleged they were abused by security services said they despaired of finding justice; several were afraid to describe what had happened to them in custody, even on condition that their identities would be kept confidential." See Human Rights Watch, "World Report: 2012," September 2012, http://www.hrw.org/sites/default/files/reports/wr2012.pdf.

"In previous research on intra-Palestinian political violence and abuses against detainees, Human Rights Watch found that the main factor underlying such human rights violations was the conflict between Hamas and its rival, the Palestinian Authority, which often prompted 'tit for tat'" abuses in Gaza and the West Bank.

See also Human Rights Watch, "World Report: 2013," 2013, http://www.hrw.org/sites/default/files/wr2013_web.pdf.

both authorities could have saved themselves the trouble. Tahrir Square, however, was an eye opener, as it revealed the extent of "people power," even in the face of a truly repressive dictatorship. Hamas, realizing that it could do little itself if such massive demonstrations in Gaza City held it to account for its abysmal performance in government, moved quickly to remedy its malfeasance and took measures to redirect energy and resources to providing services, even if a little more than minimal, to the citizenry. The PA, too, acted quickly to moderate certain policies. The youth, however, gathered on one occasion under well-managed constraints. They had only one request: that Fatah and Hamas reconcile. "The threat perception in the Hamas leadership in Gaza was huge," Palestinian pollster Khalil Shikaki, director of the Palestinian Center for Policy and Survey Research, told me.

> Far greater than the threat perception of Fatah in the West Bank, [but] both sides changed their policies to try and give potential demonstrators less things to demand domestically. Mahmoud Abbas ordered the security services to stop policies that have been used routinely before—arrest and search without warrants, arrests without courts, use of torture and the like—and these guidelines . . . were actually implemented for the most part. . . . Hamas did likewise in Gaza. Both West Bankers and Gazans would have loved to demand regime change. This would have been the natural thing for Palestinians to do, but they didn't. Instead they searched for an alternative and demanded that Fatah and Hamas end their dispute and close ranks. Hamas and Fatah grabbed it. Both were really scared, and [while] I can't say this is the only motivation for the two sides to agree to engage in a reconciliation process . . . it was part of the impact of changes in the region.[36]

Actually, reconciliation began shortly after the split in 2007. The chore of trying to effect reconciliation was handed to Azzam Ahmed, a senior member of the Fatah Central Committee. His counterpart on Hamas's side was Mousa Abu Marzouk, deputy director of Hamas's Political Bureau. Ahmed and Marzouk met frequently, in Sana and Cairo and elsewhere (the Egyptians played a prominent role as mediator), but always came up short. Committees were set; reams of paper were churned out. For a while, it looked as though the so-called Prisoner's Document[37] would provide the common ground, but it, too, was sucked into the maelstrom of rivalries, paranoia, and politicking with which both parties were rife. Ahmed and Marzouk kept talking, but there was too much distrust. In 2009 the Saudis brought the parties together in Mecca. The two sides discussed five files: the government, the PLO, the elections, social reconciliation, and security. But the talks petered out when America would not agree to any government that included Hamas. However, following the demand of the youth, when the Arab Spring broke out, Mousa Abu Marzouk and Azzam Ahmed met again in 2011. Ismail al-Ashqar, head of the Hamas-based Palestinian Legislative Council's Interior and Security Committee, joined the discussions. They now agreed to proceed on seven points in parallel: voter registration and freedom of elections, forming the technocratic government, reorganization of the PLO, political prisoners, freedom of the media, security, and creating dialogue in the PLC. But before they could agree on a document to present to their principals, there had to be agreement on the outcomes of all seven files—or there would be no agreement on any. While these discussions were ongoing, Abbas and Meshaal engineered what looked like a breakthrough when they signed the Doha Agreement in February 2012, committing the two sides to a Palestinian state on 1967 lines, with East Jerusalem as its capital, and elections to the Legislative Assembly, the PLO, and the PLC. Abbas would hold the prime minister's portfolio in the interim. But this, too, ran into difficulties and nothing became of it.

Hamas interviewees were adamant that the conflicts with Fatah and Israel are truly "existential" challenges, not just as a competition for political power but in terms of profound ideological, religious, cultural, and political differences. From Hamas's perspective, the PLO (which it equates with Fatah) has been negotiating with Israel for twenty years and, as the PLO itself has said, achieved "a big zero," giving some justification to the party-line criticism that the West Bank Palestinians were being duped, that the only way to force Israel to make concessions was as a result of armed resistance.* Hamas spews contempt at Abbas for failure to deliver the political results expected once the PLO eschewed violence. It dismisses the entire PA leadership as one that has somehow managed to hang on long past its shelf life; one that is deluded about Israel, which Hamas believes does not have any intention of "giving" the Palestinians a sovereign state. Furthermore, Hamas regards the PLO as lacking legitimacy because there have been no elections since 2006. Whether these sentiments prevail past the 2014 reconciliation is questionable.

At the same time, no Hamas interviewee could claim that Hamas's own

*The Palestinian Public Opinion Poll No. 51 reports that despite the all-too-obvious difficulties Hamas was experiencing after closing of the tunnels, 39 percent of Palestinians still believed the "Hamas" way was the better route to follow than Mahmoud Abbas's (December 2013). After the 2014 Gaza war, this rose to 88 percent. See Palestinian Center for Policy and Survey Research, "Special Gaza War Poll: 26–30 August 2014."

armed resistance had achieved anything, despite hundreds of missiles launched, lives lost, two wars,* and the near destruction of Gaza. Ismail al-Ashqar, spoke elliptically, "Everything comes with force."[38] Asked exactly what achievement he could point to that would substantiate that hypothesis, he veered into non sequiturs.

Hamas interviewees assured me that Fatah was finished as an authentic representative of the Palestinian people, even though reconciliation talks were ongoing at the time. Fatah, it said, had sold its soul at Oslo for fewer than thirty pieces of silver. Even Dr. Eyad el-Sarraj, the late Gaza psychologist who had many conversations over the years with senior officials in both Hamas and Fatah, with some resignation concurred:

> Only people in positions of leadership continue to use the label "Oslo" in order to justify their control, their benefits, their salaries, and their per diems, et cetera, et cetera. And they keep regurgitating slogans that are hollow, and they don't appreciate the fact that people know that all this is hollow and nothing is going on. If they had any shame, these people should collectively resign, from Mahmoud Abbas onward. They have not allowed young people from the younger generation to move on and take part in decision making. They continue to control the West Bank using the tools Arafat employed: money and intimidation and corruption—a potent mess. Hamas is the only player of consequence. [Mahmoud Abbas] did whatever the Americans wanted him to. Neither he nor Fatah can be taken seriously.[39]

What, Mahmoud al-Zahar, one of Hamas's founders and a senior member of its politburo, asked, had the PLO accomplished in negotiations with Israel ranging from Camp David to Annapolis? He was contemptuously disparaging: All that they had eked out of negotiations was

> a disarmed state, disconnected state, a sort of occupation, especially between the West Bank and Jordan; not anything about Jerusalem; without any linkage between West Bank and Gaza, no geographical linkage; so—no army, no security, the continued existence of Israel in this area, swapping of areas up to 5 percent. They will give you some desert here in Gaza and confiscate Jerusalem. Can anybody accept giving one inch from Jerusalem for one kilometer from another area? It's a holy place; this is the most important holy place for Muslims, every Muslim everywhere, which is the Al-Aqsa mosque. Will this state fulfill the demands of the Palestinian people inside

*Hamas interviews were conducted before the July/August 2014 Gaza war.

> and outside? It's not a matter that we would oppose such a Palestinian state package; we will not accept it.[40]

These huge differences in outlook, combined with the shared failure to make meaningful headway against the common enemy, compressed their conflict into a psychologically poisonous well of humiliation, despair, and anger that, if both parties (Hamas and Fatah) are unable to take out on the enemy, they take out on themselves. (Recall Tal Becker's observation, cited in chapter 3, that at Annapolis "the negotiations with Israel were first and foremost a weapon for Fatah in their fight with Hamas. The actual dealing with us was a secondary issue."[41])

Eyad el-Sarraj, once again, was more blunt: "What you have to remember," he said, "is that they hate each other. This is no siblings' rivalry." This éminence grise, who had extensive dealings with both Fatah and Hamas leaders, paused and chose his next words carefully. "To my regret, I have to say that I believe that the level of distrust between Hamas and Fatah is bigger than the level of distrust between Israelis and Palestinians."

Nor has the international spotlight on the West Bank and Mahmoud Abbas, as president of the Palestinian Authority, helped matters. To the contrary, it highlights how isolated Hamas is. When the World Bank and the International Monetary Fund issued their pronouncements about the readiness of the Palestinian Authority for statehood, they conflated the PA with a Palestinian state. The international community wishes this were the case, but it's not. Most Jewish Israeli interviewees mentioned Gaza only in the context of its thuggery and the threat Hamas posed to the residents of towns in southern Israel. (That changed after the 2014 war.) Most West Bank Palestinian interviewees rarely made mention of it unless I raised it specifically in a question. Moreover, the positive gloss the PA and Abbas receive in the international community and the unremittingly negative spotlight on Hamas as "terrorists" reinforce Hamas's sense of insularity and exclusion, aggravating the divisions between the two.

> > < <

Ghazi Hamad is a pragmatist who advocates reconciliation between Hamas and Fatah as not simply a matter of convenience but a necessity. "Our first priority is to unite our position as Palestinians," he said. "Otherwise, Netanyahu will take advantage of our weaknesses. We should have a common vision at two levels. The first level is political diplomacy accompanied by political action, and the second, the resistance. We should not stop the resistance against the occupation. If we use only soft tools and soft policy, the Israelis will ignore us and build more settlements." Armed resistance, he implied, would still be very much in play even in the event of reconciliation. It is only a matter of finding the optimal balance.[42] The Israelis understood the gun.

Some of the leading pacifists in both Israel and the WBG believe this too, while finding the thought of violence abhorrent. Shlomo Ben-Ami, for example, believes that nothing short of a major disruption will get the attention of the Israelis. While I was interviewing him, he pulled *Scars of War* from his loaded shelf and read a passage from an interview Henry Kissinger gave to Ahron Bregman and Jihan El-Tahri, authors of *The Fifty Years War: Israel and the Arabs*. Ben Ami wrote of this exchange that "Sadat was practically forced to go to war by the dismissive attitude prevailing, both in Israel and in the United States, toward Egypt and him personally. There was not a way he could be taken seriously. His peace overtures were defeated, not because they lacked merit, as such, but because Egypt was perceived as not having a war option to back them. Kissinger implicitly advised the Egyptians that only by starting a war would they be given credence."[43] Five years later, Sadat had his war and signed the peace treaty with Israel.

Although he stresses his commitment to nonviolence, Sari Nusseibeh, former president of Al-Quds University and himself the author of a peace plan,[44] sounded a similar note when he said, "In this present situation, armed option works. A properly carried out armed struggle, not the kind that we've been using in the past, might have a better chance to produce the two-state solution we have been struggling to in the past thirty years. If you want to make your point to Israelis, use the armed option—*assuming that you have one*, which we don't."[45]

In 2014, as we will see, Hamas had its war.

Salah al-Bardaweel, a senior leader and one of the more prominent among Hamas's spokespersons, is quite explicit regarding the eventual endgame—total liberation—but pragmatic about how it should be reached. "Even if there was a two-state solution," he told me, "as far as Hamas is concerned, this would represent one phase towards achieving the ultimate goal, and the ultimate goal is the liberation of all of Palestine. We can live together—Jews and Muslims in a binational state. There will be no Jewish state, but the Jewish population will still live in Palestine, within its borders. We are not talking about expelling them. But nobody has the right to force the Palestinians to recognize the state of Israel, as this is a sovereign decision. There is a huge difference between what you believe in deep inside of you and what you sign on the political paper. We are ready to sign this politically, on the papers, and the whole world can witness this—an end of conflict, the '67 borders, the right of return, et cetera. But what's still inside me and inside every Palestinian is not for discussion. It's not open for discussion. But political-wise, we can accept this Palestinian state."[46]

That's the "soft" side of the scale, as Hamas leaders go. Dr. Mahmoud al-Zahar speaks for the truly "hard" side. The enemy will be "eliminated sooner or later," al-Zahar said, because "Israel does not belong to the culture of this area, to the religion of this area, to the civilization of this area, to the ethnic condition of this area; it's not representing anything here. It's a foreign body."

Does he mean that Israelis will collectively flee the land, be forcibly driven into the sea, or be physically eradicated? He is a sophisticated and clever man, well versed in the sophistries of evasiveness, but if the attitude he expresses is the prevalent one within Hamas, Israeli Jews have a right to question whether a freestanding Palestinian state with an "end of claims" agreement is not the end of the conflict but the beginning of Palestinian preparation for the next phase of "liberating" all of Palestine. If the Israelis take seriously—and they do—the unequivocal declaration by Hamas's leaders that Hamas's goal is to reclaim all of Palestine, they are perfectly justified in hesitating before embracing a two-state solution.

On the question of a referendum to decide any final status agreement, should negotiations ever get that far, al-Zahar is unyielding: "Neither land [nor] religion can be subject to the mandate of a referendum. This would be contrary to a basic tenet of Islam. Is Islam the religion of the majority or not? Are we ready to accept a referendum about the nature of our religion and nationality? We can't accept that. A referendum can be used only for an *administration*, not about religion." Mukhaimer Abusada, a Fatah-aligned Gazan professor, said Gaza prime minister Ismail Haniyeh made the same point regarding a referendum on several occasions: "The people do not have the right to vote in a referendum to give part of Palestine to the Israelis, because the land does not belong to them—it's an Islamic *waqf*."[47]

To circumvent this dilemma, the pragmatic wing of Hamas has floated the idea of a *hudna*[48]—a temporary cessation of fighting for a specified or unspecified amount of time—articulated by Meshaal in the "Coexistence and Peace" document referred to earlier. A *hudna* that would last twenty-five years or more could serve as an interim solution, leaving it to the next generation to decide what to do. This is an Islamic solution Hamas is open to exploring, but it would not extend to any compromise on the question of the right of return.

A *hudna*, would, of course, put time on the Palestinians' side, but time is not much of a concern to Hamas, because it is confident in the rightness of its cause.[49] Few of the Hamas leaders I interviewed spoke in terms of urgency or immediacy in resolving the conflict with Israel. In "The Time Factor as a Barrier to Resolution of the Israeli Palestinian Conflict" in *Barriers to Peace*, Zakay and Fleisig write, "Islamic culture emphasizes and glorifies the value of waiting. Haste is a negative quality. Patience is among the most important qualities for a Muslim believer. There is no sense of 'time urgency.'"[50]

Waiting and patience are flip sides of a coin. This was a recurring catchphrase: *waiting*. This will be a *phased* liberation, with phase II deferred *indefinitely*, the work of a future generation of Palestinians.

But what about the Israelis? "The Israelis know what *hudna* means," Abusada says. "You sign it with your enemy because you are weak, but once you become stronger, you are going to violate that *hudna*."[51] Of course, in terms of this definition, it's obvious that a *hudna* in its most fundamental form is contrary to everything Israel stands for. Nevertheless, Efraim Halevy, the former head of Mossad, has written extensively encouraging Israel to explore a *hudna* "for ten, twenty, thirty, or even fifty years."[52] The idea has no traction in Israel, nor is it likely to in the near future. It would not just be nonsensical but trigger Israel's sense of existential threat to proceed under such an implicit cloud. *Hudna* is the antithesis of "never again." Nevertheless, a *hudna* raises a related issue that has not received serious attention, at least in public forums. A number of former Israeli security chiefs have gone public to assert that, at some point, Israel must talk directly with Hamas.[53] In the world of realpolitik, the "We won't talk with terrorists" line is blarney, and everyone knows it, especially those who invoke it so piously. In fact, during talks in August 2014 to end the third Gaza war, the media carried accounts of a purported Hamas proposal for a ten-year cease-fire, which in the eyes of some would have been tantamount to a *hudna*, although Israel would steer clear of ever using the word.[54]

Moreover, a *hudna* can be conceptualized in different terms, ones that do not embody the meaning that the party asking for it because it is weak will attack again once it feels strong enough but are contextualized in terms of a prolonged cease-fire after which the parties can agree to an extension or renew their attempts to achieve their ultimate aspirations, through either violence or nonviolence. The question left hanging is what Palestinians and

Israelis would opt to do after, say, fifty years of living with an interim solution that is working, that has brought about a greater degree of harmony between themselves and Israeli Jews, and that, of course, requires decisions in a world that will bear little resemblance to the one we live in today. Indeed, the Northern Ireland peace agreements could be recast in terms of a *hudna*: Each gives parity of esteem to the aspirations of the other—on this the agreements are quite specific. The Good Friday/Belfast Agreement calls for periodic referenda on whether Northern Ireland should remain in the UK or become part of a united Ireland. They call for simple majority votes.* However, after fifteen years of the two communities governing Northern Ireland on the basis of parity, a referendum is nowhere on the political radar, yet.

Another matter of potential cleavage between Islamists and secularists within the Palestinian community that has not received much attention but would undoubtedly emerge is the constitutional status of a future Palestinian state. Hamas is now tarred with labels of radical political Islam, the scourge of Arab states in the Middle East, which has made for strange bedfellows—Egypt, Saudi Arabia, Iraq, Jordan, and Israel in alignment, all committed to eradicating Islamic "terror." Indeed, Netanyahu, in August 2014, drew a straight line between the savage beheading of American journalist James Foley by ISIS (the gruesome video of the decapitation which was widely available on YouTube and other social media), and allegations that Hamas deliberately uses children as human shields.† The insinuation: Israel was out front

*A referendum can be held only if the UK secretary of state believes via the evidence (presumably of recent elections) that there would be a change of view from the balanced, power-sharing, East-West, North-South agreement of 1998. Even then, one can be held only every seven years. The Good Friday/Belfast Agreement says that Northern Ireland would remain part of the United Kingdom until a majority of the people of Northern Ireland and of the Republic of Ireland wish otherwise. Should that happen, then the British and Irish governments are under "a binding obligation" to implement that choice. For the text of the Good Friday/Belfast Agreement, see https://www.gov.uk/government/publications/the-belfast-agreement.

Some would argue that cease-fires between Hamas and Israel, brokered by the Egyptians, are in fact negotiations, and that Israel's disclaimers that it will never negotiate with Hamas as long as Hamas does not recognize Israel's existence are principled but not necessarily absolute. When I spoke with General Herzog in November 27, 2011, he bemoaned the fact that Israel had no back channel to Hamas at the time, saying that in practice it usually had one.

†"The beheading of Foley," Netanyahu declared at a press conference on August 20, "shows you the barbarism, the savagery of these people. . . . [W]e face the same savagery," he said, from Hamas terrorists. "Throw people from the sixth floor—their own people" (a reference to Hamas's seizure of Gaza from the Palestinian Authority in 2007) and "use their people as human shields" (a reference to this and other post-2007 rounds of conflict with Israel, fought from the heart of Gaza's neighborhoods). "Netanyahu Slams Ministers Criticizing His Handling of Hamas War," *Times of Israel*, August 21, 2014, http://www.timesofisrael.com/netanyahu-slams-ministers-criticizing-his-handling-of-hamas-war/#ixzz3G8mgpqzS. See also Ben Caspit, "When Will the US, Europe Wake

on the war against extreme Islamist terror, while the West slept. Would a constitutional body in Palestine endow the new state with Islamist values and rights, enshrining Sharia law? Would Israel insist on having a veto right in this matter—an Islamic state on its doorstep would undoubtedly be construed as a potential security threat. Or would Palestine enshrine in its constitution secular values and rights, emphasizing pluralist ideals and individual human rights? Would Islamists try to impose their will? Would the new state reignite rivalries that would then undermine democratic processes and degenerate into an Islamist-versus-secularist confrontation?[55]

What has happened in Egypt, where the military toppled a democratically elected government, is not necessarily an indication of what the answers might be in a future fragile Palestine, but the tumult this question has given rise to across much of North Africa and some parts of the Middle East in the embers of the Arab Spring is cautionary.[56] What is happening today in Hamas-ruled Gaza is perhaps a more valid barometer. But under the rule of the Palestinian Authority, if that ever becomes more than a surface coating, this, too, might change.

In terms of the imposition of Sharia law, on a scale of one to ten, ten being the strictest adherence, Hamas is probably an eight or nine in terms of what it would like to enforce, but only a six or seven in practice. It is Islamic, but it is no Saudi Arabia or Iran. No new law can contradict the tenets of Sharia, but Sharia is not practiced rigorously. The "morality" police, who have a significant but not pervasive presence, face a population that simply ignores some of its more severe decrees. The 65 percent of the population that is under the age of twenty-five years is a formidable barrier to enforcement of Islamic codes. Moreover, young people in Gaza are familiar with the Internet and social media, which have an added importance because they provide the youth access to the world beyond their narrow confines. Although Hamas promotes itself as the vanguard of fearless armed resistance against the occupiers, in reality it never trusted its own people, especially the younger generation, and is therefore careful to tread softly between Islamization and the norms many young people practice.[57]

Up to the Threat of Radical Islam?" *Al-Monitor*, August 21, 2014, http://www.al-monitor.com/pulse/originals/2014/08/james-foley-is-hamas-radical-islam-israel-us-europe.html; Uri Dromi, "Spot the Difference: ISIS Ideology Runs Through Hamas," *The JC*, August 21, 2014, http://www.thejc.com/news/israel-news/121585/spot-difference-isis-ideology-runs-through-hamas. A Palestinian Center for Public Opinion Poll No. 190 on August 23, 2014 indicated that 85.2 percent of Palestinians opposed ISIS, http://www.pcpo.org/index.php/polls/113-poll-no-190. See also the poll refered to in the afterword, endnote 74 page 417 "Poll : ISIS viewed positively by 24 percent of Palestinians," *Haaretz*, November 13, 2014.

"Here, most of the people are religious—conduct their prayers and keep the Ka'ba," Saleh al-Naami told me. Al-Naami is a highly respected journalist who covers Gaza for the Egyptian newspaper *Al-Ahram Weekly.* "But there are no restrictions on what a man or woman wears. The people have been influenced by television, from contacts they have with other countries. So, three years ago, if you walked down Omar Mukhtar Street, the main street, you would not see thousands of girls and women. Now you will. There's a clear change, and no one can exert a pressure on what you should wear or not wear."[58] As changes at this level trickle down, the desire for more freedom increases and support for Hamas drops. Hamas tries to enforce Sharia, but on many occasions it has the appearance of going through the motions because it fears losing the support of the youth. In 2013 it found itself at odds with much of the public when Mohammed Assaf, a Gazan, won the *Arab Idol* singing contest, an event that Hamas frowned on. Exuberant celebrations erupted spontaneously across Gaza. He was greeted ecstatically by thousands at Rafah when he returned home.

> > < <

However, this "tolerance" on the part of Hamas has helped more extreme groups draw support away from it. One example is the jihadist Salafists, one of the most puritanical and violent sects calling for an Islamic caliphate* and "pure" resistance against Israel, that is, no cease-fires, *hudnas*, or lulls in aggression. Their numbers, thought to be small, are unknown; some have tenuous links to international networks led by al-Qaeda; all have a presence in the Sinai. The Salafists have challenged Hamas's authority in Gaza, accusing it of being insufficiently diligent in applying Islamic law and chastising it for agreeing to cease-fires with Israel. They have frequently acted independently of

*"Salafism and Arab Democratization," on a Stratfor Global Intelligence blog, October 12, 2012, provides a comprehensive overview of the rise and role of Salafists in Arab Spring countries and its various ideological strains. The report concludes, "Salafists of various stripes are slowly emerging as political stakeholders across the region, especially in Libya, Tunisia, Yemen, Gaza, Lebanon, Jordan and Syria. . . . Salafist entities can be expected to complicate political transitions and undermine stability and security in the Middle East." The major challenge to stability in the Arab world thus lies only partially in the transition to democracy from autocracy. Greater than that is the challenge mainstream Islamists face from a complex and divided Salafist movement." Kamran Bokhari, "Salafism and Arab Democratization," *Geopolitical Weekly* (blog), Stratfor Global Intelligence, http://www.stratfor.com/weekly/salafism-and-arab-democratization#ixzz2mjX4lYWa. See also: Bokhari, "Salafism and Arab Democratization"; Ed Husain, "Saudis Must Stop Exporting Extremism—ISIS Atrocities Started with Saudi Support for Salafi Hate," *New York Times*, August 22, 2014, http://www.nytimes.com/2014/08/23/opinion/isis-atrocities-started-with-saudi-support-for-salafi-hate.html?hp&action=click&pgtype=Homepage&module=c-column-top-span-region®ion=c-column-top-span-region&WT.nav=c-column-top-span-region.

Hamas's leadership, drawing Hamas retaliation when it fires rockets into southern Israel, an issue that was especially acute after the 2012 cease-fire. The Salafists attract members of Hamas who believe Hamas has "gone soft." After the military coup that ousted Morsi, the Salafists have become more aggressive. Their main threat to Hamas, however, is ideological, compelling Hamas periodically to implement Sharia more stringently so that it can parade its ideological credentials.[59] In 2013, Hamas, which had cracked down hard on the Salafists on several occasions since 2007, reached an accommodation with the Salafists.[60] Nevertheless, their threat is ongoing.

The Islamic Jihad also attracts members of Hamas who believe that Hamas has gone soft. But even more troubling for Hamas is the fact that the Islamic Jihad became the beneficiary of Iran's financial largesse when Iran cut its assistance to Hamas after the latter would not side with Bashar al-Assad in the Syrian civil war.[61] And more threateningly, the Islamic Jihad has proved harder to contain and poses the biggest threat to Hamas[62] as increasing numbers of Gazans regard it as a more aggressive resistance movement than Hamas itself.[63]

Gaza interviewees had no hesitation in saying that Hamas was undergoing an intensive review of how to position itself in the political arena to deal more proactively with new realities. When Hamas and Israel agree to cease-fires, the Salafists or the Islamic Jihad or some other group—which do not feel they are bound by the terms—quickly step into the "armed resistance" void, firing some rockets into Israel and proclaiming themselves the true vanguard of the armed struggle. Irrespective of who launches rockets, Israel holds the governing Hamas responsible and targets it for the invariable retaliatory attacks.* To ensure compliance with cease-fires it reaches with Israel or to maintain "quiet for quiet,"† Hamas has to police other jihadist militias in order to assert its ultimate authority. Much as Hamas derides the Palestinian Authority for being collaborationist, it could be called the same itself. The war it conducted in 2008 against the Army of Islam[64] and its pressure on the Popular Resistance Committee[65] were strong signals in that regard, although Israel continues to view all of these organizations as one

*In Gaza's complex and, some would say, premodern social system, a number of powerful clans such as the Dormush and Samhadan exert significant influence, run their own militias, and when they can muster the wherewithal, even lob a rocket or two in Israel's direction, taxing Hamas's leadership.

†A euphemism Israel uses that essentially means that in the absence of a formal, brokered cease-fire arrangement, as in 2012, if there are no rocket attacks from Gaza, there will be no air-strikes on Gaza.

united front led by Hamas. On the other hand, policing unauthorized shelling of the Israeli enemy during cease-fires puts Hamas in an existential dilemma, because its own identity is so closely tied to armed struggle. Being outflanked on this front creates multiple problems for its constituency and brings into question its own sense of purpose.

"The political behavior of the Islamic Jihad group," says Abusada, "is that it is saying that it is different from Fatah and Hamas; it is not going to be part of the PLO and not bound by PLO restraints."[66]

Ahmad al-Dabba, a contributor to *Al Akhbar*, writes that "the missile attacks are thus also a way for the Salafists to 'impose themselves on Palestinian politics and be made partners in national decisions, even if they answer to global jihadist leaders.'"*[67] Hamas has, on occasion, resumed its own rocket fire into Israel for no better reason than to disprove the jihadists' claims to being the one true militant resistance.[68]

In September 2013, it appeared that Hamas and Islamic Jihad agreed to form a Supreme Coordination Command.[69] Such move would ease strains at most levels and hold out possibilities of a merger. Still, deep divisions, many ideological, exist among militant Islamic groups in Gaza. No matter who governs Gaza, reining in the militias currently operating as independent players—some clan based and some outliers as a consequence of the Syrian war—may simply be impossible.

Ironically, given the absence of feasible alternatives, Israel has been well served by keeping Hamas in power in Gaza. It is a known quantity. Before its invasion of Gaza in July 2014, it went to some lengths to make clear that its purpose was *not* to depose Hamas but to obliterate its armory and launch sites and render it incapable of launching rockets into Israel in the future.[70] But war, as we will see, creates its own motives as combat escalates, and it rarely follows a course that does not have unintended consequences that subordinate its original purpose.[71]

> > < <

As long as Israel enforces the blockade, Hamas is sealed off from the outside world, stuck in its tiny plot of territory, its capacity to undertake "armed resistance" limited. For Israel, it is a nuisance, although the nuisance took a murderous turn in 2014.

General (Ret.) Michael Herzog, a longtime Israeli negotiator, told me in

*Al-Dabba quoting Naji Sharab, a political science professor at Gaza's Al-Azhar University.

2011 that Israel knew Hamas had a number of more sophisticated missiles that could reach Tel Aviv if they were not intercepted by Israel's Iron Dome, "an indigenous Israeli development developed and manufactured in Israel [that] was capable of intercepting short-range rockets."[72] Israel had "three batteries deployed facing Gaza" and more were in the works. So, too, was David's Sling, a joint Israeli-American system that would be capable of intercepting longer-range missiles with a range of up to 250 kilometers (155 miles), "mostly rockets that are in the hands of Hezbollah." But it did not know how many. The threat of rockets from the West Bank, however, was a different matter. "No government would ever contemplate leaving the West Bank," he said, "until that threat was removed." Otherwise all of Israel would be exposed to attack.[73]

The "how to" is the question. One answer might be technological,[74] but technology alone, interviewees with whom I raised the issue said, would be an insufficient deterrent. Israel might have no option other than to invade Gaza and demilitarize Hamas. It could, if necessary, eviscerate Hamas, or at least reduce it to impotence for years, even though doing so would come at a heavy price.

Confinement to Gaza limits Hamas's offensive capacity to wage war, and the strategic question it faces is how to "break out" of the enclave. The most obvious way to do this would be to acquiesce to a two-state solution that would give it freedom to move between a united Gaza and West Bank, where a number of its underground cells already operate, because in a two-state arrangement, the contiguity of a Palestinian state would require a corridor, under Palestinian sovereignty, connecting the two parts of its sovereign territory. Hamas (assuming it had bought in to the settlement and Israel had accepted its bona fides—a long stretch) would be free to move between Gaza and the West Bank, to expand and solidify its presence in the latter, and to find the routes, if so disposed, for smuggling sophisticated, mobile missiles fitted with launchers and timers into the territory. Given Israel's topography, such missiles could be fired from numerous sites toward its population centers and infrastructure, including Ben Gurion Airport. This would leave Israel vulnerable to missile attacks from any number of places. A Hamas running loose in the West Bank would be an exponentially more elusive and lethal enemy for Israel.

Israel understands the threat. Rather than use its unfettered control of Gaza to improve the lives of the citizenry, Jewish Israeli interviewees uniformly said, Hamas had chosen to establish a military complex from which to wage war on Israel. How could Israel ever be certain that it would not take the same advantage of the West Bank? Given the Hamas narrative and platform, taking such advantage would be the sensible, logical thing to do. A crushing response against rocket attacks from tiny Gaza is not all that difficult, though it invariably comes with civilian casualties and levels of property destruction in Gaza unacceptable to the international community: a crushing response against both Gaza and the much larger West Bank would be another challenge entirely. Israel would face a highly mobile Hamas, more difficult to pin down, more adept at asymmetric warfare, striking perhaps from within its own population centers in the West Bank—tactics similar to Hezbollah's in the second Lebanese war—with the *Qassam* Brigades dusted off and back in business, taking on the IDF and the PASF.[75] In short measure Israel could find itself at war with the new Palestinian state, resorting to whatever measures necessary to protect itself including invasion. The regional repercussions, given the ongoing war against ISIS and Arab ambivalence regarding the role it should play, would be unpredictable but almost certainly extremely negative and the international community very definitely would not countenance an Israeli invasion of a Palestinian state in its infancy.

These considerations are the roots of Israel's security demands. All Israeli interviewees stressed that *no* Israeli government will *ever* agree to a Palestinian state on its border until satisfied beyond reasonable doubt that Hamas, Islamic Jihad, and the other splinter Islamic groups are not even remotely in a position to use the West Bank to target Israeli population centers or infrastructure with ever-more-sophisticated weaponry. A two-state solution would require that Hamas and jihadist militia groups decommission their weapons and destroy their inventories, just as the Irish Republican Army (IRA) was required by the Good Friday/Belfast Agreement to decommission its weaponry under international supervision and provide proof that all stockpiles had been rendered useless. Nor would Israel allow the decommissioning and verification to be left in the hands of any Palestinian government.

Of course, to believe that Hamas and other jihadist groups would meekly surrender their weapons to comply with an agreement they had no part in reaching is phantasmagorical. Attempts by the Palestinian security forces to enforce such orders would lead to open warfare. And in any event, even in a negotiating context, Hamas's agreement to decommission its weaponry to Israel's satisfaction would come only in return for Israel making extraordinary concessions, well beyond anything Israel would be prepared to concede.

And Israel goes even further. A number of Jewish Israeli interviewees emphatically stated that Israel would have no relationship—let alone negotiations—with any unity government in which Fatah welcomes Hamas into the ruling structure.[76] Hence the conundrum: On the one hand, Israel recognizes that any final settlement agreement that does not have the support of Hamas is probably unsustainable; on the other hand, it will not negotiate with a PLO in which Hamas has representation.[77]

How does Israel marry the self-canceling positions? For a start, by insisting that the violence cease. But when the violence does cease, Israel does not, in practice, grasp the opportunity to push ahead with negotiations. Instead, it has a proclivity to slide into complacency. Without the violence, what's the problem?[78]

> > < <

Hamas remains locked in conflict with Israel. It fired hundreds of rockets—homemade and smuggled from abroad—at southern Israel between 2007 and 2012 from its stockpile. During that period, its missiles killed a few Israeli civilians and injured several others in the vicinities of Ashkelon and Sderot and were the cause of severe psychological trauma among the residents of these cities, especially children. On every occasion, Israel retaliated with air strikes, often targeted air strikes on rocket-launching sites or on individuals identified as the perpetrators—most often with pinpoint accuracy, but too often with civilian casualties—and on every occasion the results were cycles of violence.

Hamas has also fought three wars with Israel—in 2008–09, in November 2012, and a far more deadly fifty-day-long war in July and August 2014—when some of its missiles reached Jerusalem and Tel Aviv. Israel always responded with massive force and on two occasions—in 2008–09 and 2014—it invaded Gaza, leveling much of it the first time around and practically demolishing it the second time. And while on each occasion Hamas would insist it had not been defeated, neither could it point to any tangible evidence that it had won. However, on each occasion it had to ask itself what, in terms of a cost-benefit analysis, it had achieved, other than an assertion of legitimacy for a short period of time. And on every occasion it has come up short with the answers; perhaps the 2014 war will be the exception.[79]

The first Gaza war began on December 27, 2008, when Israel invaded Gaza after an extended exchange of rocket fire from Hamas and retaliatory air strikes. The intent of Operation Cast Lead, Israel's code name for the assault, was to destroy Hamas's military capacity, and if that also required destroying infrastructure, including homes, hospitals, and schools, so be it. Israel prohibited the media from entering Gaza, but reports leaked out suggesting that little care was taken to differentiate between the militants, who composed only a tiny fraction of the population of Gaza, and everyone else. There were allegations that, among other atrocities, Israel used white phosphorous and Hamas used women and children as human shields.

On January 18, 2009, after a slew of UN resolutions, Israel unilaterally withdrew, bringing the carnage to an end. Much of Gaza was leveled, its entire infrastructure demolished, government buildings in ruins, but Hamas was still on its feet. The toll: 1,419 Palestinians dead, of whom 82 percent are estimated to have been civilians; twenty-three Israelis dead, of whom six were killed by friendly fire. Allegations made by both sides led the UN to appoint the Goldstone Commission. Its findings were scathingly critical of the IDF, which has always prided itself on being the epitome of a moral army. The commission was also critical of Hamas, but not on a scale that matched its criticisms of the IDF. The Israelis could not comprehend, much less accept, such a charge.[80] Of course, while Hamas criticizes the IDF for indiscriminate killing of civilians, there is nothing indiscriminate about its own targets—Hamas rockets are fired deliberately in the hope they will kill Israeli civilians; Palestinian civilians are deliberately used as human shields; missiles are launched from densely populated areas. It is callous and calculated: The more the IDF shells or orders air strikes on these targets, the more civilian deaths are inevitable; in the absence of discrimination, which the IDF is short on, many civilian targets come within its range, causing havoc and strewing the streets with dead bodies, sometimes of entire families, and demolished homes.

Every Jewish Israeli interviewee in a position to know affirmed that senior PA/Fatah leaders in 2008–09 practically begged Israel to finish off Hamas—not for Israel's gain but for Fatah's.* Hamas knows about that treachery (as it labels it). As far as it is concerned, Fatah collaborates with Israel, using the PASF to crack down on members of Hamas. It regards the PA/Fatah, not without justifiable reason, as an entity to which Israel subcontracted the job of clearing the West Bank of armed resistance to the occupation. The PASF, its patronage aligned to Fatah, tracks members of Hamas and arrests them in the West Bank, often with the aid of Israeli intelligence and the IDF. Under Arafat this covert collaboration, part of his Oslo

*These interviewees wished to remain anonymous.

commitment to curbing violence, was intermittent at best and rewarded, when Israel thought he was seriously going about the task, with more trappings of power and a further redeployment expanding the range of the PA's remit. Arrestees are denied due process (not that due process is something Hamas is overly familiar with), tortured, and imprisoned indefinitely. As far as Abbas is concerned, such collaboration is a prerequisite for meeting Israeli security concerns, for showing that the PASF is as professional and competent as its Israeli counterpart—a down payment on the security file when that file is opened during final settlement negotiations.[81] For Israel to buy in to a negotiated FSA, it has to be sure that it can count on the PASF to weed out terrorists in the new state with a thoroughness that matches its own.

According to Eyad el-Sarraj, who had numerous conversations with Hamas leaders in the months following Hamas's victory in the 2006 national elections, they would ask, "How can we work with these people who have provided information to the Israelis that lead to the incarceration of our members? Palestinians who were actually *arresting* fellow Palestinians on behalf of the Israelis? How can we ever trust these people?!"[82] Even today, that question lingers.

> > < <

The rise to power of the Muslim Brotherhood in Egypt promised to change everything on the *strategic* level. Hamas, the offspring of the Brotherhood, underwent a metamorphosis. It saw itself positioned with an inside track to a sympathetic Egyptian government, and surely, it believed, the close association with Egypt would carry over into the international arena, giving Hamas a voice it had hitherto lacked. In the near term, frequent openings at the Rafah crossing greatly facilitated access and traffic between Gaza and Egypt, and Hamas proposed many future projects, such as refurbishing the airport at Rafah for commercial use and establishing a free-trade zone. The fact that Hamas was now a power to be dealt with was explicitly acknowledged with the visit of the emir of Qatar—the first head of state to visit Gaza. He promised $400 million in aid. Turkey's prime minister, Recep Tayyip Erdoğan, indicated his intention to visit. Doors to the outside world were opening. Hamas had allies of stature.

The PLO watched with consternation. The scales of power and importance seemed to be shifting. In the zero-sum game of Palestinian politics, whatever benefited Hamas diminished Fatah, and vice versa.

On November 14, 2012, the IDF finally caught up with and assassinated Ahmed al-Jabari with a precision air strike on a busy street in Gaza City.[83]

Over the following eight days, Hamas responded to his assassination by unloading 1,500 rockets into southern Israel,[84] the opening salvo in the second Gaza war. On this occasion, Israel retaliated with Operation Pillar of Defense, mobilizing seventy thousand reservists, launching massive air strikes that targeted not just Qassam facilities and inventory sites but also Hamas government buildings, and moving its immense machinery of invasion north to Gaza's borders. Hamas, believing it had Egyptian president Mohamed Morsi (who had assumed his duties in June) and the Muslim Brotherhood in its back pocket, was prepared to risk the invasion. It felt either that it could drag Egypt into the war or that Islamic Jihad and the more extreme jihadist groups would grasp the opportunity to fill the vacuum or that the IDF would be unwilling or even unable to destroy it. Israel was poised to call the bluff and invade. Its citizens watched from the sidelines, once again hoping (as they had with Operation Cast Lead) that the IDF would mount a full-scale invasion and finally decapitate Hamas. But Netanyahu yielded to international pressure and disappointed them. For once, his government understood that media coverage would be detrimental to Israel, that Israel's relationship with the Muslim Brotherhood government in Egypt would be on the line—the 1978 Camp David agreement with Egypt was crucial to Israel's security—and instead opted for a cease-fire (brokered by Morsi with some involvement of U.S. secretary of state Hillary Clinton) that took effect on November 21 after six Israelis and 167 Palestinians were killed.[85] Once again the question of Israel using disproportionate force surfaced as an issue.[86] Of course, Israel and Hamas accused each other of provoking the eight-day war,[87] and each claimed victory. Some of "Hamas's demands [were] met," including "an end to targeted assassinations" (which Israel resumed some time afterward), an "easing of restrictions on movement of imports and exports, and trade," and some leverage with the Rafah crossing (which lasted only as long as Morsi lasted). Israel got a cessation of the rockets coming in from Gaza (which held, but was shaky at times until July 2014) and a promise from Egypt that it would prevent the smuggling of arms into Gaza, but without details on how this would be accomplished.[88] (When the Egyptian military sealed the tunnels after it overthrew Morsi, it took care of that detail.) Egypt assumed the role of ensuring that the cease-fire terms were adhered to, and it continued its monitoring function after ousting Morsi,[89] but with overt hostility toward Hamas.

By one measure, the war did little to advance Hamas's goals, other than to remind Israel that armed resistance remained a potent threat and jihadist groups that Gaza was Hamas's domain, but Hamas was hailed by all Palestinians for achieving a great victory. Thousands took to the streets to celebrate, both in Gaza and in the West Bank. The green flag of Hamas was everywhere, even though much of Gaza, including most government buildings, was in ruins. The image of hundreds of people standing in the rubble of their homes that had been demolished by Israeli air strikes, celebrating a "great victory" with wild enthusiasm, was an inexplicably sad and disconcerting attempt to assert dignity in the face of humiliations that exceeded what the residents of the West Bank encountered on a daily basis. Even with no Israeli soldier in sight, Israel's control is absolute, so the fact that Hamas went toe to toe with the mighty Israeli military machine and withstood the deadliest bombardment from the air and sea sealed its victory in the eyes of all Palestinians and erased for a moment the repressions of Israel's blockade. The international political payoff for Hamas after the Gaza war was exceptional but short-lived. With Morsi and the Brotherhood in control in Egypt, Hamas was the new standard-bearer for the Palestinian cause. Ramallah appeared impotent. There were murmurs of a new intifada: The gun brought results. But the moment soon faded. With other pressing world issues, the resumption of talks with the PLO was not a priority on Israel's political agenda. The Israeli blockade was eased, but not substantially. The result of a war that cost so many lives and destroyed so many homes and incapacitated Gaza is a triple irony: Hamas polices Gaza to ensure no further freelance attacks on Israel; the Palestinian Authority polices the West Bank to forestall potential terrorist (i.e., Hamas) attacks on Israel, and Israel constructs settlements more rapidly than ever. The war certainly did not spur the Israelis to try to lance this abscess by pushing for a resumption of negotiations. Instead, it only reinforced the sense that the situation is, for the ones with the real power, an irritant that does not have to be dealt with until necessity demands.

Hamas had tested how far it could push Morsi to intervene but had come up short. He worked pragmatically with the Israelis, because both Egyptians and Israelis understood that maintaining their relationship was paramount. Both played their hands deftly, ensuring that the relationship stood firm. The hard truth is that there is little that Hamas's rockets *fired from Gaza* can do to advance its goals, other than focusing the world's attention on the Palestinian cause by provoking massive retaliation from Israel and maybe setting in motion the multilateral talks that are essential to the peace process.

Since Gazans believe that official Israeli policy is to insult and humiliate them, striking back becomes a matter of honor, born of a desperation that has reached a point at which death for some—or a willingness to die—becomes a premeditated, conscious choice. Stripped of dignity, a man's willingness to act in a way that will almost certainly result in instant death is a statement of the *justness* of his cause. It is not that he thinks his death will make much difference; it is the *act* itself that counts. Launching a rocket toward southern Israel, even at the risk of almost instantaneously being killed, is seen as *a liberating act of defiance.* As a martyr, you achieve in death the dignity you were denied in life. Families hold "martyrs weddings," because "achieving martyrdom is not seen as a cause for sadness, but for gathering and celebration."[90] Our propensity to ridicule such acts as manifestations of a crazy religion that promises you the embrace of waiting virgins once you have killed yourself in such a manner in the name of the cause simply exemplifies our ignorance of Islam. Under the circumstances, such resistance is a rational act.

Israel can argue justifiably that Hamas engages in an immoral war, robbing its cause of righteousness because it *deliberately* launches rockets at civilian population centers. Israeli air strikes on Gaza do not *deliberately* target civilians, although civilians are killed—unintended "collateral damage."

> > < <

The power struggles within Hamas were recalibrated. It would not be overstating to say that both Meshaal and Haniyeh were "relieved" by Jabari's assassination. When the Political Bureau left Damascus after Hamas refused to back Assad in Syria's civil war, Meshaal ended up in Qatar, other personnel in other Arab countries. The dispersion weakened Meshaal. While he was reelected president of the Political Bureau in 2012, Gaza's Ismail Haniyeh was elected deputy president.

Meanwhile, the Morsi presidency and the ascendancy of the Brotherhood lasted slightly over a year.* In July 2013 the military deposed Morsi and

*The mayhem and violence in Egypt that accompanied the writing of a draft constitution exposed fundamental differences on "rights" among Islamists, secularists, and Coptic Christians, who felt that the whole process had degenerated into a grotesque abrogation of their rights. The Arab Spring began to shred when Morsi pushed through a referendum on a draft constitution, heavily weighted with Sharia, dividing Egypt between Islamists (the Muslim Brotherhood and the Salafists), who demanded the primacy of Sharia, and secularists, Coptics, and other religious persuasions, who wanted a pluralistic constitution with equal protection for all religions.

banned the Brotherhood. The old Mubarak regime was back, but with a new face. The military, under then-general Abdel Fattah el-Sisi, commander in chief of the Egyptian armed forces, set out to destroy the Brotherhood's infrastructure and end its participation in Egypt's political and civilian life. Soldiers swiftly arrested most of the Brotherhood's leaders, closed its offices and media outlets, banned it, and declared it a terrorist organization and its every member fair game. Almost as an afterthought, it declared Hamas a terrorist organization too. In May 2014 Sisi was elected president. The elections were legitimate, although the turnout was abysmally low.

Not open to question was the immediate impact of the coup on Hamas. In March 2014, when barrages of missiles from Gaza seemed to put the 2012 cease-fire in jeopardy, Egypt agreed to act as a mediator, not, as had always been the case, between Hamas and Israel, but between the Islamic Jihad and Israel.[91] It left Hamas twisting in the wind, to its great humiliation—a move indicative of a creeping loss of stature.[92] Matters only got worse. The Egyptian military closed and sealed the 1,400-plus tunnels that were the lifeblood of the Gazan economy during the blockade. The Gazan economy rapidly fell apart. With the supply of cheap Egyptian diesel curtailed, the Hamas government now had to purchase more expensive fuel from either the Palestinian Authority or Israel. Commerce slowly ceased; construction came to a stop; the flow of goods into Gaza was reduced to a trickle; businesses closed; unemployment skyrocketed; and the source of the bulk of Hamas's revenue suddenly no longer existed. Under siege from Israel on one side and a hostile Egypt on the other, Hamas also had to deal with a disrupted weapons supply from Syria (but was still stockpiling what it could), the lack of a financier (Iran),[93] an empty pocketbook, faltering governance (in November 2013 its 43,000 public employees were on half salary), a more aggressive Islamic Jihad, and falling popularity. It approved a budget of $784 million for 2014 with a deficit of $589 million—almost 75 percent of the whole. Unemployment hovered at 50 percent, and 60 percent of Gazan households were either food insecure or vulnerable to food insecurity.[94]

After something unprecedented happened in Gaza—public-service unions

---

Again Egypt became a vortex of instability, undermining Morsi's rule and igniting both the implosion of the revolution that had promised so much and a second "revolution" where the masses now demanded Morsi's head. The military stepped in, deposed Morsi, and instituted military rule with a veneer of civilian government and the promise of elections. The military set about crushing the Brotherhood. Unfortunately, such convolutions are not uncommon when the lid is taken off decades of repression and suppressed differences begin to emerge.

organized huge protests against the Gazan government demanding full payment of their salaries—Hamas had to reevaluate its options. With no source of financial backing, it had nowhere to turn.

Where would it find the revenue to enable it to operate as a government? Would it have to go, hat in hand, and "beg" for assistance from an already bankrupt PA? How would it curb the jihadist militias nipping at its heels? Was a "merger" with the Islamic Jihad something it should pursue? How might constraints preclude it from pursuing armed resistance? The answer to the last question came within months.

> > < <

The cleavages between Fatah and Hamas are of such a magnitude that Israel can justifiably insist that both get their houses in order before it commits to negotiating an FSA. The problem is that when Hamas and Fatah became willing to do just that, Israel shrilly condemned the arrangements they made.[95] But if Fatah and Hamas do not heal their divisions, no peace negotiated by the PLO with Israel will be realized. And even if one perchance materialized, realities on the ground would ensure that it could not be implemented. Reconciliation is a sine qua non for any process's chance of succeeding in the long term.

"I have a very pessimistic view toward Palestinian reconciliation," Professor Abusada told me in March 2012. "I don't think that there is a way to solve it, and I think what we have now is what we call conflict management instead of resolving the conflict. You have daily incitement, accusations back and forth; you have hundreds of political prisoners in the West Bank imprisoned in PA jails because they belong to Hamas, and also hundreds of Fatah people who are in jail here in Gaza in Hamas jails. You have torture and persecution taking place. . . . Fatah is afraid in the West Bank that Hamas will take control over the West Bank. Hamas is afraid that if there is reconciliation it would mean that they might lose control over the Gaza Strip."[96] But circumstances drastically changed, requiring Hamas to make decisions it otherwise would not have entertained.

Hamas had run out of money and options and resources to govern. On the one hand, it was unable to pay its employees; on the other, it found itself without friends to turn to for assistance.[97] Its options boiled down to running the risk of being overthrown or turning to the PA for financial relief. Whether the seven files Ismail al-Ashqar had referred to were closed or not became irrelevant. For Hamas, reconciliation was not just necessary; it was imperative.

Hence its turnabout: Although it had denounced the 2013–14 talks and had been unequivocal in saying that it would reject any agreement the talks might lead to,[98] within months it signed a reconciliation pact with Fatah.

The pact Azzam Ahmed and Mousa Abu Marzouk had assiduously pursued was finally signed in April 2014, immediately after the two-state talks collapsed. The pact called for the appointment of a technocratic government to administer the PA while the two parties readied themselves for elections in November 2014 and thereafter the formation of a unity government. Unity between Fatah and Hamas in governance arrangements was necessary, Mahmoud al-Zahar had stressed during our interview in 2011, "but unity regarding their respective belief systems or a shared vision as to the way forward is not. [For the] administration of governance, we have to have friendship between Fatah and Hamas. However, the respective belief systems and societal ideologies are incompatible—although they can coexist."[99] Hamas, Meshaal said, "has made concessions with Fatah. Making concessions to others is a necessity that we don't regret. . . . [Concessions] are a fundamental pillar to turn the page of division forever."[100] Implicitly he was saying that Hamas had surrendered to most of what Fatah had demanded.[101] But, in accordance with al-Zahar's formulation, it was unity in governance, not unity in belief systems. In addition, being forced to enter the pact with the PA sowed divisions in Hamas's own ranks; many in the military wing were angered at the concessions made. Strains in the fragile pact were quick to appear. The economic relief Hamas had hoped for did not materialize. Civil servants in Gaza were infuriated when Ramallah announced that workers would be vetted before being paid—a process that could take months—and the workers took to the streets again.[102] Whatever prospects there were for extending the peace talks were done with.[103]

The technocratic government was duly selected and became the PA's governing entity on June 2.[104] With its right-wing partners breathing fire, the Netanyahu government vehemently opposed the reconciliation pact from the beginning and immediately set out to undermine it. Netanyahu castigated Abbas for being willing to forge Palestinian national unity with terrorists.[105] Netanyahu was outraged. Nevertheless, the technocratic government got off to a quick start. The United States, despite cries of dissent from Israel, said it was willing to deal with the new government;[106] the EU also signaled its intentions to give it a chance. In Israel Jewish Israeli leaders were adamant: the question of negotiating with a Palestinian "consensus" government was out of the question.

So what meaning does the "reconciliation" refrain have? Rounds of on-again, off-again talks over seven years; multiple announcements made of a pact agreed; election dates announced, voter registration offices opened again; all followed by abrupt abrogation that only deepens the continuing animosity.

In April 2014, the old animosities were bottled, not buried and it remained to be seen whether what could work from the top down would work from the bottom up. The divisions between the two parties did not involve just two rival governments; they metastasized and infiltrated every segment of Palestinian society with their poison, down to the street level. In the brief but savage war in 2007, between 200 and 375 members of Fatah and Hamas were killed, with hundreds more injured and still more imprisoned and tortured. Violations of human rights were commonplace. Nevertheless, in Ramallah and Gaza City the street celebrated at news of the pact. (Less so in the West Bank, which at the best of times had a fractious relationship with Gaza.) But some caveats were expressed: While turning over a new leaf was an achievement everyone had wished for, old wounds could not easily be waved aside;[107] perpetrators of violence in 2007 would still have to face justice—none of this forgive-and-forget stuff. Compensation for losses would have to be paid. Many Palestinians demanded that Fatah and Hamas take responsibility for their actions and the consequences, much as they were demanding that Israel take responsibility for the *Nakba* and its consequences. Coming to a sustainable agreement would not be simple. Many questions as to how a unity government would function went unanswered.*

Preparations for national elections in November 2014 never got off the ground. A series of drastic changes became the catalyst for the third war

*Pertinent question: Where will a legislative assembly sit? Will Israel arrest members of Hamas running for seats in the West Bank? How would this deal affect the heretofore collaborative relationship between the IDF and the PASF? How are the PASF and Hamas's own security forces going to be integrated? What repercussions might follow if Israel refuses to allow Palestinians in East Jerusalem to participate in the elections? Will Hamas candidates who dare show their faces risk deportation? And what about the legislation passed by the groups' respective assemblies over the last seven years enacting secular laws for the West Bank and Sharia for Gaza? Amira Hass, "Unity Government Inheriting Host of Headaches from Split Palestinian Regimes," *Haaretz*, April 26, 2014, http://www.haaretz.com/news/middle-east/.premium-1.587437. "All legislation and legal amendments that were introduced to Palestinian law since Hamas took power of the Gaza Strip in 2007 will be thoroughly debated following the formation of the consensual government . . . according to Hassan Khreisheh, the second deputy speaker of the Palestinian Legislative Council PLC." Rasha Abou Jalal, "New unity government to review Hamas laws in Gaza," Al-Monitor, May 23, 2014, http://www.al-monitor.com/pulse/originals/2014/05/gaza-hamas-laws-review-unity-government-reconciliation.html. In December 2014, just 9 percent of Palestinians believed that their first and most vital goal should be to establish a democratic political system that respects freedom and rights of Palestinians. See the Palestinian Public Opinion Poll No. 54, www.pcpsr.org/en/mode/505.

between Israel and Hamas, a game changer, that would move the parameters of the conflict to a different plane and test the resilience of the pact.

> > < <

Several events converged to jump-start the third Gaza war in four years. But unlike the other two, this one, which started in July 2014, might yet be transformative. It could either entrench the status quo, with unpredictable consequences, or change it, also with unpredictable consequences. Hamas would either emerge as a political and military force to be reckoned with, or it would not. On the Israeli side, the war would determine whether Netanyahu emerges as a commanding prime minister or becomes a political has-been.

The triggering events: (1) The kidnapping of three teenage settlers in the West Bank on June 12 and Netanyahu's immediately accusing Hamas of being responsible, without any evidence to substantiate his accusation[108] and despite Hamas's vehement denials that it was involved in any way.[109] (2) Netanyahu's using the IDF's combing the West Bank to look for the boys[110] as an excuse to dismantle Hamas.[111] (3) The belligerent way the IDF conducted its search, going to one house after another, invading Palestinians' privacy, disrupting their lives, ruining their homes, rummaging through their belongings and confiscating at will, and arresting whomever they wanted (every Palestinian was held to account, leaving West Bank Palestinians angry and resentful that once again they had to submit to the arbitrary actions of the IDF).[112] During the eighteen-day operation, IDF soldiers arrested 419 Palestinians, 335 of whom were affiliated with Hamas; searched 2,218 locations; and confiscated $350,000. (4) The killing of a Palestinian Israeli boy in Jerusalem on July 2 as revenge for the murder of the Israeli teenagers, whose bodies had been found. (5) The political void left after the collapse of the 2013–14 talks. (6) Netanyahu's attempt to tie the kidnappings to the reconciliation pact.[113] (7) The failure to fully implement the provisions of the 2012 cease-fire that promised openings at the Rafah border crossing and an easing of the blockade.[114] (8) The continued nonpayment of salaries to public employees in Gaza.*

*Nathan Thrall, ICG analyst, said: "Israel and much of the international community placed a prohibitive set of obstacles in the way of the Palestinian 'national consensus' government that was formed in early June," Among these obstacles were measures they took to ensure the nonpayment of the salaries to Gaza's unpaid civil servants. Nathan Thrall, "How the West Chose War in Gaza," *New York Times*, July 17, 2014, http://www.nytimes.com/2014/07/18/opinion/gaza-and-israel-the-road to war-paved by the-west.html?_r=0. See also Nathan Thrall, "Whose Palestine?" *NYR Blog, New York Review of Books*, June 19, 2014, http://www.nybooks.com/blogs/

Hamas gambled.[115] Reacting to what it perceived as Netanyahu's trying to dismantle its structures in the West Bank, it fired volleys of rockets into southern Israel on June 29, 2014, its first rocket bombardment of Israel since the November 2012 cease-fire.*[116] Israel retaliated with air strikes, setting off a cycle of violence that became self-reinforcing. But on this occasion, for Hamas, the stakes were higher. Its recourse to armed resistance was intended to assert its identity; the war would make it relevant again, raise its resistance profile among the people; mobilize all Palestinians to its side; bring economic relief; and make it clear that Hamas would always be a formidable presence that would have to be taken into account in future peace negotiations, even if it no longer governed Gaza.[117]

Hamas missile attacks on southern Israel and the IDF air strikes moved up a level, slowly escalating and then accelerating into open warfare. Missiles launched from Gaza came in the hundreds, and hundreds of air strikes on Hamas launching sites followed.[118]

On July 8, Israel launched Operation Protective Edge. "The operation will expand and continue until the rocket firing on our cities stops, and the quiet returns," Netanyahu promised the Israeli public. However, he "consistently defined the objectives of the operation in relatively modest terms—to restore the quiet, not to topple Hamas or destroy its rocket infrastructure inside Gaza."[119]

On July 15 the Cabinet agreed to the cease-fire proposal formulated by Egypt, similar to what had been agreed to in the 2012 Cairo cease-fire. Hamas rejected the proposal because it did not meet its terms. On July 17, Hamas militants infiltrated Israel through a tunnel near Kibbutz Sufa and the IDF's Operation Protective Edge ground invasion began. The stated goal of the operation now became the destruction of tunnels from Gaza into Israel.[120] On July 20, Defense Minister Moshe Ya'alon said that it would take

nyrblog/2014/jun/19/whose-palestine/; and Elhanan Miller, "US Blocked Qatari Funds Intended for Hamas Employees," *Times of Israel*, July 15, 2014, http://www.timesofisrael.com/usblocked-qatari-funds-intended-for-hamas-employees/.

A July 29, 2014, ICG report, in which a number of Fatah leaders were interviewed, says, "No issue has been as toxic as the salaries of the employees hired under Hamas. Fatah's official position is that the PA needs to review all 40,000-plus employees, as some are said to be militants or members of Hamas-dominated security services." The ICG concludes that "the policy of trying to topple or weaken Hamas was misguided when it was designed and remains so today." See "Gaza and Israel: New Obstacles, New Solutions," Middle East Briefing No. 39, July 14, 2014, http://www.crisisgroup.org/~/media/Files/Middle%20East%20North%20Africa/Israel%20Palestine/b039-gaza-and-israel-new-obstacles-new-solutions.pdf.

*There had been sporadic rockets launched from Gaza between November 2012 and June 2014 but no sustained attacks constituting "volleys."

"two or three days" to destroy the tunnels[121]—an almost unforgivable miscalculation. Meanwhile Netanyahu's coalition partners to the right of Likud and some members of Likud itself, called for stronger measures.*

Many of Hamas's rockets had better range than in 2012. Some reached Tel Aviv and Jerusalem but were intercepted by the Iron Dome.† For the first time residents of both cities found themselves scurrying for shelter when the sirens sounded. On July 29, the mission goal changed once again: Now Netanyahu called for the demilitarization of Hamas.[122] Israel's decisions were reactive; it misread the situation from the beginning and the IDF found itself not adequately prepared for Hamas's response. One can sympathize with the IDF officers on the ground who told Israeli media that they felt that "Netanyahu and Ya'alon don't really know what their objective is."[123] Hamas's objectives remained steadfast: Lift the blockade, pay the forty-three thousand workers still unpaid, open the Rafah border crossing, and build a seaport.[124]

The IDF, as Hamas had forewarned, ran into some surprises.[125] Hamas's secret tunnel network leading into Israel was far more extensive, and sophisticated, than the IDF had previously thought. It comprised at least forty tunnels, with curved concrete walls that measured about thirty inches wide and forty-six feet deep underground, "electric lines along the walls," and rail tracks to facilitate the movement of materials; the tunnels were interconnected with one another and stretched in some cases for a mile before entering Israel, often in a field close to an adjacent town.[126]

Assaf Sharon writes, "According to expert estimates, tunnels can be dug at six to twelve meters a day, an average tunnel taking three months to complete. A former commander of an elite IDF combat engineering company estimated that a five-hundred-meter-long tunnel would take a month and a half to dig, and a longer tunnel would take several months at most."[127]

The chatter in Israel conjuring scenarios of "armed enemies popping up" in the most unexpected places, "spraying a crowd with a machine gun fire . . .

*Naftali Bennett, who opposes a Palestinian state, said that the goal should be to "forcefully root out Hamas' faith in its ability to win." Barak David, "Bennett: Destruction of Tunnels Not Enough—Hamas Must Be Completely Defeated," *Haaretz*, July 29, 2014, http://www.haaretz.com/news/diplomacy-defense/1.607836. His colleague in the Cabinet, Foreign Minister Avigdor Lieberman, said that the operation must "end with the IDF in full control of the Gaza strip." Noam "Dabul" Dvir, "Liberman Calls for Continued IDF Presence in Gaza," *YNet News*, July 15, 2014, http://www.ynetnews.com/articles/0,7340,L-4544123,00.html.

†Of the 4,700 missiles fired from Gaza during July and August, the Iron Dome intercepted 600—"Israel's Gaza War Bill: Iron Dome Intercepts of Hamas Rocket Cost $100,000 Each," *World Tribune*, September 3, 2014, http://www.worldtribune.com/2014/09/03/israeli-defense-minister-latest-gaza-war-cost-2-5-billion/.

exploding a suicide belt or snatching captives and ducking back into the dirt" went to the heart of Israeli fears, far more so than Hamas's rocketry, because it left them feeling more vulnerable, without much ability to protect themselves from sudden exposure to terrorists.[128] Hamas's fighters were able to infiltrate Israel on a number of occasions during the intensive ground invasion. Israel was also surprised by the number of underground rocket-launching sites and by the professionalism of the Hamas fighters, who were equipped to handle urban guerrilla warfare.[129] After one of Hamas's missiles fell just short of hitting Ben Gurion Airport, the United States suspended all flights to Israel for forty-eight hours, and most other countries followed suit, giving a huge psychological boost to Hamas while severely damaging Israel's economy.[130] It gave Jewish Israelis a glimpse of what the future could hold. For many it was a game changer.

Despite many attempts by the United States to arrange a cease-fire,*

*U.S. secretary of state John Kerry made a number of attempts in talks with the Egyptians and Israel to draw up a framework for a cease-fire, the terms of which were rejected out of hand by Hamas, which had no representation at the mediation table. In attempts to balance the mediating table (Sisi was vehemently anti-Hamas), Kerry tried his hand with Qatar and Turkey, especially the former. He was lambasted by Israel for trying to load the table with pro-Hamas allies. However, as the war intensified and the fallout from Hamas's targeting of Ben Gurion Airport and the extensiveness of its tunnel network into Israel emerged, Israel decided that despite the international community's increasing concern over the number of civilian casualties (including entire families) that were a direct result of Israel's targeting of Hamas's infrastructure, public opinion in Israel (which took a decidedly different view of the casualties, attributing them mostly to Hamas using civilians as human shields and stocking inventory in densely populated areas of Gaza) supported pressing ahead "to finish the job." Israel wanted no repeats of the outcomes of the 2008 and 2012 wars, viewing any future capacity of an armed Hamas as an existential threat. Besides, the law of diminishing returns applied to the horrifying scenes that live video and television coverage were bringing to the outside world. A Peace Index poll showed that over 90 percent of Jewish Israelis supported the invasion and that just 4 percent thought the IDF was using excessive force. On the home front, Netanyahu had nothing to worry about. Jodi Rudoren, "Amid Outcry Abroad, a Wealth of Backing in Israel for Netanyahu," *New York Times*, July 26, 2014, http://www.nytimes.com/2014/07/27/world/middleeast/losing-support-from-abroad-netanyahu-finds-a-wealth-of-backing-at-home.html?action=click&contentCollection=Middle%20East&module=RelatedCoverage®ion=Marginalia&pgtype=article; Michael R. Gordon and Jodi Rudoren, "In Israel, Kerry Sees 'Work to Do' to Get Deal on Cease-Fire," *New York Times*, 23 July 23, 2014, http://www.nytimes.com/2014/07/24/world/middleeast/kerry-israel-gaza.html?hp&action=click&pgtype=Homepage&version=LedeSum&module=first-column-region®ion=top-news&WT.nav=top-news&_r=0; and Michael R. Gordon "Kerry Says U.S. Would Address Hamas Demands After Cease-Fire," *New York Times*, July 22, 2014, http://www.nytimes.com/2014/07/23/world/middleeast/kerry-says-us-would-address-hamas-demands-after-cease-fire.html?rref=world/middleeast&module=Ribbon&version=con-text®ion=Header&action=click&contentCollection=Middle%20East&pgtype=article. John B. Judis, "Ending the Israeli-Palestinian Conflict Is No Longer a Vital American Interest," *New Republic*, August 10, 2014, http://www.newrepublic.com/article/119022/2014-gaza-war-why-obama-and-kerry-have-failed-end-it.

Hamas and Israel upped the ante. Hamas knew that if it agreed to anything less than the easing of border crossings and a less stringent blockade, its standing in Gaza—perhaps in the West Bank too—would plummet and it might find itself a spent political and military presence. On the other hand, Netanyahu knew that anything less than ferreting out and destroying Hamas's military assets—both its military capabilities and the tunnels it could use to enter Israel—would leave Israel in an untenable situation: Israel could expect another war in a few years, when Hamas would have acquired more sophisticated rockets capable of inflicting severe damage on cities such as Tel Aviv, Jerusalem, and Haifa, with major civilian casualties. Indeed, as the invasion continued to find more tunnels, especially tunnels into Israel—public opinion in Israel pressed for putting Hamas out of business, settling for nothing less than the demilitarization of Hamas to eliminate the threat of future attacks. On this score Netanyahu could count on 86.5 percent of Israelis in his corner.[131] The death toll was frighteningly one-sided.* Israel was not moved: The toll was horrifying, yes, but it was the result of Hamas using people in homes, schools, hospitals, mosques, and anywhere civilians might congregate, as human shields. The international community called for restraint as the Gazan civilian casualties mounted, but, in two different surveys, in Israel only 6 percent of Jewish Israelis thought the IDF was using excessive force; some 97 percent were satisfied with its performance.[132] Obama, concerned with daily reports of mounting civilian casualties in Gaza, ordered a hold on a shipment of military equipment,[133] but the shipment was cleared albeit with conditions attached with regard to the weapons' use.[134] Netanyahu weighed the cost of the international outcry against the benefits of Israel's achieving the avowed purpose of its invasion, and the latter overrode the former.[135]

Surprisingly, the reaction from Arab states was strangely moot. The political calculus in the region had changed to Hamas's detriment. No Arab state voiced its support; no Arab state even protested the mounting toll of Palestinian civilian deaths. In fact, in the most ironic twist of all, indicative of how the post–Arab Spring conflicts between political Islam and secularists that convulsed the Arab world had altered the status quo—Arab states appeared to side more with Israel than with Hamas. Hamas found itself in a lonely place.[136]

In the West Bank, the PA prevaricated before realizing that it would lose

*See casualty count on page 160.

all credibility with Palestinians unless it came out on the side of Hamas.[137] Nevertheless, after a few large protests, especially the "Day of Rage," in late July, during which five Palestinians were killed by the IDF.[138] At one point there were the usual prognostications of a third intifada, but one never materialized.[139] Many Palestinians feared that an uprising would bring a return to the chaos of the Second Intifada; there was no leadership, no plans.[140]

After Kerry tried to arrange a cease-fire that badly backfired,[141] the United States withdrew and left the stage to Sisi. A number of twenty-four-hour cease-fires broke down almost as soon as they were announced—each side, of course, blamed the other. Between August 4 and August 7, 2014, the IDF withdrew its forces—it had accomplished its mission to destroy the underground tunnels and announced that it had sufficiently degraded Hamas's military capacity.[142] But the fighting—exchanges of rocket fire and air strikes—grew more intense.

Talks finally took place in Cairo over a five-day period (August 15–19) with twenty-four-hour extensions thrown in. The Palestinians presented a united front. A PLO delegation headed by Azzam Ahmed negotiated on behalf of Hamas. Hamas, of course, sent its own delegation, headed by Mousa Abu Marzouk, which was consulted at every step by the West Bank delegation. There was never any real possibility the talks would succeed. Netanyahu would never meet a single Hamas demand, never consider lifting the siege, and never "reward" it with a chance to claim a "victory" after firing some three thousand rockets into Israel, penetrating its territory through tunnels, and killing sixty-four soldiers over close to two months of bloody battle:[143] Israel would consider concessions only in the event of Hamas demilitarizing[144]—which was never in the cards. The Egyptians were equally adamant: no concessions on Rafah crossings. When the talks collapsed,[145] Netanyahu said his government would only return fire if fired upon—"quiet for quiet," but Hamas returned to "fire for fire." In one sense it had no option: How could it face its own people with nothing to show for the devastation and death it had been instrumental in causing? All political considerations aside, it was a question of honor. On August 19, 2014, Israel dropped a one-ton bomb on a house where it believed Mohammed Deif, Hamas's military chief, was holed up.[146] The bomb demolished the house, killing Deif's wife, three-year-old daughter, infant son, and three of Hamas's top commanders.[147] Deif, Hamas said, had not been at home at the time, but his whereabouts remain a mystery.[148] In response Hamas publicly executed eighteen Gazans it accused of collaboration.[149] In one five-day period it fired 570 rockets, 168 in one day,[150] and for the first time, one of its rockets killed a child.[151]

In the final week of the conflict, Israel resorted to bombing apartment buildings, some with twelve floors, on the grounds that there was a Hamas command center operation on one of the floors.[152] In Netanyahu's cabinet Liberman and Bennett were in open revolt. In fact, Netanyahu was in a double bind.[153] On the one hand his coalition was braying for further military action; on the other hand he was well aware that Israel was losing the "hearts and minds" of the international community—especially as Israel could not compete with the scenes of carnage and wanton destruction coming out of Gaza, thanks to the efficacy of the Iron Dome, which had ensured that no apartment buildings in Tel Aviv or downtown Jerusalem were struck by an incoming Hamas rocket. On this front Israel could not win.

> > < <

And then, a cease-fire.

On August 26, Netanyahu, without consulting his war cabinet, agreed to the Egyptians' terms, which were essentially a restatement of the 2012 cease-fire, and which had been on the table for over a month, terms that Islamic Jihad and Hamas had at that point rejected. "Quiet for quiet" for a month, and then the parties would reconvene in Cairo to start addressing the serious issues—Hamas's demands for a seaport and the lifting of the blockade and Israel's for demilitarization. Hamas and Islamic Jihad agreed to the same terms. The blockade was eased to allow the entry of some materials required to begin redressing the pervasive destruction. In the meantime, restrictions on the 43,000 former Hamas employees would be lifted and they would be paid.[154] There was no talk of demilitarization.

In Israel Netanyahu faced a "storm of criticism."[155] In the space of a month his performance rating dropped from 82 percent on the eve of the invasion to 38 percent.[156] In Gaza people danced in the streets—not because Hamas's demands had been met but because the round-the-clock air strikes would stop.

Hamas, as usual, claimed "a great victory."

> > < <

To assess:

The casualty count: 2,205 Palestinians killed, of whom 722 were militants and over 500 were children on the Palestinian side; on the Israeli side, 64 IDF soldiers and 6 civilians.[157]

A total of 4,564 rockets had been fired by Hamas into Israel, with 5,226 retaliatory strikes from airstrikes and tank and gunship artillery shelling.[158] The IDF had invaded Gaza for twenty-eight days, several cease-fires were broken, and Gaza was dismembered. Over one quarter of the population was displaced (470,000 people), 280,000 Gazans took shelter in UNRWA schools, 108,000 people became homeless, 18,000 buildings were destroyed,[159] and 500,000 children were unable to start school. Estimates of the costs to restore Gaza to its previously wretched condition ran to over $6 billion[160]—more than three times Gaza's GDP.[161] (Some estimates said that reconstruction could take twenty years if one hundred tons of construction materials arrived daily in Gaza.)[162]

Negotiators in Cairo, in talks mediated by a very pro-Israel Egypt,[163] finally agreed to a one-month cease-fire, allowing both sides to claim "victory," when in reality both sides knew that at best they had reached a temporary respite.[164] "The scale of damage resulting from the fifty-day escalation in hostilities is unprecedented since the beginning of the Israeli occupation in 1967," OCHA said in a September 2014 report.[165]

Israel did a turnabout on its position on the Palestinian unity government, realizing that no matter how much it labeled Hamas a terror organization, of a kind with ISIS, it nevertheless had to acknowledge, implicitly at least, that Hamas was a player of consequence in the Palestinian-Israeli conflict—and although it was one Israel would have no dealings with, it was one Israel had to negotiate with indirectly, with the Palestinian Authority acting as its proxy.* Neither side won in terms of its demands being met†—

*Similarly, the Democratic Unionist Party in Northern Ireland would have no dealings with Sinn Féin, and the two never negotiated person to person or sat in the same room until the Good Friday/Belfast Agreement was signed. See also "Why Do Palestinians in Gaza Support Hamas?" http://www.haaretz.com/opinion/.premium-1.608906.

†According to the AP, the terms of the cease-fire included "the opening of Israeli-controlled crossings with Gaza 'that ensures the humanitarian aid and reconstruction materials' are allowed in; there will be safeguards to prevent reconstruction materials from being used for military purposes; all materials will be inspected on their way into Gaza, and will be under international supervision afterward." The fishing zone for Gaza's fishermen would be extended from three nautical miles to six nautical miles. "Israel [would] allow Gaza to export goods to West Bank for first time in eight years; Israel [would] allow the Palestinian Authority to pay salaries to civil servants employed by Hamas in Gaza, with guarantees that none of the money [went] to Hamas' military wing; an Israeli buffer zone along the Gaza border [would] be reduced from 500 meters (550 yards) to 300 meters (325 yards), and eventually down to 100 meters (110 yards)."

The Unresolved Issues were: "Hamas [wanted] Egypt to reopen the Rafah border crossing—Gaza's main gateway to the outside world—to passenger and cargo traffic. A border deal would include a role for Abbas, giving him his first foothold in Gaza since Hamas overran the area in 2007. Hamas also [wanted] a reopening of Gaza's air and seaports. Israel [wanted] Hamas to disarm. [And the] return of bodies of two Israeli soldiers killed in the war. Hamas [demanded] that dozens of Hamas prisoners arrested in a West Bank crackdown over the summer be released.

they were shuffled onto an agenda for talks to resume a month later if the cease-fire—"quiet for quiet"—held.

However, in asymmetrical warfare, whether or not "demands" are met (i.e., whether you "win" or "lose" in the conventional sense) is secondary to perception of the intangibles in the globalized world of tweets and instantaneous information and disinformation.

Hamas resuscitated itself and proved a most formidable enemy; it found chinks in Israel's security armor;[166] it emerged still standing, still defiant, still prepared to go back to war.[167] It was a source of pride for many Gazans, and compensated many for the indignities that permeated their lives, that these underdogs outperformed their superior opponent, that they were able to go head to head with one of the world's most powerful military machines and fight it to a draw.[168] Support for Hamas among Palestinians surged.[169] Seventy-nine percent believed Hamas had won the war; 59 percent were satisfied with the accomplishment gained in the agreement compared to the human and material losses sustained by the Gaza Strip; 39 percent were dissatisfied with the accomplishment. Only 30 percent thought that Hamas should have warned Israeli civilians in the specific targeted areas before launching its rockets while 68 percent believed it should not do so.[*170]

The war rattled Jewish Israelis, who were used to short wars with Hamas during which they hammered the living daylights out of it and which were more spectator sport than imminent threat to residents of Tel Aviv and Jerusalem. But the most enduring impact was psychological—among Jewish Israelis awareness of vulnerability to Hamas rocket attacks; of a threat more imminent than they had heretofore thought; of foreboding.[171]

The Jewish Israeli public not only supported the war but embraced the IDF as if its every soldier were a family member—every death was a national calamity; the funerals of soldiers attracted thousands of mourners from across the country.[172] But when the fighting stopped, the public was dissatisfied: The job had been left undone.[173] Support for Bennett and Lieberman rose sharply.[174] Jewish Israelis had little empathy with the massive humanitarian disaster the IDF had caused in Gaza; it numbed itself to the repercussions of its actions.[175] Every death, even the deaths of every member of extended families, was

---

Most had been freed in a 2011 prisoner swap." "A Look at the Gaza War and the Ceasefire Halting It," Associated Press, August 27, 2014, http://bigstory.ap.org/article/look-gaza-war-and-cease-fire-halting-it?utm_source=feedburner&utm_medium=feed&utm_campaign=Feed%3A+imeu+%28IMEU+%3A+Institute+for+Middle+East+Understanding%29.

*Of course the poll referred to was taken in the immediate aftermath of the war when the harsh realities of the extent of the devastation had not yet sunk in.

attributed to Hamas's *modus operandi*; this was symptomatic of the extent to which its "othering" of Palestinians blinded Israel to their humanity. Jewish Israelis believed that the international community was using a double standard; that it never drew attention to the fact that each of the four thousand-plus rockets fired from Gaza was targeting Jewish Israeli civilians, not military installations, and that *the aim of Hamas was to kill as many Jews as possible.* The suffering, trauma, and bewilderment of Gazans confined to tiny spaces with no escape routes was of their own making; they facilitated Hamas terror and overwhelmingly supported (88 percent) Hamas's rocket attacks on Israel, according to a poll conducted during the five-day cease-fire.[176] In short, Gazans supported the attempts to murder Jews en masse. The mantra "In the end we stand alone" assumed a more profound meaning, reinforced by Jewish Israelis' collective memories of their near annihilation, with many of those who now condemned them standing idly by. Anti-Semitism became more pronounced; Jewish Israelis were cast as the wrongdoers while it was abundantly obvious to them that the evildoers were the Hamas and Islamic Jihad terrorists. Theirs was a moral war, a war of self-defense in the face of an existential threat.[177] Nevertheless, despite what Netanyahu called a "great victory," Hamas still had a missile capacity, some underground tunnels had gone undetected, many rocket-launching sites were intact, and its inventory of weaponry, although severely depleted, had not been eliminated. Pundits had a field day: Did "they" win or didn't they? The "they" being either Hamas or Israel, depending on the context of the question and the disposition of the questioner.

The war also exposed the extent of the huge irreconcilable cleavages between Jewish Israelis and Palestinian Israelis.[178] Israel lost more clout with the Obama administration;[179] it papered over the matter as a squabble in the family but comforted itself with the knowledge that Obama would be gone in two years, it still had the overwhelming support of the American public, and it still had Congress in its pocket.[180] Abbas was either a has-been or the key to some undefined future. Netanyahu trod on thin ice, potential successors nipping at his heels but still seen as best suited to be prime minister.

> > < <

The 2014 Gaza war changed the calculus of the Palestinian-Israeli conflict, not so much in terms of its outcomes but in terms of its being the final nail in the coffin of a two-state solution.[181] If Hamas reverted to war because its demands were not met in the follow-up round of talks, as Meshaal promised[182] (this was unlikely to happen, given the magnitude of destruction in Gaza, at some point even the most Hamas-loyal Gazan would cry out:

"Enough!!"),[183] then another round of violence and more that might follow would only clobber the nail again.

During the war, Netanyahu and at least half of the members of his security cabinet called for the demilitarization of Hamas, that is, for actions that would force not only Hamas's Izz ad-Din al-Qassam Brigades but also all other militant groups in Gaza, including the Islamic Jihad—which had fought alongside Hamas—to decommission their arms.* Such talk, however, is hot air.[184] If the IDF tried to do so, it would be met with pitiless person-to-person combat and house-to-house searches, making the combat in the 2014 war look like child's play, and a united front among Gazans,[185] even if they were exhausted with the cycles of violence and economic hardships Hamas exposes them to every few years.[186]

And even if the IDF expanded the scale of its invasion and by some remarkable phenomenon demilitarized Hamas, at best Israel would buy itself a respite before it would face a rearmed Hamas—not too difficult to accomplish in a region awash in weaponry and made even easier if the purported rapprochement with Iran turned out to be real and opened the financial spigot again, and if Hezbollah's offer to help, made during the 2014 war, were still on the table.[187] *The resumption of yet another war is only a matter of time.*[188]

Of course, in this hypothetical situation, Israel could use the years of quietude that followed successful demilitarization to reengage in negotiations with the PLO. Given the unfathomable levels of distrust that exist on both sides, Israel would never sign off on an FSA for the reasons spelled out

*David D. Kirkpatrick, "A Part of Hamas Negotiates, and Another May Fight Again," *New York Times*, August 5, 2014, http://www.nytimes.com/2014/08/06/world/middleeast/part-of-hamas-talks-and-part-might-wait-to-fight-again.html?hp&action=click&pgtype=Homepage&version=HpSum&modmodule=first-column-region®ion=top-news&WT.nav=top-news&_r=0. Interviewed in Cairo on August 5, Mousa Abu Marzouk made a clear distinction between Hamas the political party and its military wing, the *Qassam* Brigades. He indicated that while Hamas still remained committed to being part of a unity government, the brigades "are completely separate. . . . Of course, they are outside the unity government."

The July 2014 poll conducted by the Israel Democracy Institute and Tel Aviv University found that, as far as "the outcome of Operation Protective Edge, a majority of Israeli Jews believed that there would be a further round of battle with Hamas (77 percent, 65 percent, and 50 percent). A minority believe that a long-term quiet, like that achieved on the northern border after [the second Lebanese war in] 2006, will be achieved (8 percent, 16 percent, and 30 percent). Polls indicated that more than 80 percent of Jewish Israelis supported expanding the war. Ya'ar and Hermann, "July 2014 Peace Index." Amos Harel, "After Israel's Unilateral Withdrawal from Gaza, What's Next?," *Haaretz*, August 3, 2014, http://www.haaretz.com/news/diplomacy-defense/israel-gaza-conflict-2014/.premium-1.608610; Raphael Ahren, "PM Wants Gaza Demilitarized, and the World Agrees—but How?," *Times of Israel*, July 20, 2014, http://www.timesofisrael.com/pm-wants-gaza-demilitarized-and-the-world-agrees-but-how/.

earlier in the chapter: because in a Palestinian state there would be free movement between the West Bank and Gaza.

A "demilitarized" Palestinian state (i.e., a state without a standing army) could not guarantee that Hamas would not remilitarize. But wouldn't the PASF ensure that Hamas did not? The PASF is a mess of corruption and patronage. Even in the aftermath of the reconciliation pact it continued to arrest Hamas members in the West Bank and clamped down on Palestinian demonstrations supporting Hamas during and after the Gaza war. In a comprehensive analysis in "Militia Patronage vs. the Diffusion of Professionalism: The Palestinian Authority Security Forces,"[189] Kimberly Marten at Barnard College and the Harriman Institute, Columbia University, concluded:

> Given the participation of PASF forces in the Second Intifada, given PASF weakness in the face of the Hamas challenge in 2007, and given the continuing problems of factionalism and corruption inside the PASF, it is completely understandable why Israeli security officials would be reluctant to trust them. It is also completely understandable why COGAT[190] might want to undercut PASF military and intelligence effectiveness by denying them equipment. . . . Israeli actions have undercut the PASF's perceived effectiveness in front of the home Palestinian population, even though the PASF is almost universally agreed to have been responsive to Israeli security requests since 2007, and to have accomplished things that Israel could not do on its own. . . .
>
> The general sense of many analysts is that the only issue area where Israeli and PASF interests have recently converged is in controlling Hamas-led terrorism.[191] That leaves PASF officers subject to accusations—sometimes even by their own family members—that they are just doing Israel's dirty work. It also undermines the ideological basis for patriotism that might have replaced patronage as the dominant norm.[192]

In a face-off between the PASF and remilitarized Qassam Brigades, it is likely that the PASF would find itself in much the same position that Hezbollah holds in relation to the Lebanese army—a non-state militia superior to the state security forces.

Which, in effect, means that even a two-state solution *acceptable to a demilitarized Hamas* would not suffice to assuage Israel's fears. In fact, there is no FSA that would be acceptable to Israel because in a new Palestinian state a neutered Hamas, always capable of rearming, would have a pervasive presence across the territory of the state. During my interview in 2012 with

Yossi Beilin, unquestionably Israel's leading dove, I asked him why Israel was so unrelentingly opposed to letting more Palestinians return to Israel than the minimal number Israel was prepared to allow on humanitarian grounds. "The Palestinians," Beilin explained, "want to show that even if we allowed them to return, it would not make much of a difference, since the best data we have indicates that at best maybe 10 percent might want to exercise such a right. So even if we allowed it, they would not come in huge numbers. This is what they say in the negotiations. *But we cannot trust this:* They may be right, *but you never know what might happen*, and if all of them decide to come, you want me to keep the door open?"

"But we cannot trust . . . you never know what might happen" encapsulates perfectly the impermeability of the Israeli position. The fact that these words are spoken by the most "dovish" of doves illustrates more than anything the depth of the Israelis' subconscious sense of potential existential threat. Given the huge stakes and the internalized suspicions, a similar line of reasoning would be invoked with a far more keenly focused skepticism by a far more distrusting Jewish Israeli public if the question of acquiescing to a demilitarized Palestinian state at its front door arose. Israel simply would not take the chance of a remilitarized Hamas emerging.

During the 2014 war, Israel's acclaimed historian Benny Morris wrote in *Haaretz* that

> As long as Hamas remains standing, it will not lay down its arms and will not let anyone else restrict its sovereignty over its territory. . . . In a few months, the tunnels leading into Israeli territory will resume operation and the missile stockpiles will be replenished, perhaps with new and improved homemade models (or even smuggled ones).
>
> Therefore, the next war will surely come. It will come in another year or two, or perhaps even sooner. . . . After 1948, 1967, 1973 and 2000–2005, the Palestinians understood that the Arabs aren't capable of destroying Israel in one blow. Thus, they adopted a tactic of taking partial but frequent bites that, over time, will gradually weaken the Jewish state. . . .
>
> Who would want to raise his children in a country under constant missile fire, even if, for the moment, very few rockets actually hit their targets? And who would want to tour or invest in a country battered by terrorism?[193]

In the 2014 war, Morris argued, Israel had the opportunity "to destroy Hamas and clean out Gaza." However, "there [was] no willingness to sacrifice soldiers." When the sixth-most-powerful military power on the planet loses less than one hundred soldiers, yet regards their deaths as some kind of national calamity, that military power seems to have lost sight of what war involves. Morris asks: "What should we do next time?" The answer, he says, is clear and well known:

> All that's needed is the courage to start down this path and the determination to finish the job. It won't be either easy or quick. We're talking about reoccupying the entire Gaza Strip and destroying Hamas as a military organization, and perhaps also as a political one. . . .
>
> This will require months of combat, during which the Strip will be cleansed, neighborhood by neighborhood, of Hamas and Islamic Jihad operatives and armaments. It will exact a serious price in lives from both Israel Defense Forces soldiers and Palestinian civilians. But that's the price required of a nation like ours, which wants to live on its own land in a neighborhood like ours. . . . The Israeli government must prepare both the Israeli people and its allies for the next round. Western leaders understand the nature of the Islamic enemy—from the Philippines through India and Pakistan, Somalia and Nigeria, Dagestan and Iraq, and all the way to Paris, Madrid and London—very well, even if they generally prefer to bury their heads in the sand and avoid using the word "Islam" explicitly.[194]

Is there such willingness? The question is not military; the question, says Yaakov Amidror, a retired general who served as Israel's national security adviser until November 2013, is what Israel wants. "To bring complete quiet to Gaza, he said, would require a takeover and occupation of the territory for six months to a year. Israel, which unilaterally withdrew its forces and settlements from the Gaza Strip in 2005, has little appetite to return."[195] In other words, there is no willingness. Israel is more comfortable with the status quo: recurring bouts of violence between itself and Hamas. Each side is attached to its addiction.

Nor is the Amidror scenario very convincing. In Northern Ireland the IRA had a membership of 1,500 at best (probably not more than 250 in active service),* well embedded in their local populations. By the time of the ceasefire in 1994, this had been reduced to around 500. Yet over a thirty-year period a British army of some 27,000 (more than Britain deployed to Iraq in 2003), augmented by the Ulster Defence Regiment (UDR) with 10,000; 3,000 UDR reservists; and a militarized police force 27,000 strong—the Royal Ulster Constabulary (RUC)—could not "defeat" the IRA—nor, for that matter, could the IRA defeat the security forces arrayed against it.[196] Engaging in urban guerrilla warfare, where Hamas members know every inch of the territory, could

*Figure ascertained from former members of the IRA.

ring the death knell for Israel's far more sophisticated conventional force, no matter how well trained. Trying to navigate street mazes—the IDF would be unfamiliar with the terrain no matter what coordinates it was provided with and unable to differentiate between civilians and members of Hamas—would be courting disaster, not defeat, just indefinite unfinished business.

But for the sake of argument, let's say Hamas and other militant groups announce that they are voluntarily going to demilitarize. Who would believe them? How would Hamas have gotten unanimity among factions within itself and brought other militant groups on board? Would Israel trust any international body capable of monitoring the process? Would Israel insist on monitoring the process itself? Would Hamas agree to this? Gazans?* And since nobody other than Hamas itself would have an exact account of its inventory, how would the monitoring body know whether it was being given the correct numbers? How would it actually verify demilitarization? What would preclude Hamas from rearming in due time? How would you prevent it from doing so? (After the signing of the Good Friday/Belfast Agreement, it took the IRA ten years to fully decommission its weapons; there was an international monitoring commission and a process of verification—and this was *after* a peace agreement was in place.)

Examine another scenario in terms of a cost-benefit analysis. On the one hand, you have a variation of the status quo: an Israel that keeps a *demilitarized* Hamas, disarmed at the cost Benny Morris lays out in stark terms, enclosed in Gaza, with more breathing room and a more robust economy, but a Hamas, nevertheless, that would always have the capacity to rearm. This Israel would always have to have contingency plans in place for dealing with periodic bouts of missiles targeting its major cities and causing severe damage and perhaps large numbers of civilian casualties, because missile technology will become a lot more sophisticated, even as missile interceptors also become more technologically advanced, and this Israel would retaliate with periodic ground invasions to smash Hamas's military infrastructure, yet again.

On the other hand, you have an Israel that would negotiate a two-state solution where Hamas, Islamic Jihad, and other jihadist groups are demilitarized but with no 100 percent ironclad guarantee that they will not rearm,

*In a poll conducted by the Palestinian Center for Policy and Survey Research (PCSR), "A majority of 51 percent wants to place the reconciliation government in charge of the Rafah crossing, but 38 percent prefer to keep it under Hamas' control. . . . 48 percent want the reconciliation government to control the border with Egypt, and 39 percent want it under Hamas' control." Palestinian Center for Policy and Survey Research, "Special Gaza War Poll: 26–30 August 2014."

and ample opportunity to scour the topological terrain and map sites to target any place of their choosing in Israel. What would that spell for the future? How many missiles would be launched from the West Bank or Gaza before Israel would intervene, creating a situation in which the fallout would scuttle the entire agreement?

Given a choice between the two, the calculus argues for sticking with the status quo.[197] As noted in chapter 2, given a choice between a known outcome (the present) and a future outcome that may be better but is uncertain, we will in all likelihood choose the former.

Moreover, while Israel would exercise considerable control over the former, it would have none over the latter. And let there be no doubt: Every time the IDF, in ground invasions or airstrikes, kills innocent Gazans, demolishes homes, kills children, and leaves bereft families to mourn their losses,* the appetite for revenge is whetted and at some point becomes insatiable.[198] Israel has nurtured a generation of recruits for Hamas.[199] Palestinians, General Herzog observes, "take a long view of history, much more than we do. 'Okay,' they say, 'we have difficulties today, but we'll prevail in 50 years from now,' and that's what drives them."[200] Foolish talk of demilitarization is the prerogative of the powerful protagonist who thinks it can "defeat" the other in asymmetrical warfare; it smacks of hubris. In 2014 the IDF found itself facing a Hamas trained to engage in open combat and use tunnel warfare, rather than the "hit and run" tactics of Hamas fighters in 2008–9 and 2012. The ingenuity of its military operations and the infrastructure supporting it caught the IDF off guard, unsure of how to act in this new theater of combat. That this entire underground edifice could be constructed under harrowing conditions, with cement and other materials that might be used for combat purposes banned, and under the eye of round-the-clock surveillance, raises serious questions about the IDF's intelligence services.

These are all points for buttressing the case for maintaining some variation of the status quo—that is, no two-state solution.†[201]

*For fatalities from the 2008–9 Gaza War up to 2014, see: B'Tselem, "Fatalities," http://www.btselem.org/statistics. For details of the 2014 Gaza War (Protective Edge) see page 160 of this chapter.

†In a poll released on October 20, 2014, 75 percent of Israeli Jews opposed a Palestinian state on 1967 lines; 76 percent if a Palestinian state included a divided Jerusalem. "Poll: 75% of Israeli Jews Oppose Palestinian State on '67 Lines," *Haaretz*, October 20, 2014, http://www.haaretz.com/news/diplomacy-defense/1.621568; Jack Moore, "Three-Quarters of Israeli Jews Oppose Creation of Palestinian State in Pre-1967 Borders," *International Business Times*, October 20, 2014, http://www.ibtimes.co.uk/three-quarters-israeli-jews-oppose-creation-palestinian-state-pre-1967-borders-1470866.

Chapter 6

Refugees and Right of Return

Of all the issues that are obstacles to a two-state solution, the refugees and their right of return have a position of preeminence. It is the one issue on which Israel takes an absolute stand, one that has hardened over the decades to the point where even the mention of five thousand refugees being allowed to return on humanitarian grounds is likely to receive a negative response.* In terms of a demographic impact, considerably more could be repatriated without threatening the Jewishness of Israel, so the question is: Why is Israel so adamant?

When we begin to probe a little deeper, a host of obstacles emerge.

> > < <

By the end of the wars of 1947–49, an estimated 750,000 Palestinians had either fled Palestine or been expelled from their homes by the Haganah. Palestinians—as noted in earlier chapters—call this seminal happening the *Nakba*, or the Great Catastrophe.[1] Over 90 percent of the Palestinian inhabitants of Haifa, Tiberias, Beit She'an, Jaffa, and Acre had vanished. Expulsions from towns and villages were common along the Tel Aviv–Jerusalem road and in the eastern Galilee. Palestinians in Nazareth and the southern Galilee for the most part stayed, and today these areas form the core of the Palestinian Israeli population. Altogether, roughly 15 percent of Palestinians remained behind and became Israeli citizens, some staying where they lived, others moving to other parts of the country, all losing their property to expropriation.

In the course of the wars, "531 villages had been destroyed, and 11 urban neighborhoods had been emptied of their inhabitants."[2] When the guns fell silent, the Israelis controlled 78 percent of Palestine, a far cry from the 55 percent mandated under the UN partition plan.[3] UN Resolution 194, passed

*"Bringing Back the Palestinian Refugee Question" Middle East Report no. 156, International Crisis Group, October 9, 2014, p. 12 and FN 37, http://www.crisisgroup.org/~/media/Files/Middle%20East%20North%20Africa/Israel%20Palestine/156-bringing-back-the-palestinian-refugee-question.pdf.

on December 11, 1948, affirmed the right of Palestinians to return to their homes once hostilities had ended. That resolution has been reaffirmed every year since then under international law.[4]

Whether the homeless individuals and families fled or were expelled is a matter of historical dispute, with the preponderance of evidence, as more archival material becomes available, coming down on the side of expulsion.[5] The refugees left with every expectation of returning home once the fighting stopped. Because President Harry Truman's recognition of Israel ensured its international recognition, in July 1949 the new state reluctantly succumbed to pressure and agreed to allow 65–70,000 Palestinians to return, but it subsequently backed off.* Ever since, Israel's position has remained unequivocal: Under no circumstances will Palestinian refugees or their descendants be allowed back to their homes or land under the rubric of the Right of Return. The number of Palestinians who remained in their homeland in the 1948 territory after the *Nakba* was estimated at 154,000 persons, and at 1.4 million on the sixty-sixth anniversary of the *Nakba* in May 2014.[6]

> > < <

When Jews constituted less than 5 percent of the population living on that land, there is now available compelling evidence that the Zionists' objective from the beginning, in the late nineteenth century, was the creation of a Jewish state in all of Palestine.[7] Even David Ben-Gurion came to Palestine in 1906 not to escape persecution but to fullfill Hertzl's dream of a national

*The United Nations Conciliation Commission for Palestine (UNCCP) was created by UN General Assembly Resolution 194 (Article III) in December 1948. Its first mission was the Lausanne Conference, held April–September 1949. The conferees never met in a general session. Rather, the UNCCP held separate meetings with the Arabs and with the Israelis over many months. "In a bid to break Arab hostility, Israel was requested to make a good will gesture towards the refugees and therefore it publicly announced its readiness to promote the payment of compensation to the Palestinian refugees for their abandoned property. But pressure was also exerted on it to accept the return of a number of refugees. Israel staunchly opposed any such move and the Lausanne discussions came to a dead end." Shelly Fried, "The Refugee Problem at the Peace Conferences, 1949–2000," *Palestine-Israel Journal of Politics, Economics, and Culture* 9, no. 2 (2002), http://www.pij.org/details.php?id=144. But in July 1949, Israel agreed to accept the return of 65–70,000 refugees ("100,00 offer") to Israel. Morris, *The Birth of the Palestinian Refugee Problem*, 295. According to Fried: "Archival sources now available show that Israel never had any intention of implementing this proposal [to allow the 65–70,000 refugees to return]. It was greeted at home by a storm of public opposition and a heated Knesset debate which underlined for Ben Gurion, and all successive governments, Israeli society's fierce opposition to the Right of Return. At the end of September 1949 the PCC, following several futile attempts to renew negotiations, was compelled to disband the Conference." Fried, "The Refugee Problem at the Peace Conferences."

Jewish home in Eretz Israel and in the years to come he was unambiguous regarding the boundaries of that nation.[8] On January 7, 1937, in evidence before the Peel Commision, he stated, "I say on behalf of the Jews, that the Bible is our Mandate, the Bible which was written by us, in our language, in Hebrew, in this very country [Palestine]. This is our Mandate, it was only the recognition of this right which was expressed in the Balfour Declaration."[9] The Zionists—worldly, pragmatic men—meticulously planned the new state from within Palestine and from safe havens far beyond. In the first half of the twentieth century, they deployed sophisticated diplomacy in Western capitals, adroitly courting their leaders. They understood that achieving their ultimate objective required the backing of a great power, and they successfully attached themselves to the greatest power at the time, Great Britain. When Britain turned from aid to obstacle, they turned on Britain and, following World War II, hitched themselves to the new greatest power, the United States.

In 1917 the Balfour Declaration announced Britain's desire to establish a "national home" for Jews.[10] The avowed motivation was altruistic: to save Jews—not Zionists—from escalating bouts of brutal pogroms in Russia. Balfour gave the veneer of legitimacy to the Zionist project, but Winston Churchill told the Peel Commission that it was promulgated because "we gained great advantage in the War. We did not adopt Zionism entirely out of altruistic love but of starting a Zionist colony; it was a matter of great importance for this country. It was a potent factor in public opinion in America."[11] Great powers do not indulge themselves in altruistic pursuits unless these serve their interests. Note Churchill's use of the word "colony"—a straightforward manifestation of the prevailing colonial mentality prior to World War II.

There are countless interpretations as to what exactly were the ultimate intentions of the Balfour Declaration, which was the culmination of years of effort by Chaim Weizmann. Regardless, it is safe to say that the Palestinians had no leader with the stature of Weizmann. He was president of the World Zionist Organization (WZO)* and later the first president of Israel. The WZO drew upon a worldwide network of Jews† to provide the financial

*The World Zionist Organization was founded at the initiative of Theodor Herzl at the First Zionist Congress, which took place in August 1897 in Basel, Switzerland. Knesset, "The World Zionist Organization," http://www.knesset.gov.il/lexicon/eng/wzo_eng.htm.

†Zionist nonprofit national funds such as Keren Kayemeth LeIsrael continued to seek global contributions; the newly established Keren Hayesod served as a fundraising vehicle for Zionist causes; and prominent individuals such as Albert Einstein were enlisted to help secure donor support. Founded by Theodor Herzl in 1901, Keren Kayemeth LeIsrael (the Jewish National

capital; established the Histadrut (1920),* the Haganah (1920),† Hebrew University (1925),‡ and the Jewish Agency§ (1929); and would finally celebrate a homeland for Jews, who had merely to immigrate, once the state was established, to receive the blessings of citizenship.[12] The emergence of a Jewish state in Palestine in less than fifty years, an achievement of unsurpassable magnitude, was the result not only of the Zionists' own persistence and perseverance but also of fortuity—the whims of powerful forces that sometimes wanted to backpedal on their promises.

Neither the Zionist project nor the state that it created ever recognized the indigenous Palestinians as a distinct people for whom Palestine had been *their* homeland for 1,500 years. Instead, they were deemed "Arabs," who would be absorbed into adjacent Arab territories. In Zionist lexicon Palestine was "a land without people for a people without a land," but when the new state of Israel declared its territorial domain at independence, Jews owned only 6.8 percent of the land. However, a plethora of new laws transferred ownership of all the land to the state of Israel.[13] Palestinians who fled or were expelled from their homes before and during the Arab-Israeli war but remained within the borders of what would become Israel were legislatively deemed "present absentees," and they were not indemnified for lost

---

Fund) was established to acquire land in Ottoman Palestine for Jewish settlements. At its London meeting in 1920, the World Zionist Conference authorized the creation of Keren Hayesod ("The Foundation Fund," or United Israel Appeal [UIA]) to purchase and settle land for the Jewish people. See "Our History," Keren Kayemeth LeIsrael/Jewish National Fund, http://www.kkl.org.il/eng/about-kkl-jnf/our-history/; "Who We Are," Keren Hayesod-UIA, http://www.kh-uia.org.il/En/Aboutus/Pages/about-kh.aspx; Walter Isaacson, "How Einstein Divided America's Jews," *Atlantic*, December 2009, http://www.theatlantic.com/magazine/archive/2009/12/how-einstein-divided-americas-jews/307763/; W. T. Mallison, Jr., "The Legal Problems Concerning the Juridical Status and Political Activities of the Zionist Organization/Jewish Agency: A Study in International and United States Law," *William & Mary Law Review* 9, no. 3 (1967–68): 554–629, http://scholarship.law.wm.edu/wmlr/vol9/iss3/3/; and Lasky, *Between Truth and Repose*. See also "About the Institute: Dr. Chaim Weizmann," Weizmann Institute of Science, http://wis-wander.weizmann.ac.il/chaim-weizmann#.U8MpOPldXPo.

*The Histadrut, Israel's organization of trade unions, was established in December 1920 during the British Mandate for Palestine. "By 1927, [the organization] claimed to serve 25,000 workers, 75 percent of the entire Jewish Palestine labor force"; https://www.jewishvirtuallibrary.org/jsource/History/histadrut.html.

†"The Haganah was a Jewish paramilitary organization in what was then the British Mandate of Palestine from 1920 to 1948, which later became the core of the Israel Defense Forces"; https://www.princeton.edu/~achaney/tmve/wiki100k/docs/Haganah.html.

‡Hebrew University was established in Jerusalem in 1925. The first Board of Governors included Albert Einstein, Sigmund Freud, Martin Buber, and Chaim Weizmann.

§The Jewish Agency was "instrumental in founding and building the State of Israel." Founded in 1929, it is the largest Jewish nonprofit organization in the world. See http://www.jewishagency.org/content/4916.

property. That is, Palestinians who retreated to a nearby village when theirs was under attack were deemed to have fled their property, even if they did so involuntarily, even if they did not intend to leave for more than a few days.[14] The property was expropriated. A not uncommon practice was the use of emergency regulations to declare land belonging to Palestinian citizens a closed military zone, forcing the population out[15] before using one of the many absentee laws to declare the land the property of the state. These laws played an enormous role in making Israel a viable state.

Among Palestinians there was the conviction that their dispossession was the price imposed on them by the West for the West's own slaughterhouses. The state of Israel was a Western creation, a "gift" to the Jews, compensation for the Holocaust, which Palestinians knew little or nothing about.*

Rural Palestinians were particularly traumatized. They believed the land belonged to them,† and the wreckage of the two wars between 1947 and 1949 and the aftermath left them discombobulated: The place called Palestine for centuries had been eviscerated; it no longer existed, leaving them without a coherent identity or sense of belonging to the community they now lived in. What had happened was beyond the scope of their understanding, just as the liquidation of Jews in the West was beyond everyone's understanding. With time, as we have seen, the events themselves, the *Nakba*, evolved into a core

*See "Afterword" in *Nakba: Palestine 1948 and the Claims of Memory*, eds, Ahmad H. Sa'di and Lila Abu-Lughod, 298, where the authors refer to Morris's work citing Ben-Gurion's referring to Western support for the partition of Palestine as "Western civilization's gesture of repentance for the Holocaust." See also Morris, *Righteous Victims*, 156. During the many interviews with Muslims/Arabs I have conducted during the last several years, I always asked about the Holocaust. Most answers were dismissive, but none denied it. Very few would concur with a figure of 6 million; a million perhaps, but nothing more. The Holocaust is a Western concern. They had nothing to do with the Holocaust, yet they had to pay the price for it. In 2014 the Anti-Defamation League reported that one in four adults were anti-Semitic, 54 percent had never heard of the Holocaust, and two out of three who had not heard of the Holocaust or thought the historical account was inaccurate believed the numbers were too high.

See ADL Global 100: An Index of Anti-Semitism, global100.adl.org/public/ADL_Global_100_Executive_summary.pdf. "ADL poll of over 100 countries finds more than one-quarter of those surveyed infected with anti-semitic attitudes," www.adl.org/press-center-press-releases-/anti-semitism-international/adl-global-100-poll.html#.VKcAkSvF9Cg See also Shibley Telhami, "2010 Israeli Arab/Palestinian Public Opinion Survey," Saban Center for Middle East Policy, http://www.brookings.edu/~/media/research/files/reports/2010/12/09%20israel%20public%20opinion%20telhami/israeli_arab_powerpoint.

†"Recent scholarship argues that the consequences of the Land Code [1858] differed from region to region in the empire and that peasants were willing to participate in and benefit from the new system." See "Land Code of 1858," Answers.com, http://www.answers.com/topic/land-code-of-1858#ixzz2gsHeG9gj.

element of the Palestinian identity, incorporating their perpetual sense of loss—a loss, they insist, that must be recognized by the perpetrator and the wrongs redressed. The loss of an important place, Marc Fried writes, "represents a change in a potentially significant component of the experience of continuity." The sense of belonging is severed; the focus of meaningful interpersonal relationships is destroyed; the sense of spatial identity and the spatial framework of social activities which is fundamental to human functioning is traumatized; the sense of group identity, of communality with other people, of shared human qualities is undermined.[16] For the bewildered Arabs who had not joined the great exodus, who had stayed behind, there was no reintegrating with friends and family whom they had expected to return, no social networks, no communities. They found it impossible to understand that their land titles, inherited from Ottoman times and respected under the British Mandate, were no longer valid.

Between 1948 and 1952, Israel absorbed almost 344,000 Jews from post-Holocaust Europe.[17] The land and villages—abandoned by Arabs by one account, or from which they had been expelled by another—were quickly populated by the new arrivals from Europe: Fields were cultivated, villages occupied or rebuilt. By 1954, more than one third of Israel's Jewish population lived on absentee property, and nearly a third of the new immigrants (250,000 people) had settled in urban areas abandoned by Palestinians. "Of the 370 new Jewish settlements established between 1948 and 1953, 350 were on absentee property."[18] These new "facts on the ground" were not questioned by the Western nations and the United States. Guilt-ridden for the breadth of their indifference to the near annihilation of European Jews, they were in no position to either impose their will or even question the morality of Israel's actions. UN Resolution 194, asserting the refugees' right of return, *haqq al-awda*, was ignored with no comment from the great powers.

The incoming survivors of the Holocaust, still traumatized by an event imaginable only because it actually happened, arrived on alien soil, often sharing little with the other new arrivals other than their status as survivors of an industry that had intended to reduce them to ashes. They were now faced with a trauma of a new kind—of adaptation, of building new communities that would bridge their cultural and linguistic differences, of forging a common identity—a Jewish identity in a "Jewish state" in which they were bombarded with Zionism and its concomitant propaganda and inculcated with the notion that the Jews were a "special" people, and the later claims to exceptionalism.[19]

Both communities were forged by trauma, which permeates much of their national narratives, and hence their very identities. On the one side were the incoming remnants of the ancient Jewish diaspora, a people decimated by close to six million lost to the gas chambers and death camps, seeking someplace in which to start over. On the other were a people who were now suddenly strangers in their own land, vassals to a new order; their neighbors and communities had literally vanished, and a new Palestinian diaspora of 750,000 was scattered across several countries, living in refugee camps, and would never be allowed to set a foot again in the place they called home. Israeli Jews should have known what Palestinians, either in exile or among them, were enduring, because in many crucial respects the Palestinian experience paralleled their own, but if they did they showed no empathy. Since 1948, the Palestinians' belief in their eventual return has persisted, every bit as strong as the belief among the Orthodox Jews of the shtetl for whom the return was, as Chaim Weizmann wrote, "vague deep-rooted in Messianism, a hope which would not die."[20]

"The Arabs loved their country as much as the Jews did," wrote Vladimir Jabotinsky, the hard man of Zionism, founder of Revisionist Zionism.* "Instinctively they understood the Zionist aspirations very well, and their decision to resist them was only natural. Every people fought immigration and settlement by foreigners, however high-minded their motives for settling. There was no misunderstanding between Jews and Arab, but a natural conflict. No agreement was possible with the Palestinian Arab; they would accept Zionism only when they found themselves up against 'an iron wall,' when armed force gave them no alternative but to accept Jewish settlement."[21]

When Golda Meir said, as late as 1969, "There is no such thing as a Palestinian people," she was speaking for all Jews. For them, the Palestinians did not exist in an existential sense. Jews had come close to not existing in a physical sense. You cannot compare one immeasurable travesty with another. Both invoke feelings that defy such a calculus. Weighing the narrative of the Jews, expelled from Palestine almost two millennia ago and then subjected to the cruelest depredations in one land after another versus the narrative of the homeless Palestinians, expelled from the land their ancestors had lived on for 1,500 years, is not a matter of arithmetic, certainly, nor

*Benjamin Netanyahu's father, Benzion Netanyahu, was Jabotinsky's secretary for a short period.

one of persecution or discrimination. It *could be* one of transcendence if the two sides were to recognize the commonality of their experiences, but one of the many tragedies of the Israeli-Palestinian conflict is that the two peoples could not find a way to convert their respective senses of loss into a common bond to help them alleviate their respective traumas and to reach accommodations. Instead, the losses festered, reinforced on the Jewish side by a determination to keep the Holocaust and the correlated hyper-vigilance of threat at the forefront of Jewish consciousness and on the Palestinian side by a determination to keep the *Nakba* at the forefront of Palestinian consciousness. Rather than becoming a path to a sense of shared suffering that might evolve into some sense of shared humanity, the losses became the basis for victimhood in a war of memories that had to be constantly invoked, so that the constancy of their presence would never allow for empathy between the two communities.[22]

> > < <

Who is a Palestinian "refugee," *exactly*? Various international agencies have their own answers, and of course Palestinians have their own definition. By their accounting, there are more than seven million refugees worldwide, with the diaspora accounting for about 64 percent of the total.[23]

When the outside world decries the plight of the refugees, it is thinking about those living in *camps*. As of January 2013, there were 2,034,641 registered refugees living in Jordan, with 369,949 living in ten camps; 441,543 registered refugees in Lebanon, with 238,528 living in twelve camps; and before the Syrian conflict almost 500,000 registered refugees living in Syria, with 159,303 living in nine camps. Within Palestine itself, the West Bank population of registered refugees was 741,409, with 216,403 living in nineteen camps; in Gaza there were 1,203,135 registered refugees, with 540,515 living in eight camps. Overall, there were 4.9 million registered refugees residing in fifty-eight camps throughout these countries or territories.[24]

Many of the camps were—and continue to be—cramped and overcrowded concrete warrens; they were designed as "temporary" little homes in which to wait for deliverance that has never come. With time, the expectation of deliverance faded into wistfulness. Most of the camps are ostensibly run by UNRWA, which constructed schools and provided some health services and aid packages of food at a little above subsistence level, but in reality they are run by militias (mostly Fatah- or Hamas-affiliated). Given the constant jingoism proclaiming the imminent demise of the Israeli state, most refugees initially remained steadfast in believing that the day would come when they would go home. In the early years, the residents were held under severe restrictions on movement and opportunities for employment. In time, in Syria and Jordan, restrictions were lifted and many went on to secure jobs in their host country, pursue education, marry, raise a family, and find accommodation outside the camps. Some melded with the general population.[25] Leaving aside the internal refugees within Palestine, Syria and Jordan appear to have the most assimilated refugee populations (taking the percentage of registered refugees not living in camps as a rough metric of assimilation). In Jordan, the only host state that grants citizenship to refugees, 82 percent live outside the camps; in Syria, 69 percent. However, in the case of Syria, the numbers are now problematic due to the Syrian civil war that erupted in 2011, which made several Palestinians refugees a second or third time: When the Assad regime exerted extraordinary pressure on the camps to support his regime, many refugees chose otherwise and made their way to Lebanon, Jordan, or Turkey, while those trapped in Yarmouk—the largest camp in Syria—have been under a tight government blockade since mid-2013.[26] Until 2010, refugees in Lebanon were confined to the camps and treated as if they lived in a foreign country. They had to apply for permits if they wished to "enter" Lebanon.[27] These policies were deemed necessary because dispersing close to 400,000 mostly Sunni Muslim Palestinians into the general population and allowing them to become integrated into Lebanese communities would upset the country's fragile power-sharing governance and the confessional arrangements that keep it just a few steps away, at best, from reverting to a new civil war rooted in various leftover grievances from the last civil war of the 1980s.[28] With the added presence of at least 1.1 million refugees, mostly Sunni Muslims who fled the Syrian civil war,[29] that tenuous confessional balance is more precarious than ever, and Lebanon, a country of about 4.4 million people, is at risk of being sucked into the Syrian war or its aftermath.[30] The Palestinian refugees, who accounted for over 20 percent of the Lebanese population in 2014, are the poorest in the region, with the highest rates of unemployment and the worst schools, and live in the greatest isolation, marginal to the cultures that surround them, but that are, so to speak, forbidden fruit. In the camps I visited, young boys and girls asked to draw a picture of home would invariably draw a picture of a house surrounded by trees—the "once upon a time" home in Palestine where they earnestly assured me they were going to live someday. Invariably, old men would take out their wallets to produce a crumpled photograph of the home in Palestine they had once lived in, expressing an implacable hope that they would return to their homes before they died. The belief that there would be a provision for their repatriation in any final settlement was pervasive. "*Haqq al-awda*, right of return," says General (Ret.) Michael Herzog, "is deeply ingrained, and if you look at their textbooks at primary-school level, you will see how this is grilled into them, and many of the refugees still walk around with the keys of their homes from '48, and it's highly important to them. So you have generation after generation educated to believe in the notion of going back."[31] Herzog, of course, fails to point out that the contradictory, centuries-old Israeli narrative (the diaspora Jews' absolute belief that one day they would return to their homeland) is written into Israeli textbooks and drilled into Israeli children.

Gilead Sher says that Palestinians "eschew engagement in a peace process because of the victimizing, the struggle over the narrative that has moved from the territories to the diaspora. Where do you hear the most voices, demands related to the right of return? In the diaspora, and from people who are not even Palestinians or Arabs. Not any more from here. Just try to research this point, and you will find out that it has shifted to a debate that is mostly in Europe and on college campuses in the West."[32]

Contrary to Sher's belief, this issue is key for refugees, and if a peace agreement leaves them in the cold—granting a token number of humanitarian repatriations but no right of return—there will be consequences.[33] Hamas has already made that clear; so, too, have militias in the camps.

Palestinians will not let go of the tragic irony and the injustice of the *Nakba*. They demand that Israel acknowledge that it is *responsible* for the Great Catastrophe. This is the heart of their historical and cultural narrative. They seek recognition and redress of their grievance, just as Jews sought redress of their own incalculable grievance.[34] The Palestinian public overwhelmingly supports this right of return for internal and external refugees and their descendants as one that cannot be abridged.[35] As Saeb Erekat once said to Dani Dayan, former chairman of the Yesha council and now its foreign envoy, "Look, it's an *individual* right. We cannot give up the right of an individual to return. It's not for us to give it up."[36]

For many members of the PLO and Fatah and other liberation movements, the importance of the right of return has added significance, because they are all stepchildren of the diaspora where their liberation movements were founded. The first "freedom fighters" came from the diaspora, not from within Palestine proper. The PLO negotiated the first Oslo Agreement from exile, and Israel recognized the diaspora-embedded PLO as the "sole representative of the Palestinian people" before one of its members had ever set foot back in Palestine after an absence of three or so decades.

Among Palestinians, loose talk about the right of return is not allowed. During an interview on Israeli television in November 2012, Abbas said that he personally had no "right" to return to Safed, his birthplace, and that the Palestinians had no territorial claims to pre-1967 Israel. Thousands of Palestinians took to the streets of Gaza and the West Bank in a demonstration organized by Hamas.[37] Signs dubbed Abbas a "traitor." One read, "The refugees will not forgive your crime, Abbas," while another asserted, "Abbas, history does not recall a worse case of treachery."

"All of Palestine, from the [Mediterranean] sea to the [Jordan] river is the property of every Palestinian," proclaimed Salah al-Bardaweel, a senior Hamas spokesperson. "No [other] entity can be recognized on our land."[38] "Youssef Rizqa, an adviser to Hamas prime minister Ismail Haniyeh, went even further, . . . equating Abbas with Palestinians who sell land to Jews—an act tantamount to treason under Palestinian and Jordanian law."[39] Criticism of Abbas poured in from the diaspora. In an op-ed titled "Please Don't Speak on Our Behalf," Abdel Bari Atwan, the editor-in-chief of the influential London-based daily *Al-Quds Al-Arabi,* chided the PLO chairman for forsaking his birthplace for political expediency. "If Abbas does not want to return to Safed and wishes to remain in Ramallah or live in his Amman home, that is his prerogative," Atwan wrote. "But in that case, he should not speak and purport to represent six million Palestinian refugees. By limiting Palestine to the West Bank and the Gaza Strip, [Abbas] is providing free concessions and compromising Palestinian principles to please the Israelis, blatantly disregarding the Palestinian people and its national sentiments."[40]

In damage-control mode, Abbas told WAFA, the official Palestinian news agency, that his detractors had not watched the interview in its entirety. "I have not and will not forgo the right of return," Abbas asserted.[41] No Palestinian leader could ever say otherwise. (This is not to say that some Palestinian leaders do not believe otherwise.) Nevertheless, a peace agreement that contains only a weak "right of return" provision could be the catalyst for unforeseeable but grim consequences.[42]

The first perspective is immutable principle: Palestinian refugees have the right to return to the homes from which they were evicted in 1948. The fact that the house no longer exists does not mean that the last legal owner is no longer eligible to go back to the village or the land, because the title deeds are still operative. The second perspective is a pragmatism that takes account of the facts on the ground in the twenty-first century. Muhammad Shtayyeh says:

> We are not asking for the return of twelve million Palestinians or eight million Palestinians to go back to what used to be called Palestine. . . . Palestinian refugees should be given the right to choose from one of the following options: first, to stay wherever they are with compensation; second, to go back to the Palestinian state-to-be with compensation; third, to choose to live in another country that is willing to take them, with compensation; and fourth, to go back to their homes, villages, cities, where it used to be, with compensation. These are the pragmatic scenarios that we have put forward.*

In this two-state solution envisioned by Shtayyeh—and in fact accepted by the Palestinian leadership but never explained to the Palestinian public—many refugees might choose to stay in Syria and Lebanon and Jordan, in the West Bank, in Gaza, wherever. Those who chose to return on humanitarian grounds to what is today's Israel would know that, while towns like Haifa and Jaffa are within historical Palestine, they would be living in *Israel*. They would need to learn Hebrew. Their children would enroll in the Palestinian Israeli education system. "This is a detailed issue," Shtayyeh concludes, "but I'm telling you, this is the pragmatic approach that we are adopting to solve the issue." To the Israelis, such talk, insofar as it implies that a substantial number of refugees or their descendants might choose to return to Israel, is delusional, a denial of a reality that Israel has adamantly adhered to since 1948: *There will be no right of return*. The refugees from the "founding wars" and their descendants have no inherent right to return to a land over which they had never

*The ICG warns that the PLO should take more account of the concerns of the refugees in the West Bank and the Gaza Strip, which, it says, have changed in recent decades. "Whenever the diplomatic process comes out of its current hiatus," the ICG says, "the Palestinian leadership will be able to negotiate and sell a deal only if it wins the support or at least acquiescence of refugees—because if it does not, it will not bring along the rest of the Palestinian population. Refugees currently feel alienated from the Palestinian Authority (PA), which they regard with suspicion; doubt the intentions of Palestinian negotiators, whom they do not believe represent their interests; and, as one of the more impoverished Palestinian groups, resent the class structure that the PA and its economic policies have produced. As a result of their isolation, refugees in the West Bank and Gaza are making demands for services and representation that are reinforcing emerging divisions within Palestinian society and politics. "Bringing Back the Palestinian Refugee Question." International Crisis Group, Middle East Report No. 156, October 9, 2014, http://www.crisisgroup.org/~/media/Files/Middle%20East%20North%20Africa/Israel%20Palestine/156-bringing-back-the-palestinian-refugee-question.pdf.

exercised *sovereign* jurisdiction. Israel is now merely exercising a prerogative of sovereignty when it prohibits them from returning to Israel. Of course, applying this topsy-turvy logic would negate the Israelis' initial claim of their own right to return to the part of the old Ottoman Empire called Palestine. But even if the Zionist version of history is accepted in full, the claim of prior sovereignty in Palestine at some point in time many centuries ago is fallacious, *as the concept of nation-state sovereignty simply did not exist until the* Peace of Westphalia in 1648.[43] In ancient times, before the Common Era, there were no political contrivances such as "nation-states." There were no conceptual notions of national sovereignty nor all the linguistic and legal paraphernalia we use today to demarcate national territories. Palestine did not exist as a geopolitical unit, nor did any other region in the Mideast (or anywhere else). There were only rulers and their fiefdoms and empires, large or small. There were no clear lines on accurate maps, only territorial smudges on inaccurate maps. The clearly delineated lines came only with the rise of nation-states in the west in the nineteenth century and in the Mideast only in the colonial era. Neither the Jews nor the Palestinians had *ever* exercised modern-style, legally recognized sovereignty over Palestine.

Today, the Palestinians' "liberation" struggle cannot be equated with wanting to *eliminate* the Jews; it seeks to *reclaim* Palestine—the land lived in during the Ottoman era—and establish a Palestinian state. Opposition to creeping colonization began in the 1920s,[44] and the fact that the Palestinians' conception of nationalism in the early part of the twentieth century did not fit the Jews' paradigm, "imported" from the West, does not abrogate their rights. The UN partition plan in 1947 called for establishing two states—one Jewish and one Palestinian, but with Palestinians comprising 46 percent of the population of what the authors of the partition called "a Jewish state."* The Jewish state would have a Palestinian minority of 325,000, making

*"To solve the problem of the future of Palestine, which was under British mandate, the General Assembly of the United Nations decided in its Resolution 181 of 29, November 1947 to divide the territory of Palestine as follows: A Jewish state covering 56.47 percent of Mandatory Palestine (excluding Jerusalem) with a population of 498,000 Jews and 325,000 Arabs; an Arab State covering 43.53 percent of Palestine, with 807,000 Arab inhabitants and 10,000 Jewish inhabitants." European Institute for Research on Mediterranean and Euro-Arab Cooperation, "UN GA Resolution 181 (Partition Plan of Palestine)," http://www.medea.be/en/themes/international-organizations-and-diplomacy/un-ga-resolution-181-partition-plan-of-palestine/.

"The plan, in its written version, set up a Jewish state that would be binational in structure, in which Palestinians would represent 46 percent of its population (498,000 Jews and 407,000 Palestinians). In reality, however, Plan Dalet contemplated removing Palestinians from that state." Walid Salem, "Legitimization or Implementation: On the UN Partition Plan the Paradox of the 1947 UN Partition Plan," *Palestine-Israel Journal* 9, no. 4 (2002), http://www.pij.org/details.php?id=99.

nonsense of the nomenclature "a Jewish state." Even allowing for the huge influx of Holocaust survivors that followed, it would have been only a matter of time before the Palestinian population eclipsed the number of Jews and the notion of a Jewish state became meaningless. Or what if the Palestinians had accepted the recommendations of the Peel Commission in 1937 and agreed to a truncated Jewish state, which would have been restricted to "Tel Aviv, the coastal plain, the northern valleys, and part of the Galilee,"[45] (about 20 percent of Palestine) a state Chaim Weizmann said would have been "skimpy," but which also recommended the transfer of several thousand Jews from their homes in the territory within the proposed Jewish state to the Arab area.[46] Would there have been room for the hundreds of thousands of Jews fleeing Nazi Germany, and then for the Holocaust survivors? We have no idea what that course might have been.[47]

Israel's historical narrative holds that the Palestinians started the 1947–49 wars, lost them, and so bear the responsibility for what has happened.* This is true if we divorce wars from expulsions. It is one thing to say that because Palestinians started the war, they are responsible for the suffering

*Lustick, "Negotiating Truth," 51–77. In negotiations among Israel, the World Jewish Congress, and the federal government of Germany in 1951, before the beginning of German reparations and the establishment of diplomatic relations, Germans strongly opposed admission of guilt and restitution: "It is important to remember that the Jews of the early 1950s who participated in these negotiations were dealing with Germans in the first decade after the war, when the experience of the Third Reich and the cataclysmic consequences of its collapse were fresh in their minds. It was with their beliefs, preferences, sensitivities, prejudices and espoused values that those Jews had to contend, not with the 'politically correct' attitudes of subsequent generations of Germans, German officials and German diplomats. . . . Indeed, only by understanding the state of mind of Germans in the period of the reparations agreement can one appreciate the powerful constraints under which the Adenauer government operated in its efforts to find any workable agreement with Jews and with Israel." Lustick says that Germans also felt victimized by Nazism, which posed challenges for Jewish negotiators in talks "that would help rehabilitate Germany as an accepted member of the civilized world, the North Atlantic Treaty Organization alliance, and the new, emerging community of Western Europe. In this context, an Israeli delegation representing a mildly apologetic, but still Zionist, government in Israel may not pose quite as different a challenge to Palestinian negotiators than that posed by Adenauer's government in its negotiations with the government of Ben-Gurion and Sharett. "If the state of mind of Germans at the time of the reparations agreement with Israel is appreciated, impressions that most Israelis would be resistant to expressing sympathy or solicitude for the suffering of Palestinians or to recognizing the extent of their own country's responsibility for that suffering may seem less decisive in judgments about agreements that may be possible between Israel and the Palestinians." Lustick says that Adenauer faced strong opposition to an agreement that included admission of guilt or generous restitution to Jews. "Indeed, German public opinion appears to have been opposed to paying much of anything to the Jews, and Adenauer's negotiations with Germans appear to have been as difficult as his negotiations with the Jews. . . . In November 1950, trying hard to reflect dominant feelings in Germany that Germans were as much the victims of Nazism as were the Jews, Adenauer continued to press demands for clemency, an end to the tribunals and an end to denazification on the American authorities as one of the highest, if not the highest, priority of his newly formed government."

and loss of their people who fled the battlefields; but it is quite another to align that argument with one that says the Palestinians also bear responsibility for the deliberate and sanctioned actions of the Haganah, which forcibly compelled them to leave their homes.

Unlike the Israeli's *meta-narratives*—based in large measure on a biblical saga—the *historical* narrative of 1947–49 can be subjected to critical scrutiny as Israeli archives of the period become open to inspection, and the preponderance of this difficult-to-refute evidence demonstrates that the Jewish narrative of that specific period is mostly a deceit. Benny Morris's groundbreaking work *The Birth of the Palestinian Refugee Problem* led the way, followed by a "new school" of Israeli historians who began to rummage through Israeli military and state archives as they became available over the years. The "discoveries" of Avi Shlaim, Tom Segev, Ilan Pappé, Benny Morris, Simha Flapan, Nur Masalha, and, more recently, books by Hillel Cohen and Ari Shavit[48] raise troubling questions about significant portions of the Israeli narrative and in some cases downright contradict the official version of events. The notion that the Palestinians were called upon by their own leaders to *voluntarily* leave their homes has been shown to be misleading, as were arguments that they undertook this mass exodus *despite appeals of the Jewish leadership for them to stay and coexist in peace.*[49] Any such appeal from the Zionists would have made nonsense of their desire and claim to be a distinctly Jewish state.[50] The fact is that when all the disputes are set aside, one fundamental fact emerges. If Israel had not forced the Palestinian expulsions and had most Palestinians not fled voluntarily, the emergent state at the war's end would not have been a Jewish state. But since a Jewish state was the objective of the Jews from the onset, Israel had to remove a sufficient number of Palestinians one way or another—and if the latter required expulsions, so be it—so that it could proclaim that Israel was a Jewish state. In fact, the standard historical narrative of that period—as accepted by a majority of Israelis and taught in their schools—obfuscates many crimes committed by the Haganah, crimes that today would be classified as war crimes, including the notorious assault on Deir Yassin, the massacre of some one hundred defenseless residents, villages pillaged and villagers fleeing at the point of a gun.[51] The state's response to the "revisionist" findings of the new historians challenging the official historical narrative? In 2010, Netanyahu, during his first term as prime minister, extended the time span materials in government and state archives could remain classified by a further twenty years.[52]

There is evidence, too, that expulsion was the aim to begin with. In his diaries, not released until 1960, Theodor Herzl, founder of the Zionist movement and the World Zionist Organization (WZO), described a two-part process that Zionists should use to expel the Arabs from their land.[53] Ben-Gurion had further territorial expansion in mind—the usurpation of the rest of Palestine and Jewish hegemony over the land stretching to the Litani River.[54] After the Peel commission's report in 1937, he raised the issue of the population transfer of all Arabs out of "all the land of our state" even though at this point he did not know how large an area might ultimately fall into Jewish hands or when. He subsequently advocated transfer on multiple occasions.[55] He noted in his diary, on the eve of Independence, "We are not obliged to state the limits of our state."[56] (Indeed, to this day, Israel, among the world's 196 countries, is the only one with no geographically fixed, internationally recognized borders.) He personally approved the expulsion of Palestinians.[57] Plan D was the keystone of a carefully designed and almost flawlessly executed project with sufficient layers of plausible deniability blanketing the text.[58] Its objective was to *cleanse* Palestine of Palestinians.[59] A Jewish state unencumbered by the presence of Arabs was from the beginning not only considered desirable, but the question on the matter of population transfer was a matter of intense discussion.[60]

Perhaps the most explicit expression of Zionist thinking on the subject can be found in the diaries of Yosef Weitz, the first director of the Jewish National Fund Land Settlement Department. In 1940, he wrote, "It must be clear that there is no room for both peoples in this country. . . . The only solution is a Palestine . . . without Arabs. The only way is to transfer the Arabs from here to the neighbouring countries, all of them, except perhaps Bethlehem, Nazareth, and old Jerusalem. Not a village, or a single tribe must be left."[61] There is also evidence to show that before 1948, "transfer"/ethnic cleansing was embraced by Zionist leaders Chaim Weizmann and Ben-Gurion.[62]

The more Israel's "new historians" intensify their search for objective source materials that confirm that Palestinians were forced out of Palestine and did not leave of their own volition, the more threatening research findings are to Israel's social cohesiveness, its ethos of itself as a moral nation and Israeli Jews as a moral people. Israeli Jews are unwilling to accept such responsibility, in spite of the evidence stored in their archives that makes a prima facie case for the Palestinians' right to return to the country from which they were forcibly expelled. For the sake of preserving its founding narrative and demanding that Palestinians recognize it as a Jewish state, official Israel *must* dismiss the evidence.

Simply put: The Israelis have placed restrictions on how the *Nakba* can be remembered.

In response to the revelations of the "new historians," therefore, officialdom has hunkered down and flatly rejected what appear to be near-irrefutable, objective facts, acknowledging grudgingly that perhaps a few Haganah commanders may have engineered unwarranted expulsions but asserting that these were inadvertent and never condoned by the Zionist leadership. Plan D is dismissed as a contingency plan that never became operational. The damning file GL-18/17028 speaks for itself.[63] In Israel there is now a "war of the historians," as traditionalists mount a counter campaign intent on debunking much of what the new historians claim to be "new," arguing that they have misinterpreted many declassified documents and reached fallacious conclusions.[64]

Collective memory, the foundation of any culture's narrative, is ahistorical; *mythology*, laced with figments of truth, is essential to forming a country's founding identity and maintaining social cohesion. In the public domain the official Zionist history portrays the near annihilation of the Holocaust, the ingathering of a persecuted people facing almost insurmountable odds on their odyssey to "reclaiming" what was legitimately theirs, the various Arab armies descending on the newly birthed state with the intention of obliterating it, the miraculously inspired courage of the small population to repulse this enemy and defeat it. This story is drummed into the children from birth, reinforced at every level during their education, with incessant reminders of the importance of the Jewishness of the state, and during their years of compulsory military service (two for females and three for males) absorbed into their beings.

The dubious narrative of what happened in 1947–49 still provides cover for what happened to the Palestinians, and it absolves the Jewish Israelis of the responsibility to either acknowledge the *Nakba* or compensate a stateless people wanting acknowledgment of their rights, a redress of historical injustice, and self-determination. With its self-justifying creative myth firmly entrenched, Israel has not moved a millimeter from its original stance:[65] Under some very specific circumstances, Israel would be prepared to allow a *small* number of Palestinians to return, but strictly on humanitarian grounds. There is nothing to suggest that there will be some sudden change of heart.

Another factor reflecting Israelis' adamant stance on the right of return is their attitude concerning the Palestinian Israelis already in their midst:

those 15 percent of the total Palestinian population who remained behind during the *Nakba*, all of whom (like their descendants, of course) are citizens of Israel. These people emerged as a group in their own right, at first with a disconnected sense of who they were, trapped between a Palestinian identity that was not recognized as sufficient by the refugees and an Israeli identity not recognized by Israelis. Even as they sought to become more assimilated into the society, Israelis persisted in seeing them as a latent fifth column.[66] For almost twenty years they were subjected to multiple restrictions on movements and constant surveillance.[67] Ben-Gurion warned his colleagues, "We cannot be guided by subversion which the Arab minority has not engaged in. We must be guided by what they might have done if they had been given the chance."[68] During his seventeen years at Israel's helm, Ben-Gurion's assessment never wavered. Close to the end of his tenure, he told his colleagues:

> Many members of the minority here do not look upon themselves as a minority but consider us a minority—a foreign usurping minority. This is the difference between the Arab minority here and minorities elsewhere. In our case the facts make it possible to think that it is not the minority but the majority who constitute a minority, since the minority is surrounded by tens of millions of his fellow countrymen beyond the borders.[69]

They are never to be trusted, because their intentions are subversive—an embodiment of Israel's paranoia regarding existential threat.* Today they

* In the tracking Interviews of Israeli youth, published in *All of the Above*, the researchers found that most of the youth thought that the Jew-Arab schism posed the greatest threat to the state of Israel, p.19. In both surveys taken in 2004 and 2010, about "two-thirds of Jewish Israeli youth believed that the Palestinian Israelis still hadn't recognized the existence of the State of Israel and would destroy it if they could," p. 122.

For more information on discrimination, see See Hexel and Nathanson, *All of the Above*, 148 fn 1.

Polls of Jewish Israeli attitudes towards Arab Israelis and Palestinians conducted between 2012 and 2014 revealed that: 74% supported separation of Israelis and Palestinians on roads in West Bank; 47% supported transferring part of the Arab-Israeli population to the Palestinian Authority and 59% believe there should be official preference for Jewish Israelis in government jobs; [1] 41% think there will be another Intifada; [2] 69% object to allowing the 2.5 million Palestinians of "Judea and Samaria" (the West Bank) to vote in Israel, if Israel were to annex those territories; [3] 33% favor legally blocking Arab-Israeli citizens from voting in the Knesset and more than 50% of Israelis do not think Arab-Israelis should be represented in the Parliament; [4] 37% of Jewish Israelis believed that long-term Palestinian aspirations are to conquer the State of Israel and destroy much of the Jewish population; [5] 62% of Israelis worry that they or their family may be harmed in their daily lives by Arabs [6]. [1] Levy, "Survey," *Haaretz*, October 2012, http://www.haaretz.com/news/national/survey-most-israeli-jews-wouldn-t-give-palestinians-vote-if-west-bank-was-annexed.premium-1.471644; [2] Palestinian Center for Policy and Survey Research

constitute close to 21 percent of Israeli citizens, yet they continue to be highly discriminated against and cannot be regarded under any circumstances as citizens who enjoy the same rights as Israeli Jews do.

In the last two decades, an educated Palestinian Israeli bourgeoisie has emerged, who define themselves as Palestinians, albeit Palestinians who want to remain in Israel in the event of a two-state solution, but who are, as a group, entitled to collective rights.*[70] In the 2007 manifesto "The Future Vision of the Palestinian Arabs in Israel" they asserted these rights.[71] But the case made eloquently for collective rights has atrophied; Palestinian Israelis are no closer to having those rights in 2015. Indeed, the attitudes of Jewish Israelis toward them have become more poisonous. Rather than implement any form of integration that might narrow the divides between the two communities, Jewish Israelis overwhelmingly opt for further segregation and would, if they had their druthers, rid Israel of the Palestinian Israelis' presence.[72] With these attitudes toward Palestinian Israelis, their fellow citizens, who have gone out of their way to voice their support for the Palestinian cause, find it hard to envisage Israeli Jews ever modifying their

---

(Jerusalem and Ramallah: December 2012). http://www.pcpsr.org/en/node/383; [3] See Gideon Levy, "Survey: Most Israeli Jews wouldn't give Palestinians vote if West Bank were annexed," *Haaretz*, October 23, 2012, http://www.haaretz.com/news/national/survey-most-israeli-jews-wouldn-t-give-palestinians-vote-if-west-bank-was-annexed.premium-1.471644. See also Arab Association for Human Rights, "2012 Israeli Jewish Public Opinion Info Sheet," October 2012, http://arabhra.files.wordpress.com/2012/11/2012-israeli-jewish-public-opinion-info-sheet.pdf. Commissioned by the Yisraela Goldblum Fund and conducted by Dialog Polling Center, news coverage of the poll, as well as its design and results, evoked considerable controversy, in part due to the sample size and references to "apartheid" and "racism." See Gabe Fisher, "Controversial survey ostensibly highlights widespread anti-Arab attitudes in Israel," *Times of Israel*, October 23, 2012, http://www.timesofisrael.com/survey-highlights-anti-arab-attitudes-in-israel/; Paul T. Karolyi, "Haaretz published poll exposing Jewish discrimination against Arabs in Israel," Arab Human Rights Association (blog), October 25, 2012, http://arabhra.wordpress.com/tag/dialog/; and Maurice Ostroff, "An open letter to the organizers of the poll about Israel that reverberated around the world," 2nd Thoughts (blog), *Jerusalem Post*, October 30, 2012, http://www.jpost.com/Blogs/2nd-Thoughts/An-open-letter-to-the-organizers-of-the-poll-about-Israel-that-reverberated-around-the-world-365213. [4] Levy, "Survey," *Haaretz*, October 2012, http://www.haaretz.com/news/national/survey-most-israeli-jews-wouldn-t-give-palestinians-vote-if-west-bank-was-annexed.premium-1.471644;[5] Harry S. Truman Research Institute for the Advancement of Peace, et al., "Joint Israeli Palestinian Poll No. 54, December 2014," Harry S. Truman Research Institute, Konrad Adenauer Stiftung, and Palestinian Center for Policy and Survey Research (Jerusalem and Ramallah: December 24, 2014), http://truman.huji.ac.il/.upload/Joint%20Poll%20Dec%202014.pdf and http://www.pcpsr.org/en/node/596. [6] Harry S. Truman Research Institute for the Advancement of Peace, et al., "Joint Israeli Palestinian Poll No. 54: 7-12 December 2014," http://www.pcpsr.org/en/node/596.

*The Palestinian-Israeli minority argues that Israel is an "ethnocracy," a regime that promotes "the expansion of the dominant group in contested territory and its domination of power structures while maintaining a democratic façade." It is pressing its case that it has inherent rights beyond individual representation; that it has corporate rights. Yiftachel, *Ethnocracy: Land and Identity Politics in Israel/Palestine*, 3.

position regarding the return of refugees. In fact, sentiment has become more obdurate.

Jewish Israelis also argue that the refugee issue has been trumped up—*manufactured*—by the surrounding Arab states. What happened to the Palestinians was no different from what happened in India and Pakistan once the subcontinent was handed over by the British, and there are numerous other examples. All wars result in displacement of people and loss of homes; in most cases few find their way back. The Arab states' concern with Palestine is hypocritical and self-serving.

"The question you must ask is why we still have these refugee camps?" Amnon Lipkin-Shahak, who was Rabin's go-between to Arafat after Oslo I, said.

> The Arab world has more than enough money to solve the problems of the refugees as far back as 1948. Is there a Palestinian strategy to keep the refugees in the camps in order to keep the Palestinian issue active all the time? We absorbed more than a million Russian Jews who came with nothing, and we didn't put them in refugee camps. We absorbed almost a million Jews coming from the Muslim states, Iraq, North Africa, Egypt when Israel was a poor state with very limited economic capabilities in the early fifties. In the beginning we had to put them in tents, because we had nothing else to offer them. But the moment we could afford to build houses, we moved them to normal accommodations. We didn't preserve them as "refugees," and again, most of them left everything behind them. They arrived with nothing and they built their lives.[73]

The PLO, he believes, wants to preserve the status quo: "If it is part of Palestinian ideology to keep the refugees in camps, to keep them in poverty, so that the Palestinian issue will remain on the front burner, that I can understand," he concluded. "It makes sense as long as you don't have your own independent state."

Other Jewish Israeli interviewees agreed. The Arab states could have absorbed the refugees from the camps and contributed substantially to their welfare. Instead, their lip-service support is coupled with contempt for Palestinian refugees within Arab societies.[74] They were marginalized, and the Arab regimes, with the exception of Jordan, took no steps to ensure that they were assimilated into the socioeconomic fabric of their societies. The contributions of the Arab states to the Palestinian cause have been and remain meager, just as their promises of contributions to various donor institutions to ensure that the Palestinian Authority keeps its head above water are rarely fulfilled.[75] Having the refugees live in wretched conditions is a deliberate ploy on the part of Arab states to use them as a bargaining chip, symbols of Palestinian suffering and victimization and dispossession, and fodder for "the street" to turn their people's attention away from their regimes' repressions and ineptitude.

Udi Dekel was Israel's front man on the right-of-return issue at Annapolis in 2007–08. When we discussed the question of the refugees, he was quick to point out, "The Palestinians could not accept the idea that their leaders were responsible also, that the Arab countries around it were responsible also, but we spoke about our responsibility for it. We said, 'Let's share responsibility—not only Israel; let everybody . . . take its part of the responsibility to the problem of the refugees.' No, they don't accept, first. Second, they cannot give up the basic right of return of refugees that everybody has."[76]

None of the Jewish Israeli interviewees I spoke with exhibited malice toward the refugees. Indeed, all acknowledged the pitifully derelict conditions in which they are forced to live, but sympathy was accompanied by an iron fist: There would never be a time when refugees would return to Israel, and Israel would never accede to the Palestinian demand that Israel acknowledge its responsibility for creating the *Nakba*—because the Palestinians had started the war, not the Israelis. It aggravates many of the interviewees that the issue persists, because the Palestinians know the irreversibility of the Israeli position.

"As an Israeli," says Pini Meidan-Shani, who served as the foreign policy adviser to Prime Minister and Minister of Defense Ehud Barak—speaking for all interviewees,

> I will insist on there being no right of return to Israel. I'm not talking about symbolic stuff and I'm not talking about compensation. I'm not Netanyahu, who wants the Palestinians to recognize us as a Jewish state, but I will not let anyone buy immigration into Israel, because this is against the concept of my idea of two homelands for the two people, in which each homeland has its permanent borders and everyone can exercise his right to return to his own homeland. And there should be no giving in to Palestinians in the diaspora who say they want to come back to Israel. Forget it! There is no deal. Let them go to their new homeland in Palestine, not to Israel. When you have two states for two people, you cannot expect me to change the characteristic of my state in order to create your own state.[77]

Also irritating for Jewish Israelis is their certainty that the Palestinian leaders know that bringing back their far-flung constituents to live in Israel is not going to happen but just won't say so publicly. Arafat himself wrote in the *New York Times* in 2002, "We understand Israel's demographic concerns and understand that the right of return of Palestinian refugees, a right guaranteed under international law and United Nations Resolution 194, must be implemented in a way that takes into account such concerns."[78] But, Gilead Sher says, "Arafat was not ready to make the compromises needed, to face his own constituency, and publicly expressed his agreement with the two-state solution, two-states-for-two-peoples solution, by delineating what the future would be for the refugees returning back to their state-to-be, Palestine, and not to Israel, and by compromising on certain aspirations that he nurtured for so many years."[79] Amnon Lipkin-Shahak, told me:

> I asked Arafat, by the way, more than once, "Do you believe that there is a real right of return to Israel?" He never answered. Even when I modified the question, like, "I don't think you understand that there is no chance to reach an agreement with the right of return for your refugees to Israel. They will have to go to the Palestinian state"—again, if I could have translated his body language, he fully understood. If I have to quote his wording, there was no answer.

Among Jewish Israeli interviewees, the issue of the right of return has long been settled. The Palestinians screwed themselves, and now they want the Israelis to solve their problem. The Jewish Israelis' frustration with the frozen peace process is often coupled with resentfulness and impatience with the seemingly endless allegations in the West that Israel is the obstacle to peace. The Palestinians' future is in their own hands. As long as they maintain their intransigent position on right of return, they are diminishing prospects for their own best future: a Palestinian state for the Palestinian people alongside a Jewish state for the Jewish people.

But their responses fit the addiction/habit paradigm: a loop with a *cue* (negotiations); a *routine* (a repeated Palestinian insistence on an Israeli apology, acknowledgment of responsibility, and willingness to accede to a right of return and Israel's copper-fastened response: no, no, and no); a *reward* (for all Palestinians, a reaffirmation of the *Nakba* as the pivotal element of their identity; for Israel, reaffirmation that Israel is a Jewish state).

> > < <

In 1995, as part of the extended negotiations following the Oslo Accords signed two years earlier, an unofficial document known as the Beilin–Abu

Mazen Understandings[80] provided Yitzhak Rabin and Yasser Arafat with a basis to consider for an FSA and end-of-claims agreement. Rabin was assassinated a few weeks before he was scheduled to review the document, and once its contents were leaked to the media, Abu Mazen (Mahmoud Abbas) quickly disassociated himself from it. The PLO and then the Israeli government followed suit. But the fact that it was negotiated has never been in dispute.

On the issue of the refugees there *was* a trade-off of sorts. The understandings read, on the one hand, that "[both sides agree that] the realities that have been created on the ground since 1948 have rendered the implementation of this right [of return] impracticable." On the other hand, they said, "the Israeli side acknowledges the moral and material suffering caused to the Palestinian people as a result of the war of 1947–1949." Note the asymmetry within the trade-off: The Palestinians concede on the right of return; the Israelis acknowledge Palestinian suffering, *but without taking any responsibility for it.* Both sides agreed to create an international organization, preferably headed by the government of Sweden, to deal with the matter of compensation. Israel would participate in financing the international fund and would continue to absorb refugees within the framework of family unification and, on occasion, on humanitarian grounds.

"In 2000," says Yossi Beilin, chief negotiator on the subject for the Israelis, "there was no agreement with respect to the origins of the refugee problem, with respect to compensation or the number of refugees who would be absorbed by Israel."[81] In one of my interviews, Nabil Sha'ath, Beilin's Palestinian counterpart, referred to the right of return only in terms of numbers he and Beilin played with.[82] At Taba they revisited the issue. According to Sha'ath but not confirmed by Beilin, the repatriation arrangement was to have a life span of twenty-one years, divided into seven periods of three years; during each period a total of 50,000 refugees would be repatriated under "family reunification" guidelines and become eligible for Israeli citizenship. After each period, the process would be revisited and decisions made on going forward, but if all went well, 350,000 refugees would have been repatriated by the end of the twenty-one years.* *But all repatriations*

*Nathan Thrall refers to an upper-limit figure of 125,000 having been discussed between Beilin and Sha'ath. "Israel & the US: The Delusions of Our Diplomacy," *New York Review of Books*, October 9, 2014, http://www.nybooks.com/articles/archives/2014/oct/09/israel-us-delusions-our-diplomacy/.

*would be on humanitarian grounds; there was no question of there being a right of return.**†

Nothing of course was concretized, and when Taba ended they went their separate ways. But Beilin is sensitive to the refugee issue and does not want to leave Palestinians empty-handed:

> We have to find a solution which will not say, "You have to give up on the right of return." From my point of view you can dream whenever you want. But what we have to speak about is implementation. So it is either you speak about a specific number, which happened in the negotiations between Olmert and [Abbas] and also between me and Nabil. Nabil spoke about something like 350,000, which is a huge number, and I said to him, "This is not realistic." I'm speaking about something between 20,000 and 30,000.

*Ambassador Miguel Ángel Moratinos, the EU's Special Envoy to the Middle East. An unofficial EU record of Taba proceedings is contained in a document known as *The Moratinos Non-Paper.* On the refugee question it says, "Non-papers were exchanged, which were regarded as a good basis for the talks. Both sides stated that 'the issue of the Palestinian refugees is central to the Israeli-Palestinian relations and that a comprehensive and just solution is essential to creating a lasting and morally scrupulous peace. Both sides agreed to adopt the principles and references [which] could facilitate the adoption of an agreement.'" Both sides suggested, as a basis, that the parties should agree that a just settlement of the refugee problem in accordance with the UN Security Council Resolution 242 must lead to the implementation of UN General Assembly Resolution 194. See: BitterLemons http://www.bitterlemons.org/docs/moratinos.html.

†In our interview Beilin recounted an anecdote that was most telling, especially in light of how former negotiators always stressed their "friendships" with their opposite numbers. Here is an excerpt: It was a conversation with Nabil Sha'ath when they were in Taba. Beilin says that he said to Nabil, "'We know each other's arguments. Let us change roles, and you will present the Israeli case, the beginning of our negotiations, and I will represent the Palestinian case, all refugees. And what is important is to check each other's presentation, and to know the real ones. Once we know that we really know the arguments of each other, then we can perhaps try to negotiate seriously about solutions.' He's also a PhD in Political Science (from a university in America), so he knows the business, and he said, 'Yes, okay, I'm ready for this . . . but I want to ask you one thing, which is very important for me to understand. You are always speaking about a Jewish majority, a Jewish majority. Why is it so important for you to have a Jewish majority?' I explained that we need the guard at the gate to enable Jews to enter a state. The sovereignty is very, very important for this very specific point to allow Jews to enter a country, and that there will not be a situation whereby all the gates are closed to Jews, as it happened before and during the Second World War. But then he said, 'You know, you don't have a majority of Jews in the United States. You have less than 30 percent, maybe 20 percent, and still you are strong; you rule everything, the politics, the media, the business community.' I said to him, 'Nabil, we are not 30 percent, we are neither 20 percent. (We are) 1.8 (percent).' I would have expected him to know, maybe not the number 1.8, but that it is a marginal percentage. And still, I mean, he spoke about 20 to 30 percent of Jews in the United States, which means tens of millions. So this was a kind of a huge surprise to me. By the way, his reaction to the number was very interesting. He said, 'You know, it grows my thesis even more so, because if with 1.8 percent you rule everything, so why do you need a majority here?' So you have such moments, which open windows to the ignorance of well-educated people. I'm sure that, again, that it is symmetric." Beilin, interview with the author.

(The Israelis, in a non-paper, suggested a possible 25,000 over three years or 40,000 over five within the context of a fifteen-year program of absorption.[83])

Two and a half years later, as I noted in chapter 4, both Israeli and Palestinian negotiators agreed to the Geneva Accord, which formulated the right of return in terms of refugees being allowed to return to Israel at Israel's discretion. Needless to say, both the Israeli government and the PLO rejected the accord. In Israel and the PLO there is some agreement on how to deal with the refugee question. Refugees would be offered a menu to choose from: a return to the new Palestinian state, with compensation for lost property and time in exile; staying put, again with a compensation package; or immigration to a third country that is willing to host them. As regards a return to Israel, Israel would accept a small quota on humanitarian grounds only, although support for the latter is falling. The PLO still wrestles with the numbers: A "small quota" is unacceptable even on humanitarian grounds, and there must be an acknowledgment of the *Nakba* and the subsequent suffering of the refugees. Four years after Geneva, at the official negotiations in Annapolis, Ehud Olmert reiterated the offer of receiving five thousand refugees, one thousand per year, on humanitarian grounds—an acknowledgment of the suffering caused but not of responsibility for the war, and no concession on the right of return.[84] Both were unacceptable to the Palestinians.

Tal Becker says:

> If an Israeli leader could bring himself to speak about Palestinian suffering, it would address the question of the indignity that Palestinian refugees feel. Palestinians have become less insistent on Israeli recognition of the right of return as a matter of principle, and more concerned with the manner of implementing an agreement on the refugee issue that they could plausibly sell to their own people. . . . No agreement will facilitate a right of return to Israel. But instead of an Israeli leader saying, "I'm against the right of return," he should say, "I am for the establishment of a Palestinian state that will be a home for refugees." You are redefining the issue, reframing it.[85]

On the question of Israel's "recognition of the right of return as a matter of principle" Becker is mistaken; for Palestinians it is the sine qua non. Recognition of the right would open ways to dealing with other aspects of the refugee issue along the lines both sides have now agreed to. How a Palestinian leader might reframe the issue for his people is tricky. What the majority of Palestinians would accept is a different matter.

> > < <

How many refugees and their descendants *would* want to return to Palestine? In a 2003 poll of a cross section of refugees in the diaspora, conducted by Dr. Khalil Shikaki, director of the Palestinian Center for Policy and Survey Research, the finding was only 10 percent.[86] The percentage varied depending on the country in which the refugees resided, but it was low in all of them. Even among those now living in the West Bank and Gaza, just 31 percent would opt for moving to the newly established Palestinian state. Only 2 percent would opt to immigrate to a European country or the United States, Australia, or Canada and obtain citizenship of that country or Palestinian citizenship.

The results surprised many observers, especially Palestinians. The refugees and their descendants know that there is no actual home to return to, that the ambience of village life and the old social setting no longer exist. As part of their compensation package they might be offered a house or apartment, but they would be returning as individuals and would find themselves strangers in towns like Lod or Ramla, with no support systems, no understanding of the language, no jobs. This is not the direst of pictures, but it does highlight the black hole in the right-of-return scenario.

The 10 percent figure was mentioned by a few Israeli interviewees, *not* in the context of the right of return but rather as a humanitarian and family-reunification gesture—and almost invariably with the caveat that just 10 percent would be 100 percent too many. For all the talk about the right of return and how the issue has stymied progress in negotiations, the Palestinian negotiators appear to care a lot more about the issue than the refugees themselves. But this jaded observation, quite common among Israelis at large, ignores the importance of the issue to the Palestinian *street*.[87] Israelis have not yet digested the fact that it is not about the numbers; it's about the *right*. Israelis should not fool themselves: non-recognition of the right of return and non-acknowledgment of responsibility for the *Nakba* would come at a price. Moreover, as a practical matter, the referendum—that is, if there can be a referendum—to approve any agreement that does not include such recognition could be doomed by resoundingly negative votes pouring in from the diaspora.

> > < <

Take the matter of the resettlement and compensation of hundreds of thousands of Palestinian refugees and their descendants. Who is eligible? Who decides? What are the different categories of compensation for the losses beginning in 1947–49, then continuing with the 1967 and 1973 wars? How in the world do you calculate the value of property expropriated over a seventy-year span, then incorporate rates of interest? Of what value are historical precedents, if they exist? The simplest questions yield answers that quickly become exponentially complicated. Most Palestinians who fled the wars of partition were tenant farmers, hence not legal owners of the land.[88] But they were the legal owners of the structures they built on the land: private versus public differentiations. What title deeds would suffice as verification? For that matter, how was land handled and registered in the Ottoman era and under the British Mandate? The answers are complicated and present additional problems.[89] Who has been compiling data?[90] Whose data is acceptable to both sides? Disputes over title deeds would flood the courts. Count on it.

Who foots the bill for all this investigation and adjudication? At the Annapolis negotiations, the Palestinians' assessment of the damages due came to an astronomical $200 billion, but the Israelis had their own assessment of damages: claims for Jewish property that was abandoned in Arab countries on the eve of or immediately following the declaration of the Israeli state. Some researchers estimate this sum to equal or exceed Palestinian claims.[91] One claim, the Israelis said, cancels the other. End of discussion.

The estimates of the *compensation* that would be required in comprehensive resettlement plans are humongous. They range from $8 billion to $19 billion; estimates for *rehabilitation programs*, from $10 billion to $14 billion; for property compensation, from $15 billion to $30 billion; and for per-capita refugee, approximately $22 billion. Estimates of the full *financial dimensions* of a resolution range from $55 billion to $85 billion[92] and even higher, to roughly $300 billion.[93]

Atif Kubursi, professor of economics at McMaster University in Ontario, comprehensively reviews the several attempts to reconcile estimates of Palestinian losses on behalf of Adam Smith International.[94] His analysis concludes that those *losses between 1948 and 2008 amounted to $300 billion* (at interest rates of zero),[95] and he suggests they could be paid in annual installments of $15 billion over a period of twenty years or installments of $20 billion annually over a fifteen-year period. The scenario, he is quick to point out, is "highly simplified and unrealistic," because the assumption of zero interest rates is unrealistic. Using a 3 percent interest would raise annual payments over twenty years to between $26.8 billion and $33.4 billion.[96] He estimates that Israel could pay this latter sum if it made a series of adjustments to tax rates, along with imposing some new taxes—all but guaranteeing revolt in Israel. At Annapolis the Palestinians sought $200 billion in compensation.[97] But, of course all these estimates and the assumptions they are based on are part of academic studies and their utility lies in the realm of the academy.[98]

"I was ambassador to Jordan in 2000," says Oded Eran, who was also a key Jewish Israeli negotiator, referring to the eve of the Camp David talks. "They gave me a letter claiming $20 billion. The Jordanian government says that Jordan hosted well over a million Palestinians for forty years; they rightly say, 'Somebody has to compensate us for doing it.' But with regards to the final figure, I estimate it will be somewhere in the region of $100 billion."[99] Other figures have been tossed around.[100]

There is no end to the permutations resulting from different sets of assumptions. Which raises an interesting question: How long would it take for negotiators and technical experts to determine—and find agreement on—the amounts that would provide parameters for negotiators? Since the Oslo process was initiated, agencies of one kind or another have been established ostensibly to find a solution to the refugee issues; few have weathered the years; fewer still made substantive progress.[101]

Yossi Beilin says, "There are many ways to find a solution, if you really want to find one." There are also many ways *not* to find a solution, as the history of the two-state negotiations has demonstrated for the two-plus decades since the first Oslo meeting. If no enduring formula *rooted in a parity of esteem* can be found regarding the right of return, if Israeli acknowledgment of responsibility remains ambiguous at best, there will be no end to this conflict. Yes, skillful negotiators may conceivably be able to conjure words sufficiently ambiguous to satisfy the other side, perhaps even their own constituency in the short run, but any agreement whose resolution of the right of return is mainly sleight of hand and obfuscation would always be a house divided against itself. Such an agreement will unleash the wrath of the street. Such an agreement might give birth to a Palestinian state, with Nobel Prizes handed out, flags raised, anthems sung, and applause for the newly installed Palestinian ambassador in the UN General Assembly. Implementation might even go hunky-dory for a number of years, but there would be unsettled business. An unsatisfied Hamas would lurk in the wings. So would jihadists. And what restrictions would apply, given the two million Syrian refugees, many of them Palestinian, who crowd camps in Jordan, and other camps in Turkey, Northern Iraq/Kurdistan, and Lebanon? Now that the Arab states of the Middle East have been corralled into a global war on the Islamic State (ISIS), restrictions on the cross-border movement of refugees and vetting for ISIS connections will become the new norm. The diaspora would remain a potent force in Palestinian politics. An Israel aware of these forces would remain an untrusting Israel, a state and a culture still on hair-trigger alert. It may have obtained its final status agreement, but it would not get its "end of claims." This will not bring *peace*.

Chapter 7

Settlers and Settlements

According to the interior ministry of Israel, there were 389,250 Jews living in Judea and Sumaria (West Bank) and another 375,000 in "disputed" neighborhoods of Jerusalem over the 1949 armistice line.[1] In the immediate aftermath of the Israeli occupation of the West Bank and Gaza Strip during the Six-Day War in 1967, the pros and cons of establishing settlements in the occupied territories were discussed at some length and often heatedly by the Israeli cabinet. Yet there are no minutes reflecting the decision of Prime Minister Levi Eshkol authorizing the settlement at Kfar Etzion in the Judean hills south of Jerusalem.[2] According to Gershom Gorenberg, who documents the history of the settlers' movement through the 1970s in *The Accidental Empire*, this first settlement happened in September 1967 (three months after the war). Without consultation or consideration of the possible implications, Eshkol alone gave the nod of approval to Hanan Porat, the charismatic leader of the settlement movement, and some of his followers to spend Rosh Hashanah at Kfar Etzion, but in language vague[3] enough to encourage them to stay on after the Holy Days, and the Kfar Etzion settlement became the bridgehead to creating *Eretz Ysrael* (Greater Israel).[4]

Shortly after the end of hostilities, Israel annexed East Jerusalem in violation of international law, and much of the surrounding area (some of it in the West Bank). Together with West Jerusalem they formed one expanded municipality. Following annexation in 1967, East Jerusalem Palestinians were given a special status as permanent residents, eligible to vote in a municipal election (something they have not much exercised)[5] but not in national ones.*

But in 1996 a new policy on residency was established, forcing Palestinians

*"Israel annexed the territory of East Jerusalem but not the Palestinians who were born and live there. It gave the territory 'full citizenship' by applying its law, jurisdiction and administration to it, anchoring that measure in basic laws that would make it difficult for any Israeli government to cede any land in East Jerusalem. But it did not grant Israeli citizenship to the Palestinians who live there. The Palestinians in question are not migrants who entered Israel but people who were born in Jerusalem and whose lives are centered here, in this city. One third of the city's residents are people without citizenship. They live in a country that views their territory as its

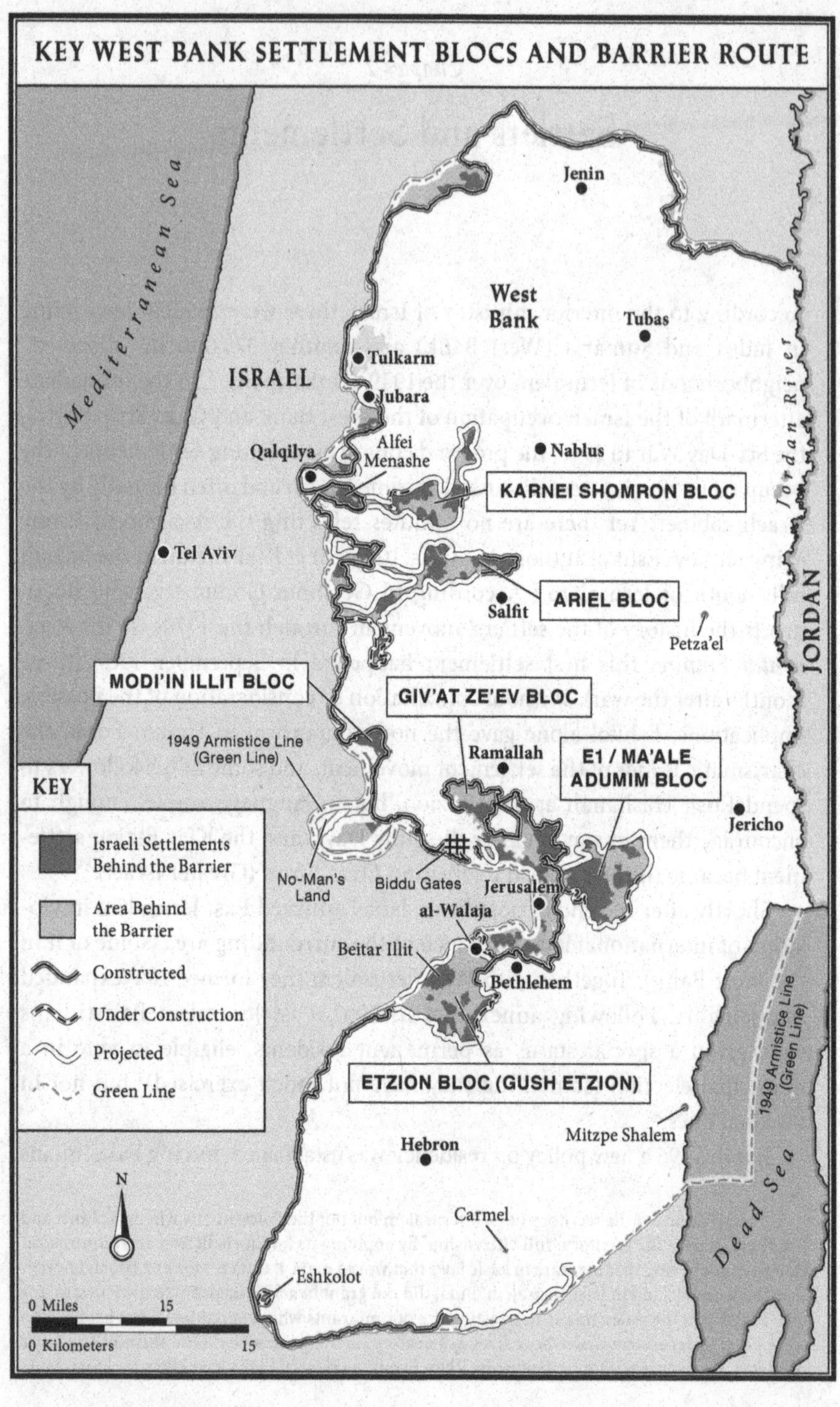
KEY WEST BANK SETTLEMENT BLOCS AND BARRIER ROUTE
Mediterranean Sea
ISRAEL
West Bank
Jenin
Tubas
Tulkarm
Jubara
Qalqilya
Alfei Menashe
Nablus
KARNEI SHOMRON BLOC
Tel Aviv
ARIEL BLOC
Salfit
Petza'el
Jordan River
JORDAN
MODI'IN ILLIT BLOC
GIV'AT ZE'EV BLOC
1949 Armistice Line (Green Line)
Ramallah
E1 / MA'ALE ADUMIM BLOC
Jericho
No-Man's Land
Biddu Gates
Jerusalem
al-Walaja
Beitar Illit
Bethlehem
ETZION BLOC (GUSH ETZION)
Mitzpe Shalem
Hebron
Carmel
Eshkolot
Dead Sea
1949 Armistice Line (Green Line)
KEY
Israeli Settlements Behind the Barrier
Area Behind the Barrier
Constructed
Under Construction
Projected
Green Line
N
0 Miles 15
0 Kilometers 15

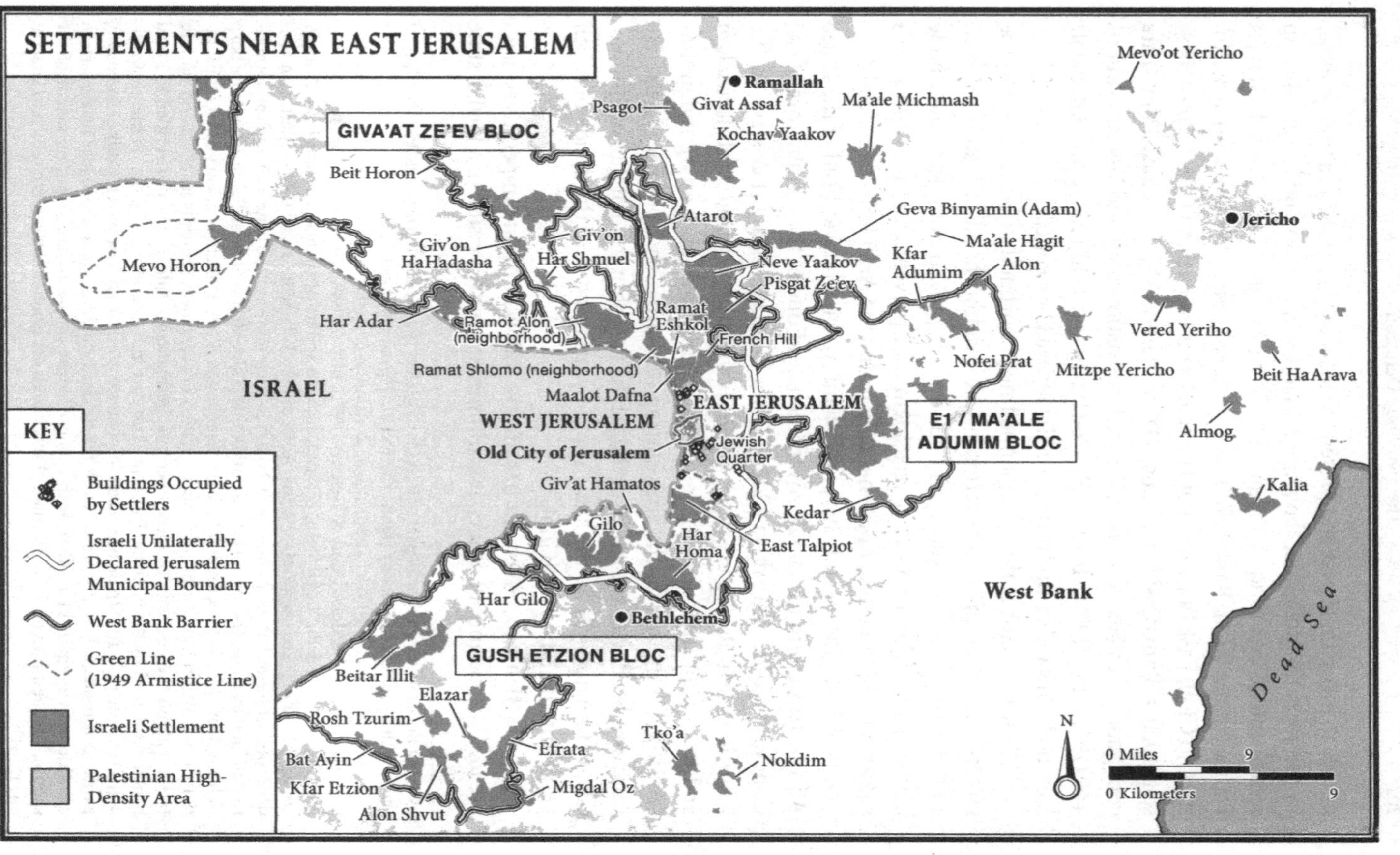
SETTLEMENTS NEAR EAST JERUSALEM
GIVA'AT ZE'EV BLOC
Beit Horon
Mevo Horon
Giv'on HaHadasha
Giv'on
Har Shmuel
Har Adar
Ramot Alon (neighborhood)
Ramat Shlomo (neighborhood)
Ramat Eshkol
French Hill
Maalot Dafna
ISRAEL
WEST JERUSALEM
Old City of Jerusalem
EAST JERUSALEM
Jewish Quarter
Psagot
Ramallah
Givat Assaf
Kochav Yaakov
Ma'ale Michmash
Atarot
Geva Binyamin (Adam)
Ma'ale Hagit
Neve Yaakov
Pisgat Ze'ev
Kfar Adumim
Alon
Nofei Prat
Mitzpe Yericho
Vered Yeriho
Mevo'ot Yericho
Jericho
Beit HaArava
Almog
Kalia
E1 / MA'ALE ADUMIM BLOC
Kedar
East Talpiot
Giv'at Hamatos
Gilo
Har Homa
Har Gilo
Bethlehem
West Bank
Dead Sea
GUSH ETZION BLOC
Beitar Illit
Elazar
Rosh Tzurim
Efrata
Bat Ayin
Kfar Etzion
Alon Shvut
Migdal Oz
Tko'a
Nokdim
N
0 Miles 9
0 Kilometers 9
KEY
Buildings Occupied by Settlers
Israeli Unilaterally Declared Jerusalem Municipal Boundary
West Bank Barrier
Green Line (1949 Armistice Line)
Israeli Settlement
Palestinian High-Density Area

unable to prove their past and present residence to leave their homes forever.* In the years that followed, the annexed land was used to build twelve Jewish settlements: Neve Ya'aqov, Pisgat Ze'ev, French Hill, Ramat Eshkol, Ma'alot Dafna, Ramot Alon, Ramat Shlomo (Rekhes Shu'afat), the Jewish Quarter (in the Old City), East Talpiot, Giv'at Hamatos, Har Homa, and Gilo. Four of these settlements (Ramat Eshkol, Ma'alot Dafna, Ramot Alon, and East Talpiot) are contiguous with East Jerusalem.[6] Under international law and UN Resolutions 446 (1979), 452 (1979), 465 (1980), 476 (1980), and 1515 (2003), all settlements have no legal validity under the Fourth Geneva Convention.[7]

"Givat Hamatos is the first planned neighborhood to be built across the Green Line since the construction of the neighborhood of Har Homah in 1997 (during the first Netanyahu administration). It completes the divide between Bethlehem and East Jerusalem and prevents any possibility of a significant diplomatic arrangement regarding the Arab Jerusalem neighborhoods of Beit Tzafafa and Sharafat," Shaul Arieli, who was head of the Peace Administration in the Barak government and one of the formulators of the Geneva Accord, told Akiva Eldar, "Givat Hamatos is another stage in the historic Israeli plan to create an urban Jewish ring around Arab Jerusalem and to disrupt the natural Palestinian urban continuum along the mountain top. To the north, the ring cutting off Ramallah from East Jerusalem was completed with the construction of the neighborhood of Ramat Shlomo. Givat Hamatos will do the same thing by bridging over the divide between Har Homah and Giloh [Gilo]."[8]

The settlement movement has always followed divine imperatives; laws are for the guidance of others. It is illuminated with a vision of a Jewish state

---

own but does not view them as part of it. As far as Israel is concerned, they reside in the place of their birth by sufferance, not by right." Klein et al., *Permanent Residency.*

*See Yael Stein, *The Quiet Deportation: Revocation of Residency of East Jerusalem Palestinians* (Jerusalem: HaMoked and B'Tselem, 1997), http://www.hamoked.org/items/10200_eng.pdf. See also B'Tselem, "Legal Status of East Jerusalem and Its Residents," January 1, 2014, http://www.btselem.org/jerusalem/legal_status. According to B'Tselem, "Israel treats Palestinian residents of East Jerusalem as immigrants who live in their homes at the beneficence of the authorities and not by right. The authorities maintain this policy although these Palestinians were born in Jerusalem, lived in the city, and have no other home. . . . Permanent residency differs substantially from citizenship. The primary right granted to permanent residents is to live and work in Israel without the necessity of special permits. Permanent residents are also entitled to social benefits provided by the National Insurance Institute and to health insurance. Permanent residents have the right to vote in local elections, but not in elections to Knesset. Unlike citizenship, permanent residency is only passed on to the holder's children where the holder meets certain conditions. A permanent resident with a non-resident spouse must submit, on behalf of the spouse, a request for family unification. Only citizens are granted the right to return to Israel at any time."

not within its internationally determined boundaries but in all of Palestine. It has clarity of purpose, its fanaticism a virtue required to clear the path. It embraces absolute devotion to rabbinical laws; it devours everything that questions the righteousness of its cause. Abraham Kook, who was chief rabbi (Ashkenazi) under the British Mandate, wrote, "[W]hat Jewish secular nationalists want they do not themselves know: The spirit of Israel is so closely linked to the spirit of God that a Jewish nationalist no matter how secularist his intentions may be, is, despite himself, imbued with the divine spirit even against his own will."[9]

Oblivious to the tumultuous trajectory of the Israeli state—wars in 1948–49, 1967, and 1973, crushing intifadas in 1987 and again in 2000, Lebanese wars, the invasions of 1978 and 1982 that led to an eighteen-year occupation of southern Lebanon; war yet again with Hezbollah in 2006, and Gaza wars in 2008–09, 2012, and 2014—the settlement movement, under the umbrella of Gush Emunim*[10] and its successor movements, "continued to build, to settle the land of Israel, and to see themselves as leading the bickering and questioning masses through the wilderness."[11] A minority of a minority, obsessed with messianic zealotry, has used every means, including narrow legalities, duplicity, connivance, political horse trading, political acumen, hypocrisy, and an utter disregard for the rights of Palestinians to create West Bank settlements that are "legal" by Israeli terms. Every millimeter of land had to be reclaimed for the vision of a Greater Israel to emerge. There are no uplifting passages here, only an example of how Israeli governments, calculating the political costs of enforcing the law, post-authorized the illegal settlements and took the settlement project itself under government control.

Ten years after the Six-Day War in 1967, 45 settlements with approximately 7,000 settlers had been established in the West Bank, primarily in the Jordan Valley.[12] There were 16 settlements built in Gaza between 1970 and 2005.[13] Within another decade—by 1987 and the First Intifada—there were 110 settlements with a population of 57,900.[14] By the eve of the Oslo I talks in 1993, the number of settlements had risen to 120, but the settler population had almost doubled to 110,900. That lower rate of growth of new settlements but definitely not of new *settlers* reflected the decision of President George H. W. Bush to apply the brakes. He was the first U.S. president to do so. In 1992

*For a summary of Gush Emunim's history, see the Knesset Web site: http://www.knesset.gov.il/lexicon/eng/gush_em_eng.htm.

James Baker, his secretary of state, announced that the United States would withdraw loan guarantees for $10 billion[15] unless settlements were halted.[16] In August 1992, three months before Bush lost his bid for reelection to Bill Clinton, Bush met with Israel's new prime minister, Yitzhak Rabin, who promised that his government would refrain from constructing further settlements, except for those already under construction.[17] While Clinton was president and before Rabin was assassinated in 1995, Rabin "undertook not to establish new settlements, *except in the Jordan Valley and the "greater Jerusalem area'."** However, he authorized "natural growth" of the settler population within the existing settlements. "Natural growth" has allowed Israel to defy multiple demands for a settlement freeze from the United Nations, the U.S. government commission headed by Senator George Mitchell, the European Union, and the Quartet's Road Map.

In the three years after Oslo I, the Israeli government established only one new settlement, but the settler population climbed to 309,200.[18] This became the new pattern for the following decade: few new settlements but thousands of new housing units built in the *existing* settlements, yielding the steadily rising settler population desired by the government. Rabin's "natural growth" doctrine was never precisely defined, but it created the template for the settlement blocs.[19]

"Altogether," Steven Rosen, who served for twenty-three years as a top official in AIPAC, says in *Foreign Policy*, "Israel completed 30,000 dwelling units in the West Bank, Gaza, and Jerusalem in the four years of Rabin's government. Even the Jan. 9, 1995, announcement of a plan to build 15,000 additional apartments in East Jerusalem neighborhoods beyond the 1967 borders (especially Pisgat Zeev, Neve Yaacov, Gilo, and Har Homa) did not stop negotiations, which resulted in the Oslo II Accords of September 28, 1995. Israeli construction continued while Arafat and Rabin signed an

*Hareuveni, *By Hook and by Crook*, 15; and Foundation for Middle East Peace, "Clinton Accepts Rabin's Expansion Policy," *Settlement Report* 3, no. 3 (May–June 1993), http://fmep.org/wp/wp-content/uploads/2015/01/3.3.pdf. "It remains unclear" the report says, "how much of Rabin's new policy—to complete construction of 11,000 publicly financed units in the West Bank and Gaza, plus an additional 1,200 to 1,500 privately financed units annually and to continue the construction boom in annexed East Jerusalem—will fall outside of Washington's undefined limits of natural growth." Natural growth under Rabin pertained to the natural growth of families. Under Netanyahu: "[The] Netanyahu government said it will deal with more than 20 illegal outposts, but is insisting on the right to build for 'natural growth.' It argues that growing families living in existing settlements must be allowed to build new homes." See Simon McGregor-Wood, "Israel Pressured by Obama's Tough Stance on Settlements," ABC News, May 28, 2009, http://abcnews.go.com/International/story?id=7694664.

historic accord."* And what was the American policy toward Rabin's construction of Jewish homes in East Jerusalem? Mild annoyance.

> > < <

In the beginning, relations between the settlers' movements and the government were riddled with contention, suspicion, and occasional confrontation. In the West Bank the early messianic settlers did not wait for government approval of their homesteading. They simply grabbed land wherever and whenever possible, staked a claim, and raised the Israeli flag, in the name of "security." When the IDF was deployed to remove them, the settlers flagrantly refused to move. The IDF found itself defending settlements created ostensibly for the purposes of security,[20] but in areas where such precautions were not necessary. Once the settlement was established on such flimsy grounds, the government would rubber-stamp the deal.[21]

Between 1977 and 1981, Ariel Sharon, then a junior minister of agriculture, created the Civil Administration to oversee the administration of the occupied territories.† Israeli settlements are in large measure Sharon's legacy from his tenure in the agriculture department, and then as minister of defense.[22] Danny Tirza, the government's "mapper," recounts flying with Sharon in a helicopter across the West Bank, with Sharon stabbing his finger repeatedly at the ground below and barking, "There . . . there . . . and there!" referring to sites where he wanted new settlements built. His selections might have seemed random but in fact were intended to make a two-state

*Steven J. Rosen, "Obama's Foolish Settlements Ultimatum," *Foreign Policy*, April 1, 2010, http://www.foreignpolicy.com/articles/2010/04/01/obama_s_foolish_settlements_ultimatum?page=0,2. "'I explained to the president of the United States,' [Rabin] said, 'that I wouldn't forbid Jews from building privately in the area of Judea and Samaria . . . I am sorry that within united Jerusalem construction is not more massive.' The same year as the famous handshake on the White House lawn, 1993, the Rabin government completed the construction of more than 6,000 units in the Pisgat Zeev neighborhood of East Jerusalem, out of a total of 13,000 units that were in various stages of completion in areas of the city that had been outside Israeli lines before 1967."

†The main task of the Civil Administration is the civil and security coordination and liaison vis-a-vis the Palestinian entities. It has regional representatives in various districts and authority over the population in Area C in matters relating to zoning, construction, and infrastructure. It is also responsible for liaising with the international community on issues relating to humanitarian aid and the promotion of various initiatives in Judea and Samaria. For more information regarding activities the Civil Administration engaged in, see Akiva Eldar, "IDF Civil Administration pushing for land takeover in West Bank," *Haaretz*, July 22, 2011, http:// www.haaretz.com/print-edition/news/idf-civil-administration-pushing-for-land-takeover-in-west-bank-1.374564; Al-Haq, "Civilian Administration in the Occupied West Bank: Analysis of Israeli Military Government Order No. 947," http://www.alhaq.org/publications/publications-index/item/civilian-administration-in-the-occupied-west-bank.

solution impossible by spreading settlements throughout the heartland of the West Bank and Gaza (WBG).[23]

In 1974 the highly disciplined settler movements were effectively incorporated into Gush Emunim,[24] the messianic right-wing movement that became a powerful force in Israeli politics between 1974 and 1986, when it was disbanded. The Gush movement pressed the government at every level to establish new settlements and to post-authorize[25] legal approval of the early, unauthorized settlements. As a result, the number of settlers and settlements proliferated at an accelerating rate—"facts on the ground"—despite repeated pro forma calls by successive American presidents and European countries for a halt to construction. The Civil Administration became a tool of Gush, and not coincidentally, the IDF and the settlers developed a close, almost symbiotic relationship that bordered on collusion, with the IDF providing on-the-ground protection.[26] "The rate of 'settlers' in IDF combat service is 80 percent higher than the country wide rate."[27] Over one hundred settler groups have been trained and armed by the IDF, ostensibly for self-defense.* During the seventies the IDF even appropriated Palestinian land on the basis of "military needs" held it for a while, and then handed it over to settlers.†

In 1981, belatedly, the government adopted the Drobles plan,‡ titled

*Chaim Levinson, "The Settlers' Army," *Haaretz*, September 24, 2012, http://www.haaretz.com/opinion/the-settlers-army-1.466454. "Over the past 20 years," he writes, "with the encouragement of the army, a civilian force armed with some 1,600 guns has arisen in the territories. In the United States, such a force is called a militia. In the Palestinian Authority, it is known as an organization's military wing. In Israel, we use the terms '*ravshatz*' (the settlement security officer, from the acronym for *rakaz bitahon shotef tzahali*, or coordinator of security with the army), and '*kitot konanut*,' the settlements' rapid-response units."

† Hareuveni, "By Hook and by Crook." Hareuveni writes that "Israel operates a complex legal and bureaucratic apparatus in the West Bank for seizing control of hundreds of thousands of dunams of Palestinian land, some privately owned. These are allocated for establishing new settlements or expanding existing ones. The main methods Israel uses are requisitioning land for 'military needs' declaring or registering land as 'state land,' and expropriating land for 'public needs.'"

‡Matityahu Drobles was head of the settlement department of the World Zionist Organization. Jad Issac explains, "In 1977 he prepared "a comprehensive plan for the establishment of colonies throughout the West Bank. Most of the colonies that were established as part of the Drobles plan were constructed on the central mountain ridge around Palestinian population centers. The Drobles plan embraced the aims of Gush Emunim. The shift coincided with the Likud Party's coming to power in Israel." Trudy Rubin further elaborates, "There were three plans. The first Drobles plan (1978) "focused on establishing small outposts populated by ideological devotees to the religious and nationalist cause of resettling key sites in Judaism's biblical history. The second Drobles plan, in 1981, aimed to amass population in the West Bank. It relied on private contractors who were handed what were defined as West Bank state lands at 5 percent of their value by the Israeli government. The plan was to establish suburban belts abutting Israeli metropolises to which young Israeli couples could be lured by bargain prices. The use of private contractors cut down on the need for government investment and sped up the building process. The aim: 100,000

"Settlement in Judea and Samaria," a master plan that called for building twelve to fifteen settlements per annum in each of the following five years, with the goal of increasing the settler population (not counting East Jerusalem) to 150,000.[28] So there were now two categories of settlements: those started without approval and then sanctioned as fait accompli and those authorized by the government as part of an official campaign.

Establishing the overall numbers for the settlements saga is difficult for a number of reasons: sometimes unclear differentiation between a new settlement and expansion of the municipal boundaries of existing settlements; an absence of clear distinctions between settlements and "neighborhoods"; possible discrepancies between the number of housing units authorized by permit and the number actually built; and numerous data baselines that pertain to overlapping time periods. In 1996, then–prime minister Netanyahu lifted a four-year freeze on new construction and expansion, abolished the ministerial committee that had reviewed building requests, and left approval of new construction up to the defense minister alone.[29] Another particularly difficult factor to itemize accurately is the unauthorized outposts.* At their zenith, outposts numbered about a hundred. Despite being illegal under Israeli law, they always managed to become attached to the electricity grid, water system, and other infrastructure requirements for survival, and no Israeli government voluntarily took action to dismantle them. Instead, governments of the day, especially Netanyahu's, engaged in protracted legal battles with Peace Now or like-minded NGOs in order to protect them. Invariably, even when courts ruled against the government and ordered dismantling, the government backdated the outpost's legal

---

settlers in five years, by 1986." The third Drobles plan called "for the establishment of another fifty-seven settlements of various kinds in the West Bank by 1987." Jad Issac, "Israeli Colonial Activities in OPT," *40 Years of Israeli Occupation, 1967–2007*, http://www.arij.org/atlas40/chapter4.2.html, and Trudy Rubin, "The Dream of a Jewish West Bank," *Christian Science Monitor*, August 17, 1983, http://www.csmonitor.com/1983/0817/081731.html/(page)/2: "The plan projects a population of 1.3 million Jews by that time." See also Foundation for Middle East Peace, "A Settlement Primer," *Report on Israeli Settlement in the Occupied Territories*, Winter 1991–92, http://www.fmep.org/reports/special-reports/special-report-on-israeli-settlement-in-the-occupied-territories/PDF.

*"An 'outpost' is, essentially, an 'unofficial' settlement established after the 1990s. In 1996, Israel responded to international pressure and announced it would no longer build new settlements, although it continued to grant permits for expansion of existing ones. However, the government looked the other way when religious settlers established their own colonies. Although these were called 'illegal' or 'unauthorized,' no punitive action was taken." Council for European Palestinian Relations, "Illegal Israeli Settlements, http://thecepr.org/index.php?option=com_content&view=article&id=115:illegal-israel-settlements&catid=6:memos&Itemid=34

standing or avoided implementing the court's orders, using every legal contrivance in the book. This still happens, and if all options are exhausted, the government simply moves the residents to adjacent state land and replicates the outpost just dismantled, and the charade starts all over again.[30]

The government was cowed by the powerful Gush Emunim and, fearing that dismantling settlements and halting construction would tear the country apart, acquiesced to the settlement movement's powerful lobby.[31] In retrospect, restricting newcomers to existing settlements was retrogressive, because it facilitated migration to settlements such as Ma'ale Adumim, Modi'in, Gush Etzion, and Beitar Illit, now mega settlement blocs built on the peripheries of Jerusalem and the West Bank that are marked by Israel for annexation in any eventual two-state-solution peace agreement. In East Jerusalem the government invested huge sums developing Jewish Israeli neighborhoods. By 2011, 486,738 of Jerusalem's residents (Jewish and Arab) lived in the areas annexed in 1967, constituting 60 percent of the total population of the city (around 804,400). The Jewish population had risen from zero to 39 percent of the total population of those areas and 38 percent of the Jewish population of the whole city.[32] Add that number to the West Bank settler population (which has almost tripled since the Oslo process began) and the total number of settlers in occupied territory* at the end of 2013 was over half a million: 520,000.[33]

> > < <

The extent even of the Israeli government's involvement in the settlements project became more transparent in 2009[34] when the English-language daily *Haaretz* published portions of the government's own classified database that included up-to-date references for all statutes relevant to the settlements and outposts in the West Bank.† An analysis of the database prepared by Dror Etkes on behalf of the Yesh Din Lands Project found within the

* Occupied territory including East Jerusalem.

†The database was compiled on behalf of the Defense Ministry by General (Ret.) Baruch Spiegel. It is available at http://www.fmep.org/analysis/reference/SpiegelDatabaseEng.pdf. Dror Etkes, Yesh Din Lands Project, provided translations of excerpts.

"The Movement for Freedom of Information and Peace Now had petitioned the courts in 2006 for access to the database. In a preliminary response to the petition, the state demanded a discussion with the court behind closed doors, without the participation of the petitioners. The state then attempted to convince the court that the information in question was secret and would likely harm the state's security. A year and a half later—in its first written response to the petition—the state agreed to transfer parts of the material that Spiegel's team had assembled but asked the court 'to reject the petition, and charge the petitioners with legal fees.'" Dror Etkes, *The Spiegel Database: An Analysis*, mondoweiss.net/files/dror-analysis.doc.

database no reference whatsoever to security concerns as a basis for authorization of the settlements. More incriminating still, the database "shows that the outposts are only the tip of the iceberg, and illegal activity is mostly taking place within official settlements—making the distinction [between settlements and unauthorized outposts] null and void for all intents and purposes."[35]

In 2008 a report[36] by Talya Sason, who had worked in the State Attorney's office, had already detailed the malfeasance of officials in the Ministry of Defense and Ministry of Housing, which conspired with the World Zionist Organization (WZO) to siphon millions of shekels from state budgets to support the outposts, a "blatant violation of the law." Little has happened since to remedy the matter, and as settlements have proliferated and constraints have loosened, the abuse of ordinary Palestinians by settlers and the IDF, which Sason also detailed, has mushroomed.[37]

The settlements drain the government's resources; their subsidies are covertly channeled through a labyrinth of government agencies. While the social protests in 2011 were not directed specifically at the cost of the settlements, there was, nonetheless, an implicit undercurrent of feeling that the Israeli taxpayer was being shortchanged: Lavish subsidies to the settlements[38] contrasted with a shortage of affordable housing for families in Israel itself.[39]

The Macro Center for Political Economics (Macro)[40] is under contract with the Israeli government to develop a database of information and estimate all of the costs associated with the settlements. Its work concludes that the cost value (i.e., the sunken cost, is $18 billion) which does *not* include security, roads between the settlements, or the subsidies required to run the settlements.[41]

The Palestinian interviewees I spoke to insisted that Netanyahu covertly breached his commitment in 2010 to forgo construction for ten months.* The moratorium was mainly, in their view, just another cynical instance of Israel's penchant for taking action at the last moment to appease its friends, rather than a sincere effort to build trust before embarking on serious negotiations. In September 2010, after the ten months had passed, it was all moot, because Netanyahu resumed construction at an accelerating pace, despite U.S. pleading to extend the freeze for another thirty days.[42]

"During its first two years in office [for part of the time constrained by

*I was in Israel at the time, and settlers I talked with laughed at the moratorium, saying they simply brought components for adding to a house or building a new one into their settlements in the trunks of their cars.

the moratorium], the Netanyahu government largely refrained from issuing tenders for construction in settlements in the West Bank, and issued only a few for construction in settlements in East Jerusalem (for a total of 833 housing units)." Then, however, the government opened the floodgates and "issued tenders for 4,469 new housing units in settlements in the West Bank and East Jerusalem."[43] In addition, in January 2013, weeks before national elections, Netanyahu's government announced its intention to issue tenders for 3,000 additional housing units. In a separate action, the Ministry of Housing and Construction published a list of tenders that included 1,216 additional units in the West Bank and East Jerusalem, which were subsequently issued."[44] Much of this construction is in especially sensitive sites like Efrat and Ariel, well inside the West Bank. And thanks to new construction, East Jerusalem is separated from the rest of the West Bank and to an increasing degree sealed off.[45]

What happened to the Road Map, the step-by-step way forward to final status negotiations, from a decade earlier, in which Israel had agreed to full compliance, including the provision to stop settlements?[46] It has not only egregiously violated that commitment; it has reconfigured the Palestinians' insistence on a freeze as a *new* demand—Abbas was left with little choice but to follow Obama's call for a freeze. It's *not* a new demand. It's the Israelis' old commitment.

In November 2012, following a string of announcements about settlement expansions, including in the highly sensitive "E1"* corridor of East Jerusalem, "the U.S. State Department issued an unusually strong rebuke of Israeli settlement policies, with a spokesperson describing them euphemistically as a 'pattern of provocation.'"[47] The E1 announcement was especially so. Undoubtedly the product of Netanyahu's pique after the United Nations awarded "observer status" to the Palestinian Authority, these tenders would, if ever brought to fruition, ensure that a future Palestinian state would be noncontiguous. Netanyahu brushed the rebuke aside and continued with business as usual. His actions were denounced even by some of his closest allies.[48] But, denunciations without teeth carry little weight. Days afterward, on a visit to Germany, he and Chancellor Angela Merkel "agreed to disagree" on the issue[49] and the EU signed off on "unprecedented mea-

*"The implementation of construction plans in E1 will create an urban bloc between Ma'ale Adumim and Jerusalem, exacerbate the isolation of East Jerusalem from the rest of the West Bank and disrupt the territorial contiguity between the northern and southern parts of the West Bank." "The E1 Plan and Its Implications for Human Rights in the West Bank," B'Tselem, November 27, 2013, http://www.btselem.org/settlements/20121202_e1_human_rights_ramifications.

sures to enhance its relations with Israel in sixty trade and diplomatic policy areas."[50]

President Obama visited Israel in March 2013 to reaffirm America's enduring support, smooth the way to a resumption of negotiations, and mend bridges with Netanyahu badly fractured during Obama's first term. As a gesture of goodwill, Netanyahu ordered a freeze on the issue of *new* tenders until mid-June. However, that freeze did not affect approved projects already in the pipeline. Obama also took time to visit Abbas and told him that insisting on a settlements freeze as a prerequisite for a resumption of talks had become counterproductive.[51] Settlement construction continued,[52] and in June tenders were issued for 3,472 new housing units in the West Bank and East Jerusalem, with plans announced for another 8,943.[53] Assuming an average settler family of five, this was housing for an additional 44,000 settlers. On this occasion however, the EU showed some muscle. In July, its foreign ministers announced that beginning January 2014, "Israeli companies and other entities based behind the 'Green Line' that marks Israel's internationally recognized borders [will not] receive any EU-sponsored grants, prizes or funding."[54] The proposed sanctions will not have a significant impact on trade relations, but the fact that the EU, Israel's largest trading partner, imposed them came as a shock to Israel.[55] Ultimately, it had little option but to comply with the constraints or else forfeit the opportunity to become part of the EU's Horizon 2020 initiative.[56]

Nothing deterred Netanyahu's settlement plans, despite widespread public concern that sanctions would harm Israel economically (67 percent) and almost half (49 percent) believing that the EU's decision regarding the settlements would endanger Israel's international status.[57] After U.S. secretary of state John Kerry had mediated a formula for negotiations acceptable to both Netanyahu and Abbas, talks between Israelis and Palestinians resumed in August. In the days preceding the talks, the Israeli government approved a further 1,200 housing units in the West Bank and 942 in East Jerusalem.[58] So, despite all the freezes and promises, settlement growth continued to accelerate. The construction doubled between 2012 and 2013.[59]

A corollary to the history of the settlements is the construction of the separation barrier, the array of trenches, electric fences, and concrete walls begun during the Second Intifada. The barrier was presented as a temporary solution in order to prevent suicide attacks in Israel.* (Suicide attacks dropped sharply

*For more on the route of the barrier and its impact, see United Nations Office for the Coordination of Humanitarian Affairs Occupied Palestinian territory, "The Humanitarian Impact of the Barrier," July 2013, http://www.ochaopt.org/documents/ocha_opt_barrier_factsheet_july

since that time.) But security wasn't the only motive. "When you check how much money was invested, and where the barrier was constructed, when it could have been constructed cheaper in other areas," Dror Etkes explains, "you realize that behind the route of the barrier, there is a very clear, long-term political doctrine: as many Israelis as possible west of the barrier, and as few Palestinians as possible . . . and, as much as possible to reserve extra land which will allow Israel to expand in the future. . . . This is the principle."

> Wherever a fence penetrates into the West Bank, it is deliberate: Israel wants to annex the area. . . . In a sense Israel has entrapped itself. On the one hand claiming that it's all ad hoc, it's all security, and it's all temporary. On the other hand it's putting facts on the ground that contradicts everything that was supposed to be temporary. These are the settlement blocs which, for the first time, have been clearly designated. Israel would have preferred not to have them identified, because as long as there is no clear map of which blocs they have their eyes on, Israel can enlarge these blocs. Here comes a fence which has established a very clear border between what is within the bloc and what is outside.[60]

In simplest terms, the barrier delineates the settlement blocs and territory that Israel intends to keep in a land swap under a two-state solution.[61]

> > < <

From the beginning, the Israeli government refused to dismantle the earliest settlements for which there was no statutory authority because it would not confront the religious settlement movement, which held that the ordained moment described in the Torah[62] had arrived, and Jews were under an

_2013_english.pdf; Legal Consequences of the Construction of a Wall in the Occupied Palestinian Territory, International Court of Justice (ICJ), http://www.icj-cij.org/docket/index.php?p1=3&p2=4&case=131&p3=4. "The planned route of barrier(s) in this area," Friedman and Etkes write, "will incorporate 10 settlements and numerous unauthorized 'outposts' on the western side of the barrier, effectively annexing more than 50,000 Israeli settlers into Israel. The settlements which are planned to be annexed this way are: Beitar Illit, Har Gilo, Efrat, Elazar, Neve Daniel, Migdal Oz, Kfar Etzion, Rosh Zurim, Bat Ayin, and Alon Shvut. By routing the barrier in this manner, the entire enclave is attached not only to Israel along the Green Line (to the west) but is incorporated into the contiguous areas of Greater Jerusalem (in much the same way that the Givat Zeev settlement bloc is being annexed in a manner that expands the contiguous Greater Jerusalem area to the north). The barrier, plus a set of bypass roads which have been already constructed over the past 15 years in this area, will allow the Israeli settler population to commute to Jerusalem in a matter of a few minutes." Lara Friedman, Americans for Peace Now, and Dror Etkes, Peace Now, "The Etzion Bloc and the Security Barrier," November 2006, http://peacenow.org.il/eng/content/etzion-bloc-and-security-barrier.

obligation to complete their divine mission to populate the land and establish *Eretz Ysrael* throughout all of Palestine.[63] Etkes explains: "Ideologically speaking, we're looking at two different worlds in terms of our attitudes to Zionism. The *ultraorthodox* world, in general, has rejected Zionism and any active attitude to collective Jewish history; the *national orthodox* has adopted a very proactive attitude toward helping God to shape the Jewish collective history."

The national religious orthodox (wooed assiduously by Naftali Bennett, head of Jewish Home) are more connected to the settlements than any other sector in Israeli society; in the early years there were only a few ultraorthodox settlements in the West Bank. Shas, the influential ultraorthodox political party, blocked funding in the Knesset for settlements and outposts.[64] (However, in the last ten years it is the ultraorthodox who have become the main growth factor in the settler movement in the West Bank, where housing is cheaper.) The religiously motivated settlement movement holds tenaciously to the belief that it had and continues to have a mandate to complete the Jewish return to their homeland, fulfilling prophetic prognostications and scriptural prescience. While others dithered, it answered the call, elevating itself to a position where the sacredness of its cause, it righteously asserted, superseded the authority of governments that queried its actions or called it to account. Enveloped in its impermeable mantle of virtue, it was intolerant of everything or person that stood in its way.*

The settlers live among Palestinian populations. When their numbers were fairly small, they were undoubtedly unfriendly to one another, but not overtly hostile. But after the 2005 Gaza withdrawal, as the settlers' numbers grew in the West Bank, a certain "critical mass" was reached; harassment of local Palestinians became more frequent and intrusive and violent.[65] Settlers routinely overturn Palestinian stalls in the marketplace. They cut down their precious olive trees—over 800,000 since 1967, the equivalent of razing all of the 24,000 trees in New York City's Central Park thirty-three times.†

*The irony is that messianic Judaism and radical Islam share so much in common that the words, or at least the sentiments, of a virulent rabbi are interchangeable with the words of a rabble-rousing extremist imam. Both lay claim to all of Palestine in the name of their particular divinities; both preach hatred of the other as a legitimate tool to advance their goals.

†"Since 1967 Israel Has Razed over 800,000 Palestinian Olive Trees, the Equivalent to Destroying Central Park 33 Times Over," *Mondoweiss*, October 10, 2013, http://mondoweiss.net/2013/10/palestinian-equivalent-destroying.html; Jodi Rudoren, "In a Harvest, Palestinians Cast a Light on Hardship," *New York Times*, October 22, 2013, http://www.nytimes.com/2013/10/23/world/middleeast/in-a-harvest-palestinians-cast-a-light-on-hardship.html?_r=0.

In short, settlers believe they can act with impunity because they live and work under the IDF's protective umbrella. From 2007 through 2011, according to the Jerusalem Fund for Education and Community Development, there was a 315 percent increase in violent incidents. Over 90 percent of *all* Palestinian villages have experienced multiple instances of arson, stone throwing, vehicular attack, shootings, and physical attacks by settlers.[66] "[A]rmed settlers in areas surrounding settlements and outposts . . . create de facto 'no go zones' which often include private Palestinian land. This ensures that the land will be virtually abandoned by its fearful owners. In recent years, settlers have launched their 'price tag'* campaign . . . , in which they retaliate during attempts to dismantle outposts by carrying out violent attacks on nearby Palestinian villages,"[67] often desecrating their mosques. As recently as February 2014 Reuters reported that "Israeli forces are using excessive, reckless violence in the occupied West Bank, killing dozens of Palestinians over the past three years (2011–2013) in what might constitute a war crime," according to Amnesty International.[68] "The Israeli army dismissed the allegations, saying security forces had seen a 'substantial increase' in Palestinian violence and that Amnesty had revealed a 'complete lack of understanding' about the difficulties soldiers faced. . . . Amnesty said that in none of the cases it reviewed did the Palestinians appear to be posing any imminent threat to life."[69] In the years in question, Reuters also reported that 22 Palestinians were killed, 4 of whom were children, and 261 Palestinians, at least 67 of whom were children, were shot and seriously injured by live ammunition fired by Israeli soldiers, citing Amnesty International's data.[70] In the same period eleven Israeli settlers and two IDF soldiers were

*This term refers to random acts of violence aimed at Palestinians and Israeli security forces by radical settlers, who, according to the *New York Times*, "exact a price from local Palestinians or from the Israeli security forces for any action taken against their settlement enterprise." The *Wall Street Journal* states that the term refers to "a campaign of retribution by fundamentalist Israeli youths against Palestinians in the West Bank." Between 2012 and 2013 there were 788. See: "price tag" attacks. "Price Tag Epidemic" *YNet News* June 18, 2013 www. ynetnews.com/articles/0,7340,L-4394072,00htm; Ethan Bronner and Isabel Kershner, "Resolve of West Bank Settlers May Have Limits," *New York Times*, September 13, 2009, http://www.nytimes.com/2009/09/14/world/middleeast/14settlers.html?pagewanted=all&_r=0; Joshua Mitnick, "Mosque Is Torched in Israel," *Wall Street Journal*, October 4, 2011, http://online.wsj.com/news/articles/SB10001424052970204612504576608994254954306.

According to *Haaretz*, "The 'price-tag' policy was adopted by Israeli settlers and right-wing activists, intended to pressure the government away from making concessions regarding settlement building in the West Bank. Attacks of the sort usually occur after the dismantling of an outpost or similar event, and are often directed at Israeli Arabs, Palestinians and left-wing organizations." "Price Tag," *Haaretz*, http://www.haaretz.com/misc/tags/Price%20tag-1.477120.

killed. Eight Israeli settlers were killed and thirty-seven others injured by Palestinians in 2011. In 2012, for the first time since 1973, there were no casualties.[71] In 2013 three settlers and two members of the IDF were killed.[72]

In almost all circumstances, Palestinians, who know that they have little legal recourse and that the settlers are armed and protected by the IDF, either cannot or will not retaliate, trapping them into passively accepting insult and humiliation. In a series of reports, Yesh Din, a human rights organization, found that 90 percent of the complaints filed by Palestinians with the West Bank Israeli police force are either lost or closed.[73] "When convictions are made, Israeli citizens involved in such violent acts are handed light sentences."[74] Another report concludes that "the IDF does not view the protection of the Palestinian civilians as one of its missions.... Settlers perpetuating violence against Palestinians and their property know they are not likely to face any punitive action from the Israeli authorities for their crimes."[75] The Yesh Din report concludes that the violence is part of a "sophisticated, wider strategy designed to assert territorial domination over Palestinians in the West Bank.... According to international humanitarian law, as the occupying power in the Occupied Palestinian Territories (OPT), Israel is charged with ensuring the security and safety of the residents of the OPT. It has neglected this obligation for decades."*[76]

Indeed, there is no dearth of reports by high-profile organizations like Amnesty International and Human Rights Watch that have catalogued IDF and settler violations in the West Bank. Israel trashes such reports as biased, distorted, and, when necessary, anti-Semitic. There is no call within Israel itself for commissions to investigate the thousands of complaints filed and left to collect dust.[77] No report of any kind, no matter how damning of the indisputable and ongoing history of the settlements has more than a passing impact on Israeli public opinion, which is prone to believe that most complaints are simply concocted by Palestinians in their ceaseless efforts to be perceived as victims. Of course, Israeli Jews resent being called "occupiers," and worse still, "colonialists," but their actions and behaviors are well documented as characteristic of a colonial/settler society mentality.[78] Whatever

*"According to Yesh Din, the IDF and police are neither prepared nor willing to provide the necessary protection to Palestinians attacked by violent settlers. Law enforcement agencies display repeated failure to conduct proper investigations of these incidents. When convictions are made, Israeli citizens involved in such violent acts are handed light sentences." Yesh Din, "Criminal Accountability of Israeli Citizens," http://www.yesh-din.org/cat.asp?catid=3.

the argument, the fact remains that Palestinians are subject to the laws of occupation, applied judiciously, arbitrarily, or capriciously and with little accountability.*

No Jewish Israeli interviewees—religious or secular—regarded the settlements as a breach of international law. They accepted the arguments of successive governments that the provisions in the Geneva Convention IV Relative to the Protection of Civilian Persons in Time of War 1949 ("Fourth Geneva Convention")† and the UN charter that forbid an occupying power from moving its people into occupied territories are applicable *only* when the territory in question had prior status as a sovereign entity in its own right. They also do not see the ongoing construction as an obstacle to reconciliation. They repeated many times: Neither the Camp David nor the Annapolis initiatives set the halting of new construction settlement as a precondition for a resumption of negotiations; Mahmoud Abbas's demand was simply a red herring. If Palestinians were really serious about establishing their own state, Gilead Sher asks, why put *any* obstacles in the way, especially as the issue of settlements will be negotiated? On the basis of this logic, the Israelis conclude that Abbas's actions are designed to scuttle negotiation progress on all fronts, and they accept none of the blame. Jewish Israeli interviewees rejected out of hand the very idea that Israel could be the impediment to the peace process. On the contrary, Israel has actively promoted a final resolution to the conflict for over two decades. They did not see any contradiction between their efforts to promote the peace process and the construction of settlements for up to 500,000 Israeli Jews in the West Bank and the Judaization of East Jerusalem; no contradiction with the

*A Yesh Din study on law enforcement in the IDF reported in 2012 that "240 complaints and other reports ('notifications') were submitted to the Military Police Criminal Investigations Division (MPCID) regarding criminal offenses allegedly committed against Palestinians and their property in the West Bank and Gaza Strip by IDF soldiers . . . of the 240 complaints submitted, 103 investigations were opened—and one indictment served." Yesh Din, "Law Enforcement upon IDF Soldiers in the Territories: Figures for 2012," January 2013, http://www.yesh-din.org/userfiles/file/datasheets/Law%20Enforcement%20upon%20-%202012.pdf.

†Article 49(6) of the Fourth Geneva Convention also prohibits an occupying power from transferring parts of its own civilian population into the territory that it occupies. This prohibition has attained the status of customary international law. "A situation of military occupation prevails in the OPT. As the occupying power, Israel is bound under international humanitarian law by a set of obligations provided for in the Hague Regulations of 1907 (annexed to the Hague Convention IV Respecting the Laws and Customs of War on Land 1907), which are recognized as forming part of customary international law, and the Fourth Geneva Convention, to which Israel is a High Contracting Party." See "Convention (IV) relative to the Protection of Civilian Persons in Time of War, Geneva, 12 August 1949," International Committee of the Red Cross ICRC, https://www.icrc.org/applic/ihl/ihl.nsf/INTRO/380?OpenDocument.

acceleration of both developments during Netanyahu's first term and the even greater acceleration during his second term.[79]

Neither were Jewish Israeli interviewees well informed on the actual number of settlers in East Jerusalem and the West Bank around Jerusalem or in the West Bank itself and sometimes were unable to differentiate among them. All were at a loss to seriously pursue a conversation about the illegal "outposts" spread across the West Bank and the government's reluctance to dismantle them, even under the order of Israel's own courts. None condoned the outposts, and all agreed that they should be dismantled if so ordered by the court, but none suggested that the government should dismantle in the absence of a court ruling. Once land is swapped and borders set in a final status agreement, they assumed settlements outside the new Israel would be dismantled and settlers evacuated.

Estimates of how many settlers would have to be evacuated under any plausible agreement range from 60,000 to 150,000. The most commonly cited number is 100,000.*[80]

A large majority of Israeli Jews now oppose the land swaps that would necessitate evacuations. In the July 2013 Peace Index poll, some 62.5 percent of Jewish Israeli respondents said they would *not* support a permanent peace deal even if it included security arrangements for Israel, the creation of a demilitarized Palestinian state, international guarantees, a declaration by Palestinians that the conflict was over, and withdrawal to the 1967 borders with territorial swaps.† Even if it is specified that Israel would keep its major

*In October 2013, the UN estimated there were 500,000 to 650,000 in the West Bank, including East Jerusalem. The settler population living in the West Bank (excluding East Jerusalem) had almost tripled since 1993. During the past decade (2003–13), it grew at an average yearly rate of 5.3 percent, compared with 1.8 percent for the Israeli population as a whole. The settler population in East Jerusalem also grew by approximately one third between 1993 and 2012. Since the signature of the Oslo Accords, there has been an increase of approximately 270,000 settlers in the West Bank, including East Jerusalem. UN General Assembly, Sixty-seventh Session, Offical Records, Item 53, *Israeli Settlements in the Occupied Palestinian Territory, Including East Jerusalem, and the Occupied Syrian Golan*, prepared by the Office of the United Nations High Commissioner for Human Rights pursuant to General Assembly resolution 66/78, A/67/375, September 18, 2012.

†"Under the conditions of a permanent peace agreement with security arrangements, a demilitarized Palestinian state, international guarantees and a Palestinian declaration of the end of conflict, 77 percent of Israeli Jews oppose recognition of the Palestinian 'right of return' involving the return of a small number of refugees and financial compensation for the rest; 63 percent oppose withdrawal to the 1967 borders with land swaps; 58 percent oppose dismantling settlements while leaving Ariel, Ma'ale Adumim, and the Gush Etzion bloc intact; and 50 percent oppose transferring Arab neighborhoods in Jerusalem to the Palestinian Authority along with a special arrangement for the Holy Places." Democracy Institute, "Peace Index: July 2013," http://en.idi.org.il/media/2668402/Peace%20Index-July%202013.pdf.

West Bank settlement blocs as well as Ma'ale Adumim and the city of Ariel, 58 percent said they were still opposed to land swaps. (Only three years earlier, in the 2010 poll, 51 percent had *supported* such a swap.)[81] Moreover, about half of the Jewish Israeli respondents in 2013 opposed a deal that would include the transfer of the Palestinian neighborhoods of Jerusalem to Palestinian control with "special arrangements" for the Old City holy places (i.e., would reject the Clinton Parameters).

In fact, another poll, conducted on behalf of Ariel University by Geocartography Knowledge Group (GCKG), shows "The overwhelming majority of Israeli Jews support Israel extending its sovereignty over some or all of the West Bank, either unilaterally or as part of an agreement."[82] Specifically, the survey found that 35 percent of respondents favored the government annexing the *entire* West Bank, 24 percent only the settlement blocs, 20 percent no annexations without an agreement with the Palestinians, and 12 percent no sovereignty over any of the West Bank. A poll conducted a year earlier had almost identical results. In the wording of the pollsters, "about 80 percent of the public supports extending Israeli sovereignty to the territories of Judea and Samaria."

Most Israeli Jews believe that any peace deal that involves evacuating settlements should be submitted to voters in a referendum for approval,[83] and only 49 percent of Israeli Jews think Palestinian Israeli citizens should be permitted to vote in such a referendum.[84] The increasingly hard-line, uncompromising attitudes of Israeli Jews reveal the demographic shift toward right-leaning populations, especially among the ultraorthodox and West Bank settlers.

For Palestinians, every tender for settlement construction deepens their resentment and compounds their distrust as Israeli leaders seem to say one thing and do another. General Ephraim Sneh could not have put the point better. Not even trying to hide his contempt for Netanyahu and the settlements, he said, "I am a medical doctor. I'm a specialist in internal medicine. The West Bank is the lungs. The settlements are the metastases of the cancer. There is a point, if the lungs are full of metastases, you can't breathe anymore. That's what they want to achieve. The metastases will replace the breathing tissue of the lungs, so it will collapse. That's an analogy. They want to expand the metastases so much that the lungs will not be viable any more. That's it! That's what they want to achieve. Are they going to achieve it? Not yet. There is still time to stop it."[85]

For at least a dozen years, one pundit after another has warned that unless the settlements are halted soon, the window for a two-state solution will close. They have been saying this for years, and they still are. The late Ron Pundak, one of the architects of Oslo II, told me in November 2011, "We are getting closer to the tipping point. I've always said that we still have time, that we still are not there, and now I'm asking myself whether we are very close to it, or maybe, again, with hindsight we'll understand that we already passed it, because it's true that at some point of time the ability to cut the two nations demographically and geographically from each other will be so difficult that everyone will do everything in order to prevent or preempt it."[86]

Pundak believed it might be too late—but he also believed that there is no viable alternative to the two-state solution, so it is never too late, it *cannot be* too late. Every Israeli interviewee agreed with that sentiment. General Sneh also agreed, but he worried about the disposition of some settlers: "The radical minority of the settlers, the radical violent minority, maybe anywhere in the region of ten thousand to thirty thousand, will not go easily. Many of them are registered members of the Likud. In the primaries they have a critical mass of votes. . . . Every MK [member] of the Likud who wants to be reelected needs the votes of the settlers . . . so they take hard-line positions, just because they want their votes. So [Netanyahu] is the slave of the MKs, who are the slaves of party members, and he is surrounded by hard-liners. This government will dig us deeper into isolation and, down the road, to becoming a pariah state."

Within Likud, Netanyahu's influence is waning.[87] In 2012 settlers accounted for 30 percent of *new* Likud party members.[88] The politics are daunting. If no Israeli leader will stand before his public and say there will be no undivided Jerusalem, is there one who will say that Israel has to evacuate perhaps up to a hundred thousand of its citizens from their homes in the West Bank and repatriate them to Israel? Who knows how many members of the Knesset have family members who are settlers or are the offspring of settlers? Who realizes that the network of state ministries, institutions, NGOs and assorted agencies, even the Jewish Agency and the World Zionist Organization, have been instrumental in channeling billions of dollars to Israel, encouraging its citizens to become settlers, subsidizing the settlements and new construction? Such networks do not suddenly dissolve. The bureaucracies they have relied on will not suddenly self-immolate; rather, they will find ways to wage bureaucratic "warfare," obfuscating evacuation agendas, putting obstacles in the way of orderliness, jamming the works. What may appear achievable when it is outlined before any action is taken will turn out to be a labyrinth of bewilderments. Who pauses for a moment and reflects that 70 percent of Jewish Israelis were born into a country in which close to 4.4 percent of its citizens (closer to 10 percent if you include East Jerusalem) live in territories another people claim as their homeland?[89] After almost fifty years of occupation, most Jewish Israelis* consider it as normal as the Uzis the teenage soldiers nonchalantly carry around. Since the Second Intifada most Jewish Israelis have rarely† set foot in the occupied territories and rarely see West Bank Palestinians—a people they have been trained to kill. Who sees the similarities in the behaviors of two people, each with some of the land but wanting all of it, pursuant to their respective divine mandates? Pinchas Wallerstein, one of the most influential settler leaders, sees and understands all of this. Mayor of the Binyamin Regional Council from 1979 to 2008, the former head of the Yesha Council, the umbrella organization for an estimated 350,000 settlers, and one of the early founders of the right-wing, ultraconservative Gush Emunim, he now works for the Amana settlement.[90] "If this new Palestinian state," he says, "insisted on there being no settlements within its borders on the West Bank and an undetermined number of settlers would have to be evacuated, it will not pass parliament." Wallerstein blames "the intervention of the international community" for a lot of the problems, because it gives Palestinians and their Arab sponsors "false hopes."[91] Israel will not divide Jerusalem and it will not evacuate settlers from the West Bank. Period.

Dani Dayan,[92] the chairman of the Yesha Council until 2013, and presently its foreign envoy, seconds his predecessor's view. Dayan loses no sleep worrying about the fate of the settlements. He says bluntly, "Evacuation of settlers is simply not in the cards. . . . If an agreement is signed along the lines of the so-called two-state solution with some land swaps, the minimum of Jewish persons that will be affected is, in my opinion, at least 150,000, more or less. I don't believe any agreement, for instance, will be reached that includes Ariel. But an agreement is impossible to achieve; it's purely theoretical. The Yeshiva is aware of the chatter that two-state proposals bandied about could call for evacuation of some 100,000; it's in the back

*The percentages of Israeli Jews born during the occupation (measured from 1967 to 2012) are as follows: 0–14 years old: 27.1 percent; 15–24 years old: 15.7 percent; 25–54 years old: 37.8 percent. Index Mundi, "Israel Demographics Profile 2014," http://www.indexmundi.com/israel/demographics_profile.html.

†After the separation barrier was erected, it became illegal for Israeli Jews to enter that part of the West Bank within its encirclement.

of our minds, but it has never been formally discussed because we sincerely believe it's not a feasible solution."[93]

Asked whether their vision and their future might possibly be in jeopardy, Wallerstein and Dayan sympathetically dismiss such political naïveté. And why should they waste time wondering about the daunting technical problems of evacuation, or the possible use of violence by opponents of any ordered evacuation, or the overall impact on Israeli culture? Such concerns are *beyond* hypothetical. The settlements are a fire wall, and they will hold. Such adamancy is the reason most interviewees agreed that the constellation of political parties that would be required to approve the evacuation of settlers—at the very least, a moderate right/center consortium that could withstand vociferous opposition from the National Orthodox, perhaps the ultraorthodox, and various Greater Israel parties—is not yet in our galaxy.

Surveying the political scene prior to the Israeli elections in January 2013, Sneh wasn't sure that Netanyahu would win reelection. He did win, easily, but his coalition limited his ability to impose his will on the cabinet, and he no longer had the clout to unilaterally deal with Palestine as he wished. Netanyahu's Likud party is generally labeled right-wing, but among the right wing there are many factions, each with a differing agenda, all contending for the same broad bloc of votes. Their politics is therefore driven not by party platforms but by opportunism: To what degree will a party betray its platform in order to join a governing coalition and enjoy the whiffs of power in the air, including, most importantly, ministerial posts? Other parties, either center or left, are not immune from the same expediency. In 2013 thirty-four parties contested 120 seats in the Knesset. Each party in the Knesset, no matter how miniscule its representation, could be the decisive one for the coalition. This coalition that emerges does not reflect a majority consensus on any given issue. It is a hybrid, perhaps a number of hybrids, connected by the perfume of power. And it is always in flux. Hence the frequency of elections. It is a repetitious cycle, one that called for some reform, and in March 2014 the threshold for a party's representation in the Knesset was raised to 3.25 percent of the vote.

> > < <

Dani Dayan says he told Netanyahu's predecessor, Ehud Olmert, before Olmert flew to Annapolis in 2007 that "from a technical point of view, it is possible to evacuate 150,000 people. But that will shatter the backbone of Israeli society."[94]

"It's not just [settlers] leaving their homes," Dayan said when I spoke with him.

> There were many fourth-generation settlers. It's the only thing they know. More than that, we are more committed than any other segment in the society to our mission. The mission is establishing Greater Israel, what we see as the raison d'être of Israel, of our lives. The despair that we will feel, a betrayal by Israel will have tremendous consequences. Our plan is we're not moving from our homes, and if you want to bring us out, you're going to have to send in somebody from the IDF to say, "Here, move," and when people in Jerusalem and other places see the IDF with guns to our heads, you are not going to be in government—you, the prime minister; you, the minister of housing; you, the member of Knesset. The list is long. We will not collaborate in any way with the implementation, but you have to also know one additional thing. After the disengagement from Gaza of 2005, the whole leadership in Yesha Council for Judea and Samaria has changed. The fringe elements that do not respect any local leadership are larger than ever. You will have to take account of that. You do not give an order and 100,000 obey. We have our limits, our moral red lines on how can you oppose, but they are not everyone's red lines. They have no formal or other obligation to obey my leadership.

What about violence? "We're arming ourselves," Dayan continued, "and we are not moving from our community. It will never be on the table. There is no political will."[95]

Like Dani Dayan, Tamar Asraf is a card-carrying member of the political elite of the settlement movement, the spokeswoman for the Binyamin Regional Council. She lives in Eli, one of a number of communities in Psagot, a settlement about twenty minutes from Jerusalem. Binyamin is the largest regional council in Israel, comprising forty-four communities and 55,000 residents in the hills and mountains north of Jerusalem, from the border of the West Bank to the Jordan Valley. Asraf reports and the visitor's eye corroborates that most of the Jewish residents are young couples with children. Asraf and her community are not attached to material goods, which are luxuries that only impede dedication to the profound cause for which they have been chosen to be the foot soldiers. She says, "99.9 percent of the people who live in Judea and Samaria live here because they are connected deeply to our historical narrative; they are Zionist pioneers doing whatever it takes to ensure the safety of Israel. People came here because they feel they are a part of the Israeli state."[96]

The settlers' life may be simple in its outward manifestations, but not in its social complexity and unity. Small communities run with all the appurtenances of local democracy, comradeship, a common sense of purpose, and always the magnificent lure of the seemingly empty land.

The communities that would be targeted for evacuation in a two-state solution believe there is nothing the government could give them that would compensate for losing what they have. And what they have is worth fighting for. Asraf says the numbers supporting the "price tag" movement are growing.[97] They will struggle to the end to stay where they are, "demonstrating, taking political actions, whatever it would take. That would be the majority. A really small percentage would agree to leave their homes, perhaps no more than one hundred or two hundred families, if they got compensation in return." For decades the settlers have moved onto the land with the encouragement and financial backing of successive governments. Today the growth continues. Asraf says, "The members of our government live on another planet. No one in Israel has any illusion that seventy thousand people will just pack and leave. Whoever is talking about achieving peace now is a dreamer, or hallucinatory."

She believes that if Israel abandons the settlers in these hills (of course, this is not the way an evacuation would be organized), surrounded by Palestinians, they would be slaughtered the following day. "In every community surrounding us," she says, "you will find that people have been slaughtered, killed, shot at; we know our Palestinian neighbors, what they are capable of doing." (Here is more testimony of the sustaining power of myth, embedded fear masquerading as reason. Recall B'Tselem's casualty data in chapter one: from the first intifada in 1987 until April 2014, nearly 10,000 Palestinians and approximately 1,636 Israelis were killed.[98] So much for Palestinians rampantly "slaughtering" Jews.)

Asraf proposes a different solution to the conflict, a different "peace," one seen as naive in the eyes of those outside the settlement community. It is unyielding on the issue of land but sufficient, she believes, to keep Palestinians content with what they have.

Asraf's solution is based on the tripartite division of the West Bank as established by the Oslo II agreement, described in chapter 3. (The data she used in her configuration was invariably incorrect.) Her idea of a fair and just settlement: expand the autonomy of Areas A and B "so that a Palestinian can drive freely"—no army checkpoint, roadblocks, or circuitous routes, never having to be aware of an Israeli army presence—and "giving Palestinians more civil rights and better lives than they can get today." Under her scenario no Israeli should live in Area A or B, and they should not be able to enter without permits; the IDF should enter Area B only for "security" purposes (which is the law at present but has not prevented the proliferation of illegal outposts according to Israeli law).[99] She believes that in Area C, which comprises 61 percent of the West Bank, about 50,000 Palestinians and 350,000 Israelis live on threads of land winding in and out of Areas A and B. (This is incorrect, as 297,900 Palestinians and some 320,000 settlers live in Areas A and B.)[100] Since most of the settler communities are in Area C, and all of Area C is under the military *and civil* control of Israel, Area C is de facto Israel. Thus Asraf believes the best two-state solution is obvious: Israel goes ahead and *annexes* Area C. De facto is then de jure (under Israeli law). In exchange, the fifty thousand Palestinians (an incorrect number, of course) living in Area C would be offered full Israeli citizenship equivalent in all respects to that of the other Palestinian Israeli citizens. She doesn't feel that these additional Palestinians would interfere with the demographic balance and pose a risk to the Jewishness of Israel. She says, "[This annexation] will do away with any semblance of apartheid, because in the C territories Palestinians have fewer rights than their brothers in Areas A and B. But if they were citizens they would have the same rights as every Israeli. If they are willing to agree to such an arrangement, they are welcome to go to the A and B territories. This situation will make everyone's life better and no one would be forced out of their homes."

Tamar Asraf's plan would yield Palestine just 39 percent of the 22 percent earmarked for a Palestinian state, seven million people packed into a space no larger than Washington DC's Beltway. Her plan for Israel to annex 61 percent of the West Bank is extremely improbable—but not out of step with the third-largest party in the Knesset, Jewish Home, which advocates annexing 60 percent of the West Bank.

There is no doubt that Asraf believes passionately in her proposal. There are no theatrics in her presentation or personality, no messianic zealotry, just a core unshakable belief. It is sad that she thinks of Palestinians as a people whose humanity extends only to slaughtering other people, especially people like her, and believes that their aspirations for self-determination should be satisfied by accepting Areas A and B (and Gaza) as their "state," one without actual sovereignty or any geographical contiguity at all.

> > < <

The settlers and their avid supporters are a powerful force in Israeli politics and society, but they are by no means an absolute majority. Many Israeli interviewees took a more pragmatic, less ideological view of the settlements, assuming that those outside the perimeters of the large settlement blocs might have to be abandoned someday, and their inhabitants relocated. There was an implicit undercurrent of resentment about the cost of the settlements (an annual financial subsidy in the range of two billion shekels, or half a billion dollars), especially in light of Israel's own harsh economic realities, dramatically brought home when over 400,000 Israelis took to the streets of Tel Aviv in 2011—the biggest turnout for anything in Israel's history—to peacefully protest the high cost of living and shortage of affordable housing.[101] But even these more pragmatic observers did *not* condemn the settlements as a moral blight on the land, nor did they condemn the frequent seizure of privately owned Palestinian land. For most, the settlements are simply part of the Israel they grew up with.

For decades, settlers were perceived as securing the land of Israel, living in idyllic communities with a sense of togetherness, and there was a bond between Israelis living inside and outside the recognized borders. Today they are just as likely to be considered as bargaining chips at best, facts on the ground that strengthen Israeli leaders' hand in negotiations. In fact, the settlers are rarely referred to as *people* living in *homes*, second- and third-generation *communities* with a social nexus providing common values and a sense of purpose and aspiration, gathered together in their synagogues and giving thanks for the privilege of doing God's work. Instead, they are prone to be viewed as a monolithic, impersonal mass, no longer sacrosanct. Surveys confirm this shift in attitudes regarding settlements and settlers.[102]

Danny Tirza, who lives in Kfar Adumim, a small community in the same council as Tamar Asraf's Psagot, disagrees with Asraf on the settlers' willingness to move. "We said to the Palestinians, 'Don't look for the settlements,'" he said, referring to the Annapolis negotiations during the tenure of Ehud Olmert. "We promise you that on the day that we will have an agreed border, we will evacuate these settlements . . . because we know that Israelis cannot live in Palestine for security reasons. It will be difficult, but as a man that lives on the ground, I meet many Israelis, most of the Israelis that are living in these settlements, and most of them are ready to get evacuated from their houses for a real peace agreement."[103]

For Hagit Ofran, one of the Peace Now leaders, context is everything. She said:

> If the majority of the Knesset and the majority of the public support an FSA, and Israelis understand the benefits they will reap when Israel makes peace with the Arab world, Israel would be hailed across the world as

peacemakers. In such circumstances, the Israeli public would be very supportive of the necessary evictions. Settlers who are ideologically or religiously motivated may say, "We will protest against it." But they have to deal with the fact that they are protesting the decision of the majority of Israelis. Eventually, they will pack their things and move back. Only a minority will not accept it. We saw it in Gaza and they did not use violence. If some use violence against the IDF, whatever support they have in Israel will quickly evaporate.[104]

"I can promise you," says Dov Weisglass, a key Netanyahu adviser during his first government, "that the majority of Israeli public opinion would stand behind the government in an effort to evacuate the settlers."[105] He even believes that the Israelis will say "good riddance" to the settlers, seeing them more as parasites than as the citizens called on to make the greatest sacrifice for the greater good.

The settlers were enticed by successive governments to move to the rough-and-tumble West Bank; now they would be called upon to leave it all behind. Can we reasonably expect them to embrace a resolution of this issue without being consulted and drawn into the process—without granting respect to their *narrative*? Excluding them from any peace process would be a grievous omission. Successful negotiations require having *all* the players at the table. Excluding the settlers because some of them are "extreme" is a prescription for making more of them extreme. Their inclusion must *not* be contingent on their meeting a range of preconditions.

Gilead Sher is a founding member of Blue White Future,[106] a group on the center left of the Israeli political spectrum dedicated to an Israel that is "Jewish *and* democratic"* and actively working on an initiative to provide housing for evacuated settlers. Sher believes that dealing with the settlements is a straightforward "intellectual exercise." Every single one of the 125 settlements[107] can be easily demarcated as being on one side of a negotiated border or the other, and then swapped accordingly. Sher ignores the distinction between settlements—infrastructure—and the people whose lives would be radically changed if such a heartless division were made. And

* According to Tal Herman, Director of the Democracy Institute, in the last four years Peace Index polls reveal there has been a decline in the importance of the three components to Israeli Jews. Now only 37 percent say both components are equally important to them; about 33 percent say the Jewish component is most important and about 33 percent say "being democratic" is the most important component.

"Tamar Hermann on Israeli Public Opinion," Israel Policy Forum, October 10 2013, http://www.israelpolicyforum.org/news/tamar-hermann-israeli-public-opinion.

Tal Becker suggests that since the problem is the extremes on each end of the political spectrum, the answer is to bring together the two centers—left and right—in which case "we're home free."[108] He assumes that the marginalized extremes will somehow get lost in the political wilderness while the two centers hold firm—a dynamic that is not confirmed by history. More likely is that the extremes will consume the middle, because at the end of the day it's the extremes that are more motivated, prepared to sacrifice more and to pursue their ends with relentless persistence.[109]

All in all, the responses of pragmatic Jewish Israeli interviewees were surprisingly desultory, occasionally close to hand-wringing but with an implicit confidence that any government would sign an FSA only after a stringent cost-benefit analysis of the called-for evacuations and that the failure of any set of parameters to pass that test would sink that agreement. Most Israelis seem to be confident that Israeli ingenuity will come up with some solution, once the chips are really down. Some wondered about finding appropriate work for the settlers, given that their skill base is limited and that they would be moving from a small, hermetic environment to a more dynamic and individualistic society. What kinds of counseling would be provided? Most interviewees talked dispassionately about how the evacuations could be conducted on the ground, with estimates of the time necessary to complete the job ranging from ten months to five years. A few wondered about the monumental costs. Who would run the evacuations on the ground? The IDF? Palestinian security forces? Both working together? How well would that work? And what about collusion between the settlers and some members of the IDF? "The settlements," Robert Danin says, "provide a disproportionate role in providing the Elite Officer Corps of the IDF."[110] (By one estimate, the rate at which settlers join the IDF is 60 percent higher than the countrywide rate.[111]) "And you have to be careful what you can ask of them. Like the debate about the ultraorthodox: Do you really want them in the army? The ultraorthodox used to be resented for their exemption from military service, but now that they have lost their exemption,* people are wondering where their ultimate allegiance might

*"The compulsory draft, even in its limited scope applying to a minority of yeshiva students, will only take effect in four years (after the next elections) and will start off with large-scale exemptions. Close to 30,000 yeshiva students ages 22–28 will be immediately exempted from army service. Similarly, close to 20,000 additional yeshiva students who are currently between 18 and 22 years old will receive full exemptions at age 24." Uri Regev, "Haredi Draft Law: Problems and Concerns," *Jerusalem Post*, March 19, 2014, http://www.jpost.com/Opinion/Op-Ed-Contributors/Haredi-draft-law-Problems-and-concerns-345905. For background information on the issue, see Library of Congress,

come down in a crunch. Which is supreme, the law of the land or the dictates of their rabbis and their religion? The question would pose serious problems for any evacuation." But for Danin, most disturbing are the "whispers" he hears in the corridors of power. He asks, "At what point do the internal politics of Israel [coalesce] . . . so that an Israeli prime minister is in a position to order the military to evacuate by force a certain number of Israelis, and be confident that the army will carry out the order?" The question raises nightmarish scenarios.

How would daily media coverage affect public support for evacuations? The Heisenberg uncertainty principle states that the act of observation changes the nature of the thing being observed. Streaming video coverage of evacuees being forced out of their homes, Twitter and social media and ancillary distortions and misinformation, settler demonstrations, settlers lined up protecting their properties and facing a formidable IDF with all its paraphernalia, confrontations—all the stuff of video images will impact Israeli viewers, *even those who agree with the evacuations*, in unpredictable ways. The political fallout would also be highly unpredictable.* Several Israeli interviewees accepted the likelihood that a minority within the settler community might resort to violence, a prospect that they viewed with disgust but believed would have to be answered with violence. But once violence is met with violence, things have a nasty habit of getting out of control. Nevertheless, despite all the questions and caveats and concerns and even fear, they disagreed with Dani Dayan's belief that the strife of evacuations would "shatter the backbone of Israeli society." Macro estimates, Roby Nathanson told me, that 30 percent of the West Bank settlers are ideological. (It is actually closer to 40 percent.[112]) "Ideological settlers," says Oded Eran, "are the toughest because they were further away from the '67 line [that is, deeper inside the West Bank], for ideological reasons. . . . There will be a fierce opposition, meaning that there will be a small number who will take the law into their own hands. You could see violence between the settlers and the

---

"Israel: Supreme Court Decision Invalidating the Law on Haredi Military Draft Postponement," http://www.loc.gov/law/help/il-haredi-military-draft/haredi-military-draft.php.

*In the "people's revolt" in Egypt and the massive demonstrations in Tahrir Square calling for the resignation of Hosni Mubarak, social media as a tool of mass organization and communication played the decisive role in instigating the protests in the first place. Since then social media have been used to orchestrate "spontaneous" mass demonstrations for political change in other countries and have changed the relationship between the governed and their government. The latter must gauge the possible extent of "the people's" response to actions, usually repressive, that they would otherwise have simply imposed.

IDF and violence between settlers and Palestinian population. This is going to be a long, painful and expensive operation."[113]

A Macro poll conducted on behalf of Blue White Future in August 2013 found that 30 percent of the residents of West Bank settlements outside the major blocs would evacuate for compensation even if there were no peace deal with the Palestinians. Nearly 50 percent of the hundred thousand settlers living in areas likely to become part of a Palestinian state under a peace agreement would voluntarily evacuate after an agreement, while 40 percent would not.[114]

Among the settlers willing to evacuate voluntarily without a peace agreement, the survey found that three quarters would relocate to areas within the pre-1967 borders and the rest to the settlement blocs. After an agreement, 55 percent would relocate to the settlement blocs and 45 percent within the pre-1967 borders. The age group of settlers most willing to relocate voluntarily before a peace agreement in exchange for compensation is fifty to fifty-nine. The age group least willing to do so is eighteen to twenty-nine. Of those willing to relocate prior to a peace deal, 12.6 percent define themselves as religious and 45.4 percent as secular. Some 22.4 percent identify as ultraorthodox and 35.5 percent as traditional. The results are broadly similar to polls taken in 2008 and 2012.[115]

Polls, surveys, and surmises aside, an Israeli prime minister contemplating an evacuation of settlers would have to ask: What arrangements have been made for their accommodation and how will they find employment? Do I fully understand the economic and social consequences of evacuating anywhere between sixty to a hundred thousand settlers? Of the unavoidable reconfigurations of the national polity? Of the cost? Of possible social upheavals? Have I fully thought through the security implications? Can I be absolutely sure that I can rely on *all* of the IDF falling into line, come what may? Have I fully considered the possible emotional backlash that could pose hard to predict and contain challenges to the country's social fabric? Have I found a way to balance the risks and uncertainties? Am I prepared to cash in my political career? And when you aggregate these considerations, wouldn't a prime minister not be inclined to ask himself/herself: Why, exactly, should I take such a huge risk, and for what?

Furthermore, what party leader, trying to form a governing coalition, would put the evacuation of settlers on the front burner? Will there ever be such a leader? Such a coalition? Before trying to assemble such a coalition, the presumptive prime minister would have to have the stature to activate all the institutional levers at his disposal, some of which have been sitting on the peace shelf for decades, and put into motion the initial steps that *might* eventually lead to evacuations. He would have to test the resolve of his generals down the chain of command to the troop level and have the unambiguous and aggressive support of all key international players, who together would form a board of overseers who could set a time frame for each component of the process; establish a multinational police force that would work side by side with the IDF and the PASF to monitor the process itself; and create feedback mechanisms so that problems with implementation would be identified before they began to ensure that both the Israeli prime minister and Palestinian leadership are singing from the same songbook.

Complex and complicated? Beyond calculation. Career threatening? Definitely. Necessary anyway? Only if the cost-benefit analysis clearly comes out on the plus side—and how can it, since the peace benefits would be possible but by no means certain, while the social and monetary costs would be huge and potentially crippling?

Netanyahu resolved the matter to his own satisfaction in March 2014. Although Israel, he said, would not be able to extend its sovereignty under an FSA to encompass all of the settlements, he was adamant that "there will be no act of evacuation." In short, settlers would have a choice, either to stay put or voluntarily evacuate.[116] However it is difficult to differentiate between what Netanyahu says for political expedience and what he really believes.

> > < <

Any discussion of settlements encompasses two that pose particular difficulties: Ma'ale Adumim and Ariel. For Israelis, Ma'ale Adumim is not even a "settlement" in the traditional sense. With a population of forty thousand Jewish residents, it's effectively a suburb four miles east of Jerusalem. Its boundaries stretch almost all the way to Jericho, approximately 10.9 miles away. As part of what is sometimes called the "Jerusalem envelope,"* it serves as "high ground" protection for Jerusalem, creating "defensible borders." Israel is adamant: Ma'ale Adumim is nonnegotiable. It must remain as part

*"East Jerusalem and the adjacent West Bank 'settlement blocs' of Giv'at Ze'ev (extending to the edges of the Palestinian city of Ramallah) and Ma'ale Adumim (extending almost halfway to Jericho) are all on the west side of Israel's Barrier in what is sometimes referred to as the 'Jerusalem envelope.' This means that Palestinian East Jerusalem is separated and to an increasing degree sealed off from the rest of the West Bank." Americans for Peace Now, "Settlements 101," http://peacenow.org/settlements-101.html.

of Israel.* In 1994, while in the midst of hammering out the details of the Oslo Accords, Prime Minister Yitzhak Rabin declared that a "united Jerusalem" as the capital of Israel, would include Ma'ale Adumim under Israeli sovereignty,† and every prime minister since, including Netanyahu (in both tenures), has reiterated this position. To fortify Ma'ale Adumim and put the issue to rest, the government wants to build a residential complex with thousands of homes along the Expanded E1 corridor, a largely empty patch of the West Bank that would connect suburb and city. (Rabin "provided then-mayor Benny Kashriel with the annexation documents.")[117] With E1 in place—Ma'ale could be grouped with other large settlements like Alfei Menashe, Modi'in Illit, and Beitar Illit in a land swap with the Palestinians.

Palestinian interviewees insisted that there will be no agreement that deeds Ma'ale Adumim to Israel, because without it the Palestinian state

*For a comprehensive overview of Ma'ale Adumim, see Palestine Liberation Organization Negotiations Affairs Department, Negotiation Support Unit, "On-going Settlement Activity in the Adumim 'Bloc' and the E-1 Area," December 2012, http://www.nad-plo.org/userfiles/file/fact%20sheet/Maale_Adumim_E1_Dec2012_en.pdf.

According to the PLO's Negotiations Affairs Department: (NAD)—"Since 1975, when Ma'ale Adumim was first established . . . Israel has built an elaborate road network to connect Ma'ale Adumim and its satellite settlements with one another and with West Jerusalem, as well as a major transnational highway (Road #1) running through Ma'ale Adumim eastward to the Jordan Valley.

"In order to strengthen these settlements and facilitate their future expansion, Israel is currently building a Wall around Ma'ale Adumim and its satellite settlements. Penetrating 14 [kilometers] (8.6 miles) east of the 1967 border, the Wall will effectively annex the Adumim settlements to Israel, incorporating 58 kilometers of Palestinian land, complete the encirclement of Palestinian East Jerusalem, and cut the West Bank in half. . . . Israel has developed an ambitious expansion plan known as 'E-1.' The plan is to be built on 12,442 dunams (3,110 acres) of Palestinian land belonging to the villages of Anata, At-Tor, Issawiya, Abu Dis, and Al-Eizariya." The PLO's NAD document goes on to say that Building housing units in E1, connecting the Ma'ale Adumim bloc to Jerusalem, would make it impossible to connect the West Bank cities of Ramallah and Bethlehem to East Jerusalem. In short, it would effectively bisect the West Bank and sever the physical link between the Palestinian territories and Jerusalem, ensuring that a Palestinian state would be noncontiguous, an almost-fatal blow to its viability and in all likelihood the end of a two-state solution. For Israel, building on E1 is crucial to consolidating its hold over the whole of Jerusalem and having a security buffer in the east.

Steve Erlanger, "West Bank Land, Empty but Full of Meaning," *New York Times*, December 17, 2012, http://www.nytimes.com/2012/12/18/world/middleeast/e1-on-west-bank-is-empty-but-full-of-meaning.html?pagewanted=all&_r=0.

†"Jerusalem and outlying areas cannot be defined by us as a political issue or as a security issue," Rabin declared soon after taking office in 1992. "United Jerusalem under Israeli sovereignty will remain our capital forever. For us it is the heart and the soul of the Jewish people." Foundation for Middle East Peace, "Rabin Builds on the Vision of a Permanent Jewish City," *Settlement Report* 4, no. 7 (February 1994), http://www.fmep.org/reports/special-reports/special-report-on-israeli-settlement-in-the-occupied-territories-1/rabin-builds-on-the-vision-of-a-permanent-jewish-city.

cannot be contiguous.* "Ma'ale Adumim," Sabri Saidam says, "destroys the topography of Jerusalem, encircles Arabs and cuts Jerusalem into a number of entities. There is a link [E1] associated with Ma'ale Adumim, which Israel wants to build, creating a greater Ma'ale Adumim. And Israel wants to expand other settlements so Jerusalem is totally isolated from the West Bank. Ramallah and Bethlehem would be cut off from the capital, making the contiguous Palestinian state . . . virtually impossible."[118]

At Annapolis, Abu Ala stood his ground on Ma'ale Adumim and added a new argument. "In one track of our negotiations with Condoleezza Rice," he says, "Rice said in front of Tzipi Livni: 'Abu Ala, I can understand your position regarding Ariel, but why is it the same regarding Ma'ale Adumim?' I told her, 'Ma'ale Adumim is even more of a danger for us than Ariel.' She said, 'Why?' I told her, 'Look, Jerusalem is not a holy place for us only. Jerusalem also is the most important resource for our economy. We call it our petrol. If Jerusalem is open to the east, I expect no less than 1,500,000 tourists to come to East Jerusalem each year. Now, all of them will come through Israel [by way of the E1 corridor] and will not even spend one shekel for a bottle of Coca-Cola in the Palestinian areas, and then they will leave. Without Ma'ale Adumim, no Palestinian state will be viable. She didn't respond."[119†]

Danny Yatom dismisses the Palestinians' arguments. "It's a question of a few kilometers," he says. "What we suggested is that by building bridges and tunnels, the Palestinians will be able to drive through the Jewish area. It is very easy to build infrastructure that you will be able to drive freely through those places without meeting or seeing any Israeli."[120]

Of course, building infrastructure is not the main point for the Palestinians. For them it is not about bricks and mortar. Even if East Jerusalem is the Palestinian capital in a two-state solution, one can say with a fair degree of certainty that Ma'ale Adumim will fall within Israel's borders and the

*Saed Bannoura, "E.U. Warns Israel Against Connecting Ma'ale Adumim with Jerusalem," IMEMC, December 23, 201 http://www.imemc.org/article/6272. The article provides EU commentary on "Israeli intentions to create two networks of roads that would separate Palestinian and Israeli traffic from each other. One network would link West and East Jerusalem from Jerusalem to Ma'ale Adumim in East Jerusalem, and would also run from the north to the south in order to link settlements in the northern part of the West Bank with Jerusalem and other settlements in the south. The experts also believe that the second network of roads would be used by the Palestinians linking Ramallah with Bethlehem, and in the future linking the southern areas of West Jerusalem with the Jericho area via a bypass road that keeps Palestinian traffic from approaching Ma'ale Adumim. The EU said that such projects would foil any chances for the two-state solution.

†In the first draft of a letter to Condoleezza Rice on August 25, 2008, Abu Ala sets out in detail the PLO's understanding of where the negotiations stood.

Palestinians are going to come out with the short end of the stick. An expectation that Palestinians would forgo their claim to Ma'ale Adumim, which they regard as being integral to the continuity of their state, is indicative of the embedded asymmetry of power in this conflict. At the end of the day Israel holds all the instruments of power. If the government does not get its way in negotiations, it can impose its will in other ways. Even when the 2013–14 talks were under way, the government had begun to reconfigure the E1 corridor by demolishing the Bedouin village of Az Za'ayyem in September 2013, displacing forty-seven Bedouins.[121] Not a word from the State Department, even though Obama, in an answer to a question specifically about the E1 corridor during his visit to Ramallah six months earlier, had been unequivocal: "I think that is an example of at least a public statement by the Israeli government that would be very difficult to square with a two-state solution. And I've said that to Prime Minister Netanyahu. I don't think that's a secret."[122]

Roby Nathanson says: "If you divide the areas in Jerusalem's surroundings, you will create huge problems in terms of infrastructure. Attempting to resolve the status of Jerusalem and the adjacent areas requires you to make a big distinction between the *political* arrangements and the *practical* arrangements on how to share the infrastructure we depend on to live there. If East Jerusalem is under absolute Palestinian control in the future Palestinian state, it doesn't mean necessarily that they will put borders there. Jerusalem should be an open city. Otherwise, it will suffocate the Palestinian, as well as the Jewish populations there. It's a lose-lose situation. The interdependence between both populations would be virtually impossible to untangle."[123]

Ariel is a different situation altogether. A Jewish settlement of eighteen thousand residents and another ten thousand students, it forms part of the Ariel-Elkana bloc, which has a total population of at least fifty thousand and is located near the middle of the West Bank.* It was founded in 1978 on land

*Shalom Yerushalmi, "Israeli Settlements Are Irreversible," *Al-Monitor*, January 14, 2013, http://www.al-monitor.com/pulse/politics/2013/01/the-situation-in-the-territories.html#; "About Ariel," Ariel: The Healthy Lifestyle City, http://www.ariel.muni.il/?CategoryID=457: "With the collapse of the Soviet Union the state of Israel received a large influx of new immigrants from the F.S.U. More than 6,000 new immigrants chose Ariel as their new home in Israel and doubled the city's population. As a direct result of the growth in population Ariel was declared a city in October 1998 by Prime Minister Netanyahu. This growth in population took Ariel to the next step in development of the city with more houses built, more employment available for new immigrants and a boost in the cultural activities in town. Today around 40% of the residents are former new immigrants from the F.S.U. During the disengagement from the Gaza

seized for security purposes (that old story), cheek to jowl with Palestinian villages. It is the fourth-largest settlement, and the original plan for the separation barrier called for extending the barrier all the way from the Green Line to Ariel, twelve miles away. International pressure squelched that idea, but the plan indicates the importance the Israeli government places on keeping Ariel under Israeli sovereignty. To drive home the point, Netanyahu declared Ariel the "capital of Samaria" and was instrumental in having university status conferred on its postsecondary-education college, over the objections of Israel's elite universities. Some Jewish Israeli interviewees suggested that Israel could concede Ariel in return for a concession on Ma'ale. For their part, Palestinian negotiators *cannot* concede Ariel, which would bifurcate the West Bank in ways that would make a Palestinian state look like arbitrarily sawed-off branches of a tree or, to switch metaphors, a hasty, makeshift construction, tattooed with the presence of Israel at its core.

There is no better manifestation than Ariel of the success of the settlements project in limiting Palestinian options. The Palestinians may well hold a losing hand on Ma'ale Adumim, with the engineered solution inelegant at best, and it would be a loss but not an insuperable one. Losing on Ariel would be catastrophic and unacceptable to Palestinians. If Ariel should be swapped, the evacuation *might* not be as difficult as with some other settlements, according to Nathanson, who said, "People [in Ariel] are far less ideological and far more economic oriented. They are more practical, and if a peace agreement called for voluntary evacuation, they would be far more open to compensation." On the other hand, it's a city of nineteen thousand and, as part of a bloc of fifty thousand people, quite an impediment to orderly evacuation. "So you have a plus and a minus."[124]

> > < <

Until June 27, 2012, Ulpana was a small outpost north of Jerusalem, fifteen miles into the West Bank. On that day, the thirty families of Ulpana were moved by the government down the hillside to Beit El, pursuant to a Supreme Court ruling that the outpost had been illegally built on Palestinian land and must be dismantled.[125] The Yesha Council had opposed the

---

strip in 2005 a group of 40 families from the community of Nezarim were welcomed to the city of Ariel. Their arrival in the city together with the arrival of many new families from North America and South Africa strengthened the religious community of the Ariel which since has been growing constantly together." Ariel is 16 kilometers (9.9 miles) east of the Green Line. There is a direct motorway to Tel Aviv, less than 40 kilometers (roughly 25 miles) away, and Jerusalem 50 kilometers (31 miles) away. The average apartment in Ariel costs roughly $280,000 and in Tel Aviv $600,000.

court order in every possible way—indicative of the lengths to which the government was and is prepared to go in attempting to thwart the judiciary's rulings—and the settlers refused to comply until they finally ran out of options. In the weeks prior to evacuation day, Ulpana was flooded with outsiders, "well-wishers bringing homemade cakes; a food charity truck filled with fresh cherries; yeshiva boys poring over sacred texts in a 24-hour vigil; and a small tent city reminiscent of the Occupy movement. Some have strategically placed tires on pathways, ready to be set ablaze to block the police; others stand guard at driveways entering the neighborhood with makeshift weapons."[126]

In the end, though, the bubble of unadulterated support burst; the government could not figure out a way to legalize Ulpana and voted to evacuate.[127] The settlers then walked peacefully out of their old homes and down the hill to their new homes in Beit El under the watchful eyes of a thousand IDF soldiers. This was nominally a defeat for Netanyahu, which he minimized in several ways, including an offer to remove the buildings of Ulpana from their foundations and move them, rather than demolish them.[128] He also agreed to build an additional three hundred housing units in Beit El, and he promised that Ulpana would not be used as a precedent for policy on settlements elsewhere in the West Bank.[129]

Ulpana was not a fight about Ulpana. At stake was the future of the settlers' movement. Says Roby Nathanson: "The lessons of Ulpana are, first, you must establish a dialogue with the settlers, and try to come to a reasonable agreement of withdrawal through dialogue. Most of them will accept some kind of compensations or other avenues of resettling, not necessarily in the occupied territory areas, but also inside the Green Line. The second lesson from Ulpana is that they moved without violence."[130]

The case of the outpost at Migron, another red-line outpost for right-wing settlers,[131] is closely analogous. When it was ordered dismantled on February 12, 2007,[132] the push-back lasted five years. As in Ulpana, the full resources of the government were devoted to finding ways to somehow get around the order rather than how to oversee its implementation. On the eve of the final order of the Supreme Court to dismantle the outpost no later than March 31, 2012, the settlers sought a restraining injunction on the grounds that they had discovered evidence that the land was not Palestinian owned. That move failed—the government had already conceded the ownership issue—and the government moved the few hundred Migron residents a few hundred yards away, onto land owned by the state on September 2, 2012. There was no violence.

Nathanson notes that Netanyahu would not go along with a last-ditch move to take the decision on the Migron outpost out of the hands of the Supreme Court. Netanyahu said he would abide by the court's final decision, much as he might dislike it. Nathanson said: "Adhering to this [decision] is essentially speaking for the Israeli democratic system and a far more important decision than moving those houses from a couple of hundred meters. . . . The fact that in Israel once it is established that settlers in the West Bank are building on privately owned Palestinian land* and could produce authentication of ownership and seek remedy in the courts is a small victory in the larger scheme of things, it is still a move in a direction that people must understand. There are laws and if the law obliges settlers or the government to move in a certain way, the government ultimately has to comply with the decision of the high court."[133]

Nathanson overlooks the lengths to which the government and settlers' movement went in trying to thwart the court's ruling. Considering all the resources poured into protecting illegal outposts, dismantling them only in extremis, we could wonder what message was sent to the settler community in general. Regardless, Netanyahu skillfully positioned himself between the courts and the settlers, so that when he did yield ever so reluctantly to the Supreme Court, he was able to stay within the norms of Israel's democratic values while minimizing the wrath of the settlers. Soothing their feelings he told them, "I tell those who think they can use the judicial system to hurt settlement that they are mistaken, because in practice, the exact opposite will occur. Instead of shrinking Beit El, Beit El has expanded. Instead of hurting settlement, settlement has been strengthened."[134]

> > < <

How much would evacuation cost? $20 billion? $30 billion? At least. As Hagit Ofran, one of the more prominent leaders of Peace Now, points out, "The eight thousand evicted from Gaza each received one million shekels per person, and still more has been added for their rehabilitation. This is about eight

*Hareuveni, *By Hook and By Crook*. Using Civil Administration records, the settlements jurisdictional area, and aerial photos of the settlements taken in 2009, B'Tselem found that 21 percent of the built-up area of the settlements is land that Israel recognizes as private property owned by Palestinians. According to Spiegel's database, the status of land in at least sixty-seven settlements is not uniform and is made up of various combinations: land requisitioned by military orders, areas declared "state land," survey land, and private Palestinian land. Some private Palestinian lands have become enclaves within settlements. Some land was taken as a result of negligent implementation of military requisition orders and demarcation of "state land," and some was unlawfully seized by settlements or individual settlers. This document is also a resource for court decisions and legalities involving settlements.

billion shekels, about two billion dollars, a very large sum of money for Israel." Doing the math, equivalent compensation for 68,000 settlers, much less 100,000 or more, from the West Bank and perhaps East Jerusalem, would be mind-boggling for Israel, whose annual budget is on the order of $100 billion. Even with lower compensation, the cost is still overwhelming.

Of course, Israel, which has ignored every call from the international community at every level for close to fifty years to halt construction of settlements, would ask that same international community to come to its assistance and bear a considerable part of the costs associated with evacuations and relocation. Israel would tell the international community that if it wants to give real meaning to all those pro-Palestinian UN votes, it will have to cough up the resources to turn resolution into living reality and, in effect, compensate Israel for its illegal actions. A field day for exceptionalism.

In the end, the rest of the world would contribute probably the lion's share of the cost, although Nathanson says Israel could "easily" finance 100,000 evacuees.[135] These costs, of course, would be on top of the huge numbers required to finance the compensation and relocation of the five million Palestinian refugees, whose fate would be determined by the same final status agreement that determines the fate of the settlers. Palestinians believe that as continuing victims for more than half a century, they are entitled to donor assistance, and they will get it. But how much? The answer might surprise everyone. Israel and the new Palestine could encounter an international community very enthusiastic about resolving this conflict at last, but less than enthusiastic about paying the full fare.

Economists predict a peace dividend for both economies, but there will also be a security *surcharge*, especially for Israel, because a new Palestinian state alongside Israel would be met with great apprehension by many Israelis, and security measures and costs would rise accordingly and eat into the peace dividend. The simple truth is that no one has any good idea what would happen with evacuations, or how much they would ultimately cost, or what the unintended consequences would be. We know only that there would be consequences, possibly grave.

But evacuations and their consequences would arise only if there were a two-state solution. The 2014 Gaza war, however, makes such an outcome highly problematic, a delusion whose time has come.

Chapter 8

The Economics of Sustainability

Would the economy of a Palestinian state created by a two-state "solution" be viable? The answer is all-important, because a peace agreement would be of no *lasting* value if the new state only became the ward of the international community and, to some extent, of Israel. In such circumstances, political instability would prevail, a recipe for inevitable violence.

The only way to predict what that economy might look like is to examine the *present* viability and the near-term *capacity* to grow. Are there good metrics suggesting that a Palestinian economy might "take off" with a durable peace agreement in place, or will it just get mired in slow- or even no-growth stagnation? And if the economy is to all appearances viable, the question is whether it is *sustainable* with sufficient potential to ensure it will *endure*.

Its viability will be measured by a number of key technical parameters.[1] Among the most important: Would the state be along the borders of 1967, with East Jerusalem as its capital, real contiguity, geographical cohesiveness, access to water, etc.? Would the state be able to wean itself off donor assistance and meet its own financial needs, especially with regard to the ability to *manage* its financial affairs (a budget with deficits at reasonable levels relative to GDP)? Would it be able to maintain a level of debt where interest costs did not eat significantly into the budget, while possessing a plan to provide for what undoubtedly would be the country's burgeoning needs as refugees return, adding to the level of services the state needs to provide? Would it be able to ensure that donor assistance for capital and infrastructure development was not siphoned off to meet operational expenditures or did not disappear in a miasma of corruption? Would it attract inward investment? Expand the tax base? Ensure that taxes were paid? Achieve educational and skill standards, develop human and social capital, and strengthen resiliency in the face of change? Would it maintain competitiveness in any given field and a rate of growth to create sufficient jobs for the more than a quarter of a million unemployed[2] *and* the returnees? Would it build and sustain an independent legal sector where prosecutors and judges were not patronage appointees, where due process was followed, and where respect for human rights was part of the fabric of the society?

To these add the integration of the Gaza, West Bank, and East Jerusalem economies—a sine qua non for success. Certainly the economies of the separated West Bank and Gaza, under occupation, have never come close to meeting even some of these conditions. The Second Intifada shattered an already dysfunctional economy, adding 120,000 people to the already bloated unemployment rolls and destroying all government institutions. GDP numbers were negative in 2002–3 and again in 2004–5. There was a further decline in 2006, after Hamas emerged as the winner in the Palestinian national elections and took control in Gaza, leading to United States and OECD countries' financial restrictions, and Israel installed its blockade.

Today the West Bank and Gaza are separate entities. One, the West Bank, is functional, although it depends on donor support to maintain its viability. The other, the Gaza Strip, is for all intents and purposes a non-economy.

> > < <

In 2005 Abbas announced that the PLO had abandoned armed resistance and committed itself to a peaceful resolution of the conflict. Under the tutelage of Lt. General Keith Dayton, the U.S. head of the security coordination program, the PASF made remarkable strides policing terrorism (the arrestees being mostly Hamas members) and earning the plaudits of the IDF.[3]

Abbas's 2007 appointment of Salam Fayyad as prime minister had a perceptible impact on the performance of the economy. Fayyad, a highly respected economist and former employee of the International Monetary Fund (IMF) who belonged to no political faction, embarked on transformational change. He drew up the Palestinian National Development Plan,[4] which outlined how the PA would convince the UN that Palestine met the standards for statehood within three years. He purged the PA of political hacks, professionalized its public institutions, and began to eliminate corruption. He succeeded to a considerable degree in both respects. Government ministries, institutions, and agencies were overhauled.

Fayyad put strict financial controls in place; inefficiencies were identified and eliminated and phases of the five-year national development plan were implemented. The West Bank began to post positive rates of growth as the impact of the Second Intifada waned and security improved markedly due to an overhauled and better-trained PASF. The more secure environment encouraged development policies that focused on small community projects, and Israeli "security" closure restrictions eased somewhat. In the dozen years from 2002 (the height of the intifada) to 2013, per-capita income more than doubled from $1,215.20 to $2,669.70. (Israel's per-capita income is thirty times greater.)*

Fayyad's administration was a success: The economic environment became conducive to inward investment, and the economy responded with quite exceptional results—reaching double-digit growth rates in 2011.

Reports produced since 2007 by the IMF, the World Bank, the United Nations Conference on Trade and Development (UNCTAD), the UN's Ad Hoc Liaison Committee (AHLC), and others agree that the main challenge inhibiting further Palestinian recovery remains Israel's comprehensive restrictions that stunt economic growth: "Beyond movement within and across the Palestinian Territories, [Israeli] policies (and procedures also) restrict access to domestic and international markets, land, water and other natural resources."[5] They acknowledge the legitimacy of Israel's security concerns but find these hard to reconcile with access restrictions and the protection and expansion of Israeli settlement activity in the West Bank. The commitments entered into by Israel under the 2005 Agreement on Movement and Access (AMA) remain as unfulfilled as they are critical. The AMA must be implemented immediately.[6] "Moving forward, the full implementation of the AMA must be seen as an important step toward stability, not a consequence of it."[7]

With monotonous regularity, economists and governments in the West and the United States call on Israel to dismantle some of its five hundred checkpoints and reduce closures, but Israel simply ignores their reports. In February 2014, there were 99 permanent roadblocks in the West Bank; 59 were internal, including 33 that were manned at all times. In addition, there are hundreds of portable temporary roadblocks that go up in a flash, some 450 permanent unmanned barriers on the roads, and 232 kilometers (144 miles) of segregated roads for Israelis only.

> > < <

Following the boomlet of 2007–10, growth in the West Bank dipped from 9 percent to 6 percent in 2012. Though that level of growth in an EU country would be regarded as phenomenal, the base in the West Bank is very low, and despite the growth, unemployment reached 27 percent. Among youth it reached roughly 50 percent. Real wages and productivity also declined. In 2011

*Agencies such as the IMF, World Bank, the International Labour Organization, and the Palestinian Census Bureau all use different starting points or different sets of data as starting points, which results in discrepancies.

poverty rates were 18 percent in the West Bank and 30 percent in Gaza. Without social assistance from UNRWA, the numbers would have been worse.

Nonetheless, in April 2011, six months prior to the Palestinian bid for statehood, the UN declared that the PA was ready to run an independent state, *as long as restrictions imposed by Israel were addressed.*[8] The UN report came on the heels of two other endorsements, from the International Monetary Fund and the World Bank: The PA was ready to manage a sovereign economy. The IMF effusively praised the Western-backed PA for a "solid record" of increasing fiscal transparency and discipline, reducing dependence on donor aid, and boosting supervision of local banks. "The PA," the IMF report concluded, "is now able to conduct the sound economic policies expected of a future well-functioning Palestinian state."[9] The World Bank was supportive but more cautious in its assessment, prepared for the AHLC. It acknowledged Palestinian progress in strengthening institutions, providing public services, and promoting needed reforms, "and this progress must be sustained and bolstered."[10] It also noted that "Ultimately, sustainable economic growth in WB&G ([the West Bank and Gaza)] can only be underpinned by a vibrant private sector. The latter will not rebound significantly while Israeli restrictions on access to natural resources and markets remain in place."[11]

UNWRA was the first to question the findings of the international agencies, arguing in its June 2011 report, that the Palestinian economy was not as healthy as it was being made out to be.[12] The ILO, also in June 2011 was next to raise further doubts.[13] And finally, in March 2012, the Israeli government weighed in with its own analysis of the PA economy. It claimed, according to *Haaretz*, which had obtained a copy of the report, "that the Palestinian economy is not stable enough to meet the standards of a well-functioning state . . . the fiscal crisis is especially acute because much of the West Bank economy still depends on the public sector and on construction projects, both still heavily financed by foreign aid. . . . It also serves as an alarming warning sign for the stability of the Palestinian economy," while pointing to "a long line of actions by Israel to aid the Palestinian economy in the West Bank and Gaza Strip." Economic growth in the West Bank, it concluded, "has foundered."[14] While much of the international community looked askance at the Israeli report raising questions about the sustainability of a Palestinian economy because that lack of sustainability was due to the policies of successive Israeli governments, it simply bolstered the conclusions both UNWRA and the ILO had come to.

> > < <

In 2012 the World Bank backpedaled: Its previous "ready for statehood" assessment of the PA was downgraded to not ready.[15] In 2015, it is still "not ready." In September 2012 the UN reported that long-term economic development prospects were becoming "more unattainable," that previous growth was "deceptive," and that further deterioration would occur due to mobility restrictions, aid reductions, agricultural decline, and fiscal crisis.[16] By then, debt amounted to $1.5 billion, and the immediate budget shortfall of cash was $500 million. Growth in GDP was driven not by the private sector or some form of restructuring of Palestinian production but by an unsustainable level of government expenditure. (Foreign aid and borrowing are not drivers of real economic growth.) Donor assistance for capital projects was being used to meet everyday operating expenses. Six months later, in March 2013, the World Bank reported to the AHLC that the West Bank and Gaza (WBG) was in danger of losing its capacity to compete in the global market.[17] Rather damningly, it disclosed that the structure of the economy had deteriorated since the late nineties as the value-added of the tradable sectors declined; "the productivity of the agriculture sector [had] roughly halved and the manufacturing sector [had] largely stagnated."[18] The share of exports in the Palestinian economy, the world bank said, dropped to 7 percent in 2011, one of the lowest in the world. The labor force was deemed in danger of losing its long-term employability. Although "increased employment in the public sector has provided some short-term relief," the World Bank stressed that "this is unsustainable and does little to prepare employees for future private sector jobs."[19] And the bank concluded there were other problems leading to deteriorating economic competitiveness, which affected social cohesion.[20]

"At the beginning of 2013, Palestine experienced a severe fiscal crisis which was the result of donor shortfalls, higher-than-expected expenditure and lower-than-expected revenue," the European Commission reported. This was exacerbated, it said, "by measures imposed by Israel in response to Palestine's successful bid at the U.N." The fiscal shortfall was more than 200 million USD, which had to be covered by further accumulation of arrears and increased indebtedness to the banking sector."[21]

Nothing new in this analysis: It just confirms what every international agency monitoring the West Bank said year after year.[22]

What had happened, in just a few years, to the good news and numbers and optimism engendered by Salam Fayyad's first years as prime minister? A number of factors, including the role Israel played, prevented Fayyad from carrying out the agenda he had in mind. The first fact of life for the economies of the West Bank and Gaza is that Israel enjoys a stranglehold over both; as such, it is the *principal determinant* of whether Palestinians can claw their way back to per-capita levels of income that existed fifteen years ago.

In any examination of the viability and sustainability of a Palestinian economy within the framework of a two-state solution, it is imperative to differentiate between the PA's (read West Bank's) readiness for statehood in terms of structural reform of the institutions of governance and the degree to which a Palestinian state has sovereignty over its territory but *not* over its economy. A state whose economy can be manipulated externally by a vastly wealthier and more powerful state is not a "free" state; rather, it is an appendage to an economy on which it is dependent for the bulk of its imports and exports.

Since the tradable-goods sector—manufacturing and agriculture—is vital to a resuscitated Palestinian economy, the severity of the closures by the Israeli government cripples the competitiveness of these sectors by putting a brake on the extent to which the economy can recover from its 1994 base. The efficacy of foreign donor support is affected, and the purposes for which it is given cannot "be sufficiently realized until the Israeli closure policy and blockade of Gaza are lifted."[23] In the simplest terms, the long-term source of stability will be "the loosening of restrictions on people and products."[24] Deaf to these calls to ease restrictions, Israel can and does play the Palestinian economy like an accordion, squeezing tightly to reduce growth and employment or expanding to facilitate growth and employment. According to Naser Tahboub, former deputy minister of national economy in the PA, "Israel routinely violates the 1994 Paris Accords on the free movement of goods and services, but is not held to any standards of accountability. We buy through Israel or from Israel $3.5 billion. We sell to Israel, at best, at the peak, $600 million. So we have a trade deficit of $2 billion. If Israel tried to alleviate this trade balance, we would be able to create more jobs in Palestinian industries."[25]

A closely related issue is Area C—the 61 percent of the West Bank that remains under the absolute control of the IDF.* Here, in 2011, the IMF was unequivocal: "Restrictions on private investment in "Area C" . . . should be promptly removed."[26] In October 2013 the World Bank estimated that

*See chapter 7, endnote 98.

allowing Palestinian businesses and farms to develop in Area C would add $3.4 billion—as much as 35 percent—to the Palestinian GDP."[27] The World Bank said again access to Area C would go a long way toward solving the PA's economic problems and substantially improve the prospects for sustained growth. Since 326,400 dunams, or 80,620 acres, are "notionally available to Palestinians," agriculture, specifically, "could deliver an additional USD 704 million in value added to the Palestinian economy" if restrictions on movement and access to water supplies were eased."[28] Moreover, the Dead Sea is in Area C. "The Palestinian economy," the World Bank said, "could earn as much as $918 million if minerals such as potash and bromine were harvested from the water,"[29] and the tourism sector could be boosted by $126 million annually by building Dead Sea resorts similar to those in Israel and Jordan. The World Bank also estimated that access to the stone and quarry sector of Area C would double the contribution of that sector to the economy.[30] In short, without access to Area C, the Palestinians' economy is *necessarily* fragmented and stunted, and the outlook bleak. Israel also collects tax revenues on the PA's behalf.* These monies account for almost 70 percent of the PA's revenue; external grants and aid make up a little over 30 percent. The PA always faces a fiscal cliff, with limited remedies at its disposal when Israel withholds the tax revenues on "collective punishment" grounds whenever the PLO engages in actions Israel disapproves of. This results in serious budgetary constraints and adversely affects the livelihoods of the close to two million people living in the West Bank. When Abbas failed in his gambit for UN recognition in 2011, Israel withheld $100 million in custom fees (and the U.S. Congress curtailed aid).[31] A year later, Israel again withheld $100 million in tax revenue after the UN General Assembly overwhelmingly endorsed observer-state status for Palestine (and the U.S. Congress did not release the aid it had approved in 2012 until March 2013).[32] In 2013, the PA's budget deficit was $1.7 billion, 17 percent of GDP,[33] and significant donor assistance from Arab states did not materialize to make up

*Article III of the 1994 Protocol on Economic Relations (Paris Protocol) agreement between Israel and the PLO stipulates that Israel can collect customs and taxes on West Bank border terminals but must transfer them to the PA within six working days. Israel can collect a 3 percent interest fee for doing so. The full text of the protocol can be viewed at http://www.nad-plo.org/userfiles/file/Document/ParisPro.pdf. The Paris Protocol later was incorporated, with small adjustments, into the September 1995 Oslo Accords as Annex V. Its full text can be viewed at http://www.mfa.gov.il/mfa/foreignpolicy/peace/guide/pages/the%20israeli-palestinian%20interim%20agreement%20-%20annex%20v.aspx. For a brief overview of the Paris Protocol, see Konrad-Adenauer-Stiftung, "The Paris Protocol: Historical Classification," December 12, 2012, http://www.kas.de/palaestinensische-gebiete/en/pages/11895/.

the difference, one small glimmer of relief emerged when a UN-commissioned report estimated that Israel had retained some $300 million in tax revenue due to "fiscal leakages"—equivalent to 17 percent of total tax revenue, in addition to 4 percent of lost GDP and about ten thousand jobs a year.[34] Israel, of course, questioned the findings, and it is not yet clear that the matter has been satisfactorily disposed of.

While the consequences of a collapse of their economy would be disastrous for Palestinians in the short run, they would also be extremely costly for Israel, which would have to assume the headaches and costs of administering the functions that had fallen under the PA's purview, with all kinds of unintended repercussions, not least the fact that it would be a giant step backward to a pre-Oslo-like political situation, certainly not an outcome in the best interests of any of the players. So whenever Israel withholds customs taxes, it does so knowing that it could set in motion actions leading to the collapse of the PA, thus endangering itself.[35] It's playing Russian roulette with the West Bank. Whatever the shortfall between what the PA needs and what international donors are willing to provide must be met by desperate pleas for emergency assistance, further domestic borrowing, or a cutback in service—all of which have follow-on effects. The current situation highlights the irony that the same international community that condemns Israel's occupation of the West Bank underwrites most of the costs associated with it; hence the Palestinian complaint that the occupation is almost cost-free to Israel.* Hence, too, the pragmatism expressed by Saleh Elayan, PA cabinet secretary and aide to Palestinian legislative speaker Abu Ala: "As much as the PLO may decry the US and bias to Israel," he says, "it has to keep its criticisms within bounds, because otherwise the PA would collapse."†[36]

> > < <

Israel isn't the only cause of the West Bank's all-too-common economic and budget crises. Also culpable is the structural imbalance in its economy. Apart from the boomlet in 2007–10, growth in GDP has been increasingly

*Gershon Gorenberg, writing in *The American Prospect*, says, "[Oslo] has become the lasting means by which Israel outsources its rule over Palestinians in occupied territory. Donor countries foot the budget." "Rebellion in Ramallah?," http://prospect.org/article/rebellion-ramallah.

†"From FY2008 to [FY2014], annual regular-year U.S. bilateral assistance to the West Bank and Gaza Strip has averaged around $500 million, including annual averages of approximately $200 million in direct budgetary assistance and $100 million in non-lethal security assistance for the PA in the West Bank." Jim, Zanotti. "U.S. Foreign Aid to the Palestinians." Congressional Research Service, January 18, 2013, http://fpc.state.gov/documents/organization/217502.pdf.

driven by government spending and private consumption, remittances, and donor aid. Foreign investment is minimal; hence there is no base for a self-sustaining economy. The impact of the recession in the West, especially in the European Union, which is Israel's export base, slowed growth in Israel, which in turn slowed growth in the PA. The private sector shrank. Young people entered a private-sector labor market that was shedding jobs. As the employer of last resort, the Palestinian Authority picks up the employment cudgel one more time, employing far more workers than it needs and can afford. Although Fayyad had some success in reducing this excess employment to levels more acceptable to the international community—and received accolades from the World Bank and the IMF for doing so—the cutbacks could not be indefinitely sustained because the private sector could not pick up the slack.

The result: Public-sector employment in the West Bank has grown by 60 percent since 1999; by 2011, it had absorbed over 50 percent of the budget*—a prohibitive level by all international yardsticks. In addition, the tax base is small, collection practices are lax, and many businesses receive generous exemptions. In July 2011 Fayyad announced that the PA would cut its employees' pay by half.[37] The result was a mass demonstration—bigger than any the PLO could muster for political action—and the government quickly backed down.[38] It tried again the following year with an announcement that there would be some tax increases, and in 2012 the backlash was the same, only on this occasion protesters burned effigies of Fayyad.[39] The PA government lacks popular support[40] and is, in fact, illegitimate because its electoral mandate has run out. As a result of the public's alienation from the governing authorities, the PA operates in fear of the unpredictability of the street. It sees every demonstration as a possible precursor to a Tahrir Square–like situation.

So in the end, as matters now stand with the West Bank economy, it's all about donors' willingness to keep the Palestinian Authority afloat. Hazem Shunnar, the assistant deputy minister of the Ministry of the National Economy, one of the most forthcoming of all my interviewees, made no attempt to spin the truth or muddy the water. He stated bluntly that the PA

*"The PA Wage bill as a share of GDP is at least twice the average share for the Middle East & North Africa (MENA) region" from "Stagnation or Revival? Palestinian Economic Prospects Economic Monitoring Report to the Ad Hoc Liaison Committee," March 21, 2012, http://siteresources.worldbank.org/INTWESTBANKGAZA/Resources/WorldBankAHLCreportMarch2012.pdf.

had relied on the donor assistance to "run the public sector."[41] In Paris in 2007, eighty-seven countries and international organizations pledged $7.4 billion over three years to support implementation of the PA's program, outlined in "Building the Palestinian State: Sustaining Growth, Institutions, and Service Delivery."[42] Shunnar labeled those years a "splurge." But the donors' enthusiasm waned and their contributions fell. By 2012, the PA's budget was a little more than $4 billion. Aid required to meet the shortfall was $1.2 billion. Altogether, the PA had accumulated almost $5 billion in internal and external debt[43]; it owed 1.3 billion to local Palestinian banks, which were no longer prepared to extend further credit.[44] Similarly, much of the private sector, which supplies the government with a variety of services, had not been paid, and it, too, was now unwilling to extend further credit.[45] (Total accrued interest accounted for 19 percent of the budget, a huge chunk of revenue not available to provide services or improve infrastructure.) This lethal combination of elements triggered the worst fiscal crisis in the PA's eighteen-year existence; the cutbacks in jobs and pay and pensions all but triggered revolt.[46]

In the course of our interview in June 2012, Oussama Kanaan, who is in charge of the Palestinian portfolio at the IMF, summarized the situation.

> Because the Palestinian private sector is so small, the domestic tax base is inadequate, the restrictions on the movement of goods and people are so severe Palestinian products are noncompetitive in world markets. The PA has no access to either a seaport or an airport, and the result was a shift from a tradable to a nontradable economy. Once you get to the point where the private sector is not getting paid, and when there are instances when the wage payments are delayed, this creates uncertainty among the population that affects confidence overall in the economy. It spreads to investors; it affects the whole population, which is trying to make decisions on where to put its money. Ultimately it can affect banks. So the donor aid shortfall, that is aid that is below what the budget requires, has been disruptive. This is the situation we face now.[47]

Along with everyone else, Kanaan decried the situation within Area C, which is off limits to Palestinian investment; the arbitrary withholding of the revenue taxes by the Israelis; the checkpoints and closures; a bloated public sector; a private sector that has almost no place to go, figuratively and literally, since it is without a seaport or major airport; and skittish banks. And the addiction to donor contributions as the "fix" is pervasive.[48] However, going cold turkey on the contributions would not work. Kanaan sees no choice but reliance on the donors for the "medium term." Of course, that's a phrase for all seasons, an amorphous concept that resides in the ethereal.

During our interview in July 2012, then–Prime Minister Salam Fayyad played down the extent of the financial crisis the PA faced. "A few hundred million dollars can make a difference between us continuing to chug along with the greatest difficulty, in a crisis mode, or being able to get out of the buzzard's neck," he said.

> The hole is not that deep, but everything is relative. We are not getting enough money to fill it. It's causing us all kinds of problems. Critics are thinking, "This guy is preaching readiness for statehood when in fact he can't even pay salaries." But there are a number of other countries around the world with severe financial problems, and they have existed not only for decades. People should know that we have been actually reducing our reliance on aid as a matter of policy since 2008. We have been enhancing our own capabilities. Our revenues have been increasing. We continue to reform our institutions, tightening administration practices and raising taxes. But this is a financial crisis. *We definitely should get some assistance to get us out of it.* The problem is that a weary donor community is no longer prepared to cough up the money needed to cover the full extent of the shortfall in the deficit.[49]

He acknowledged the public's concerns. Although the PA's performance may have improved and it may operate under more responsible management, the people didn't see an improvement in their lives and were worried about the future. "People cannot eat GDP," he continued.

> I understand that. . . . Dependence on aid today is less than it was last year, and last year it was less than in the year before. 2008 was big. Since 2008, we have improved our own capabilities to the tune of 60 percent difference in GDP. Unemployment has declined somewhat over the past five years, but is still high. Poverty, on the other hand, has declined quite significantly over the same time period. It's not enough. We really need to do more, obviously, in order for that to reach people, but I can tell you five consecutive years of growth have had an impact. It is happening, in fact, albeit not to an extent felt by the public when it comes to improvement of opportunities.

In January 2013, Fayyad again publicly squeezed the donor nations and stated bluntly that the crisis was due solely to the failure of "some Arab donors not fulfilling their pledge of support in accordance with Arab League resolutions."* He was correct in his charge, but the short-term solution doesn't address the long-term structural issues. As a result, the PA staggers from one year and one crisis to the next, soliciting sufficient assistance to preclude a free fall and warning of what might happen should it collapse. These not-too-implicit forebodings of what dire consequences might follow the PA crashing usually work, because as long as the Middle East roils in turmoil, unwilling donors can be nudged into reluctant contributors.

The increasingly fatigued donors have urged ad nauseam that the PA reassess its priorities: lower the public-sector wage bill and redirect assistance to investment in education and public infrastructure to ensure future financial and economic viability. But the PA is in an invidious position. The *backbone* of the economy is the 180,000 public employees. Any attempt to reduce those public-sector costs sets up a self-perpetuating crisis of unemployment, lower tax revenues, slow or no growth, covering operational costs with money designated for investments, and social and political unrest. *The PA can cut back on the size of public sector employment only to a politically acceptable level*; attempts to raise revenues backfired.[50] Accordingly, whenever the PA fails to receive donor aid already promised, its future becomes more uncertain. However, when the donors do come through, they attach stiffer conditions, and these remedies just add fuel to self-perpetuating crises of unemployment, recession, and simmering unrest.

The IMF's prescriptions for Palestine to put its house in order are replicas of the austerity-based measures voluntarily adopted by the Conservative Party in Britain and imposed by the EU banking system on European countries like Ireland, Greece, and Spain, which needed help to avoid default on their sovereign debt. Such antistimulus measures, rather than Keynesian stimulus formulas, were met by massive street demonstrations against which the police often used truncheons and tear gas to disperse crowds and defend government buildings. (The austerity measures have had negative impacts and the EU appears unable to lift itself out of chronic recession.) But at least the nexus of the European societies' governance and civil-society institutions is strong enough to absorb the shocks. The PA lacks such foundations. It is highly unlikely it would withstand similar crowd assaults. Its institutions are simply not strong enough. For the first time in a decade, the West Bank economy shrank in the first half of 2013.[51]

*"Palestinian PM Fayyad slams Arab donors for failing to deliver aid to PA," Associated Press, in *Haaretz*, January 6, 2013, http://www.haaretz.com/news/diplomacy-defense/palestinian-pm-fayyad-slams-arab-donors-for-failing-to-deliver-aid-to-pa-1.492288.

The West Bank "street" does not blame Israel or the United States or the EU or the IMF or the World Bank or the Arab donors for the Palestinian crises. It *blames the Palestinian Authority.* Despite Fayyad's best efforts, corruption is still pervasive, which adds to people's alienation from their government.[52] The street believes the politicians in the PA skim donor money, that there is little accountability and no transparency.[53] Fayyad's message that Palestinians need to build the institutions of state prior to achieving statehood did not find much resonance on the street. The vision he outlined of a people joining together, willing to sacrifice together to achieve a common purpose, had little traction. His vision failed to become their vision. With the distresses of the Second Intifada still vivid, Palestinians want to fill their bellies; they are engaged with their lives, not with matters outside the scope of everyday living. Street protesters demand more services, but they are not prepared to pay additional taxes to receive them. Which raises a question: Has the Palestinian public become so dependent on donor assistance that it believes that whenever its demands on the PA government exceeds the PA's resources, the donors should automatically chip in, that the people themselves have no responsibility in the matter, that the occupation relieves them of any obligation? If so—and all indicators point in that direction—weaning them off foreign assistance will be like successfully detoxing an addict.

In April 2013, because of a dispute with Abbas,[54] Fayyad resigned as prime minister, to the delight of his many enemies in Fatah, who saw him as opportunistic, excelling at self-promotion and taking credit for improvements in the PA that should properly be attributed to others.[55] He was replaced by Rami Hamdallah, for fifteen years president of An-Najah National University in Nablus. Hamdallah's problem is the same as Fayyad's: A Palestinian state economy is not viable now, and it is impossible to predict when it might be. The IMF's "bucket list" for improving the West Bank economy has twenty-three items, all considerable, none easily solved, some impossible to solve without serious Israeli cooperation.[56] And all require *Palestinian* cooperation.

> > < <

Separated from the West Bank by only twelve miles, the Gaza Strip is another world. Pummeled by wars in 2008–09, 2012, and 2014, crippled by the closure of the 1,400 tunnels that had been its economic lifeline, unable to pay its public servants, and with no outlet at the Rafah crossing, it is an impoverished enclave. Three quarters of Gazans are classified as refugees.

According to a declassified military document, between 2008 and 2010

"Israeli authorities blockading the Gaza Strip went so far as to calculate how many calories would be needed to avert a humanitarian disaster."[57] The answer was 2,279 calories per person each day, a figure in line with World Health Organization (WHO) guidelines. That became the benchmark. Gazans were allotted a survival-level diet. "During that time," the Associated Press reported, "Israel limited food supplies entering Gaza and maintained a baffling list of items that were banned or permitted as part of a broader effort to topple the violently anti-Israel Hamas by squeezing the economy." The declassified document "broke down the calorie allocation by various food groups, and in minute details. It said that males aged 11 to 50 required 316.05 grams of meat per day, and women in the same age group needed 190.47 grams of flour."[58]

There is a single power plant, which frequently malfunctions or goes dead because the Hamas government cannot cough up the resources needed to keep it running; or it has not been adequately repaired after being bombed during the war: portable generators are used to take up the slack. "If you honestly evaluate the situation here," says Dr. Ahmed Yousef, a Hamas leader who is close to Ismail Haniyeh, "you can only conclude that the Israelis are continually provoking us to react. You have to keep at least five hundred meters from the border. This denies us access to some of the most productive land for agriculture."[59] After the 2014 Gaza War, Israel stretched the buffer zone to 3 kilometers (1.8 miles), eating up approximately 44 percent of Gaza's territory.[60]

Without the tunnels, Gaza's only source of relief is the UNRWA. So we have this irony: The world body that has labeled Hamas a "terrorist" government is also its main benefactor. Without UNRWA, the West Bank would struggle even more than it has done and Gaza might not function at all. The relationship between Hamas and UNRWA is complicated.*

Some 800,000 people rely on the agency for housing and food allowances. Eighty percent of its budget is allocated to education in grades kindergarten through nine; almost all of the schools run double shifts. Gaza's universities—eight in such a small area—continue to churn out graduates, a very high proportion of them women who face a jobless future; some end up as teachers at UNWRA schools, completing the cycle back to the schools where they began their educations. Twenty health clinics providing primary care attend to a caseload of 850,000. A jobs program guarantees a job of some sort—sorting

*UNRWA is a U.S.-designated organization, and with the United States being UNRWA's largest funder, questions arise regarding interaction between the two, given that Hamas is designated a terrorist organization by the United States.

garbage, cleaning the streets, and the like—to 100,000 people, so most households have some income coming in for some period of the year.

Despite UNWRA's efforts, the UN says, Gaza's jobless rate is among the most severe in the world and a "reversal of deepening poverty and aid dependency among ordinary people in Gaza is unlikely."[61] The UN report warns that unless remedial measures are taken immediately to alleviate problems in water and electricity, education, and health, the situation will only get worse. By 2020 the economy could collapse. For all intents and purposes it already has.[62] In a U.S. diplomatic cable released by WikiLeaks in 2013, American diplomats quoted their Israeli colleagues as saying the blockade was meant to push the area's economy "to the brink of collapse."[63] Take your own meaning from that phrase, but this is certain: The word "de-development," which Sara Roy used to describe the Israeli manipulations of the West Bank economy, does not begin to cover the situation in Gaza.[64] Of course, Israel has a legitimate right to protect its citizens from the rocket attacks emanating from Gaza, but it has no valid pretext for restrictions on humanitarian assistance—the blockade is, in effect, collective punishment of 1.7 million people.

Before the ad hoc "tunnel economy" kicked in,[65] the blockade ensured that Israel was in full control of this statelet, with the Gazans living in total dependency, "locked in a situation of degradation, to be pushed to self-degradation by need, fulfils the definition of humiliation."[66] And it is more humiliating still for Hamas to be dependent on Israel, the country it is bent on destroying, for the supply of goods to ensure that it and the enclave it purportedly governs do not collapse.[67]

Without the full cooperation of Israel, which presumably will not be forthcoming without an FSA in place, neither the West Bank nor Gaza has prospects for a viable, freestanding economy.

But what if the two were united under a two-state solution?

> > < <

A separate West Bank economy would be landlocked. Numerous studies show that such economies are among the poorest in the world.[68] Among the thirty landlocked countries of middle and low income, twenty countries are classified as "poor."*[69] Any final status agreement would provide for a linkage

*"The landlocked economies' performance is lower than that of coastal countries on all components of the human development index (HDI). The average GNP per capita in landlocked economies is 57% below its coastal countries counterparts; the average life expectancy is 3.5 years less; and the education index is also lower." The more inland the country, the lower the

between the two entities, either an above-the-ground corridor or an underground tunnel.

Mazen Sinokrot, one of the West Bank's most successful businessmen, who exports agriculture-related commodities to many countries around the world, including the United States, Russia, and the UK, begins his analysis of the Palestinian future with this requirement:

> You cannot have two separate states. You cannot have two separate economies. And they have to complement each other, because Gaza is on the seaside of the Mediterranean while the West Bank is not. Gaza will have the gas.[70] The West Bank will not have the gas. We don't have fuel here in the West Bank. Gaza also has very highly skilled labor, especially in agriculture, while the West Bank does not have much of that. Gaza has very good skilled labor in the manufacturing of furniture, while the West Bank does not. Gaza has the sea—a tourist attraction, a Sharm el-Sheik in Gaza.[71]

Though the integration of the two economies is necessary, it would be painstakingly slow, given the scale of reconstruction required in Gaza after the 2014 war and the ongoing need for humanitarian aid, beset with problems and tensions. Since the occupation began, each of the two parts of Palestine has essentially gone its own way, thanks mainly to the web of Israeli checkpoints, multiple restrictions on movement, and the blockade. They have very different social networks and norms. There are psychological barriers and mutual suspicions.[72] All agree with the World Bank's assessment that "the strategic goal of an economically viable Palestine is achievable only if Gaza and the West Bank are maintained as an integral economic entity."[73] Ironically, if the two Palestinian entities did function separately but also freely, without Israeli constraints, the West Bank would enjoy the demographic "pull" and would start from a higher economic base, but the overall advantage in the long run would go to Gaza for three reasons: deepwater access, a port, and the development of offshore gas fields. Disparities in trade—exports and imports between Gaza and the West Bank—would take time to correct.[74]

And, of course, there is also the matter of integrating yet another economy, that of East Jerusalem, with the economies of the West Bank and Gaza. East Jerusalem, the presumed capital of a Palestinian state, is a cesspool of poverty. According to the Association for Civil Rights in Israel (ACRI), its

---

HDI. Nu'man Kanafani, "The Palestine State: Economic Integration Despite Geographic Discontinuity," 12.

360,000 Palestinian residents constitute 38 percent of Jerusalem's population yet garner just a 10 percent allocation of the municipality's budget.[75] An estimated 78 percent of its residents live under the poverty line, including 84 percent of children. About 40 percent of Palestinian males and 85 percent of Palestinian females do not participate in the Jerusalem labor market; the separation barrier cuts East Jerusalem off from the West Bank and it has gone from being a central urban hub that provided services and opportunities to wide portions of the West Bank to having limited access. The once-thriving commerce between the two is gone, as "the route of the Separation Barrier, which winds its way along 142-kilometer," divides one Palestinian from another.[76] "Only 4 percent of those living beyond the wall have continued to do their shopping in Jerusalem," the ACRI notes, "whereas 18 percent did so before. Conversely, their consumer purchasing in areas that do not require passing through the Barrier or checkpoints has jumped from 25% to 50%." East Jerusalem is dilapidated, mostly falling apart, with crumbling infrastructure, its needs unattended to for decades.

Nu'man Kanafani, who is the research director at the Palestine Economic Policy Research Institute in Ramallah and professor at the Department of Resource Economics, University of Copenhagen, prescribes five conditions necessary for the economic cohesion of the West Bank and Gaza: equality of economic opportunity; convergence of standards of living between the two; a high degree of financial integration (an efficient system to transfer financial resources from the West Bank to Gaza); complementary production processes on the basis of the comparative advantage of each; and measures to curb the persistent tendency of labor to move from Gaza to the West Bank in search of higher-paying jobs and more opportunity.[77]

None of these goals would be easy to achieve; each would require priority status. Also requiring priority status would be bridging the housing, employment, and income gap *within* each entity in parallel with bridging the gap between them.[78] Given the fact that Gaza's economy is virtually nonexistent and in dire need of immediate attention after the 2014 war, it will absorb the greater part of whatever donor assistance is forthcoming, and additional assistance targeting integration of the two economies simply might not materialize. Add to this the fact that a Palestinian state would be divided ideologically by rivalries within Fatah and Hamas and between the two; by cleavages between internal refugees and returnees from the camps in the neighboring countries; and between fundamentalists and secular Muslims. Militias would continue to proliferate, and so would guns under the bed.

Uncertainty scares investors. Nevertheless, the Palestinian interviewees join the World Bank, the IMF, and all the others in a fundamental optimism: Remove *all* the barriers to the movement of people, goods, and services *within* and *between* the West Bank and Gaza, open Area C in the West Bank, let the Palestinians collect their own customs taxes and be released from dependence on Israel in that important regard, and abundance would flow. Naser Tahboub suggested that one path to viability would be financial compensation for the refugees and an Israeli commitment to providing working permits to 200,000 members of the Palestinian labor force. A related idea, likely to be palatable to all parties, is industrial zones along the border of Israel and the new Palestine, which the PA and Israel are already exploring with a plan of using Palestinian labor and Israeli capital. Hazem Shunnar told me, "We started projects like this before the intifada, which at that point in time Israelis found acceptable." Palestine must also have trade and preferential labor treatment and favored-nation status.

At present UNRWA provides services for about half the population of WBG, and although there probably would be a transitional process before it departed,[79] an increasing proportion of the services it provides would become the responsibility of a Palestinian government. It would have to build the schools and train the teachers for the explosive growth in the number of young people. Would the rich Arab countries provide the wherewithal for a new state to begin its life as a stable one, or would they, as they have so often done in the past, pass the buck back to the West? It's hard to believe that they would take on this responsibility given that they are so unwilling to live up to their donor commitments now.

Tahboub says, "Palestine must be weaned off donor reliance, and improvements in the standard of living must be driven by a dynamic, high-value-added export sector." He also points out the comparative advantage the Palestinians would have in a different sector, tourism; most of the holy sites would be in Palestine, which would be a major boost to the related craft industries.

> We have an unlimited number of businessmen and capital around the world. When the political conditions change, they will enable us; they will contribute. I am a very strong believer in my brother Arabs. If 10 percent of what they have accumulated in these years was directed to Palestine, we are Monaco. I estimate the Palestinian diaspora wealth to be not less than $200 billion. In reality, the best estimate is $70 billion. If something like 5

percent of this money will come to Palestine in the first ten years, we will be in good shape.*[80]

This "if" is wildly optimistic, because Palestinian capital is just like all other capital: It wants a safe harbor; it is driven by profit, not patriotism, and most certainly not by altruism.

Jamil Hilal, a sociologist at Birzeit University and a senior research fellow at the Palestinian Institution for the Study of Democracy, notes that Palestinian expatriate capital was very interested in the opportunities that opened up following the recognition of the Palestinian Authority in 1993, and some of that capital did flow back, but after the Second Intifada a lot of it was withdrawn and new investors' interest disappeared. "Even today there is significant Israeli capital invested in projects in the West Bank," Tahboub, always optimistic, reminds me. "We have never prevented Israeli investment in Palestine. We know that they have many projects inside Palestine financed by Israeli venture capital. We know that big projects in Palestine, which are supposedly owned by Palestinians, are in fact owned by Israelis. We never prevented that. We welcome Israeli investments as far as it does not affect ownership of land."[81]

Tahboub aims high: "We shoot to be a Monaco, a Singapore, or similar countries." His vision should be an inspiring one, but it is riddled with assumptions and dubious propositions.[82] Tourism and craft-based industries are not high-value-added job bases; services are low value-added. The Palestinian manufacturing sector is composed of small companies. The high-tech sector does show promise, but it is in its infancy and will have to compete in the global marketplace, where Israel's high-tech sector is already among the most sophisticated. His assumptions regarding the level and sources of capital inflow are untested. Right now Tahboub's "brother Arabs" have more capital invested in Israel than in the occupied West Bank.†

Per-capita income differences between Israel and WBG highlight what might well be the most difficult task for establishing the independent

*According to a World Bank article, "7.2 million Palestinians currently live beyond the boundaries of Palestine. These Palestinians are estimated to hold an aggregate wealth of more than $70 billion." See http://archive.thisweekinpalestine.com/details.php?id=4174&ed=226&edid=226.

†Private Palestinian investment in the West Bank was $1.5 billion in 2011, compared with at least $2.5 billion in Israel. Amira Hass, "Study: Palestinians Invest Twice as Much in Israel as They Do in West Bank," *Haaretz*, November 22, 2011, http://www.haaretz.com/print-edition/features/study-palestinians-invest-twice-as-much-in-israel-as-they-do-in-west-bank-1.396979.

Palestinian economy: weaning itself off the Israeli economy while recognizing, paradoxically, that this link must be cultivated as a source of job creation. In the short run, continued dependence on Israel as the major export and import market for Palestine is a foregone conclusion, but a developmental model for the economy should prioritize finding access to other markets. Otherwise, the West Bank would become an adjunct of the Israeli economy.

Mazen Sinokrot believes that because Israel has, in essence, hijacked the Palestinian economy, a united Palestinian economy freed of Israeli domination would boom almost by definition. He rattles off innumerable reasons why a new Palestinian state would attract foreign direct investment. He sees a market for government-issued bonds sold to investors outside Palestine (a major tool used by Israel in the early years). "But before people would invest," he adds, "they must be assured that their investments are safe. In the postindependence phase, the bonds could encourage the private sector to invest, because they are sure they will have a guaranteed return. . . . There is quite a good surplus of money. Rates of return on investment in Palestine would be great. If the return of investment in some countries now is within 3 percent to 5 percent, I can assure you in Palestine it can be more than 10 percent on some strategic projects."

Palestinian Banks have about $8 billion in deposits.[83] "Private investment [in the West Bank] has averaged a mere 15 percent of GDP over the past seven years, compared with rates of over 25 percent in vigorous middle-income countries.[84] Needless to say, there is virtually no private investment in Gaza. Even given a two-state solution, investors are not going to rush in blindly. They would take a wait-and-see approach, measuring the degree of uncertainty. Moreover, Palestine would have to find a balance between trying to attract capital-intensive economic activities and labor-intensive ones. Given the huge levels of unemployment, labor-intensive industries/services should take precedence over capital-intensive ones; the latter are conducive to higher levels of per-capita productivity, and while this may generate higher rates of growth, it is also conducive to increasing income inequality. In the last thirty years capital has become increasingly "footloose": The activities it generates can easily be moved from one place to another. Many countries, all hungry for capital, offer companies huge tax breaks and subsidies to attract them. And many found that once these special benefits ran out, some companies simply walked after finding yet another country willing to offer attractive packages of benefits. One should temper the belief that expatriate capital will flow into a new Palestine. And, throw into the pot the exponentially increasing uncertainty in the region as Arab states supposedly commit themselves to a coalition that ultimately may require them to provide the "boots on the ground" to combat the Islamic State (ISIS) in Syria, and perhaps Jordan, if ISIS probes, as it has, for an opportunity;[85] the complexities inherent in the overall Obama strategy and wide-scale doubt among regional experts as to whether it has a chance of succeeding; an Iraq that has slid into a Sunni/Shia/Kurdistan divide that defies a lasting reconciliation; the shifting pattern of regional alliances; and, of course, a recalcitrant Iran, increasingly unwilling to denuclearize in line with the West's conditions.

Sinokrot joins Tahboub in highlighting the prospects for the tourism industry, and for the same reasons, and he adds another industry in which the new, freed economy would have a competitive advantage: farming. "Because of weather and the climate in the Jordan Valley, Palestine has the competitive advantage for being a very important food basket for Europe. Palestine will be in a position to offer fresh produce for Europe." Perhaps climate change may throw a wrench into that sunny scenario.

Nor is it a given that agriculture would be the finely tuned engine of growth. Agribusiness is capital intensive, not labor intensive. "Small" farm agriculture is not among the higher-value-added industries, with limitations on the extent that its output can move upstream into value-added activities generating employment; and still more limitation if its produce is mainly for direct export to overseas markets. Besides, the more sophisticated the technology used to cultivate the land, the smaller the workforce required. The shortage of water, already a concern, will require that a Palestinian state (like its neighbors in the Levant) build desalination plants, which are very capital intensive. Israel is a pioneer in this field and already uses desalinated water, even for household drinking. Given the huge sums of capital involved, it would almost necessarily have to import water from Israel, which has the necessary resources and expertise in the field, but water dependency devalues sovereignty.

> > < <

Hazem Shunnar foresees monumental but not insurmountable difficulties for a united, free Palestinian economy in the beginning, when expectations will be sky-high and the ability to meet them far more modest. The PA's debt crisis will persist. Shunnar believes a Palestinian state would be a ward of the international community and reliant on donor aid for some indefinite period. Whether or not the Fatah-Hamas pact holds (and since we are talking about some unspecified time in the future, all references to a Hamas–Fatah pact may be irrelevant), the outlook for even maintaining existing levels of aid are poor. The EU is still wrestling with economic recession and austerity-imposed economies. The Obama administration has cut foreign assistance by at least 15 percent.[86] In an increasingly partisan United States, with Republicans' likely grip on Congress unshakable for years to come and their obsession with lowering the debt ceiling and not raising taxes and larger defense budgets, the variables of most importance for underwriting the economy of a sovereign Palestine would still not be under the control of its government.

"We have to start a transition period from half occupation to total freedom," Shunnar says. "The main resources we have are human resources. We have a higher rate of education than in most Arab countries, but we will have to adjust educational curricula to match the needs of the economy, emerging industries and services." He, too, puts most of his eggs in the tourism basket. He insists that returning refugees would not be a burden on the new state[87]—the opposite, in fact, assuming a well-managed and staggered process for repatriating them. Shunnar dismisses concerns about friction between the indigenous population and returnees, who may be given preferential treatment and who may arrive with substantial compensation packages enabling them to build or purchase homes better than those of the local population. The boom in the construction industry would benefit everyone, he says. The multiplier effect would kick in. Of course, all this optimism assumes that refugee compensation will come in large sums. "We will have to gradually absorb them and gradually adjust ourselves and our economy according to their needs and to their contributions. The estimates of the compensation they will receive are in the area of $100 billion.[88] Refugees would bring their compensation with them and the skills they learned from their living outside. Some will have businesses and assets that they will relocate."

As for immigration aside from returning refugees, it is safe to assume that citizens of higher-income countries would *not* migrate to the homeland. They would, of course, come smiling and proud and do the tourist route with all its trappings. Immigrants would most likely only come from countries with lower standards of living. Nevertheless, Shunnar is confident that once Area C is opened up, returning refugees will settle and create jobs. "Agricultural and rural development will be one of the main ways of development after getting independence,"[89] he says. But will the returnees want to build their new, liberated lives in Area C?

Robert Danin has a different take on the future. "In any real settlement," he says, "Israel would *not* want the basic concept of one unified economic space. The Palestinians would, because there's the dependency; Israel is a wealthy country which they can benefit from in the short term. But they will be looking for greater economic opportunities. In the longer run, the Palestinian orientation will be to the East, not to the West, or at least not into Israel."[90] He is skeptical that there will be massive trade between the two, even in sectors that seem to be win-win, such as tourism. Both sides would benefit, but "there's a tendency in the Israeli tourism industry" he says, "to see the conflict or to see the opportunities more in zero-sum terms." A peace agreement will do little to change entrenched mind-sets. He expects that Israeli tourist interests would lobby hard for protection.

If Danin's explication is a weather vane, Israel intends to hold all that it has, yield little, and for the most part let a Palestinian state fend for itself. Israel will measure economic cooperation more in terms of a win-lose equation, pressing for arrangements of which it is the main beneficiary and putting obstacles in the way of arrangements that might be detrimental to its own interests. Palestine may already have a fledgling high-tech sector, but Israel will do all it can to ensure that it does not become a viable competitor to its own "very formidable high-tech industries." Indeed, more so now than ever because the high-tech sector in Israel like high-tech sectors in other countries, faces an increasingly competitive environment.

High tech is the ultimate in "human capital," and Palestinian interviewees always stressed that such capital is their people's greatest asset. They repeatedly—and with great pride—referred to having the most educated workforce in the Arab world.[91] Often in oppressed-oppressor relationships, the oppressed, once free, are prone to adopt many of the practices that were instrumental in their oppressors' success, and to emulate their habits.[92] Over the length of its forty-five-year occupation, Israel has become an economic powerhouse.[93] Palestinians would like to develop the attributes to emulate such entrepreneurship, innovation, and use of cutting-edge technology.

The optimism, palpable as it may be, should come with a caveat: the long time lags between producing (1) teachers who can impart mastery of the subjects that form the core of a skills-oriented curriculum; (2) graduates who have the skill sets required; (3) industries/services, whether start-ups (which require investment) or preexisting, that can draw on this pool of skilled workers; and (4) a market for their products. The competition is *worldwide* in the knowledge industry. Every developing nation wants to establish this beachhead, but the shoreline is short and can accommodate only a few. The best, as has happened elsewhere, will be offered opportunities and remuneration packages far superior to what Palestine can offer in many other countries, especially in the West, eager to grab their talents.

Palestinians can rightfully—and proudly—point to the fact that their literacy rates rank among the highest in the world: Illiteracy rates are just 4.7 percent in Gaza and 4.9 percent in the West Bank. But pedagogical methodology is lacking. Surveying the situation, Rana Baker, who had been studing for a masters degree at London's School of Oriental and African Studies, writes in *Al Monitor* that

> The Palestinian education system relies heavily on traditional means of teaching where students are silent receivers. . . . Internet-empowered technology and computer systems are hardly employed in any of Gaza's schools. The Internet continues to be stressed as a source of distraction rather than a platform to develop a broader outlook on all kinds of subjects.
>
> Although technology is a basic subject at public and private schools alike, it continues to be presented in theoretical terms. The topics discussed in this subject range from information systems to engineering, and even carpentry. Naturally, these topics stress practical applications and experiments, but students do nothing beyond memorizing the theories so as to answer the questions in the exam.[94]

In 2006, the Peres Center for Peace and the Palestine Trade Center commissioned a detailed study of economic activity[95] between Israel and the PA that estimated the benefits to both entities from maximizing the opportunities for future cooperation and development over a five-to-ten year period.[96] It concluded that the Palestinian employment market would benefit to the tune of half a million new jobs (a doubling of the total jobs in the economy), a "dramatic" increase. However, the report continues, "our analysis shows that this increase in employment opportunities would barely enable the Palestinian economy to contain the current alarming unemployment rate, of close to 25% . . . the creation of 500,000–600,000 new jobs will be necessary just in order to keep Palestinian unemployment rate under the 25% line." In other words, the conclusions of this best-of-possible scenarios the study envisages come up short on the question of a self-sustaining and viable Palestinian economy.

In December 2007, a report prepared on behalf of the Palestine International Business Forum examined in depth a number of Palestinian-Israeli trade scenarios. The team of international experts concluded that a "cooperative trade arrangement," specifically an "enhanced" Free Trade Agreement (FTA+) would maximize benefits to both. With 2005–2007 as a base, it projected that over a ten-year period, "Palestinian jobs would grow by 120 percent," more than 25 percent of which would be in tourism; revenue from tourism would "potentially rise by a factor of 30," from agriculture by "more than a factor of 20," and "overall export earnings would increase by a factor of 18." Heady stuff.[97] Amid all the different predictions, numerous international organizations have made, one comprehensive and disarmingly short list of what has to happen in order for the Palestinian economy to be viable and sustainable emerges. These are not numbers and percentages and other technical benchmarks but rather the intangible conditions that would allow for those metrics to be achieved: genuine, well-meaning Israeli cooperation; good governance; successful social and political integration of Gaza and the West Bank (especially a rapprochement between Fatah and Hamas); international and Arab support, initially, and then a slow but steady weaning of the economy from that support; successful integration of returning refugees and their compensation; investment from the Palestinian diaspora; a well-functioning and independent legal system; a professional and capable police force; cooperation from the world economy (a coincidental twenty-year boom would be helpful); a deep commitment from the whole society to accept austerity if necessary to make this work; and *real* peace based on parity of esteem. In short a wish list.

At the end of 2013, the PA was in its accustomed situation: facing a severe financial crisis and still awaiting previously pledged donor aid. In September 2013 the International Monetary Fund reported that the PA's recurrent fiscal deficit had widened to 14.2 percent of gross domestic product last year and was likely to be bigger in 2014. GDP growth had slowed to 2.7 percent in the West Bank and Gaza while unemployment reached 17 percent in the West Bank alone.[98]

In 2014 the situation got worse, even though much could be excused on the Gaza war.

The downward spiral:

"The recent conflict in Gaza will put further stress on an already struggling Palestinian economy," the World Bank warned in September 2014, "with falling income per capita in 2013, projected to contract further by the end of 2014."

One in six Palestinians in the West Bank labor force was unemployed; nearly every second person in Gaza, "even before the recent conflict." The situation was unsustainable.

Although the average yearly economic growth exceeded 8 percent between 2007 and 2011, it declined to 1.9 percent in 2013, and reached minus 1 percent for the first quarter of 2014. A quarter of the Palestinian population was living in poverty, with the rate in Gaza twice as high as that in the West Bank. The constraints on the private sector were such that "only 11% of formal firms have more than 20 workers compared to 35% in comparable lower-middle income countries."

And as regards the PA's efforts to strengthen its fiscal position? In September 2014, the World Bank in yet one more stark report warned that the Palestinian economy had begun to contract: "falling income per capita in 2013," was projected to fall further in 2014. Growth had declined to 1.9 percent in 2013 and reached minus 1 percent in the first quarter of 2014.[99]

And then came the Gaza War, accelerating decline in the West Bank and leaving the Gaza economy in rubble.

Everyone who has studied or simply mulled the prospects for the hypothetically united and free Palestinian economy agrees on one thing: Such an economy could not possibly be worse than the current one. Moreover, a West Bank economy that survives on donor assistance and a Gaza economy that is virtually nonexistent hardly suggest that an integrated economy would be anywhere close to being either viable or sustainable.

Chapter 9

Demographics: The Enemy Within

In Jerusalem, on May 28, 2013, Netanyahu addressed the Global Forum for Combating Anti-Semitism and railed against the rise of anti-Semitism worldwide and the efforts by many countries to delegitimize Israel.[1] At other forums he has described an Iranian nuclear bomb as an "existential" threat to his nation. However, notwithstanding either persistent and perverse anti-Semitism or the implications of an Iranian bomb, the gravest existential threat Israel faces as a *Jewish* state is not a security threat in the traditional sense but the silently creeping, inexorably irreversible changes in Israel's demographic profiles. Even as polls unanimously confirm that Jewish Israelis' primary cultural and political concern is preserving the culture's Jewishness, at the expense of some of their democratic norms, if necessary,[2] the numbers are working the other way. Non-Jews, including Christians, Bedouins, Druze, Palestinian Israelis, and the "Others,"[3] together with the Palestinian populations in the West Bank and Gaza, either will outnumber Jews within a few years or already have.

Jewish Israelis therefore have three choices: a two-state solution that gives the Palestinians in the West Bank and Gaza their own state, leaving an Israeli state in which Jews, according to 2014 data, account for, at best, 75 percent of the population; or, as demographics change, an unmistakably apartheid state (along the lines of the old South Africa) if it refuses to extend the voting franchise to the non-Jewish residents of the West Bank and the Gaza Strip; or becoming some form of a binational/consociational state that is, by definition, *not* a Jewish state.

These choices are not news to Israelis. The Israel they live in today will not be the Israel of tomorrow. Still, for most, "threat" is understood in terms of militarism and "security" is whatever it takes to protect them from "terrorists." Besides, Israelis have been living on the edge of an existential precipice for sixty-five years. The country's collective narrative inoculates Israeli public consciousness against placing a premium on expectations about the future. So when yet another round of peace negotiations falls apart, Israelis shrug. Do they know the demographic clock is at one minute to midnight?

Almost certainly. But to a people who have already *known* midnight, demographics are just another problem.[4] Israelis live as much as possible in the present, which is one of prosperity, a well-deserved global reputation for entrepreneurship and technological innovation, and economic numbers that qualify it for membership in "exclusive" organizations such as the OECD. When the issue of demographics starts to be taken seriously and reduced to sound bites that are easily absorbed by the general public, the real battle for the soul of Israel will get under way.[5] The conventional wisdom is that the only way to avoid demographic entrapment is a two-state solution. One would think that should concentrate Israeli minds, but it has not. When the 2013–14 talks collapsed in April 2014, just 9 percent of Jewish Israelis regarded the resumption of talks and finalization of an FSA as being among their major priorities.[6] The impending demographic threat is not sufficiently immediate, the imperative for two states not sufficiently grounded in their consciousness.

> > < <

Sergio DellaPergola is Israel's preeminent demographer of world Jewry.[7] Here is a small sampling of the key numbers that he reeled off during our four extensive interviews[8] and that he also reeled off to Aaron David Miller, who interviewed him before President Obama's trip to Israel in March 2014:[9]

- A little over twelve million people live in the area between the Mediterranean shore and the Jordan River, which encompasses the territories of Israel and the Palestinians.
- Just about half—six million—are Jewish citizens who live either within Israel's internationally recognized borders or in East Jerusalem, the Golan Heights, or the occupied West Bank.
- Just about all of the other half are Palestinian: 1.7 million Palestinian Israeli citizens of Israel, 2.3 million Palestinians in the West Bank, *not* including East Jerusalem, and a further 1.6 million in the Gaza Strip. About 300,000 documented or undocumented foreign workers and refugees, mostly from African countries, also reside in the country.
- Among OECD countries, Israel has the highest fertility rate by far: 3 children per woman on average compared to a 1.7 OECD average.[10] During the last decade and a half, fertility has been slowly increasing, and not only among observant Jews. It is above five children among Jewish settlers in the West Bank. Among Israel's Palestinian population, fertility has been stable or slowly declining but still stands at a very high 3.5 children per household.

- While annual population growth around the world is estimated at 1.2 percent, among Jews in Israel, it is 1.8 percent (including immigration and births). Among Palestinian Israelis, it is 2.3 percent. For Palestinians in the West Bank and Gaza it is 2.7 percent.
- Both Jews and Muslims throughout Palestine are growing more religious. In DellaPergola's surveys 21 percent of Jews said they are more religious than they were earlier in life; 14 percent are less religious. Among Muslims, 41 percent said they are more religious; only 4 percent said they are less religious.
- The ultraorthodox, or Haredim, the most religious and self-segregated component of Israeli society, accounts for slightly above 10 percent of the population and is growing; among Jews under twenty years old, this ultraconservative cohort accounts for 20 percent; *between 25 percent and 33 percent of Israeli schoolchildren attend Haredim schools.*
- Within Israel proper, Jews constitute 79 percent of the population, a number that will diminish by a few percentage points by 2030. But if you include the occupied West Bank and Gaza, the present roughly fifty-fifty split becomes an estimated 56 percent Palestinian majority by 2030.

In demography, slight changes in fertility rates, marriage rates, mortality rates, economic circumstances, religious observance, ethnic makeup, and other factors produce dramatic changes in the raw numbers in just a few decades. And changes demographers themselves make in their *assumptions* about the variability of changes in those factors yield dramatically different predictions about the future. Changes in the raw numbers can result in changes in political affiliation. If Russian Jews, for example, emerge as the dominant group in Israel, one set of outcomes can be expected; if the ultraconservative cohort becomes dominant, another. Nor is the emerging demographic profile of the Palestinian population either homogeneous or stable. One set of outcomes can be expected if Islamists predominate, another if a combination of moderate Muslims, secularists, and Christians become a dominant coalition. Differentials in these variables between the West Bank and Gaza are important, as are internal migration rates between the two Palestinian entities. If political competition between Fatah and Hamas mutates into intercommunal war, or if Gaza is cast adrift and allowed to run its own statelet, demographic balances for the whole would shift.

When all the talking and calculating is done, demographics will go a long way toward determining the success or failure of any resolution of the Israeli-Palestinian conflict. Any final outcome must take into account not just the facts on the ground, including politics, today, but also *the facts that are likely to be on the ground,* including politics driven by demographics, *thirty to fifty years from now.*

"The Jewish majority is constantly decreasing—if it exists at all, over the whole territory between the Mediterranean Sea and the Jordan River," DellaPergola says. "The crucial point is the rate of growth of every [cohort] which is *not Jewish.* The population growth of the Palestinians in the West Bank and Gaza, as well as among the Palestinian Israeli citizens, is higher than it is for the Jewish population. The slight but steady percentage differential is moving inexorably in one direction."

In 2009 the Palestinian Israeli cohort accounted for 30 percent of the total *natural* increase in Israel's population. *The share of Palestinian Israeli children under fifteen will likely be 30 percent of the total in 2030.* Jewish Israelis comprised 91 percent of all Israelis who are seventy-eight years of age and 77 percent of those aged forty-eight. The aging Jewish population requires a higher birthrate just to stay in place. "You are witnessing," DellaPergola summarizes, "a gradual transformation in structural identity within Israeli society, as you move from the older to the younger age cohorts. [As a result] there will be a transformation from a national into a binational state."[11]

The Palestinian Israeli minority argues that Israel is an "ethnocracy"—a regime that promotes "the expansion of the dominant group in contested territory while maintaining a democratic façade."[12] It is pressing its case that it has inherent rights beyond individual representation; that it has *corporate* rights; that there must be a more equitable distribution of power and allocation of resources, i.e., some form of governance, some consociation that reflects the Palestinian Israeli weight in the total population. Today Palestinian Israelis have equitable representation in the Knesset, but no party would dare ask them to become part of a ruling coalition; hence they exercise no power in government. They can participate in most levels of Israel's civic life but few hold positions in the upper echolons of public administration. Thus they have little say in the decisions that affect their community. Israel discriminates against them at most levels of economic and social activity. They are largely shut out of the job market for the high-technology sector and security-related industries. They face formidable barriers when trying to purchase land. And Jewish Israelis, rather than wanting to see these inequities narrowed, favor instead further discrimination.[13] The percentage of Palestinian Israelis in universities is low: 11.3 percent of undergraduate students, 7 percent of master's degree students, 3 percent of doctoral students, and 2 percent of the academic faculty.[14] "The gaps are closing—there have been some improvements in the last decade, including an increase in the number of departmental director generals," according to Mohammad Darawshe, codirector of the Abraham Fund, "but on most social and economic indicators Palestinian Israelis continue to lag and face discrimination and racism."*

DellaPergola admits that "the gap is huge." Within the Jewish state, he says, "you have enough potential for conflict with a minority now large enough to break the chains of being regarded as a lurking fifth column, increasingly assertive in its own right." With regard to Palestine itself, "can you pretend that you can administer Israel as a 100 percent Jewish state, if 50 percent of the people are non-Jewish? That would be untenable. You can be a Democratic president who governs the United States with 51 percent versus 49 percent over Republicans, but there is a certain basic consensus about what the United States *is*. . . . That is not the situation here."

Of course, we all manipulate numbers to meet our particular agendas, and even when the agendas change, we convince the figures to come along

*Mohammad Darawshe, interview with the author, February 20, 2012. All quotes from Darawshe in this chapter are from this interview unless otherwise noted. The fund, according to Darawshe, "is the largest organization in Israel that works on the Jewish-Arab relations in Israel with the goal of creating what we call the 'shared society'—trying to restructure the relationship of the state of Israel with its Arab minority in a way that is sustainable and in a way that it can create what we consider is to become a cohesive society, which is not cohesive enough today and not sustainable enough." According to Adalah, the Legal Center for Arab and Minority Rights in Israel, currently there are more than fifty laws that discriminate against Palestinian citizens of Israel. These laws affect Israeli Arab civil and political rights; criminal justice; prisoners' and detainees' rights; economic, social, and cultural rights; land and planning rights; and rights within the Occupied Palestinian Territories. Most of these were enacted after the February 2009 Knesset elections, when "Members of Knesset (MKs) immediately introduced a flood of discriminatory legislation that directly or indirectly targets Palestinian Arab citizens of Israel, as well as Palestinians in the Occupied Palestinian Territory (OPT) and the Palestinian refugees." See Adalah, "New Discriminatory Laws and Bills in Israel"; and Adalah, "Index of Currently Pending Discriminatory Bills." A comprehensive picture of rights violations and efforts to secure them can be obtained at Adalah, Discriminatory Laws in Israel (database), http://adalah.org/eng/Israeli-Discriminatory-Law-Database.

See also the report of the Or Commission, established in 2000, to investigate the deaths of twelve Arab and one Jewish citizen following riots within the Israeli Arab sector. Among the commission's findings: the plight of Israel's Arab citizens constitutes the "most sensitive and important domestic issue facing Israel today" and that the state must "initiate, develop, and operate programs emphasizing budgets that will close gaps in education, housing, industrial development, employment, and services." For more on the Or Commission, see Jewish Virtual Library, "The Official Summation of the Or Commission Report," http://www.jewishvirtuallibrary.org/jsource/Society_&_Culture/OrCommissionReport.html. For more on the levels of discrimination that Palestinian Israelis face, see the publications of Sikkuy (Association for the Advancement of Civic Equality) at http://www.sikkuy.org.il/?lang=en, particularly the Equality Index; and Pappé, *Forgotten Palestinians*.

with us. Israel is no different. There is a small school of demographers who dismiss the demographic threat and produce sets of data to support their assertions. Like people everywhere, the Israeli public treats any set of demographic data with suspicion unless it supports their prejudices. (Netanyahu has been careful not to get involved in the demography wars, at least publicly. He has not embraced any one set of figures.)

Pinchas Wallerstein has a very different perspective. "As regards the so-called demographic threat," he says, "Yoram Ettinger and his research fellows—some from the U.S.—have shown very convincingly that the accepted demography is extremely inaccurate and that demography is not a threat. Arab birthrates are falling as they become more educated, while the birthrate of the Jews is going up. Demography will be less of a problem in the future than it even is today."[15]

Yoram Ettinger, whose predictions Wallerstein alludes to with such confidence, is not a demographer.* He heads an organization called "2nd Thought: US Israel Initiative," runs a Web site called The Ettinger Report, and regularly rebuts the "political correctness" of the establishment's demographic profiles.[16] He strenuously opposes any suggestion that Israel should, as the phrase goes, concede Jewish geography in order to secure Jewish demography. Doing so, according to Ettinger, would ignore the correct demographic trends in Israel, the Muslim world in general, and west of the Jordan River in particular. These trends, he argues, work in *favor* of Israel's Jewish demographics, and will continue to do so. Ettinger is not taken seriously by professional demographers, who dismiss his work as bordering on quackery, but he has an audience that reaches well beyond the one that professional demographers reach. They may have the facts, but he has the influence, writing for *Israel Today* (a newspaper financed by ultra-right wing American billionaire Sheldon Adelson[17] and distributed free on a daily basis) and provided with ample opportunities by the Right, including the settlement movement, to promulgate his views and support them with the "correct" data that is ignored by large segments of the political elite and its constituencies.

In 2013 Ettinger wrote in his report that "in sharp contrast with projections issued by the demographic establishment, there is a 66 percent Jewish

*"Ambassador (ret.) Ettinger—who did his graduate studies at UCLA and undergraduate at University of Texas at El Paso—served as minister for congressional affairs at Israel's embassy in Washington, Israel's consul general in Houston, and director of Israel's Government Press Office." See his bio at http://www.docstoc.com/docs/88482399/Yoram-Ettinger.

majority (6.3 million Jews) in the combined area of Judea, Samaria (1.66 million Arabs) and pre-1967 Israel (1.65 million Arabs), compared with a 40 percent Jewish minority in 1948 and a 9 percent Jewish minority in 1900. "The Jewish majority benefits from a robust tailwind of fertility rate and migration, which could produce an 80 percent Jewish majority by 2035 [in all of Palestine][18]. . . ." After much discussion of fertility rates and the other tools of the trade, Ettinger concludes, "Anyone suggesting that Jews are doomed to become a minority west of the Jordan River is either dramatically mistaken or outrageously misleading."[19]

Ettinger's function is to obfuscate, to raise doubt about the demographers' political correctness, and to shore up the claims of the right wing.

"The relationship of the Israelis and their Palestinian neighbors is one of great significance to Israeli demographers," Arnon Soffer, who holds the Reuven Chaikin Chair of Geostrategy at the University of Haifa, says.[20] "The issue is simply posed: Who will 'prevail,' demographically? The professionals conclude that it will be the Palestinians, unless they have their own state; Yoram Ettinger says it is the Jews, and they won't need a two-state solution in order to retain the Jewishness of the state of Israel."[21]

I interviewed him twice, once in 2011 and again in 2012. Much of what he related to me reflects the research of him and his late colleague, Evgenia Bystrov, addressing the implications of the current distributions of the Jewish population.

He paraphrases Ettinger in this manner: "'We don't have Arabs anymore. They are leaving the country and all the census data is wrong. The demographic future is rosy. There are just one and a half million Arabs.' He is easy to listen to and leaves you with an optimistic smile. Open the Web site of the Israeli minister of information and you will find the handiwork of Ettinger. If you take the figures from the Israeli minister of information, there are no more refugees and there are no more Arabs. Therefore, we can annex the West Bank without endangering our majority. This is the information the minister of information wants you to buy into. Ettinger is the winner."[22]

Roby Nathanson is more skeptical about projections on both sides. "Demographic prognosis is always based on statistics," he contends. "But you never know how they could be affected by external shocks that we didn't consider; the statistics cannot catch what will happen in twenty or thirty years. I don't think a politician in Israel now will take decisions, major decisions, because of demographic considerations; it's something always in the back of our minds, but it's still a long way off."[23]

> > < <

The proportion of different segments of the Jewish populations—the ultraorthodox, the National Religious Party, and the secular—and the relationships among them are also matters of great interest to demographers. To a great extent, religious affiliation reflects political leaning: the more orthodox, the further right, the more secular, the further left.

On this matter DellaPergola and Soffer agree: Both see an increasingly religious Israel on the horizon. "It's hard not to, when the Haredim, or ultraorthodox, already comprise 10 percent of the Israeli population," Soffer says, "and the number could be 20 percent by 2030." According to Soffer and Bystrov in 2010 about one third of infants in Israel were born to ultraorthodox families and about one fifth more to religious families. Almost 50 percent of first-grade children go to schools that have a religious affiliation, each with a very different religious education curriculum.[24] In December 2013 the ultraorthodox population lay somewhere between 444,000 and 700,000.[25] It is expected to pass one million by 2030, most of them children.[26] "The inescapable conclusion," write Bystrov and Soffer, "is that about half of Israel's population is likely to be religious by 2030. The proportion of non-religious people will accordingly presumably fall," and beyond 2030 Israeli society will have a pronounced religious character."[27] The prospect leaves Soffer less than brimming with optimism about the future. "If my grandchildren, secular children, will be ready to stay in Israel in a religious country, they will not be able to drive on Saturday; they will not be able to swim in the beach, in a bikini," say Soffer with a laugh. "The dressing will be like the ultra-Orthodox Jews, with thousands of other restrictions; I'm not sure they will stay in this environment. Israel is going, deterministically, to be an ultra-religious country. I don't know about the ultra-secularists, whether they will accept it, or will they take their luggage and go to the airport."[28]

According to Israel's Central Bureau of Statistics, the Haredim will account for 41 percent of the population in 2059.[29] This leaves Israel with a conundrum. Although it will continue its effort to integrate the ultraorthodox Jews into the workforce and to cut back on the subsidies they receive, which the nation cannot afford, the very high birthrate in the ultraorthodox sector acts as a bulwark of sorts and slows the drift to a Palestinian majority in Palestine. This "advantage" is nullified in the event of a two-state solution and becomes a *disadvantage* as the ultraorthodox cohort in Israel outgrows the other Jewish subgroups. The almost exponential growth in the ultraorthodox population will have enormous consequence for Israeli society, Soffer and DellaPergola believe, because the ultraorthodox yeshiva system of education does not provide graduates with the skills necessary for the modern labor market, and this cohort has a low rate of participation in the labor force to begin with. Furthermore, it is subsidized by the state. About 60 percent of the ultraorthodox are poor, according to a study by the Bank of Israel.[30] Every year in the last decade, 8 percent to 10 percent of Israel's GNP was remitted directly to ultraorthodox households.[31] In 2014, according to UNICEF, Israel was ranked fourth in child poverty in the developed world.[32]

The Bank of Israel concludes that unless the Haredim receive more higher education, Israel will fall from sixteenth to twenty-sixth in OECD rankings.[33] The strain on the working cohort to support this underemployed or non-working cohort has reached a level where it called for lower subsidies and greater ultraorthodox participation in the workforce. However, because the importance of the ultraorthodox vote for forming coalitions is paramount, no Israeli government has cut back on the subsidies. But if more ultraorthodox do enter the workforce, as is beginning to happen—ultraorthodox youth are now required, like other Israeli Jewish youths, to perform military service*—subsidies will be phased out and birthrates *should* begin to fall, thus hastening Israel's decline into a minority status in all of Palestine, in the absence of a peace agreement.

Within Israel proper (that is, within the pre-1967 borders), "you are going to have a genuine cultural split," Soffer predicts.[34] "The seculars and the national religious Jews share the same Western style of life. They are very modern, although for the latter there are huge differences between them and seculars regarding settlements—they believe in the Promised Land and a Greater Israel. With the ultra-Orthodox Jews there is a clash of values. Although the ultra-Orthodox and the national religious have some common denominator as far as religion is concerned, they have their own quarrels. As a result, there are clashes between the national religious and secular but not regarding cultural norms; a clash between the secular and the ultra-Orthodox, definitely about cultural norms, and a clash between

*Ruth Levush, a senior foreign law specialist, writes: "The draft deferment for Haredi youth has been recognized as a violation of the right of the majority of Israelis to equal treatment under the law. It has also been continuously linked to the poverty rate in the Haredi community and its impact on the state budget." "Israel: Supreme Court Decision Invalidating the Law on Haredi Military Draft Postponement," Law Library of Congress, March 2012, http://www.loc.gov/law/help/il-haredi-military-draft/haredi-military-draft.php.

the national religious and the ultra-Orthodox, also about cultural norms." Moreover, he continues, "there is a very wide gap between them and the ultra-Orthodox on the meaning of God and how to pray. They are on the same ground as far as Saturday and kosher food; they are split as far as the occupation of the West Bank and cultural aspects. It's unbearable, and they are intolerant to each other. They both have very high birth rates. It's like a triangle between the secular and the ultra-Orthodox, between the secular and the national religious groups and between the national religious groups and the ultra-Orthodox. And within the ultra-Orthodox, you have Shas, the Sephardim, and the Jews of North Africa who are in a conflict among themselves."[35] Not surprisingly, Soffer and Bystrov's research projects an Israel that is very divided along religious lines.

Hence the scenario they predict: political polarization at all levels of society and the disappearance of the political space in which to forge a consensus—especially on matters relating to settler relocation.

> > < <

The third issue of greatest concern for demographers is the structural imbalances between Jewish Israelis and Palestinian Israelis due to accelerating rates of difference in the geographic distribution of the population. In mid-2014, "just under half of the Jewish population lived in the center of the country, either Jerusalem or the Tel Aviv metropolitan area, 60 percent of the Arab population lives in the north."[36] In short, the country is becoming increasingly self-segregated and impoverished.[37]

Soffer's analysis of the trends in population growth rates among different segments of Israeli society, using the 2012 population as a base, leads him to conclude that the probable outcomes threaten to tear the social fabric of Jewish Israeli society and its relationships with both Palestinian Israelis and Palestinians in the West Bank, that could fundamentally alter the nature of an ongoing Palestinian-Israeli conflict. Different population trends among Israel's subgroups are pulling the country in different directions. Different population groups have different agendas and different political dispositions regarding the conflict. *Israel,* he repeatedly said, *is on its way to becoming a religious society where the ultraorthodox will exercise undue influence.* Both Nathanson and DellaPergola agree with this assessment.

Soffer's data suggests that by 2025 80 percent of Israel's population will be living in the greater Tel Aviv area,[38] which already has a population density of 7,522 persons per square kilometer,[39] and a limit on spatial expansion in a country that is ranked as one of the most densely populated areas in the developed world.[40] Ultraorthodox with large numbers of children will increasingly be packed into Tel Aviv's metropolitan area. Tel Aviv's absorptive capacity, he believes, would be overstretched and its physical infrastructure incapable of meeting the demands placed on it. "The result will be more poverty, infrastructure issues, poor schools, environmental degradation and a weak social fabric." "The combination," Soffer and Bystrov write, "of a periphery of the poor, the foreign, and the alienated, and decline in the quality of life in the Tel Aviv space, creates the conditions for the collapse of the Zionist entity in very short time frames."[41] They wrote the "Tel Aviv State: The Threats to Israel," in 2006. In the course of our interviews, several years later, Soffer was more emphatic than ever about their ominous prediction.

There are three areas where Palestinian Israelis are in the majority and increasingly so—the Galilee Mountains, the northern Negev, and the Triangle. The Triangle is a hundred-square-mile area northeast of Tel Aviv, in the "narrow waist" of Israel,* with a population of 300,000, almost entirely Palestinian Israeli citizens. "When people look at the Arab citizens in Israel," says Mohammad Darawshe, "they think 20 percent, and they think of them as concentrated in pockets, but once you take the Tel Aviv district, which is the heart of the country, out of the formula, suddenly you see that Arab citizens are around 40 percent everywhere else in the country." Soffer concurs. This concentration of Palestinian Israelis in the north is a matter of considerable concern to the Israeli government; hence its attempts to Judaize the Galilee through initiatives like community committees that vet Palestinian Israelis who wish to live there and can prevent them from purchasing a dwelling if they are not a "fit" (do not meet "community's norms"). Palestinian Israeli interviewees repeatedly referred to the innumerable laws and regulations that make it virtually impossible for Palestinian Israelis to purchase land.[42]

Dr. Alon Liel, a former director general in the Israeli Ministry of Foreign Affairs, drew my attention to the explosive ethnic cocktail in the north, where, he says, "there is always the potential for an innocuous-looking flare-up between Jews and Palestinian Israelis to erupt into open confrontation, especially in the 'mixed cities.'"[43]

Tensions already exist between Jewish and Palestinian Israeli populations in cities such as Ramla, Lod, Acco, Haifa, Jaffa, upper Nazareth, and

*"The Triangle, inhabited for the most part by Palestinian Israelis, extends from Um al-Fahm in the North to Kafr Qasim in the South."

Beersheba.[44] Inflows of Palestinian Israelis from rural villages and their higher rates of fertility are changing the demographic profiles of these cities, and with their increasing numbers come obstacles to their further demographic penetration. The Palestinian Israelis, Bystrov and Soffer write, "complain of deprivation at the hands of the State and of displays of racism by their Jewish neighbors." On the other hand, Jewish residents maintain that Arab proximity turns mixed towns into zones of violence, drug trafficking, a culture of poverty, disorder, and falls in property values[45]—attitudes that approximate all too closely those of whites in American cities where African Americans begin to live in increasing numbers in heretofore exclusively white areas. In short, as Palestinians move into a neighborhood, Jews move out.[46] Gerrymandering keeps Jewish Israelis in control of municipal councils. Few have master plans for development. Municipal services, funding for separate schools, public amenities, and public spaces are allocated disproportionally. Palestinian Israelis have more limited access to the services the municipality provides. There are innumerable restrictions—zoning regulations in particular—that make it practically impossible for Palestinian Israelis migrating to these cities to purchase land. The restrictions squeeze the land on which they can build. The local-population Palestinian Israelis find it next to impossible to get municipal permits to make additions to their residences or build on other parts of their property. If they do purchase land, they face interminable bureaucratic delays in getting building permits. Some simply tire of waiting and build anyway, but if the municipality learns they have, even years later, the buildings or additions in question are demolished.

The scales of the divisions and their impacts vary from city to city. In Lod clashes between Israeli Jews and Palestinian Israelis have occurred;[47] in Safed and Acco there are standoffs; in Haifa the situation, although picture perfect on the surface, includes a growing number of problems. To date, the authorities have responded to the growing polarization in mixed cities with measures that make intermingling more unlikely (i.e., policies that promote segregation). "In many cases," Nicolas Pelham writes in an unpublished paper titled "From Backwater to Frontline," "municipalities have erected physical obstacles, such as bypass roads, army bases and industrial zones, creating at their extremes—Arab ghettoes side by side with Jewish gated communities. 'Left to fester, Arabs would comprise an increasingly large proportion of the population until Israel no longer exists,' says Uri Shani, Prime Minister Sharon's former chief of staff. As pressures mount, so too do the separation barriers."[48]

Competition for land between Jewish Israelis and Palestinian Israelis will intensify, and further land restrictions imposed on Palestinian Israeli citizens by future Knesset and Jewish-controlled municipalities will exacerbate latent tensions and strain relations between the two communities. In "mixed" cities clashes between the two communities are likely to become more frequent and become intertwined with the myriad accumulated grievances Palestinian Israelis harbor as a result of the discriminatory practices they face at virtually every level.[49]

Adding to the brew in the boiling pot is the explosive growth in the Bedouin population, which will alter the character of southern Israel at the same time that many geographical areas in the north will have Palestinian Israeli majorities.

The nomadic Bedouin are a distinct cohort within Israeli culture. Bedouin shepherds discovered the Dead Sea Scrolls; over a thousand serve in the IDF, many of them as elite trackers. The proportion of children among them "breaks world records," as Soffer puts it. "Among Jews, the proportion of children aged up to 18 years approaches 30%. Among the northern Arabs of Israel it is around 40%; for the Bedouin it reaches 63%." Families on average, have 11.6 children. Their fertility rates are roughly equivalent to those of the ultraorthodox Jews. However, Jewish men no longer take multiple wives, and Bedouins do. "Today," says Soffer, "you have anywhere from 12 to 25 children per father."[50]

In 2011 the Bedouin population accounted for about 14 percent of all Muslims in Israel; by 2030 it will account for 23 percent to 25 percent.[51] Many of the Bedouin settlements are illegal and without governance. The Prawer Plan,[52] drawn up in 2011, calls for relocating thirty thousand to seventy thousand Bedouin from thirty to forty unrecognized villages* into urban zones with modern facilities. Another way to look at it is that the government wants to confiscate 700,000 dunams (about 270 square miles) to make way for development and Judaization of the vacated lands. The Prawer Plan was met with great resistance by the Bedouin, who saw the attempt to "modernize" them as a threat to their way of life. When their protests drew international media attention, the government backed down, at least for the moment.[53]

"Integrating the Bedouin community into Israeli society," Bystrov and

*"Unrecognized villages" do not appear on maps; there are no roads leading to them, and they are cut off from water and electricity grids. They lack any feature of what we would call a "modern" community.

Soffer write, "is a great challenge for Israeli society, the most problematic question being how to advance their lot and integrate them after 80 years of disregarding their existence and spread (both numerical and territorial)."[54]

Finally, there is the question of demographics in Jerusalem, the largest of Israel's cities in area and population. According to the Association for Civil Rights in Israel (ACRI), in 2012, 38 percent (360,882) of its total population were Palestinians who live in the east of the city. Only 5 percent of Palestinians in East Jerusalem are Israeli citizens.* Almost all of the rest are "permanent residents." They are, for the most part, impoverished, with limited employment opportunities, a severely depleted educational system, and a systematic lack of physical and economic infrastructures. Of those living in East Jerusalem, 78 percent, including 84 percent of children, live below the poverty line. Over 40 percent of the male Palestinian population in Jerusalem does not participate in the labor market, and the number for the women is drastically higher: approximately 85 percent. "Nearly all Palestinian neighborhoods lack development plans," says the ACRI. "The building ratio allowed in Palestinian neighborhoods is generally between 35 percent and 75 percent, while in Jewish neighborhoods it stands between 75 percent and 150 percent." Furthermore, "a third of Palestinian land in Jerusalem has been expropriated since 1967, upon which thousands of apartments have been built for the city's Jewish population;... 35 percent of the planned areas in Palestinian neighborhoods have been designated as 'open landscape areas' on which it is forbidden to build ... Between 2005–2009, only 13% of the Jerusalem housing units granted building permits were in Palestinian neighborhoods; in Jewish neighborhoods, there is an average of 20 square meters of housing per resident, compared to 11 square meters in Palestinian neighborhoods."[55]

In East Jerusalem building permits issued to Jews have increased to the point where, if one envisions a Palestinian state with East Jerusalem as its capital, the Clinton Parameters guidelines that Arab areas are Palestinian and Jewish ones are Israeli may have lost its relevance. Jerusalem is one of

*Linda Gradstein, "East Jerusalem's Identity Crisis," *Jerusalem Post*, October 4, 2012, http://www.jpost.com/In-Jerusalem/Features/East-Jerusalems-identity-crisis. (The population data that Gradstein and the Association for Civil Rights in Israel use to calculate the 38 percent cited in the last paragraph, come from different databases.) "In 1967, when Israel annexed east Jerusalem, it offered Palestinians citizenship. Most declined, saying that east Jerusalem must eventually be the capital of the Palestinian state. They insist that accepting Israeli citizenship is equivalent to accepting Israeli control over Jerusalem. Even today, only about 5 percent of East Jerusalem Arabs have Israeli citizenship."

the poorest cities in Israel. Nevertheless, despite the breadth of the dire statistics, polls suggest that a majority of Palestinians in East Jerusalem would rather stay in an Israeli state than be in a Palestinian state with East Jerusalem as its capital.[56] Each of the three conflicts the demographers study—Israelis versus Palestinians, religious Israelis versus less-religious and secular Israelis, Palestinian Israelis versus Jewish Israelis—portends trouble for Israel, within the 1967 borders, as a "Jewish state." Together this collage of demographic challenges threatens to tear the social fabric of Israeli society across the board and make political fissures unmanageable, further paralyzing decision-making systems. The rise of radical Islam in neighboring countries and in Palestine could result in a rise in the level of terror; accelerated urbanization inside Israel and around its borders will require the IDF to adopt new and complex forms of warfare. Any of these outcomes would leave the Palestinian-Israeli conflict fundamentally altered.

The real menace to Israel is the demographic "enemy within," or rather, multiple enemies. The conventional wisdom holding that the Israeli-Palestinian conflict should be the major preoccupation of the Israeli government has obscured "facts on the ground" that have nothing to do with refugees and settlements but may be *more threatening.*

However, both Soffer and DellaPergola are categorical when they say that in the absence of a Palestinian state in the West Bank, the Jewish Zionist state will abort at some point, if Israel has to give the vote to the Palestinians, who are inexorably destined to become the voting majority. If Israel chooses otherwise in order to maintain its Jewishness, it will become an apartheid state, a pariah state, a state that has lost its legitimacy.

Soffer has briefed Netanyahu, members of his cabinet, and Knesset members. "Even Bibi [Netanyahu] told me he's behind me and my vision," he says, "but he's a politician. He has to deal with his coalition and all his life he compromises. Soon there will be nothing to compromise over. We are engulfed with problems: Jews among themselves; Jews and Arabs within Israel, and Israel vis-à-vis the West Bank. The winners are the settlers. They have a lot of backing. They will control the Knesset and we are heading in the direction of annexation. Israel will have a problem. . . . The political establishment doesn't want me in the news and to tell the reality to the public. Some of them told me, 'Listen, you can ruin the *bosa*, the money, the atmosphere, the cheerful atmosphere in the shopping centers. Don't disturb the people; they are having a good life.' The defense branches are completely behind me. But you have to understand, the army cannot play politics. It must prepare itself for wars. They have no time for Ettinger, and therefore, they are behind these figures. But they don't interfere in the public debate."[57]

No matter what turn the public debate takes, any resumption in negotiations, in addition to core protected values, must take account of the dynamics of internal demographic change, urbanization, and the concentration of Palestinian Israelis in the north—where they already have majorities in many villages and towns, a trend unlikely to be reversed—and possible calls for autonomy.

Ethnocracy cannot last. Among the many permutations of consociational governance and different forms of binational/federal states there are models that would still provide Israel with the space to maintain almost exclusive Jewishness.[58] Otherwise, as demographics move in one direction, old grievances harbored by Israel's once-too-small-to-count minority will reach a critical mass where they can no longer be ignored.

Chapter 10

Facing the Truth

Between August 2010, when I began research for *The Two-State Delusion*, and 2014, Jewish Israelis and Palestinians went through their routine of familiar engagements, always with the same outcomes, entrapped by their various addictions to replay the past in new guises, ensuring that the distrust of each for the intentions of the other increased exponentially, deepening and hardening as though there were no bottom to arrest their descent.

In the four years that elapsed, the Middle East underwent cataclysmic change, and it still reverberates with its aftershocks. Political standoffs are rife; political Islam and secularists vie for power. Regimes toppled and in many cases their replacements toppled, too. Some simply imploded; others were overwhelmed by the tsumani-like waves of wrath of their long-repressed masses. "People power" came and went. Regional alignments unraveled and were replaced by new ones intent on crushing political Islam. The juggernaut of ISIS was poised to swallow more of Syria and much of Iraq before the United States woke up to the Islamic State's global threat and belatedly stepped in. The region, perennially engulfed in a maelstrom of violence and instability, became a haven for jihadists. Bashar al-Assad shrugged off efforts to oust him in a civil war then into its fourth year. Abdel Fattah el-Sisi, Egypt's new strongman, moved assertively to reestablish Egypt's hegemony among Arab states and emerged as a key player in the Israeli–Palestinian conflict. Iraq threatened to come apart. Negotiations on the denuclearization of Iran stalled. Yet despite the political convolutions that tore apart the countries that surrounded it, the Israeli-Palestinian conflict moved further from resolution rather than toward it. The parties did not move an iota closer to reaching an FSA. Indeed, in the view of most observers—even more so after the 2014 Gaza war—a two-state solution has become a blur on a disappearing horizon, despite the plethora of voices warning that time is running out.[1] All the issues we have addressed in previous chapters continue to pose insurmountable obstacles—the power of the narratives still subsumes everything in its path. Moreover, unaddressed and rarely mentioned has been the underlying dynamic driving the conflict: The ethos of conflict has over the decades become a catalyst for an ethos of hatred.

> > < <

From birth, almost all Jewish Israelis are inculcated with negative images of Palestinians and Palestinian Israelis, both of whom are perceived as enemies because in the Israeli narrative they seek only the destruction of Israel and hence the Jewish people; Jewish Israelis believe that the missiles indiscriminately launched from Gaza are expressions of Palestinians' intentions to erase them. For their part, most Palestinians are imbued with a hatred of Israeli Jews because they witness from a very young age the humiliations, such as arbitrary arrests and detentions—that they, their families and friends are subjected to on a daily basis; they become aware that the occupation rules every aspect of their lives, that the proliferation of Jewish Israeli settlements is a manifestation of their impotence and loss of dignity, that the Israelis' disproportionate use of force shows their disregard for the lives of Palestinians.

The roots of the hatreds on both sides are embedded in their one-sided worldviews and mutual fear of "the other."[2] The failure of the Oslo Accords has reinforced these fears. Each side has a tool kit of ready-made explanations of how "the other" is the party responsible for the shambles. The "othering" of the opposing side is done in the schools of both cultures.[3] Well before young people become adults, their brains are almost hardwired by their textbooks, the hatred, the ethos of conflict indelibly imprinted; individual attitudes are rock hard, reinforced, virtually impervious to change, and strengthened by social cohesion. The landmark study "'Victims of Our Own Narratives?' Portrayal of the 'Other' in Israeli and Palestinian School Books" (2013) could hardly be more discouraging.[4] Its conclusions buttress the ethos of conflict. Israel refused to participate in the study. However, when "Victims of Our Own Narratives" was released, the Israeli Ministry of Strategic Affairs issued a harsh detailed response rejecting out of hand the study's findings regarding incitement in Israeli school textbooks.[5]

One small sliver of hope, "Victims of Our Own Narrative?" finds that neither side uses textbooks to describe the "other" in terms that dehumanize or demonize but there is an absence of information that legitimizes the presence and humanizes the other. Moreover, the architecture of how the "other" is portrayed uses "unilateral national narratives that present the other as enemy, chronicle negative actions by the other directed at the self-community, and present the self-community in positive terms with actions aimed at self-protection and goals of peace."[6]

Thus school textbooks, tailored to reflect national narratives, provide the material for generating the "truths"—or "usable pasts"—that evolve into young people's values and norms; they provide the cues for developing lifelong habits. The recurring emphasis on the justice of students' own cultural narratives results in attributes that sustain the habits/addictions they slip into, the patterns of behavior that become routine (seamlessly fitting into the societal norms of their community), and actions that become reflexive. "Israeli school maps feed into the Palestinian narrative that Israel wants to grab more and more land, and Palestinian school maps feed an Israeli narrative that Palestinians want to throw them into the sea," says Bruce Wexler,[7] a Jewish American Yale professor, who directed the study told the *Economist*.*

In *Palestine in Israeli School Books*,[8] Dr. Nurit Peled-Elhanan, a lecturer at Hebrew University, explores the content of schoolbooks in Israeli classrooms. She quotes from the findings of other studies. Caroline Coffin, Professor of English and Linguistics at the Open University in the UK, argues that "students learn not only from the discourse of historians in their textbooks but also from the discourse of politicians, lawyers, and other manipulators of discourse. They learn to present interpretations as facts, to insert personal views into seemingly neutral representations, in short they learn the language of power."[9] As a result of this "imposition of the official 'truth,'" she goes on to say, students are "not only alienate[d] from disciplinary discourse,"[10] but there emerges what the late Paul Ricoeur, former John Nuveen professor of philosophical theology at the University of Chicago, called a

*Israeli textbooks, ""Victims of Our Own Narrative?"'" said: "concentrate on examples of violent attacks against Israel: Palestinians are the enemy at Israelis' doorstep and want to destroy rather than to dominate Israel. Palestinian textbooks teach youngsters that Palestine was taken from them by stealth and handed over to the Jews by "'international powers'" and that the Jews have appropriated Palestinian land and resources. Their textbooks, however, are more likely to describe "Israelis as seeking to dominate rather than to destroy, Palestinians.Historical events, while not false or fabricated, are selectively presented to reinforce each community's national narrative." There is little information of any kind about the 'other.' Palestinian maps are drawn to simply deny evidence of the existence of Israel, to deny the legitimacy of the other. In a study of Israeli maps, "76 percent did not indicate any borders (i.e., line, color, or other demarcation) between Israeli and Palestinian areas, although borders were indicated between Israel and neighboring countries (e.g., Egypt, Jordan, Lebanon, Syria) and the labels 'Palestine' or 'Palestinian Authority' did not appear anywhere on the maps. Since these maps are presented as maps of Israel, the absence of borders between Israel and Palestine and the absence of the label 'Palestinian Authority' can be seen as implying that the Palestinian areas are part of the State of Israel." Regarding the texts themselves, the study's researchers found that 49 percent of text dealing with Palestinians in Israeli state-issued schoolbooks was negative. In Palestinian textbooks 84 percent of the references to Israelis were negative, a singularly significant contrast to the Israeli textbooks. In both Palestinian and Israeli state schools the books teach "'martyrdom-sacrifice through death.'" The *Economist* notes that. "Each side glorifies itself while denigrating the other."

"wanting not to know."[11] This "wanting not to know," Peled-Elhanan asserts "inculcated into Israeli youth, through education, is in fact 'not wanting to teach.'"[12] Her study concludes that "[t]he representation of Palestinians in Israeli school books enhances ignorance;" that "[t]he past three generations of Jewish Israelis are, for the most part, not aware of the geopolitical or social realities of their country;" that "Israeli Jewish students are drafted into the army, to carry out Israeli policy vis-à-vis Palestinians, whose life-world is unknown to them and whose very existence they have been taught to resent and fear."[13] And furthermore, Professor Dan Rabinowitz, in the department of sociology and anthropology at Tel Aviv University, writes, the lack of contact, enhanced by physical and mental barriers, between Israeli-Jewish and Israeli-Palestinian youth keeps these youngsters ignorant of each other's lives, that "[t]he image of the Palestinians as potentially 'bloodthirsty desperados, yearning for violent revenge, pushed to act against their own interests if they can only harm as many Israelis as they can'[14] is still prevalent in textbooks as in the general discourse." "Textbooks and curricula are political tools."[15] Surveying yet another set of studies, Peled-Elhanan finds that they conclude that "textbooks that are meant to change fixed ideas do not always succeed in doing so, but as Israeli youth's attitudes towards Palestinians may prove, textbooks that seek to ingrain dominant ideas, biased and fraudulent as they may be, do succeed, as they are part of an all-encompassing promulgation of an anti-Arab myth."[16]

> > < <

Some studies have concluded that about one third of Jewish youth hate Palestinians[17] and that a little over a third of Jewish adults harbor medium-level hatred,[18] a figure that has remained stable even after periods of conflict,[19] even after the IDF pulverized Gaza in the 2008 war with minimal Israeli casualties.[20] When the issue is framed implicitly rather than explicitly, however, 64 percent of Jews expressed high levels of hate toward Palestinians[21]—three years after the Second Intifada ended, three years *without* a terrorist attack. And undergirding the hate is the level of fear. A slew of surveys cited in "The Socio-Psychological Barriers to Resolving the Israeli Conflict: An Analysis of Jewish Israeli Society" in *Barriers to Peace* suggests that since 2000 "fear is a stable and central psychological characteristic of the entire Jewish society in Israel. . . . A large majority of Israeli Jews still believe that ongoing terrorist attacks might cause a strategic, and even existential, threat to the state of Israel."[22]

The Dialog poll on behalf of *Haaretz* is a catalogue of Israelis' racist attitudes. Some of its more disturbing findings: "42 percent [of Jewish Israelis] don't want to live in the same building with Arabs and 42 percent don't want their children in the same class with Arab children. A third of the Jewish public wants a law barring Israeli Arabs from voting for the Knesset."[23]

In his review of Daniel Bar-Tal's book *Living with Conflict*, on behalf of the Arab Center for Research and Policy, Professor Mahmoud Muhareb, former head of Al-Quds University, says,

> Bar-Tal asserts that the Jewish Israeli society has developed a self-sustaining web of racist values and beliefs [that]. . . keep it psychologically primed for a continued conflict with the Arabs. These racist beliefs and values, which have become part of the psyche of Israeli Jewish society, focus on Israel's "moral" right to expand, and on the "nobleness and justice" of such objectives. Collective and individual security, and that of the state, were placed above all other considerations with Israel assuming the role of the "victim," albeit a victim that kills and oppresses. A positive image of the collective self was created in contravention to facts, and was endowed with values of ethical supremacy and pacifism; while at the same time a "siege mentality" [was] fostered, rallying patriotic sentiment and national unity in the face of external threat. The assumption was that the state is in constant threat and this imagined existential threat was linked to the holocaust. In the face of that, the legitimacy of the Arabs' existence—along with their humanity, was denied; they were cast at a lower place and excluded from the ranks of humane society. Bar-Tal explains how these socio-psychological beliefs and values "manufacture" the racist Israeli subject and shape his worldview from cradle to grave.[24]

Palestinians are also adept at hatred; the incitement they propagate in their schools is no less insidious.[25] Dr. David Pollock, a fellow at the Washington Institute for Near East Policy, investigated what accounts for the 84 percent negative representations of Israeli Jews in Palestinian textbooks. He published his findings in "Beyond Words: Causes, Consequences and Cures for Palestinian Authority Hate," a comprehensive and meticulously researched documentation of incitement on the part of PA officials and in PA media outlets.[26] The study's cover illustration: "Bridge of Return: Palestinians will return to Israel via the barrel of a gun." Its source is the Facebook page of Fatah, a party committed to nonviolence. Imagine what Hamas's Facebook page would look like.

In addition to examining textbooks, Pollock's study itemizes a litany of incitements (hate speech) emanating from every media outlet that the PA controls, either officially or unofficially, and statements of senior PA officials. The message, in essence, is that Jews must be driven from Palestine and Palestine reclaimed by the Palestinian people.[27] There is not a word about peace, about reconciliation, about two states for two people living side by side in harmony. The Palestinians' insistence that they would not want *any* Jewish presence in their new state[28] stokes the undercurrents of animosity. Likewise, Israel's insistence on being recognized as a Jewish state is designed to nurture animosity rather than rapprochement.

In January 2014, the Israeli cabinet spent two hours discussing the findings of the annual "Palestinian Incitement Index," which the government prepares from statements of PA officials, religious, educational, and media outlets, and even people close to Abbas himself to show "the culture of hatred in the PA." Even while peace talks were being conducted, the government's index showed that not only did incitement not lessen but the same themes were reiterated again and again: "Israel has no right to exist, certainly not as the state of the Jewish People, which, in any case, have no link to the holy Land; the disappearance of Israel is unavoidable and is expected soon the Jews are sub-human creatures and must be dealt with accordingly; in principle, all forms of struggle, including terrorism are legitimate in order to realize the final goal."[29]

Academic studies are abstract and cannot convey the visceral nature of hatred; that only becomes apparent when it suddenly explodes, as it did in late June and the early weeks of July 2014.

It began on June 12 with the kidnapping of three Israeli teenagers from settler families—Eyal Yifrach, nineteen; Naftali Fraenkel, sixteen; and Gilad Shaar, also sixteen—while they were hitchhiking at Mount Etzion in the West Bank. The kidnappings triggered an outpouring of grief in Israel the likes of which the country had not experienced, some said, for decades.[30] On June 30 the bodies of the three boys were found, close to where they had been kidnapped. At their funerals on July 1 the three were wrapped in Israeli flags and buried side by side, eulogized by Israel's president, Shimon Peres, Prime Minister Netanyahu, Chief Rabbi David Lau, and Minister of Defense Moshe Ya'alon, who said they were killed just because they were Jews.

In his eulogy, Netanyahu said, "The light you radiate shines even brighter in contrast to the horrific darkness of those who seek our destruction—despicable kidnappers of children, heinous murderers whose brothers rejoice at the spilling of innocent blood. A deep and wide moral abyss separates us from our enemies. They sanctify death while we sanctify life. They sanctify cruelty while we sanctify compassion. Throughout the history of our people, we have proven time and again that . . . the force of life that pulses in us overpowers the murderous aspirations of our enemies."[31]

> > < <

Thousands of mourners from across the country flooded the cemetery in Modi'in. The calls for more punitive action to be taken against Hamas ratcheted up.[32] The thirst for blood was in the wind.[33]

"During funerals for the boys, hundreds of extreme-right-wing protesters blocked roads in Jerusalem, chanting "Death to Arabs," the *New York Times* reported. A Facebook page named "People of Israel Demand Revenge" gathered 35,000 "likes" before being taken down; a blogger gave prominence to a photo, also on Facebook, that featured a sign saying: "Hating Arabs is not racism, it's values."[34]

A day later, on July 2, the body of Muhammad Abu Khdeir, a teenager from Shuafat in East Jerusalem, was found beaten and burned in a forest. By all accounts the murder was a revenge attack.[35] Rioting spread in the West Bank.[36] On July 4, Muhammad was given a martyr's funeral. "Young Palestinian men, some with faces covered by kaffiyehs, filled the main street, chanting about blood and guns, sacrifice and struggle. . . . The body, wrapped in a Palestinian flag . . . was greeted with firecrackers, whistling and calls of Allahu akbar, God is great," according to another report in the *Times*, "[T]he crowd carried Muhammad, in an open-topped green wooden box, down the main road, past the Israeli police line at Shuafat's edge, and finally to the cemetery. There, automatic rifle fire into the air marked the burial in a grave not far from a relative, Amjad, who had been fatally shot outside the Old City at age thirty-three by a Jewish Israeli five years earlier. . . . Earlier, the throngs had chanted an old Hamas slogan and sung a fighting song from Fatah, the more moderate faction that dominates the P.L.O. 'The gun lives on' [and] 'To Jerusalem we are going, martyrs in millions.' There were calls for suicide bombings, a third intifada, a revenge attack in the Jewish settlement of Gilo, in South Jerusalem." And then the chant: "Explode the skull of the Zionist!"[37]

Rioting in East Jerusalem and a harsh police response continued over the next several months as Palestinian youth confronting police were arrested in droves, minors jailed for months before their trials.[38]

The shortest and most telling summary conveyed the raw sentiments academic studies can't: "Death to Arabs" versus "Explode the skull of the Zionist"—each side dehumanizing the other.[39] For days the hate between the youth on the two sides was palpable, a living, throbbing, insidious, and malignant presence.[40] But the two protagonists are afraid to call it for what it is. Denial is more comforting, obviates the need for soul-searching, and distracts negotiators from having to come to grips, yet again, with the imponderables standing in the way of a two-state solution. But if the most important player—Hamas—is not represented using the formula along the lines of the Cairo 2014 cease-fire model, further talks will once again add another layer of delusion.

The Israeli newspaper *Haaretz* editorialized that the country's leaders "must begin raising the next generation, at least, on humanist values, and foster a tolerant public discourse"[41]—on the one hand, observing the painfully banal; on the other, blissfully oblivious to its improbability. Until Israelis and Palestinians address the manner in which they educate their children, hatred will continue to churn and breathe its bile, and all talk of two states living side by side in harmony will be a fantasy. Facts in the heart count for more than facts on the ground.[42]

Addressing hatred is a necessary prerequisite to *any* solution. Unless both Palestinians and Israelis scrub the textbooks they use in their schools of "othering," stop instilling hate at the earliest age, and agree that incitement is destructive and opens the floodgates to dehumanization, they will be perennially stuck in their respective lairs of self-incubating misanthropic malignancy. Is this likely to happen soon? Not very.* But then, neither is a two-state solution. Undoing the legacy of hatred would take at least a generation. The common thread weaving together what every interviewee said was the repeated references to "lack of trust." But they should dig a little deeper and engage in a little more introspection. Lack of trust is just a surface manifestation of latent hatred. Hatred precludes respect; without respect, there can be no trust. The math is simple.

> > < <

But say—leaving aside for a moment all the reasons I have laid out why Israel will not agree to a two-state solution—an FSA is negotiated that provides for an independent Palestinian state. Is the conflict over? Far from it. The hurdles implementation faces are virtually insurmountable. For starters, how many years would be required to reach the finality of an "end of claims" agreement, which would be signed only upon resolution of the differing interpretations of

*According to a study reported in *Haaretz* on January 2, 2015, half of all Palestinian Israeli and Jewish Israelis want no contact with each other. See Dr. Kashti, "Study: Half of Israel's Jewish, Arab Pupils Want No Contact with Each Other, *Haaretz*,January 2, 2015.

all the mistakes, inadequacies, outright evasions, and obfuscations incorporated into the FSA are resolved?[43] That would be an incredibly complicated process—that is, it would require more rounds of incredibly complicated negotiations. Different interpretations of every clause would be given, with potential for conflict at every turn.[44]

A two-state solution would require uniting a ward of the international community (the West Bank) with a failed statelet (Gaza) and the pivot of an impoverished urban community (East Jerusalem) into a reasonably healthy polity and economy. The prospects of a nominally unified Hamas and Fatah being capable of running a country on a day-to-day basis are problematic, if the past is a performance guide. Myriad problems would be posed by the return of tens of thousands of refugees, even if those returns are phased in over a number of years. And the records of the Palestinian Authority and Hamas—in terms of being competent to govern, honoring human rights, and being corruption free—make it unlikely that a new Palestine would suddenly be transmogrified into a culture respecting the primacy of individual freedoms and earn the public's trust in policing and due process to protect their personal safety. In the absence of the public's feeling safe from the vagaries of personal violence, studies show economic growth would be stunted.[45] How would a Palestinian state eradicate the endemic, entrenched cronyism and corruption and the lack of transparency and accountability that characterized governance in both the PA and Gaza? And what of possible clashes between secularists and Islamists, not to mention Fatah and Hamas? No one should doubt that these practical implementation issues would be a grave challenge for any agreement to overcome.

But I am moving ahead of myself. Even greater challenges would continue to impede the two parties' reaching an agreement in the first place, as they have for two and a half decades. Though on the surface impediments like the right of return and the questions of borders and settlements might be overcome through courageous leadership and complex trade-offs that could be marketed to their publics as "win-win" outcomes, on a deeper level it seems that the impasse relates to human nature and the nature of social structures that have been the source of the two peoples' habits/addictions, not the least of which is an impenetrable adherence to national narratives.

> > < <

Meanwhile, the behaviors they generate are reflected in this startling collage, all data from before the Gaza war of 2014:[46]

- 50 percent of Jewish Israelis and 63 percent of Palestinians do not believe they can coexist peacefully in two states.
- "45 percent of Palestinians are more likely to say armed struggle is the best way for their people to achieve statehood"; just 15 percent say negotiations.
- 47 percent of Palestinians and 74 percent of Israelis support a two-state solution; 34 percent of Palestinians and 36 percent of Israelis think it is no longer feasible.
- 58 percent of Jewish Israelis see the Hamas-Fatah reconciliation pact as dangerous or moderately dangerous and reject the claim that the unity pact will help peace.
- 69 percent of Jewish Israelis would object to giving Palestinians the right to vote if Israel annexes the West Bank.
- 48 percent of Jewish Israelis say a final agreement will never be reached; 47 percent of Palestinians say the same.
- 55 percent to 63 percent of Jewish Israelis would never acknowledge the Palestinians' right of return, even if all other issues were resolved to their satisfaction; 59 percent of Palestinians would never accept an agreement that would not acknowledge their right of return and allow them to return to their homes.
- 77 percent of Jewish Israelis say that in the absence of a two-state solution there will be intense conflict and instability for years ahead; 76 percent of Palestinians share a similar view.
- 71 percent of Jewish Israelis believe the status quo as indefinite with little change; 81 percent of Palestinians share a similar view.
- 9 percent of Jewish Israelis put reaching a peace agreement as their major priority after talks collapsed in April 2014.
- 58 percent of Palestinians think that Israel's goals in the long run are to extend its borders to cover all the area between the Jordan River and the Mediterranean Sea and expel its Arab citizens.
- 59 percent of adolescents and 69 percent of young Israeli adults believe that Palestinian Israelis seek the destruction of Israel.
- 37 percent of the Israelis think that the Palestinian aspirations in the long run are to conquer the state of Israel and destroy much of the Jewish population in Israel; 18 percent think the goals of the Palestinians are to conquer the state of Israel.
- 50 percent of Israelis and 38 percent of Palestinians support a permanent settlement package along the Clinton parameters.
- 60 percent of Palestinians say that the five-year goal (2014–2019) "should be to work toward reclaiming all of historic Palestine, from the river to the sea."
- 41 percent of Palestinian Israelis would support and 56 percent would not support a proposal calling for mutual recognition of Israel as the state of the Jewish people and Palestine as the state of the Palestinian people "after the establishment of a Palestinian state and the settlement of all issues of the conflict."

- 22 percent of Israeli Jews believe that negotiations between Israel and the Palestinian Authority will lead to peace between Israel and the Palestinians.
- 68 percent of Israelis believe Palestinians benefitted from the Oslo Accords; 64 percent of Israelis believe it harmed Israeli interests.
- 75 percent of Palestinians believe Israelis benefitted from the Oslo Accords; 49 percent believe it harmed Palestinian interests.

Add to this bewildering picture the hatred that precludes finding common ground, and the conclusion is clear: There is not even a glimmer of hope for a two-state solution here. The Palestinians know it,[47] and the Jewish Israelis are moving inexorably to this truth as well. How could we possibly expect successful negotiations when Israelis and Palestinians teach their children the value of demonization, racism, and hatred? Negotiation in such a context is a waste of time. You cannot build where there are no foundations to begin with. As the December 2013 Zogby poll succinctly sums up: "The ground today is also less fertile than it was the first time around, having been polluted during the past 20 years by the ill-will created and negative behaviors of both sides that sapped confidence and trust of both Palestinians and Israelis."[48]

Surveys showing that Palestinian support of a two-state solution either is underwhelming or no longer exists, that over 60 percent of Palestinians do not believe peaceful coexistence is possible, and that only 46 percent of Jewish Israelis and just one third who describe themselves as religious think it is possible should give their leaders pause. They can spend as much time as they like at the negotiating table but, it seems, it would be in vain. And after reviewing the reams of data available, it is pertinent to ask whether they are so far out of touch with the evolving aspirations of their respective constituencies that they are trying to negotiate an outcome that no longer truly reflects what their constituencies consistently believe is in their interests.

The time has come to consider other options; none are palatable, but serious attention to all may break the stranglehold of thinking only in terms of a two-state solution.[49] Uri Savir, an architect of Oslo, says that officials in many Israeli and Palestinian circles are already planning for a binational state.*

*Uri Savir, in *Al-Monitor* in August 2014, writes: "Netanyahu will not speak of a binational state, although that seems to be the direction his policies will take the country. The Palestinian leadership is well aware of this trajectory and never suspected anything else. In Ramallah as well, there is talk of a policy that leads to a binational state. It exists in the following circles: Fatah veteran leaders, who see no hope for a two-state solution; officials close to Abbas, who want to use the eventuality of a binational state as tactical pressure on Israel and the United States; and

> > < <

What about the alternative of a *one*-state, or binational, solution?[50] Some eminent Palestinian scholars say a one state/binational state is the *only* feasible option,[51] perhaps the inevitable one, unpalatable though it may appear to both Israelis and Palestinians. A substantial body of literature makes the case,[52] but such a state could only eventuate once the principals—and their publics—put aside their delusional obsession with the two-state solution; recognize that their chronic inability to reach agreements on any of the core issues has run its course; acknowledge that on this well-traveled road their shoes are frayed and coming apart at the soles; concede that continuing to ply the same negotiating tools and going through the same motions ad nauseam is setting a course of endless futility; and, most important, come to understand that only fundamental changes in understanding of the respective national narratives can break their addictions and substantially weaken the ethos of conflict on both sides. That, too, would take a generation.

But where, friends who read the manuscript of *The Two-State Delusion* asked, is my vision for the future? "You can't just end the book and leave the reader with no alternative to a two-state solution if you are so sure one is delusional. You have to give the reader hope that something is possible, that there exists some route to setting a new course." But why should I be so presumptuous as to dare to provide a vision for people who refuse to provide one for themselves, not just in the here and now, but in the future too? For

---

hard-liners in Fatah's young guard, who actually believe in such a vision and count on the Arab demographic edge."

"This eventuality in Palestine is not ruled out by some and is preferred by others. Palestinian policy planning experts have begun to prepare for a binational state process. These plans focus on the share of authorities and powers between the Israeli and Palestinian parts of the binational state. They are consulting experts on international law as to how to ensure, through the international community, equal rights for Palestinian citizens. An anti-apartheid state campaign is envisioned, adopting the South African model to Palestine." Uri Savir, "Israel-Palestine, a Binational State in the Making," *Al-Monitor*, August 24, 2014, http://www.al-monitor.com/pulse/originals/2014/08/israel-palestinians-binational-state-right-wing-netanyahu.html.

In "Israel: The Alternative," published in the *New York Review of Books*, the historian Tony Judt, once an ardent Zionist, called Israel an "anacronysism," dimissed a two-state solution, and advocated a binational state. Tony Judt," Israel: The Alternative," *New York Review of Books*, October 23, 2003, http://www.nybooks.com/articles/archives/2003/oct/23/israel-the-alternative/.

In his last interview, one month before his death from ALS in July 2010, with the *Atlantic*'s Merav Michaeli, he reiterated his support for a binational state along the lines of the federal state, with two autonomous communities with crossover priviliges and rights for both. Merav Michaeli, "Tony Judt's Final Word on Israel," *The Atlantic*, September 14, 2011, http://www.theatlantic.com/international/archive/2011/09/tony-judts-final-word-on-israel/245051/. The late Tony Judt was founder and director of the Remarque Institute at New York University.

people who have no faith in the possible? Who themselves believe the conflict will take generations to resolve? Who are content to live their hatreds? Who are so resolutely opposed to the slightest gesture of accommodation? Who revel in their mutual pettiness? Why delude you into thinking that there is a magic bullet? Why trot out platitudes or list what both parties must do to reach a two-state FSA? These have been laid out in depth in numerous books and other publications.

I can, however, offer a few observations, although in this conflict everything that appears new is obvious, but these observations should be seen through a lens that takes a generation as its baseline; they are at best palliatives but are germane to putting in place prerequisites for trying to hammer out a shared Palestine. They may ease the path to negotiating a future when the time is "ripe."

Forget about talk of FSAs and the like. First, both sides must address their respective habits/addictions, understand their nature, how they manifest themselves, and begin the arduous process of addressing them. Is there a point at which they will be *willing* to? For without *willingness* they're on a fool's errand. I have mentioned "parity of esteem" on a number of occasions and turn to it again as a sine qua non: parity of esteem for each other's narratives. This must begin in the classroom. Again, if there is no *willingness* to start here, the two sides may as well throw in the towel. Without Hamas and the Islamic Jihad agreeing to an accommodation, all caveats in chapter 5 aside, there can be no accommodation.

Here, however, Israel faces an existential dilemma. If it *really* wants a two-state solution—which the polling data I have plied you with leaves open to question, and distinguishing between *wanting* and being *prepared* to pay the price—and if it believes, as my interviews with Jewish Israelis suggest, that a buy-in from Hamas, despite their reservations, is imperative, then it knows that a strong Fatah-Hamas reconciliation pact is a necessary first step.

But the interviews I drew on for this book were conducted before the 2014 war. Many attitudes in Israel are very different now. Before 2014, Jewish Israelis could at least accept at some level that Hamas would have to be part of any FSA resulting in a two-state solution, but that has changed. With Hamas within a hair's breadth of being able to target Israeli citizens, raining terror on their cities and towns, they know that had it not been for the exceptional performance of the Iron Dome as a missile interceptor during the 2014 war, hundreds of them—in cities like Tel Aviv and Jerusalem and Beersheba—would likely have been casualties. Given their range, the missiles coming out of Gaza are no longer a "nuisance" for cities such as Sderot and Ashkelon in southern Israel but an existential threat to all of Israel.[53] The right in Israel continues to move further to the right; to say that "the center will not hold" is simply to quote poetry. Translation: Israel would not be prepared to have a Palestinian state as a neighbor in which even a demilitarized Hamas is free to roam.

Furthermore, nothing that Hamas says will move Israel to believe it. Nothing will convince Israel to agree to any arrangement that would give Hamas access to the West Bank.

The April 2014 pact between Fatah and Hamas was put to a severe test regarding its resiliency during the 2014 war. Up to three hundred Fatah members were confined to their homes by Hamas for the duration of the Gaza conflict.* Many believe that the pact is one of expediency, a wily ruse on the part of Hamas, which wants to use it for the purpose of overthrowing the PA and taking control of the West Bank (a plot Shin Bet says it foiled).[54]

*Within days of the August 27 ceasefire Fatah and Hamas were at each other's throats. Abbas accused Hamas of having needlessly prolonged the war; in a confrontation with Mashaal in Doha he said he believed the Shin Bet reports of a Hamas plot that had been in the making to overthrow the PA; he accused Hamas of running a shadow government in Gaza; that Hamas was preventing PA ministers from entering Gaza. "Palestinian security apparatuses summoned Hamas members who were participating in festivals celebrating the end of the Gaza war in the cities of Ramallah and Tulkarm, on the evening of Aug. 30. Hamas immediately issued a statement calling on Fatah to immediately intervene to prevent these arrests." "Abbas Blames Hamas for Prolonged Battle with Israel," http://www.timesofisrael.com/abbas-blames-hamas-for-prolonged-battle-with-israel/; "Hamas, Fatah Trade Accusations as Gaza War Ends," http://www.maannews.net/eng/ViewDetails.aspx?ID=726327; "Fear and Loathing Mar Fatah-Hamas Ties in Gaza," http://www.dailystar.com.lb/News/Middle-East/2014/Sep-09/270005-fear-and-loathing-mar-fatah-hamas-ties-in-gaza.ashx#axzz3CqJrD8Ao; "Unity Government at Crossroads as Fatah and Hamas Bicker," http://www.al-monitor.com/pulse/originals/2014/09/abbas-pa-hamas-fallout-ties-war-israel.html.

According to the news report, on September 6, 2014, Abbas warned Arab journalists in Cairo that the unity government with Hamas was on the brink of collapse. The account has Abbas saying that "if the government will not be unified, [in terms of] the weapons and laws in the West Bank and Gaza, there won't be any partnership or discussion with the [Hamas] organization." Furthermore, he did not trust Hamas "because they change their words all the time. There must be a unified Palestinian Authority." He confirmed reports of the "stormy meeting" he had with Meshaal in Qatar in August, "in which he slammed the Hamas leader for his organization's coup attempt" in the West Bank. "You are smuggling weapons, explosives and money to the [West] Bank," he supposedly said at that meeting, "not to fight Israel, but to hold a coup against the Palestinian Authority." Commenting on the meeting with Meshaal, Abbas remarked, "Hamas has been trying to cause the Palestinian Authority to fail since the day it was formed." Hamas confined "dozens of Fatah members to effective house arrest for the duration of the conflict." "Abbas Threatens to End Hamas Unity Deal," http://www.israelnationalnews.com/News/News.aspx/184815. Khaled Abu Toameh, "Palestinian Authority Steps Up Crackdown Against Hamas Activists in the West Bank," *Jerusalem Post*, September 6, 2014, http://www.jpost.com/Arab-Israeli-Conflict/Palestinian-Authority-steps-up-crackdown-against-Hamas-activists-in-the-West-Bank-374600.

When Abbas confronted Khaled Meshaal on the issue, Meshaal told him that he was being duped, calling it Israeli trickery to sow disunity in the unity government. But Abbas was not so easily mollified. He told Meshaal to his face that he believed the Shin Bet reports.[55] In the weeks preceding his "We knew all along that this deal is just on paper," Khalil Shikaki said of the reconciliation, "and Abbas seems to be on the verge of allowing it to fall apart."[56] The November elections, part of the pact agreement, went the way of other elections that were supposed to have been held.

Israel and Palestine are about to enter a new era. The end of Netanyahu's tenure as prime minister, whether or not he manages a fourth term, and Abbas's stepping down as president of the PA will bring fresh faces—and, one hopes, fresh ideas. However, if trends in *All of the Above*[57] are harbingers of more hard-line Israeli governments, relations between Palestinians and Jewish Israelis will be further poisoned and the future more ominous. My money is on a continuing deleterious deterioration of relations.

One option, touched upon in chapter 5, is to explore whether Israel would be willing to examine with Hamas and Islamic Jihad how a long-term *hudna* would be agreed and implemented.* A *hudna* for ninety-nine years would push the question of the future of Israel into a century that has no certainties. Recall that Khaled Meshaal at least had a plan that purported to allow the two peoples to coexist. Look at it. Bring it into the discussion. The peace agreements in Northern Ireland, as I have suggested, are not to be taken as something duplicable, but they can, nevertheless, be construed—or explored—as a *hudna* in different parlance. Look at them afresh. There is no downside to considering an idea—even if it has already expeditiously been given the once-over—and asking whether, in considered terms, there are ways their modalities can be adapted or reimagined. *But there must be willingness.* That said, one comes back to reality. Israel would never believe that Hamas would adhere to the terms of a *hudna*.

There is little hope for advance on any front until both Jewish Israelis and Palestinians begin to think in terms of the long view *and differentiate between what they can accomplish in the here and now and what they can leave to future generations to decide.* They and their neighbors and countries the world over are on the threshold of a new global era. New variables outside their control will shape the way they live. Inculcate this ethos: We cannot live apart; we cannot live together; what must we do to change the matrix

*See chapter 5, p. 135–36.

of possibilities? Demography is a long way down the road; so is squeezing out the hatred; so, too, is educating both publics about the costs of living apart and the benefits of living together. But of the utmost importance is *respect*. The accommodation of aspirations will, as in Northern Ireland, belong to the future. And from the deepest recesses of their respective collective consciousnesses, both Palestinians and Jewish Israelis *must* find leadership, that elusive, almost ephemeral, intangible attribute. If both eschew consideration of this path, the next best step is war, à la Kissinger's prescription. Intifadas are last century's insurrections. The nature of warfare has changed and we will have to learn to live with its consequences.

There is nothing "new" in the limited steps I have outlined. All "newness" at one time or another has had its day. Time is on the side of the Palestinians.

Hamas and Islamic Jihad, for the sake of analogy, are like the Viet Cong in the 1960s and 1970s and the Israelis like the Americans. During the Vietnam War, the Americans believed that if they poured up to half a million soldiers into the Vietnamese countryside, ferreted out every Viet Cong "terrorist," destroyed their tunnels, disrupted their supply routes, and, most important, pulverized North Vietnam with incessant bombing and much of South Vietnam with "targeted" air strikes, then the Viet Cong would eventually fold under such withering onslaughts—realizing that it could not withstand the massive devastation and destruction of much of the country, it would see the futility of continuing to infiltrate South Vietnam and surrender. But the Viet Cong were familiar with every inch of the terrain of South Vietnam, knew how to use it to their advantage, and were easily able to replace one network of tunnels the Americans destroyed with another, while young American soldiers were carrying out missions in territory they were utterly unfamiliar with and were hopelessly lost in the vast stretches of underbrush. No matter how much the Americans scorched the earth and laid waste the land, the Viet Cong and North Vietnamese always rebounded—a cautionary tale for the Israelis.

During the 2014 war, Israel unleashed over five thousand air strikes on Gaza in fifty days and invaded with tanks and artillery bombardments that resulted in astronomical levels of mass destruction and over two thousand deaths across the Gaza Strip. But Hamas was unbowed and will rebuild and will, in matters of war, have the support of most Gazans.[58]

> > < <

Israel is already "losing" Europe,[59] the label "apartheid" being more frequently invoked.[60] Labels stick.[61] An emerging generation is declaring that "the Holocaust is over."* These young people do not deny or forget the scale of the genocide perpetrated by the Nazis during World War II, but they do not accept being held hostage to the sense of guilt of their parents or the actual guilt of their grandparents. These young people also do not see Jewish Israelis as victims. They do not believe that the Holocaust validates Israel's claim to exceptionalism or serves as justification for holding another people hostage. What they see is an Israel that is among the world's most developed countries, a global military power, an Israel that is among the most innovative and entrepreneurial countries. The youth mainly know about the Start-Up Nation, they have not yet felt the impact of the other economy.† During the

*In Western Europe, where 54 percent of those polled by the Anti-Defamation League were aware of the Holocaust, there is a "gap between older adults who know their history and younger men and women who, more than 70 years after the events of World War II, are more likely to have never heard of or learned about what happened to the six million Jews who perished." Anti-Defamation League, "ADL Poll of Over 100 Countries Finds More Than One-Quarter of Those Surveyed Infected with Anti-Semitic Attitudes" (press release), May 13, 2014, http://www.adl.org/press-center/press-releases/anti-semitism-international/adl-global-100-poll.html. See also Burg, *Holocaust Is Over.*

†Israeli society is undergoing significant change: an aging population that is living longer (an Israeli born today has a life expectancy of eighty-nine years); higher dependency ratios—larger numbers under fourteen and over sixty-five; almost half of Jewish Israeli schools in Haredim entering the labor force with no marketable skills; a severe housing shortage that led to the largest demonstration in Israeli history—more than 400,000 people in Tel Aviv on the streets in April 2011. Reducing socio/economic differences is the primary concern of most people (47 percent). Employment among men in the prime age cohort (thirty-five to fifty-four) is relatively low and continues to decline. Workers work longer hours than in the West, but their productivity is lower. Of the world's thirty-four economically developed countries, Israel is the most impoverished, with a poverty rate of 21 percent—a higher percentage of poor people than Mexico, Turkey, or debt-ridden Spain and Greece. Surveys show people's greatest concern is ending up in poverty. On the other hand, you have the "Start-Up Nation," one of the most innovative and entrepreneurial on the planet. You have two economies; the second economy is the large and growing segment of the population with neither the tools nor the conditions to work in the modern, competitive, global economy. This underachieving cohort has and will have a very significant impact on the future prospects for the economy.

See Dan Senor and Saul Singer, *Start-Up Nation: The Story of Israel's Economic Miracle* (Toronto: McClelland & Stewart, 2011); Gershom Gorenberg, *The Unmaking of Israel*, chapter 6, "The Labor of the Righteous is Done by Others"; Ronny Linder-Ganz, "Israel Facing Rapidly Aging Population, Says OECD," *Haaretz*, May 19, 2011, http://www.haaretz.com/business/israel-facing-rapidly-aging-population-says-oecd-1.362663; Shaul Amsterdamski, "Israel Is Aging Too Fast," *Al-Monitor*, May 2, 2014, http://www.al-monitor.com/pulse/business/2014/05/agin-population-demographics-yong-generation-retired-burden.html#ixzz30vyoBEQv; Taub Center, "Israelis Working More, Making Less," September 2013, http://taubcenter.org.il/index.php/publications/e-bulletin/israelis-working-more-making-less/lang/en/; "Aging," The Center for Research on Aging, Myers-JDC-Brookdale Institute, http://brookdale.jdc.org.il/?CategoryID=176; Nadav Neuman, "Bank of Israel: Growth Will Slow Down Unless More Haredi Education," *Globes*, February 12, 2013, http://www.globes.co.il/en/article-1000898306; Moti Bassok, "Israel's Growth Will Slow Down Unless Ultra-Orthodox Start Working, Bank of Israel Warns," *Haaretz*, December 3, 2013, http://www.haaretz.com/business/.premium-1.561418; Jesse Colombo, "Why Israel's Boom Is

2014 war, in many major European cities there were widespread demonstrations against Israel. In some, anti-Semitism raised its ugly face.[62] Talk of boycotts of Israeli products—unthinkable ten years ago—is gaining international traction, and if the status quo does not change, at some point in the not-too-distant future the still fledgling BDS (boycott, divestment, and sanctions) movement will move into the mainstream.[63] The UN commission to investigate the war in Gaza will undoubtedly find that both Israel and Hamas were guilty of crimes against humanity, findings that Israel will vehemently dispute but that will cost it in the international arena and threaten its legitimacy.

> > < <

Finally, there are certain variables beyond the control of either party. Nature may be the key determinant of how the Palestinians and Israelis are ultimately *compelled* to govern themselves.

In December 2013 Israel suffered its driest winter on record, so bad that the country's chief rabbis called for daily recitation of the traditional Torah prayer for rain. God answered with the heaviest snowstorm in at least a half century, bringing the country to a standstill.[64] Afterward, the drought promptly returned.

Whether we would wish it away or not, climate change is with us,[65] and we are already feeling its impacts.[66]

Despite decades of ominous warnings, "The world is now on track to more than double current greenhouse gas concentrations in the atmosphere by the end of the century. This would push up average global temperatures by three to eight degrees Celsius" and the end of civilization as we know it.[67] "To meet the UN goal of keeping global temperatures from rising more than two degrees Celsius above preindustrial levels[68] would require a worldwide reduction in greenhouse gas emissions of 40 to 70 percent by midcentury, according to the Intergovernmental Panel on Climate Change (IPCC)." The odds of meeting that goal are increasingly discouraging. In September 2013, the World Meteorological Organization (WMO) reported that emissions in 2013 were the highest in thirty years,[69] "reflecting ever-rising emissions

---

Actually a Bubble Destined to Pop," *Forbes*, April 29, 2014, http://www.forbes.com/sites/jessecolombo/2014/04/29/why-israels-boom-is-actually-a-bubble-destined-to-pop/2/; and Yuval Goren, "Poll Shows 43% of Israelis Fear They'll Fall into Poverty (More than Other Threats)," *Al-Monitor*, November 7, 2012, http://www.al-monitor.com/pulse/tr/contents/articles/business/2012/11/fearful-of-poverty.html#ixzz2NvEOFVj9.

from automobiles and smokestacks but also, scientists believe, a diminishing ability of the world's oceans and plant life to soak up the excess carbon put into the atmosphere by humans."[70]

The Middle East, according to the reports of the IPCC, will be among the regions most affected by climate change.

Water is a preeminent threat.[71]How, where, and when it flows will have profound implications for the future of the land "between the river and the sea."

Indeed, already the two sides are at each other's throats on this issue. Israel is down-gradient of West Bank aquifers (of which the Western Aquifer is the main one), which means that the groundwater flows from the recharge areas and upland aquifers of the West Bank down to those on the Israeli side of the Green Line on its way to the sea. "Israel has been tapping up to 270 million cubic meters of the aquifer from its side of the Green Line since 1955.[72] It claims "ownership" of the water and invokes legal precedents that the legitimate claim of ownership lies with the party into which the water flows.[73] Outraged Palestinians hotly dispute this. Palestinians argue that the point of origin of the water is what counts, and of course they invoke a different set of legal references. The Oslo Accords provided for water protocols between Israel and the PA that are today hopelessly outdated.[74] And Israel has either ignored or abused many of its provisions according to human rights organizations.[75] Water consumption in Israel is three times the consumption in the West Bank, where it does *not* meet WHO standards.[76] In Gaza the availability and quality of water are among the factors that cause the UN to say Gaza will be unlivable by 2020, and after the 2014 war, the water is mostly undrinkable.

Israel has a water crisis[77] (at the moment it has a surplus because the amount of water produced by its desalination plants exceeds its current needs, but reliance on desalination plants is unsustainable);[78] so too do the Palestinians, Jordan,[79] Syria (or what is left of it), and Lebanon.[80] These crises will remain because they all share the same diminishing resource in the face of rapidly increasing populations. The Jordan River itself has already become a puddle, a trickle, rather than the river that made the valley so fertile and the produce from the valley the envy of other countries a mere decade ago. Jordan finds itself frequently unable to provide Israel with the allotted water as per their 1994 peace treaty.[81] The Levant will get a lot hotter as a result of climate change[82] and with less precipitation; we know, too, that the limited water supply, notwithstanding the large-scale, capital-intensive, carbon-emitting desalination plants Israel can build, will hardly suffice in the face of accelerating population growth. We know that a Palestinian economy, even under the most advantageous circumstances, will be hard-pressed or unable to generate the capital needed to build desalination plants; we know that if it cannot, it will become water dependent on Israel's desalinated water, the ultimate form of dependence because any delay or reduction would be life threatening. Water sources in the Levant and beyond are interconnected and will have to be addressed on a regional basis. There is no other option. Scientists warn that the Mediterranean could rise by several feet over the coming centuries as a result of the irreversible melting of western Antarctica;[83] the Israeli and Gaza (or, in the future, Palestinian) coastline will be pushed inland, along with the population, with indeterminable consequences dictated by nature, not politics.[84] Climate change as a catalyst for global political conflict—with the Middle East as one of the primary targets—is on the radar among U.S. military researchers.[85] And a ready example is the Syrian civil war, which had its roots in a six-year drought that scorched much of the country and forced hundreds of thousands of farmers and their families to abandon their land and seek refuge in cities.[86] In Iran, drought, coupled with a potential water crisis, is becoming a major political problem.[87]

We know there will be frequent and extreme weather, less precipitation, prolonged droughts, and heavier storms.* We know it will affect crop yields and ecosystems.†[88] For those negotiators engaged with this issue,

*"A severe storm that blanketed Israel with snow and brought flurries to parts of the Middle East for the first time in over 100 years was an example of extreme weather caused by man-made climate change, a report by a United Nations agency charged Monday." Associated Press and *Times of Israel* staff, "UN: December Blizzard Example of Human-Induced Extreme Weather," *Times of Israel*, March 24, 2014, http://www.timesofisrael.com/un-report-says-climate-change-led-to-snow-storm/.

Ruth Schuster, "Forecast for 2014: El Nino—and Grain Famine," *Haaretz*, June 18, 2014, http://www.haaretz.com/life/nature-environment/.premium-1.599397. "Scientists are predicting another El Nino weather pattern this year. If it hits hard, it could ruin grain crops—and the world is ill prepared, says Israeli scientist Hendrik Bruins." Israel imports 90 percent of its grain; effects of climate change on grain growing in either Australia or the United States (or both) could leave Israel and Palestine in a dire situation, especially as China and India would leave the bread basket empty. See also: Justin Gillis, "Looks Like Rain Again. And Again," *New York Times*, May 12, 2014, http://www.nytimes.com/2014/05/13/science/looks-like-rain-again-and-again.html.

†I would be remiss not to draw attention to a study conducted over a nine-year period by a team of international scientists that, in contrast to previous predictions, found no measurable changes in the vegetation even after nine years of rainfall manipulations. None of the crucial vegetation characteristics, neither species richness and composition, nor density or biomass—a particularly important trait for these ecosystems traditionally used as rangelands—changed appreciably in the rainfall manipulations. These conclusions were reached regardless of whether the sites were subjected to more or less rain. The plants in this community proved to be

connecting the dots may lead to awkward conclusions. Who on either side links the resolution of this conflict with the inescapable consequences of climate change—availability of resources and food security—that in 2030 onward will be very different than they are today?[89] The inside-the-box obsession with core-protected values—borders, security, refugees, settlers, Jerusalem—has deafened almost everyone to the freight train around the bend.

Zafrir Rinat, one of Israel's most respected journalists on environmental matters, was the only interviewee, other than Arnon Soffer, who linked demography and resource scarcity with the Israeli-Palestinian conflict. "We are already facing very difficult problems from both perspectives relating to water and demography," Rinat says. "It is going to get worse because the trends are very clear. Even if, miraculously, the Arab society at large and the Jewish society at large change their habits and their way of life and start producing smaller families, the time it will take to change the impact of what already has gone on will take so long that demography will still be a big issue. I don't see the trend changing."[90]

Water will either be shared and managed or fought over. There are no other choices: Nothing, not even food, is more basic.

Countries will be required by nature and necessity to collaborate extensively and share the diminishing resource. It is the only way to assure mutual viability. Palestine and Israel will be no exception.

> > < <

The Palestinian-Israeli conflict, which has its antecedents in the last decades of the nineteenth century, is now entering the second decade of the twenty-first century. The parameters of both the conflict and the efforts to resolve it were defined in the circumstances and "facts on the ground" in the twentieth century. But a century has moved geopolitics, populations, land mass, and availability of resources and created ineluctable interdependencies: History has moved, but the contours of how to address the Palestinian-Israeli question have remained immovable, frozen in time. Both protagonists are still fiddling

remarkably resilient to a long-term decrease in rainfall. The study, "Middle-Eastern Plant Communities Tolerate 9 Years of Drought in a Multi-Site Climate," covering the Eastern Mediterranean Basin, a global biodiversity hotspot, was conducted by a team of international scientists headed by Dr. Katja Tielbörger (University of Tübingen) and was published in *Nature Communications* on October 6, 2014. "Based on our study, the going hypothesis that all arid regions will react strongly to climate change needs to be amended," Dr. Tielbörger said. The study can be found at http://www.nature.com/ncomms/2014/141006/ncomms6102/pdf/ncomms6102.pdf.

with variations of recommendations proposed some eighty years ago by the Peel Commission that tried to accommodate facts on the ground as they were at the time. Few ask: After eighty years of fruitless preoccupation with every permutation of the same model, is it not time for Israelis and Palestinians—and the United States—to climb out of the decrepit two-state box and open their minds to the realities of the century in which they live? Or are they intent on staying in the box, ensuring the "integrity of their quarrel,"* preferring to produce another generation that will be taught to hate, live with fear, and ultimately aspire to kill?

Ultimately, it is their choice.

*A phrase Winston Churchill used in 1922 to describe the political state of Northern Ireland.

Afterword

The unforgiving realities in Israel and Palestine crystallized in the six months after the completion of this book. The situation in Israel/Palestine careened from one crisis to the next, reinforcing the argument of *The Two-State Delusion* that a two-state solution is obsolete.

What was described as a "leaderless" intifada broke out in Jerusalem, bringing home to Jewish Israelis that the Separation Barrier was an insufficient deterrent to Palestinian terror attacks and heightening their sense of personal insecurity. Violence between Palestinian youth and the police erupted in East Jerusalem; the nightly bouts of rock throwing by the youth and retaliation by the police had the media talking of a third intifada in the making.[1] Shortly afterwards, an attempt of right-wing Jews to pray on the Temple Mount/*Haram al-Sharif* led to explosive confrontations between Palestinian youth and Jewish extremists. Jews praying in Temple Mount/*Haram al-Sharif* is a prescription for a religious war, not just between Israel and Palestine, but Israel and the Muslim world.[2] Jordan recalled its ambassador and thousands marched in Amman, calling for ending the 1994 treaty with Israel.* Netanyahu, pressured by John Kerry, went to Amman and reassured King Abdullah that the status quo on the Mount would remain in place,[3] but this only led to more calls from incensed right-wing members of

*Suleiman Al-Khalidi, "Thousands march in Jordan calling to end Israel-Jordan peace treaty" *Haaretz*, November 7, 2014; http://www.haaretz.com/news/diplomacy-defense/1.625249 Israel annexed East Jerusalem, which is home to The Old City, where most of the Holy sites are located, including the Al Aqsa Mosque/Temple Mount after the 1967 Six-Day War—a move never recognized internationally. The Hashemite have a long and storied relationship with Al Aqsa. In March 2013, Palestinian Authority President Mahmoud Abbas signed a deal with King Abdullah, entrusting him with the defense of Muslim holy sites in Jerusalem. The deal confirmed a verbal agreement dating back to 1924 that gave the kingdom's Hashemite leaders custodial rights over the Muslim holy sites. These arrangements are reaffirmed in the Israel/Jordanian Treaty (1994). Dalia Hatuqa, "UNESCO to Inspect Jerusalem's Old City," *Al Monitor*, April 25, 2013; http://www.al-monitor.com/pulse/tr/originals/2013/04/unesco-inspect-jerusalem-old-city-walls.html; Muusa Hattar, "Fearing backlash, Jordan asserts al-Aqsa custodianship," *Times of Israel*, November 16, 2014; http://www.timesofisrael.com/fearing-backlash-jordan-asserts-al-aqsa-custodianship/ "Temple Mount unrest is a threat to Hashemite regime's legitimacy in the eyes of its subjects, pushing it to take tough stance against Israel."

the Likud and Jewish Home for Jews to have the right to pray on the Mount.[4] The ingredients of an imminent combustion were in place.*

A new pattern of violence soon emerged. In Jerusalem, individual Palestinians began to attack and kill or injure Jews—not police or IDF, but civilians going about their days. These Palestinians did not belong to Hamas or Fatah; they did not receive instructions from either. The acts were random, sporadic outbursts, personal intifadas. A car plowed into a crowd waiting for the light rail train, killing two riders. Its Palestinian driver was shot by security forces.† An Israeli woman and soldier were killed in Tel Aviv in knife attacks, which had become unaffiliated Palestinians modus operandi. The attackers were shot by security forces.[5] The Minster of Home Security, Yitzhak Aharonowitz, declared publicly that he did not want any terrorist to survive after an attack.[6]

On November 18, matters took a turn for the worse. Two Palestinian cousins, Ghassen and Uday Abu Jamal, neither with any affiliation with Hamas or Fatah, walked into a synagogue in Har Hof, a neighborhood in West Jerusalem, armed with meat cleavers, and killed five people in cold

*In a December 2014 poll, an overwhelming majority (86 percent) of Palestinians believed that *al Haram al Sharif* was in grave danger: 56 percent believed that Israel intended to destroy al Aqsa Mosque and the Dome of the Rock and replace them with a Jewish temple; 21 percent believed that Israel intended to divide the plateau on which the two mosques sat so that Jews would have a synagogue alongside the Muslim holy places; and 9 percent believed that Israel intended to change the status quo prevailing in the plateau since 1967 by allowing Jews to pray there. Only 6 percent believed that Israel was interested in maintaining the status quo without change. Half of the Palestinian public believed that Israel would succeed in implementing its plans for *al Haram al Sharif.* "Palestinian Public Opinion Poll No.54," December 3-6 2104; http://www.pcpsr.org/en/node/505; for further information contact Dr. Khalil Shikaki, at pcpsr@pcpsr.org.

Jodi Rudoren, "Mistrust Threatens Delicate Balance at a Sacred Site in Jerusalem," *New York Times* November 22 2014; http://www.nytimes.com/2014/11/23/world/middleeast/mistrust-threatens-delicate-balance-at-a-sacred-site-in-jerusalem-.html Rudoren reported that the PLO had declared that the name used for the site by Jews, the Temple Mount, was "null and void." Instead, the group said, the compound—"a symbol for all Palestinians"—must be called Al Aqsa Mosque or the Noble Sanctuary.

†"The route of the train runs from the national cemetery at Mount Hertz," the *Washington Post* reported, "past the embankments of the Old City, through the Arab neighborhoods of East Jerusalem to the Jewish settlement of Pisgat Zeev." Hailed at the time it was built as a symbol of Jerusalem as an undivided city, it only exposed its divisions. Now it is a target of Palestinian fury. "Ticket booths in Palestinian areas have been smashed with hammers and torched with gasoline . . . Fifteen of the twenty three trains are damaged . . . In Palestinian neighborhoods protesters tried to rip the rails from the ground." William Booth and Ruth Eglash, "Jerusalem train line destined to connect Jews and Arabs has widened bitter divide," *Washington Post,* November 3, 2014. http://www.washingtonpost.com/world/middle_east/jerusalem-train-line-destined-to-connect-jews-and-arabs-has-widened-bitter-divide/2014/11/01/331d11ea-5f73-11e4-9f3a-7e28799e0549_story.html

blood, including four rabbis, wounding seven others.[7] It was hatred, Jewish Israelis said; unadulterated evil.[8] "A cartoon of a bloody meat cleaver like the one used in the attack that killed four Orthodox Jews circulated on social media [in the PA and Gaza]" *The New York Times* reported. "Residents of the Gaza Strip paraded in the streets singing victory songs, giving out candy, waving flags."[9]

Hamas and Islamic Jihad praised the killers and urged Palestinians to attack more Jews. It ridiculed Abbas and called for an intifada in the West Bank.[10] In Jerusalem, Palestinians were assaulted by right-wing Jewish Israeli youth; in the West Bank, Palestinians targeted settlers. The Knesset succumbed to openly expressed hatreds, vitriolic diatribes—every party on the right calling for more extreme measures: Jews should have the right to pray on Temple Mount, the residency of Palestinians in East Jerusalem should be revoked. Some Jews would not ride in buses or take taxis driven by Palestinian Israelis.[11] Barricades crisscrossed Jerusalem; neighborhoods were sealed. The random attacks unnerved Jewish Israelis and shattered their sense of personal safety.[12] The events resurrected memories of the suicide bombings of the second intifada; as these traumas resurfaced, emotions were relived, irrationality gripped minds,[13] and any measure taken against Palestinians was seen as justified. For many Jerusalemites, Palestinians and Palestinian Israelis became objects of openly expressed hatred, proof of their endemic suspicions that Palestinians residing in Israel were the enemy within, waiting for the opportune moment to turn murderously on them.[14] Vengeance was in the air; extremist Jewish youth began to prowl the streets, encouraged by hate-crazed adults who conjured up for the umpteenth time the shibboleths that all Palestinians aspired to the elimination of Jews. "Draped in Israeli flags," *Haaretz* reported "they were carrying banners proclaiming, 'There can be no coexistence with cancer.'"[15] Israel's president, Reuven Rivlin, told a conference that "it is time to honestly admit that Israel is sick, and it is our duty to treat this illness. We have all witnessed the shocking sequence of incidents and violence taking place by both sides."[16] Just as vociferously, youth in Gaza and the West Bank called for "Death to the Jews," whom they believed were conspiring to destroy one of their holiest of sites by imposing their alien religious practices. In Jerusalem and the West Bank, the IDF routinely detained scores of Palestinians in night raids,[17] adding to the 80 percent increase in the number of detainees in prison at year's end over the number of detainees in 2013 and including a 47 percent increase in the number of children detained.[18] Settler attacks on civilian Palestinians continued to escalate.[19]

Addiction to ethos of conflict had both Israelis and Palestinians in its grip.[*] One more spark and the fuse for igniting holy war would unfold. The distant dream of a two-state solution was again swamped in the detritus of mutual loathing. In Israel, incitement was stoked by right-wing political parties, rivals for the same support base; in the PA and Gaza, incitement was exploited by Hamas and the PA competing for the support of the Palestinian street. Both used mainstream and social media to solicit incitement;[20] feeding off hatred, they thrived.

> > < <

Confident that he would prevail in a new election and be able to form a more like-minded ideological coalition, in early December, Netanyahu peremptorily fired Yair Lapid, his finance minister, and Tzipi Livni, the justice minister. New elections were scheduled for March 2015.

Meanwhile, Abbas, under pressure from senior Fatah officials and seeking to bolster his flagging support among the public,[†] authorized Jordan to submit a draft resolution of the PLO's plan for a peace deal to the United Nations Security Council (UNSC).[‡] Although the UNSC almost immediately rejected it even without the United States having to exercise its veto, Abbas signed the necessary documents to join the International Criminal Court (ICC), asking it to investigate Israel for war crimes during the 2014 Gaza war[21] and formally recognizing the court's jurisdiction to do so.[§] Within days, the UN ratified the PA as a member of the court.[22] Israel in

*Carolina Landsmann, "Hysterical Knesset legislation is the harbinger of total chaos," *Haaretz*, November 28, 2014, http://www.haaretz.com/opinion/.premium-1.628955. "It's frightening," she wrote, "to see a society that removes the masks from itself and exposes its ugliness."

†The level of satisfaction with the performance of Abbas in December 2014, before he authorized the UNSC resolution, had dropped to 35 percent, compared to 39 percent three months earlier. Satisfaction with Abbas stood at 50 percent before the Gaza war. If elections were held in December 2014, polls indicated that Hamas would come out on top. "Palestinian Public Opinion Poll No.54," December 3-6 2104, http://www.pcpsr.org/en/node/505.

‡On December 29, 2014, a draft resolution to the UNSC that called for peace with Israel within a year and an end to the occupation within three years. Among its provisions: a Palestinian state to have borders congruent with the '67 borders, East Jerusalem as its capital, an end to settlement building, settlement of the refugee question in accordance with UN resolution 194, and the release of political prisoners.

§In the absence of viable negotiations, 80 percent supported joining more international organizations; 73 percent supported joining the International Criminal Court; and 60 percent favored resort to popular non-violent resistance; 56 percent supported a return to an armed intifada, and 49 percent supported dissolving the PA. "Palestinian Public Opinion Poll No. 54," December 3-6, 2104, http://www.pcpsr.org/en/node/505; "Palestinians recognize ICC jurisdiction for period covering Gaza war," *Al Monitor*, January 6, 2015, http://www.al-monitor.com/pulse/contents/afp/2015/01/cpi-conflit-palestiniens-isra%C3%ABl.html.

turn threatened to file charges against the PA, accusing it of crimes of inhumanity during the Gaza war.[23]

The PA application for membership in the ICC only escalated the conflict, with the United States and Israel promising harsh responses.[24] Israel promptly withheld $127 million in tax revenues belonging to the PA.[25]* The PA's formal membership in the ICC became effective on April 1, 2015.

Making a case to have the ICC investigate allegations of a war crime would be an immensely complicated, time-consuming process. And even if the court decides there are grounds for an investigation, Israel would never cooperate. There would be adjudication of findings, evaluation of the evidence, and the appointment of a prosecutor to conduct a trial. There would also be issuance of warrants, bringing the accused to The Hague, and evidentiary proceedings at the trial—reversible at several points—and then a judgment by the court.† If the ICC concluded that an investigation is warranted, Israel will stonewall and proceedings grind to a halt. Israel, of course, would be poisoning its own well, inviting harsh international condemnation. But well ahead of such an eventuality, Israel undoubtedly would file counterclaims of war crimes perpetrated by Hamas during the Gaza war, when missiles were fired deliberately

*The United States has legislation in place prohibiting financial aid to the PA—currently about $400 million annually—if it initiates any action against Israel at the ICC. Barak Ravid, "Israel to ask U.S. congressmen to halt aid to Palestinians," *Haaretz*, January 5, 2015, http://www.haaretz.com/news/diplomacy-defense/1.635316.

The law in question is H.R.5013—Department of State, Foreign Operations, and Related Programs Appropriations Act, 2015: "Prohibits the availability of Economic Support Fund assistance under this Act for the PA if the Palestinians: obtain the same standing as a United Nations (U.N.) member state or full membership in the U.N. or any specialized U.N. agency outside an agreement negotiated between Israel and the Palestinians; or initiate an International Criminal Court (ICC) investigation or actively supports such an investigation, that subjects Israeli nationals to an investigation for alleged war crime against Palestinians."

†"Understanding the International Criminal Court," http://www.icc-cpi.int/iccdocs/PIDS/publications/UICCEng.pdf; "ICC: Situations and Cases," http://www.icc-cpi.int/en_menus/icc/situations%20and%20cases/Pages/situations%20and%20cases.aspx

Among the multiple provisions involved are also stipulations that The Prosecutor will initiate an investigation unless there are "substantial reasons to believe that an investigation would not serve the interests of justice" when "taking into account the gravity of the crime and the interests of victims." Furthermore, even if an investigation has been initiated and there are substantial facts to warrant a prosecution and no other admissibility issues, the Prosecutor must determine whether a prosecution would serve the interests of justice "taking into account all the circumstances, including the gravity of the crime, the interests of victims and the age or infirmity of the alleged perpetrator, and his or her role in the alleged crime." Charges are filed against individuals, not states or institutions, the State in which the accused live—in this case Israel—has the responsibility to enforce warrants of arrest; the accused must be present at their trial. See also Alex Whiting, "Palestine and the ICC: An 'Imagined' View from inside the Court," Lawfare January 5, 2015, http://www.lawfareblog.com/2015/01/palestine-and-the-icc-an-imagined-view-from-inside-the-court/.

targeting Israel's civilian population.[26] In fact, even before the PA had been formally accepted as a member of the ICC, an Israeli NGO had filed charges of war crimes against leading members of the PA.* (Months later, following its own investigation, Amnesty International reported that "Palestinian armed groups, including the armed wing of Hamas, repeatedly launched unlawful attacks during the conflict killing and injuring civilians.")[27]

Netanyahu's reaction to these events as they unfolded? As usual, rather than attempt to compromise he took a punitive stance, promising that if reelected he would not evacuate any settlements in the West Bank.[28]

Although the PLO failed to attain statehood at the UN, it nonetheless achieved its intended "paradigm shift"—internationalizing the conflict by putting it under the umbrella of the UN, and hoping to dilute the influence of the United States—all goals the Palestinians interviewed had articulated in 2011 and 2012.† Of course, the UN cannot mandate a sovereign state into being, nor would any resolution it passes end the occupation of the West Bank. But the more Israel ignores the demands of the international community, the more it leaves itself open to being delegitimized, giving a huge impetus to a Boycott, Divestment and Sanctions (BDS) that is gaining ground.‡ The scenario suggests that the sooner Israel gets back into bilateral

*Avi Lewis, "Israeli group files war crimes suits against Palestinian leaders," *Times of Israel*, January 5, 2015, http://www.timesofisrael.com/group-files-war-crimes-lawsuits-against-palestinian-leaders/.

On January 5 2015, the Israeli legal group Shurat HaDin, the Israel Law Center, filed indictments at the International Criminal Court (ICC) against PA Prime Minister Rami Hamdallah, Abbas's deputy; minister Jibril Rajoub; and PA intelligence chief Majed Faraj, all of whom belong to Abbas's Fatah party, for alleged war crimes, terrorism, and human rights offenses. It also pursued existing litigation filed against Abbas last November, as well as a case against Gaza-based terror group Hamas and its leader Khaled Mashaal, filed at the ICC on September 2014.

†The French are ready to move forward. See: Somini Sengpta, "France Seeks U.N. Security Council Resolution on Mideast Talks," *New York Times*, March 27, 2015; Sengpta reported that "France signaled on Friday [March 27] that it would press the Security Council to adopt a resolution soon to spur talks between Israel and the Palestinians, a step that the United States resisted last year." French Foreign Minister Laurent Fabius told reporters at the UN that "if we want to have a two-state solution, and if we want to avoid a complete crash, we must go in the same direction. I hope the partners who were reluctant will not be reluctant." The move, according to the *Times*, was intended to put pressure on the U.S. to act. http://www.nytimes.com/2015/03/28/world/middleeast/france-security-council-peace-talks-resume.html?ref=world.

‡Debra Nussbaum Cohen, "The year BDS became the number one concern for American Jews," *Haaretz*, December 27, 2015, http://www.haaretz.com/jewish-world/jewish-world-features/.premium-1.633972.

A Knesset report, however, said that BDS was having no impact on the economy; that exports to Europe had in fact doubled since the launch of the BDS movement. Ora Coren and Zvi Zrahiva, "Knesset report: BDS movement has no impact on economy," *Haaretz*, January 9, 2015, http://www.haaretz.com/news/diplomacy-defense/.premium-1.636172.

negotiations, the more successful it might be in staving off the mounting international pressure. But no matter what diplomatic maneuvering is afoot, no matter whether Israel may be *compelled* to negotiate for a two-state solution, no matter what the heretofore moribund Quartet might conjure and no matter the number of UN resolutions calling for a Palestinian state, the solution all parties (except Hamas) are so unwaveringly committed to is no longer feasible. One more unforgiving reality.

Problems for Israel mounted on other fronts. Among European countries, the heretofore immalleable support which had begun to falter during the Gaza war had collapsed into near freefall.[29] The ferocity of Israel's latest assault on Gaza and the devastation it caused were a tipping point. Muted concern on the Palestinian issue was replaced with actions designed to put pressure on Israel to end the occupation, acknowledge its unequivocal commitment to Palestinian self-determination, and engage in negotiations to eventuate that outcome. The EU agreed to accept "in principle" the establishment of a Palestinian state—a decision that followed Sweden's recognition of Palestine—and parliaments in Britain, Ireland, Spain, and France passed symbolic resolutions recognizing Palestine.[30] The European Court took Hamas off the EU's terrorist list,[31] and the conference of the Geneva Convention—emphasizing the prohibition on colonizing occupied land—declared that international humanitarian law should be applied to the West Bank, calling for "all serious violations" to be investigated and for those responsible for breaches to be brought to justice.[32] Facing this negative perception abroad, a majority of Jewish Israelis resorted to denial, an absence of introspection and soul searching that typifies their reaction to any form of international censure. The December Dialog poll found 56 percent of the electorate blamed the Americans, Europeans or Palestinians for Israel's wretched international status. Only a third of the country's public was prepared to name Netanyahu's government as being mainly responsible.[33]

Relations between Netanyahu and Obama further deteriorated in October after Netanyahu again expedited plans for the construction of more housing units in East Jerusalem[34] and stood aside when 200 Israeli settlers moved into Silwan, a predominantly Palestinian neighborhood south of the Old City, triggering riots in East Jerusalem and the Old City.[35] The Israeli cabinet backed a bill extending Israeli civil law to the settlements, coming one step closer to outright annexation.[36] To shore up his right-wing credentials in advance of the election, Netanyahu approved the government's appropriation of 1000 acres in the West Bank, near Bethlehem and close to

Bitar Ilit—one of the biggest Israeli settlements in the West Bank—another kiss of death to a contiguous Palestinian state, as if more were needed.[37] To mollify Naftali Bennett, he approved another 1,060 units of housing in east Jerusalem.[38]

Then, Netanyahu blindsided the Obama administration by accepting an invitation from Republican Speaker John Boehner to address a joint session of Congress on March 3, 2015—two weeks before Israel's election—without informing the White House. In alignment with congressional Republicans, he used the occasion to warn of the folly of an agreement on denuclearization the administration was pushing for with Iran. Netanyahu used the occasion to reenergize his electoral base, probably giving "the kiss of death" to relations with Obama, infuriating Democrats.[39]

> > < <

Meanwhile, the reconciliation pact between Hamas and Fatah continued to unravel amid staccato-like accusations and counteraccusations—Abbas that Hamas was intent on overthrowing him; Hamas that Abbas wanted to destroy it.[40] The 43,000 unpaid Hamas public employees, one of the factors that precipitated the 2014 Gaza war, continued to go unpaid.[41] Hamas refused to hand over control of checkpoints to the PA.[42] The PA appears to govern, but Hamas rules. Elections were put on hold.[43] The pact could be resuscitated, but only, Hamas said, under a new set of conditions, which Hamas did not do much to clarify.* The PASF, along with the IDF, scoured the West Bank for Hamas militants.[44] A week before Israel's elections the PASF rounded up fifty Hamas and Islamic Jihad activists in the West Bank to thwart any last-minute terror attack that might throw the election to Likud.[45] The bad blood is as fresh as ever; the rivalry as bitter.

The PA has become more authoritarian than ever; dissent is stifled, leaving open to question the kind of Palestine that would emerge if a two-state solution ever saw the light of day. The lip service to democratic norms, respect for human rights, due process, and the primacy of the rule of law still effortlessly roll off the tongues of PA officials, but the situation on the ground

*Sami Abu Zuhri, Hamas spokesman, said at a press conference in Gaza City on November 30 that the six-month span of the unity government had expired and that talks would take place regarding a future government according to the Palestinian Ma'an news agency. According to the *Jerusalem Post*, Abbas said earlier that Hamas is completely responsible for Gaza, and not the joint Fatah-Hamas unity government. "Islamic Jihad slams PA-Israel security coordination as unity gov't expires," *Alakhbar*, November 30, 2014, http://english.al-akhbar.com/node/22696.

tells a different story: The largest union in the West Bank is banned because it tried to organize strikes; security agents monitor social media, Fatah continues to purge suspected supporters of Hamas; two thirds of the public say it is afraid to criticize Abbas for fear of the possible repercussions. Dissent comes at a high price.[46] Fatah itself faces internal divisions, which will prove difficult to reconcile.*

Hamas faces its own troubles. The Cairo talks that were supposed to resolve the outstanding issues between itself and Israel when the ceasefire was announced in August 2014 never really got off the ground. Egypt, still convinced that arms were being smuggled through Gaza to the Sinai, finally demolished the town of Rafah on its side of the border, creating an extended buffer zone, a formidable obstacle to constructing the tunnels that were Hamas's supply route for weapons, but not one that Hamas regarded as insurmountable.[47] The Rafah gate became a prison gate. Openings were periodic, leaving the Eretz gate the only point of exit for Gazans. When it came to Hamas, the Egyptians were doing for Israel what the Israelis could not itself do. Sisi could demolish Hamas, if that became his liking.[48]

At the donors' conference convened by Norway in October, donors pledged $5.4 billion to rebuild Gaza[49] (Qatar alone promised $1 billion), but it's unlikely to reach the people who need it. The money pledged would be channeled to the PA, half to provide budgetary assistance and help stabilize the West Bank—and supposedly about to assume the additional task of governing a bankrupt Gaza; and half for reconstruction in Gaza. What is more,

*Besides the persistent infighting over Abbas's successor, pressing issues included: what policies to adopt after taking steps to join the International Criminal Court (ICC); whether to be open to further negotiations with Israel after twenty years of failed negotiations; the future of nonviolent protest; countering perceptions that the party was too closely aligned with the PA and hence its all-too-comfortable accommodation with successive Israeli governments and the public's belief that the PA itself was almost insatiably corrupt; a course of action should the PA collapse; whether the PA should collapse itself; the role of imprisoned Marwan Barghouti, by far the public's choice for president; after twenty years of failed negotiations under what conditions, if any, it should negotiate with the Israeli government again; the need for new blood, especially at the leadership level, which would be determined by the outcome of elections to the party's twenty-member Central Committee and hundred-member Revolutionary Council; a redefinition of itself as a national liberation organization; how to reengage the diaspora, which believed that Fatah only paid lip service to the right of return; rifts between supporters of Mohammed Dahlan, former Gaza security chief, who was booted out of Fatah by Abbas but had now reemerged on the political scene, and Fatah members who wanted no dealing with him; Dahlan's coy responses to Hamas's overtures; the future of reconciliation with Hamas . . . and more. See also, Daoud Kuttab, "West Bank refugee camp threatens Palestinian leadership," *Al Monitor*, March 16, 2015, http://www.al-monitor.com/pulse/originals/2015/03/west-bank-balatta-camp-security-trouble-government.html.

if the track record of international donors between money pledged and pledges honored is a guide, the omens are not encouraging. The interminable confrontations between Hamas and Fatah only add to donors' hesitancy. And corruption of course will have its cut.[50]

> > < <

On March 17, 2015, Israelis went to the polls. All parties, except for Likud, ran on platforms that for the most part eschewed the Palestinian question and focused almost exclusively on domestic socioeconomic issues—the priority concern of the electorate, or so it seemed.[51] The election was a referendum on Netanyahu's tenure, whether after seven years Israelis had their fill of his strident right-wing policies, which had all but emasculated the prospect of a two-state solution and damaged Israel's position with the one indispensable ally whose support was crucial to its survival, or whether, despite their disenchantment, a sufficient number of voters still believed he was best qualified to lead the country. His opponents spoke from the same playbook: "anyone but Bibi," but offered little in the way of substance to prove that an alternative would have more to offer. They relied on "Netanyahu fatigue," which numerous polls suggested encapsulated voters' sentiments.

Once again, Netanyahu ran a campaign that sold him as Mr. Security, trying to shift the focus of the electorate to the preeminent existential threat of a nuclearized Iran and the Fatah-Hamas terrorist nexus.* Polls indicated

*Two weeks after the election, on April 2, the P5 +1—the five permanent UN Security Council members plus Germany—and Iran after marathon negotiations reached agreement on a Framework Agreement. A final agreement will have to address many of the most contentious issues that were put aside. Both U.S. President Barak Obama and Iranian Foreign Minister Mohammad Zarif called the agreement "historic." "We have reached a historic understanding with Iran, which, if fully implemented, will prevent it from obtaining a nuclear weapon," Obama said from the White House Lawn after the deal was announced. European Union foreign policy chief Federica Mogherini was a little more circumspect, calling it a "decisive step." The joint statement issued after agreement was finalized said Iran and the P5+1 "have reached solutions on key parameters" that would form the basis for reaching the detailed final Iran nuclear accord by the end of June. Among the measures agreed, the most important would lengthen the amount of time it takes to produce enough fissile material for one nuclear weapon—to at least one year and for Iran the lifting of sanctions once compliance with the measures agreed was verified. For full details of the agreement see "Details of Agreement to Limit Iran's Nuclear Program," *New York Times*, April 2, 2015, http://www.nytimes.com/interactive/2015/04/02/world/middleeast/iran-nuclear-agreement.html

Netanyahu lambasted the agreement as a historic sellout, saying that it legitimized Iran's nuclear program, threatened Israel's survival, and would set off a nuclear arms race in the Middle East. Any final deal, he insisted, would have to include Iran's recognition of the State of Israel. Most analysts agreed that Obama faced a hard sell with the Republican-controlled Congress, seen as being closely aligned with Netanyahu. Should Netanyahu's continuing adamantine

that after seven years the public had tired of him, that he should no longer be prime minister, and a majority believed the country was headed in the wrong direction. Still, when it came to naming who was best qualified to be prime minister, he bested his nearest rival by double digits.[52] Israelis, like him or not, still believed that he was best equipped to safeguard Israel's interests and navigate the increasingly treacherous terrain of global geopolitics.

Nevertheless, in the weeks before the election, support for Likud hemorrhaged. Smaller right-wing parties picked off disenchanted Likud voters, while support surged for the center left Zionist Union (ZU), formed after the merger of Isaac Herzog's Labor party and Tzipi Livni's Hatnuah party. Days before the election opinion polls showed the ZU with at least a four-seat advantage over Likud. Pundits began to write Netanyahu's political obituary: he had lost the political plot, his actions were desperate and bizarre; there was panic in the ranks.

Two days before the election, Netanyahu resorted to scorched earth campaigning: under his watch, he declared, there would be no Palestinian state;[53] he would build thousands of new housing units in East Jerusalem, despite international pressure.[54] Palestinian Israeli voters, he warned his base, were going to vote in droves, throwing the election to the center left ZU.[55] Likud better get to the polls if it wanted its interests safeguarded.

To the consternation of all—pundits, pollsters, the international community, and certainly the ZU—Netanyahu's Likud came from behind to win thirty seats to the ZU twenty-four seats—a swing of ten seats in forty-eight hours.[56] Prime minister again for a historic fourth term, Netanyahu and his hard-line positions on Iran and the Palestinian issue were vindicated.* The media on the center left and left in Israel decried the race baiting tactics he had used and excoriated him for doing a turnabout on his support for a two-state solution.[57] Pundits in the U.S. were no less censorious.[58] In the international community, however, responses were more tempered, more accepting of realpolitik.[59] Obama's criticism was harsh,[60] and there were even intimations of retribution from the White House: hints that should a resolution endorsing a Palestinian state reach the UNSC, the US might withhold its veto,†[61] a move that would seriously undermine Israel's international stand-

---

objections, promulgated vociferously from every global pulpit he can find, stiffen Republican opposition to a point of scuppering the deal, Netanyahu could pay a heavy price.

*In the 2009 elections Likud won twenty-seven seats; in the 2013 elections it won twenty seats.

†Complicating matters further is the fact that after the Iran nuclear deal reached on April 2, most analysts agreed that Obama faced a hard sell with the Republican-controlled Congress, seen as being closely aligned with Netanyahu. Should Netanyahu's continuing adamantine objections, promulgated vociferously from every global pulpit he can find stiffen Republican opposition to a

ing and threaten a self-perpetuating erosion of its legitimacy. For Republicans, not surprisingly, Obama was the problem.[62]

Netanyahu, never a politician to let one statement of intent get in the way of its opposite, immediately began to backpedal. Days after the elections, he told NPR's Steve Inskeep that "the dramatic changes that have occurred in the last few years in the region has [sic] brought the rise of militant Islam in any territory that is being vacated. By the way, that's true of Iraq and Syria with ISIS as it's true of us in Gaza. We vacated and we got—we didn't get peace. We got, in fact, an Iranian-backed terrorist enclave that is using the territory for launching pads against us. I don't want a one-state solution, but I certainly don't want a zero-state solution—a no state solution where Israel's very existence would be jeopardized. And that's what the people of Israel overwhelmingly elected me to do."*[63] He apologized profusely to Palestinian

---

point of scuppering the deal, Netanyahu will pay a heavy price. Hence the theater of realpolitik: The French resolution to have the UNSC endorse the plan it outlined for a Palestinian state, evolved into a trade-off between Netanyahu and the administration. Tone down the opposition and agree to work within its parameters and influence the final agreement in return for the U.S. vetoing a SC vote on the French proposal or continue to vociferously object to the framework agreement and enlist the Republican Congress on his side and risk the U.S. allowing the SC vote to pass. At this point in time copper-fastening a final agreement with Iran takes precedence over the Palestinian issue. On one issue Obama cannot risk alienating Netanyahu to the point where his opposition threatens to undermine the deal; on the other, Netanyahu must sufficiently appease Obama so as not to risk a U.S. pass in the SC. See Eric Lipton, "G.O.P.'s Israel Support Deepens as Political Contributions Shift," *New York Times*, April 4, 2015, http://www.nytimes.com/2015/04/05/us/politics/gops-israel-support-deepens-as-political-contributions-shift.html?hp&action=click&pgtype=Homepage&module=first-column-region®ion=top-news&WT.nav=top-news&_r=0; Jodi Rudoren, "Israeli Response to Iran Nuclear Deal Could Have Broader Implications," *New York Times*, April 3, 2015, http://www.nytimes.com/2015/04/04/world/middleeast/israeli-response-to-iran-nuclear-deal-could-have-broader-implications.html.

*Netanyahu's promise that there would be no two-state solution "on his watch" was little more than an iteration of what most Jewish Israelis had already internalized. According to the December 2014 Peace Index, 70 percent of Israelis did not believe that negotiations between Israel and the Palestinian Authority would lead to peace "in the coming years." Monthly Peace Index Poll, December 9, 2014, http://en.idi.org.il/about-idi/news-and-updates/monthly-peace-index-poll/. According to the March 2015 Peace Index, published a week before the elections, 64 percent of Israeli Jews agreed with the statement that no matter which party formed the next government the peace process with the Palestinians would not advance because there was no solution to the dispute; 32 percent disagreed with this statement. http://en.idi.org.il/about-idi/news-and-updates/monthly-peace-index/.

Moreover, according to a survey in the West Bank and Gaza immediately following Netanyahu's reelection 68 percent of Palestinians in the West Bank and Gaza said they support launching rockets from Gaza at Israel if Israel does not lift its Gaza blockade; 48 percent said they supported returning to an armed intifada, in the absence of viable peace negotiations. A majority of 74 percent favors Hamas's way of resisting occupation; 56 percent favored the transfer of Hamas's armed approach to the West Bank and 40 percent opposed. As regards a two-state solution, opinion was almost evenly split: 51 percent favored and 49 percent opposed. While the U.S. and the EU might continue to insist on a two-state solution it didn't appear at the time of the Israeli elections that a substantial number of Palestinians shared their insistence—on the contrary just

Israelis: "I know that my comments last week offended some Israeli citizens and offended members of the Israeli Arab community. This was never my intent. I apologize for this."[64] In a further conciliatory gesture, Israel resumed the transfer of tax revenues it had withheld since December.*[65]

None of these efforts did anything to ameliorate the White House's antagonism. The White House was unmoved. The occupation, the White House Chief of Staff told the annual J Street conference, "must end,"[66] reiterating Obama's earlier comment "that from our point of view the status quo is unsustainable."[67] However, Israel's support in the U.S. Congress is still rock solid, with both the House and the Senate having substantial Republican majorities.[68] Heading into the presidential primary season, support for Netanyahu among the would-be contenders for the Republican nomination for president is absolute.[69]

> > < <

Mostly lost in the furor over Netanyahu's ugly, divisive, race-baiting campaign tactics designed to tap into the most primal fears of Jewish Israelis is the fact that the positions he promulgated with such pugnacity accurately reflect the views of the millions who flocked to the polls to stamp them with

---

about as many opposed one as supported one. Perhaps the West should take a time out. The fact that the same poll indicated that just 39 percent of Palestinians surveyed supported recognizing Israel as the state for the Jewish people in return for an Israeli recognition of Palestine as the state for the Palestinian people. It is time, perhaps, for a pause; time perhaps to take more account of what the Palestinian street thinks and who the PA elite and its longtime negotiators who have been wedded to a two-state solution for decades represents. Of course, should the UNSC endorse a UNGA resolution endorsing a Palestinian state the Palestinian street will celebrate: in the zero sum context of Israeli/Palestinian a "victory" for one is celebrated as much for being a "defeat" of the other. See Palestinian Public Opinion Poll no 55, Palestine Center for Policy and Survey Research, Ramallah, West Bank, www.pcpsr.org/en/node/603; see also, Raghida Dergham, "ISIS: A Priority in the Region at the Expense of Palestine and Other Issues." *Huffington Post* March 20, 2015 http://www.huffingtonpost.com/raghida-dergham/isis-a-priority-in-the-re_b_6912544.html?

Asher Schechter, "Netanyahu's victory is forcing the world to face reality—and that's a good thing," *Haaretz*, March 25, 2015, http://www.haaretz.com/news/israel-election-2015/.premium-1.648780. "Instead of waiting for the center-left to hit the wall of the Israeli consensus," Schechter wrote, "the world can finally acknowledge that the two-state solution is all but dead and continue from there."

*Close to $500 million is involved. For a period of time the PA had to cut PA employee salaries by 40 percent. Although the Israeli government said the monies were being handed over "on humanitarian grounds," the IDF had recommended the release of the impounded money because of fears that impoundment was contributing to instability in the West Bank and posed security concerns for Israel itself. In fact in such situations the withheld tax revenues are always eventually returned to the PA when the impact of the collective punishment threatens the survival of the PA—its collapse would definitely not be in Israel's interest as it would then have to assume the costs and burden of administering and governing the West Bank.

their approval. More than ever, the election results confirmed the depth of polarization among Jewish Israelis. On the one hand, one Israel more right wing, more religious, more aggressive, more starkly apparent now the depth of its opposition to a two-state solution. On the other hand, one Israel more left leaning, more secular, with a passive commitment to a two-state solution. The schism is threatening Israel's social cohesiveness. Writing in the *Times of Israel*, contributor Haviv Rettig Gur called the new Knesset "[the] parliament of a splintered, tribal Israel . . . a new legislature of alienated, antagonistic factions."[70]

But why the surprise and recriminations and finger pointing over what had been abundantly apparent to any careful observer for decades?

The *Haaretz* columnist Gideon Levy, no right winger by any yardstick, put Netanyahu's reelection in context describing his opposition to a two-state solution as "Israel's truth."

> For at least 25 years [he wrote] most Israeli statesmen have been lying, misleading the world, the Israelis and themselves until Netanyahu arose and told the truth. Netanyahu said . . . that if he were to be reelected, a Palestinian state would not be established on his watch. Plain and simple, loud and clear. This simple, pure truth was the case for all his predecessors as well—all the prime ministers, peace lovers and justice seekers from the center and the left, who gave false promises. But who thought to admit it before him? Who had the courage to reveal the truth?
>
> After all, one had to deceive the Americans, bluff the Europeans, and cheat the Palestinians, fudge things for the Mideast Quartet and lie to some Israelis. One also had to play for time, to build settlements and get rid of every possible Palestinian partner—Yasser Arafat, who was too strong; President Mahmoud Abbas, who is too weak; and Hamas, which is too extreme. One has to play for time, so the Palestinians become more extreme and everyone understands that there's no one to talk to.
>
> Now comes the man who is considered a bluffer, and only he tells the fateful, historic truth: there will be no Palestinian state. Not during his term, this now seems eternal. And not after it, because by then it will be too late. The end of negotiations, the end of games. No more shuttle diplomacy, Quartets, emissaries, processes, outlines, mediators and plans. That's it; it will not happen.
>
> It had no chance from the very beginning. In Israel, there was not one single prime minister—including the two Nobel Peace Prize laureates—who intended for one second to let a Palestinian state be established. But the bluff of the century was convenient for everyone. Now Netanyahu has put an end to it.[71]

> > < <

As noted in Chapter 10, the June 2014 Pew Global Poll found that 63 percent of Palestinians and 50 percent of Jewish Israelis say peaceful coexistence is impossible.[72] The same Pew Poll also sampled public opinion in Lebanon, Tunisia, Egypt, Turkey, and Jordan. It reported that "in the wake of yet another breakdown in the Middle East peace process (the 2013-2014 talks), publics in the region have little faith that a way can be found for Israel and an independent Palestinian state to coexist peacefully with each other. Majorities or pluralities in countries across the region voice the view that peaceful coexistence is not possible. And such pessimism is on the rise among many Middle Eastern publics."

The preponderance of opinion, then, both within Israel and Palestine and among their neighbors, is that Israelis and Palestinians cannot coexist in two independent states. Yet everyone is still advocating a solution that all agree is unworkable.

To find common ground, Israelis and Palestinians would have to address the hate so viscerally on display in the later months of 2014, that much abused word, "trust," would somehow have to emerge from the rubble of Gaza and the debilitations of the occupation of the West Bank, and Israel would have to face the ugly truths about itself. Hamas and the Islamic jihad as well as the multitudinous minor jihadist groups in the Gaza Strip would have to agree to decommission their weapons and destroy their stockpiles of arms under conditions that would ensure rearmament impossible, and the requisite transformative leadership on both sides would have to materialize. Each "would have to" is extremely unlikely; all of them converging is phantasmagorical. The new generations in both countries are less tolerant, not more—the Israelis hard, unforgiving, and moving inexorably to the right; the Palestinians more and more inclined to believe that violence is the only means that will bring the occupation and its accrued humiliations to an end.[73]

Some polling now suggests that one quarter of Gazans may be sympathetic to ISIS,[74] a figure that can be expected to increase if reconstruction in Gaza proceeds at a snail's pace and the IDF continues to ride roughshod over Palestinians in the West Bank. The door to the religious war that opened in October 2014 remains permanently ajar. The "peace process," the indulgent misnomer that had served as a useful euphemism for thirty-five years, is over. The PA is hunkered down, declaring the PASF would no longer cooperate with the IDF on security matters,[75] but intent on intensifying its pursuit of statehood at the UN and pressing the ICC to bring Israel to trial for war crimes.[76] The IDF prepares for war in the West Bank.[77] The rift between Fatah and Hamas continues to deepen.[78] In Gaza teenagers flock to Hamas to prepare to fight in the next war with Israel.[79] Hamas hoards its resources to reconstruct destroyed tunnels to be used for weapons trafficking rather than to alleviate the plight of impoverished and homeless Gazans.*[80]

Hatred is calcifying and all sides are provoking one another and readying for war. But even if a Palestinian state were on the horizon, what are its prospects? Contrast: on the one side a one party PA statelet, which last had elections ten years ago led by an aging, unpopular autocrat with power-hungry successors nipping at his heels,[81] corrupt to a fault, and an entrenched elite for whom the occupation has been a source of power and privilege; on the other side is a one party Gaza statelet under the iron thumb of a global pariah, an internationally tarred terrorist movement; it, too, with entrenched elites and the noveau riche merchants of the tunnels. The PA is on a life support system provided by the international donor community; Gaza has a brain-dead economy. Neither adheres to democratic norms, although both pay prolific lip service to the aspirations of democratic ideals; neither has much regard for human rights, although both give prolific expressions of its fealty to such.† One is secular Islamist; the other Islamist. The sum of the two does not a nation state make; rather, it suggests the rudiments of a failed state already in place.

Nothing is etched in infinity. The Middle East is being reshaped, and neither Israel nor Palestine can escape indefinitely the repercussions of that reshaping.[82] Neither can they simply brush aside the realities that now define them, realities that eviscerate the notion that there will ever be two states for two people. History does not indulge illusions; it is time to seek another way forward.

Padraig O'Malley
April 1, 2015

*According to Musa Abu Marzouk, Hamas rejected an offer for a five-year ceasefire with Israel in exchange for lifting the Israeli blockade to facilitate reconstruction. "Hamas rejected 5-year Israel truce in return for end to Gaza blockade, says Abu Marzouk," *Haaretz*, March 11, 2015, http://www.haaretz.com/news/diplomacy-defense/.premium-1.646479.

See also: Jack Khoury, "Hamas rejected 5-year Israel truce in return for end to Gaza blockade, says Abu Marzouk," *Haaretz*, March 11, 2015, http://www.haaretz.com/news/diplomacy-defense/.premium-1.646479.

†According to the PCPSR Palestinian Poll No. 54, just 9 percent of Palestinians believe that the first and most vital goal for Palestinians should be to establish a democratic political system that respects freedoms and rights of Palestinians. http://www.pcpsr.org/en/node/505.

Acknowledgments

In the writing of *The Two-State Delusion*, there are numerous people to thank for assistance and encouragement. Without the assistance of Nancy Riordan, my colleague and friend, the book would not have crossed the finishing line. Her skills, editorial gifts, research abilities, hours of work more than what one should reasonably ask of anyone, tenacious persistence, and the huge amounts of time she invested in the project were remarkable, and just expressing my gratitude does not adequately express the depth of my feelings.

For bringing order to a manuscript that rambled, was far too long, and in need of restructuring, my thanks to Mike Bryan, whose expertise was stretched to its fullest capacity as he toiled at bringing an enormous bulk of a manuscript to manageable proportions; thanks, too, for the editorial assistance of Tom Mashberg, who chipped away at excess verbiage, of which there was much; Alex Lay and Kathleen Adams for meticulous and always timely research of inestimable value, done voluntarily and with enthusisatic willingness; Marcy Murninghan for digging out hard-to-find data, and for her impeccable research, mapping skills, knack for always finding creative solutions to innumerable technical problems, due diligence in the bibliographical compilation, and, most importantly, her unflagging encouragement over four years; Ward Williamson for helping in the compilation of the bibliography and cataloguing my scattered papers, reports, years of research materials, and innumerable documents.

In Jerusalem, gratitude to Tal Kligman and Avner Haramati for making Jerusalem a home; Sam Bafour for introducing me to the West Bank; Ibrahim Alkhteel for whisking me around the West Bank, driver par excellence, and for his friendship; and the staff at the Jerusalem YMCA for their courtesy and help during my long stays.

Thank you to Paul Aaron, without whom Gaza would have remained a mystery, and Jonathan Moore for introducing us; Nathan Thrall, the International Crisis Group's man in the middle of it all, for feeding me invaluable material; the late Dr. Eyad el-Sarraj, the Gazan psychiatrist, for long insightful conversations; my Jewish Israeli, Palestinian Israeli, West Bank, and Gazan interviewees for always making themselves available, despite disruptions to their schedules; Dr. Alon Liel for encouragement and friendship; Saro

Nakashian for taking the time to track down contact details for many interviewees; Quintin Oliver for introducing me to Kamel Husseini, who also tracked down details for many interviewees; Natalie Flanagan, Cheryl Broderick, and Rhett Nichols for being there; Mariska Kappmeier for company at the Cambridge City Library; and my University of Massachusetts Boston colleagues Steve Crosby, former dean of the John W. McCormack Graduate School of Policy and Global Studies, and his successor, Dean Ira Jackson, whose unbridled enthusiasm and infectious can-do spirit provided a lift on the many occasions I grappled to make sense of everything in a region of the world where sense has no place; the staff at the school, including Candyce Carragher, who left for brighter lights; Eduardo Luciano for keeping phones on connected; my brother, Peter, for the type of encouragement only a brother can give, and for always coming up with an aphorism that puts a situation in perspective; my nephew Gabriel for his ongoing interest and encouragement; my sister, Mary Kelly, and her husband, John, who allowed me to turn their home in Dublin into an office; the staff at Au Bon Pain, at the corner of Massachusetts Avenue and Mount Auburn Street in Cambridge, especially Mani Rayamajhi Yubaraj Subedi, Sudari Maharjan, who had a fresh cup of coffee ready at six every morning and allowed me the unencumbered occupancy of a booth; Derek Gaul, Gnomon Copy, and Elmekki Akroud whose spontaneous good humor and eagerness to be of assistance always lifted my spirits, and Lee F. Lawyer, also at Gnomon, who ensured I didn't erase everything I was about to print; Jim Demo for keeping track of my movements; and numerous friends throughout the Levant, where I conducted much of my research between 2008 and 2012, and the many who spoke to me under conditions of anonymity—their willingness to be so forthcoming shed light on some events and added to my understanding of the history in Israel and Palestine. With respect to Jonathan Moore and his wife, Katie, it is difficult to express the affection I have, which they return in abundance, fortifying me throughout the years I worked on this book. And thanks to Jonathan, again, for the many spirited conversations we enjoyed over lunch at the Charles Hotel. We will enjoy more in the years ahead.

I would be remiss if I did not express both my appreciation of and gratitude to Shlomi Eldar for access to the portions of *Lehakir et Hamas* ("To Know Hamas") that were translated into English and for the time he put aside to be interviewed when he was a fellow at the Wilson Center in Washington DC.

The Two-State Delusion took many different turns and forms throughout four years, and I will always be indebted to Kathryn Court, my editor at Viking Penguin, for again keeping the faith, knowing that the book would eventually come home, and later for the editorial input of Lindsey Schwoeri and Emily Hartley. And finally, there is Pat Keefer, my other half in Washington DC, and Ntombikayise Gladwin Gilman, the South African child we became guardian of eons ago in South Africa, who is now on her way to graduating from Mount Holyoke College.

All conclusions reached and opinions expressed in this book are mine alone and I take full responsibility for their content.

Padraig O'Malley
October 2014

Notes

Introduction

1. Helene Cooper, "Washington Memo; Weighing an Obama Plan to End a Mideast Logjam," *New York Times*, April 8, 2010, http://query.nytimes.com/gst/fullpage.html?res=9F05E7D8173CF93BA35757C0A9669D8B63.

2. Senator George Mitchell, interview with the author, August 3, 2011. All quotes from Senator Mitchell in this chapter are from this interview unless otherwise noted.

3. Barack Obama, "Remarks by the President on a New Beginning" (speech, Cairo University, Cairo, Egypt, June 4, 2009), http://www.whitehouse.gov/the_press_office/Remarks-by-the-President-at-Cairo-University-6-04-09.

4. Benjamin Netanyahu, "Full Text of Netanyahu's Foreign Policy Speech at Bar Ilan," June 14, 2009, *Haaretz*, http://www.haaretz.com/news/full-text-of-netanyahu-s-foreign-policy-speech-at-bar-ilan-1.277922.

5. Barak Ravid, "Netanyahu Declares 10-Month Settlement Freeze 'to Restart Peace Talks,'" *Haaretz*, November 25, 2009, http://www.haaretz.com/news/netanyahu-declares-10-month-settlement-freeze-to-restart-peace-talks-1.3435.

6. Avi Issacharoff and Barak Ravid, "In Jerusalem, Clinton Hails 'Unprecedented' Israeli Settlement Concessions," *Haaretz*, October 31, 2009, http://www.haaretz.com/news/in-jerusalem-clinton-hails-unprecedented-israeli-settlement-concessions-1.5060.

7. "Abbas Insists on Settlement Freeze," *AP Arkansas Online*, November 21, 2010, http://www.arkansasonline.com/news/2010/nov/21/abbas-insists-jerusalem-settlement-freeze/?print.

8. Adrian Blomfield, "Obama Snubbed Netanyahu for Dinner with Michelle and the Girls, Israelis Claim," *Telegraph*, March 25, 2010, http://www.telegraph.co.uk/news/worldnews/barackobama/7521220/Obama-snubbed-Netanyahu-for-dinner-with-Michelle-and-the-girls-Israelis-claim.html; Jeffrey Heller and Matt Spetalnick, "Obama, Netanyahu Seek to Diffuse U.S.-Israeli Tensions," Reuters, March 24, 2010, http://www.reuters.com/article/2010/03/24/us-israel-usa-idUSTRE62L2JN20100324.

9. Katie Zezima, "A Short History of Awkward Encounters Between Obama and Netanyahu," *Washington Post*, October 1, 2014; Adam Taylor, "Netanyahu Humiliated After US Trip Goes Awry," *Huffington Post*, May 26, 2010 (updated May 25, 2011), http://www.huffingtonpost.com/2010/03/26/netanyahu-humiliated-afte_n_514816.html; Akiva Eldar, "Obama's Jewish Minefield Is Israel's Bomb," *Haaretz*, May 24, 2010, http://www.haaretz.com/print-edition/opinion/obama-s-jewish-minefield-is-israel-s-bomb-1.291841.

10. Brian Whitaker, "How a Man Setting Fire to Himself Sparked an Uprising in Tunisia," *Guardian*, December 28, 2010, http://www.theguardian.com/commentisfree/2010/dec/28/tunisia-ben-ali. For a chronological overview, see Gary Blight, Sheila Pulham, and Paul Torpey, "Arab Spring: An Interactive Timeline of Arab Protests," *Guardian*, January 5, 2012, http://www.theguardian.com/world/interactive/2011/mar/22/middle-east-protest-interactive-timeline.

11. The *Washington Post* maintains an interactive time line on the Syrian situation from March 23, 2011, to the present. See Anup Kaphle, "Timeline: Unrest in Syria,"

Washington Post, January 20, 2014, http://apps.washingtonpost.com/g/page/world/timeline-unrest-in-syria/207/.

12. For one account of how jihadists cannot easily be equated with extremism, see Ben Hubbard, "In Jordan Town, Syria War Inspires Jihadist Dreams," *New York Times*, April 13, 2014, http://www.nytimes.com/2014/04/13/world/middleeast/in-jordan-town-syria-war-inspires-jihadist-dreams.html, which provides an account of a Jordanian Muslim who left his family and went to Syria to become part of the jihad. See also Raja Abdulrahim and Ken Dilanian, "Foreign Fighters Answer Calls to Join Syrian Conflict," *Los Angeles Times*, January 2, 2014, http://www.latimes.com/world/la-fg-syria—foreign-fighters-20140102-story.html#page=1.

13. As profiled by the BBC, "Under its former name Islamic State in Iraq and the Levant (ISIS), it was formed in April 2013, growing out of al-Qaeda in Iraq (AQI). It has since been disavowed by al-Qaeda, but has become one of the main jihadist groups fighting government forces in Syria and Iraq." See "Syria Iraq: The Islamic State Militant Group," *BBC Middle East*, August 2 2014, http://www.bbc.com/news/world-middle-east-24179084.

14. For a comprehensive overview of the Arab Spring see: Noueihed and Warren, *Battle for the Arab Spring*.

15. In his May 19, 2011, speech, Obama called for two states along the 1967 borders, but he was ambiguous about Jerusalem. Much controversy arose out of that speech. Barack H. Obama, "Remarks by the President on the Middle East and North Africa" (speech, State Department, Washington, DC, May 19, 2011), http://www.whitehouse.gov/the-press-office/2011/05/19/remarks-president-middle-east-and-north-africa. For live blog coverage, see "Barack Obama's Middle East Speech—Thursday, 19 May 2011," *Guardian*, May 19, 2011, http://www.theguardian.com/world/middle-east-live/2011/may/19/barack-obama-middle-east-speech-live. See also Reuters, "Instant View: Middle East Reaction to Obama's Speech," May 19, 2011, http://www.reuters.com/article/2011/05/19/us-obama-mideast-reaction-idUSTRE74I5O620110519.

16. The State Department maintains an interactive online record of Secretary of State John Kerry's travel schedule at http://www.state.gov/secretary/travel/2013/.

17. David Remnick, "Going the Distance: On and Off the Road with Barack Obama," *New Yorker*, January 27, 2014, http://www.newyorker.com/reporting/2014/01/27/140127fa_fact_remnick?currentPage=all.

18. Ian S. Lustick, "Two-State Illusion," *New York Times*, September 14, 2013, http://www.nytimes.com/2013/09/15/opinion/sunday/two-state-illusion.html?pagewanted=all.

19. An "ethos of conflict" has several components that interplay and reinforce one another relating to societal beliefs: about the justness of the society's own goals; about security; about having a "positive collective self-image" (e.g., to encourage the "ethnocentric tendency to attribute positive characteristics" to one's societal values and behaviors); about victimhood; about delegitimizing the enemy; about patriotism that propagates the virtues of loyalty and sacrifice; about cohesiveness while the conflict persists to ensure that internal differences are set aside in the face of external threat; and about peace as being ultimately desirable. See Daniel Bar-Tal, "Societal-Psychological Foundations of Intractable Conflicts," and Bar-Tal et al., "Ethos of Conflict."

20. Fishman and Lavie, *Peace Process: Seventeen Plans in Ten Years*.

21. See www.nelsonmandela.org/omalley/.

Chapter 1 **Early History: The Two Narratives**

1. O'Brien, *Siege*, 34–40, 96–98, 107–16, 146, 170–71.
2. Ibid., 33.

3. For the impact of the Hebron Massacre on the Jewish community see Hillel Cohen, "How the 1929 Hebron Massacre Invigorated the Zionist Movement," *+972*, March 5, 2013, http://972mag.com/how-the-1929-hebron-massacre-invigorated-the-zionist-movement/67101/. The text used is from a translation from Cohen, *1929: Year Zero of the Jewish-Arab Conflict*.

4. For more on the disorders of August 1929 and the political history of Palestine under the British, see UK Delegation to the UN, "Ad Hoc Committee on the Palestinian Question—Communication from the United Kingdom Delegation to the United Nations," letter dated August 18, 1947, to the United Nations General Assembly, October 2, 1947, UN Doc. A/AC.14/8, http://unispal.un.org/UNISPAL.NSF/0/16B8C7CC809B7E5B8525694B0071F3BD. "There can, in our view, be no doubt," the Shaw commission concluded, "that racial animosity on the part of the Arabs, consequent upon the disappointment of their political and national aspirations and fear for their economic future, was the fundamental cause of the outbreak of August last. In less than ten years three serious attacks have been made by Arabs on Jews. For eighty years before the first of these attacks there is no recorded instance of any similar incidents. It is obvious then that the relations between the two races during the past decade must have different [*sic*] in some material respect from those which previously obtained. The Arabs have come to see in the Jewish immigrant not only a menace to their livelihood but a possible overlord of the future." See Great Britain and Shaw, *Report of the Commission*, 40–43, originally published 1930. The full report can be viewed at Pinhas Ofer, "The Commission on the Palestine Disturbances of August 1929: Appointment, Terms of Reference, Procedure and Report," *Middle Eastern Studies* 21, no. 3 (1985), doi:10.1080/00263208508700633.

5. Ibid.

6. O'Brien, *Siege*, 186.

7. Cohen, "How the 1929 Hebron Massacre."

8. Ibid.

9. See Aviva Halamish, Israel Studies An Anthology: "The Yishuv: The Jewish Community in Mandatory Palestine," *Jewish Virtual Library*, September 2009, http://www.jewishvirtuallibrary.org/jsource/isdf/text/halamish.html; Kimmerling and Migdal, *Palestinians*, 96–123; O'Brien, *Siege*, 234–41; Khalidi, *Iron Cage*, 105–22; Krämer, *History of Palestine*, 264–95.

10. According to the BBC, "Jewish representatives in Palestine (the Jewish Agency) accepted the plan tactically—though with reluctance—because it implied international recognition for their aims of establishing a state, but on lesser territory than they considered a legal and historical right to. Palestinians and Arabs felt that it was a deep injustice to ignore the rights of the majority of the population of Palestine. The Arab League and Palestinian institutions rejected the partition plan, and formed volunteer armies that infiltrated into Palestine beginning in December of 1947." The BBC maintains a platform with links to key documents and Web sites. See "UN Partition Plan," Israel and the Palestinians: Key Documents, BBC News, http://news.bbc.co.uk/2/hi/in_depth/middle_east/israel_and_the_palestinians/key_documents/1681322.stm.

According to the Israel Ministry of Foreign Affairs (MFA), "United Nations General Assembly Resolution 181 called for the partition of the British-ruled Palestine Mandate into a Jewish state and an Arab state. It was approved on November 29, 1947, with 33 votes in favor, 13 against, 10 abstentions and one absent (see list at end of document). The resolution was accepted by the Jews in Palestine, yet rejected by the Arabs in Palestine and the Arab states." For more on Resolution 181, including an audio recording of the UN vote, see Israel Ministry of Foreign Affairs, "UN General Assembly Resolution 181."

11. Haganah was founded in 1920, http://www.encyclopedia.com/topic/Haganah.aspx. For details of Haganah operations, see Benny Morris, "The First Wave," in *The Birth of the Palestinian Refugee Problem, 1947–1949* (Cambridge: Cambridge University Press, 1987); see also O'Brien, *Siege*, 232–33.

12. O'Brien, *Siege*, 232.

13. According to Moshe Naor, the Yishuv had mobilized 30,000 men on the eve of independence. The population of the new state was approximately 660,000. *Social Mobilization in the Arab/Israeli War of 1948: On the Israeli Home Front* (London: Routledge Press, 2013), 33.

14. See "Palestinian Refugees: An Overview," Palestinian Refugee ResearchNet (PRRN), http://prrn.mcgill.ca/background/.

15. For a background on Palestinians who remained in Israel and became citizens, visit the World Directory of Minorities and Indigenous Peoples, Minority Rights Group International, http://www.minorityrights.org/5007/israel/palestinians.html.

16. Zochrot and other Israeli NGOs have been raising the *Nakba*, the destruction of hundreds of villages and resulting hundreds of thousands of Palestinian refugees in the 1948 War, to an awareness of the broad Jewish public. See www.zochrot.org as well as the social media application iNakba. Christa Case Bryant, "iNakba Reminds Israelis of Palestinian Towns Erased from the Map," *Christian Science Monitor*, May 15, 2014, http://www.csmonitor.com/World/Middle-East/Olive-Press/2014/0515/iNakba-reminds-Israelis-of-Palestinian-towns-erased-from-the-map.

17. Nurit Peled-Elhanan, *Palestine in Israeli School Books: Ideology and Propaganda in Education* (London: I. B. Tauris, 2012), 8–12.

18. Bar-Siman-Tov, *Barriers to Peace*.

19. Since the beginning of the Israeli Offensive on Gaza (Protective Edge) in July 2014, 2,008 Palestinians were killed, of whom 1,670 were civilians, including 471 children and 252 women; and 8,150 people wounded. See the Palestinian Centre for Human Rights, http://pchrgaza.org/portal/en/. There were also 64 IDF soldiers killed and 3 civilians (one a foreign worker from Thailand), with hundreds wounded. See United Nations Office for the Coordination of Humanitarian Affairs, "Occupied Palestinian Territory: Gaza Emergency: Situation Report (as of 15 August 2014, 0800 hrs)," produced by OCHA oPt in collaboration with humanitarian partners, http://www.ochaopt.org/documents/ocha_opt_sitrep_15_08_2014.pdf.

20. For the difference between a meta narrative and a historical narrative, see Yehudith Auerbach, "National Narratives in a Conflict Identity," in Bar-Siman-Tov, *Barriers to Peace*, 99–104.

21. Gisha, an Israeli human rights organization, whose goals are to protect the freedom of movement of Palestinian residents of the Gaza Strip and West Bank as rights guaranteed by international and Israeli law. The organization labels the occupation of Gaza "closure" because Israel's total control of the movement of people and commercial goods into and out of Gaza does not fit the legal definition of siege, blockade, or sanctions. Israel also uses closure in the West Bank, periodically restricting the movement of commercial goods and people. Gisha, "Gaza Closure Defined: Collective Punishment," December 2008, http://www.gisha.org/UserFiles/File/publications/GazaClosureDefinedEng.pdf.

22. See World Bank, "Fiscal Crisis." See also data maintained by the Jerusalem-based B'Tselem: The Israeli Information Center for Human Rights in the Occupied Territories, on its Web site, including "Effect of Restrictions on the Economy," B'Tselem.org, January 1, 2011, http://www.btselem.org/freedom_of_movement/economy.

23. Oded Na'aman, "The Checkpoint: Terror, Power, and Cruelty," *Boston Review*, November 13, 2012, http://www.bostonreview.net/world/checkpoint-oded-naaman.

24. Akram Hanieh, interview with the author, October 22, 2011. All quotes from Hanieh in this chapter are from this interview unless otherwise noted.

25. Issa Kassissieh, interview with the author, October 27, 2011. All quotes from Kassissieh in this chapter are from this interview unless otherwise noted.

26. Abu Ala, interview with the author, November 13, 2011. All quotes from Ala in this chapter are from this interview unless otherwise noted.

27. Jabril Rajoub, interview with the author, October 29, 2011. All quotes from Rajoub in this chapter are from this interview unless otherwise noted.

28. Saeb Erekat, interview with the author, February 17, 2012. All quotes from Erekat in this chapter are from this interview unless otherwise noted.

29. The wars they were witnesses to were the December 2008–January 2009 war (Operation Cast Lead) and the eight-day war (Operation Pillar of Defense) in November 2012. Interviews were completed before the third war in 2014—the fifty-day war between Hamas and Israel between July 7 and August 26, 2014—hence the lack of comment.

30. Amira Haas, "Palestinian Reconciliation: Real Unity, or Tactic?," *Haaretz*, April 24, 2014, http://www.haaretz.com/news/diplomacy-defense/.premium-1.587004.

31. *In The Much Too Promised Land*, Aaron David Miller, reflecting on a twenty-year involvement with the peace process, observes that "Mahmoud Abbas barely controlled Fatah, let alone the West Bank," 355.

32. Roy, *Failing Peace*, 67–75.

33. For examples of gross violations of human rights in the West Bank and Gaza, see the HRW 2014 report. In Gaza, it said, Hamas committed executions after unfair trials. "The authorities permitted some local human rights organizations to operate, but suppressed political dissent, free association, and peaceful assembly. . . ." In the West Bank, it said, "Palestinian Authority (PA) security services beat peaceful demonstrators, detained and harassed scores of journalists and online activists, and arbitrarily detained hundreds. . . . Credible allegations of torture committed by the PA's security services increased." Ongoing coverage of human rights issues is provided by Human Rights Watch at https://www.hrw.org/middle-eastn-africa/israel-palestine.

34. Blumenfield, "On the Brink," a report sponsored by the Middle East Forum. For more, see the work of the Geneva Centre for the Democratic Control of Armed Forces (DCAF), which maintains an Assistance Programme on Palestinian Security Sector Reform. Its work can be viewed at http://www.dcaf.ch/Project/Assistance-Programme-Palestinian-Security-Sector-Reform. See also the "Palestinian Security" Web page hosted by Marsad, the Palestinian Security Sector Observatory, http://www.marsad.info/en/tags/palestinian-security.

35. Hiba Husseini, interview with the author, June 25, 2012. All quotes with Husseini in this chapter are from this interview unless otherwise noted. See also Ginges and Atran, "Humiliation and the Inertia Effect."

36. Hanan Ashrawi, interview with the author, November 3 2011. All quotes from Ashrawi in this chapter are from this interview unless otherwise noted.

37. See Adrian Blomfield and Alex Spillius, "Arab Fury at Obama UN Speech," *Telegraph*, September 22, 2011, http://www.telegraph.co.uk/news/worldnews/barackobama/8782527/Barack-Obama-UN-speech-Arab-fury-over-Palestinian-statehood-speech.html.

38. Barbara Opall-Rome, "US Experts Forecast Military Aid Hikes for Israel," *Defense News*, June 17, 2013, http://www.defensenews.com/article/20130617/DEFREG04/306170028/US-Experts-Forecast-Military-Aid-Hikes-Israel.

39. Connie Bruck, "Friends of Israel," *New Yorker*, September 1, 2014, http://www.newyorker.com/magazine/2014/09/01/friends-israel. "I think there is a growing sense among

members," John Yarmuth, congressman from Kentucky, told Bruck, "that things are done just to placate AIPAC, and that AIPAC is not really working to advance what is in the interest of the United States. We all took an oath of office. And AIPAC, in many instances, is asking us to ignore it." See also Stephen M. Walt. "AIPAC Is the Only Explanation for America's Morally Bankrupt Israel Policy," *Huffington Post*, July 22, 2014.

40. Sharp, *U.S. Foreign Aid to Israel*, 2.

41. Opall-Rome, "US Experts Forecast Military Aid."

42. Zanotti, *U.S. Foreign Aid to the Palestinians.*

43. Ibid.

44. Indyk, *Innocent Abroad*, 289–92, 294–97, 313–15, 326. For various references to Indyk's perceived "bias toward Israel," see Editorial, "Israeli-Palestinian Talks: Perpetual Motion," *Guardian*, January 1, 2014, http://www.theguardian.com/commentisfree/2014/jan/01/israeli-palestinian-talks-editorial. For Habil Shaath's quote see Philip Weiss, "How Fair Is Martin Indyk, Who Says He Was Motivated by '. . . My Connection to Israel'?" *Mondoweiss*, July 22, 2013, http://mondoweiss.net/2013/07/how-fair-is-martin-indyk-who-says-he-was-motivated-by-my-connection-to-israel.html; and Nathan Guttman, "Martin Indyk Brings Baggage to Mideast Talks—and That's the Point," *Jewish Daily Forward*, July 30, 2013, http://forward.com/articles/181400/martin-indyk-brings-baggage-to-mideast-talks-and/. See also Isi Leibler, "Indyk: A Disastrous Choice for Mediator," *Jerusalem Post*, July 25, 2013, http://www.jpost.com/Opinion/Columnists/Indyk-A-disastrous-choice-for-mediator-321096; and Danny Danon, "Definition of Insanity: Failed Negotiators Trying Yet Again," *Jewish Press*, August 8, 2013, http://www.jewishpress.com/indepth/opinions/definition-of-insanity-failed-negotiators-trying-yet-again/2013/08/08.

By the spring of 2014, before Indyk stepped down as peace envoy, even the Israeli government disagrees with him, according to a Reuters report: "Israel Slams Indyk Accusations on Peace Talks," *YNetNews.com*, May 9, 2014, http://www.ynetnews.com/articles/0,7340,L-4517947,00.html. See also Shimon Shiffer, "It's Hard Being a Jewish American Official," *YNet News.com*, May 20, 2014, http://www.ynetnews.com/articles/0,7340,L-4521617,00.html.

45. Martin Indyk, interview with the author, August 8, 2011. All quotes from Indyk in this chapter are from this interview unless otherwise noted.

46. Saeb Erekat, interview with the author, December 5, 2011.

47. See for example Nusseibeh, *What Is a Palestinian State Worth?*, 221–24.

48. Tal Becker, interview with the author, October 3, 2011. All quotes from Becker in this chapter are from this interview unless otherwise noted.

49. See UN General Assembly and Security Council, "Letter Dated 18 November 1988." A/43/827S/20278 http://unispal.un.org/UNISPAL.NSF/0/6EB54A389E2DA6C6852560DE0070E392.

50. Akram Hanieh, interview with the author, October 22, 2011.

51. Sentiments expressed by Shlomo Ben-Ami, interview with the author, March 9, 2012; these are more fully explored in Ben-Ami, *Scars of War.*

52. The International Criminal Court (ICC) is the one instrument that can on occasion prosecute individuals or countries for committing "crimes against humanity." Being hauled before the ICC is the one thing Israel fears, and as an observer member state at the UN, the PLO is slowly trying to achieve that outcome.

53. For an examination of how the country's policies are undermining Israel's democracy and its existence as a Jewish state, see Gorenberg, *Unmaking of Israel.*

54. The Holocaust was the systematic, bureaucratic, state-sanctioned persecution and murder of approximately six million Jews by the Nazi regime and its collaborators. To learn more, go to the United States Holocaust Memorial Museum, http://www.ushmm.org/wlc/en/

article.php?ModuleId=10005143. See also Cebulski, "Memory of the Holocaust"; Klar et al., "The 'Never Again' State of Israel"; Brison, "Trauma Narratives"; Yablonka, "The Development of Holocaust Consciousness"; Sagi, "The Holocaust and the Foundation of Jewish Identity."

55. Keissar-Sugarmen, "A Portrait of Israeli Jews."

56. Roughly 3 percent of survivors are still alive and reside in Israel. At the end of 2008, there were some 233,700 Holocaust survivors living there. Of course, that number of survivors continues to decrease. The projection for 2015 is 143,900 survivors, with two thirds of the group over eighty years old. See Brodsky et al., "Holocaust Survivors in Israel."

57. Anat Hoffman, interview with the author, September 13, 2011. All quotes from Hoffman in this chapter are from this interview unless otherwise noted.

58. See Cohen, *Identity and Pedagogy*, described at the Bar-Ilan School of Education Web site, http://education.biu.ac.il/en/node/5104. A summary of findings from Dr. Cohen's survey on coverage of the Holocaust in Israeli schools can be viewed at Abe Seleg, "Holocaust Education Important to Israeli Educators, Students," *Jerusalem Post*, January 27, 2010, http://www.jpost.com/Israel/Holocaust-education-important-to-Israeli-educators-pupils. See also Hexel and Nathanson, *All of the Above.*

59. Lerner, *Embracing Israel/Palestine*, 273–74.

60. Ibid., 274.

61. Aryeh Savir of Tazpit, "'Witnesses in Uniform': IDF Officers in Auschwitz," *YNet News.com*, April 7, 2013, http://www.ynetnews.com/articles/0,7340,L-4364761,00.html.

62. Lerner, *Embracing Israel/Palestine*, 274–75.

63. Ibid., 261–62.

64. See Margalit, *Ethics of Memory*, 107–46. See also Cathy Caruth, ed., *Trauma: Explorations in Memory* (Baltimore: John Hopkins University Press, 1995); Cathy Caruth, *Unclaimed Experience: Trauma, Narrative and History* (Baltimore: John Hopkins University Press, 1996); Daniel Schacter, *Searching for Memory: The Brain, the Mind, and the Past* (New York: Basic Books, 1996).

65. The United States persuaded Abbas not to have the Goldstone Report tabled at the UNHRC. See S. Farhan Mustafa, "PA Stonewalled the Goldstone Vote," The Palestinian Papers, Al Jazeera, January 26, 2011, http://www.aljazeera.com/palestinepapers/2011/01/2011126123125167974.html; and Israel Ministry of Foreign Affairs, "Initial Response to Report of the Fact Finding Mission on Gaza," Israel MFA Web page, September 24, 2009, http://mfa.gov.il/mfa/foreignpolicy/terrorism/pages/initial-response-goldstone-report-24-sep-2009.aspx.

66. See Amnesty International, "Impunity for War Crimes in Gaza and Southern Israel a Recipe for Further Civilian Suffering," Amnesty.org, July 2, 2009, http://www.amnesty.org/en/news-and-updates/report/impunity-war-crimes-gaza-southern-israel-recipe-further-civilian-suffering-20090702.

67. See Carter, *Palestine: Peace Not Apartheid.* Desmond Tutu described Israel as being worse than an apartheid state. Any comparison with apartheid arouses extreme ire in Israel. After the Kerry-sponsored talks failed, Kerry, speaking to a closed-door meeting of the Trilateral Commission in April 2014, said Israel was on its way to becoming an apartheid state. Following the immediate uproar that followed in Israel, he apologized profusely for using the word and went to great lengths to praise Israel for being such a staunch ally, stating that America would always be at its side. Michael R. Gordon, "Kerry Expresses Regret After Apartheid Remark," *New York Times*, April 28, 2014, http://www.nytimes.com/2014/04/29/world/middleeast/kerry-apologizes-for-remark-that-israel-risks-apartheid.html?_r=0.

68. B'Tselem, "47 Years of Occupation," www.btselem.org/publications/47-year-long-temporary-occupation.

69. UN Department of Public Information, "General Assembly Votes Overwhelmingly."

70. Gabe Fisher, "Government Pushes Ahead in New West Bank Housing," *Times of Israel*, January 16, 2013, http://www.timesofisrael.com/government-pushes-ahead-with-new-west-bank-housing/.

71. "Merkel Meets Netanyahu amid New Strains in Relations," France24.com, last modified December 6, 2012, http://www.france24.com/en/20121205-israel-germany-netanyahu-merkel-frosty-diners-strained-relations-un-vote. The call between Merkel and Netanyahu was in February 2011. See Harriet Sherwood, "Merkel Rebukes Israeli PM Netanyahu for Failing to Advance Peace," *Guardian*, February 25, 2011, http://www.theguardian.com/world/2011/feb/25/merkel-rebukes-netanyahu-peace-israel. For more on the December 2012 meeting, see Matthias Gebauer and Ulrike Putz, "Touchy Talks in Berlin: Netanyahu Airs Complaints Ahead of Germany Visit," *Spiegel Online International*, December 5, 2012, http://www.spiegel.de/international/world/netanyahu-airs-complaints-ahead-of-visit-to-berlin-a-871199.html. www.germany.info/vartreting/USA/en/-pr/p-wash/2014/02/25-GermanyIsrael.htm.

72. As for governmental sanctions—comprising economic, diplomatic, and military actions—thus far the European Union has not taken action. "Europe has carried a very small stick indeed and encouraged Israel to gorge on the juiciest carrots it has available in its bilateral relations hamper—free trade, visa-free travel, and joint scientific cooperation," proclaimed *Haaretz* in early February, and by mid-2014 this remained the case. "Future EU Sanctions Against Israel? Real, Imagined, and Somewhere in Between," Jerusalem Center for Public Affairs, March-April 2014, http://jcpa.org/article/future-eu-sanctions-against-israel/; and Daniel Levy, "On Sanctions, Israel Hasn't Seen Anything Yet," *Haaretz*, February 6, 2014, http://www.haaretz.com/opinion/.premium-1.572776.

73. Miller, *Much Too Promised Land*, 224–29.

74. Shlomo Cesana et al., "Israel Furious at US Support for Palestinian Unity Government," *Israel Yahom*, June 3, 2014, http://www.israelhayom.com/site/newsletter_article.php?id=17947.

75. Stuart Winer, "Netanyahu: Geneva Offer to Iran Is a 'Historic Mistake,'" *Times of Israel*, November 7, 2013, http://www.timesofisrael.com/netanyahu-geneva-offer-to-iran-is-a-historic-mistake/.

76. See Halperin et al., "Socio-Psychological Barriers," 28–57. This chapter can be viewed at http://www.kas.de/upload/dokumente/2011/03/barriers_to_peace/chapter1.pdf.

77. Nathanson's demography study: Hexel and Nathanson, *All of the Above*. For more on ultranationalism, see 124; for more on propensity to hatred, see 220.

78. See Asher Zeiger and Times of Israel staff, "Netanyahu at Shoah Ceremony: 'We Won't Leave Our Fate in the Hands of Others,'" *Times of Israel*, April 7, 2013, http://www.timesofisrael.com/the-holocaust-is-still-with-us-peres-says-at-memorial-ceremony/; Yanir Yagna et al., "There Will Never Be Another Holocaust, Netanyahu Vows at Yad Vashem," *Haaretz*, April 7, 2013, http://www.haaretz.com/jewish-world/holocaust-remembrance-day/there-will-never-be-another-holocaust-netanyahu-vows-at-yad-vashem.premium-1.514156.

79. Israel Ministry of Foreign Affairs, "Suicide and Other Bombing" (accessed on April 4, 2015).

80. On Israeli casualties in the Gaza strip between 1967 and 2005, see Israel Ministry of Foreign Affairs, "Exit of IDF Forces from the Gaza Strip Completed," September, 12, 2005, http://www.mfa.gov.il/mfa/pressroom/2005/pages/exit%20of%20idf%20forces%20from%20the%20gaza%20strip%20completed%2012-sep-2005.aspx.

81. For information on the Islamic State (IS) also known as the Islamic State in Iraq and Syria (ISIS) see the Council on Foreign Relations, "Islamic State in Iraq and Syria,"

Backgrounders, last updated August 8, 2014, http://www.cfr.org/iraq/islamic-state-iraq-syria/p14811.

82. "Where jargon turns living issues into abstractions, and where jargon ends by competing with jargon, people don't have causes. They only have enemies; only the enemies are real." V. S. Naipaul, *The Return of Eva Perón*. The quote is from Naipaul's Nobel Lecture delivered on receiving the Nobel Prize in Literature in 2001.

83. Shlomo Ben-Ami, interview with the author, March 9, 2012. All quotes from Ben-Ami in this chapter are from this interview unless otherwise noted.

84. See Adnan Abu Amer, "Study Shows Dire Consequences if Palestinian Authority Collapses," *Al-Monitor*, February 14, 2014, trans. Sahar Ghoussoub, http://www.al-monitor.com/pulse/originals/2014/02/palestinian-authority-report-pcpsr-israel.html.

85. Tzipi Livni, who served as Minister of Foreign Affairs from 2006 to 2009, said, "I believe that the solution of two nation states serves the interests of both sides. Not every celebration of ours is cause for sorrow on the other side, and vice versa. I say to my Palestinian colleagues: Do not bemoan the establishment of the State of Israel; establish your own state, rejoice in its establishment and we will rejoice with you, since for us the establishment of the Palestinian state is not our *Nakba* or disaster—provided that upon its establishment the word '*Nakba*' be deleted from the Arabic lexicon in referring to Israel." Israel Ministry of Foreign Affairs, "Address by FM Livni to the Annapolis Conference," November 27, 2007, http://www.mfa.gov.il/mfa/pressroom/2007/pages/address%20by%20fm%20livni%20to%20the%20annapolis%20conference%2027-nov-2007.aspx.

86. Khaled Diab, "Israel's Missed Opportunities," *Haaretz*, October 22, 2012, http://www.haaretz.com/opinion/israel-s-missed-opportunities.premium-1.471479.

87. Israel Ministry of Foreign Affairs, "Disputed Territories."

88. For an overview of the July 2011 B'Tselem report "No Minor Matter: Violation of the Rights of Palestinian Minors Arrested by Israel on Suspicion of Stone-Throwing," go to http://www.btselem.org/publications/summaries/2011-no-minor-matter. The full report can be downloaded at http://www.btselem.org/publications/fulltext/201107_no_minor_matter.

89 Settlement construction was 70 percent greater in the first six months of 2013 than during the same period in 2012. Ori Nir, "Settlement Surge Looms Large over Netanyahu-Obama Meeting," Americans for Peace Now press release, March 3, 2014, https://peacenow.org/entry.php?id=3695#.UzQpaPldW0c; Israel Central Bureau of Statistics, "Construction Begun and Construction Completed in 2013," http://www.cbs.gov.il/reader/newhodaot/tables_template_eng.html?hodaa=201404052.

90. See Yossi Ginossar, "Factors That Impeded Negotiations," *The Camp David Summit, 2000: What Went Wrong?* eds., S. Shamir and B. Maddy-Weitzman, 51–59.

Chapter 2 **Dueling Narratives and Addiction to Narrative**

1. Adwan et al., *Side by Side*, x.

2. Ibid.

3. Ibid., xv.

4. Ibid. "This tension between two contradictory symmetries is well known to those of us who are experienced with working with small groups under fire," writes Maoz in "Coexistence Is in the Eye of the Beholder."

The "double minority" syndrome expressed here is somewhat analogous to the double minority syndrome in Northern Ireland. Catholics saw themselves as a minority in Northern Ireland; Protestants, on the other hand, saw themselves as a minority in *all* of Ireland.

Hence, both saw themselves as the "real" minority and used that prism to determine their worldview. In the Israel-Palestine conflict this translates into both sides seeing themselves as the "real" victims. In Northern Ireland, as in Israel, it did nothing to ameliorate Protestants' sense of superiority to and condescension toward Catholics. Israel overcompensates for this "*feeling* inferior" by asserting its authority over an occupied people, through the strength of its military, through its claims to exceptionalism, etc.

5. Building on Tel Aviv University psychology professor Arie Nadler's work on instrumental and socioeconomic paths to reconciliation, Columbia University's Jennifer S. Goldman and Peter T. Coleman examine how the emotional experience of humiliation contributes to the enduring nature of some conflicts. Their work is part of a broader research agenda on the relationship between moral emotions and behavior. Goldman and Coleman, "How Humiliation Fuels Intractable Conflict." See also Nadler and Schnabel, "Instrumental and Socio-Emotional Paths to Intergroup Reconciliation and the Needs-Based Model of Socio-Emotional Reconciliation." This article appears in Nadler et al., *Social Psychology of Intergroup Relations.*

6. Clovis Maksoud, "Netanyahu Stuck on Repeat in Palestine," Lebanon Pulse, *Al-Monitor,* October 15, 2013, http://www.al-monitor.com/pulse/originals/2013/10/netanyahu-knesset-negotiations-peace-palestine-israel.html.

7. Jodi Rudoren, "Sticking Point in Peace Talks: Recognition of a Jewish State," *New York Times,* January 1, 2014, http://www.nytimes.com/2014/01/02/world/middleeast/sticking-point-in-peace-talks-recognition-of-a-jewish-state.html?_r=0.

8. Ibid.

9."Netanyahu's AIPAC Speech: The Full Transcript," *Haaretz,* March 4, 2014, http://www.haaretz.com/news/diplomacy-defense/1.577920.

10. Sayigh, "The Palestinian Identity," 3–22; Sa'di, "Catastrophe, Memory and Identity," 175–200; Barbara Landau and George Awad, "Shrinking the Gap: Our Fears About the Middle East and Our Identity Group," CommonGroundNews.org, July 9, 2009, http://www.commongroundnews.org/article.php?id=25871&lan=en&sp=1.

11. Muhammad Shtayyeh, interview with the author, October 29, 2011. All quotes from Shtayyeh in this chapter are from this interview unless otherwise noted.

12. Bar-Tal, "Sociopsychological Foundations of Intractable Conflicts."

13. Lerner, *Embracing Israel/Palestine,* 256.

14. Ibid.

15. Ibid.

16. Garth Stevens, Gillian Eagle, Debra Kaminer, and Craig Higson-Smith, "Continuous Traumatic Stress: Conceptual Conversations in Contexts of Global Conflict, Violence and Trauma," *Peace and Conflict: Journal of Peace Psychology* 19, no. 2 (May 2013), doi: 10.1037/a0032484.

17. Ibid.

18. Ibid.

19. Ibid.

20. Ignacio Martin-Baro, "Political Violence and War as Causes of Psychosocial Trauma in El Salvador," *International Journal of Mental Health* 18, no. 1 (1989): 3–20.

21. Noa Schori, Yechiel Klar, and Sonia Roccas, "'In Every Generation, They Rise Up Against Us to Annihilate Us': Perpetual Ingroup Victimhood Orientation (PIVO) and Behavior in a Current Intergroup Conflict" (paper presented at the International Society of Political Psycology [ISPP] 32nd Annual Scientific Meeting, Trinity College, Dublin, Ireland, December 12, 2012), http://citation.allacademic.com/meta/p310159_index.html.

22. Ibid.

23. Bar-Tal, "Sociopsychological Foundations of Intractable Conflicts."

24. See Bar-Tal and Salomon, "Israeli-Jewish Narratives." See also Bar-Tal et al., "Ethos of Conflict," 41. Since 1998 Bar-Tal, along with colleagues, has developed and refined the "ethics of conflict" idea, which is "the configuration of central societal shared beliefs that provide particular dominant orientation to a society and give meaning to the societal life under the conditions of intractable conflict."

25. Bar-Tal et al., "A Sense of Self-Perceived Collective," 241.

26. Bar-Tal and Salomon, "Israeli-Jewish Narratives," 24–25.

27. Ibid., 19–46.

28. Bar-Tal, *Shared Beliefs in a Society: Social Psychological Analysis* (Thousand Oaks, CA: Sage, 2000).

29. The views expressed here encapsulate the themes explored in Bar-Tal et al., "A Sense of Self-Perceived Collective."

30. International Crisis Group, "The Emperor Has No Clothes." See also Akiva Eldar, "Israel's New Politics and the Fate of Palestine," *National Interest*, June 28, 2012; and Tal Herman, "How the Peace Process Plays in Israel," *Current History*, December 2010.

31. See for example Marc H. Ellis, "Is the Peace Process a Dangerous Addiction?," *Mondoweiss*, July 31, 2013, http://mondoweiss.net/2013/07/is-the-peace-process-a-dangerous-addiction.html; Roger Cohen, "Cycles of Revenge in Israel and Palestine," *New York Times*, July 4, 2014, http://www.nytimes.com/2014/07/04/opinion/roger-cohen-cycles-of-revenge-in-israel-and-palestine.html.

32. Duhigg, *Power of Habit*, 19.

33. In *Soldiering Under Occupation*, Grassiani analyzed confessions collected by Breaking the Silence, a group that exposes the conduct of Israeli troops, as well as interviews that she conducted herself. Erella Grassiani, *Soldiering Under Occupation: Processes of Numbing Among Israeli Soldiers in the Al-aqsa Intifada* (New York: Berghahn Books, 2013).

34. Grassiani found that IDF soldiers get excited when military operations break the monotonous routines.

35. Hedges, *War Is a Force*, 4, 9, 25; see also chapter 4, and 83–221, 162–64, 173.

36. Lindner, *Making Enemies*, 127–40.

37. Ibid., 133.

38. For an examination of the relationship between humiliation and humiliation as an addiction, see Lindner, ibid., 127–40. See also the Human Dignity and Humiliation Studies Network Web site at http://www.humiliationstudies.org.

39. Sari Nusseibeh, interview with the author, February 18, 2012. All quotes from Nusseibeh in this chapter are from this interview unless otherwise noted.

40. Raja Shehadeh, "Checkpoint Jitters," *New York Times*, June 22, 2012, http://latitude.blogs.nytimes.com/2012/06/22/israeli-checkpoint-willies/.

41. Goldman and Coleman, "How Humiliation Fuels Intractable Conflict."

42. Ibid.

43. See Lerner, 259-65; Burtonwood, "The Holocaust Memorial Day in Schools," 69–82; Ben-Amos and Bet-El, "Holocaust Day and Memorial Day in Israeli," 258.

44. Halperin et al., "Socio-Psychological Barriers."

45. See Vojko Strahovnik, "Beyond the Culture of Fear: Fear and Responsibility," in *From Culture of Fear to Society of Trust*, Janez Juhant, Bojan Zalec eds., LIT Verlag Münster, December 28, 2013, 93; and Bar-Tal, "Why Does Fear Override Hope."

46. Bar-Tal, "Why Does Fear Override Hope"; and Shlomo Ben Ami, "Israel's Victory of Fear," *Huffington Post*, March 20, 2015, http://www.huffingtonpost.com/shlomo-benami/israel-netanyahu-victory-fear_b_6912188.html.

47. Duhigg, *Power of Habit*, 20.

48. Ibid., 25.

49. Thórisdóttir and Jost, "Motivated Closed-Mindedness."

50. Lindner, *Making Enemies*, 127–40.

51. Marris, *Loss and Change*.

Chapter 3 **Two-State Paradigm, Decades of Failure, and Addiction to Process**

1. Sixty-two percent of Israelis and 54 percent of Palestinians support a two-state solution, according to a June 2014 joint poll conducted by the Harry S. Truman Research Institute for the Advancement of Peace at the Hebrew University of Jerusalem and the Palestinian Center for Policy and Survey Research (PCPSR) in Ramallah, available at http://www.pcpsr.org/en/node/467. A similar poll by the Truman Institute and the PCPSR, released in December 2013, revealed that 63 percent of Israelis and 53 percent of Palestinians support a two-state solution. See Harry S. Truman Research Institute for the Advancement of Peace et al., "Joint Israeli Palestinian Poll, December 2013." A listing of other joint Israeli Palestinian polls conducted by the Truman Research Institute and the PCPSR, conducted with the support of the Konrad Adenauer Stiftung in Ramallah and Jerusalem, and going back to 2000, can be viewed at http://www.pcpsr.org/en/joint-polls and http://truman.huji.ac.il/?cmd=joint_polls.256.

Another poll released in the summer of 2014 showed a majority of Israelis (60 percent) view a two-state solution as preferable in the long term, even though they mistrust their prime minister in achieving it, and even though they don't know its conditions. That's the finding of a June 2014 Dialog Institute survey, conducted for *Haaretz*'s Israel Conference on Peace, held on July 8, 2014, in Tel Aviv. See Nir Hasson, "Despite It All, Most Israelis Still Support the Two-State Solution," *Haaretz*, July 7, 2014, http://www.haaretz.com/news/diplomacy-defense/israel-peace-conference/1.601996. For more on the Israel Conference on Peace, go to http://www.haaretz.com/news/diplomacy-defense/israel-peace-conference/1.603480 and http://www.haaretz.co.il/st/inter/Hheb/conference/luz3.pdf. However, in still another poll in October 2014, a majority of Jewish Israelis opposed a two-state solution. Mairav Zonstein, "Most Jewish Israelis Oppose Palestinian State, New Poll shows," *+972*, October 19, 2014.

2. Negotiation tracks presented to respondents in the June 2014 Joint Israeli Palestinian Poll included the "Saudi Plan" and the "Israeli-Palestinian Track." Components of the Saudi Plan include calls for Arab recognition and normalization of relations with Israel after it ends its occupation of Arab territories occupied in 1967 and after the establishment of a Palestinian state; Israeli retreat from all territories occupied in 1967 including Gaza, the West Bank, Jerusalem, and the Golan Heights; and the establishment of a Palestinian state. "The refugee problem will be resolved through negotiations in a just and agreed upon manner and in accordance with UN resolution 194. In return, all Arab states will recognize Israel and its right to secure borders, will sign peace treaties with Israel and establish normal diplomatic relations."

The Israeli-Palestinian Track features dismantling settlements, mutual recognition, and a two-state solution. See Harry S. Truman Research Institute for the Advancement of Peace et al., "Joint Israeli Palestinian Poll, June 2014."

In the *Haaretz* 2014 poll, the range of peace deal scenarios presented to survey respondents included: unilateral annexation of territories; a boycott of the Palestinians; revitalized efforts to resume the negotiations; unilateral withdrawal from the territories; a freeze on settlement construction; or do nothing.

3. Supporters of the options presented in "Joint Israeli Palestinian Poll, June 2014" display misgivings about certain conditions attached to a peace agreement. According to researchers, "29 percent of the Israelis and 50 percent of the Palestinians support the Saudi peace plan, while 64 percent of the Israelis and 46 percent of the Palestinians oppose it. In December 2013, 47 percent of the Palestinians supported the Saudi plan and 50 percent opposed it, while 33 percent of the Israelis supported and 64 percent opposed it."

As for the Israeli-Palestinian Track, "44 percent of the Israelis support and 51 percent oppose the dismantling of most of the settlements in the West Bank as part of a peace agreement with the Palestinians." With respect to mutual recognition, "52 percent of the Israeli public supports such a mutual recognition and 38 percent opposes it. Among Palestinians, 40 percent support and 59 percent oppose this step. In December 2013, 58 percent of the Israelis supported and 34 percent opposed this mutual recognition; among Palestinians, the corresponding figures were similar to the current poll (43 percent support and 56 percent oppose)." See summary results, Harry S. Truman Research Institute for the Advancement of Peace et al., "Joint Israeli Palestinian Poll, June 2014."

Underlying beliefs continue to influence attitudes: each side continues to view the other as posing an existential threat. The findings of the June 2014 poll show that "55 percent of Palestinians think that Israel's goals in the long run are to extend its borders to cover all the area between the Jordan River and the Mediterranean Sea and expel its Arab citizens. Twenty-six percent think the goals are to annex the West Bank while denying political rights to the Palestinians. Thirty-one percent of the Israelis think that the Palestinian aspirations in the long run are to conquer the State of Israel and destroy much of the Jewish population in Israel; 20 percent think the goals of the Palestinians are to conquer the State of Israel."

According to the 2014 *Haaretz* poll, "Overall, it would seem the Israeli public is more apprehensive about granting equal rights to the Palestinians than about returning territories. Fifty-six percent said they are against granting the Palestinians full rights in the event of annexation." See Hasson, "Despite It All."

4. Fishman and Lavie, *Barriers to Peace.*

5. For example, even during the 2013–14 talks, the Islamic State (ISIS) had no bearing on the talks regarding security. In October 2014, the Islamic State is at the top of the international agenda. The U.S.-led global war on ISIS will necessarily involve the Muslim states of the Middle East. Fear of radical Islam has resulted in a realignment of alliances, including Israel's. The threat of ISIS emerging in Jordan is a threat to Israel. Hence, in the future, one can expect Israel to take a much tougher stand on keeping troops in the Jordan Valley.

6. Tal Becker, interview with the author, October 3, 2011. All quotes from Becker in this chapter are from this interview unless otherwise noted.

7. Akram Hanieh, interview with the author, October 22, 2011. All quotes from Hanieh in this chapter are from this interview unless otherwise noted.

8. Swisher, *Truth About Camp David*; and Shamir et al., *Camp David Summit.*

9. Saeb Erekat, "The Political Situation in Light of Developments with the U.S. Administration and Israeli Government and Hamas' Continued Coup d'Etat," Al Jazeera Investigations, Palestine Papers, December 2009, http://www.ajtransparency.com/en/projects/thepalestinepapers/201218211239109728.html. Erekat's views also were expressed during a

meeting with George Mitchell and others on October 2, 2009, according to meeting minutes released as part of the Palestine Papers. "It is the last time for the two states," he said. "My option, the BATNA [best alternative to a negotiated agreement], if all goes down, is the one state." See "Meeting Minutes: Saeb Erekat and George Mitchell," Al Jazeera Investigations, The Palestine Papers, n.d., http://transparency.aljazeera.net/en/projects/thepalestinepapers/20121821919875390.html; and David Poort, "The Threat of a One-State Solution," *Al Jazeera*, January 26, 2011, http://www.aljazeera.com/palestinepapers/2011/01/201112612953672648.html. For more, see Juan Cole, "Erekat Sees One-State Solution If Settlements Are Not Halted," *Informed Comment*, November 5, 2009, http://www.juancole.com/2009/11/erekat-sees-one-state-solution-if.html (in which a translation of Erekat's interview with Al-Hayat appears). See also Akiva Eldar, "Palestinians Threaten to Adopt One-State Solution," *Haaretz*, February 26, 2010, http://www.haaretz.com/print-edition/news/palestinians-threaten-to-adopt-one-state-solution-1.266295.

10. In an article appearing in *Al-Quds Al-Arabi*, on March 17, 2012, Ahmed Qurei (Abu Ala) wrote, "We must seriously think about closing [the book on] the two-state solution and turning over a new leaf." A one-state solution would allow Palestinians "to expand our manoeuvering room and to continue [our] comprehensive diplomatic campaign to take [back] the basic rights of freedom, independence and human honour that we have been denied." Quoted in Harriet Sherwood, "Look Beyond the Oslo Accords, Say Architects of Middle East Peace Plan," *Guardian*, April 24, 2012, http://www.theguardian.com/world/2012/apr/24/middle-east-two-state-solution. See also Khaled Abu Toameh, "Qurei Calls for Reconsidering One-State Solution," *Jerusalem Post*, March 17, 2017, http://www.jpost.com/Middle-East/Qurei-calls-for-reconsidering-one-state-solution.

11. "Israel is singlehandedly destroying the two-state solution with the continuation of its expansionist settlement policies in and around Jerusalem, the confiscation of Palestinian land, the demolition of Palestinian homes, the eviction of Palestinian residents of Jerusalem, and the closure of Palestinian institutions in Jerusalem. . . . All of these illegal actions are in direct violation of signed agreements and international conventions. . . . [W]ithout Jerusalem as the capital of Palestine, there will be no Palestinian state, and without a Palestinian state, there will be no peace or stability in the region," said Ashrawi. Quoted in Elad Benari, "PLO Official Says Israel 'Destroying Two-State Solution,'" August 15, 2012, *Arutz Sheva*, http://www.israelnationalnews.com/News/News.aspx/158925. "We are witnessing the end of the two-state solution, and if Israel is not held to account, chances of peace and stability in the region will be destroyed indefinitely," said Ashrawi, as quoted in Ma'an News Agency, "Ashrawi: We Are Witnessing the End of the Two-State Solution," Ma'an News Agency, November 21, 2013, http://www.maannews.net/eng/ViewDetails.aspx?ID=649776.

12. "The current Israeli negotiating position is the worst in more than 20 years," said Yasser Abed Rabbo in a statement released in October 2013. "They want security first, and that the borders of the state of Palestine should be set out according to Israeli security needs that never end, and that will undermine the possibility of establishing a sovereign Palestinian state." Quoted in Ma'an News Agency, "PLO: Israel's Stance in Talks Harshest in 20 Years," Ma'an News Agency, October 29, 2013, http://www.maannews.net/eng/ViewDetails.aspx?ID=642424. "Israel did not commit to stopping settlements and we see the continuation of the settlement policy as destroying any possible chance of [a deal]," Rabbo said. Quoted in Reuters, "Senior PA Official: Peace Talks with Israel Going Nowhere," *Jerusalem Post*, September 4, 2012, http://www.jpost.com/Diplomacy-and-Politics/Senior-PA-official-Peace-talks-with-Israel-are-going-nowhere-325267; and Khaled Abu Toameh, "For the Palestinians, Peace Process with Israel Is Dead," *Jerusalem Post*, May 27, 2011, http://www

.jpost.com/Features/In-Thespotlight/For-the-Palestinians-peace-process-with-Israel-is-dead.

13. Miller, *Much Too Promised Land*, 369.

14. See ICG, "The Emperor Has No Clothes," 29–30.

15. Background on the history of the PLO, see home page of the Permanent Observer Mission of the State of Palestine to the United Nations, http://palestineun.org/about-palestine/palestine-liberation-organization/.

16. For a history of the PLO, organizations besides Fatah that were members, and why many left the organization, see: O'Brien, *Siege*, 480; and "Profile: Fatah Palestinian Movement," *BBC*, June 16, 2011, http://www.bbc.com/news/world-middle-east-13338216. The charter of the PLO can be found at http://www.iris.org.il/plochart.htm and at https://www.fas.org/irp/world/para/plo.htm.

17. Bickerton and Klausner, *History of the Arab-Israeli Conflict*, 145.

18. Hanan Ashrawi, interview with the author, November 3, 2011. All quotes from Ashrawi in this chapter are from this interview unless otherwise noted.

19. Why did the Palestinians reject the Peel Commission's recommendation? Because they never deviated from saying that *all* of Palestine was theirs and rejected anything that involved less.

20. George Mitchell, interview with the author, August 3, 2011. All quotes from Mitchell in this chapter are from this interview unless otherwise noted.

21. See Muhareb, "An Analysis of Israeli Public Opinion"; and Harriet Sherwood, "Israeli Poll Finds Majority Would Be in Favour of 'Apartheid' Policies," *Guardian*, October 23, 2012, http://www.theguardian.com/world/2012/oct/23/israeli-poll-majority-apartheid-policies. See PCPSR polls on Israeli and Palestinian opinion regarding final borders in an FSA, http://www.pcpsr.org/en/node/210l; http://www.pcpsr.org/en/node/381.

22. Ghassan Khatib, interview with the author, July 1, 2012. All quotes from Khatib in this chapter are from this interview unless otherwise noted.

23. Tamar Hermann, "How the Peace Process Plays in Israel," *Current History*, December 2010, http://www.openu.ac.il/Personal_sites/download/Tamar-Hermann/how-the-peace-process.pdf.

24. Jena McGregor, "Remembering James MacGregor Burns and His Leadership Wisdom," *Washington Post*, July 17, 2014, http://www.washingtonpost.com/blogs/on-leadership/wp/2014/07/17/remembering-james-macgregor-burns-and-his-leadership-wisdom/.

25. Samih Al-Abed, interview with the author, November 28, 2011. All quotes from Al-Abed in this chapter are from this interview unless otherwise noted.

26. Abu Ala, interview with the author, November 13, 2011. All quotes from Ala in this chapter are from this interview unless otherwise noted.

27. Raphael Ahren, "Kerry Focuses Blame on Israel for Collapse of Talks; Secretary of State Highlights Both Sides' 'Unhelpful Moves' but Indicates Crisis Began with Failure to Release Prisoners," *Times of Israel*, April 8, 2014, http://www.timesofisrael.com/kerry-focuses-blame-for-impasse-in-talks-on-israel/. Kerry, as quoted in the article: "The prisoners were not released by Israel on the day they were supposed to be released and then another day passed and another day, and then 700 units were approved in Jerusalem and then poof—that was sort of the moment."

28. Husam Zumlot, interview with the author, February 21, 2012. All quotes from Zumlot in this chapter are from this interview unless otherwise noted. "So the crux of the issue is that how do you use all the cards that you have? The crux of our thinking right now is the issue of nonviolence. Nonviolence has taken a long time, but I refuse to say that nonviolence

is something that Palestinians are thinking about. Nonviolence is the Palestinian method par excellence over the century. The exception was the armed period. That's the exception because ever since Palestinians started their resistance against the British Mandate in 1919, the White Paper, and what have you, and then the Great Strike in 1936 that lasted for six months, one of the longest national strikes in the history of mankind, it all was civil, peaceful, nonviolent mass mobilization. Throughout our history, for almost one hundred years now, nonviolence has been enshrined in our activities and action. And nonviolence is not just protests and demonstrations. Nonviolence, or mass movements, or popular resistance, call it the way you want, popular resistance is a nice and accurate term for it, it takes so many creative shapes, used in fostering and preserving on your land, knowing that your removal is a victory for your opponent and a defeat, and your ability to stay on the land despite the adverse circumstances is the biggest resistance there is."

29. Palestinian Center for Policy and Survey Research, "Palestinian Public Opinion Poll No. 50."

30. "Poll: Palestinians Overwhelmingly Reject Two-State Solution, Want Palestine 'from River to Sea,'" *Haaretz*, June 30, 2014, http://www.haaretz.com/news/diplomacy-defense/.premium-1.601938.

Chapter 4 **Specific Failures**

1. Savir, *Process*, 15.

2. For these photographs, see "1993: Rabin and Arafat Shake on Peace Deal," "On This Day 1950–2005," BBC News, http://news.bbc.co.uk/onthisday/hi/dates/stories/september/13/newsid_3053000/3053733.stm.

3. Nabil Sha'ath, interview with the author, October 18, 2011. All quotes from Sha'ath in this chapter are from this interview unless otherwise noted.

4. Ian J. Bickerton and Carla L. Klausner, *History of the Arab-Israeli Conflict* (Boston: Prentice Hall, 2010), 263.

5. Bar-Siman-Tov, "Justice and Fairness as Barriers," in *Barriers to Peace*, 199–202.

6. Ibid, 199.

7. Qurei, *From Oslo to Jerusalem*, 296–97.

8. Bar-Siman-Tov, "Justice and Fairness as Barriers," 196–222.

9. Ibid., 201.

10. Ibid.

11. Ghassan Khatib, interview with the author, July 1, 2012. All quotes from Sha'ath in this chapter are from this interview unless otherwise noted.

12. These dates come from Frontline, "The Negotiations," from *Shattered Dreams of Peace: The Road to Oslo* video, PBS, June 27, 2002, http://www.pbs.org/wgbh/pages/frontline/shows/oslo/negotiations/. This source also offers more information on implementation of the DOP, especially the redeployments of IDF. (The main page for the *Shattered Dreams of Peace* program can be viewed at http://www.pbs.org/wgbh/pages/frontline/shows/oslo/.)

13. Hussein Agha and Ahmd Samih Khalidi, "Yasser Arafat: Why He Still Matters," *Guardian*, November 13, 2014, http://www.theguardian.com/news/2014/nov/13/-sp-yasser-arafat-why-he-still-matters.

14. Hanan Ashrawi, interview with the author, November 3, 2011. All quotes from Ashrawi in this chapter are from this interview unless otherwise noted

15. Miller, *Much Too Promised Land*, 60.

16. "1994: Yasser Arafat Ends 27-Year Exile," On This Day 1950–2005, BBC News, http://news.bbc.co.uk/onthisday/hi/dates/stories/july/1/newsid_2489000/2489631.stm.

17. Savir, *Process*, 180.

18. Uri Savir, interview with the author, February 14, 2014. All quotes from Savir in this chapter are from this interview unless otherwise noted.

19. Ron Pundak, interview with the author, November 6, 2011. All quotes from Pundak in this chapter are from this interview unless otherwise noted.

20. For more on reasons why Hamas opposed Oslo, see Wendy Kristianasen, "Challenge and Counterchallenge: Hamas's Response to Oslo," *Journal of Palestine Studies* 28, no. 3 (Spring 1999): 19–36.

21. Roy, *Failing Peace*, 195–96.

22. Ibid., See Sara Roy's review of Oslo, 233-249, and for the crisis within Palestinian society, 191-211.

23. Jacob Perry, interview with the author, February 6, 2012. All quotes from Perry in this chapter are from this interview unless otherwise noted.

24. For the details of the Sharm el-Sheikh agreement, see "The Sharm el Sheikh Memorandum," https://www.knesset.gov.il/process/docs/sharm_eng.htm.

25. Present for the PLO were Abu Ala, Hasan Asfour, and Hiba Husseini; from the Israeli government, Shlomo Ben-Ami, Elan Shapira, and Gilead Sher. See Qurei, *Beyond Oslo*, 114.

26. In the "Swedish Track" there were two rounds of talks. The first round of talks (May 12-15) was aborted due to leaks; the second beginning on May 18 and ending on June 3 in Tel Aviv. See Qurei *Beyond Oslo*, 108–24. For his account of the Stockholm talks, see 108–60.

27. Hiba Husseini, interview with the author, June 28, 2012. All quotes from Husseini in this chapter are from this interview unless otherwise noted.

28. An extract from Shlomo Ben-Ami's diary quoted in Ari Shavit, "End of a Journey," *Haaretz*, September 13, 2011, http://www.haaretz.com/end-of-a-journey-1.288142.

29. Ben-Ami, *Scars of War*, 282.

30. Sher, *Israel-Palestinian Peace Negotiations*, 30.

31. See Qurei, *Beyond Oslo*, 133.

32. Ibid., 266–67.

33. Barak's coalition was composed of strange bedfellows and was in trouble soon after it took government. Ehud Barak (Labor Party) was elected prime minister in May 1999 after putting together a broad-based coalition. However, in the summer of 2000 he had a number of crises: three parties quit the coalition, leaving him with a minority government that barely succeeded in surviving a vote of confidence in July. The failure at Camp David and outbreak of the Second Intifada further weakened him. In December 2000 he called for elections that took place in February 2001, losing to Likud leader Ariel Sharon by a margin that was the largest in Israeli electoral politics.

34. Sher, *Israeli-Palestinian Peace Negotitations*, 56; Gilead Sher, interview with the author, October 26, 2012.

35. Gilead Sher is quite scathing when he talks about the lack of preparation on the part of the Americans. Sher, interview with the author, 2012. See also Miller, *Much Too Promised Land*, 298–301.

36. Malley and Agha, "The Palestinian-Israeli Camp David Negotiations," 62-85.

37. Ibid.; see also Miller, *Much Too Promised Land*, 289–314.

38. Malley and Agha, "The Palestinian-Israeli Camp David Negotiations," 62–85.

39. Ibid., 67 ("A third Palestinian request—volunteered by Clinton, rather than being demanded by Arafat—was that the U.S. remain neutral in the event the summit failed and not blame the Palestinian.") and 68 ("Clinton assured Arafat on the eve of the summit that he would not be blamed if the summit did not succeed. 'There will be,' he pledged, 'no finger-pointing.'"). According to Baruch Kimmerling, in a review of Ran Edelist's book on

Barak, the same thing was agreed with the Israelis. Baruch Kimmerling, "Tragic for Us All, Our Own Greek Hero" (review of Ran Edelist and Ilan Kfir, *Ehud Barak: Fighting the Demons*), *Haaretz*, April 4, 2003, http://www.haaretz.com/culture/books/tragic-for-us-all-our-own-greek-hero-1.13973.

40. Miller, *Much Too Promised Land*, 280.

41. Sher, *Israeli-Palestinian Peace Negotiations*, 52.

42. Throughout Camp David, no matter what proposal regarding the division of Jerusalem, disposition of the holy places, or issues relating to the Temple Mount/Haram al-Sharif, Arafat never budged from his initial position: full sovereignty over east Jerusalem. Nothing would dissuade him from settling for anything less. With regard to Barak's proposals, he replied, according to Abu Ala, his response to President Clinton was "I cannot accept Barak's proposals, and I invite your Excellency to attend my funeral if you stick to this position on Jerusalem." Ahmed Qurei (Abu Ala), *Beyond Oslo: The Struggle for Palestine*, 217.

43. Miller, *Much Too Promised Land*, 306–7.

44. Shamir and Maddy-Weitzman, *Camp David Summit*, 225.

45. Shamir and Shikaki, "Determinants of Reconciliation," 190.

46. Ibid., 185.

47. For an exhaustive analysis of Camp David (which often means settling scores) see the extended exchanges in the *New York Review of Books* between 2001 and 2002. See also Swisher, *Truth About Camp David*; Malley and Agha, "The Palestinian-Israeli Camp David Negotiations"; Dennis Ross, "Camp David: An Exchange," *New York Review of Books*, September 20, 2001; Agha Hussein and Robert Malley, "Reply to Dennis Ross," *New York Review of Books*, September 20, 2001; Benny Morris, "Camp David and After: An Interview with Ehud Barak," *New York Review of Books*, June 13, 2002; Hussein Agha and Robert Malley, "An Exchange: A Reply to Ehud Barak," *New York Review of Books*, June 13, 2002; Benny Morris and Ehud Barak, "Camp David and After—Continued," *New York Review of Books*, June 27, 2002; Agha Hussein and Robert Malley, "Camp David and After—Continued," *New York Review of Books*, June 27, 2002; Helga Baumgarten, *The Myth of Camp David or the Distortion of the Palestinian Narrative*, comments by Martin Beck and Suleiman Rabadi (Birzeit: Birzeit University, March 2004); Shamir and Maddy-Weitzman, eds., *Camp David Summit*; Balaban, *Interpreting Conflict*; "Nicholas Kristof: Arafat and the Myth of Camp David" (a reprint of Kristof's May 17, 2002, op-ed column from the *New York Times* titled "Is Arafat Capable of Peace?"), displayed on the PLO's Negotiations Affairs Department Web site at http://www.nad-plo.org/etemplate.php?id=187; and Bruce Hirst, "Don't Blame Arafat," *Guardian*, July 16, 2004, http://www.theguardian.com/world/2004/jul/17/comment.davidhirst; Enderlin, *Shattered Dreams*; Dan Meridor, "Camp David Diaries," *Haaretz*, July 29, 2011; Hanieh, "The Camp David Papers."

48. Sher, interview with the author, October 26, 2011; Shlomo Ben-Ami, interview with the author, March 9, 2012. All quotes from Ben-Ami in this chapter are from this interview unless otherwise noted. See also Morris, "Camp David and After: An Interview with Ehud Barak."

49. Ben-Ami, *Scars of War*, 250.

50. Shlomo Ben-Ami, interview with the author.

51. Amnon Lipkin-Shahak, interview with the author, October 23, 2011. All quotes from Lipkin-Shahak in this chapter are from this interview unless otherwise noted.

52. Shimon Shamir, "The Enigma of Camp David," in Shamir and Maddy-Weitzman, eds., *Camp David Summit*, 12.

53. Ephraim Sneh, interview with the author, October 6, 2011; General Amnon Lipkin-Shahak, interview with the author, October 23, 2011, regarding security; Eyyad Sarraj,

interview with the author, December 3, 2011, regarding Arafat; and General Jacob Perry, interview with the author, February 6, 2012, regarding Arafat.

54. Nusseibeh, *What Is a Palestine State Worth?*, 173.

55. Deborah Sontag, "And Yet So Far: A Special Report; Quest for Mideast Peace: How and Why It Failed," *New York Times*, July 26, 2001, http://www.nytimes.com/2001/07/26/world/and-yet-so-far-a-special-report-quest-for-mideast-peace-how-and-why-it-failed.html.

56. Gilead Sher, interview with the author, October 26, 2011.

57. For an outline of what the parties agreed to see President Bill Clinton, "Sharm El-Sheikh Summit concluding statement by President Clinton" (statement, Sharm el-Sheikh, Egypt, October 17, 2000), http://unispal.un.org/UNISPAL.NSF/0/46B79961630ECA3F85256E3700653CBF#sthash.8y3sJ5N4.dpuf.

58. Esther Pan, "Middle East: Peace Plans Background," February 7, 2005, *Council on Foreign Relations*, http://www.cfr.org/israel/middle-east-peace-plans-background/p7736#p3.

59. Bill Clinton, *My Life* (New York: Farrar, Straus & Giroux, 2005), 725, excerpted at https://www.jewishvirtuallibrary.org/jsource/Peace/ClintonMyLife.html.

60. For the PLO's reaction, see Negotiations Affairs Department, Palestine Liberation Organization, "Official Palestinian Response to the Clinton Parameters (and Letter to the International Community)," January 1, 2001, http://www.nad-plo.org/etemplate.php?id=98.

61. The White House confirmed on December 29 that "both sides have now accepted the president's ideas with some reservations." Here's how Ben-Ami describes the event: "Clinton wanted a yes-or-no answer by 27 December. The Israeli government met the deadline. But Arafat lingered. He refused to respond. He resumed his journeys throughout the world. Instead he asks to come to Washington to see the President, 'I accept your ideas,' and then proceeded to tick off a number of reservations, each of which vitiated those ideas. He never formally said no, but his 'yes' was a 'no.'" Ben-Ami, interview with the author; and Ben-Ami, *Scars of War*, 272–73.

62. See "Bush Administration Rejects Clinton Mideast Deal," *CNN*, February 8, 2001, http://cgi.cnn.com/2001/US/02/08/us.mideast/.

63. See Israeli Committee Against House Demolitions, "Map: The 'Judaization' of the Old City," http://www.icahd.org/node/448.

64. Danny Yatom, interview with the author, November 2, 2011. All quotes from Yatom in this chapter are from this interview unless otherwise noted.

65. Ben-Ami, cited in Bar-Siman-Tov, "Justice and Fairness as Barriers to the Resolution of the Israeli Palestinian-Conflict," in *Barriers to Peace*, 207.

66. Suzanne Goldenberg, "Rioting as Sharon Visits Islam Holy Site," *Guardian*, September 28, 2000, http://www.theguardian.com/world/2000/sep/29/israel.

67. Zertal and Eldar, *Lords of the Land*, 404–12.

68. Suha Arafat, Yasser Arafat's wife, confirmed in a television interview on Dubai TV that he planned the Second Intifada; http://www.jpost.com/Middle-East/Suha-Arafat-admits-husband-premeditated-Intifada, December 29, 2012.

69. Zertal and Eldar, *Lords of the Land*, 404–15.

70. Ibid.

71. Ben-Ami, *Scars of War*, 267.

72. Efraim Sneh, quoted in Zertal and Eldar, *Lords of the Land*, 412–13.

73. Efraim Sneh, interview with the author, October 6, 2011. All quotes from Sneh in this chapter are from this interview unless otherwise noted.

74. Benny Morris, "Camp David and After: An Exchange (1. An Interview with Ehud Barak)," *New York Review of Books*, June 13, 2002, http://www.nybooks.com/articles/archives/2002/jun/13/camp-david-and-after-an-exchange-1-an-interview-wi/.

75. Lipkin-Shahak, interview with the author. The United Nations Commission on Human Rights report found the Israeli government in violation of the Fourth Geneva Convention but also of the laws of armed conflict, specifically the principle of proportionality. Swisher, *Truth About Camp David*, 386.

76. See Morris, "Camp David and After"; a response by Robert Malley and Hussein Agha in the same issue; and the rejoinder, "Camp David and After—Continued," by Morris and Barak, Malley and Agha.

77. Then again, Anwar al-Sadat and Menachem Begin never went one-on-one at Camp David 1979 until after an agreement was reached.

78. See Halperin et al., "Socio-Psychological Barriers," *Barriers to Peace*, 44–46.

79. Ben-Ami, interview with the author, March 9, 2012. At Taba, the Israeli delegation, led by Foreign Minister Shlomo Ben-Ami, included Yossi Beilin, Israel Hassoun, Amnon Lipkin-Shahak, Yossi Sarid, and Gilead Sher. The Palestinian delegation was headed by Ahmed Qurei (Abu Ala), speaker of the Palestinian Council, and included Yasir Abid Rabbuh, Hassan Asfour, Mohammad Dahlan, Saeb Erekat, and Nabil Sha'ath. See "Special Document File, The Taba Negotiations (January 2001)," *Journal of Palestine Studies* 31, no. 3 (Spring 2002): 79–89.

80. Danny Yatom, interview with the author, February 6, 2012; Danny Yatom is more categorical. "I was in the room," Yatom says, "when Barak told Ben Ami and Yossi Beilin, 'You do not have a mandate to decide. You should bring it to me' . . . so Barak did not accept the mutual understanding that was achieved between Ben Ami and Abu Ala."

81. Danny Yatom, interview with the author, February 6, 2012.

82. See "Special Document File, The Taba Negotiations (January 2001)," 88.

83. Ibid., 86. "The Israeli side, informally, suggested a three-track fifteen-year absorption program, which was discussed but not agreed upon. The first track referred to the absorption to Israel. No numbers were agreed upon, but with a nonpaper referring to 25,000 in the first three years of this program (40,000 in the first five years of this program did not appear in the nonpaper but was raised verbally). The second track referred to the absorption of Palestinian refugees into the Israeli territory that shall be transferred to Palestinian sovereignty, and the third track referr[ed] to the absorption of refugees in the context of a family reunification scheme. The Palestinian side did not present a number, but stated that the negotiations could not start without an Israeli opening position. It maintained that Israel's acceptance of the return of refugees should not prejudice existing programs within Israel such as family reunification."

84. Ibid., 83–85.

85. Tal Becker, interview with the author, October 3, 2011. Gidi Grinstein, interview with the author, October 30, 2011. All quotes from Becker and Grinstein in this chapter are from these interviews unless otherwise noted.

86. For more on the proposal, see "Text: Arab Peace Plan of 2002," BBC News, last modified March 22, 2005, http://news.bbc.co.uk/2/hi/middle_east/1844214.stm.

87. For more, see the Negotiations Affairs Department Web page hosted by the Palestinian Liberation Organization. See PLO Negotiations Affairs Department, "The Arab Peace Initiative, Frequently Ask Questions," 2014, http://www.nad-plo.org/etemplate.php?id=157.

88. Greg Myre, "Israelis and Palestinians Join in Peace Draft," *New York Times*, October 14, 2003, http://www.nytimes.com/2003/10/14/international/middleeast/14MIDE.html.

89. Yoav Peled and Nadim N. Rouhana, "Transitional Justice and the Right of Return of the Palestinian Refugees," in *Israel and the Palestinian Refugees*, ed. Eyal Benvenisti, Chaim Gans, and Sari Hanafi, Max Planck Institute for Comparative Public Law and International

Law (Berlin: Springer Berlin Heidelberg, 2007), 141–57, http://link.springer.com/chapter/10.1007/978-3-540-68161-8_5. In the *Virginia Journal of International Law*, Lewis Saideman makes the point that acceptance of "new nationality" means waiving the right of return, and he devotes a whole section to it. See Lewis Saideman, "Do Palestinian Refugees Have a Right of Return to Israel? An Examination of the Scope of and Limitations on the Right of Return," *Virginia Journal of International Law* 44 (2003–4): 829.

The Palestinian negotiators were Yasser Abed Rabbo, former minister of information and culture; Prisoners Affairs Minister Hisham Abd el Razek; Nabil Qassis, former minister of tourism; Qadoura Fares and Mohamed Horani, members of the PLC associated with the Fatah/Tanzim movement; Ghadi Jarei, member of the Prisoners Committee and Fatah member; General Zoheir Manasra, former governor of Jenin and head of preventative security in the West Bank; Samih Al-Abed; Bashar Jum'a; Dr. Nazmi Shuabi; Gheith al-Omri; Jamal Zakut; Nazmi Jub'a. The Israeli negotiators were former Meretz head Yossi Beilin, former IDF Chief of Staff Amnon Lipkin-Shahak, then-Labor Knesset members Amram Mitzna and Avraham Burg, Brigadier-General (Res.) Gideon Shefer, Police Commander Elik Ron, and the Likud's Nehama Ronen; http://www.mideastweb.org/geneva1.htm.

90. "The Roadmap: Full Text," BBC News, April 30, 2003, http://news.bbc.co.uk/2/hi/middle_east/2989783.stm.

91. The official version of Yasser Arafat's death in a Paris hospital on November 2004 is that it was the result of a stroke suffered due to a "blood disorder"—even though Parisian doctors couldn't specify the cause of the disorder. Because of subsequent suspicions and controversy, his body was exhumed in 2012, so that Swiss, French, and Russian investigators could examine tissue samples. According to an account in the *Guardian*, "Yasser Arafat died of natural causes, French investigators have concluded. The team of scientific and medical experts found his death in 2004 was due to 'old age following a generalized infection,' ruling out allegations he was poisoned, it was reported on Tuesday. Swiss scientists had previously reported 'unexpectedly high activity' of radioactive polonium-210 in Arafat's body and personal effects, including his clothing, leading to accusations that he was assassinated. On Tuesday, it was reported that the French investigators had ruled out poisoning in their report but that traces of polonium had been found. A source told Reuters: 'The results of the analyses allow us to conclude that the death was not the result of poisoning.'" See Kim Willsher and Harriet Sherwood, "Yasser Arafat Died of Natural Causes, French Investigators Say," *Guardian*, December 3, 2013, http://www.theguardian.com/world/2013/dec/03/yasser-arafat-died-natural-causes-french-investigators.

92. Udi Dekel, interview with the author, July 3, 2012. All quotes from Dekel in this chapter are from this interview unless otherwise noted.

93. Swisher, *Palestine Papers.*

94. See Bernard Avishai, "A Plan for Peace That Still Could Be," *New York Times Magazine*, February 7, 2011. Aaron David Miller, however, told me, discussing Avishai's article, that "there was never a moment in *any* negotiation—and I've participated in most of the government-to-government negotiations—where in fact any or all of the issues parties were prepared to sign, or they had negotiated with a level of specificity and detail, which would have stood up to the test of what would be required to actually sign an agreement. The second interim agreement in Oslo was three hundred pages. Israelis and Palestinians have not engaged in that kind of negotiation and produced those kinds of documents on permanent status. And even if they had, they're not close to signing them, not on the core issues. The Israelis have added a fifth element, which is recognition of Israel as the nation-state of the Jewish people. Right now they're not serious about a comprehensive agreement. They've

never been that close. I'm not suggesting that creative fixes on each of these issues may not have materialized. What I'm suggesting is that the degree of specificity required to actually incorporate solutions to all of these problems (security, borders, Jerusalem, settlements, right of return) in an actual document that an Israeli prime minister is prepared to take to the Knesset or even his cabinet or a Palestinian president is prepared to subject to the Palestinian Legislative Council is not real." Aaron David Miller, interview with the author, July 10, 2011. See also Aaron David Miller, "How to Break the Mideast Deadlock," *New York Times*, April 4, 2011, http://www.nytimes.com/2011/04/05/opinion/05iht-edmiller05.html.

95. Aluf Benn and Shmuel Rosner, "PM: 20,000 Palestinians Could Enter over Decade," *Haaretz*, August 14, 2008, http://www.haaretz.com/print-edition/news/pm-20-000-palestinian-could-enter-over-decade-1.251731.

96. Samih Al-Abed, interview with the author, November 28, 2011: "Neither in 2000, 2001, or when Clinton gave us his parameter, nor when we met in Taba. But the Israelis don't want to have a deal. That's the bottom line. There's not a single prime minister who came after Rabin who is willing to come up with any, or to strike a deal with the Palestinians. We cannot see it. We tried Peres, we tried Ehud Barak, we tried Netanyahu before, and then Olmert, and then Netanyahu again. God knows who's coming. And we used to tell the Israelis, please let us know which government you think that they can make an agreement with us." All quotes from Al-Abed in this chapter are from this interview unless otherwise noted.

97. George Mitchell, interview with the author, August 3, 2011. All quotes from Mitchell in this chapter are from this interview unless otherwise noted.

98. Salam Fayyad, interview with the author, July 8, 2012. All quotes from Fayyad in this chapter are from this interview unless otherwise noted.

99. Jonathan Lis, "Israel Passes Law Requiring Referendum on Land Concessions," *Haaretz*, http://www.haaretz.com/news/national/.premium-1.579475. Israel passed a law requiring that any withdrawal from sovereign Israeli territory be approved by referendum. "Under the law," he writes, "any government decision to give up part of Jerusalem or the Golan Heights, which Israel annexed, would require approval in a referendum before it could be carried out. But the law would not apply to withdrawals from the West Bank, which was not annexed. The Knesset first passed a referendum law in 2010 as a regular law, which can be overturned by a simple majority of Knesset members or the High Court of Justice. Now that the referendum law is a Basic Law, the Israeli equivalent of a constitutional provision, it is beyond the purview of the High Court, and can only be overturned by an absolute Knesset majority of 61 votes. The bill was sponsored by Habayit Hayehudi, and widely supported by the right wing as an obstacle to withdrawals from Jerusalem or the Golan Heights. Its passage follows that of the other two bills in the package deal—the Haredi draft law, and the law raising the electoral threshold." For more, see Stuart Winer, "Cabinet Approves Referendum Bill on Relinquishing Territory," *Times of Israel*, July 28, 2013, http://www.timesofisrael.com/cabinet-approves-referendum-bill-on-peace/#ixzz32ZnV3Nmd.

100. Peace Now, Settlement Watch, "The Voting Patterns of the Settlers—2013 Knesset Elections," http://peacenow.org.il/eng/sites/default/files/VotingPatterns2013.pdf.

101. "Elections 2013: 19th Knesset to See Right, Left Virtually Tied," *YNetNews*, January 23, 2013, http://www.ynetnews.com/articles/0,7340,L-4335946,00.html.

102. The ministry responsible for economics, trade, and Jerusalem affairs went to Naftali Bennett, who wants to annex 60 percent of the West Bank; the ministry of housing, which oversees matters relating to settlements, went to Uri Ariel, one of the most prominent leaders of the settlers' movement and a director of the Keren Kayemeth—Jewish National Fund—a major arm of the settlement enterprise. In 2012 he authored a paper making the

case that Israel could annex all of the West Bank and still remain Jewish and democratic. Following his cabinet appointment, he told Channel 10 television that "the idea of a settlement freeze is dreadful," and that building in Judea and Samaria would continue as usual. He would work, he said, to encourage settlements building in the West Bank. "New Housing Minister Rejects Settlement Freeze as 'Dreadful' Idea," *Times of Israel*, March 17, 2013, http://www.timesofisrael.com/new-housing-minister-rejects-settlement-freeze-as-dreadful-idea/#ixzz3G3qU8Wee.

Moshe Ya'alon became minister of defense. He served as the Israeli army's chief of staff between 2002 and 2005 and is considered to be a hawk on the Palestinian issue. He once said that "the Palestinian threat harbors cancer-like attributes" and has called the left-wing Peace Now group, which monitors settlement activities in the West Bank, "a virus." "Ya'alon Calls Peace Now 'a Virus,'" *YNetNews*, August 19, 2009, http://www.ynetnews.com/articles/0,7340,L-3764439,00.html. The deputy minister, Dani Danon, is a settler; so, too, is the Knesset's speaker, Yuli Edelstein. Nissan Slomiansky is chairman of the Knesset Finance Committee. Beytenu honcho Avigdor Lieberman is foreign minister and Ze'ev Elkin, who is standing in for Lieberman as deputy foreign minister, is also a settler who shares Ariel's desire to annex the entire West Bank. "For twenty years, we talked about what to give and why. Now the time has come for an entirely different discourse," Elkin declared at a conference in March 2012. "This is our land, and it's our right to apply sovereignty over it. Regardless of the world's opposition, it's time to do in Judea and Samaria what we did in [East] Jerusalem and the Golan." Raphael Ahren, "The Newly Confident Israeli Proponents of a One-State Solution," *Times of Israel*, July 16, 2012, http://www.timesofisrael.com/at-hebron-conference-proponents-of-the-one-state-solution-show-their-growing-confidence/.

103. William Booth, "Mideast Peace Talks Set to Begin After Israel Agrees to Free 104 Palestinian Prisoners," *Washington Post*, July 28, 2013, http://articles.washingtonpost.com/2013-07-28/world/40859181_1_peace-talks-israeli-prisoners; Michael R. Gordon and Jodi Rudoren, "Kerry Achieves Deal to Revive Mideast Talks," *New York Times*, July 19, 2013, http://www.nytimes.com/2013/07/20/world/middleeast/kerry-extends-stay-in-mideast-to-push-for-talks.html; Ainav Weisberg, "Reopening Negations, at a Price," *Jerusalem Online*, June 25, 2013, http://www.jerusalemonline.com/news/politics-and-military/reopening-negations-at-a-price-880.

In April 2014, when talks were faltering—Israel had refused to release the last batch of prisoners until the Palestinians agreed to an extension of the talks—the Palestinians went to some lengths to separate the issue of the release of prisoners from whether or not they would agree to an extension of talks when they expired on April 29, 2014. In a statement released by the PLO Negotiation Affairs Department on April 2, 2014, Saeb Erekat said:

"In July 2013, the PLO took the difficult decision to postpone accession to multilateral treaties and conventions in exchange for the release of 104 pre-Oslo prisoners in four stages. In fact, release of pre-Oslo prisoners is a commitment Israel had already made 20 years ago as part of the Palestinian Israeli interim accords (Oslo accords), again in 1999 through the Sharm al-Sheikh Agreement and a third time at the beginning of this negotiations process.

"The release of prisoners was not formally linked to the negotiations process.

"The fourth and final release of 30 prisoners was set to take place on March 29th 2014. As Israeli officials indicated that Israel would not go through with the release, the PLO requested that the US administration ensure that Israel fulfill its commitment. Since Israel failed to release the last group of prisoners, the State of Palestine is no longer obliged to postpone its rights to accede to multilateral treaties and conventions." nad-plo.org/userfiles/file/fact%20sheets/Q8A&20Accession.pdf.

104. Harriet Sherwood, "Israeli Cabinet Split over Palestinian Prisoner Release," *Guardian*, July 28, 2013, http://www.theguardian.com/world/2013/jul/28/israeli-cabinet-split-palestinian-prisoner-release.

105. Ibid.

106. Barak Ravid, "Israel Advancing Plan for Some 5,000 New Homes in West Bank and East Jerusalem," *Haaretz*, October 30, 2013, http://www.haaretz.com/news/diplomacy-defense/premium-1.555373.

107. Lahov Harkov, "Netanyahu Lowers Expectations for Israeli-Palestinian Peace," *Jerusalem Post*, October 7, 2013, http://www.jpost.com/Diplomacy-and-Politics/Netanyahu-puts-a-damper-on-Israeli-Palestinian-peace-process-at-2013-Bar-Ilan-speech-328052. The root [of the conflict], the *Jerusalem Post* reported Netanyahu as saying, was not the "so-called territories or West Bank settlements. Palestinian Arabs had attacked Jews in Jaffa in 1921 and massacred Jews in Hebron, destroying an ancient community. It wasn't a territorial conflict then; Jews didn't have any territory." The *Post* said the prime minister hammered the point home, noting that "Grand Mufti Haj Amin al-Husseini was a partner and consultant to Hitler and Eichmann; the latter even called the leader of Arabs in Mandatory Palestine a friend. The mufti offered up Muslims as SS soldiers and broadcast Nazi propaganda. Jews still didn't have a state then. There were no West Bank settlements. . . ." After countless statements and conferences and letters opposing the current round of peace talks and its goals," the *Jerusalem Post* continued, "Likud hard-liners like deputy ministers Danny Danon, Ze'ev Elkin and Tzipi Hotovely can let out a sigh of relief, even though none of them—nor any other Likud MK—sat in the audience to show support for the prime minister. . . . He may not have done what the no-show protesters were praying for—renounce his commitment to a Palestinian state—but he said settlements are not the enemy."

108. Khaled Abu Toameh, "Former PLO Negotiator Calls On PA to Endorse 'Resistance' Against Israel," *Jerusalem Post*, January 23, 2014, http://www.jpost.com/Diplomacy-and-Politics/Former-PLO-negotiator-calls-on-PA-to-endorse-resistance-against-Israel-339194.

109. "Peace Talks with Israel Going Nowhere: Senior Palestinian," Reuters, Ramallah, September 4, 2013, http://www.reuters.com/article/2013/09/04/us-palestinians-israel-idUSBRE9830AV20130904.

110. Ben Caspit, "Netanyahu, Unscathed by Peace Talks Collapse, Finds New Agenda," *Al-Monitor*, May 4, 2014, http://www.al-monitor.com/pulse/originals/2014/05/netanyahu-abbas-iran-basic-law-jewish-independence.html#ixzz3G3yX7J5J.

111. As more demands were attached to the agreement, talks started to fall apart. See Herb Keinon and Khaled Abu Toameh, "Kerry's 'Framework' Expected to Be 'Outline' of Future Agreement," *Jerusalem Post*, January 2, 2014, http://www.jpost.com/Diplomacy-and-Politics/Kerrys-framework-expected-to-be-outline-of-future-agreement-336840; Jodi Rudoren, "Standoff over Prisoner Release Threatens Mideast Talks," *New York Times*, March 23, 2014, http://www.nytimes.com/2014/03/24/world/middleeast/standoff-over-prisoner-release-threatens-mideast-talks.html; John B. Judis, "John Kerry's Peace Process Is Nearly Dead—and the Fault Is Mostly Netanyahu's," *New Republic*, March 25, 2014, http://www.newrepublic.com/article/117141/john-kerrys-peace-process-nearly-dead.

112. For a comprehensive overview of the talks, See Nathan Thrall, "Israel & the US: The Delusions of Our Diplomacy," *New York Review of Books*, October 9, 2014, http://www.nybooks.com/articles/archives/2014/oct/09/israel-us-delusions-our-diplomacy/. For a longer version, which includes new details on the negotiations led by John Kerry and why they collapsed, see Thrall, "Faith-Based Diplomacy."

113. Jodi Rudoren and Isabel Kershner, "Arc of a Failed Deal: How Nine Months of Mid-east Talks Ended in Disarray," *New York Times*, April 28, 2014, http://www.nytimes.com/2014/04/29/world/middleeast/arc-of-a-failed-deal-how-nine-months-of-mideast-talks-ended-in-dissarray.html; Ben Birnbaum and Amir Tibon, "The Explosive, Inside Story of How John Kerry Built an Israel-Palestine Peace Plan—and Watched It Crumble," *New Republic*, July 20, 2014, http://www.newrepublic.com/article/118751/how-israel-palestine-peace-deal-died.

114. Jodi Rudoren and Michael R. Gordon, "Palestinian Rivals Announce Unity Pact, Drawing U.S. and Israeli Rebuke," *New York Times*, April 23, 2014, http://www.nytimes.com/2014/04/24/world/middleeast/palestinian-factions-announce-deal-on-unity-government.html.

Chapter 5 **Hamas: Spinning Wheels**

1. Avishai et al., "Israel and Palestine," *Harper's*, September 2014, 30–43.

2. A translated text of the Hamas charter can be found in *Journal of Palestine Studies* 22, no. 4 (Summer 1993): 122–34, http://www.palestine-studies.org/sites/default/files/jps-articles/1734.pdf. Hroub, *Hamas: Political Thought and Practice*; Hroub, *Hamas: A Beginner's Guide*; Milton-Edwards and Farrell, *Hamas*; Roy, *Hamas and Civil Society in Gaza*; "The Covenant of the Islamic Resistance Movement," August 18, 1988, http://avalon.law.yale.edu/20th_century/hamas.asp; Zachary Laub, "Hamas," Council on Foreign Relations, updated August 1, 2014, http://www.cfr.org/israel/hamas/p8968.

3. The United States designated Hamas as a foreign terrorist organization (FTO) in 1997; the EU designated it as such in 2003.

4. Barak Ravid, "Sharon Was Planning Diplomatic Moves Beyond Gaza, Leaked Documents Reveal," *Haaretz*, January 13, 2014, http://www.haaretz.com/news/diplomacy-defense/.premium-1.568192. "A series of cables from the U.S. embassy in Tel Aviv to the State Department that were leaked to WikiLeaks show that in fact, even before the Gaza withdrawal, Sharon was planning his next big diplomatic move. Moreover, leaked Palestinian documents show that after Yasser Arafat's death in November 2004, and even more so once Mahmoud Abbas was elected Palestinian president the following January, Sharon made efforts to coordinate the Gaza withdrawal with the Palestinian Authority. . . . On February 8, 2005, Sharon and Abbas held a summit at Sharm al-Sheikh that was meant to mark the end of the second intifada and a new start between Israelis and Palestinians. The six-page Arabic protocol of the meeting shows that the encounter was positive and the atmosphere almost playful at times."

5. Ibid.

6. Ibid.

7. "Khaled Mesh'al Lays Out New Hamas Policy Direction," *Middle East Monitor*, September 5, 2010 (reprint of Khaled Meshaal interview with the Jordanian newspaper *Al-Sabeel* in July 2010), https://www.middleeastmonitor.com/articles/middle-east/1491-khaled-meshal-lays-out-new-hamas-policy-direction.

8. Steven Erlanger, "Victory Ends 40 Years of Political Domination by Arafat's Party," *New York Times*, January 26, 2006, http://www.nytimes.com/2006/01/26/international/middleeast/26cnd-hamas.html?pagewanted=all.

9. For text of the Mecca Accord, see "Fatah-Hamas Mecca Agreement." For all previous and current reconciliation documents up to the Gaza 2014 agreement, see al-Saadi, "Palestinian Reconciliation."

10. Knudsen and Ezbidi, "Hamas and the Quest for Palestinian Statehood." The PLO and Fatah at first accepted the results of Hamas's winning the elections. See Scott Wilson,

"Hamas Sweeps Palestinian Elections, Complicating Peace Efforts in Mideast," *Washington Post*, January 27, 2006, http://www.washingtonpost.com/wp-dyn/content/article/2006/01/26/AR2006012600372_2.html.

Abbas asked Hamas to form a new government and appointed Ismail Haniyeh prime minister. See Greg Myre, "Hamas Is Formally Asked to Form a New Government," *New York Times*, February 22, 2006, http://www.nytimes.com/2006/02/22/international/22mideast.html. The West and Israel could not accept a Hamas-led government and responded by cutting contact with and aid to the PA.

11. Gershon Baskin, interview with the author, November 11, 2011, detailed how the back channel between him and Ghazi Hamad of Hamas played a key role in Shalit's release. All quotes from Baskin in this chapter are from this interview unless otherwise noted.

12. Shlomi Eldar in "Without Hamas, Palestinians and Israelis Can Find Peace," *Al-Monitor*, August 12, 2014, http://www.al-monitor.com/pulse/originals/2014/08/hamas-gaza-peace-oslo-accords-terror-palestinians.html.

13. The Amnesty International Annual Report 2012 writes on the Palestinian Authority: "The West Bank, including East Jerusalem, and Gaza remained under Israeli occupation, but two separate non-state Palestinian authorities operated with limited powers—the Fatah-led PA government in the West Bank and the Hamas de facto administration in Gaza." See http://www.amnesty.org/en/region/palestinian-authority/report-2012. In addition, some 61,000 Palestinian Authority employees stayed in Gaza and received their monthly salaries, despite the fact that they had nothing to do. "The European Union should stop paying the salaries of Palestinian civil servants in Gaza who don't work, EU auditors recommended Wednesday. The findings were made public by the European Court of Auditors, which scrutinized how 1 billion euros ($1.3 billion) in EU financial support to the Palestinian Authority has been used." "Audit: EU Pays Palestinians in Gaza to Not Work," *YNetNews*, November 12, 2013, http://www.ynetnews.com/articles/0,7340,L-4464239,00.html.

14. Steven Erlanger, "Abbas Plays on Hamas Boycott to Keep His Cabinet in Place," *New York Times*, July 12, 2007.

15. "Karni: Formerly the main transit point (via truck) for goods between Israel and Gaza, this crossing was partially closed in 2007 save for the movement of grain and animal feed via conveyer belt. The conveyer belt was shut down in 2011. Kerem Shalom: The sole operational transit point into Gaza for goods and humanitarian aid (via truck). It has less capacity than Karni did at its peak." See Neri Zilber, "Using Gaza's Border Crossings to Cement a Ceasefire," The Washington Institute: Policy Watch 2300, August 7, 2014, http://www.washingtoninstitute.org/policy-analysis/view/using-gazas-border-crossings-to-cement-a-ceasefire.

16. For Israeli control in the Gaza Strip, see B'Tselem, "The Scope of Israeli Control in the Gaza Strip," http://www.btselem.org/gaza_strip/gaza_status, updated January 5, 2014. See also "Gaza 2013: Snapshot," Gisha Legal Center for Freedom of Movement, June 2, 2013, http://gisha.org/en-blog/2013/06/02/gaza-2013-snapshot/.

17. Jon Donnison, "Palestinian Unity Undermined by Geographic Divide," BBC News, February 24, 2012, http://www.bbc.com/news/world-middle-east-17140711.

18. Akiva Eldar, "Israel Must End Gaza-West Bank Separation Policy," *Al-Monitor*, August 20, 2014, http://www.al-monitor.com/pulse/originals/2014/08/separation-policy-israel-west-bank-gaza-olmert-government.html.

19. CIA, "2014 Demographic Data for Gaza," The World Factbook, https://www.cia.gov/library/publications/the-world-factbook/geos/gz.html.

20. "Under Cover of War: Hamas Political Violence in Gaza," Human Rights Watch, April 2009, http://www.hrw.org/sites/default/files/reports/iopt0409web.pdf.

21. "UN Independent Panel Rules Israel Blockade of Gaza Illegal," *Haaretz*, September 13, 2011, http://www.haaretz.com/news/diplomacy-defense/un-independent-panel-rules-israel-blockade-of-gaza-illegal-1.384267.

22. Associated Press, "Rebuilding Gaza Will Take 20 Years, Housing Group Says," *Huffington Post*, August 30, 2014, http://www.huffingtonpost.com/2014/08/30/rebuilding-gaza_n_5740884.html.

23. "Lack of Sufficient Services in Gaza Could Get Worse Without Urgent Action, UN Warns," UN News Centre, August 27, 2012, http://www.un.org/apps/news/story.asp?NewsID=42751.

24. Abu Shahla, interview with the author, November 30, 2011. All quotes from Shahla in this chapter are from this interview unless otherwise noted.

25. Robert Danin, interview with the author, June 5, 2012. All quotes from Danin in this chapter are from this interview unless otherwise noted.

26. According to Hamas interviewees, states recognize states, and as a political party or resistance movement, Hamas is not required to recognize the existence of Israel. Salah al-Bardaweel, interview with the author, March 6, 2012; Mohammad Awad, interview with the author, December 1, 2011; Ghazi Hamad, interview with the author, March 7, 2012; Mahmoud al-Zahar, interview with the author, March 5, 2012.

27. Khaled Meshaal reiterated this point ad nauseam in an interview with Charlie Rose on July 27, 2014. *Charlie Rose: The Week*, PBS, http://video.pbs.org/video/2365297457/.

28. Israel Defense Forces, "New Hamas School Textbook Denies Israel's Existence, Calls Jewish Holy Books 'Fabricated,'" http://www.idfblog.com/hamas/2013/11/07/new-hamas-school-textbook-denies-israels-existence-calls-jewish-holy-books-fabricated/; Fares Akram and Jodi Rudoren, "To Shape Young Palestinians, Hamas Creates Its Own Textbooks," *New York Times*, November 3, 2013, http://www.nytimes.com/2013/11/04/world/middleeast/to-shape-young-palestinians-hamas-creates-its-own-textbooks.html?_r=0; Sharona Schwartz, "'Meant to Brainwash': Hamas Blasts U.N. Agency over Textbooks Featuring MLK, Rosa Parks and Gandhi," *Blaze*, February 12, 2014, http://www.theblaze.com/stories/2014/02/12/meant-to-brainwash-hamas-blasts-u-n-agency-over-textbooks-featuring-mlk-rosa-parks-and-gandhi/; "Hamas Rejects UN Textbooks in Gaza Schools," *Haaretz*, February 13, 2014, http://www.haaretz.com/news/middle-east/1.574208.

29. "Yale: Accords Research," http://www.yale.edu/accords/israel.html; Porter Speakman, "Netanyahu's Party Platform 'Flatly Rejects' Establishment of Palestinian State," *Mondoweiss*, November 3, 2011, http://mondoweiss.net/2011/11/netanyahu%E2%80%99s-party-platform-flatly-rejects-establishment-of-palestinian-state.html. See also Barak Ravi and Jonathan Lis, "Likud Officials Call to Omit Netanyahu's Two-State Declaration from Party Platform," *Haaretz*, December 25, 2012, http://www.haaretz.com/news/national/likud-officials-call-to-omit-netanyahu-s-two-state-declaration-from-party-platform.premium-1.489731; and Frank Barat, "Likud Charter Does Not Recognize Palestine," *Palestine Chronicle*, January 31, 2009, http://palestinechronicle.com/old/view_article_details.php?id=14772.

30. Zvika Krieger, "Welcome to 'Fortress Gaza,' Home of the Newly Radicalized Hamas," *Atlantic*, September 25, 2012, http://www.theatlantic.com/international/archive/2012/09/welcome-to-fortress-gaza-home-of-the-newly-radicalized-hamas/262811/.

31. "Erosion of Gaza's Economy Accelerates amid Israeli Military Operations, Ongoing Blockade," UN News Centre, September 3, 2014, http://www.un.org/apps/news/story.asp?NewsID=48631#.VBHf6_ldXlg.

32. Kurz, "The Israeli-Palestinian Political Process: Dead End Dynamics." In this review of negotiations during the Netanyahu era, there is scarcely a mention of Hamas.

33. Anne Barnard, "Questions About Tactics and Targets As Civilian Toll Climbs in Israeli Strikes," *New York Times*, July 21, 2014, http://www.nytimes.com/2014/07/22/world/middleeast/questions-about-tactics-and-targets-as-civilian-toll-climbs-in-israeli-strikes.html.

34. Of course, these interviews were conducted before the Obama-sponsored talks in 2013–14.

35. Ghazi Hamad, interview with the author, December 1, 2011.

36. Khalil Shikaki, interview with the author, September 28, 2011. All quotes from Shikaki in this chapter are from this interview unless otherwise noted.

37. Text of the numerous reconciliation documents, including the June 2006 Prisoner's Document, can be found in al-Saadi, "Palestinian Reconciliation."

38. Ismail al-Ashqar, interview with the author, July 18, 2012. All quotes from al-Ashqar in this chapter are from this interview unless otherwise noted.

39. Eyad el-Sarraj, interview with the author, July 19, 2012. All quotes from el-Sarraj in this chapter are from this interview unless otherwise noted.

40. Mahmoud al-Zahar, interview with the author, December 1, 2011. All quotes from Zahar in this chapter are from this interview unless otherwise noted.

41. Tal Becker, interview with the author, October 3, 2011. All quotes from Becker in this chapter are from this interview unless otherwise noted.

42. While Bobby Sands was on hunger strike in 1981, a seat for the Westminster parliament opened up and Sinn Féin selected him as a candidate, convinced that if he won, Prime Minister Margaret Thatcher would not allow an elected MP to die in a hunger strike. In this they were mistaken; Sands died on May 5, 1981. Thereafter, members of Sinn Féin, who previously had either avoided running for election or if elected did not take their seats, now contested elections at every opportunity and slowly eroded much of the Social Democratic and Labour Party's electoral base. The new policy adopted at the 1981 Ard Fheis (annual conference) was succinctly summarized in the movement's publication, *An Phoblacht*, with the bold headline "By Ballot and Bullet" as the way to prevail in the Republican struggle for a united Ireland. See O'Malley, *Uncivil Wars*, 274.

43. Shlomo Ben-Ami, *Scars of War*, 144–45, and interview with the author, March 9, 2012. All quotes from Ben-Ami in this chapter are from this interview unless otherwise noted.

44. The text of the Nusseibeh-Ayalon Agreement (September 3, 2002) can be found at http://www.nad-plo.org/etemplate.php?id=274.

45. Sari Nusseibeh, interview with the author, February 18, 2012. All quotes from Nusseibeh in this chapter are from this interview unless otherwise noted.

46. Salah al-Bardaweel, interview with the author, March 6, 2012.

47. Mukhaimer Abusada, interview with the author, November 30, 2011.

48. Tuastad, *The Hudna: Hamas's Concept of a Long-Term Ceasefire*. The concept of a *hudna* stems from the Arab Muslim tradition and refers to a reciprocal truce under agreed-upon conditions and for a specified time period. Reut Institute, "Hudna," April 20, 2005, http://reut-institute.org/Publication.aspx?PublicationId=287.

49. Abusada, interviews with the author, November 30, 2011, and March 6, 2012.

50. Zakay and Fleisig, "The Time Factor as a Barrier to Resolution" *Barriers to Peace*, 278.

51. Abusada, interview with the author, November 30, 2011.

52. Efraim Halevy, "Israel's Hamas Portfolio," *Israel Journal of Foreign Affairs* 2, no. 3 (2008), http://www.israelcfr.com/documents/issue6_hamas.pdf.

53. Key officials called for talks with Hamas. Nehemia Shtrasler, "Talk to Hamas," *Haaretz*, March 4, 2008, http://www.haaretz.com/print-edition/opinion/talk-to-hamas-1.240584; Amos

Harel, "Former Defense Officials Call for Indirect Talks with Hamas," *Haaretz*, May 18, 2008, http://www.haaretz.com/print-edition/news/former-defense-officials-call-for-indirect-talks-with-hamas-1.246039; Orly Halpern, "Experts Question Wisdom of Boycotting Hamas," *Jewish Daily Forward*, February 9, 2007, http://forward.com/articles/10055/experts-question-wisdom-of-boycotting-hamas/; Mike Gapes, "Time to Talk to Hamas," *Guardian*, August 12, 2007, http://www.theguardian.com/commentisfree/2007/aug/13/foreignpolicy.israel; James P. Rubin, "Hypocrisy on Hamas," *Washington Post*, May 16, 2008, http://www.washingtonpost.com/wp-dyn/content/article/2008/05/15/AR2008051503306.html?hpid=opinionsbox1; Richard N. Haass and Martin S. Indyk, "A Time for Diplomatic Renewal: Toward a New U.S. Strategy in the Middle East," Brookings Paper, December 2008, http://www.brookings.edu/research/papers/2008/12/middle-east-haass.

54. Nicolas Pelham, "Israel Should Consider Hamas' Cease-fire Offer More Seriously," *Haaretz*, July 28, 2014, http://www.haaretz.com/opinion/.premium-1.607604; Zvi Bar'el, "Internationalizing Gaza Disadvantages Israel," *Haaretz*, August 25, 2014, http://www.haaretz.com/news/diplomacy-defense/.premium-1.612192.

55. Johnson and Sergie, "Islam: Governing Under Sharia." Abbas is quoted as telling the emir of Qatar in August 2014—at the height of the Gaza war—that "[Former PLO leader Yasser] Arafat invited them [Hamas] to join the Palestinian Authority and the 1996 elections, but they refused and said that democracy is forbidden because it is the rule of the people, while we Hamas want the rule of Shari'a." Abbas was also quoted as saying, "They issue fatwas as they like and use religion to serve their interests." Khaled Abu Toameh, "PA Chief Abbas: Hamas Leader Mashaal Is a Liar," *Jerusalem Post*, September 1, 2014, http://www.jpost.com/Middle-East/Abbas-Hamas-leader-Mashaal-is-a-liar-374113; "Hamas Invited to Join Arafat's Government," CNN, June 13, 1998, http://www.cnn.com/WORLD/meast/9806/13/arafat.hamas/.

For a comprehensive account of the torrent of change that came in the wake of the Arab Spring as competing forces vied for domination in the region, with confrontation between secular parties and Islamists, see Noueihed and Warren, *Battle for the Arab Spring*.

56. "Twice in the last seven days," the *New York Times* reported on August 25, 2014, "Egypt and the United Arab Emirates have secretly launched airstrikes against Islamist-allied militias battling for control of Tripoli, Libya, four senior American officials said, in a major escalation of a regional power struggle set off by Arab Spring revolts." David D. Kirkpatrick and Eric Schmitt, "Arab Nations Strike in Libya, Surprising U.S.," *New York Times*, August 25, 2014, http://www.nytimes.com/2014/08/26/world/africa/egypt-and-united-arab-emirates-said-to-have-secretly-carried-out-libya-airstrikes.html?hp&action=click&pgtype=Homepage&version=HpSum&module=first-column-region®ion=top-news&WT.nav=top.

57. "Gaza Youth Breaks Out with a 'Manifesto for Change,'" *Mondoweiss*, January 2, 2011, http://mondoweiss.net/2011/01/gaza-youth-breaks-out-with-a-manifesto-for-change.

58. Saleh al-Naami, interview with the author, December 3, 2011. All quotes from al-Naami in this chapter are from this interview unless otherwise noted.

59. For a comprehensive overview of the growth of the Salafists in Gaza 2007 and the scope of their activities, see Yoram Cohen, "Jihadist Groups in Gaza: A Developing Threat," Washington Institute, January 5, 2009, http://www.washingtoninstitute.org/policy-analysis/view/jihadist-groups-in-gaza-a-developing-threat; Daniel Williams, "Salafism: A New Threat to Hamas," *New York Times*, October 27, 2009, http://www.nytimes.com/2009/10/28/world/middleeast/28iht-letter.html?_r=0. Benedetta Berti, "Salafi-Jihadi Activism in Gaza:

Mapping the Threat," May 2010, https://www.ctc.usma.edu/posts/salafi-jihadi-activism-in-gaza-mapping-the-threat; Jon Donnison, "Salafist Ideological Challenge to Hamas in Gaza" BBC News, May 13, 2011, http://www.bbc.com/news/world-middle-east-13387859; Benedetta Berti, "Hamas's Internal Challenge: The Political and Ideological Impact of Violent Salafist Groups in Gaza," Strategic Studies, Vol. 14, No. 2, July 2011, 33-84, http://www.inss.org.il/index.aspx?id=4538&articleid=2363.

60. Adnan Abu Amer, "Hamas reconciles with Gaza Salafists" *Al Monitor*, November 5, 2013; http://www.al-monitor.com/pulse/originals/2013/11/hamas-salafist-gaza-reconciliation.html#.

61. Peter Beaumont and Patrick Kingsley, "Violent Tide of Salafism Threatens the Arab Spring," *Guardian*, February 9, 2013, http://www.theguardian.com/world/2013/feb/09/violent-salafists-threaten-arab-spring-democracies. Robert Tait, "Iran Cuts Hamas Funding over Syria," *Telegraph*, May 31, 2013, http://www.telegraph.co.uk/news/worldnews/middleeast/palestinianauthority/10091629/Iran-cuts-Hamas-funding-over-Syria.html. Tait reported that Hamas leaders had admitted that Iran had cut up to £15 million a month in funding as punishment for the movement's backing of the uprising in Syria.

62. Steven A. Cook, "Social Work, Violence and Palestinian Nationalism," *From the Potomac to the Euphrates* (blog), Council on Foreign Relations, May 8, 2014, http://blogs.cfr.org/cook/2014/05/08/social-work-violence-and-palestinian-nationalism/; Adnan Abu Amer, "Iran Seeks to Retain Influence in Palestinian Affairs," *Al-Monitor*, April 4, 2013, http://www.al-monitor.com/pulse/originals/2013/04/iran-hamas-ties.html#.

Amer reports that: "In the months that preceded the Israeli war on Gaza [2012], when the Iran-Hamas relationship was at its nadir, Iran provided unprecedented military support for Islamic Jihad. In fact, Israeli intelligence noted that Islamic Jihad's military capabilities may be approaching, or have even exceeded, those of Hamas. While strengthening Islamic Jihad to fight Israel, Iran was also punishing Hamas." The 2014 Gaza war proved otherwise.

63. Rasha Abou Jalal, "Islamic Jihad Gains Support in Gaza as Hamas Declines," *Al-Monitor*, April 10, 2014, http://www.al-monitor.com/pulse/ru/originals/2014/04/islamic-jihad-support-gaza-expense-hamas.html. Jalal refers to a recent poll by the Watan Center for Studies and Research in the Gaza Strip. "It suggests," he wrote, "increased support for the Islamic Jihad movement amid reports of declining popularity for Hamas. Among Gazans, 23.3% expressed support for Hamas, while 13.5% preferred Islamic Jihad. Fatah, however, was more popular than the Islamist movements individually, with the support of 32.9% of Gazans. Backing for the Popular Front for the Liberation of Palestine stood at 4.2% and 1.5% for the Democratic Front for the Liberation of Palestine. Of all those surveyed, 24.6% had no opinion." In a 2010 poll, Islamic Jihad registered an insignificant 1 percent.

See also Jodi Rudoren, "Islamic Jihad Gains New Traction in Gaza," *New York Times*, May 3, 2014; http://www.nytimes.com/2014/05/04/world/middleeast/islamic-jihad-gains-new-traction-in-gaza.html?_r=0; Asmaa al-Ghoul, "Hamas Isolated as Iran Boosts Ties with Islamic Jihad, Fatah," *Al Monitor*, February 12, 2014, http://www.al-monitor.com/pulse/originals/2014/02/islamic-jihad-fatah-hamas-iran-palestinians.html#.

64. Zvi Bar'el, "Giving Israel a New Look at Hamas" (review of *Lehakir et Hamas* ["To Know Hamas"] by Shlomi Eldar), *Haaretz*, September 19, 2012, http://www.haaretz.com/culture/books/giving-israel-a-new-look-at-hamas-1.465584.

65. Ibid.

66. Abusada, interview with the author, November 30, 2011.

67. Ahmad al-Dabba, "Gaza Escalation: Sabotaging Hamas," *Al-Akhbar*, September 18, 2012, http://english.al-akhbar.com/node/12374.

68. Amos Harel and Avi Issacharoff, "Hamas' Change of Strategy: Rocket Fire Directed at Israeli Military Targets," *East Side Story* (blog), *Haaretz*, June 20, 2012, http://www.haaretz.com/blogs/east-side-story/hamas-change-of-strategy-rocket-fire-directed-at-israeli-military-targets.premium-1.439939.

69. Kifah Ziboun, "Disagreement Continues over Claims of Hamas-PIJ Joint Command," *Asharq Al-Awsat*, September 18, 2013, http://www.aawsat.net/2013/09/article55317254. Ziboun writes: "Controversy continues to surround statements by senior Hamas official Mahmoud Al-Zahar that Hamas and Palestinian Islamic Jihad (PIJ) intend to form a joint command, with some movement officials confirming the news, and others denying it."

70. The purpose of Protective Edge was to restore security to Israeli civilians living under Hamas rocket fire; dismantle the Hamas tunnel network used to infiltrate Israel. See the IDF's Web site: http://www.idfblog.com/operationgaza2014/#Genralinformation.

71. Dan Bilefsky illustrates how an extraneous variable can have consequences that affect the conduct of war taking place thousands of miles away. See Dan Bilefsky, "Israel's Gaza Incursion Sets Off Protests in Europe," *New York Times*, July 21, 2014, http://www.nytimes.com/2014/07/22/world/europe/israels-gaza-incursion-sets-off-protests-in-europe.html.

72. Michael Herzog, interview with the author, November 27, 2011. All quotes from Herzog in this chapter are from this interview unless otherwise noted.

73. Jonathan Ferziger and Amy Teibel, "Israel Minister Says Annexing West Bank 'Only Sane Plan,'" *Bloomberg*, June 9, 2014, http://www.bloomberg.com/news/2014-06-08/annexation-plan-sparks-threat-to-topple-israel-government.html.

74. Morris, *One State, Two States*, 164–65.

75. Adnan Abu Amer, "Hamas Not Giving Up Military Wing, Despite Agreement," *Al-Monitor*, May 2, 2014, http://www.al-monitor.com/pulse/originals/2014/05/qassam-weapons-hamas-fatah-reconciliation.html.

76. Akiva Eldar, "Bibi Uses Gaza as Wedge Between Abbas and Hamas," *Al-Monitor*, September 1, 2014, http://www.al-monitor.com/pulse/originals/2014/09/israel-netanyahu-abbas-gaza-war-disengagement-sharon.html. Even after a PLO delegation negotiated indirectly on behalf of Hamas during cease-fire talks in Cairo in August 2014 while a unity government, agreed between Hamas and Fatah in April 2014, was still in place, Eldar writes: "Israeli Prime Minister Benjamin Netanyahu will accept Palestinian president Mahmoud Abbas's rule in Gaza only if the unity government was dissolved."

77. At the cease-fire talks in Cairo during the 2014 war, the PA negotiated with Israel, with Egypt mediating, while Hamas occupied its own suite for consultations between itself and the PA negotiators—perhaps a template for the future.

78. Noam Sheizaf, "Israel's Addiction to the Status Quo," *Al-Monitor*, December 5, 2012, http://www.al-monitor.com/pulse/ar/politics/2012/12/we-have-become-addicted-to-the-s.html.

79. The cease-fire arrangements were predicated upon Hamas's being able to keep "quiet for quiet" on for a month, after which the parties would reconvene in Cairo and start negotiating the substantive issues. The war began on July 8 and lasted fifty days, until August 26, 2014. Aaron Lerner, "PM Netanyahu to Hamas: Quiet for Quiet Is Goal," *Independent Media Review Analysis*, July 11, 2014, http://www.imra.org.il/story.php3?id=64296.

80. United Nations General Assembly, "Human Rights in Palestine and Other Occupied Arab Territories."

81. Ghassan Khatib, interview with the author, July 1, 2012.

82. El-Sarraj, interview with the author, July 19, 2012.

83. Gershon Baskin, "Israel's Shortsighted Assassination," *New York Times*, November 16, 2012, http://www.nytimes.com/2012/11/17/opinion/israels-shortsighted-assassination.html.

84. "Gaza: Palestinian Rockets Unlawfully Targeted Israeli Civilians," *Human Rights Watch*, December 24, 2012, http://www.hrw.org/news/2012/12/24/gaza-palestinian-rockets-unlawfully-targeted-israeli-civilians.

85. U.S. Secretary of State Hillary Clinton played a small role in arranging a cease-fire. See Clinton, *Hard Choices*, 476–87.

86. Matt Spetalnick, "Obama: 'Preferable' to Avoid Israeli Ground Invasion of Gaza," Reuters, November 18, 2012, http://www.reuters.com/article/2012/11/18/us-asia-obama-mideast-idUSBRE8AH07Z20121118.

87. International Crisis Group, "Israel and Hamas: Fire and Ceasefire," http://www.crisisgroup.org/~/media/Files/Middle%20East%20North%20Africa/Israel%20Palestine/133-israel-and-hamas-fire-and-ceasefire-in-a-new-middle-east.

88. Ibid.

89. Ibid.

90. Ben Hubbard, "In Jordan Town, Syria War Inspires Jihadist Dreams," *New York Times*, April 12, 2014, http://www.nytimes.com/2014/04/13/world/middleeast/in-jordan-town-syria-war-inspires-jihadist-dreams.html?_r=0.executions.html?action=click&contentCollection=Middle%20East&module=RelatedCoverage®ion=M.

91. "Egypt 'Intentionally' Ignored Hamas on Gaza Ceasefire," Ma'an News Agency, March 13, 2014, http://www.maannews.net/eng/ViewDetails.aspx?ID=681373.

92. See EN 66.

93. Ali Hashem, "Iran-Hamas Rebuild Ties Following Morsi's Ouster," *Al-Monitor*, August 12, 2013, http://www.al-monitor.com/pulse/originals/2013/08/iran-hamas-rebuild-ties-after-morsi.html.

94. "Food Insecurity in Palestine Remains High," joint press release by the Palestinian Central Bureau of Statistics (PCBS), the Food and Agriculture Organization (FAO), the United Nations Relief and Works Agency for Palestine Refugees in the Near East (UNRWA), and the World Food Programme (WFP), June 3, 2014, http://www.unrwa.org/newsroom/press-releases/food-insecurity-palestine-remains-high." Food insecurity in Palestine remains at very high levels, with a third of households—33 percent, or 1.6 million people—food insecure, according to the 2013 annual food security survey, a collaborative effort between the Palestinian Central Bureau of Statistics and United Nations (UN) agencies in the food-security sector. In Gaza, food-insecurity levels remained at 57 percent, while in the West Bank, food insecurity remained at 19 percent—both unchanged from 2012 levels. The high food-insecurity levels in 2012 and 2013 reversed the improvement that took place over the 2009–11 period, when overall food insecurity in Palestine fell to 27 percent.

95. "Netanyahu: Mideast Peace Talks 'Essentially Buried' If Hamas-Fatah Deal Stands," Fox News, April 24, 2014, http://www.foxnews.com/politics/2014/04/24/netanyahu-hamas-fatah-deal-blow-to-peace/.

96. Abusada, interview with the author, July 19, 2012.

97. Zvi Bar'el, "Hamas Is Looking for a Way Out," *Haaretz*, July 8, 2014, http://www.haaretz.com/news/national/.premium-1.603847.

98. "Hamas Rejects Any PA-Israeli Pacts as Not Binding," Alalam News Network, December 5, 2013, http://en.alalam.ir/news/1541712://www.haaretz.com/news/national/.premium-1.603847.

99. Al-Zahar, interview with the author, December 1, 2011.

100. Khaled Meshaal, speech on Nakba Day, Qatar, May 20, 2014; see Adnan Abu Amer, "Hamas Leader Stresses 'Concessions' in Reconciliation Deal," *Al-Monitor*, May 27, 2014, http://www.al-monitor.com/pulse/originals/2014/05/gaza-hamas-leader-meshaal-reconciliation-fatah.html#.

101. It retained the same prime ministers, deputy prime ministers, finance minister, and foreign minister. Nathan Thrall, "How the West Chose War in Gaza," *New York Times*, July 18, 2014, http://www.nytimes.com/2014/07/18/opinion/gaza-and-israel-the-road-to-war-paved-by-the-west.html.

102. Nidal al-Mughrabi, "Hamas Government Workers in Gaza Launch Strike in Test of Unity Deal," *Haaretz*, June 26, 2014, http://www.haaretz.com/news/diplomacy-defense/1.601438; Reuters, "Gaza Public Servants Strike over Pay Dispute," Al Jazeera, June 27, 2014, http://www.aljazeera.com/news/middleeast/2014/06/gaza-public-servants-strike-over-pay-dispute-2014626162613667541.html; Nidal al-Mughrabi, "Palestinian Reconciliation Pact Threatened by Disunity," *Chicago Tribune*, June 10, 2014, http://articles.chicagotribune.com/2014-06-10/news/sns-rt-us-palestinian-rivals-unity-20140610_1_hamas-activists-palestinian-islamist-group-hamas-fatah.

103. "Netanyahu: Mideast Peace Talks 'Essentially Buried' If Hamas-Fatah Deal Stands," Fox News, April 24, 2014, http://www.foxnews.com/politics/2014/04/24/netanyahu-hamas-fatah-deal-blow-to-peace/.

104. Jodi Rudoren and Isabel Kershner, "Palestinian Premier Says New Government Lacks Power in Gaza," *New York Times*, June 13, 2014, http://www.nytimes.com/2014/06/13/world/middleeast/palestinian-authority-premier-says-unity-government-lacks-power-in-gaza.html?_r=0.

105. "Netanyahu Warns of Hamas Rise in W. Bank," CBN News, June 8, 2014, http://www.cbn.com/cbnnews/insideisrael/2014/June/Netanyahu-Warns-of-Hamas-Rise-in-W-Bank/.

106. Ibid.

107. Hazem Balousha, "Palestinians Seek to Heal Wounds from Hamas-Fatah Clashes," *Al-Monitor*, May 9, 2014, http://www.al-monitor.com/pulse/originals/2014/05/palestine-reconciliation-hamas-fatah-social-healing.html.

108. Zvi Bar'el, "Israel Struggling to Tie Hamas to West Bank Kidnappings," *Haaretz*, June 22, 2014, http://www.haaretz.com/news/diplomacy-defense/.premium-1.600229; "Israel Names Hamas as Behind Killings Despite Anomalies," *Geopolitical Diary* (blog), Stratfor Global Intelligence, June 30, 2104, http://www.stratfor.com/geopolitical-diary/israel-names-hamas-behind-teenagers-killings-despite-anomalies#axzz36Dy1j9Ua.

109. Adnan Abu Amer, "Hamas Denies Role in Kidnapping," *Al-Monitor*, June 16, 2014, http://www.al-monitor.com/pulse/originals/2014/06/hamas-israel-confrontation-hebron-kidnapping; Jack Khoury, "Meshal—Hamas Not Responsible for Kidnapping, Wants Calm with Israel," *Haaretz*, July 3, 2014, http://www.haaretz.com/news/middle-east.premium-1.602871; Associated Press, "Hamas Admits Kidnapping Israeli Teens," *Washington Post*, August 21, 2014, http://www.washingtonpost.com/world/middle_east/hamas-admits-kidnapping-israeli-teens/2014/08/21/6e70b51e-2957-11e4-8b10-7db129976abb_story. About two months later, Hamas learned that a number of its operatives had been involved. Palestinian leader Khaled Meshaal told a news conference on August 22 that the kidnappers were Hamas members, which it had learned only from the Israeli investigation, but that the kidnappings had not been authorized by the Hamas leadership, which bore no responsibility in the matter. "Meshaal Admits Hamas Members Kidnapped and Murdered Naftali, Gilad and Eyal," *Jerusalem Post*, August 23, 2014, http://www.jpost.com/Arab-Israeli-Conflict/Meshaal-admits-Hamas-members-kidnapped-and-murdered-Naftali-Gilad-and-Eyal-371997. See also Shlomi Eldar, "Accused Kidnappers Are Rogue Hamas Branch," *Al-Monitor*, June 29, 2014, http://www.al-monitor.com/pulse/originals/2014/06/qawasmeh-clan-hebron-hamas-eadership-mahmoud-abbas.html; Steven Erlanger, "Arrest by Israel in Abduction

of 3 Youths Is Made Public," *New York Times,* August 5, 2014, http://www.nytimes.Com/2014/08/06/world/middleeast/israeli-arrest-made-public-in-abduction-of-3-youths.html. *The New York Times* reported on August 5 that Hussam Qawasmeh, who was arrested on July 11, said in court documents that Hamas had funded the operation.

110. "Hamas Slams Palestine Helping Israel Locate Missing Teenagers," *TwoCircles.net*, June 15, 2014, http://twocircles.net/2014jun15/israel_arrests_80_palestinians_over_missing_teenagers.html#.U9foP_ldX; Jodi Rudoren, "Fate of 3 Kidnapped Israelis Raises Tensions on Many Fronts," *New York Times*, June 22, 2014, http://www.nytimes.com/2014/06/23/world/middleeast/fate-of-3-kidnapped-israelis-twists-tensions-on-many-fronts.html?action=click&contentCollection=Middle.

111. "Is the IDF Overreacting to West Bank Abductions?," Middle East Policy Council, http://www.mepc.org/articles-commentary/commentary/idf-overreacting-west-bank-abductions?print.

112. Gideon Levy, "West Bank Operation Turns from Farce into Tragedy," *Haaretz*, June 22, 2014, http://www.haaretz.com/opinion/.premium-1.600214.

113. Zvi Bar'el, "Israel Struggling to Tie Hamas to Kidnappings," *Haaretz*, June 22, 2014; http://www.haaretz.com/news/diplomacy-defense/.premium-1.600229.

114. For the terms of that cease-fire, see International Crisis Group, "Israel and Hamas: Fire and Ceasefire."

115. Michael R. Gordon and Jodi Rudoren, "In Israel, Kerry Sees 'Work to Do' to Get Deal on Cease-fire," *New York Times*, July 23, 2014, http://www.nytimes.com/2014/07/24/world/middleeast/kerry-israel-gaza.html?hp&action=click&pgtype=Homepage&version=LedeSum&module=first-column-region®ion=top-news&WT.nav=top-news&_r=0; Zvi Bar'el, "Hamas Has Been Looking for Allies, So Far in Vain," *Haaretz*, July 25, 2014, http://www.haaretz.com/news/diplomacy-defense/.premium-1.607178; Anne Barnard, "Hamas Gambled on War As Its Woes Grew in Gaza," *New York Times*, July 22, 2014, http://www.nytimes.com/2014/07/23/world/middleeast/hamas-gambled-on-war-as-its-woes-grew-in-gaza.html.

116. Avi Issacharoff, "Hamas Fires Rockets for First Time Since 2012, Israeli Officials Say," *Times of Israel*, June 30, 2014, http://www.timesofisrael.com/hamas-fired-rockets-for-first-time-since-2012-israeli-officials-say.

117. "What Led to Protective Edge," *IDF Blog*, June 28, 2014, http://www.idfblog.com/blog/2014/06/28/live-updates-gaza-terrorists-fire-rockets-israel/.

118. Shlomi Eldar, "Hamas Surprises Israel," *Al-Monitor*, July 9, 2014, http://www.al-monitor.com/pulse/originals/2014/07/hamas-protective-edge-rockets-idf-gaza-tel-aviv.html.

119. Herb Keinon, "Netanyahu: Israel to Expand Operation Protective Edge," *Jerusalem Post*, September 7, 2014, http://www.jpost.com/Diplomacy-and-Politics/Netanyahu-Israel-to-expand-Operation-Protective-Edge-362110.

120. Associated Press (contrib.), "Israeli Troops Push into Gaza As Netanyahu Warns of Expanded Ground Assault," Fox News, July 18, 2014, http://www.foxnews.com/world/2014/07/18/netanyahu-tells-israeli-military-to-prepare-for-significant-expansion-in-gaza-offensive/.

121. "The Tunnel Threat Gives Israel's Gaza Offensive Its Legitimacy," *Haaretz*, July 30, 2014, http://www.haaretz.com/opinion/1.607903.

122. Raphael Ahren, "PM Wants Gaza Demilitarized and the World Agrees—but How?," *Times of Israel*, July 29, 2014, http://www.timesofisrael.com/pm-wants-gaza-demilitarized-and-the-world-agrees-but-how/.

123. Assaf Sharon, "Failure in Gaza," *New York Review of Books*, September 25, 2014, http://www.nybooks.com/articles/archives/2014/sep/25/failure-gaza/.

124. Oslo II had called for a seaport. Donald Neff, "Israel Never Honored the Oslo Peace Accords Signed at White House," first published in *Washington Report on Middle East Affairs*, September 1998, http://www.wrmea.org/1998-september/israel-never-honored-the-oslo-peace-accords-signed-at-white-house.html; Mirak-Weissbach, "Who Murdered the Oslo Accords?"

125. Shlomi Eldar, "Hamas Surprises Israel," *Al-Monitor*, July 9, 2014, http://www.al-monitor.com/pulse/originals/2014/07/hamas-protective-edge-rockets-idf-gaza-tel-aviv.html; Paul Rogers, "Israel vs Hamas, a War of Surprises," *Open Democracy*, July 24, 2014, https://www.opendemocracy.net/paul-rogers/israel-vs-hamas-war-of-surprises; Isabel Kershner, "In Tunnel War, Israeli Playbook Offers Few Ideas," *New York Times*, August 1, 2014, http://www.nytimes.com/2014/08/02/world/middleeast/an-old-playbook-leaves-israel-unready-for-hamass-tunnel-war-.html; "Five Must-Read Articles About Terror Tunnels from Gaza to Israel," *Haaretz*, July 22, 2014, http://www.haaretz.com/news/diplomacy-defense/1.606682.

126. Amos Harel, "Hamas' Terror Tunnels: A National Strategic Failure for Israel," *Haaretz*, July 22, 2014, http://www.haaretz.com/news/diplomacy-defense/.premium-1.606510; Avi Bar-Eli, "Millions Down the Tunnel: How Israel Botched the Battle Against Hamas," *Haaretz*, July 21, 2014, http://www.haaretz.com/business/.premium-1.606434; Jodi Rudoren, "Tunnels Lead Right to the Heart of Israeli Fear," *New York Times*, July 28, 2014, http://www.nytimes.com/2014/07/29/world/middleeast/tunnels-lead-right-to-heart-of-israeli-fear.html?hp&action=click&pgtype=Homepage&version=HpSum&module=photo-spot-region®ion=photo-spot&WT.nav=photo-spot.

127. Quoted in Assaf Sharon, "Failure in Gaza," *New York Review of Books*, September 25, 2014, n. 6, http://www.nybooks.com/articles/archives/2014/sep/25/failure-gaza/.

128. Rudoren, "Tunnels Lead Right to the Heart of Israeli Fear."

129. Noah Browning, "Hamas Guerrilla Tactics Are Tailored to Israel's Ground War," Reuters, July 23, 2014, http://www.businessinsider.com/hamas-guerrilla-tactics-are-tailored-to-israels-ground-war-2014-7; Jonathan Ferziger and Saud Abu Ramadan, "Retooled Hamas Bloodies Israel with Help from Hezbollah," *Bloomberg*, August 21, 2014, http://www.bloomberg.com/news/2014-08-20/retooled-hamas-bloodies-israel-with-help-from-hezbollah.html.

130. Anshel Pfeffer, "Will the Threat to Israel's Only International Airport be a Game-Changer?," *Haaretz*, July 22, 2014, http://www.haaretz.com/news/diplomacy-defense/.premium-1.606685; Alan M. Dershowitz, "Hamas' Threat to Israel's Airports Threatens Two-State Solution," *Haaretz*, July 22, 2014, http://www.haaretz.com/opinion/.premium-1.606701.

131. Gil Hoffman, "Poll: 86.5% of Israelis Oppose Cease-fire," *Jerusalem Post*, July 28, 2014, http://www.jpost.com/Operation-Protective-Edge/Poll-865-percent-of-Israelis-oppose-cease-fire-369064?utm_source=Sailthru&utm_medium=email&utm_term=%Oper2ASituation%20Report&utm_campaign=SitRep0728.

132. Ya'ar and Hermann, "August 2014 Peace Index"; "Poll: Overwhelming Majority of Jewish Israelis Say Gaza Op Justified," *Haaretz*, August 22, 2014, http://www.haaretz.com/news/diplomacy-defense/1.611987.

133. Marissa Newman, "Israeli Official Confirms US Nixed Arms Sale; Pols Argue over Who's to Blame," *Times of Israel*, August 14, 2014, http://www.timesofisrael.com/israeli-official-confirms-us-nixed-missile-sale-pm-blamed-for-soured-ties/. Sudarsan Raghavan and Ruth Eglash, "In Deaths of Civilians in Gaza, U.S. Weapons Sales to Israel Come Under Scrutiny," *Washington Post*, August 23, 2014, http://www.washingtonpost.com/world/mid

dle_east/in-deaths-of-civilians-in-gaza-us-weapons-sales-to-israel-come-under-scrutiny/2014/08/23/4f6565e7-da0f-4ecb-b005-5b2202463d1f_story.html.

134. Barak Ravid, "Obama's Message to Netanyahu: Weapons with Strings Attached," *Haaretz*, August 15, 2014; http://www.haaretz.com/news/diplomacy-defense/.premium-1.610748. Gili Cohen, "U.S. Missile Shipment Delay Over: Israeli Official," *Haaretz*, August, 26, 2014, http://www.haaretz.com/news/diplomacy-defense/.premium-1.612424.

135. Jodi Rudoren, "Amid Outcry Abroad, a Wealth of Backing in Israel for Netanyahu," *New York Times*, July 26, 2014, http://www.nytimes.com/2014/07/27/world/middleeast/losing-support-from-abroad-netanyahu-finds-a-wealth-of-backing-at-home.html?action=click&contentCollection=Middle%20East&module=RelatedCoverage®ion=Marginalia&pgtype=article.

136. Rachael Levy, "What People on the Arab Street Are Saying About Hamas," *Vocativ*, July 23, 2014, http://www.vocativ.com/world/israel-world/people-arab-street-saying-hamas/?utm_campaign=June1&utm_medium=cpc&utm_source=outbrain; David D. Kirkpatrick, "Arab Leaders, Viewing Hamas as Worse Than Israel, Stay Silent," *New York Times*, July 30, 2014, http://www.nytimes.com/2014/07/31/world/middleeast/fighting-political-islam-arab-states-find-themselves-allied-with-israel.html?ref=world. Kirkpatrick writes: "After the military ouster of the Islamist government in Cairo last year, Egypt has led a new coalition of Arab states—including Jordan, Saudi Arabia and the United Arab Emirates—that has effectively lined up with Israel in its fight against Hamas, the Islamist movement that controls the Gaza Strip. That, in turn, may have contributed to the failure of the antagonists to reach a negotiated cease-fire even after more than three weeks of bloodshed." Zvi Bar'el, "Hamas Has Been Looking for Allies, So Far in Vain," *Haaretz*, July 25, 2014, http://www.haaretz.com/news/diplomacy-defense/.premium-1.607178; Zvi Bar'el, "Hamas Wages a Lonely War, Giving Israel the Opportunity to Boost Abbas' Standing," *Haaretz*, July 18, 2014, http://www.haaretz.com/news/diplomacy-defense/.premium-1.605873/.premium-1.605873.

137. "Abbas was not a fan of Hamas' strategy and actions when the current war Gaza in began.... [But he] has made a major change that was reflected in his speech in Ramallah on July 23 to members of the Palestinian leadership that brought him praise from even Islamic Jihad.... In his meeting with the Palestinian leadership, Abbas' change of mind was clear in both text and tone. In his July 23 speech, the Palestinian president said: 'It is time that we all raise our rightful voices in the face of Israel's killing and destruction machine. Israeli forces have crossed all lines and broken all international laws and humanitarian values with the utmost brutality. We know we do not have planes or artillery tanks, but what we have is stronger than this firepower and arrogance. We have the strength of righteousness and justice.'... The president came to see that the cease-fire agreement was meant to stop resistance without any relief to the major problems facing Gazans. 'It became clear to him that despite the good intentions of the Egyptians, none of the changes regarding lifting the siege would be accomplished, [Abbas Zaki, a senior member of the Fatah Central Committee] told *Al-Monitor* by phone from his home in Hebron." Daoud Kuttab, "What Made Abbas Change His Position on Gaza War?" *Al-Monitor*, July 28, 2014, http://www.al-monitor.com/pulse/originals/2014/07/gaza-israel-war-mahmoud-abbas-hamas-resistance-ceasefire.html; Ben Lynfield, "One Blood, One Enemy: Solidarity for Gaza Boils Over in the West Bank," *Christian Science Monitor*, July 19, 2014, http://www.csmonitor.com/World/Middle-East/2014/0719/One-blood-one-enemy-Solidarity-for-Gaza-boils-in-West-Bank.

138. Isabel Kershner and Michael R. Gordon, "Israel Agrees to Pause in Assault on Gaza as Cease-fire Deal Is Pursued," *New York Times*, July 25, 2014, http://www.nytimes.com/2014/07/26/world/middleeast/israel-gaza-strip.html?_r=0; "West Bank Protests over Gaza

Turn Deadly," *Al Jazeera*, July 25, 2014, http://www.aljazeera.com/news/middleeast/2014/07/israel-kills-palestinian-west-bank-clashes-2014724213831750431.html; "Violent Protests Erupt as Palestinian Authority Officials Call for 'Day of Rage,'" *CBSDC/AP*, July 25, 2014, http://washington.cbslocal.com/2014/07/25/palestinian-authority-officials-call-for-day-of-rage-in-west-bank-following-deadly-protests/; B'Tselem, "13 Palestinians Killed by Israeli Security Forces in West Bank Since Operation Protective Edge Began: Excessive Use of Live Fire Suspected," July 29, 2014, http://www.btselem.org/press_releases/20140729.

139. "Palestinian Authority Opposes Hamas's Call for Intifada but Potential Triggers Include Collapse of Security Forces," *IHS Jane's Intelligence Review*, September 1, 2014, http://www.janes.com/article/42645/palestinian-authority-opposes-hamas-s-call-for-intifada-but-potential-triggers-include-collapse-of-security-forces.

140. Ghassan Khatib, interview with the author, July 1, 2012.

141. Michael R. Gordon, "Even Gaza Truce Is Hard to Win, Kerry Is Finding," *New York Times*, July 27, 2014, http://www.nytimes.com/2014/07/28/world/middleeast/kerry-finds-even-a-truce-in-gaza-is-hard-to-win-cease-fire-hamas.html?&hp&action=click&pgtype=Homepage&version=LedeSum&module=first-column-region®ion=top-news&WT.nav=top-news; Associated Press, "Netanyahu to U.S.: Don't Second-Guess Me on Hamas," *Politico*, August 2, 2014, http://www.politico.com/story/2014/08/netanyahu-to-us-dont-second-guess-me-on-hamas-109664.html. According to the latter article, "Following the quick collapse of the cease-fire [one in many] in Gaza, Israeli Prime Minister Benjamin Netanyahu told the White House not to force a truce with Palestinian militants on Israel. . . . The Israeli leader advised the Obama administration 'not to ever second guess me again' on the matter. The officials also said Netanyahu said he should be 'trusted' on the issue and about the unwillingness of Hamas to enter into and follow through on cease-fire talks."

142. "Operation Protective Edge, Day 26," *Haaretz*, August 3, 2014, http://www.haaretz.com/news/diplomacy-defense/1.608426; "IDF Destroys Hamas Tunnels into Israel," *Haaretz*, July 21, 2014, http://www.haaretz.com/news/video/1.606443; Gili Cohen, "Israeli Military Withdraws Bulk of Troops from Gaza," *Haaretz*, August 3, 2014, http://www.haaretz.com/news/diplomacy-defense/.premium-1.608590.

143. Daoud Kuttab, "Israel Ignores Calls to Lift Gaza Siege," *Al-Monitor*, August 21, 2014, http://www.al-monitor.com/pulse/originals/2014/08/fail-cease-fire-israel-refuse-lift-gaza-siege.html.155.

144. Among Jewish Israelis, 0.4 percent believe Hamas demands to stop rocket fire; 58 percent believe none of Hamas's demands should be met and that it should be fought until it surrenders; 41 percent believe that some Hamas demands that are not a threat to national security should be met; 66 percent believe that the best way to deal with Hamas is through a combination of military and political diplomacy; 63 percent think "the world is against Israel"; 60 percent trust Sisi as a mediator; 71 percent believe that chances of things being quiet for three years are low. Gil Hoffman, "Poll Finds Almost No Support for Accepting Hamas's Demands," *Jerusalem Post*, August 19, 2014, www.jpost.com/Arab-Israeli-conflict/Polls-finds-almost-no-support-for-accepting-Hamass-demands-371486.

145. Just three rockets were fired. Hamas denied firing them—they may have come from one of the fringe militia groups. Nevertheless, adhering to its policy that Hamas is responsible for any missiles fired from Gaza, Israel retaliated and the cycle began again. Isabel Kershner and Jodi Rudoren, "Rockets from Gaza and Israeli Response Break Cease-Fire," *New York Times*, August 19, 2014, http://www.nytimes.com/2014/08/20/world/middleeast/israel-gaza-strip.html?_r=0.

146. Ari Yahsar, "Report: Israel Refrained from Attack on Mohammed Deif, Due to Ceasefire," *Arutz Sheva*, August 24, 2014, http://www.israelnationalnews.com/News/News.aspx/184372#.U_pgr_ldVCg. "According to the report, Israel was bound by a ceasefire with Hamas. . . . Israel's political echelon last week was presented with incriminating, irrefutable evidence that Deif had taken advantage of the ceasefire to visit his wife and children in a building in the Sheikh Radwan neighborhood in northwest Gaza, the report claims. They were asked to make a decision whether to give a strike on the building the go-ahead or to block the rare opportunity to assassinate the slippery arch-terrorist responsible for planning numerous lethal attacks; they chose the latter option."

147. William Booth and Ruth Eglash, "Israeli Airstrikes Kill 3 Top Hamas Commanders in Gaza Strip," *Washington Post*, August 20, 2014, http://www.washingtonpost.com/world/middle_east/israeli-airstrikes-kill-3-top-hamas-commanders-in-gaza-strip/2014/08/21/627e90b8-2930-11e4-958c-268a320a60ce_story.html. Jodi Rudoren, "Israel Kills 3 Top Hamas Leaders as Latest Fighting Turns Its Way," *New York Times*, August 21, 2014; http://www.nytimes.com/2014/08/22/world/middleeast/israel-gaza-strip.html.

148. Gili Cohen, "Despite Hamas' Denial, Still Unclear Whether Mohammed Deif Assassinated," *Haaretz*, August 20, 2014, http://www.haaretz.com/news/diplomacy-defense/.premium-1.611689.

149. "Hamas Executes 18 Suspected Informants for Israel in Gaza," World News, August 22, 2014, http://article.wn.com/view/2014/08/22/Gunmen_execute_alleged_collaborators_in_Gaza/.

150. Tova Dvorin, "570 Rockets Fired on Israel in 5 Days," *Arutz Sheva*, August 24, 2014, http://www.israelnationalnews.com/News/News.aspx/184355#.U_pkd_ldVCg; Yoav Zitun, "Gaza Rocket Fire Hits New Heights: 168 Launched in One Day," *YNetNews*, August 20, 2014, http://www.ynetnews.com/articles/0,7340,L-4560729,00.html.

151. "Parents of Israeli Boy Killed by Hamas Rocket Criticize U.N. in Letter to Ban," *JTA*, September 4, 2014, http://www.jta.org/2014/09/04/news-opinion/israel-middle-east/parents-of-boy-killed-by-hamas-rocket-criticize-u-n-in-letter-to-ban.

152. "Lost Homes and Dreams at Tower Israel Leveled," *New York Times*, September 14, 2014, http://www.nytimes.com/2014/09/15/world/middleeast/at-gaza-tower-israel-leveled-lost-homes-and-dreams.html; "Israel Bombs Two Gaza City Tower Blocks," *Guardian*, August 26, 2014, http://www.theguardian.com/world/2014/aug/26/israel-bombs-two-gaza-city-tower-blocks; Reuters, "Israel Levels More Gaza Apartment High-Rises," *Jewish Daily Forward*, August 26, 2014, http://forward.com/articles/204683/israel-levels-more-gaza-apartment-high-rises.

153. Gregg Carlstrom, "Forget Hamas: The Israeli Prime Minister Is Now Facing a War Within His Own Government," *Foreign Policy*, September 3, 2014, http://www.foreignpolicy.com/articles/2014/09/03/bibis_next_battle_benjamin_netanyahu_naftali_bennett_avigdor_lieberman_israel?utm_content=bufferb631e&utm_medium=social&utm_source=twitter.com&utm_campaign.

154. Khaled Abu Toameh, "Hamas Says Will Settle Gaza Salary Dispute and Pay Employees in Strip," *Jerusalem Post*, September 10, 2014, http://www.jpost.com/Middle-East/Hamas-says-will-pay-salaries-to-employees-in-Gaza-374977.

155. Spencer Ho, "Ceasefire Sparks Storm of Criticism Against Netanyahu: Disapproval from Allies, Opposition Exposes Rifts in Prime Minister's Coalition," *Times of Israel*, August 27, 2014, http://www.timesofisrael.com/ceasefire-sparks-storm-of-criticism-against-netanyahu/.

156. "Israel Premier's Approval Ratings Drop: Poll," *PressTV*, August 26, 2014, http://www.presstv.ir/detail/2014/08/26/376578/bibi-approval-ratings-drop-dramatically/.

"According to a poll published by Israel's Channel 2, on Monday, Netanyahu's approval ratings plunged to 38 percent from 82 percent at the beginning of the Israeli war on Gaza."

157. United Nations Office for the Coordination of Humanitarian Affairs, "Gaza Emergency Situation Report," http://www.ochaopt.org/content.aspx?id=1010361, accessed on April 14, 2015.

158. "A Look at the Gaza War and the Ceasefire Halting It," Associated Press, August 27, 2014, http://bigstory.ap.org/article/look-gaza-war-and-cease-fire-halting-it?utm_source=feedburner&utm_medium=feed&utm_campaign=Feed%3A+imeu+%28IMEU+%3A+Institute+for+Middle+East+Understanding%29; Ben Hartman, "50 Days of Israel's Gaza Operation, Protective Edge—by the Numbers," *Jerusalem Post*, August 28, 2014, http://www.jpost.com/Operation-Protective-Edge/50-days-of-Israels-Gaza-operation-Protective-Edge-by-the-numbers-372574.

159. United Nations Office for the Coordination of Humanitarian Affairs, "Gaza Emergency Situation Report" http://www.ochaopt.org/content.aspx?id=1010361, accessed on April 14, 2015; "Assessing the Damage and Destruction in Gaza," *New York Times*, August 14, 2014, http://www.nytimes.com/interactive/2014/08/03/world/middleeast/assessing-the-damage-and-destruction-in-gaza.html?ref=world.

160. Associated Press, "Housing Group: 20 Years to Rebuild Gaza After Fighting with Israel," *Haaretz*, August 30, 2014, http://www.haaretz.com/news/diplomacy-defense/1.613194.

161. United Nations Office for the Coordination of Humanitarian Affairs, "Occupied Palestinian Territory: Gaza Emergency: Situation Report (as of 25 August 2014, 08:00 hrs)"; "Assessing the Damage and Destruction in Gaza," *New York Times*, August 15, 2014. www.ochaopt.org/documents/ocha_opt_sitrep_25_08_2014.pdf. OCHA, "Occupied Palestinian Territory: Gaza Emergency Situtation Reports," August 22–25, 2014.

162. Associated Press, "Housing Group: 20 Years to Rebuild Gaza After Fighting with Israel."

163. "Egypt and Gaza: No Longer a True Mediator," *Economist*, July 23, 2014, http://www.economist.com/blogs/pomegranate/2014/07/egypt-and-gaza.

164. Yoel Marcus, "See You in the Next Round," *Haaretz*, August 15, 2014, http://www.haaretz.com/news/video/.premium-1.612800; "Is Gaza War Really Over?" *Haaretz*, August 27, 2014, http://www.haaretz.com/opinion/.premium-1.610657.

165. United Nations Office for the Coordination of Humanitarian Affairs, "Occupied Palestinian Territory: Gaza Emergency: Situation Report Covering the Period from 28 August (08:00 hrs) to 4 September 2014 (08:00 hrs)," http://www.ochaopt.org/documents/ocha_opt_sitrep_04_09_2014.pdf.

166. Amos Harel, "Hamas' Terror Tunnels—A National Strategic Failure for Israel," *Haaretz*, July 22, 2014, http://www.haaretz.com/news/diplomacy-defense/.premium-1.606510; Isabel Kershner, "In Tunnel War, Israeli Playbook Offers Few Ideas," *New York Times*, August 1, 2014, http://www.nytimes.com/2014/08/02/world/middleeast/an-old-playbook-leaves-israel-unready-for-hamass-tunnel-war-.html?ref=world; Avi Bar-Eli, "Millions Down the Tunnel: How Israel Botched the Battle Against Hamas," *Haaretz*, July 21, 2014, http://www.haaretz.com/business/.premium-1.606434; Amos Harel, "The Summer Israel's Security Bubble Wrap Burst," *Haaretz*, August 29, 2014, http://www.haaretz.com/news/diplomacy-defense/1.613053.

167. Jack Khoury, "Meshal: Hamas Will Go Back to War Against Israel If Upcoming Truce Talks Fail," *Haaretz*, August 28, 2014, http://www.haaretz.com/news/diplomacy-defense/.premium-1.613015. See also Palestinian Center for Policy and Survey Research, "Special Gaza War Poll: 26–30 August 2014."

168. Jodi Rudoren, "In Gaza, Grief, Anger—and No Small Measure of Pride," *New York Times*, August 10, 2014, http://www.nytimes.com/2014/08/11/world/middleeast/gaza-strip

-palestinians-are-exhausted-but-hold-on-to-hope-war-brings-change.html?hp&action=click&pgtype=Homepage&version=HpSum&module=first-column-region®ion=top-news&WT.nav=top-news&_r=0.

169. Daniel Estrin (Associated Press), "After 50-Day Gaza War with Israel, Poll Shows Dramatic Rise in Palestinian Support for Hamas," *U.S. News & World Report*, September 2, 2014, http://www.usnews.com/news/world/articles/2014/09/02/after-gaza-war-poll-finds-support-for-hamas-rises.

170. Palestinian Center for Policy and Survey Research, "Special Gaza War Poll: 26–30 August 2014": "79% believe that Hamas has won the Gaza War. . . . 79% believe Israel was responsible for the eruption of the Gaza War. . . . 63% believe that the ceasefire agreement satisfies Palestinian interests, but 34% disagree with that. Moreover, 59% are satisfied with the accomplishment gained in the agreement compared to the human and material losses sustained by the Gaza Strip. . . . 39% are dissatisfied with the accomplishment. An overwhelming majority of 86% support the launching of rockets from the Gaza Strip at Israel if the siege and blockade are not ended. 60% say that Hamas does not launch rockets from populated areas, but 30% say it does. 49% think it is justified for Hamas to launch rockets from populated areas and 46% disagree with that. Percentage of those who believe that launching rockets from populated areas is unjustified increases to 59% among Gazans while standing at 38% among West Bankers. Only 30% believe that Hamas should warn Israeli civilians in the specific targeted areas before launching its rockets; 68% believe it should not do so. 57% oppose disarming armed groups in the Gaza Strip while 25% support such a measure after the ending of the siege and the conduct of elections; 13% support this measure but only after reaching a peace agreement with Israel. In our June 2014 poll, only 33% said it opposed disarming and dissolving armed groups in the Gaza Strip. . . . Moreover, only 25% describe Egypt's role in the ceasefire negotiations as positive while a majority of 52% describe it as negative and 22% as neutral. 94% are satisfied with Hamas' military performance in confronting Israeli forces; 78% are satisfied with its defense of civilians in Gaza; and 89% are satisfied with its media and communication performance." Estrin, "After 50-Day Gaza War with Israel, Poll Shows Dramatic Rise in Palestinian Support for Hamas."

171. Sixty percent said they felt personally more unsafe; just 19 percent felt more secure; a majority felt the war would resume within a year, 37 percent within six months. Gil Hoffman, "Polls—Israelis Unhappy with Truce, Feel Less Secure Than Before Gaza Operation," *Jerusalem Post*, August 28, 2014, http://www.jpost.com/Israel-News/Politics-And-Diplomacy/Protective-Edge-began-with-huge-support-ended-with-Israel-shamed-and-confused-says-Likud-MK-372472.

172. Daniel Ben Simon, "Why Israelis Saw the Gaza War Differently," *Al-Monitor*, August 29, 2014, http://www.al-monitor.com/pulse/originals/2014/08/israeli-society-gaza-war-idf-soldiers-solidarity-protest.html.

173. Only 29 percent of Jewish Israelis felt Israel had defeated Hamas; 27 percent felt that it had not. Seventy-five percent wanted to see Hamas toppled. Gil Hoffman, "Poll: 86.5% of Israelis Oppose Cease-fire," *Jerusalem Post*, July 28, 2014, http://www.jpost.com/Operation-Protective-Edge/Poll-865-percent-of-Israelis-oppose-cease-fire-369064; Joshua Mitnick, "Israelis Frustrated with Outcome of Gaza Conflict," *Wall Street Journal*, August 29, 2014, http://online.wsj.com/articles/israelis-frustrated-with-outcome-of-gaza-conflict-140934848; Gil Hoffman, "Polls—Israelis Unhappy with Truce, Feel Less Secure Than Before Gaza Operation," *Jerusalem Post*, August 28, 2014, http://www.jpost.com/Israel-News/Politics-And-Diplomacy/Protective-Edge-began-with-huge-support-ended-with-Israel-shamed-and-confused-says-Likud-MK-372472.

174. Ibid.

175. Asher Schechter, "Israel's Terrifying Descent into Numbness," *Haaretz*, August 4, 2014, http://www.haaretz.com/news/diplomacy-defense/.premium-1.608690. "While it remains to be seen if the operation makes Israelis any safer, we can already discern one legacy. It seems to have brought Israel one step closer to an emotional numbness that blocks out any suffering but our own, as attested by a new, violent voice in the public discourse."

Although Western television viewers were seeing daily scenes of carnage in Gaza, hearing accusations that the IDF was targeting UN facilities, and learning of the horrific numbers of Palestinian casualties, less than 4 percent of Israeli Jews thought the IDF was using excessive firepower in Gaza, according to a poll taken by the Israel Democracy Institute and Tel Aviv University on July 14, 16–17, and 23. Moreover, 95 percent of Jewish Israelis believed Operation Protective Edge was just. On a scale where 1 was very poor and 10 was excellent, Israeli Jews gave the behavior of the Israeli Jewish public on average a grade of 8.9; they gave the behavior of the Palestinian Israelis on average a grade of 4. Israeli Jews supported agreeing to a cease-fire only after an agreement on the conditions for "sustaining quiet" was reached (64 percent, 60 percent, and 56 percent; the result of three consecutive surveys). Ya'ar and Hermann, The Israel Democracy Institute, press release regarding "July 2014 Peace Index," http://en.idi.org.il/about-idi/news-and-updates/july-2014-peace-index/.

176. Palestinian Center for Policy and Survey Research, "Special Gaza War Poll: 26–30 August 2014." Eighty-six percent support the launching of rockets from the Gaza Strip at Israel if the siege and blockade are not ended.

177. Raphael Ahren, "Netanyahu Lays Out Israeli Case for Morality of Gaza Campaign," *Times of Israel*, August 6, 2014, http://www.timesofisrael.com/netanyahu-lays-out-case-for-legality-of-gaza-campaign/.

178. For the July Israel Democracy Institute poll, when asked to score on a scale of 1 to 10, where 1 was very poor and 10 was excellent, Jewish Israelis rated the behavior of Israeli Jews at 8.9, 8.2, 8.7; they rated Arab Israelis at 4.0, 3.4, 3.4. In the August poll, 44 percent of Israeli Jews said Operation Protective Edge had achieved all or most of its goals; 48 percent said it had achieved some. In contrast, 64 percent of the Arab public said it had not achieved any, 13 percent said it had achieved all, and 13% said it had achieved some. As regards satisfaction with the outcome, 32 percent of Israeli Jews were satisfied with the outcome, 41 percent were neither satisfied nor dissatisfied, 27 percent were dissatisfied. Among the Arab public, 64 percent were dissatisfied with the outcome, 18 percent neither satisfied nor dissatisfied, and 8 percent satisfied. On unity among Jewish Israelis during the conflict, Israeli Jews rated themselves at 9.0; Israelis Arabs rated them at 4.3. Seventy-one percent of Israeli Jews and 49 percent of Israeli Arabs thought chances were low that Operation Protective Edge would lead to three years or more of complete quiet from Gaza. Twenty-five percent of Israeli Jews and 38 percent of Israeli Arabs thought chances for complete quiet of at least three years was high. Ya'ar and Hermann, "July 2014 Peace Index"; Ya'ar and Hermann, The Israel Democracy Institute, "August 2014 Peace Index."

179. "Report: US Halted Weapons Transfer to Israel During Gaza Offensive," *Jerusalem Post*, August 14, 2014, http://www.jpost.com/Diplomacy-and-Politics/Report-US-halted-weapons-transfer-to-Israel-during-Gaza-offensive-371062; *Times of Israel* staff and Rebecca Shimoni Stoil, "Hold Up of US Missile Shipment to Israel Reportedly Resolved," *Times of Israel*, August 21, 2014, http://www.timesofisrael.com/hold-up-of-us-missile-shipment-to-israel-reportedly-resolved/#ixzz3DDnxN0DQ.

180. Pew Research, "As Mideast Violence Continues, a Wide Partisan Gap in Israel-Palestinian Sympathies," *People Press*, July 15, 2014, http://www.people-press.org/2014/07/15/as-mideast-violence-continues-a-wide-partisan-gap-in-israel-palestinian-sympathies/.

In July 2014, 51 percent of Americans sympathized more with Israel. Fourteen percent sympathized more with the Palestinians, while 15 percent sympathized with neither side. These views were little changed from an April Pew poll. "The share of Republicans who sympathize more with Israel has risen from 68 percent to 73 percent; 44 percent of Democrats express more sympathy for Israel than the Palestinians," compared with 46 percent in April. "The share of independents siding more with Israel than the Palestinians slipped from 51 percent to 45 percent. Just 17 percent of Democrats, 17 percent of independents, and 6 percent of Republicans sympathized more with the Palestinians than Israel." Over-65s backed Israel over the Palestinians by nearly seven to one. Among young adults aged 18 to 29, however, that support was two to one in favor of Israel. Chris McGreal, "Relations Are Strained over Gaza but US Support for Israel Remains Strong," *Guardian*, August 10, 2014, http://www.theguardian.com/world/2014/aug/10/united-states-israel-strained-relations-gaza.

181. "Netanyahu: Gaza Conflict Proves Israel Can't Relinquish Control of West Bank," *Times of Israel*, July 11, 2014, http://www.timesofisrael.com/netanyahu-gaza-conflict-proves-israel-cant-relinquish-control-of-west-bank/.

182. Jack Khoury, "Meshal: Hamas Will Go Back to War Against Israel If Upcoming Truce Talks Fail," *Haaretz*, August 28, 2014, http://www.haaretz.com/news/diplomacy-defense/.premium-1.613015.

183. Hamas cited the suffering Gazans had endured as its reason for agreeing to the monthlong cease-fire in late August 2014.

184. Amos Harel, "As Gaza War Winds Down, War over Narrative Begins," *Haaretz*, August 4, 2014, http://www.haaretz.com/news/diplomacy-defense/.premium-1.608739; Spencer Ho, "Ceasefire Sparks Storm of Criticism Against Netanyahu," *Times of Israel*, August 27, 2014, http://www.timesofisrael.com/ceasefire-sparks-storm-of-criticism-against-netanyahu/.

185. Rasha Abou Jalal, "Gazans Reject Israel's Calls to Disarm," *Al-Monitor*, September 2, 2014, http://www.al-monitor.com/pulse/originals/2014/09/disarming-gaza-resistance-after-end-israel-occupation.html. *Al-Monitor* quotes from what it called an "unprecedented" statement made by Abbas Zaki, a member of Fatah's Central Committee, to the television channel Al Mayadeen on August 14: "The Palestinian leadership has agreed that disarming the resistance is [akin to] betrayal," http://www.almayadeen.net/ar/news/palestine-nq1aawdIbEy5gqOHAPk9Wg/.

186. Itamar Sharon, "Cabinet Told Purging Gaza of Terror Would Take 5 Years, Cost Hundreds of Soldiers' Lives," *Times of Israel*, August 6, 2014, http://www.timesofisrael.com/purging-gaza-of-terror-would-take-5-years-cabinet-was-told/; Amir Oren, "Mohammed Deif's Mole in Jerusalem," *Haaretz*, August 17, 2014, http://www.haaretz.com/opinion/.premium-1.610878; "Israel Will Not Move on Demilitarization," *Haaretz*, Operation Protective Edge, Day 31, August 8, 2014, http://www.haaretz.com/news/diplomacy-defense/1.609323.

187. Nasser Chararah, "Gaza War Brings Hamas, Hezbollah Closer," *Al-Monitor*, August 8, 2014, http://www.al-monitor.com/pulse/originals/2014/08/hamas-hezbollah-relations-meshaal-normalization.html; Nasser Chararah, "Hezbollah, Hamas Repair Political Ties During Breakup," *Al-Monitor*, July 24, 2014, http://www.al-monitor.com/pulse/originals/2014/07/hezbollah-hamas-repair-ties.html; Adnan Abu Amer, "Iran, Hezbollah Break with Assad to Support Hamas," *Al-Monitor*, July 25, 2014, http://www.al-monitor.com/pulse/originals/2014/07/nasralla-relation-renewed-hamas.html. An example of the PASF's antipathy toward Hamas: Barak Ravid and Jack Khoury, "PA Security Questions Salam Fayyad's Aid NGO over Campaign to Help Gazans," *Haaretz*, August 26, 2014, http://www.haaretz.com/news/diplomacy-defense/.premium-1.612458.

188. Jonathan Lis, "Both Right and Left Blast Israel's Unilateral Gaza Pullout," *Haaretz*, August 3, 2014, http://www.haaretz.com/news/national/.premium-1.608689 ("Hamas has not been defeated and the countdown to the next round of fighting has already begun, one critic says"); Yoel Marcus, "See You in the Next Round," *Haaretz*, August 15, 2014, http://www.haaretz.com/opinion/.premium-1.610657.

189. Marten, "Militia Patronage vs. the Diffusion of Professionalism."

190. COGAT—Coordination of Government Activities in the Territories—"is responsible for implementing the government's policy in Judea and Samaria and vis-à-vis the Gaza Strip. In addition, COGAT constitutes the civilian authority for residential zoning and infrastructure and is responsible for addressing the needs of Israeli settlements in the West Bank," http://www.cogat.idf.il/894-en/Matpash.aspx.

191. International Crisis Group, "Squaring the Circle: Palestinian Security Reform under Occupation," Middle East Report No. 98, September 7, 2010, http://www.crisisgroup.org/en/regions/middle-east-north-africa/israel-palestine/98-squaring-the-circle-palestinian-security-reform-under-occupation.aspx.

192. Charles Levinson, "Palestinian Support Wanes for American-Trained Forces," *Wall Street Journal*, October 15, 2009, http://online.wsj.com/news/articles/SB125547035200183335.

193. Benny Morris, "We Must Finish Off Hamas—Next Time," *Haaretz*, July 30, 2014, http://www.haaretz.com/opinion/.premium-1.607984.

194. Ibid. "The Israeli government must prepare both the Israeli people and its allies for the next round against Hamas, and be prepared to deliver the killer blow."

195. Isabel Kershner, "In Tunnel War, Israeli Playbook Offers Few Ideas," *New York Times*, August 1, 2014, http://www.nytimes.com/2014/08/02/world/middleeast/an-old-playbook-leaves-israel-unready-for-hamass-tunnel-war-.html?_r=0.

196. Martin Melaugh, "Violence: Membership and Arsenals of Paramilitary Groups," in "Security Forces in the Troubles," *BBC History*, February 2013, http://www.bbc.co.uk/history/topics/troubles_security_forces. Before the Troubles, the number of RUC members was at a constant of around 3,500. During the 1970s, this figure rose to 8,500—the second-largest police force in the UK after the London Metropolitan Police. When the RUC was replaced by the Police Service of Northern Ireland in 2001, the number of serving officers stood at 8,450.

At its inception the UDR had a membership of around 6,000, which rose to 10,000 in 1972. Between 1985 and 1994, there were roughly 3,000 part-time and 3,000 full-time members. In 1972 there were 27,000 British army servicemen in Northern Ireland (1,000 more soldiers than Britain deployed to the invasion of Iraq in 2003). By the time of the cease-fire, this had been reduced to 17,000. Since 2007, when Operation Banner was concluded, only 5,000 troops remain in Northern Ireland for training purposes. Vincent Kearney, "Security Forces in the Troubles," *BBC History*, February 2013, http://www.bbc.co.uk/history/topics/troubles_security_forces. Martin Melaugh, Fionnuala McKenna, and Brendan Lynn, "Background Information on Northern Ireland Society: Security and Defence," CAIN Web Service, http://cain.ulst.ac.uk/ni/security.htm.

197. Noam Sheizaf, "This Is Netanyahu's Final Status Solution," *+972*, August 4, 2014, http://972mag.com/this-is-netanyahus-final-status-solution/94938/; Roger Cohen, "Israel's Bloody Status Quo," *New York Times*, July 14, 2014, http://www.nytimes.com/2014/07/15/opinion/roger-cohen-israels-bloody-status-quo.html?hp&action=click&pgtype=Homepage&module=c-column-top-span-region®ion=c-column-top-span-region&WT.nav=c-column-top-span-region&_r=0.

198. Avishai Margalit, "The Suicide Bombers," *New York Review of Books*, January 16, 2003, http://www.nybooks.com/articles/archives/2003/jan/16/the-suicide-bombers/.

199. Gideon Levy and Alex Levac, "'Israel Has Stolen Gaza's Future, and Its Hope,'" *Haaretz*, July 2, 2014, http://www.haaretz.com/weekend/twilight-zone/.premium-1.608239.

200. Michael Herzog, interview with the author, February 28, 2012.

201. Akiva Eldar, "Bibi Uses Gaza as Wedge Between Abbas and Hamas," *Al-Monitor*, September 1, 2014, http://www.al-monitor.com/pulse/originals/2014/09/israel-netanyahu-abbas-gaza-war-disengagement-sharon.html.

Chapter 6 **Refugees and Right of Return**

1. United Nations Conciliation Commission, "Final Report of the United Nations Economic Survey Mission for the Middle East," December 28, 1949, UN Doc. A/AC.25/6/Part.1, 21; Morris, *Birth of the Palestinian Refugee Problem, 1947–1949*, 297–98; official UN estimates put the number at 750,000; Khalidi, *Iron Cage*, 225n2; see also Pappé, *Ethnic Cleansing of Palestine*.

2. Pappé, *Ethnic Cleansing of Palestine*, xiii.

3. "The Partition Plan: Background and Overview," September 1947, *Jewish Virtual Library*, http://www.jewishvirtuallibrary.org/jsource/History/partition_plan.html. Text of the Partition Plan may be found in United Nations General Assembly, "Resolution 181 (II): Future Government of Palestine," November 29, 1947, UN Doc. A/RES/181(II), http://unispal.un.org/unispal.nsf/0/7F0AF2BD897689B785256C330061D253.

4. Resolution 194 states: "[T]he refugees wishing to return to their homes and live at peace with their neighbours should be permitted to do so at the earliest practicable date, and . . . compensation should be paid for the property of those choosing not to return and for loss of or damage to property which, under principles of international law or in equity, should be made good by the Governments or authorities responsible." Resolution 194 has been reaffirmed by the UN more than 110 times since its introduction in 1948, with universal consensus except for Israel and the United States. This resolution was further clarified by UN General Assembly Resolution 3236, subsection 2, which "reaffirms also the inalienable right of Palestinians to return to their homes and property from which they have been displaced and uprooted, and calls for their return." "Factsheet on Palestinian Refugees: The Right to Return, a Basic Right Still Denied," Al-Awda, October 8, 2012, http://www.al-awda.org/facts.html.

5. Morris, *Birth of the Palestinian Refugee Problem*, 62–65. For an in-depth examination of Plan Dalet (also called Plan D), see Pappé, *Ethnic Cleansing of Palestine*, 126.

6. See Palestinian Central Bureau of Statistics, "On the 66th Anniversary of the Palestinian Nakba," May 12, 2014, http://www.pcbs.gov.ps/site/512/default.aspx?tabID=512&lang=en&ItemID=1111&mid=3171&wversion=Staging.

7. Pappé, *Ethnic Cleansing of Palestine*, 37–126.

8. Anita Shapira, *Ben Gurion: Father of Modern Israel* (New Haven: Yale University Press, 2014), translated from the Hebrew by Anthony Berris, 1-42.

9. O'Brien, *Siege*, 225.

10. "The Jewish Coercion Administration," *Haaretz*, May 22, 2013, http://www.haaretz.com/opinion/the-jewish-coercion-administration-1.525281.

11. Quoted in O'Brien, *Siege*, 130.

12. Law of Return Act (1950), found at Israel Ministry of Foreign Affairs, http://www.mfa.gov.il/mfa/mfa-archive/1950-1959/pages/law%20of%20return%205710-1950.aspx;

Israeli Nationality Act (1952), found at Israel Law Resource Center, http://www.israellawresourcecenter.org/israellaws/fulltext/nationalitylaw.htm.

13. Reactivation of the Defence (Emergency) Regulations, Law and Administration Ordinance (Amendment) Law (1948), Article 125 of the Defence (Emergency) Regulations; Absentees' Property Law, 5710-1950, which replaced Emergency Regulations (Absentees' Property) Law, 5709-1948 (December), Emergency Regulations (Requisition of Property) Law, 5709-1949; Land Acquisition Law (1953); Prescription Law, 5718-1958; Land (Settlement of Title) Ordinance; Land Acquisition (Validation of Acts and Compensation) Law (1953), Ordinance (Amendment) Law, 5720-1960; Land (Settlement of Title) Ordinance (New Version), 5729-1969, and the Land Law, 5729-1969; Prescription Law (1958), amended in 1965.

14. Segev, *1949: The First Israelis*, 68–91. For the text of the original 1950 Absentees' Property Law, see http://unispal.un.org/UNISPAL.NSF/0/E0B719E95E3B494885256F9A005AB90A.

15. In 2013 there was a battle in Israel's Supreme Court over the 1950 absentee law. See Yonah Jeremy Bob, "A-G: Israel to Stop Using 1950 Law to Confiscate East Jerusalem Arab Properties for Jews," *Jerusalem Post*, August 28, 2013, http://www.jpost.com/National-News/AG-Israel-to-stop-using-1950-law-to-confiscate-east-Jerusalem-Arab-properties-for-Jews-324540.

16. Mark Fried, quoted in Marris, *Loss and Change*, 43.

17. Israel Ministry of Foreign Affairs, "Aliyah," October 29, 2002, http://www.israel.org/MFA/MFA-Archive/2002/Pages/Aliyah.aspx.

18. Joseph Ginat and Edward J. Perkins, *The Palestinian Refugees: Old Problems—New Solutions* (Brighton: Sussex Academic Press, 2001), 93.

19. David Rosenberg, "Israeli Exceptionalism," *Jerusalem Post*, September 29, 2014, http://www.jpost.com/Magazine/Lifestyle/Israeli-exceptionalism; Jonathan Cook, "Israel's 'Exceptionalism' and the UN," Al Jazeera, November 18, 2013, http://www.aljazeera.com/indepth/features/2013/11/israel-exceptionalism-un-2013111710465371468.html; Stein, "The Holocaust, the Uncanny and the Jewish Sense of History"; Goldman, "The Vicissitudes of Jewish Exceptionalism"; Alam, "Israeli Exceptionalism"; Adesanmi, "'Nous les Colonisés,'" 35–58; Ami Kaufman, "Poll: 70% of Israeli Jews Believe Jews Are 'Chosen People,'" +972, January 27, 2012, http://972mag.com/poll-shows-israel-slowly-but-surely-turning-into-a-theocracy/33989/; David N. Myers, "Is There Still a 'Jerusalem School'? Reflections on the State of Jewish Historical Scholarship in Israel," *Jewish History* 23, no. 4 (December 2009), 389–406, doi: http://dx.doi.org/10.1007/s10835-009-9094-y; Joseph B. Maier, "Vico's View of Jewish Exceptionalism," in *Ethnicity, Identity, and History: Essays in Memory of Werner J. Cahnman*, ed. Joseph Maier and Chaim Isaac Waxman, 81–92 (New Brunswick: Transaction, 1983).

20. Weizmann, *Trial and Error*, 10–11.

21. Quoted in O'Brien, *Siege*, 679, from Jabotinsky's Russian-language newspaper, *Razsvyet*, November 11, 1923.

22. Lerner, *Embracing Israel/Palestine*, 255–90.

23. How the Palestinian definition differs from that of the UNRWA and others: "Today the total Palestinian refugee population is estimated at around 7.4 million (about 64 percent of the worldwide Palestinian population, making Palestinians the largest single group of refugees in the world). These refugees include: 5.3 million persons registered with the UNRWA; 335,000 internally displaced persons in Israel (from 1948) and their descendants; some 940,000 displaced persons from 1967; and over one million refugees who are not registered because of UNRWA's narrow definition of who is a Palestinian refugee: only persons whose normal place of residence was Palestine during the period 1 June 1946 to 15 May

1948 and who lost both home and means of livelihood as a result of the 1948 conflict" and who took refuge in Jordan, Lebanon, Syria, the Jordanian-ruled West Bank, or the Egyptian-administered Gaza Strip. This fourth category of refugees comprises those who fled to countries where the UNRWA does not operate, plus those who fled but were not in need of assistance, or missed the deadline to register. The majority of refugees live in the West Bank and Gaza (where they account for 44.2 percent of the total population)." "Endless Injustice: Palestinian Refugees 66 Years On," Palestinian Academic Society for the Study of International Affairs, http://www.passia.org/images/meetings/2014/may/Refugees_2014.pdf.

24. United Nations Relief and Works Agency for Palestine Refugees in the Near East, "In Figures: As of 1 January 2013," January 1, 2013, http://www.unrwa.org/sites/default/files/2013042435340.pdf.

25. Before the Syrian civil war, Palestinian refugees in Syria shared many of the characteristics of the indigenous population, according to a report issued by the Norwegian group Fafo in 2006. See Åge A. Tiltnes, *Human Capital*; Tiltnes, "Keeping Up: A Brief on the Living Conditions of Palestinian Refugees in Syria," Fafo Report 2007–13 (Oslo: Fafo Institute for Applied International Studies, 2007), http://www.fafo.no/pub/rapp/20013/20013.pdf. Palestinian refugees in Jordan are less integrated than their counterparts in Syria, according to Fafo. See Khawaja and Tiltnes, eds., "On the Margins."

26. The situation of Palestinian refugees in the Yamouk camp is one of the most horrific humanitarian disasters of the Syrian civil war; see "The Crisis in Yarmouk," United Nations Relief and Works Agency for Palestine Refugees in the Near East, http://www.unrwa.org/newsroom/emergency-reports/yarmouk-situation-update-15.

27. In 2010, "amendments to Lebanese law grant permits to Palestinians to work in the private sector, and provided them with some welfare benefits, and are an important step in the right direction," according to UNRWA, but many Palestinians say they fall short of what they had hoped for. "Lebanon: Palestinians Still Dissatisfied Despite Labour Law Changes," *IRIN*, August 30, 2010, http://www.irinnews.org/report/90327/lebanon-palestinians-still-dissatisfied-despite-labour-law-changes.

28. Lebanon is a parliamentary democracy that relies on the "confessionalism" form of electoral representation, in which certain religious and ethnic groups are allocated proportional standing based on their percentage in the population. Elections are structured according to the provisions of the Ta'if Agreement, reached in 1989 among former members of the 1972 Lebanese parliament after the Lebanese civil war (1975–89). It diminished the role of the state by transferring power away from the president to a cabinet composed of equal numbers of Christians and Muslims. Eleven religious groups within both Christian (Maronite, Greek Orthodox, Greek Catholic, Armenian Orthodox, Armenian Catholic, Protestant, other Christians) and Muslim (Sunni, Shi'ite, Alawite, Druze) faith traditions are accorded status, which often leads to gridlock. See "Lebanese MPs Fail to Pick New President," *Al Arabiya News*, April 23, 2014, http://english.alarabiya.net/en/News/middle-east/2014/04/23/Lebanon-parliament-to-vote-on-new-president-.html. For a concise description, see Imad Harb, "Lebanon's Confessionalism: Problems and Prospects," United States Institute of Peace, March 30, 2006, http://www.usip.org/publications/lebanons-confessionalism-problems-and-prospects.

29. Stephanie Nebehay, Reuters, "U.N.: Syrian Refugees, Sectarian Tensions Endanger Lebanon," *Al Arabiya News*, July 14, 2014, http://english.alarabiya.net/en/News/middle-east/2014/07/14/U-N-Syrian-refugees-sectarian-tensions-endanger-Lebanon-.html.

30. During a midsummer 2014 meeting in Beirut among Lebanese and UN officials and donor countries, Lebanese prime minister Tammam Salam called upon the international

community to step up and provide more help, as Lebanon could not deal with the burden of 1.12 million Syrian refugees on its own. According to the UN, 12,000 Syrian refugees have fled to Lebanon every week; at that rate, the influx would reach 1.6 million by the end of 2014. "We fear [tensions] will expand even further and not only result in Syrian-Lebanese interactions but also unfortunately raise the specter of Lebanese-Lebanese inter-sectarian problems," said Ross Mountain, the UN resident and humanitarian coordinator. Lebanon needs $1.6 billion in donor support, but as of July had received less than a quarter of that. See Stephanie Nebehey, "Syrian Refugees, Sectarian Tensions Endanger Lebanon: U.N.," Reuters, July 14, 2014, http://www.reuters.com/article/2014/07/14/us-syria-crisis-lebanon-un-idUSKBN0FJ1RJ20140714; Nohad Topalian, "Lebanon Pleas for Aid, As Syrian Refugee Crisis Deepens," *Al-Shorfa*, July 16, 2014, http://al-shorfa.com/en_GB/articles/meii/features/2014/07/16/feature-02; "Lebanon Cannot Bear the Brunt of the Syrian Crisis Alone, UN Relief Official Warns," UN News Centre, March 18, 2014, http://www.un.org/apps/news/story.asp?NewsID=47379#.U_4e9TJdVZE.

31. Michael Herzog, interview with the author, November 27, 2011. All quotes from Herzog in this chapter are from this interview unless otherwise noted.

32. Gilead Sher, interview with the author, October 26, 2011. All quotes from Sher in this chapter are from this interview unless otherwise noted.

33. See, for example, Thrall's observations in "Faith-Based Diplomacy."

34. Ian S. Lustick, "Negotiating the Truth: The Holocaust, Lehavdil, and Al-Nakba," *Journal of International Affairs* 60, no.1 (September 22, 2006), 51.

35. Rex Brynen, "The Past as Prelude?"

36. Dani Dayan, interview with the author, February 28, 2012. All quotes from Dayan in this chapter are from this interview unless otherwise noted.

37. A lot of media spin followed. See "The Palestine Papers: Abbas Admits Refugee Return 'Illogical,'" *Guardian*, January 24, 2011, http://www.theguardian.com/world/palestine-papers-documents/4507; Khaled Abu Toameh, "PA: Abbas Did Not Relinquish Right of Return," *Jerusalem Post*, November 3, 2012, http://www.jpost.com/Middle-East/PA-Abbas-did-not-relinquish-right-of-return.

38. Elhanan Miller, "Arab Street Lambastes Abbas for Moderate-Sounding Remarks," *Times of Israel*, November 4, 2012, http://www.timesofisrael.com/arab-street-lambastes-abbas-for-moderate-sounding-remarks.

39. Ibid.

40. Ibid.

41. Ibid. At Camp David, according to General Lipkin-Shahak, in the course of a conversation, Abu Mazen said, "I have an idea how to solve the refugee problem. Bring the refugees in buses to the old places, and they will see in their own eyes that there is nothing there that they can go back to. I was born in Safed. I went there, and I saw that Safed is no longer a place I recognized. It invalidated my memories. The fact is it will be the responsibility of the Palestinian leadership to tell their people, 'We have a Palestinian state, it is our homeland.'" General Lipkin-Shahak, interview with the author, October 23, 2011.

42. Muhammad Shtayyeh, interview with the author, October 29, 2011. All quotes from Shtayyeh in this chapter are from this interview unless otherwise noted.

43. The Peace of Westphalia comprised two 1648 peace treaties, signed in Osnabruck, Lower Saxony, and Munster, Westphalia, which marked the end of decades of religious wars throughout most of Europe: the Thirty Years' War in the Holy Roman Empire (1618–1648) and the Eighty Years' War between Spain and the Netherlands (1568–1648). The concept of Westphalia marked a transition from the medieval world of faith, politics, and continued warfare to the modern idea of a secular, sovereign state, serving as a foundation of world

politics for roughly 350 years. It also established a principle of nonintervention—"one risked both chaos and war if the barriers against intervention were lowered," writes J. Bryan Hehir—that came to serve as the basis of international law and diplomacy. However, contemporary policy makers and scholars such as Hehir write that the Westphalian concept of domestic sovereignty—and how the states should relate to each other in the world of war, power, and politics—"does not exist in a geopolitical vacuum . . . and must share the stage of history with other actors." For the past fifty years, bolstered by the collapse of the Cold War, the Westphalian legacy of state sovereignty has eroded, giving way to an increasingly interdependent international system. A combination of political, economic, ethnic, demographic, and environmental forces—including the challenges of a nuclear age—now directly affect a sovereign state's control of its destiny, policy, and politics. Therefore, Hehir says, "the wisdom of Westphalia" needs to be revised as "the appropriate response to a changing pattern of world politics." See "Treaty of Westphalia," The Avalon Project, Lillian Goldman Law Library, Yale Law School, http://avalon.law.yale.edu/17th_century/westphal.asp. See also Hehir, "Expanding Military Force"; Hehir, "Just War Theory," 237–57; Hehir, "Intervention," 1–13; and Hehir, "Military Intervention," 29–54.

44. O'Brien, *Siege*, 132–95.

45. Segev, *One Palestine Complete*, 402.

46. O'Brien, *Siege*, 224–37. See Jewish Virtual Library, "The Partition Plan: Background & Overview" (September 1947), http://www.jewishvirtuallibrary.org/jsource/History/partition_plan.html. According to the Jewish Virtual Library: "The Peel Commission in 1937 concluded [that] the only logical solution to resolving the contradictory aspirations of the Jews and Arabs was partition of Palestine into separate Jewish and Arab states. The Arabs rejected the plan because it would have forced them to accept the creation of a Jewish state and required some Palestinians to live under 'Jewish domination.' The Zionists opposed the Peel Plan's boundaries because they would have been confined to little more than a ghetto of 5,000 out of the 26,700 square kilometers [roughly 20 percent] remaining in Palestine. Nevertheless, the Zionists decided to negotiate with the British, while the Arabs refused to consider any compromises." According to the Palestinian Academic Society for the Study of International Affairs (PASSIA), *100 Years of Palestinian History* (2005), 57–58, "Ben-Gurion accepted the proposal after judging its shortcomings vis-à-vis Zionist territorial ambitions to be outweighed by the immense value of a non-Zionist plan which endorsed the concept of 'forced transfer.'" He wrote of the Peel Plan in his diary: "This will give us something we never had, even when we were under our own authority, neither in the period of the First Temple nor in the period of the Second Temple . . . forced transfer." See also Segev, *One Palestine*, 403–7.

47. Twenty years later, Ben Gurion wrote, "Had partition been carried out, the history of our people would have been different and six million Jews in Europe would not have been killed—most of them would be in Israel." Segev and others have pointed out the Jewish community in Palestine would not have been able to absorb millions of Jews. Segev, *One Palestine*, 414.

48. Among their most important publications are: Flapan, *Birth of Israel*; Segev, *1949*; Avi Schlaim, *Collusion Across the Jordan: King Abdullah, the Zionist Movement and the Partition of Palestine* (Oxford: Clarendon Press, 1988); Pappé, *Britain and the Arab-Israeli Conflict*; Pappé, *Making of the Arab-Israeli Conflict*; Pappé, *Ethnic Cleansing of Palestine*; Morris, *Birth of the Palestinian Refugee Problem*; Morris, *Righteous Victims*; and Benny Morris, *After: Israel and the Palestinians* (Oxford: Clarendon Press, 1990); Nur Masalha, *Expulsion of the Palestinians: The Concept of "Transfer" in Zionist Political Thought*, 1882-1948, Washington, DC, Institute for Palestine Studies, 1992; Shavit, *My Promised Land*; Cohen, *1929: Year Zero of the Jewish-Arab Conflict*.

49. Walid Khalidi, "Why Did the Palestinians Leave, Revisited," *Journal of Palestinian Studies* 34, no. 2 (2005), 42–54; Rosemarie Esber, "The 1948 Palestinian Arab Exodus from Haifa," *Arab World Geographer/Le Géographe du monde arabe* 6, no. 2 (2003), 112–41.

50. Sa'di, Afterword, in *Nakba: Palestine 1948 and the Claims of Memory*, eds., Ahmad H. Sa'di and Lila Abu-Lughod, quoting Morris, 298; Benny Morris, "Falsifying the Record: A Fresh Look at Zionist Documentation of 1948," *Journal of Palestinian Studies* 24, no. 3 (Spring 1995).

51. Chris McGreal, "Israelis Learn of a Hidden Shame in Its Early Years: Soldiers Raped and Killed Bedouin Girl in the Negev," *Guardian*, November 4, 2003, http://www.theguardian.com/world/2003/nov/04/israel1. See the Deir Yassin Remembered Web site, http://www.deiryassinremembered.org/#/the-story-of-deir-yassin/4571175003.

52. David Barak, "State Archives to Stay Classified for Twenty More Years, PM Instructs," *Haaretz*, July 29, 2010, http://www.haaretz.com/print-edition/news/state-archives-to-stay-classified-for-20-more-years-pm-instructs-1.304449.

53. Theodor Herzl, *The Complete Diaries of Theodor Herzl*, ed. Raphael Patai. New York: Herzl Press and Thomas Yoseloff, 1960. Chaim Simons, "A Historical Survey of Proposals to Transfer Arabs from Palestine, 1895-1947," http://www.archive.org/stream/AHistoricalSurveyOfProposalsToTransferArabsFromPalestine1895-1947/simons_djvu.txt; Theodor Herzl, handwritten diary, entry June 12, 1895 (CZA H ii B i); *The Complete Diaries of Theodor Herzl*, trans. Harry Zohn (New York, 1960) henceforth Herzl Diaries, vol. 1, 88; Theodor Herzl, *The Jewish State*, trans. Sylvie D'Avigdor (London, 1946), henceforth Herzl Jewish State, 30; Desmond Stewart, *Theodor Herzl* (London, 1974), 191-92. Herzl noted in his diary on June 12, 1895: "We must expropriate gently. We shall try and spirit the penniless population across the border by procuring employment for it in the transient countries, while denying any employment for it in our own country . . . Both the process of expropriation on the removal of the poor must be carried out discreetly and circumspectly." Quoted in Morris, "Revisiting the Palestinian Exodus of 1948," in Eugene Rogan and Avi Shlaim, eds, *The War for Palestine* (Cambridge University Press, 2007), 41.

54. See: O'Brien, *Siege*, 230. O'Brien quotes a letter Ben-Gurion wrote to his son at the time of the Peel Commission. Ben-Gurion wrote: "A . . . Jewish State in part of Palestine is not the end but the beginning. The establishment of such a Jewish State will serve as a means in our national efforts to redeem the country in its entirety." Camille H. Habib, *Consociationalism and the Continuous Crisis in the Lebanese System* (Beirut: Madj 2009), 85.

55. Benny Morris, "Revisiting the Palestinian Exodus of 1948," in Eugene Rogan and Avi Shlaim, eds., *The War for Palestine*, 37–56, http://communication.ucsd.edu/fields/comm158/Benny%20Morris%20Palestinian%20Exodus.pdf. In "Revisiting the Palestinian Exodus of 1948," Benny Morris quotes extensively from entries in Ben Gurion's diaries, especially an entry on 12 July 1937 and another entry on 20 July 1937, following publication of the Peel Commission's report, in which Ben Gurion expounded at length on the merits of population transfer as a way of achieving a "pure" Jewish state. He even advanced the idea publicly at the 20th Zionist Congress called in Zurich specifically to debate the Peel Commission's recommendations (although all references to it in his speech were deleted from the "official proceedings," as transfer was not an idea the Zionists were anxious to associate themselves with in the public arena). Nor was he alone. Weizmann was another proponent. Indeed, transfer was the prevalent view among leading Zionists. After reviewing new archival material, declassified after publication of *The Birth of the Palestinian Refugee Problem, 1947–1949*, Morris concluded, "Without doubt the crystallization of the consensus in support of transfer among the Zionist leaders helped to pave the way for the precipitation of the

Palestinian exodus in 1948." He also concluded after examining the newly declassified material that, "For good or ill, the newly opened material tends to reinforce the version of events of those who would stress the Yishuv's and Israel's part in the propulsion of the Palestinian Arabs out of the areas that became the State of Israel rather than those who would reduce Israel's responsibility for what happened," 38.

56. David Ben-Gurion, quoted in Khalidi, *Nakba*, 291–92. Acclaimed Jewish Israeli historian Anita Shapira writes in her biography, *Ben Gurion: Father of Modern Israel*, that "during Operation Danny, two Arab cities in the middle of the country were conquered, and their residents did not have time to flee. A brief uprising by the residents of Lydda (Lod) exposed the danger inherent in leaving a hostile population behind the advancing army, midway between Tel Aviv and Jerusalem. The commanders, Allon and Yitzhak Rabin, who were considering a large scale population evacuation, went to consult with Ben Gurion. At the end of the discussion, Ben Gurion waved his hand and said, according to Rabin: Expel them." Anita Shapira, *Ben Gurion: Father of Modern Israel*.

57. Adam Horowitz, "'We Must Expel Arabs and Take Their Place': Institute for Palestine Studies Publishes 1937 Ben-Gurion Letter Advocating the Expulsion of Palestinians," *Mondoweiss*, March 28, 2012, http://mondoweiss.net/2012/03/we-must-expel-arabs-and-take-their-place-institute-for-palestine-studies-publishes-1937-ben-gurion-letter-advocating-the-expulsion-of-palestinians.html.

See also Pappé's reference in note 4 to the preface of *The Ethnic Cleansing of Palestine*, which documents the various sources in IDF and Hagana archives and presents hard-to-refute evidence of what Plan Dalet was intended to achieve. Indeed, Pappé quotes from Leo Motzkin, regarded as one of Zionism's more liberal thinkers, who wrote in 1917, "Our thought is that the colonization of Palestine has to go in two directions: Jewish settlement in Eretz Israel and the settlement of Arabs in areas outside the country. The transfer of so many Arabs may seem at first unacceptable economically, but is nonetheless practical. It does not require too much money to resettle a Palestinian village on another land." Pappé, 7–8. And, if one were to look for icing on the cake, how better than to quote from former Prime Minister Menachem Begin, once leader of the Irgun, a terrorist militia, responsible for among other atrocities the bombing of the King David Hotel, wrote in *The Revolt*: "Arabs throughout the country, induced to believe wild tales of 'Irgun butchery' were seized with limitless panic, and started to flee for their lives. This mass flight soon developed into a maddened, uncontrolled stampede. Of the 800,000 who lived on the present territory of Israel, only some 165,000 are still there." Quoted in Pappé, *Ethnic Cleansing of Palestine*, 272n8.

58. Morris, *Birth of the Palestinian Refugee Problem*, 62–63.

59. Pappé, *Ethnic Cleansing of Palestine, 28.*

60. Ibid., 63.

61. Quoted in Masalha, *Palestinian Nakba*, 5–6.

62. Masalha, *Expulsion of the Palestinians.*

63. Shay Hazkani, "Catastrophic Thinking: Did Ben-Gurion Try to Rewrite History?" *Haaretz*, May 16, 2013, http://www.haaretz.com/weekend/magazine/catastrophic-thinking-did-ben-gurion-try-to-rewrite-history.premium-1.524308: "The file in the State Archives contains clear evidence that the researchers at the time did not paint the full picture of Israel's role in creating the refugee problem."

64. Efraim Karsh, "Rewriting Israel's History," *Middle East Quarterly* 3, no. 2 (June 1996), 19–29, http://www.meforum.org/302/rewriting-israels-history; Avi Shlaim, "The War of the Israeli Historians," *Annales* 59, no. 1 (January–February 2004), 161–67, http://users.ox.ac.uk/~ssfc0005/The%20War%20of%20the%20Israeli%20Historians.html.

65. While one poll suggests that a significant number of Israelis may believe that many Palestinians were expelled ("Study Surprisingly Finds 47% of Israeli-Jews Believe That the 1948 Palestinian Refugees Were Expelled by Israel," Teachers College, Columbia University, April 6, 2009, http://www.tc.columbia.edu/news.htm?articleID=6811), they will still stand by the official narrative. Moreover, there is no significant body of evidence that Israelis have, in fact, changed their attitudes—indeed, the preponderance of evidence still indicates otherwise—or whether, if they have, it has any bearing on their position either on accepting responsibility for the *Nakba* or on the right of return. Given the degree to which Israel has swung to the right since Annapolis, the Teachers College poll has to be read in the context of the time of its taking. In short, Israelis will not publicly deviate from their official narrative. See Halperin, Oren, and Bar-Tal, "Socio-Psychological Barriers to Resolving the Israeli-Palestinian Conflict."

66. O'Brien, *Siege*, 421–24.

67. Ibid.

68. Lustick, *Arabs in the Jewish State*, 66. He attributes the quote to Shmuel Divon, Ben-Gurion's second Arab affairs adviser.

69. Quoted in Jiryis, *Arabs in Israel*, 45.

70 The idea of "corporate rights" is related to "corporatism," a concept in political theory that applies to political systems comprising many and varied ethnic, ideological, economic, and social groups. With its Latin roots in *corpus*, meaning "body," the idea of "corporate rights" accrues to the "body politic" and a political system that advances certain ideals shared by all constituent "parts." There are many structural forms "corporatism" can take in politics, ranging from authoritative to cooperative, from centralized to defined social partners, or more pluralist. The concept has evolved, over centuries, and continues to, affecting different kinds of interest association, participation, and representation. Corporatism's essential feature is that it transcends formal politics and parties—it involves "standing" for certain groups, beyond parties—and offers a more holistic view of community, political, and economic well-being. In other words, state, society, and economic agents participate in political exchange and power relations. For more on corporatism, see Oscar Molina and Martin Rhodes, "Corporatism: The Past, Present, and Future of a Concept," *Annual Review of Political Science* 5, no. 1 (2002), 305–31, doi. 0.1146/annurev.polisci.5.112701.184858. For background on the evolution of corporatism within an Israeli context, see Guy Mundlak, "Addressing the Legitimacy Gap in the Israeli Corporatist Revival," *British Journal of Industrial Relations* 47, no. 4 (December 2009), 765–87, doi: 10.1111/j.1467-8543.2009.00754.x. For more on the history of the Palestinian-Israeli interpretation, see Grinberg, *Split Corporatism in Israel*.

71. National Committee for the Heads of the Arab Local Authorities in Israel, "The Future Vision of the Palestinian Arabs in Israel"; see also "Haifa Declaration," Alternatives International, http://www.alterinter.org/spip.php?article855. In the declaration, Palestinians are defined as "the original inhabitants"—a "homeland minority" in the place where Jewish Israelis claim ownership.

72. See Lieberman's statements about population transfer and polls: "Might They Want to Join Palestine? Avigdor Lieberman's Radical Ideas for Population Transfers Are Gaining Ground," *Economist*, January 18, 2014, http://www.economist.com/news/middle-east-and-africa/21594353-avigdor-liebermans-radical-ideas-population-transfers-are-gaining-ground-might; Stewart Winer, "Lieberman Defends His Population Transfer Plan," *Times of Israel*, January 8, 2014, http://www.timesofisrael.com/liberman-defends-his-population-transfer-plan/; Peter Beaumont, "Plan to Transfer Arab-Israelis to New Palestinian State

Seeks Legal Approval," *Guardian*, March 25, 2014, http://www.theguardian.com/world/2014/mar/25/transfer-arab-israeli-citizens-palestinian-state; Barak Ravid, "Lieberman Presents Plans for Population Exchange at UN," *Haaretz*, September 28, 2010, http://www.haaretz.com/news/diplomacy-defense/lieberman-presents-plans-for-population-exchange-at-un-1.316197; Alex Kane, "Palestinian Citizens Slam Lieberman's Support for Transfer," *Mondoweiss*, January 7, 2014, http://mondoweiss.net/2014/01/palestinian-citizens-liebermans.html.

73. Amnon Lipkin-Shahak, interview with the author, October 23, 2011. All quotes from Shahak in this chapter are from this interview unless otherwise noted.

74. Shahak, interview with the author. Herzog, interview with the author.

75. Data from the July 2014 Congressional Research Service records the following: Until the 1990s, Arab states made no contributions to UNRWA. Since then several have made "modest annual contributions toward UNRWA's core activities," although "Saudi Arabia, and Kuwait have given very generously to emergencies like Syria today, and Gaza and Lebanon in the past." The US accounts for 26 percent of UNRWA's budget; European countries for 56 percent; and Muslim countries in aggregate 9 percent. [A]ccording to Reuters, "a high of $1.8 billion in foreign aid in 2008 plunged to $600 million [in 2012]." The Arab League countries contributed approximately $443 million in 2007; that slipped to $429 million in 2013 and to $206 million in 2014. Jim Zanotti, "U.S. Foreign Aid to the Palestinians," Congressional Research Service, July 3, 2014, http://fas.org/sgp/crs/mideast/RS22967.pdf. See also Julie Stahl, "Arabs Not Honoring Financial Pledges to Palestinians," CNS News, July 29, 2008, http://cnsnews.com/news/article/arabs-not-honoring-financial-pledges-palestinians; Glenn Kessler, "Arab Aid to Palestinians Often Doesn't Fulfill Pledges," *Washington Post*, July 27, 2008, http://www.washingtonpost.com/wp-dyn/content/article/2008/07/26/AR2008072601797.html. In the course of my interview with then Prime Minister Saleh Fayyad, he told me that as the PA was experiencing once again a significant deficit shortfall, "We have been reducing our deficit. It's just that there have been in recent years, over the past two years, significant shortfalls in aid relative to commitments. That's where we find ourselves."

76. Udi Dekel, interview with the author, July 3, 2012. All quotes from Dekel in this chapter are from this interview unless otherwise noted.

77. Pini Meidan-Shani, interview with the author, October 5, 2011. All quotes from Meidan-Shani in this chapter are from this interview unless otherwise noted.

78. Yasser Arafat, "The Palestinian Vision of Peace," *New York Times*, February 3, 2002, http://www.nytimes.com/2002/02/03/opinion/the-palestinian-vision-of-peace.html.

79. Gilead Sher, interview with the author, June 26, 2012.

80. Framework for the conclusion of a final status agreement between Israel and the Palestine Liberation Organization: "The Beilin-Abu Mazen Document 31/10/1995," Reut Institute, http://www.reut-institute.org/data/uploads/ExternaDocuments/20050328%20-%20The%20Beilin-Abu%20Mazen%20Document.pdf.

81. Beilin, *Path to Geneva*, 169.

82. Nabil Sha'ath, interview with the author, October 18, 2011. All quotes from Sha'ath in this chapter are from this interview unless otherwise noted.

83. See "The Moratinos 'Non-Paper,'" BitterLemons, http://www.bitterlemons.org/docs/moratinos.html. See also Brynen, "The Past as Prelude?"

84. Bernard Avishai, "A Plan for Peace That Still Could Be," *New York Times Magazine*, February 7, 2011, http://www.nytimes.com/2011/02/13/magazine/13Israel-t.html?pagewanted=all&_r=1&. Ibid., regarding Olmert. For the Palestinian position, see "The Palestinian Papers and the Right of Return," Christians for Fair Witness on the Middle East, February 22, 2011, http://www.israelbehindthenews.com/library/pdfs/Palestine_Papers_Right_of_return

_memo.pdf: "While there have been claims in the media that the Palestinian Authority was willing to offer great compromises on refugees, the Papers reveal that this was not the case."

85. Tal Becker, interview with the author, February 13, 2012. All quotes from Becker in this chapter are from this interview unless otherwise noted.

86. The International Middle East Media Center (IMEMC) interpretation of Dr. Shikaki's PCPSR data, "Palestinian Survey Center: Only 10% of Refugees Will Choose To," IMEMC, http://www.imemc.org/article/6759. "Responding to how each will use his right to return; only 10% said that they are willing to return and live inside Israel. 31% expressed willingness to live in the future Palestinian state, 23% preferred to move to areas which will be provided by Israel in the suggested future swap of territories, 17% preferred to stay in their current country of residence, 13% rejected all suggested options, and 5% expressed no opinion. 23% of Palestinian refugees from Lebanon expressed interest in returning to live in Israel, 13% from West Bank and Gaza, and only 5% from Jordan. Dr. Shikaki said that the high percentage of Palestinian refugees in Lebanon who are willing to live in Israel could be explained by their close family ties with Palestinians currently residing inside Israel."

Dr. Shikaki, speaking with NPR radio host Robert Siegel, expanded on this: "The overwhelming majority wanted to live in a Palestinian state; only a small minority wanted to live in the state of Israel. That minority that wanted to have the state of Israel as the place of permanent residency was only 10 percent. But even in those 10 percent, only 10 percent of them wanted to have Israeli citizenship or Israeli passports. Ninety percent of those who wanted to have Israel as a permanent place of residence said that they would rather have a Palestinian citizenship and a Palestinian passport." See Robert Siegel, "Interview: Khalil Shikaki Discusses a New Poll on How Palestinian Refugees View the Right of Return," *All Things Considered*, *NPR*, July 14, 2003, http://www.npr.org/programs/atc/transcripts/2003/jul/030714.shikaki.html.

At the time of this writing, the Palestinian Center for Policy and Survey Research report, "Data Concerning Palestinian and Israeli Public Opinion on the Issue of the Palestinian Refugees and the Right of Return," was not available on the PCPSR Web site. A copy can be obtained, however, through Tel Aviv University, at http://spirit.tau.ac.il/socant/peace/psp/downloads/Symposium1E.doc, or Zochrot, at http://www.zochrot.org/en/content/poll-refugees-preferences-and-behavior-palestinian-israeli-permanent-refugee-agreement.

The report was, and remains, very controversial, igniting a frenzy around the right-of-return debate—so much so that about a hundred people stormed the press conference at which Dr. Shikaki announced the results and pelted him with eggs and wrecked his office. See Max Abrahms, "The 'Right of Return' Debate Revisited," Washington Institute, August–September 2003, http://www.washingtoninstitute.org/policy-analysis/view/the-right-of-return-debate-revisited, and "Palestinian 'Right of Return' Poll Sparks Mob Attack," *All Things Considered*, *NPR*, July 14, 2003. The latter appears alongside the aforementioned *NPR* interview with Dr. Shikaki.

87. When the results of Shikaki's 2003 poll were released, his office in Ramallah was stormed. Figures in a poll might say one thing, but they did not reflect embedded Palestinian wisdom. The poll's findings were outrageously out of sync with street sentiment. For results of the 2003 poll and subsequent controversy, see Abrahms, "The 'Right of Return' Debate Revisited"; Reuters, "Poll on Right of Return to Israel Provokes Furor," *Los Angeles Times*, July 14, 2003, http://articles.latimes.com/2003/jul/14/world/fg-mideast14.

88. Aumann, "Land Ownership in Palestine"; Reiter, "Family Waqf Endowment Entitlements," 173–93. Aumann makes the argument that "Until the passage of the Turkish Land Registry Law in 1858, there were no official deeds to attest to a man's legal title to a parcel of

land; tradition alone had to suffice to establish such title." Palestinians lived on land passed down through generations even though the property right was not recognized by any legal entity. Although they did not have legal deeds, property was transmitted through traditional "familial property" patterns. Islamic inheritance law pertaining to familial property imposes compulsory rules for the distribution of property.

89. "Half the territory . . . was registered during Ottoman times as state property and during the British Mandate as public lands divisible among all residents of the country." See Reiter and Lehrs, *Sheikh Jarrah Affair*, 44n118.

90. Reiter and Lehrs, *Sheikh Jarrah Affair*. This report provides a wealth of references regarding the use of symbols of heritage and holiness, proprietary and legal issues behind the displacement of Palestinian families, legal issues related to the properties in East and West Jerusalem, Jewish settlement in the heart of Arab neighborhoods in East Jerusalem, and the opening of the "1948 files" regarding restitution of Palestinian properties in West Jerusalem and Israel.

"Since the 1980s," they write, "the PLO has been collecting documentation about Arab property in West Jerusalem. In 1982 the PLO requested access to documents in the archives of the United Nations Conciliation Commission for Palestine (UNCCP). The commission, which was established by the UN in December 1948 in order to promote a peaceful resolution of the Israeli-Arab conflict, gathered documentation about Palestinian property within Israeli territory in two phases. The first phase, in 1951, involved a quick, preliminary survey of the scope of properties abandoned and their value on the basis of British Mandate maps and reports. During the second phase, beginning in 1952, the Technical Office of the Conciliation Commission undertook a more comprehensive effort, which continued until 1964. This project led to a report detailing the estimated value of Arab properties in Israeli territory, but most of the contents of this report have long remained concealed from the public. In the mid-1980s the PLO requested and received copies of this archival material, which was then filed with the PLO's Economic Division in Damascus. In the 1990s the PLO and the United Nations led a project for the preservation and computerization of the archival material, making it more accessible. . . . In the 1990s, in preparation for negotiations towards a final status agreement, the PLO began building a database of Palestinian properties in West Jerusalem. Two Palestinian institutions led the effort: The Institute for Research and Legal and Services on Issues on Land and Water and the Association for the Defense of Human Rights," pp. 47, 48.

91. See ibid., 44n11 and 119.

92. See Arnon and Bamya, eds., *The Arab Peace Initiative and Israeli-Palestinian Peace.* The original figures for refugee compensation appear in Arie Arnon and Saeb Bamya, eds., *Economic Dimensions of a Two-State Agreement Between Israel and Palestine* (Aix Group, November 2007), http://www.aixgroup.org/sites/default/files/publications_pdf/economic_dimensions_english_website%20%281%29.pdf.

93. Discussants at a December 2013 Chatham House workshop on the Palestinian refugee issue estimated refugee compensation costs at $30 billion to nearly $300 billion. Each of three working groups generated several scenarios, featuring lump-sum payments of $2,000 to $50,000 each, made to an estimated five million refugees. In addition, each of the working groups was asked to evaluate how well refugee compensation would be addressed by different funding levels: $3 billion to $5 billion; $20 billion; $10 billion to $50 billion; or unlimited funding. See: "Chatham House Working Group," *Palestinian Refugee Issue*.

94. Kubursi, "Palestinian Losses in 1948," 5–8.

95. Ibid, 27.

96. Ibid.

97. "Terms of Reference: Israel's Ability to Compensate Palestinian Refugees," "The Palestine Papers," Al Jazeera Investigations, http://www.ajtransparency.com/en/projects/thepalestinepapers/201218231237343868.html.

98. For Israel, an end of claims is embraced as part of the demand to close accounts arising from the *Nakba*, including UN Resolution 194. For Palestinians, an end of claims is promoted as a vehicle for realizing Palestinian demands for a just resolution to Palestinian losses—national, personal, and territorial—over the last seventy years. See Aronson, "A Never-Ending End to Claims," 266.

99. Oded Eran, interview with the author, June 25, 2012. All quotes from Eran in this chapter are from this interview unless otherwise noted.

100. See, for example, the various estimates from different sources cited by Michael Fischbach in *The Peace Process and Palestinian Refugee Claims: Addressing Claims for Property Compensation and Restitution* (Washington, DC: United States Institute of Peace, 2006). See also Thrall, "Israel and the US: The Delusions of Our Diplomacy," who refers to a 2003 survey that he says showed "that among those refugees willing to choose compensation instead of returning to Israel, 65 percent believed a fair amount would be $100,000–$500,000 per family. Prior to the Camp David negotiations in 2000, US officials estimated that a combined total of up to $20 billion might be available to Palestinian refugees and Jewish refugees from Arab countries, meaning that Palestinians could expect to receive no more than $1,000–$3,000 per refugee. All neglect how unacceptable their proposals are to refugees, whose support will be indispensable for a lasting agreement."

101. Among them was the Refugee Working Group, in which Canada played a leading role. Participation was open to any interested state. It met eight times in plenary sessions between 1992 and 1995, became largely dysfunctional in 1997, but has continued to conduct "lower-level work," addressing the immediate needs of refugees and exploring prospects for a mutually acceptable resolution of the refugee issue. A Continuing (or "Quadripartite") Committee was established in 1994 after the peace agreement between Israel and Jordan, with a remit to address issues relating to "displaced" persons, but it, too, became dysfunctional and stopped working in 2000. Provisions in the Oslo Accords relating to the refugee problem created by the exodus of Palestinians from the West Bank and Gaza during the Six-Day War were never implemented. The "Ottawa Process," involving Canada and the International Development Research Centre, has explored technical issues that would have to be resolved and engaged refugees themselves in forums to discuss possible futures. The Aix Working Team Group, which has examined the refugee issue, proposed an International Agency for the Palestinian Refugees (IAPR) in 2007, but there were no takers. See Arnon et al., "Framework for Permanent Agreement," 14–17.

Chapter 7 **Settlers and Settlements**

1. Ahuva Balofsky, "Jewish Population in Judea & Samaria Growing Significantly," *Breaking Israeli News*, January 5, 2015, http://www.breakingisraelnews.com/26966/jewish-population-in-judea-and-samaria-growing-significantly/#UbkOjzyX7P6yPRDB.97.

2. Gorenberg, *Accidental Empire*, see pages 112–13 for the pithy and ambiguous conversations between charismatic settlers' movement leader Hanan Porat and Prime Minister Levi Eshkol, which resulted in the birth of the settlers' movement.

3. Ibid., 113.

4. Ibid.

5. The PA and PLO have upheld a boycott of municipal elections in East Jerusalem: "The PLO said the municipality supports settlements in east Jerusalem and is turning it into a

Jewish city, 'which is a national and political issue and not an issue of providing services.' 'Participating in these elections will be considered normalization with the Israeli occupation authority, which means legitimizing the annexation of Jerusalem,' read the statement. The call on Palestinians not to participate will certainly be heeded. In no previous elections have Palestinians in Jerusalem participated with numbers more than single digits." Daoud Kuttab, "Palestinians to Continue Boycott of Jerusalem Elections," *Al-Monitor*, October 11, 2013, http://www.al-monitor.com/pulse/originals/2013/10/jerusalem-municipal-election-palestinians.html#ixzz3144VcrV8.

6. PLO Negotiations Affairs Department, "East Jerusalem Today," August 2013, http://www.nad-plo.org/userfiles/file/Factsheet%202013/EJ%20TODAY_FINAL%20REPORT_II.pdf, 4. See also B'Tselem, "Statistics on Building Starts in East Jerusalem," January 1, 2012, http://www.btselem.org/jerusalem/building_starts_statistics; and Yehezkel Lein, *Land Grab: Israel's Settlement Policy in the West Bank*, B'Tselem.org, May 2002, http://www.btselem.org/sites/default/files/publication/200205_land_grab_eng.pdf.

7. United Nations Human Rights Council, "Report of the Independent International Fact-Finding Mission," 5. See also UN General Assembly, Sixty-eighth Session, Offical Records, Agenda Item 52, "Israeli Settlements in the Occupied Palestinian Territory, Including East Jerusalem, and the Occupied Syrian Golan," prepared by the Office of the United Nations High Commissioner for Human Rights pursuant to General Assembly Resolution 67/120, A/68/513, October 9, 2013, http://unispal.un.org/UNISPAL.NSF/0/0E780293F13D3AB785257C16004C5E78.

8. Akiva Eldar, "The Facts About Buying Land in Jerusalem's Latest Settlement," *Al-Monitor*, October 6, 2014, http://www.al-monitor.com/pulse/originals/2014/10/israeli-arabs-apartments-east-west-jerusalem-national-lands.html.

9. Tepe, *Beyond Sacred and Secular*, 11.

10. According to the Knesset Web site, "Gush Emunim [translated as 'Bloc of the Faithful'] was an extra-parliamentary national-religious movement advocating Israeli sovereignty in the Golan Heights, Gaza Strip, Judea, and Samaria by a massive civilian presence in these territories. For this purpose, the movement not only promoted settlement, but acted to promote education, social projects, immigrant absorption, and propaganda. Gush Emunim called for coexistence with the Arab population and negated the principle of transfer as advocated by Meir Kahane. Its ideological inspiration was derived from the teachings of Rabbi Zvi Yehuda Kook, according to which the purpose of the Jewish people is to gain physical and spiritual salvation through living in and developing Eretz Yisrael [the Land of Israel]; the sanctity of Eretz Yisrael obligates seizing it after it was freed from foreign rulers, and therefore it must be settled even against governmental policy." See http://www.knesset.gov.il/lexicon/eng/gush_em_eng.htm.

11. Mitch Ginsburg, "For Settler Ideologues, PM Is the Impious King Saul Failing to Follow the Divine Path," *Times of Israel*, June 6, 2012, http://www.timesofisrael.com/settlers-lead-flock-fails-to-follow/.

12. "In July 1977, Begin refused President Jimmy Carter's request to freeze settlement activity. At the time, there were about 50,000 Israelis living in annexed East Jerusalem, but only 7,000 settlers in forty-five civilian outposts in the West Bank and Gaza." Foundation for Middle East Peace, "Israeli Settlements in the Occupied Territories: A Guide," *Settlement Report* 12, no. 7 (March 2002), http://fmep.org/wp/wp-content/uploads/2015/01/12.7.pdf.

13. For background on the settlements, see B'Tselem, "Land Expropriation and Settlements," January 23, 2014, http://www.btselem.org/settlements.

14. Hareuveni, *By Hook and by Crook*, 9. See also A/36/341s/14566, June 19, 1981, "Letter dated 19 June 1981 from the Acting Chairman of the Committee on the Exercise of the

Inalienable Rights of the Palestinian People to the Secretary-General" (UNSC) regarding lands being seized for the purpose of establishing settlements and cutting off the Arab population in order to make it difficult for it to form a territorial and political continuity, http://unispal.un.org/UNISPAL.NSF/0/3E5D731750EEB69E8525696600663AD0.

15. Loan guarantees: U.S. Department of State, Office of the Historian, "Milestones: 1989–1992: The Madrid Conference, 1991," https://history.state.gov/milestones/1989-1992/madrid-conference. According to the U.S. Department of State site, "Between March and October 1991, Baker succeeded in getting Arab leaders and Palestinian representatives from the occupied territories to drop their demands that PLO officials and Palestinians from East Jerusalem participate in an international peace conference. Instead, the Arab parties agreed that the Palestinians would only be represented by delegates from the occupied territories, and as part of a joint Palestinian-Jordanian delegation. Simultaneously, Baker and Bush put pressure on Shamir to drop Israel's insistence on bilateral negotiations by withholding $10 billion in loan guarantees that he had requested to help settle Jewish immigrants from the Soviet Union. The President insisted that Shamir would have to promise that the funds would not be used to finance new settlement activity in the occupied territories. Shamir refused to accept Bush's demand, but it undoubtedly played a role in his decision to come to Madrid."

16. John M. Goshko, "Baker Firm on Guarantees as Mideast Talks Resume," *Tech* (MIT), February 25, 1992, http://tech.mit.edu/V112/N8/baker.08w.html.

17. Lein, "Land Grab." "The exceptions in the government's guidelines effectively became the main tool permitting the continued building of settlements and growth of the Israeli population in the settlements. According to the basic guidelines, 'Greater Jerusalem area' encompassed not only those areas annexed in 1967 and included in the municipal boundaries of the city but also considerable areas beyond these limits. In addition, during the term of the Rabin government, 9,850 new housing units were completed throughout the West Bank (not only in the government's priority areas). Construction of these units had begun under previous governments, though no mention of them is made in the government's basic guidelines."

18. Foundation for Middle East Peace, "Israeli Settler Population 1972–2006," http://www.fmep.org/settlement_info/settlement-info-and-tables/stats-data/israeli-settler-population-1972-2006.

19. Hareuveni, *By Hook and by Crook.*

20. Geoffrey Aronson, "The Settlers and the Army Are One," *Foundation for Middle East Peace* 22, no. 1 (January-February 2012), http://www.fmep.org/reports/archive/vol.-22/no.-1/the-settlers-and-the-army-are-one. "The settlements and the IDF, on the other hand, are locked in a symbiotic embrace. The army is duty bound to protect settlements and their residents and to promote their welfare—missions that preclude the effective protection of Palestinians and their property despite being mandated by international law. The mission of protecting settlements and settlers allows the IDF to be seen by Israelis (if not by Palestinians and the international community) as something other than a foreign army of occupation."

21. Lein, "Land Grab," 16. "Another method employed in order to expand the settlements was the seizure of a new location by a group of settlers who erected a number of caravans on the site. While this method was the settlers' initiative, without approval from the relevant authorities, the government generally refrained from evicting the settlers or demolishing the buildings they erected without permits. Some received retroactive approval. Overall, contrary to the expectations raised by the Oslo Process, the Israeli governments have implemented a policy leading to the dramatic growth of the settlements. Between September 1993, on the signing of the Declaration of Principles, and September 2001 (the time of the outbreak

of the al-Aqsa intifada), the number of housing units in the settlements in the West Bank (excluding East Jerusalem) and Gaza Strip rose from 20,400 to 31,400—an increase of approximately fifty-four percent in just seven years."

22. Ibid., 14. See also Zertal and Eldar, *Lords of the Land*, 56–67.

23. "For most of his life, Ariel Sharon was among the hardest of hard line Israelis," Benjamin Studebaker writes. "But late in his political career, Sharon came to the conclusion that if Israel was to survive as a Jewish state it would have to withdraw from most of the occupied territories and leave the Palestinians with enough land to create a viable state, i.e., he would have to evacuate tens of thousands of settlers, for many of whose settler status he was responsible in the first place. Hence his withdrawal from Gaza in 2005 and his intended withdrawal from large parts of the West Bank before he was felled by a stroke in 2007." Benjamin Studebaker, "The Legacy of Ariel Sharon," *Benjamin Studebaker* (blog), January 12, 2014, http://benjaminstudebaker.com/2014/01/12/the-legacy-of-ariel-sharon/. See also Henry Siegman, reviews of *The Accidental Empire* by Gershom Gorenberg and *Lords of the Land* by Idith Zertal and Akiva Eldar, *London Review of Books* 30, no. 7 (2008), 15–17, http://www.lrb.co.uk/v30/n07/henry-siegman/grab-more-hills-expand-the-territory; and Hammes, *Sling and the Stone*, 121.

24. See EN 9.

25. Lein, "Land Grab," 14.

26. Seth Freedman, "Israeli Military Gives Settlers Free Rein," *Guardian*, October 29, 2009, http://www.theguardian.com/commentisfree/belief/2009/oct/29/israeli-military-settlers-pdf; Zertal and Eldar, *Lords of the Land*, 287–331; "Israel's Policy of Arming Israeli Settlers Endangers Palestinians in the Territories," *Settlement Report* 4, no. 3 (May–June 1994), http://www.fmep.org/reports/archive/vol.-4/no.-3/israels-policy-of-arming-israeli-settlers-endangers-palestinians-in-the-territories.

27. Tzvi Ben Gedalyahu, "Who Fights More for the IDF, Settlers or Others?" *Arutz Sheva*, January 8, 2012, http://www.israelnationalnews.com/News/News.aspx/151500#.VA21F_ldXlg. "The rate of 'settlers' in IDF combat service is 80 percent higher than the country-wide rate, contrary to the image in mainstream media."

28. Drobles, "Settlement in Judea and Samaria."

29. See Neil MacFarquhar, "Israel Will Allow Settlers to Build," *New York Times*, August 3, 1996, http://www.nytimes.com/1996/08/03/world/israel-will-allow-settlers-to-build.html.

30. See Shalev, "Under the Guise of Legality," and Hareuveni, "By Hook and by Crook."

31. Zertal and Eldar, *Lords of the Land*, 44–79.

32. "Table III/10: Population of Jerusalem, by Age, Religion, and Geographic Spreading, 2011," *Statistical Yearbook of Jerusalem, 2013* (Jerusalem: Jerusalem Institute of Israel Studies, 2013), http://www.jiis.org.il/.upload/yearbook2013/shnaton_C1013.pdf. In September 2014, the "Jerusalem municipality has approved plans to build a Jewish religious school in the heart of occupied East Jerusalem." "Israel Approves Jewish Yeshiva in Heart of East Jerusalem," Ma'an News Agency, August 28, 2014, http://www.maannews.net/eng/ViewDetails.aspx?ID=724005.

33. Nick Cumming-Bruce and Isabel Kershner, "U.N. Panel Says Israeli Settlement Policy Violates Law," *New York Times*, January 31, 2013, http://www.nytimes.com/2013/02/01/world/middleeast/un-panel-says-israeli-settlement-policy-violates-law.html; United Nations Human Rights Council, "Report of the Independent International Fact-Finding Mission."

34. Uri Blau, "Secret Israeli Database Reveals Full Extent of Illegal Settlement," *Haaretz*, January 1, 2009, http://www.haaretz.com/secret-israeli-database-reveals-full-extent-of-illegal-settlement-1.266936.

35. Dror Etkes, *The Spiegel Database: An Analysis*, mondoweiss.net/files/dror-analysis.doc; Yesh Din Volunteers for Human Rights, "'Spiegel Database' *of West Bank Settlements and Outposts*," http://www.fmep.org/analysis/reference/SpiegelDatabaseEng.pdf.

36. Talya Sason, "Summary of the Opinion Concerning Unauthorized Outposts," Israel Ministry of Foreign Affairs, March 10, 2005, http://www.mfa.gov.il/mfa/aboutisrael/state/law/pages/summary%20of%20opinion%20concerning%20unauthorized%20outposts%20-%20talya%20sason%20adv.aspx.

37. The publication of *Our Harsh Logic: Israeli Soldiers' Testimonies from the Occupied Territories 2000–2010* did little to move public consciousness.

38. For the level of subsidies in the 2011–12 budget, see Akiva Eldar, "New State Budget Gives Settlements NIS 2 Billion—and More," *Haaretz*, December 31, 2010, http://www.haaretz.com/print-edition/news/new-state-budget-gives-settlements-nis-2-billion-and-more-1.334390. Other relevant data can be found in Ofran, "The Price of Maintaining the Territories"; and Peace Now, "Instead of Tax Hikes, Stop Indulging the Settlements," proposal, July 2012, http://settlementwatcheastjerusalem.files.wordpress.com/2012/07/peacenowsavingsplan.pdf. For information on how outposts are handled, see Communications Department, Israel Prime Minister's Office, "Summary of the Opinion Concerning Unauthorized Outposts," March 10, 2005, http://unispal.un.org/UNISPAL.NSF/0/956AA60F2A7BD6A185256FC0006305F4#sthash.XRztJ3nh.dpuf.

The Sason Report found that the Ministry of Housing and Construction created a special budgetary clause called "general development misc," which was used to finance unauthorized outposts. "In 2001 the amount in this section was 17 million shekels. . . . According to information the Ministry of Construction & Housing supplied (referring to a partial list it had been given), between 2000 and 2004 the Ministry has spent 71,870,000 on unauthorized outposts." A report from the Adva Center in September 2014 showed that "settlements have received a disproportionate amount of state funds over the past twenty years." Tali Heruti-Sover, "Report: Settlements Receive Disproportionate State Funding," *Haaretz*, September 9, 2014, http://www.haaretz.com/business/.premium-1.614765.

39. Heruti-Sover, "Report: Settlements Receive Disproportionate State Funding."

40. Roby Nathanson's Macro inventory of settlements and table documents on file, 2011, upon request from Dr. Nathanson.

41. Roby Nathanson, interview with the author, October 9, 2011. All quotes from Nathanson in this chapter are from this interview unless otherwise noted.

42. Joel Greenberg, "Construction Resumes in West Bank," *Washington Post*, September 28, 2010, http://www.washingtonpost.com/wp-dyn/content/article/2010/09/27/AR2010092706300.html.

43. Peace Now, "Settlements & the Netanyahu Government: A Deliberate Policy of Undermining the Two-State Solution," http://www.peacenow.org/images/Summary%20of%20the%204%20years%20of%20Netanyahu%20Government.pdf.

44. Ibid.; Jodi Rudoren, "Israeli Decree on West Bank Settlements Will Harm Peace Talks, Palestinians Say," *New York Times*, August 4, 2013, http://www.nytimes.com/2013/08/05/world/middleeast/palestinians-assail-israeli-settlement-decree.html.

45. Americans for Peace Now, "Settlements 101," http://peacenow.org/settlements-101.html.

46. Phase 1 of the Road Map provided: "Israel also freezes all settlement activity, consistent with the Mitchell report." The full text of the Road Map is available at http://news.bbc.co.uk/2/hi/middle_east/2989783.stm.

47. Institute for Middle East Understanding, "Does Netanyahu Really Support the Two-State Solution?" March 19, 2013, http://imeu.net/news/article0023751.shtml.

48. Jeffrey Heller and Justyna Pawlak, "Israel Pushes Settlement Plan Ahead; EU Summons Envoy," Reuters, December 5, 2012, http://www.reuters.com/article/2012/12/05/us-palestinians-israel-netanyahu-idusbre8b40ns20121205. "EU mulls response to settlement building plans," *Jerusalem Post*, December 5, 2012, http://www.jpost.com/International/EU-mulls-response-to-settlement-building-plans.

49. "Merkel, PM 'Agree to Disagree' on Settlements," *Jerusalem Post*, December 6, 2012, http://www.jpost.com/Diplomacy-and-Politics/Merkel-PM-agree-to-disagree-on-settlements.

50. Steven Rosen, "A European Boycott of Israel?" *The Middle East Quarterly* (Spring, 2014), http://www.meforum.org/3747/europe-boycott-israel. Regarding details of the measures agreed, see "Annex: Support to the European Neighbourhood Policy (ENP.) Israel-European Union (EU) Action Plan, 2013," Europa, European Union, Brussels, accessed, January 21, 2014. http://eeas.europa.eu/enp/pdf/2014/country-reports/israel_en.pdf.

51. Jack Khoury, "Palestinians Lowering Expectations Ahead of Renewed Talks with Israel," *Haaretz*, March 27, 2013, http://www.haaretz.com/news/middle-east/palestinians-lowering-expectations-ahead-of-renewed-talks-with-israel.premium-1.511518.

52. Hagit Ofran, "The Compensation Package for the Settlers: 851 Units to Undermine the Two States Solution," *Huffington Post*, June 22, 2012, http://www.huffingtonpost.com/hagit-ofran/israel-west-bank-settlements_b_1616793.html.

53. Peace Now (Israel) and Americans for Peace Now, "Bibi's Settlements Boom: March–November 2013," November 7, 2013, http://peacenow.org/Bibis%20Settlements%20Boom%20-%20March-November%202013%20-%20FINAL.pdf. Full details of Netanyahu's construction plans during 2013 are available at http://archive.peacenow.org/entries/updated_new_peace_nowapn_report_bibis_settlements_boom_—_even_bigger_than_was_known and http://mondoweiss.net/2013/11/unnecessary-confrontation-internationalhtml.

54. Ehab Zahriyeh and Renee Lewis, "Israel Approves More Settler Homes in East Jerusalem," *Al Jazeera America*, August 13, 2013 http://america.aljazeera.com/articles/2013/8/13/israel-approves-another900settlerhomesinoccupiedeastjerusalem.html.

55. Joshua Chaffin in Brussels and John Reed, "EU to Block Funding of Entities in Israeli Settlements," *Financial Times*, July 16, 2014, http://www.ft.com/intl/cms/s/0/96304cdc-ee01-11e2-816e-00144feabdc0.html?siteedition=uk#axzz3XgqlKL9v; Barak Ravid, "EU: Future Agreements with Israel Won't Apply to Territories," *Haaretz*, July 16, 2012, http://www.haaretz.com/news/diplomacy-defense/.premium-1.535952.

56. Annie Robbins, "In 'Earthquake' Diplomatic Move, EU Calls on Israel to 'Recognize in Writing That the West Bank Settlements Are Not Part of Israel," *Mondoweiss*, July 16, 2013, http://mondoweiss.net/2013/07/in-earthquake-diplomatic-move-eu-calls-on-israel-to-recognize-in-writing-that-the-west-bank-settlements-are-not-part-of-israel.

57. Barak Ravid, "Israel Agrees to Recognize EU Ban on Funding Institutions in Settlements," *Haaretz*, November 13, 2014, http://www.haaretz.com/news/diplomacy-defense/.premium-1.557726; "Israel, EU Sign Horizon 2020 Scientific Cooperation Agreement," *Haaretz*, June 9 2014, http://www.haaretz.com/news/national/1.597705.

58. Ya'ar and Hermann, "Peace Index: August 2013."

59. "Israel Says It Doubled New Settlement Building in 2013," March 3, 2013, Reuters, http://uk.reuters.com/article/2014/03/03/uk-israel-palestinians-settlements-idUKBREA221DU20140303.

60. Dror Etkes, interview with the author, February 27, 2012.

61. In his introduction to *Atlas of the Conflict: Israel-Palestine*, having mapped the conflict from 1040 BCE to 2010, Malkit Shoshan writes: "Israel's dynamic spatial maneuvers are tied to fluctuations in borders and to patterns of settlements. They result in a unique and ever

evolving spatial practice of temporality, which can be detected in settlements typologies, from a Wall and a Tower (1930s) to Caravillas (2005). The settler is, until this day, used as an occupying power, creating a fact on the ground, a living wall, a keeper of the land and of its natural resources; always placed strategically, according to a national agenda.

"The constant intensive movements in space and time of the Zionist project have no precedent.

"Shaping the state territories and widening its boundaries, pushing and intensifying undesired demographic fragments out or into enclaves, settling and foresting, covering up the traces of the past while evacuating other layers under; all together these define a fluid state of existence, a new Israeli and Palestinian reality."

62. Zertal and Eldar, *Lords of the Land*, 32, 55, 63. See also Christa Case Bryant, "How Some Israelis See the Sacred in Settlements": "The expansion of Israeli settlements in the West Bank is driven by more than politics and security concerns. Religious Zionists say settling the land is ushering in a messianic age." *Christian Science Monitor*, December 18, 2012, http://www.csmonitor.com/World/Middle-East/2012/1218/How-some-Israelis-see-the-sacred-in-settlements.

63. Zertal and Eldar, *Lords of the Land*, 32, 55, 63.

64. Marissa Newman writes, "The government allocated nearly NIS 600 million ($172 million) to West Bank settlements since last October, outside of the annual budget and at the expense of Israeli citizens," Labor MK Stav Shaffir charged on Sunday. "Of the funds transferred, NIS 133 million ($38 million) were given to the World Zionist Organization Settlement Division; NIS 24 million ($6.8 million) were dispensed for projects encouraging younger people to settle in the West Bank; NIS 28 million ($8 million) were allotted to the settlement of Beit El to complete building projects; and NIS 36 million ($10.3 million) went for compensation for the settlement construction freeze, according to Shaffir." Marissa Newman, "Labor MK: State Quietly Giving Huge Sums to Settlements," *Times of Israel*, March 23, 2014, http://www.timesofisrael.com/labor-mk-state-quietly-giving-millions-to-settlements/. A new law is being debated for transparency on this funding; see Tovah Lazaroff, "Knesset Law Committee to Debate Transparency of Funding for Settlements," *Jerusalem Post*, March 31, 2014, http://www.jpost.com/National-News/Knesset-Law-Committee-to-debate-transparency-of-funding-for-settlements-346985.

65. Yousef Munayyer, "When Settlers Attack," Palestine Center, 2012, http://www.thejerusalemfund.org/ht/a/GetDocumentAction/i/32678; Harriet Sherwood, "Jewish Settler Attacks on Palestinians Listed as 'Terrorist Incidents' by US," *Guardian*, August 19, 2012, http://www.theguardian.com/world/2012/aug/19/jewish-settler-attack-terrorist-us-palestinian.

66. Ibid.

67. Yesh Din, "Criminal Accountability of Israeli Citizens," http://www.yesh-din.org/cat.asp?catid=3.

68. Crispian Balmer, "Amnesty Says Some Israeli West Bank Killings May Be War Crimes," Reuters, February 26, 2014, http://www.reuters.com/article/2014/02/27/us-palestinians-israel-amnesty-idUSBREA1Q00G20140227. For the actual report, see Amnesty International, "Trigger-Happy," https://www.amnesty.org/en/articles/news/2014/02/trigger-happy-israeli-army-and-police-use-reckless-force-west-bank/.

69. Ibid.

70. Ibid.

71. Gili Cohen, "Shin Bet: No Israelis Killed in West Bank Terror in 2012, First Year Since 1973," *Haaretz*, http://www.haaretz.com/news/diplomacy-defense/shin-bet-no-israelis-killed-in-west-bank-terror-in-2012-first-year-since-1973.premium-1.496253.

72. Ben Hartman, "Shin Bet: West Bank Terror Attacks More Than Doubled in 2013," *Jerusalem Post*, January 27, 2014, http://www.jpost.com/Defense/Shin-Bet-West-Bank-terror-attacks-more-than-doubled-in-2013-339522.

73. Lior Yavne, "A Semblance of Law: Law Enforcement upon Israeli Civilians in the West Bank," *Yesh Din*, June 2006, http://www.ochaopt.org/documents/opt_prot_yeshdin_semblance_law_june_2006.pdf.

74. See Yesh Din, "Criminal Accountability."

75. Munayyer, "When Settlers Attack."

76. Yesh Din, "Criminal Accountability."

77. Breaking the Silence, *Our Harsh Logic*. Breaking the Silence is an Israeli NGO established in Jerusalem in 2004 by Israel Defense Forces veterans to document the testimonies of Israeli soldiers who have served in the occupied territories.

78. Attributes of colonial societies: These characteristics include power differentials within the dominant/subordinate relationship, depending on the nature of different societies involved. Nevertheless, for purposes of analysis, a "colonial/settler framework" includes forced displacement of the indigenous population; imposition of various systems of control (socio-economic, political, bureaucratic, cultural, and what Menachem Klein calls an "ethno-security regime"); and, despite attempts at reintegration, continued differentiation and structural inequalities between dominant and subordinate populations. Although the "settler mentality" varies according to whether one looks at the pre-1948, 1948 to 1967, or post-1967 periods, it dominates the current relationship to Palestinians. For more, see Menachem Klein, *The Shift: Israel-Palestine from Border Struggle to Ethnic Conflict*, trans. Chaim Weitzman (New York: Columbia University Press, 2010); and Veracini, "The Other Shift," 26–42. See also Omar Jabary Salamanca, Mezna Qato, Kareem Rabie, and Sobhi Samour, "Past Is Present: Settler Colonialism in Palestine," *Settler Colonial Studies* 2, no. 1 (2012), 1–8, doi: 10.1080/2201473X.2012.10648823; Zureik, *Palestinians in Israel*; and F. De Jong, review of *The Palestines in Israel: A Study of Internal Colonialism*, by Elia Zureik, *International Journal of Middle East Studies* 12, no. 4 (December 1980), 547–49, http://www.jstor.org/stable/163140.

79. Reuters, "Israel Says It Doubled New Settlement."

80. Blue White Future states: "The 2005 evacuation of the Gaza Strip settlers was performed without proper planning. Israel's failure to absorb the settlers suitably led many to the general conclusion that Israel is not capable of properly evacuating settlers; in light of the fact that Israel failed in evacuating 8,000 settlers from the Gaza Strip, how would it succeed in evacuating 100,000 from the West Bank?" See http://bluewhitefuture.org/planning/.

Roby Nathanson, interview with the author. Nathanson, Macro's director, explains the origin of one of the lowest numbers, 68,000: "In all we have 450,000 settlers, including East Jerusalem. If you take out East Jerusalem, then you will have about 250,000. Out of this 250,000, 68,000 are in 72 settlements which are in the eastern side of the fence." Nathanson was speaking in 2011; in October 2013, the picture had changed considerably.

81. Ya'ar and Hermann, "Peace Index: July 2013."

82. Ilan Ben Zion, "'Most Israeli Jews Would Annex Part of West Bank,'" *Times of Israel*, April 21, 2013, http://www.timesofisrael.com/most-israeli-jews-would-annex-part-of-west-bank/.

83. Legislation was passed requiring a referendum only on the question of Jerusalem. Stuart Winer, "Cabinet Approves Referendum Bill on Relinquishing Territory," *Times of Israel*, July 28, 2013, http://www.timesofisrael.com/cabinet-approves-referendum-bill-on-peace/; "Knesset Endorses Withdrawal Referendum Bill," *Times of Israel*, August 1, 2013, http://www.timesofisrael.com/knesset-endorses-peace-referendum-bill/.

84. Edmund Sanders, "Most Israelis Oppose Peace Deal with Land Swaps, Poll Finds," *Los Angeles Times*, August 6, 2013, http://articles.latimes.com/2013/aug/06/world/la-fg-wn-israelis-oppose-peace-deal-poll-20130806.

85. Ephraim Sneh, interview with the author, November 6, 2011. All quotes from Sneh in this chapter are from this interview unless otherwise noted.

86. Ron Pundak, interview with the author, November 6, 2011. All quotes from Pundak in this chapter are from this interview unless otherwise noted.

87. Barak Ravid and Jonathan Lis, "Likud Officials Call to Omit Netanyahu's Two-State Declaration from Party Platform," *Haaretz*, December 25, 2012, http://www.haaretz.com/news/national/likud-officials-call-to-omit-netanyahu-s-two-state-declaration-from-party-platform.premium-1.489731; Harriet Sherwood, "How a Rattled Netanyahu Outflanked Likud's Militant Settler Faction," *Guardian*, May 9, 2012, http://www.theguardian.com/world/2012/may/09/netanyahu-likud-settlers.

88. Chaim Levinson writes that "30 percent of the Likud's new members last year were settlers." See "Israeli Settlers Make Up 30 Percent of New Likud Members," *Haaretz*, January 27, 2012, http://www.haaretz.com/print-edition/news/israeli-settlers-make-up-30-percent-of-new-likud-members-1.409387.

89. Elior Levy, "123 Percent Rise in New Settlement Construction in 2013," *YNetNews*, March 3, 2014, http://www.ynetnews.com/articles/0,7340,L-4494635,00.html. Ofer Aderet, "Israeli Population Exceeds 8 Million on Eve of Independence Day," *Haaretz*, http://www.haaretz.com/news/national/israeli-population-exceeds-8-million-on-eve-of-independence-day.premium-1.515455.

90."Interview with Pinchas Wallerstein," Ariel Zellman: Research, Publications, Information, September 19, 2010, http://arielzellman.wordpress.com/2010/09/19/interview-with-pinchas-wallerstein/.

91. Pinchas Wallerstein, interview with the author, September 22, 2011. All quotes from Wallerstein in this chapter are from this interview unless otherwise noted.

92. For the text of the Dayan Plan, see "The Dayan Plan for a New Reality in Yehuda and Shomron," *Yeshiva World News*, June 10, 2014, http://www.theyeshivaworld.com/news/headlines-breaking-stories/238155/the-dayan-plan-for-a-new-reality-in-yehuda-and-shomron.html#sthash.PfMNvoAz.dpuf; David Lev, "Dani Dayan to Resign Yesha Council Chairmanship," *Arutz Sheva*, January 8, 2013, http://www.israelnationalnews.com/News/News.aspx/164001#.U6G65fldW0c. The new chairman is Avi Roeh, chairman of the Yesha Council; Dayan is now playing an international role for the council. Dani Dayan, "Peaceful Nonreconciliation Now," *New York Times*, June 8, 2014, http://www.nytimes.com/2014/06/09/opinion/peaceful-nonreconciliation-now.html?hpandrref=opinionand_r=1.

93. Dani Dayan, interview with the author, February 28, 2012. All quotes from Dayan in this chapter are from this interview unless otherwise noted.

94. Ibid.

95. Ibid.

96. Tamar Asraf, interview with the author, February 26, 2012. All quotes from Asraf in this chapter are from this interview unless otherwise noted.

97. Lara Friedman, "'Price Tag' Escalation Timeline: January 1, 2011–Present," Americans for Peace Now, October 14, 2014, http://peacenow.org/entry.php?id=1077#.VDQoIfldXlg.

98. B'Tselem, "Statistics: Fatalities," http://www.btselem.org/statistics.

99. Akiva Eldar, "West Bank Outposts Spreading into Area B, in Violation of Oslo Accords," *Haaretz*, February 18, 2012, http://www.haaretz.com/print-edition/news/west-bank-outposts-spreading-into-area-b-in-violation-of-oslo-accords-1.413390.

100. United Nations Office for the Coordination of Humanitarian Affairs Occupied Palestinian Territory, "In the Spotlight: Area C Vulnerability Profile." In March 2014, OCHA estimated that 297,900 Palestinians lived in "532 residential areas in Area C, comprising some of the most vulnerable communities in terms of humanitarian needs."

101. Isabel Kershner, "Summer of Protest in Israel Peaks with 400,000 in City Streets," *New York Times*, September 3, 2011, http://www.nytimes.com/2011/09/04/world/middleeast/04israel.html?_r=0.

102. Attitudes toward settlements differ, mostly with regard to money going to settlements. Talila Nesher, "Poll: Most Israelis Support Heavy Cuts to Settlement Funding," *Haaretz*, January 14, 2013, http://www.haaretz.com/news/poll-most-israelis-support-heavy-cuts-to-settlement-funding.premium-1.493961; Michael Grumer, "Netanyahu Receives Letters from More than 700 Jewish Clergy Protesting Settlement Expansion," *Haaretz*, January 7, 2013, http://www.haaretz.com/news/diplomacy-defense/netanyahu-receives-letters-from-more-than-700-jewish-clergy-protesting-settlement-expansion.premium-1.492483; Adam Chandler, "Israel Freezes All Government Funds for West Bank Settlements," *Wire*, February 1, 2014, http://www.thewire.com/global/2014/02/israel-freezes-all-government-funds-west-bank-settlements/357629/.

103. Danny Tirza, interview with the author, October 23, 2011. All quotes from Tirza in this chapter are from this interview unless otherwise noted.

104. Hagit Ofran, interview with the author, September 15, 2011. All quotes from Ofran in this chapter are from this interview unless otherwise noted.

105. Dov Weisglass, interview with the author, November 27, 2011. All quotes from Weisglass in this chapter are from this interview unless otherwise noted.

106. Quoted from the group's Web site: "Blue White Future seeks to help resolve the Israeli-Palestinian conflict on the basis of a 'two states for two peoples' solution by facilitating the relocation of settlers so that all Israel's citizens reside within secure permanent borders that guarantee a Jewish majority. BWF also seeks to advance the processes necessary to meet this goal, through the projects it runs and through its proposed policy plan, and thus provide security and prosperity for generations to come." See http://bluewhitefuture.org/.

107. As of 2013, there were 125 government-sanctioned Israeli settlements in the West Bank (not including East Jerusalem and settlement enclaves within Hebron). In addition, there were approximately 100 "settlement outposts" located throughout the West Bank. The outposts do not have official government recognition, although many of them were established with governmental assistance. B'Tselem, "Land Expropriation and Settlements," January 23, 2014, http://www.btselem.org/settlements.

108. Tal Becker, interview with the author, February 13, 2012.

109. In Northern Ireland, the Social Democratic and Labour Party (SDLP) and the Unionist Party were the most prominent mainstream parties and commanded the largest share of their respective communities' vote in local and national elections. Sinn Féin, spokesparty for the IRA, did not begin to participate in the electoral process until it put forward Bobby Sands, while he was on hunger strike, as a candidate for an open seat at Westminster Parliament. Sands was elected, but that did not save his life. Thereafter Sinn Féin participated in local and national elections, always getting a larger share of the Nationalist/Republican vote, to the SDLP's detriment, and by the time of the negotiation of the Good Friday Agreement it had overtaken the SDLP. Similarly, the Democratic Unionist Party (DUP), more right-wing than the Unionist Party, under the charismatic leadership of the Reverend Ian Paisley, played second fiddle to the Unionist Party again, until the time of the Good Friday negotiations. After the agreement was signed, both Sinn Féin and the DUP

dominated the electoral process. Today the first minister, Peter Robinson, is leader of the DUP; Martin McGuinness, who is regarded by many sources as having been the chief of staff of the IRA and who was Sinn Féin's chief negotiator, is deputy first minister. The Unionist Party has fallen apart, and while the SDLP still commands a significant percentage of the Nationalist vote, it plays second fiddle to Sinn Féin.

110. Robert Danin, interview with the author, June 5, 2012. All quotes from Danin in this chapter are from this interview unless otherwise noted.

111. Tzvi Ben Gedalyahu, "Who Fights More for the IDF, Settlers or Others?" *Arutz Sheva*, August 1, 2012, http://www.israelnationalnews.com/News/News.aspx/151500#.UrCkq_RDvG8.

112. Hagit Ofran and Noa Galili, "West Bank Settlements: Facts and Figures, June 2009," Peace Now, June 2009, http://peacenow.org.il/eng/node/297.

113. Oded Eran, interview with the author, November 10, 2011. All quotes from Eran in this chapter are from this interview unless otherwise noted.

114. Blue White Future and Macro Center for Political Economics, "The Feasibility of Voluntary Evacuation of Settlers Living East to the Security Barrier Prior to an Agreement: Findings of the 2013 Survey," February 2014, http://bluewhitefuture.org/wp-content/uploads/2014/03/Survey-booklet-voluntary-evacuation-final.pdf. Similar surveys were conducted in 2008 and 2012. See "Poll: 30 Percent of Settlers Outside Blocs Would Evacuate Without Peace Deal," *Haaretz*, March 18, 2014, http://www.haaretz.com/news/diplomacy-defense/1.580414.

115. Blue White Future and Macro Center for Political Economics, "Feasibility of Voluntary Evacuation."

116. Raphael Ahren, "Netanyahu: I Won't Forcibly Evacuate Settlements," *Times of Israel*, March 9, 2014, http://www.timesofisrael.com/netanyahu-i-wont-forcibly-evacuate-settlements/.

117. Larry Derfner, "The Settlement That Broke the Two-State Solution," *Foreign Policy*, December 26, 2012, http://www.foreignpolicy.com/articles/2012/12/26/the_settlement_that_broke_the_two_state_solution.

118. Sabri Saidam, interview with the author, February 7, 2012. See also Palestine Liberation Organization, Negotiations Affairs Department, "The Adumim 'Bloc' and the E-1 Expansion Area," background paper, February 2009, http://www.ajtransparency.com/en/projects/thepalestinepapers/20121820444631953.html.

119. Abu Ala, interview with the author, November 13, 2011. All quotes from Ala in this chapter are from this interview unless otherwise noted.

120. Danny Yatom, interview with the author, February 6, 2012. All quotes from Ala in this chapter are from this interview unless otherwise noted.

121. Philip Weiss, "Israel Demolishes Bedouin Village in E1 That Obama Declared Was Key to Two-State Solution," *Mondoweiss*, September 23, 2013, http://mondoweiss.net/2013/09/israel-demolishes-bedouin-village-in-e1-that-obama-declared-was-key-to-two-state-solution.html/comment-page-1.

122. "Remarks by President Obama and President Abbas of the Palestinian Authority in Joint Press Conference, Muqata Presidential Compound, Ramallah, West Bank," March 21, 2013, http://www.whitehouse.gov/the-press-office/2013/03/21/remarks-president-obama-and-president-abbas-palestinian-authority-joint-.

123. Roby Nathanson, interview with the author, July 3, 2012.

124. Ibid.

125. Jodi Rudoren, "Forced Move Raises Anger in West Bank Villages," *New York Times*, June 19, 2012, http://www.nytimes.com/2012/06/20/world/middleeast/forced-move-raises-anger-in-west-bank-villages.html.

126. Ibid.

127. Tovah Lazaroff and Lahav Harkov, "Knesset Rejects Ulpana Bill 69–22," *Jerusalem Post*, June 6, 2012, http://www.jpost.com/Diplomacy-and-Politics/Knesset-rejects-Ulpana-bill-69-22. After the Knesset vote, Netanyahu stated in a press conference, "Passing this bill would have hurt Beit El. The plan I outlined—relocating the disputed homes, bolstering the settlement movement and providing legal protection against legal precedents—reinforces the settlement movement. Nevertheless, this is not an easy day. The decision to relocate homes is never an easy one, even when only five homes are involved. This is not something the government relishes doing, but the court has rendered its ruling and we must respect it. Those who think the legal system was used to ram the settlement movement are wrong." He continued, "Beit El is not getting smaller—it's getting bigger. Beit El will be expanded, with 300 new families joining it." See Attila Somfalvi, "Netanyahu Defends Voting Down 'Ulpana Bill,'" *YNet-News*, June 6, 2012, http://www.ynetnews.com/articles/0,7340,L-4239211,00.html.

128. Tovah Lazaroff, "Ulpana Residents Agree to Voluntary Evacuation," *Jerusalem Post*, June 20, 2012, http://www.jpost.com/Diplomacy-and-Politics/Ulpana-residents-agree-to-voluntary-evacuation.

129. Jodi Rudoren, "Forced Move Raises Anger."

130. Nathanson, interview with the author, July 3, 2012.

131. Tovah Lazaroff, "Police Complete Largely Peaceful Migron Evacuation," September 2, 2012, *Jerusalem Post*, http://www.jpost.com/Diplomacy-and-Politics/Police-complete-largely-peaceful-Migron-evacuation.

132. For more information on the issues related to the Migron outpost, see the Migron Petition, October 2006, at Peace Now's Web site, http://peacenow.org.il/eng/content/migron-petition; and B'Tselem, "3 August '11: High Court Orders State to Dismantle Migron Outpost," August 3, 2011, http://www.btselem.org/settlements-land/3-aug-11-high-court-orders-state-dismantle-migron-outpost. See also Hareuveni, "By Hook and by Crook."

133. Nathanson, interview with the author, July 3, 2012.

134. "Full remarks by Netanyahu on Beit El Now Released," *Arutz Sheva*, June 16, 2012.

135. Jonathan Ferziger, "Removing West Bank Settlers Would Cost $10 Billion: Peace Group," *Bloomberg*, March 18, 2014, http://www.bloomberg.com/news/2014-03-17/removing-west-bank-settlers-would-cost-10-billion-group.html. Gilead Sher, cofounder of Blue White Future, which is working on this problem, estimates that 100,000 settlers, or 25,000 households, could be evacuated at a cost of $10 billion.

Chapter 8 **The Economics of Sustainability**

1. The OECD's 2011 Policy Guidance Supporting Statebuilding in Situations of Conflict and Fragility provides key strategically important functions for state building. They include "security and justice, revenue and expenditure management, economic development—especially job creation—and service delivery." Organisation for Economic Co-operation and Development, "Supporting Statebuilding."

2. According to International Labour Organization data, the numbers increased from 275,100 in the third quarter of 2013 to 301,200 in the fourth quarter of 2013. See Palestinian Central Bureau of Statistics (PCBS), "The Labour Force Survey Results Fourth Quarter (October–December [2013])," press release, February 12, 2014, http://www.pcbs.gov.ps/site/512/default.aspx?tabID=512&lang=en&ItemID=1022&mid=3171&wversion=Staging.

"It is been estimated that in 2012–15 about 250 thousand young Palestinians will enter the labor market," about 62,000 per year. Kock et al., "West Bank and Gaza."

3. For more on PASF reform, see Marten, "Militia Patronage vs. the Diffusion of Professionalism"; Ethan Bronner, "U.S. Helps Palestinians Build Force for Security," *New York Times*, February 26, 2009, http://www.nytimes.com/2009/02/27/world/middleeast/27palestinians.html?_r=0.

4. Palestinian National Authority, "National Development Plan 2011–13."

5. World Bank, "Two Years After London." See also Raja Khalidi and Sahar Taghdisi-Rad, "The Economic Dimensions of Prolonged Occupation: Continuity and Change in Israeli Policy Towards the Palestinian Economy," United Nations Conference on Trade and Development, August 2009, http://unctad.org/en/docs/gds20092_en.pdf.

6. "Negotiators from Israel and the Palestinian Authority November 15 achieved an agreement on facilitating the movement of people and goods within the Palestinian Territories and on opening an international crossing on the Gaza-Egypt border that will put the Palestinians in control of the entry and exit of people." See more at http://unispal.un.org/UNISPAL.NSF/0/C9A5AA5245D910BB852570BB0051711C#sthash.saYAGTJy.dpuf.

7. World Bank, "Two Years After London." See also Hartberg, "Beyond Ceasefire." "Under the AMA and the accompanying Technical Elaboration, the Israeli government agreed to principles and standards for the *continuous operation* of the crossings, whereby any single crossing would only be closed if there was a clear, direct and exceptional threat to security. The Israeli government also agreed that in the event of a security incident at one crossing, goods and people would be diverted to other crossing points, thereby limiting disruptions to Palestinian civilians. In order to support the AMA, the US government invested millions of dollars in sophisticated security technology, which the World Bank, USAID and the Quartet agreed would enable trucks to be scanned in seconds and drive directly from Gaza to the West Bank without the need for further security checks or lengthy procedures."

8. United Nations Office of the Special Coordinator for the Middle East Peace Process, "Palestinian State-Building: A Decisive Period."

9. International Monetary Fund, "West Bank and Gaza," October 25, 2011.

10. World Bank, "Building the Palestinian State."

11. Ibid.

12. Kevin Murphy, "West Bank Economy Not As Healthy As Perceived," IMEMC and Agencies, June 8, 2011, http://www.imemc.org/article/61402.

13. "The Situation of Workers of the Occupied Arab Territories," International Labour Conference, 100th Session, June 2011, ilo.wbgjune 2011wcms_155419.pdf.

14. Barak Ravid, "Israel: Palestinian Economy Not Stable Enough for Independent State," *Haaretz,* March 18, 2012, http://www.haaretz.com/blogs/diplomania/israel-palestinian-economy-not-stable-enough-for-independent-state-1.419358.

15. "Palestinian Economy Not Ready for Statehood: World Bank," *Al Arabiya*, July 25, 2012, http://english.alarabiya.net/articles/2012/07/25/228348.html. See also World Bank, "Fiscal Challenges and Long Term Economic Costs."

16. United Nations Conference on Trade and Development, "Report on UNCTAD Assistance to the Palestinian People." See also United Nations Development Group, "Occupied Palestinian Territories: Comprehensive Analysis" (draft), November 2012, http://www.undg.org/docs/13107/oPt-UNDAF—CA-draft2.pdf.

17. World Bank, "Fiscal Challenges and Long Term Economic Costs," Economic Monitoring Report to the Ad Hoc Liaison Committee, March 19, 2013, http://siteresources.worldbank.org/INTWESTBANKGAZA/Resources/AHLCMarchfinal.pdf; World Bank, "Economic Monitoring Report to the Ad Hoc Liaison Committee," January 21, 2014, http://www.worldbank.org/en/news/feature/2014/01/21/economy-monitoring-ahlc.

18. World Bank, "Palestinian Economy Is Losing Long-Term Competitiveness," press release, March 11, 2013, http://www.worldbank.org/en/news/press-release/2013/03/11/palestinian-economy-losing-long-term-competitiveness. The press release also stated that the economy "has deteriorated" since the late 1990s with "the productivity of the agriculture sector having roughly halved and the manufacturing sector having largely stagnated." When Israel controls 80 percent of Palestinian water resources, it is not surprising that Palestinian farmers are struggling to irrigate their crops.

19. Ibid.

20. World Bank, "Fiscal Challenges and Long Term Economic Costs." Another report from the Ad Hoc Liaison Committee, issued in September 2013, further reinforces these conclusions: World Bank, "Economic Monitoring Report."

21. European Commission, "The EU's Neighbouring Economies: Managing Policies in a Challenging Global Environment," *European Economy—Occasional Papers*, No. 160 (August 2013): 123–26, http://ec.europa.eu/economy_finance/publications/occasional_paper/2013/pdf/ocp160_en.pdf.

22. "The situation of workers of the occupied Arab territories," International Labour Office, Geneva, 2013, http://www.ilo.org/public/english/standards/relm/ilc/ilc93/pdf/rep-i-ax.pdf.

23. "Palestinian economy in modest growth amid Israeli occupation—UN," UN News Centre, August 31, 2010; http://www.un.org/apps/news/story.asp?NewsID=35780#.VSaOR_nF_lh. See also "Report on UNCTAD Assistance to the Palestinian People: Developments in the Economy of the Occupied Palestinian Territory," July 13, 2010. http://unctad.org/en/Docs/tdb57d4_en.pdf.

24. Ibid.

25. Naser Tahboub, interview with the author, September 28, 2011. All quotes from Tahboub in this chapter are from this interview unless otherwise noted.

26. International Monetary Fund, "Macroeconomic and Fiscal Framework for the West Bank and Gaza: Seventh Review of Progress, April 13, 2011."

27. World Bank, "Area C and the Future of the Palestinian Economy," Report No. AUS2922, October 2, 2013, https://openknowledge.worldbank.org/bitstream/handle/10986/16686/AUS29220REPLAC0EVISION0January02014.pdf?sequence=1.

28. Ibid.

29. Ibid.

30. World Bank, "Palestinians Access to Area C Key to Economic Recovery and Sustainable Growth," press release, October 8, 2013, http://www.worldbank.org/en/news/press-release/2013/10/07/palestinians-access-area-c-economic-recovery-sustainable-growth.

31. See DPA, "Abbas: Palestinians to Continue Efforts to Seek Full UN Membership," *Haaretz*, November 12, 2011, http://www.haaretz.com/news/diplomacy-defense/abbas-palestinians-to-continue-efforts-to-seek-full-un-membership-1.395143; Barak Ravid, "Israel to Continue Freeze on Palestinian Tax Money, Says Senior Official," *Haaretz*, November 21, 2011, http://www.haaretz.com/news/diplomacy-defense/israel-to-continue-freeze-on-palestinian-tax-money-says-senior-official-1.396794; Donald McIntyre, "Abbas Is Punished by $200M Cut in Aid from US," *Independent*, October 1, 2011, http://www.independent.co.uk/news/world/middle-east/abbas-is-punished-by-200m-cut-in-aid-from-us-2363976.html; Associated Press, "Palestinians [*sic*] Economy Affected by U.S. Aid Cut, PA Officials Say," *Haaretz*, October 3, 2011, http://www.haaretz.com/news/diplomacy-defense/palestinians-economy-affected-by-us-congress-aid-cut-pa-officials-say-1.387961.

32. See Reuters, "West Bank Palestinians Strike in Protest of Israeli Sanctions," *Haaretz*, December 19, 2012, http://www.haaretz.com/news/middle-east/west-bank-palestinians-strike

-in-protest-of-israeli-sanctions.premium-1.485865; Yoel Goldman, "US Unblocks $500 Million in Aid to Palestinians," *Times of Israel*, March 23, 2013, http://www.timesofisrael.com/us-unblocks-500-million-in-aid-to-palestinians/.

33. "IMF Urges the Palestinian Authority and Donors to Reassess Priorities," 2013 https://www.imf.org/external/country/WBG/RR/2013/071013.pdf.

34. See also United Nations Conference on Trade and Development, "Occupied Palestinian Territory Loses Estimated US$300 Million/Year in Public Revenue 'Leakage' to Israel, UNCTAD Report Says," press release, September 3, 2013, http://unctad.org/en/pages/newsdetails.aspx?OriginalVersionID=593. "Arab States 'Completely Incapacitated' PA by Withholding Aid, Fayyad Says," *Times of Israel*, January 2013, http://www.timesofisrael.com/pa-prime-minister-blasts-arab-countries-for-with-holding-donations/.

35. Adnan Abu Amer, "Study Shows Dire Consequences If Palestinian Authority Collapses," *Al-Monitor*, February 14, 2014, http://www.al-monitor.com/pulse/originals/2014/02/palestinian-authority-report-pcpsr-israel.html.

36. Sarah Elyan interview with the author, November 13, 2011.

37. Bassam Abu Eid, "Is the PA's Financial Crisis Genuine?," Ma'an News Agency, July 4, 2011, http://www.maannews.net/eng/ViewDetails.aspx?ID=402110.

38. Fadi Abu Saada, "Palestine Protests: Occupation Economy Falters," *Al-Akhbar*, September 7, 2012, http://english.al-akhbar.com/node/11855.

39. "Palestinian Authority Suspends Plans to Raise Taxes," Ma'an News Agency, January 29, 2012, http://www.maannews.net/eng/ViewDetails.aspx?ID=456422.

40. A Palestinian public opinion poll released in March 2014 showed that "a positive evaluation of the Haniyeh government stands at 37% and positive evaluation of the performance of Al Hamdallah stands at 41 percent. . . . We asked West Bank and Gaza publics about their expectations regarding economic conditions in their respective areas in the next few years: 19 percent expected better conditions and 52 percent expected worse conditions. In the Gaza Strip, 28 percent expected better conditions and 34 percent expected worse conditions." Palestinian Center for Policy and Survey Research, "Palestinian Public Opinion Poll No. 51."

41. Hazem Shunnar, interview with the author, July 5, 2012. All quotes from Shunnar in this chapter are from this interview unless otherwise noted.

42. "International Donors' Conference for the Palestinian State: Final Statement of the Chair and Co-chairs," December 17, 2007, http://unispal.un.org/UNISPAL.NSF/0/4CB6C31B95E505B7852573B500568508#sthash.XRa7tv7g.dpuf.

43. "Minister: Palestinian Authority Facing Financial Crisis," Ma'an News Agency, August 21, 2013, http://www.maannews.net/eng/ViewDetails.aspx?ID=622062.

44. Karin Laub and Mohammed Daraghmeh, Associated Press, "Financial Crisis Strains Palestinian Government," *USA Today*, January 6, 2013, http://www.usatoday.com/story/news/world/2013/01/06/palestine-fayyad-arab-donors/1812007/.

45. Ibid.

46. In the years 2010–11 the West Bank experienced an economic slowdown, with real GDP growth declining to about 5 percent from an annual average rate of 9 percent in 2008–10. "Unemployment has reached 19 percent in the West Bank and as much as 30 percent in Gaza. The authority's severe financing difficulties over the past 20 months have led to a substantial rise in domestic payment arrears and debt to commercial banks. Although the authority has reduced its reliance on international aid after economic reforms—to $1.1 billion in 2010 from $1.8 billion in 2008—the amount received since then has not been sufficient to fulfill requirements. Much of the shortfall is due to a drop in aid from Arab

countries, according to officials. In both 2008 and 2009, Arab donors disbursed $500 million, but in 2011 and so far in 2012, the amount dropped to more like $200 million." Isabel Kershner, "Financial Strains Said to Threaten Stability of Palestinian Authority," *New York Times*, September 17, 2012, http://www.nytimes.com/2012/09/18/world/middleeast/palestinian-authoritys-stability-threatened-by-financial-strains.html?pagewanted=all.

47. Oussama Kanaan, interview with the author, June 4, 2012. All quotes from Kanaan in this chapter are from this interview unless otherwise noted.

48. Sarah Marusek, "Foreign Aid to Palestine Exists Only to Support the 'Peace Process' Industry," *Middle East Monitor*, September 25, 2013, https://www.middleeastmonitor.com/articles/activism/7514-foreign-aid-to-palestine-exists-only-to-support-the-qpeace-processq-industry. "Some donors," Marusek writes, "are becoming increasingly frustrated to find that much of their aid is rebuilding what Israel had previously destroyed, only to be destroyed yet again. A 2012 report from the Displacement Working Group compiled by a group of local and international NGOs and chaired by the UN Office for the Coordination of Humanitarian Affairs found that in 2011 alone, Israel had demolished 62 European-funded structures out of a total of 620 structures destroyed that year, and that 110 additional structures remained at risk."

49. Salam Fayyad, interview with the author, July 8, 2012. All quotes from Fayyad in this chapter are from this interview unless otherwise noted. In a scathing op-ed in the *New York Times*, Ian Lustick wrote that the Palestinian Authority supports the "peace talks" only because the accompanying economic aid subsidizes "the lifestyles of its leaders, the jobs of tens of thousands of soldiers, spies, police officers and civil servants," and helps to secure "the authority's prominence in a Palestinian society that views it as corrupt and incompetent." "The Two State Illusion," *New York Times*, September 14, 2013, http://www.nytimes.com/2013/09/15/opinion/sunday/two-state-illusion.html?pagewanted=all&_r=0.

50. Isabel Kershner, "Financial Strains Said to Threaten Stability of Palestinian Authority."

51. Noah Browning, "West Bank Economy Shrinks for First Time in Decade—World Bank," Reuters, October 8, 2013, http://www.reuters.com/article/2013/10/08/israel-palestinians-economy-idUSL6N0HY1O120131008.

52. According to a December 2013 PCPSR poll, 77 percent believe that the government in the West Bank is corrupt and 68 percent the government in Gaza. Palestinian Center for Policy and Survey Research, "Palestinian Public Opinion Poll No. 50," www.pcpsr.org/survey/polls/2013/soe.html. According to Poll No. 54, 81 percent of the Palestinian public believe that PA institutions are corrupt, www.pcpsr.org/en/node/505.

53. The Palestinian opinion poll for March 2014 indicated that just 31 percent of West Bank residents were satisfied with the way things were going, while the percentage of those who believed conditions in the West Bank were bad or very bad stood at 42 percent. "Perception of corruption in PA institutions in the West Bank stands at 80 percent." Palestinian Center for Policy and Survey Research, "Palestinian Public Opinion Poll No. 51." See also http://bbcwatch.org/tag/pa-budget-deficit/.

54. Jack Khoury and Reuters, "Palestinian President Abbas Accepts PM Fayyad's Resignation," *Haaretz*, April 14, 2013, http://www.haaretz.com/news/middle-east/palestinian-president-abbas-accepts-pm-fayyad-s-resignation-1.515285; Elhanan Miller, "As Fayyad Resigns, Palestinian Politics Face the Unknown," *Times of Israel*, April 14, 2013, http://www.timesofisrael.com/as-pm-resigns-palestinian-politics-face-the-unknown/.

55. Azzam Ahmed, interview with the author, November 13, 2011. All quotes from Ahmed in this chapter are from this interview unless otherwise noted.

56. International Monetary Fund, "Recent Experience and Prospects of the Economy of the West Bank and Gaza," staff report prepared for the meeting of the Ad Hoc Liaison

Committee by Christoph Duenwald, Udo Kock, and Anna Unigovskaya, March 19, 2013, http://www.imf.org/external/country/WBG/RR/2013/031913.pdf.

57. Amy Teibel, "Israel Counted Gaza Calorie Needs During Blockade," Associated Press, October 17, 2012, http://bigstory.ap.org/article/israel-counted-food-needs-gaza-blockade.

58. Associated Press, "Document on Calorie Figures in Gaza Blockade Stirs Dispute," *New York Times*, October 17, 2012, http://www.nytimes.com/2012/10/18/world/middleeast/israel-counted-calories-needed-for-gazans-in-blockade.html; Amira Hass, "2,279 Calories per Person: How Israel Made Sure Gaza Didn't Starve," *Haaretz*, October 17, 2012, http://www.haaretz.com/news/diplomacy-defense/2-279-calories-per-person-how-israel-made-sure-gaza-didn-t-starve.premium-1.470419. A translation of the declassified document can be viewed at the *Haaretz* Web site: State of Israel Ministry of Defense, "AAA 3300/11 Ministry of Defense v. Gisha 'Food Consumption in the Gaza Strip—Red Lines' Presentation," http://www.haaretz.com/resources/Pdf/red-lines.pdf. "The analysis also included adjustments for locally grown farm products." Since calorie count was the key consideration, "the blockade allowed frozen salmon and low-fat yogurt into the Hamas-ruled territory, but not cilantro or instant coffee. . . . The guidelines recommend allowing 300 calves into Gaza each week to fulfill the territory's meat needs. In a September 2008 court case, the government rejected a request by an importer to bring more calves into Gaza, saying 300 animals were sufficient, using an identical figure from the guidelines."

59. Ahmed Yousef, interview with the author, December 3, 2011. All quotes from Yousef in this chapter are from this interview unless otherwise noted.

60. Jesse Rosenfield, "Israel Creates No Man's Land in Gaza," *The Daily Beast*, July 28, 2014, http://www.the daily beast.com/articles/2014/07/28/as_israel_enforces_its_buffer_zone_guza_shrinks_by_40_per_cent.html.

61. United Nations Relief and Works Agency, "Economic Situation of Refugees in Gaza Remains of Concern Despite Improved Indicators," press release, December 7, 2011, http://www.unrwa.org/newsroom/press-releases/economic-situation-refugees-gaza-remains-concern-despite-improved-indicators. See also Reuters, "Gaza's Thriving Tunnel Imports Unleash Building Boom," *Haaretz*, December 24, 2011, http://www.haaretz.com/news/diplomacy-defense/gaza-s-thriving-tunnel-imports-unleash-building-boom-1.403357.

62. United Nations Country Team in the occupied Palestinian territory, "Gaza in 2020: A Liveable Place?" August 2012, http://www.unrwa.org/userfiles/file/publications/gaza/Gaza%20in%202020.pdf.

63. Josef Federman, "Israel Said It Would Keep Gaza Near Collapse: WikiLeaks," *Huffington Post*, January 5, 2011, http://www.huffingtonpost.com/2011/01/05/israel-gaza-collapse-wikileaks_n_804583.html.

64. Sara M. Roy, *The Gaza Strip: The Political Economy of De-Development* (Beirut: Institute for Palestine Studies, 1995).

65. Reuters, "Gaza's Thriving Tunnel Imports Unleash Building Boom." "UN estimates for the import of building materials in September show that 46,500 tons of aggregate arrived via the Kerem Shalom crossing from Israel into Gaza, whereas 90,000 tons came through the tunnels. Some 9,195 tons of cement came through Kerem Shalom, against 90,000 through the tunnels. For steel rods, 1,418 tons transited Kerem Shalom versus 15,000 via the underground routs."

66. Lindner, *Making Enemies*, 73.

67. Before Israel invaded, the IDF said it was allowing two hundred trucks of cargo, including 200,000 liters of oil, into Gaza. See Yoav Zitun and Roi Kais, "Israel Allows Fuel, Aid into Gaza Despite Fighting," *YNetNews*, July 10, 2014, http://www.ynetnews.com/articles/0,7340,L-4541153,00.html.

Problems arose almost immediately after the monthlong cease-fire in August 2014. The Israeli blockade had not been lifted. Moreover, under the reconciliation pact, the PA was expected to pay the 40,000-plus Gaza civil servants and take over the civil administration of Gaza from Hamas, including the borders, a move that would help with monitoring and the flow of goods into the enclave. Yet relations between Hamas and Fatah had deteriorated, with tensions over the payment of salaries to Hamas workers still a matter of contention. Nor did Hamas appear overly eager to allow PA ministers entry into Gaza—all of which hampered the flow of aid, as donors waited until it was established who would monitor the border crossings. As of September 10, 2014, the payment of the then-40,000 employees had not been resolved. See Adnan Abu Amer, "Hamas Frustrated by Israel's Flouting of Cease-Fire Deal," *Al-Monitor*, September 12, 2014, http://www.al-monitor.com/pulse/originals/2014/09/hamas-demands-not-achieved-gaza-war-end.html.

68. Nu'man Kanafani, "The Palestine State: Economic Integration Despite Geographic Discontinuity," MAS Annual Conference Papers, January 23–24, 2011, http://library.mas.ps/files/400.aspx?down=1, 11; Jean-François Arvis, Gael Raballand, and Jean-François Marteau, "The Cost of Being Landlocked: Logistics Costs and Supply Chain Reliability," World Bank Policy Research Working Paper 4258, June 2007, http://elibrary.worldbank.org/doi/book/10.1596/1813-9450-4258.

69. L. MacKellar, A. Wörgötter, and J. Wörz, *Economic Development Problems of Landlocked Countries*, Transition Economics Series, no. 14 (Vienna: Institute for Advanced Studies, 2000), 6, https://www.ihs.ac.at/publications/tec/te-14.pdf. A World Bank pilot study and working paper summarized the negative qualities experienced by landlocked economies: They trade with a lower rate (30 percent below average); they grow at a slow pace (1.5 points lower than the average growth); and they remain for a longer period under the supervision and support of the International Monetary Fund. Faye et al., "The Challenges Facing Landlocked Developing Countries," 31–68. A survey of seventy-eight nontropical countries found that the absence of the sea leads to a reduction of per-capita income by $5,190 per year. Gallup et al., "Geography and Economic Development," 8.

70. "Gaza Marine gas field is located 30 km off the coast of the Gaza Strip . . . , at a water depth of 603 m. The development of the Gaza field has been on hold for several years due to disputes between Israel and the Palestinians. Backed by the US, the Palestinian National Authority commenced discussions with Israel in September 2012 over the possible development. The development, if undertaken, is expected to take three to four years to complete. British Gas (BG) holds a 90% interest in the field. BG's stake will reduce to 60 percent if the Palestinian Investment Fund (PIF) and Consolidated Contractors Company (CCC) choose to exercise their options. PIF and CCC would subsequently hold 30% and 10% interests, respectively." An Israeli Foreign Ministry report stated that "development of the Gaza Marine gas field will generate revenues that could contribute dramatically to Palestinian fiscal sustainability." The field is estimated to hold one trillion cubic feet of gas, it is estimated to have a life of 15 years. "Gaza Marine Gas Field, Palestine," *Offshore Technology*, http://www.offshore-technology.com/projects/gaza-marine-gas-field/.

71. Mazen Sinokrot, interview with the author, October 17, 2011. All quotes from Sinokrot in this chapter are from this interview unless otherwise noted.

72. Khalil Shikaki drew these conclusions after studying the case of the twenty thousand Gazans who moved to the West Bank between 1967 and 1971 and lived in Tulkarm and Qalqilya. See Jonathan Schanzer, "A Gaza-West Bank Split? Why the Palestinian Territories Might Become Two Separate States," *Middle East Intelligence Bulletin*, July/August 2001, http://www.meforum.org/333/a-gaza-west-bank-split.

73. World Bank, "Palestinian Economic Prospects: Gaza Recovery and West Bank Revival," Economic Monitoring Report to the Ad Hoc Liaison Committee, June 8, 2009, http://siteresources.worldbank.org/INTWESTBANKGAZA/Resources/AHLCJune09Reportfinal.pdf.

74. Ibid.

75. Mya Guarnieri, "Fact sheet: Israel's tightening control over Jerusalem," *+972*, December 7, 2011, http://972mag.com/jerusalem-fact-sheet/29115/.

76. Alyan et al., "Policies of Neglect in East Jerusalem."

77. Nu'man Kanafani, "The Palestinian State: Economic Integration Despite Geographic Discontinuity."

78. Ibid.

79. Bob Bowker, "The Political Management of Change in UNRWA," Palestinian Refugee ResearchNet, http://prrn.mcgill.ca/research/papers/bowker.htm.

80. Naser Tahboub, interview with the author, September 28, 2011.

81. Jamil Hilal, interview with the author, October 18, 2011. All quotes from Hilal in this chapter are from this interview unless otherwise noted.

82. Mitt Romney rode the wave of "If I am elected president I will create twelve million new jobs in four years" without ever specifying how he would accomplish this. The promise was the policy.

83. Bernard Avishai, "'The Hand of Providence,'" *Bernard Avishai Dot Com*, July 30, 2012, http://bernardavishai.blogspot.com/2012_07_01_archive.html; Bernard Avishai, "The West Bank Through Chinese Eyes," *Daily Beast*, March 19, 2012, http://www.thedailybeast.com/articles/2012/03/19/the-west-bank-through-chinese-eyes.html.

84. Niksic, Eddin, and Cali, "West Bank and Gaza: Area C and the Future of the Palestinian Economy."

85. David Schenker, "Preventing ISIS Inroads in Jordan," Washington Institute, September 3, 2014, http://www.washingtoninstitute.org/policy-analysis/view/preventing-isis-inroads-in-jordan; King Abdullah of Jordan, interviewed on *60 Minutes*, CBS, September 21, 2014.

86. Jeremy Kadden, "U.S. Lawmakers Quietly Propose Foreign Aid Cuts," *The Hill*, May 29, 2013, http://thehill.com/blogs/congress-blog/economy-a-budget/302299-us-lawmakers-quietly-propose-foreign-aid-cuts.

87. For building the new state, see "Assisting Palestine Independence Through Trade: Trends and Prospects of Economic and Social Development in the Occupied Palestinian Territory," prepared by the national team headed by Dr. Hazem Shunnar, to be presented at the Fourth United Nations Conference on the Least Developed Countries, Istanbul, May 2011, http://www.hebroninvestment.com/pdf/STUDIES/Foriegn%20Trade/assisting%20palestine%20Through%20Tade.pdf.

88. Hazem Shunnar, interview with the author. See also Brynen, "Financing Palestinian Refugee Compensation." For estimates that are in the $300 billion range, see chapter 10; every set of estimates begins from a different starting point and a different set of assumptions.

89. Shunnar, interview with the author, July 12, 2012.

90. Robert Danin, interview with the author, June 2012. All quotes from Danin in this chapter are from this interview unless otherwise noted.

91. Naser Tahboub, interview with the author, September 28, 2011. Although the country is highly educated, the World Bank's 2014 Systems Approach for Better Education Results (SABER) rated Palestine as emerging and latent in categories of workforce development. World Bank, "Workforce Development," SABER Country Report 2013, http://wbg

files.worldbank.org/documents/hdn/ed/saber/supporting_doc/CountryReports/WFD/SABER_WfD_Palestine_CR_Final_%202014.pdf.

92. See a variety of far-ranging sources: P. Freire, *Pedagogy of the Oppressed* (New York: Continuum Publishing Co., 2011), http://www.ebookdb.org/item/52219/Pedagogy-of-the-Oppressed-30th-Anniversary-Edition; Glenn Frank, "The Tide of Affairs: Comments on the Times," *Century* magazine, Vol. 99, 1920, 787–802; Lawrence R. Alschuler, "Jung and Politics," in *The Cambridge Companion to Jung*, Polly Young-Eisendrath and Terence Davison, eds. 299–314 (Cambridge: Cambridge University Press, 2008); Charlotte Baker-Shenk, "Characteristics of Oppressed and Oppressor: Their Effect on the Interpreting Context," Characteristics-of-the-Oppressed-_110314 pdf.

93. "Start-Up Nation: An Innovation Story," *OECD Observer*, no. 285, Q2 2011, http://www.oecdobserver.org/news/fullstory.php/aid/3546/Start-up_nation:_An_innovation_story.html; see also Senor and Singer, *Start-Up Nation*.

94. Rana Baker, "Palestinian Education Methods Require Revamp," *Al-Monitor*, February 4, 2013, http://www.al-monitor.com/pulse/originals/2013/02/palestinian-education-standards.html.

95. "The Untapped Potential: Palestinian-Israeli Economic Relations: Policy Options and Recomm[e]ndations," Paltrade, 2006, http://old.paltrade.org/en/publications/other/Untapped%20Potential%20-%20Dec%202006%20PRINTED%20(Arabic-English).pdf.

96. Ibid.

97. "Future Economic Relations Between the Palestinian and Israeli Economies," Palestinian International Business Forum, December 2007, http://www.pibf.net/wp-content/PIBF-Report-on-Future-Economic-Relations-Dec-2007.pdf, 18.

98. International Monetary Fund, "West Bank and Gaza," staff report prepared for the September 11, 2013, meeting of the Ad Hoc Liaison Committee, http://www.imf.org/external/country/wbg/rr/2013/091113.pdf.

99. World Bank, "Palestinian Economy in Decline and Unemployment Rising to Alarming Levels," press release, September 14, 2014, http://www.worldbank.org/en/news/press-release/2014/09/16/palestinian-economy-in-decline-and-unemployment-rising-to-alarming-levels.

Chapter 9 **Demographics: The Enemy Within**

1. Sam Sokol, "PM: Israel's Hope for Peace Not Reciprocated," *Jerusalem Post*, May 28, 2013, http://www.jpost.com/Jewish-World/Jewish-News/PM-Prepared-to-compromise-for-peace-but-not-reciprocated-314636.

2. Gideon Levy, "Survey: Most Israeli Jews Wouldn't Give Palestinians Vote If West Bank Was Annexed," *Haaretz*, October 23, 2012, http://www.haaretz.com/news/national/survey-most-israeli-jews-wouldn-t-give-palestinians-vote-if-west-bank-was-annexed.premium-1.471644.

3. "Others (i.e., non-Jews who are members of Jewish households and Israeli citizens by the provisions of the Law of Return) [about 325,000] . . . and foreign workers and refugees [300,000]." See DellaPergola, "Demographic Trends," in *Jewish Studies at the Central European University*, 37–62.

4. Zafrir Rinat, "In Israel, Population Growth Is an Issue to Be Avoided at All Costs," *Haaretz*, October 2, 2013, http://www.haaretz.com/news/national/.premium-1.550169.

5. Olga Khazan, "Why Demography Is Still a Problem for Some Jews," *Washington Post*, January 1, 2013, http://www.washingtonpost.com/blogs/worldviews/wp/2013/01/01/why-demographics-are-still-a-concern-for-some-israeli-jews/.

6. Israel Democracy Institute, "April 2014 Peace Index," May 7, 2014, http://en.idi.org.il/about-idi/news-and-updates/april-2014-peace-index.

7. See, for example, DellaPergola, "Demographic Trends."

8. Sergio DellaPergola, interviews with the author, November 18, 2010; September 26, 2011; July 2 and 12, 2012. All quotes from DellaPergola in this chapter are from these interviews unless otherwise noted.

9. Miller, "Israel's Demographic Destiny"; Pini Herman, "Israel's 65th Demographics," *Jewish Journal*, April 22, 2013, http://www.jewishjournal.com/demographic_duo/item/israels_65th_demographics.

10. Organisation for Economic Co-operation and Development, "Society at a Glance 2011: OECD Social Indicators," 2011, http://www.oecd.org/berlin/47570005.pdf, 44.

11. DellaPergola, "Israel's Existential Predicament: Population, Territory, and Identity," *Current History*, 109, no. 731 (December 2010), 13, http://www.bjpa.org/Publications/details.cfm?PublicationID=13561.

12. Yiftachel, *Ethnocracy*, 3.

13. For information on the discriminatory land-allocation policies applied to Palestinian Arab citizens of Israel, see Adalah: The Legal Center for Arab Minority Rights in Israel, Discriminatory Laws in Israel (database), http://adalah.org/eng/Israeli-Discriminatory-Law-Database.

14. Talila Nesher, "Israel to Launch Campaign to Attract More Arab Students to Universities," *Haaretz*, October 21, 2012, http://www.haaretz.com/news/national/israel-to-launch-campaign-to-attract-more-arab-students-to-universities.premium-1.471184.

15. Pinchas Wallerstein, interview with the author, September 22, 2011. All quotes from Wallerstein in this chapter are from this interview unless otherwise noted.

16. *Ettinger Report*, http://www.theettingerreport.com/Demographic-Scare.aspx; Yoram Ettinger, "2nd Thought: US Israel Initiative," http://yoramettinger.tumblr.com/.

17. Sheldon Adelson made his fortune from hotels and casinos in Las Vegas. In the United States he is well known for contributing large, often huge, donations to extreme right-wing Republican candidates running for congressional office, and he advocates right-wing causes.

18. Yoram Ettinger, "Israel's Jewish Demography Defies Conventions," *Ettinger Report*, April 5, 2013, http://www.theettingerreport.com/Demographic-Scare/Israel%E2%80%99s-Jewish-Demography-Defies-Conventions.aspx.

19. Ibid.

20. Arnon Soffer, interview with the author, November 7, 2011. All quotes from Soffer in this chapter are from this interview unless otherwise noted.

21. Bystrov and Soffer, "Israel: Demography and Density 2007–2020"; Bystrov and Soffer, "Israel: Demography 2013–2034".

22. Soffer, interview with the author. See also Uri Sadot, "Israel's Time Bomb Is a Dud," *Foreign Policy*, December 18, 2013, http://www.foreignpolicy.com/articles/2013/12/18/israel_s_demographic_time_bomb_is_a_dud_israel_arab_two_state_solution.

23. Roby Nathanson, interview with the author, July 3, 2012. All quotes from Nathanson in this chapter are from this interview unless otherwise noted.

24. Bystrov and Soffter, "Israel: Demography 2013–2034."

25. When David Ben-Gurion, one of the founding fathers of Israel, was persuaded that a certain number of Jewish men should be excluded from the workforce so that they could devote themselves to the study of the Torah, he had in mind 400 or so, total. Today there are about 60,000. Isabel Kershner, "Some Israelis Question Benefits for Ultra-Religious," *New*

York Times, December 28, 2010, http://www.nytimes.com/2010/12/29/world/middleeast/29israel.html?pagewanted=all.

26. Bystrov and Soffer, "Israel: Demography 2013–2034."

27. Bystrov and Soffer, "Israel: Demography 2012–2030. See also Elazar, "How Religious Are Israeli Jews?" At the time of Oslo I, only 20 percent of Israeli Jews fell into the secular category.

A 2009 survey titled "A Portrait of Israeli Jews: Beliefs, Observance, and Values of Israeli Jews, 2009," conducted by the Israel Democracy Institute in conjunction with the Avi Chai Foundation, examined local levels of Jewish religiosity compared with those over the past twenty years. According to the study, involving face-to-face interviews with 2,803 local Jews above the age of twenty, Jewish Israelis' affinity for their religion and its traditions has increased notably since 1999: "In 2009, one can say that many Israeli Jews have an interest in the place that religion occupies in the State of Israel and in the meaning of a 'Jewish State,' they are sympathetic toward manifestations of religion and tradition in the public sphere." Keissar-Sugarmen, "A Portrait of Israeli Jews." See also Yair Ettinger, "Four Surveys Yield Different Totals for Haredi Population," *Haaretz*, April 21, 2011, http://www.haaretz.com/print-edition/news/four-surveys-yield-different-totals-for-haredi-population-1.357117.

28. Arnon Soffer, interview with the author, October 31, 2010.

29. Elad Benari, "Population Forecast: More Haredim by 2059," *Arutz Sheva*, December 13, 2013, http://www.israelnationalnews.com/News/News.aspx/150670#.U2vbVvldWhE.

30. Jodi Rudoren, "Israel Prods Ultra-Orthodox to 'Share Burden,'" *New York Times*, June 6, 2013, http://www.nytimes.com/2013/06/07/world/middleeast/israels-ultra-orthodox-fight-to-fit-in.html?pagewanted=alland_r=0.

31. Bystrov and Soffer, "Israel: Demography 2013–2034," 60–61.

32. "Israel Is Fourth in Child Poverty in Developed World," UNICEF Says, *Haaretz*, October 28, 2014.

33. Nadav Neuman, "BoI: Growth Will Slow Without More Haredi Education," *Globes*, February 12, 2013, http://www.globes.co.il/en/article-1000898306: "'Long-term growth forecasts show that the demographic changes currently taking place in Israel are expected to slow the growth rate of the economy compared to previous decades,' warns the Bank of Israel. 'An accepted and practical way to measure the stock of human capital in the economy involves looking at the average years of schooling among the population and combining it with estimates of the returns to schooling—the extent to which the number of years of schooling affects human capital and income in the economy.'"

34. Soffer, interview with the author, November 7, 2011..

35. Ibid.

36. Jewish Virtual Library, "Vital Statistics: Latest Population Statistics for Israel," updated September 2014, https://www.jewishvirtuallibrary.org/jsource/Society_&_Culture/newpop.html.

37. See for example the analysis of Bystrov and Soffer, "Israel: Demography 2013–2034," 34,78.

38. Hagai Amit, "Israelis Moving en Masse to Tel Aviv Area by 2025," *Haaretz*, March 28, 2013, http://www.haaretz.com/business/israelis-moving-en-masse-to-tel-aviv-area.premium-1.512096.

39. Jewish Virtual Library, "Vital Statistics: Latest Population Statistics for Israel," updated September 2014, https://www.jewishvirtuallibrary.org/jsource/Society_&_Culture/newpop.html.

40. Bystrov and Soffer, "Israel: Demography 2013–2034."

41. Arnon Soffer and Evgenia Brystrov, *Tel Aviv State: The Threat to Israel*, 11.

42. For more on this topic, see Adalah, "Land and Planning Rights," http://adalah.org/eng/category/7/Land-and-Planning-Rights/1/0/0/.

43. Alon Liel, interview with the author, June 23, 2011. All quotes from Liel in this chapter are from this interview unless otherwise noted. The mixed cities are Akko (Acre), Haifa, Jaffa (the southern quarter of Tel Aviv), Ramla, and Lod.

44. Bystrov and Soffer, "Israel: Demography 2013–2034."

45. Ibid.

46. Sawsan Zaher, interview with the author, October 12, 2011. All quotes from Zaher in this chapter are from this interview unless otherwise noted.

47. Tova Dvorin, "Vandalism in Lod: Local Jews Complain of Arab Harassment," *Arutz Sheva*, December 24, 2013, http://www.israelnationalnews.com/News/News.aspx/175491#.U2uPXPldWhE.

48. Nicolas Pelham, "From Backwater to Frontline: Urban Conflict in Israel's Arab--Jewish Cities and Its Impact on Israel's Israeli-Palestinian Relations," unpublished paper, 2012.

49. Zaher, interview with the author.

50. Soffer, interview with the author. See also Bystrov and Soffer, "Israel: Demography 2013–2034," 36–39.

51. Bystrov and Soffer, "Israel: Demography 2013–2034."

52. Adalah, "Demolition and Eviction of Bedouin Citizens of Israel in the Naqab (Negev): The Prawer Plan," http://adalah.org/eng/Articles/1589/Demolition-and-Eviction-of-Bedouin-Citizens-of-in; Noam Sheizaf, "Report: 40,000 Bedouins Will Be Evicted from Homes Under Prawer Plan," +972, December 8, 2013, http://972mag.com/report-40000-bedouin-will-be-evicted-from-homes-under-prawer-plan/83238/. In June 2013, the Knesset passed a law that would involve "the mass expulsion of the Arab Bedouin community in the [Negev] Desert in the south of Israel." The Prawer-Begin Plan would "result in the destruction of 35 'unrecognized Arab' Bedouin villages, the forced displacement of up to 70,000 Bedouin citizens of Israel, and the dispossession of their historical lands in the [Negev]."

53. Jodi Rudoren, "Israel Shelves Plan to Move Bedouins amid Outcry," *New York Times*, December 12, 2013, http://www.nytimes.com/2013/12/13/world/middleeast/israel-shelves-plan-to-move-bedouins-amid-outcry.html. The protests coincided with P5+1 talks with Iran. Netanyahu objected to discussion of the proposed formula to deal with the nuclear issue and did not want international media attention on the protests.

54. Bystrov and Soffer, "Israel: Demography 2013–2034."

55. Alyan et al., "Policies of Neglect in East Jerusalem."

56. See Jacob Berkman, "Jerusalem Is Israel's Poorest City," *JTA*, May 11, 2010, http://www.jta.org/2010/05/11/fundermentalist/jerusalem-is-israels-poorest-city; and Nir Hasson, "Israeli Plan for East Jerusalem: A Trial Run in Annexation," *Haaretz*, June 30, 2014, http://www.haaretz.com/news/.premium-1.602097. The municipality has belatedly woken up to this fact and is now injecting huge sums for development into East Jerusalem in order to take this part of the city off the diplomatic agenda and further secure Jewish enclaves.

57. Soffer, interview with the author, November 7, 2011.

58. Consociationalism, or "consensus democracy," is a form of power sharing in which all interest groups are represented within an institutional framework that brings them together. It is found in societies divided along ethnic, religious, ideological, cultural, and other lines. Arend Lijphart provides modern analytic and empirical models of consociational

governance in his classic *Patterns of Democracy*; a full, free copy of the 1999 edition can be downloaded at http://digamo.free.fr/lijphart99.pdf.

Chapter 10 **Facing the Truth**

1. Jodi Rudoren, "50 Days of War Leave Israelis and Palestinians Only More Entrenched," *New York Times*, August 29, 2014, http://www.nytimes.com/2014/08/30/world/middleeast/50-days-of-war-leave-israelis-and-palestinians-only-more-entrenched.html?hp&action=click&pgtype=Homepage&version=HpSumSmallMediaHigh&module=second-column-region®ion=top-news&WT.nav=top-news&_r=0.

2. For a review of the relentlessly negative behavioral patterns that typified Israeli and Palestinian attitudes between 2003 and 2009, see Sammy Smuha, *Index of Arab-Jewish Relations 2003–2009* (Haifa: Jewish-Arab Center, University of Haifa, 2010), http://soc.haifa.ac.il/~s.smooha/uploads/editor_uploads/files/IndexOfArabJewishRelations2003_2009.pdf; Muhareb, "An Analysis of Israeli Public Opinion"; Ben Meir and Bagno-Moldavsky, *Vox Populi*; Shamir, *Public Opinion in the Israeli-Palestinian Conflict*; Bar-Tal, "Why Does Fear Override Hope?," 601–27.

3. Moore and Aweiss, "Hatred of 'Others,'" 151–72.

4. Wexler et al., "'Victims of Our Own Narratives?'"

5. Ron Kampeas, "Study Elicits Harsh Response from Israel," *Jewish Exponent*, February 6, 2013, http://jewishexponent.com/study-elicity-harsh-response-from-Israel.

6. Wexler et al., "'Victims of our own Narratives?," 1.

7. "Israeli and Palestinian Textbooks Teaching Children to Hate Each Other," *Economist*, February 8, 2013.

8. Nurit Peled-Elhanan, *Palestine in Israeli School Books: Ideology and Propaganda in Education* (London: I. B. Tauris, 2012).

9. Ibid., 231. Coffin fully referenced on 253.

10. Ibid.

11. Ibid. She cites (Ricoeur, Paul. *Memory, History, Forgetting*, trans. Kathleen Blamey and David Pellauer (Chicago: University of Chicago Press, 2004 (2000), 448.

12. Peled-Elhanan, 232.

13. Ibid.

14. Rabinowitz, Dan, professor, Department of Sociology and Anthropology, Tel Aviv University; fully referenced in ibid., 257.

15. Bekerman and Zembylas, fully referenced in ibid., 253.

16. Ibid., 235.

17. Kupermintz et al., "Perception of the Other Among Jewish & Arab Youth in Israel: 2004-2005," Center for Research on Peace Education, University of Haifa, 2007 (translated from Hebrew).

18. Halperin, "Emotional Barriers to Peace: Negative Emotions & Public Opinion about the Peace Process in the Middle East," *Journal of Peace Psychology*, 17, 22–45 2011.

19. Eran Halperin, Daphna Canetti-Nisim, and Sivan Hirsch-Hoefler, "Emotional Antecedents of Political Intolerance: The Central Role of Group-Based Hatred," *Political Psychology* 30, no. 1 (February 2009), 93–123.

20. Halperin and Gross, "Intergroup Anger in Intractable Conflict: Long-term Sentiments Predict Anger Responses During the Gaza War," *Group Processes & Intergroup Relations*, Vol. 14 (4), 2010, 477–488, http://scholar.google.com/scholar_url?url=http://www.researchgate.net/profile/Eran_Halperin/publication/241648500_Intergroup_anger_in

_intractable_conflict_Long-term_sentiments_predict_anger_responses_during_the_Gaza_War/links/0a85e52da9fe0885a4000000.pdf&hl=en&sa=X&scisig=AAGBfm25nd6sxh0gEgsLmYzb7nz51vODzw&nossl=1&oi=scholarr.

21. For the role of fear in the conflict, see E. Halperin, "Group-Based Hatred in Intractable Conflict in Israel," *Journal of Conflict Resolution*, 52, 713–736, 2008. In "Socio-Psychological Barriers to Resolving the Israeli-Palestinian Conflict" in *Barriers to Peace*, 47, Halperin et al, refer to a study by Halperin and Canetti-Nisim, 2008, which found that 63.9 percent of Jews in Israel expressed high levels of hatred toward Palestinians, etc. However, there is no reference to the Halperin, Canetti-Nisim study in the references accompanying the study, 53–57. I am assuming that the ommission was an error on their part as the authors are all highly regarded academics.

22. Halperin et al., "Socio-Psychological Barriers to Resolving the Israeli Conflict," 45. See also Nimrod Rosler, "Fear and Conflict Resolution Theoretical Discussion and a Case Study from Israel," the Gildenhorn Institute for Israel Studies (GIIS), University of Maryland, November 2013.

23. Gideon Levy, "Survey: Most Israeli Jews Wouldn't Give Palestinians Vote If West Bank Was Annexed," *Haaretz*, http://www.haaretz.com/news/national/survey-most-israeli-jews-wouldn-t-give-palestinians-vote-if-west-bank-was-annexed.premium-1.471644.

24. Mahmoud Muhareb, "An Analysis of Israeli Public Opinion" (review of Daniel Bar-Tal, *Living with the Conflict: Socio-Psychological Analysis of the Israeli Jewish Society* (Jerusalem: Carmel, 2007, in Hebrew), Arab Center for Research & Policy Studies Book Reviews (Doha Institute), February 2011, 4–5, http://english.dohainstitute.org/file/get/bb9adc0c-2e8a-4341-925a-b146c765b7a0.pdf. See also Seth Freedman, "Culture of Fear," *Guardian*, June 22, 2008, http://www.theguardian.com/commentisfree/2008/jun/22/israelandthepalestinians.fear; and Ravit Hech, "Israelis Have Become Exactly What They Fear," *Haaretz*, June 12, 2014, http://www.haaretz.com/opinion/.premium-1.598239.

25. See Moore and Aweiss, "Hatred of 'Others,'" *Palestinian Media Watch* (PMW; http://www.palwatch.org/home.aspx) is a media watchdog that monitors and analyzes the PA through media and schoolbooks and in messages used by Palestinian leaders from the Palestinian Authority, Fatah, and Hamas. See Michael Sharnoff, "Palestinian Attitudes Toward Israel," Foreign Policy Research Institute, May 2012, http://www.fpri.org/articles/2012/05/palestinian-attitudes-toward-israel.

26. David Pollock, "Beyond Words: Causes, Consequences, and Cures for Palestinian Authority Hate Speech," Washington Institute: Policy Focus 124, September 2013, http://www.washingtoninstitute.org/policy-analysis/view/beyond-words-causes-consequences-and-cures-for-palestinian-authority-hate-s.

27. Ibid. See also Palestinian Center for Policy and Survey Research, "Palestinian Public Opinion Poll No. 50." Here one finds contrary sentiments: A majority of 77 percent are worried that they might be hurt by Israelis in their daily life, and 83 percent believe that Israel's long-term aspiration is to annex all Palestinian territories and expel the population or deny them their political rights.

28. Reuters, "Abbas: 'Not a Single Israeli' in Future Palestinian State," *Jerusalem Post*, July 30, 2013, http://www.jpost.com/Middle-East/Abbas-wants-not-a-single-Israeli-in-future-Palestinian-state-321470.

29. Gil Ronen, "PA Incitement: Jews Are 'Subhuman,'" *Arutz Sheva*, January 5, 2014, http://www.israelnationalnews.com/News/News.aspx/175949#.VCGV7PldVCg.

30. Jodi Rudoren, "Fate of 3 Kidnapped Israelis Raises Tensions on Many Fronts," *New York Times*, June 22, 2014, http://www.nytimes.com/2014/06/23/world/middleeast/fate-of-3-kid

napped-israelis-twists-tensions-on-many-fronts.html?action=click&contentCollection=Middle; Dalit Halevi and Elad Benari, "Hamas Leader: Bless Whoever Kidnapped the Youths," *Arutz Sheva*, June 24, 2014, http://www.israelnationalnews.com/News/News.aspx/182085#.VGgm7smKUQA.

Hamas leader Khaled Meshaal denied that his group was behind the kidnappings but welcomed the abductions. In August, he acknowledged that the three men charged with the kidnapping were in fact Hamas members, but went to lengths to reiterate that the kidnappings had not been ordered by the Hamas leadership: they were the work of local operatives acting on their own without official authorization. "Mashaal Admits Hamas Members Kidnapped and Murdered Naftali, Gilad and Eyal," *Jerusalem Post*, August 23, 2014, http://www.jpost.com/Arab-Israeli-Conflict/Mashaal-admits-Hamas-members-kidnapped-and-murdered-Naftali-Gilad-and-Eyal-371997.

31. "Israeli Prime Minister Netanyahu's Eulogy at the Funerals of Eyal Yifrach, Naftali Frankel and Gilad Shaar," *Algemeiner*, July 2, 2014, http://www.algemeiner.com/2014/07/02/full-transcript-israeli-prime-minister-netanyahu%E2%80%99s-eulogy-at-the-funeral-for-eyal-yifrach-naftali-frankel-and-gilad-shaar/.

32. "Israel Searches for Teens Kidnapped in West Bank, IDF Arrests 50 Prisoners Released in 2011 Shalit Swap," *Haaretz*, June 17, 2014, http://www.haaretz.com/news/diplomacy-defense/1.599302.

33. "Israeli Incitement: Fueling Intolerance & Hate Crimes," Institute for Middle East Understanding, August 6, 2014, http://imeu.org/article/israeli-incitement-fueling-intolerance-hate-crimes?utm_source=feedburner&utm_medium=feed&utm_campaign=Feed%3A+imeu+%28IMEU+%3A+Institute+for+Middle+East+Understanding%29.

34. "Can Israeli and Palestinian Leaders End the Revenge Attacks?" *New York Times*, editorial, July 7, 2014, http://www.nytimes.com/2014/07/08/opinion/can-israeli-and-palestinian-leaders-end-the-revenge-attacks.html.

35. Isabel Kershner, "Arab Boy's Death Escalates Clash over Abductions," *New York Times*, July 2, 2014, http://www.nytimes.com/2014/07/03/world/middleeast/israel.html?_r=0; Ahmad Melhem, "Israelis Accused of Torturing Palestinian Child Detainees," *Al-Monitor*, July 25, 2014, http://www.al-monitor.com/pulse/originals/2014/07/israel-torture-children-prisons-detainees.html.

36. Jack Khoury, Gili Cohen, Shirly Seilder, and Associated Press, "Police Arrests 20 Protesters as Riots Spread to Arab Towns," *Haaretz*, http://www.haaretz.com/news/diplomacy-defense/.premium-1.603263.

37. Jodi Rudoren, "Tensions High in Jerusalem as Palestinian Teenager Is Given a Martyr's Burial," *New York Times*, July 4, 2014, http://www.nytimes.com/2014/07/05/world/middleeast/israel.html?_r=0.

38. "E. Jerusalem: Hundreds of Youths Arrested in Riots," i24 News, September 9, 2014, http://www.i24news.tv/en/news/israel/diplomacy-defense/44342-140919-e-jerusalem-hundreds-of-youths-arrested-in-riots; Nir Hasson, "Jerusalem Prosecution Hardens Stance on Palestinian Minors Suspected of Rioting," *Haaretz*, September 22, 2014, http://www.haaretz.com/news/diplomacy-defense/.premium-1.617090.

39. "Crowd Shouts 'Death to the Arabs' at an Israeli Wedding of Jew and Muslim," Reuters, August 17, 2014, http://www.newsweek.com/crowd-shouts-death-arabs-israeli-wedding-jew-and-muslim-265150; Adam Horowitz, "Video: Jewish Mob Chanting 'Death to Arabs!' Stops Cars in Jerusalem to Check Drivers' Ethnicity," *Mondoweiss*, July 6, 2014, http://mondoweiss.net/2014/07/chanting-jerusalem-ethnicity#sthash.Mhf90gvO.dpuf; "'Death to Arabs' Sprayed on Arab-Jewish School in Capital," *Times of Israel*, October 30, 2014, http://www

.timesofisrael.com/death-to-arabs-sprayed-on-arab-jewish-school-in-capital/#ixzz3WwDzVER3; Jodi Rudoren, "Tensions High in Jerusalem as Palestinian Teenager Is Given a Martyr's Burial"; Isabel Kershner and Jodi Rudoren, "Teenagers' Deaths Raise Fears of Shift from Political Struggle to Blood Feud," *New York Times*, July 3, 2014, http://www.nytimes.com/2014/07/04/world/middleeast/palestinian-militants-and-israel-trade-attacks.html?action=click&content; Melhem, "Israelis Accused of Torturing Palestinian Child Detainees."

40. Roger Cohen, "Cycles of Revenge in Israel & Palestine," *New York Times*, July 4, 2014, http://www.nytimes.com/2014/07/04/opinion/roger-cohen-cycles-of-revenge-in-israel-and-palestine.html.

41. "Jewish Hate of Arabs Proves: Israel Must Undergo Cultural Revolution," *Haaretz*, July 7, 2014, http://www.haaretz.com/misc/iphone-article/.premium-1.603451.

42. On the hatred that manifested itself among Israeli and Palestinian youth after the kidnapping and killing of the three Israeli teens and the subsequent murder of the Palestinian youth who was burned to death after being forced to drink gasoline, see David Shulman, "Palestine: The Hatred and the Hope," *New York Review of Books*, August 2, 2014, http://www.nybooks.com/blogs/nyrblog/2014/aug/02/palestine-hatred-and-hope/?insrc=rel.

43. "We think differently, we attach different meanings to the same words." Shlomo Ben-Ami, interview with the author, March 9, 2012.

44. Aronson, "A Never-Ending End to Claims," in *The Palestinian Refugee Problem*, 266–84. For Israel, an end of claims is embraced as part of the demand to close accounts arising from the *Nakba*, including UN Resolution 194. For Palestinians, an end of claims is promoted as a vehicle for realizing Palestinian demands for a just resolution to Palestinian losses, national, personal, and territorial, over the last seventy years.

45. Haugen and Boutros, *Locust Effect*.

46. "Mounting Pessimism About Two State Israeli-Palestinian Solution." Pew Global Poll, June 9 2014, http://www.pewglobal.org/2014/06/25/mounting-pessimism-about-two-state-israeli-palestinian-solution/; "Despite Their Wide Differences, Many Israelis and Palestinians Want Bigger Role for Obama in Resolving Conflict," Pew Global Poll May 2013, http://www.pewglobal.org/2013/05/09/despite-their-wide-differences-many-israelis-and-palestinians-want-bigger-role-for-obama-in-resolving-conflict/; Zogby Research Services, "Israel and Palestine: 20 Years After Oslo," January 2014, https://www.google.com/webhp?sourceid=chrome-instant&rlz=1C1JPGB_enUS634US634&ion=1&espv=2&ie=UTF-8#q=zogby%20research%20services%2C%20%E2%80%9Cisrael%20and%20palestine%3A%2020%20years%20after%20oslo%2C%E2%80%9D%20january%202014%2C; Ephraim Ya'ar and Tamar Hermann, "Peace Index Column April 2014," Israel Democracy Institute, http://en.idi.org.il/media/3164001/Peace_Index_April_%202014-Eng.pdf; "Survey: Most Israeli Jews Wouldn't Give Palestinians Vote If West Bank Was Annexed" *Haaretz*, October 23, 2012, http://www.haaretz.com/news/national/survey-most-israeli-jews-wouldn-t-give-palestinians-vote-if-west-bank-was-annexed.premium-1.471644; Telhami, Kull, et al., "Israeli and Palestinian Public Opinion on Negotiating a Final Status Peace Agreement," http://public-consultation.org/pdf/is-pal-report.pdf; Palestinian Center for Policy and Survey Research. Poll #54 (http://www.pcpsr.org/en/node/596); "All of the Above: Identity Paradoxes of Young People in Israel," Dr. Ralf Hexel and Dr. Roby Nathanson, Israel: Friedrich-Ebert-Stiftung, 2010, 146; The Washington Institute, http://www.washingtoninstitute.org/policy-analysis/view/new-palestinian-poll-shows-hardline-views-but-some-pragmatism-too; Matt Duss, ThinkProgress, March 2014, http://thinkprogress.org/world/2014/03/05/3328171/palestinian-recognition-of-israel-as-a-jewish-state/.

47. According to pollster Khalil Shikaki, among Palestinians between ages eighteen and thirty-four there is "solid support" for a one-state solution. Bernard Avishai, Dani Dayan,

Forsan Hussein, Eva Illouz, Bassim Khoury, Erel Margalit, Danny Rubinstein, and Khalil Shikaki, "Israel and Palestine: Where to Go from Here," *Harper's*, September 2014, 35, http://harpers.org/archive/2014/09/israel-and-palestine/.

48. According to the previously cited Zogby poll, "68 percent of Israelis are convinced that Palestinians were the main beneficiaries of Oslo while 64 percent of Israelis say that they were harmed by the Accords. On the other side, 75 percent of Palestinians maintain that the Israelis were Oslo's big winners, with 49 percent of Palestinians asserting that their interests were harmed by the Accords." Zogby Research Services, "Israel and Palestine: 20 Years After Oslo."

49. Sari Nusseibeh, "How Israel Can Avoid a Hellish Future," *Haaretz*, June 25, 2014, http://www.haaretz.com/news/diplomacy-defense/israel-peace-conference/1.599063.

50. For a stimulating debate between Uri Avnery and Ilan Pappé, Avnery making the case for two states and Pappé the case for one, see Uri Avnery and Ilan Pappé, "Two States or One State," CounterCurrents.org, June 11, 2007, http://www.countercurrents.org/pappe110607.htm. See also Morris, *One State, Two States.*

51. Chemi Shalev, "Leading Palestinian Intellectual: We Already Have a One-State Solution," *Haaretz*, December 5, 2011, http://www.haaretz.com/news/diplomacy-defense/leading-palestinian-intellectual-we-already-have-a-one-state-solution-1.399629. This is the view of Rashid Khalidi, Edward Said Professor of Arab Studies, Columbia University, a member of the Palestinian delegation at Madrid and one of the first proponents of a two-state solution. Among other scholars and "prominents" who advocate or advocated a unitary or binational state are Ali Abunimah, Jamil Hilal, Ilan Pappé, Sharif Elmusa, As'ad Ghanen, Jack Strawson, Sari Nusseibeh, Jamal Dajani, Caroline B. Glick, Tony Judt (deceased), and Edward Said (deceased).

52. See Abunimah, *One Country*; Hilal, *Where Now for Palestine?*; Pappé, "The Two State Solution Died over a Decade Ago"; Sharif Elmusa, "Alternative Approaches for Resolving the Israeli-Palestinian Conflict," in Hilal, *Where Now for Palestine?*; Bavly and Ghanem, *One State, Two Peoples*; Jack Strawson, *Legal Fundamentalism in the Palestinian-Israeli Conflict* (London: Pluto Press, 2010); Nusseibeh, *What Is a Palestinian State Worth?*; Jamal Dajani, "Israel: Occupation or Apartheid?" *Huffington Post*, April 7, 2010, http://www.huffingtonpost.com/jamal-dajani/israel-occupation-or-apar_b_450817.html; Glick, *The Israeli Solution*; Tony Judt, "Israel: The Alternative," *New York Review of Books*, October 23, 2003, http://www.nybooks.com/articles/archives/2003/oct/23/israel-the-alternative/; Edward Said, "The One-State Solution," *New York Times Magazine*, January 10, 1999, http://www.nytimes.com/1999/01/10/magazine/the-one-state-solution.html; Mark LeVine and Mathias Mossberg, eds. *One Land, Two States: Israel and Palestine as Parallel States* (Berkeley: University of California Press, 2014).

53. Akiva Eldar, "Netanyahu Convinces Israelis of Existential Threat," *Al-Monitor*, July 28, 2014, http://www.al-monitor.com/pulse/originals/2014/07/israel-protective-edge-right-left-support-avri-gilad.html.

54. Yaakov Lapin, "Hamas in West Bank 'Planned to Topple Palestinian Authority,'" *Jerusalem Post*, August 18, 2014, http://www.jpost.com/Arab-Israeli-Conflict/Massive-Hamas-infrastructure-in-West-Bank-planned-to-topple-the-Palestinian-Authority-371409; "Shin Bet Chief Met Abbas to Update Him on Hamas Plot to Topple PA," *Jerusalem Post*, September 1, 2014, http://www.jpost.com/Arab-Israeli-Conflict/Shin-Bet-chief-met-Abbas-to-update-him-on-Hamas-plot-to-topple-PA-373097.

The IDF and Shin Bet announced on August 18—just after cease-fire talks had begun between Israel and the Palestinian Authority, acting on behalf of Hamas in Cairo—that they had uncovered "a large-scale Hamas terrorist formation in the West Bank and Jerusalem [that had] planned to destabilize the region through a series of deadly terrorist attacks in Israel and then topple the Fatah-ruled Palestinian Authority." Nonsense, Hamas said, of course. "Shin Bet Chief Met Abbas to Update Him on Hamas Plot to Topple PA," *Jerusalem Post*, September 1, 9014, http://www.jpost.com/Arab-Israeli-Conflict/Shin-Bet-chief-met-Abbas-to-update-him-on-Hamas-plot-to-topple-PA-373097.

The *New York Times* reported that although Abbas had praised the "Palestinian resistance" during the fighting, his attitude is somewhat different after the cease-fire. It cites Arab news reports that he "criticized Hamas for prolonging the hostilities and running a shadow government in Gaza, and accused it of plotting a coup against him in the West Bank. Hamas leaders in Gaza were dismissive of Mr. Abbas and his new diplomatic initiative [at the UN] demanding a three-year deadline for ending Israel's occupation, renewing doubts about the durability of their reconciliation." Jodi Rudoren, "Hamas Emerges Buoyant Despite Bloodshed and Devastation in Gaza," *New York Times*, September 3, 2014, http://www.nytimes.com/2014/09/04/world/middleeast/israel-gaza-hamas-fatah.html?hp&action=click&pgtype=Homepage&version=LargeMediaHeadlineSum&module=photo-spot-region®ion=top-news&WT.nav=top-news.

Shlomi Eldar was more skeptical. See his "Despite Reconciliation, Abbas in No Position to Negotiate for Hamas," *Al-Monitor*, August 25, 2014, http://www.al-monitor.com/pulse/originals/2014/08/mahmoud-abbas-hamas-plot-topple-down-khaled-meshaal-qatar.html.

55. Khaled Abu Toameh, "PA Chief Abbas: Hamas Leader Mashaal Is a Liar," *Jerusalem Post*, September 1, 2014, http://www.jpost.com/Middle-East/Abbas-Hamas-leader-Mashaal-is-a-liar-374113. See also Shlomi Eldar, "Despite Reconciliation, Abbas in No Position to Negotiate for Hamas," *Al-Monitor*, August 25, 2014, http://www.al-monitor.com/pulse/originals/2014/08/mahmoud-abbas-hamas-plot-topple-down-khaled-meshaal-qatar.html.

56. Jodi Rudoren, "Palestinian Leader Assails Hamas, Calling Unity Pact into Question," *New York Times*, September 7, 2014, http://www.nytimes.com/2014/09/08/world/middleeast/gaza-strip-palestinian-leader-assails-hamas-calling-unity-pact-into-question.html.

57. See Hexel and Nathanson, "All of the Above."

58. Daniel Estrin, "After 50-Day Gaza War with Israel, Poll Shows Dramatic Rise in Palestinian Support for Hamas," *U.S. News & World Report*, September 2, 2014, http://www.usnews.com/news/world/articles/2014/09/02/after-gaza-war-poll-finds-support-for-hamas-rises.

59. Hirsh Goodman, "Losing the Propaganda War," *New York Times*, January 31, 2014, http://www.nytimes.com/2014/02/01/opinion/sunday/how-israel-is-losing-the-propaganda-war.html?_r=0.

60. Peter Beaumont, "Israel Risks Becoming Apartheid State If Peace Talks Fail, Says John Kerry," *Guardian*, April 28, 2014, http://www.theguardian.com/world/2014/apr/28/israel-apartheid-state-peace-talks-john-kerry. "It is believed to be the first time a U.S. official of Kerry's standing used the term 'apartheid' in the context of Israel." His remarks provoked an angry response from Israel, which is extraordinarily sensitive to the charge. So, being the diplomat on the spot and hoping that he might have another shot at a peace process, Kerry backed off. Aaron Blake, "Kerry Backs Off 'Apartheid State' Comment," *Washington Post*, April 29, 2014, http://www.washingtonpost.com/blogs/post-politics/wp/2014/04/29/kerry-backs-off-apartheid-state-comment/. "Kerry says he wishes he would have used different words when he said that Israel could become an 'apartheid state' without a peace deal with Palestinians."

61. Oren Yiftachel, "Neither Two States nor One: The Disengagement and 'Creeping Apartheid' in Israel/Palestine," *Arab World Geographer/Le Géographe du monde arabe* 8, no. 3 (2005):

125–29, http://www.geog.bgu.ac.il/members/Yiftachel/new_papers_eng/Yiftachel%20in%20Arab%20World%20Geographer.pdf; Richard Rogers and Anat Ben-David, "Coming to Terms: A Conflict Analysis of the Usage, in Official and Unofficial Sources, of 'Security Fence,' 'Apartheid Wall,' and Other Terms for the Structure Between Israel and the Palestinian Territories," *Media, War & Conflict* 3, no. 2 (August 2010), 202–29, http://mwc.sagepub.com/content/3/2/202.short; Carter, *Palestine: Peace Not Apartheid*; Tyler Levitan, "Head of Canada's Israel Lobby Claims Israeli Apartheid Week Renamed Islam Awareness Week," *Mondoweiss*, June 5, 2014, http://mondoweiss.net/2014/06/apartheid-renamed-awareness.html.

62. Melissa Eddy, "Anti-Semitism Rises in Europe Amid Israel-Gaza Conflict," *New York Times*, August 1, 2014, http://www.nytimes.com/2014/08/02/world/europe/anger-in-europe-over-the-israeli-gaza-conflict-reverberates-as-anti-semitism.html?_r=0.

63. A Dutch pension conglomerate in December 2013 divested "from Israel's five largest banks because of their ties to occupation." According to [Israel's] finance minister, even a partial European boycott would cost Israel [about $5.7 billion] in exports annually and almost 10,000 jobs. Goodman, "Losing the Propaganda War."

64. Associated Press and *Times of Israel* staff, "UN: December Blizzard Example of Human-Induced Extreme Weather," *Times of Israel*, March 24, 2014, http://www.timesofisrael.com/un-report-says-climate-change-led-to-snow-storm/.

65. "Climate Change 2014: Impacts, Adaptation, and Vulnerability," Intergovernmental Panel on Climate Change, http://ipcc-wg2.gov/AR5/; Intergovernmental Panel on Climate Change, "Report Overview: Climate Change 2013: The Physical Science Basis," http://www.climatechange2013.org/report/.

66. J. J. Goldberg provides an excellent encapsulation of the IPPC reports released in 2014. J. J. Goldberg, "Flood of Reports Point to a Warming Earth—but Concern Drops," *Jewish Daily Forward*, May 30, 2014, http://forward.com/articles/198771/flood-of-reports-point-to-a-warming-earth-but-co/; Justin Gillis, "U.N. Draft Report Lists Unchecked Emissions' Risks," *New York Times*, August 26, 2014, http://www.nytimes.com/2014/08/27/science/earth/greenhouse-gas-emissions-are-growing-and-growing-more-dangerous-draft-of-un-report-says.html?ref=world&_r=0. A draft of the UN report, writes Gillis, found that: "Runaway growth in the emission of greenhouse gases is swamping all political efforts to deal with the problem, raising the risk of 'severe, pervasive and irreversible impacts' over the coming decades. Global warming is already cutting grain production by several percentage points, the report found, and that could become much worse if emissions continue unchecked. Higher seas, devastating heat waves, torrential rain and other climate extremes are also being felt around the world as a result of human-produced emissions, the draft report said, and those problems are likely to intensify unless the gases are brought under control. . . ." 'Human influence has been detected in warming of the atmosphere and the ocean, in changes in the global water cycle, in reduction in snow and ice, and in global mean-sea-level rise; and it is extremely likely to have been the dominant cause of the observed warming since the mid-20th century,' the draft report said. 'The risk of abrupt and irreversible change increases as the magnitude of the warming increases.'"

67. "Climate Realities," *New York Times*, September 21, 2014, http://www.nytimes.com/2014/09/21/opinion/sunday/climate-realities.html?_r=0.

68. Ibid.

69. "Greenhouse Gas Emissions Rise at Fastest Rate for 30 Years," *Guardian*, September 9, 2014, http://www.theguardian.com/environment/2014/sep/09/carbon-dioxide-emissions-greenhouse-gases. Karl Ritter, "UN Climate Talks In Lima Reach Agreement" *Huffington*

Post, December 15, 2014. http://www.huffingtonpost.com/2014/12/14/un-climate-talks-in-lima-_n_6321950.html

Ritter reported that the UN climate change talks in Peru were saved from collapse at the last moment. "The U.N. talks were still far away from reaching any agreement on reducing emissions of carbon dioxide and other greenhouse gases to a level that scientists say would keep global warming in check. But the Paris agreement would be the first to call on all countries to control their emissions."

70. Joby Warrick, "CO2 Levels in Atmosphere Rising at Dramatically Faster Rate, U.N. Report Warns," *Washington Post*, September 8, 2014, http://www.washingtonpost.com/national/health-science/co2-levels-in-atmosphere-rising-at-dramatically-faster-rate-un-report-warns/2014/09/08/3e2277d2-378d-11e4-bdfb-de4104544a37_story.html. "The latest figures from the World Meteorological Organization's monitoring network are considered particularly significant because they reflect not only the amount of carbon pumped into the air by humans, but also the complex interaction between man-made gases and the natural world."

71. See Oli Brown and Alec Crawford, "Rising Temperatures, Rising Tensions: Climate Change and the Risk of Violent Conflict in the Middle East," International Institute for Sustainable Development (IISD), 2009, https://www.iisd.org/pdf/2009/rising_temps_middle_east.pdf.

72. Youssef Bassil, *Journal of Science*, Vol. 2, No. 3, 2012, 163.

73. Israel uses 183 liters per capita per day; the part of the West Bank connected to the water grid uses 73 liters and a further 20–25 liters from sources not connected to the grid; Gaza uses 70–90 liters from the coastal aquifer—overpumped for decades—and some 180 million cubic meters (mcm) are pumped from the coastal aquifer, although the replenishment rate is only 50–60 mcm per year; the water is saline and polluted and 95 percent unfit for drinking, compelling residents to purchase treated water. Even with its low per-capita consumption, even with rationing, the Palestinian Authority has to purchase water from Mekorot, the Israeli national water company, at a price well above what Israelis pay. B'Tselem, "Background: Water Crisis," February 25, 2014, http://www.btselem.org/water; Palestine Liberation Organization, Negotiations Affairs Department, "Israel's Exploitation of Palestinian Water Sources," media brief, February 13, 2014, http://www.nad-plo.org/userfiles/file/media%20brief/Water%20Statement.pdf; Israeli Ministry of Foreign Affairs, "The Water Issue in the West Bank and Gaza," June 24, 1999, http://www.mfa.gov.il/mfa/foreignpolicy/peace/guide/pages/the%20water%20issue%20in%20the%20west%20bank%20and%20gaza.aspx; Adri Nieuwhof, "Crimes Against Humanity: Stealing Palestine's Water Resources," Global Research, February 2013, http://www.globalresearch.ca/crimes-against-humanity-stealing-palestines-water-resources/5321547; "Troubled Water: Palestinians Denied Fair Access to Water," 2009.

74. For an excellent exposition of issues relating to the Jordan River, see Daene McKinney, "The Jordan River Valley Under Climate Change," University of Texas, Austin, April 20, 2010, http://www.caee.utexas.edu/prof/mckinney/ce397/Topics/Jordan/Jordan(2010).pdf.

75. For issues relating to water and the Accords, see B'Tselem, "Water Crisis: Issues Under the Oslo Accords," April 23, 2014, http://www.btselem.org/water/oslo_accords.

76. Amira Hass, "Just How Much Do Palestinians Rely on Israel for Water?" *Haaretz*, February 13, 2014, http://www.haaretz.com/news/middle-east/.premium-1.573976.

77. "As far back as 1919, the Zionists began a determined effort to ensure that southern Lebanon up to the Litani River would be included in a future Israeli state." They coveted the water. Habib, *Consociationalism and the Continuous Crisis*, 84–88. Hence their alignment with Maronite Christians in the Lebanese civil war. Indeed, it appears the Zionists were aware

of possible water shortage in Palestine as early as 1919. See United Nations Security Council Official Records, Thirty-sixth year, 2320th Meeting, December 18, 1981, New York, Section 58, http://unispal.un.org/UNISPAL.NSF/0/4A0B0E83E246E43205256800005CA622.

78. For a comprehensive overview of water distribution and the problems with water supply, see Brooks, Trottier, and Doliner, "Changing the Nature of Palestinian Transboundary Water Agreements," 674–75. "Israel has been pushing to the limits of the sustainable water resources available to it and, all too often, beyond those limits. Though desalination has provided some relief from concerns for drinking water supplies, it comes with a high dollar and energy cost, as well as raising new environmental problems." Ironically, desalinated water is too pure for irrigation, which remains, by far, the largest use of water throughout MENA [Middle East and North Africa]—even in Israel, where agriculture is a minor element in the economy. "Palestinians, too, push against and exceed the limits of sustainable water resources, particularly in the Gaza Strip." David B. Brooks and Julie Trottier, "An Agreement to Share Water Between Israelis and Palestinians: The FoEME proposal, Revised Version," EcoPeace/Friends of the Earth Middle East, March 2012. See also Zafrir Rinat, "Israel's National Water Carrier: Both Boom and Bane," *Haaretz*, June 26, 2014, http://www.haaretz.com/life/nature-environment/.premium-1.601284; Yuval Elizur, "Over and Drought: Why the End of Israel's Water Shortage Is a Secret," *Haaretz*, January 24, 2014, http://www.haaretz.com/news/national/1.570374; Peretz Darr, "Israel Is Digging Its Own Watery Grave," *Haaretz*, December 26, 2013, http://www.haaretz.com/opinion/.premium-1.565762.

79. Avi Bar-Eli, "Jordan, Palestinians Seek to Buy Israel's Excess Desalinated Water," *Haaretz*, January 9, 2014, http://www.haaretz.com/business/.premium-1.567667.

80. Bou-Zeid and El-Fadel, "Climate Change and Water Resources in Lebanon and the Middle East," 343.

81. See "Israel, the West Bank, and Gaza," United Nations University (old Web site), http://archive.unu.edu/unupress/unupbooks/80859e/80859E08.htm; Gidon Bromberg, "Will the Jordan River Keep On Flowing?" September 18, 2008, http://e360.yale.edu/feature/will_the_jordan_river_keep_on_flowing/2064/; Akiva Eldar, "Israel-Palestinian Peace Requires Realism on Jordan Valley," *Al-Monitor*, February 5, 2014, http://www.al-monitor.com/pulse/originals/2014/02/jordan-valley-dead-sea-natural-resource-middle-east-peace.html.

Eldar writes: "How does a two-state solution reconcile with the status quo in which 85% of the Jordan Valley and the northern Dead Sea—which constitute more than one-quarter of the West Bank area—are off-limits to Palestinians, and 83.4% of the valley lands are under the jurisdiction of the local Jewish councils? Is it really possible to instill in the hearts of the region's Palestinian residents hope for a just peace while the Israeli regime prevents many Palestinian villages from hooking up to the water infrastructure and forces them to make do with a daily consumption of a mere 20 liters (5 gallons) per person, a tiny portion of the daily consumption of their neighbors in the adjacent settlement? With 28 of the 42 Israeli water wells in the West Bank located in the Jordan Valley, is there any sane Israeli who believes that Palestinian President Mahmoud Abbas will deed the area over to Israel?"

Daene McKinney, "The Jordan River Valley Under Climate Change," University of Texas, Austin, April 20, 2010, http://www.caee.utexas.edu/prof/mckinney/ce397/Topics/Jordan/Jordan(2010).pdf; Zafrir Rinat, "Israel Basks in Longest Winter Heat Wave in Almost 40 Years," *Haaretz*, February 15, 2010, http://www.haaretz.com/print-edition/news/israel-basks-in-longest-winter-heat-wave-in-almost-40-years-1.265995.

82. See Oli Brown and Alec Crawford, "Rising Temperatures, Rising Tensions Climate Change and the Risk of Violent Conflict in the Middle East."

83. Brian Clark Howard, "West Antarctica Glaciers Collapsing, Adding to Sea-Level Rise," *National Geographic*, May 12, 2014, http://news.nationalgeographic.com/news/2014/05/140512-thwaites-glacier-melting-collapse-west-antarctica-ice-warming/; Chris Mooney, "This Ice Sheet Will Unleash a Global Superstorm Sandy That Never Ends," *Mother Jones*, May 23, 2014, http://www.motherjones.com/environment/2014/05/inquiring-minds-richard-alley-antarctica-greenland-sandy; Suzanne Goldenberg, "Western Antarctic Ice Sheet Collapse Has Already Begun, Scientists Warn," *Guardian*, May 12, 2014, http://www.theguardian.com/environment/2014/may/12/western-antarctic-ice-sheet-collapse-has-already-begun-scientists-warn; Justin Gillis, "U.N. Draft Report Lists Unchecked Emissions' Risks," *New York Times*, August 26, 2014, http://www.nytimes.com/2014/08/27/science/earth/greenhouse-gas-emissions-are-growing-and-growing-more-dangerous-draft-of-un-report-says.html?ref=world&_r=0. "Sea levels could rise by 2.3 meters for each degree Celsius that global temperatures increase, and they will remain high for centuries to come, according to a new study by the leading climate research institute." Erik Kirschbaum, "Seas May Rise 2.3 Meters per Degree of Global Warming: Report," Reuters, July 15, 2013; http://www.reuters.com/article/2013/07/15/us-climate-ice-study-idUSBRE96E0GQ20130715.

84. Sharon Udasin, "'Climate Change Puts 5m. Israelis at Risk of Severe Flooding Events,'" *Jerusalem Post*, November 5, 2013, http://www.jpost.com/Enviro-Tech/Climate-change-puts-5m-Israelis-at-risk-of-severe-flooding-events-330695.

85. Coral Davenport, "Climate Change Deemed Growing Threat by Military Researchers," *New York Times*, May 13, 2014, http://www.nytimes.com/2014/05/14/us/politics/climate-change-deemed-growing-security-threat-by-military-researchers.html; Mitch Ginsberg, "A Parched Syria Turned to War, Scholar Says, and Egypt May Next," *Times of Israel*, May 9, 2013, http://www.timesofisrael.com/lack-of-water-sparked-syrias-conflict-and-it-will-make-egypt-more-militant-too/; Brown and Crawford, "Rising Temperatures, Rising Tensions"; Barnett and Adger, "Climate Change, Human Security and Violent Conflict"; John Vidal, "Water Supply Key to Outcome of Conflicts in Iraq and Syria, Experts Warn," *Guardian*, July 2, 2014, http://www.theguardian.com/environment/2014/jul/02/water-key-conflict-iraq-syria-isis.

86. "Syria: Drought Is Driving Farmers to Cities," *Transatlantic Dialogue on Climate Change and Security*, September 30, 2009, http://climatesecurity.blogspot.com/2009/09/irin-middle-east-middle-east-syria.html; Thomas L. Friedman, "Without Water, Revolution," *New York Times*, May 18, 2013, http://www.nytimes.com/2013/05/19/opinion/sunday/friedman-without-water-revolution.html?pagewanted=all; "Assad Regime's Drought Response Triggered Syrian War," Environment News Service, February 28, 2014, http://ens-newswire.com/2014/02/28/assad-regimes-drought-response-triggered-syrian-war/; Kieran Cooke, "Climate Change Drought Adding to Syria's Misery," *Global Climate Change News & Analysis*, April 22, 2014, http://www.rtcc.org/2014/04/22/climate-linked-drought-adding-to-syrias-misery/; Brad Plumer, "Drought Helped Cause Syria's War. Will Climate Change Bring More Like It?" *Wonkblog*, *Washington Post*, September 10, 2013, http://www.washingtonpost.com/blogs/wonkblog/wp/2013/09/10/drought-helped-caused-syrias-war-will-climate-change-bring-more-like-it/; Shahrzad Mohtadi, "Climate Change & the Syrian Uprising," *Bulletin of the Atomic Scientists*, August 16, 2012, http://thebulletin.org/climate-change-and-syrian-uprising; Francesco Femia and Caitlin Werrell, "Syria: Climate Change Drought & Social Unrest," Center for Climate and Security, n.d. [ca. February 2012], http://climateandsecurity.org/2012/02/29/syria-climate-change-drought-and-social-unrest/.

87. "Drought Triggers Protests in Iran," *Al-Monitor*, September 10, 2014, http://www.al-monitor.com/pulse/originals/2014/09/esfahan-zayandeh-rood-protest-water-crisis.html;

Jason Rezaian, "Iran's Water Crisis the Product of Decades of Bad Planning," *Washington Post*, July 2, 2014, http://www.washingtonpost.com/world/middle_east/irans-water-crisis-the-product-of-decades-of-bad-planning/2014/07/01/c050d2d9-aeeb-4ea1-90cc-54cef6d8dd10_story.html.

88. "Massive Malnutrition May Come with Climate Change," *Israel21c*, June 22, 2014, http://israel21c.org/environment/massive-malnutrition-may-come-with-climate-change.

89. "Climate Change Will Reduce Crop Yields Sooner Than We Thought," Phys.org, March 16, 2014, http://phys.org/news/2014-03-climate-crop-yields-sooner-thought.html; Sowers et al., "Climate Change, Water Resources, and the Politics of Adaptation," 1.

90. Zafrir Rinat, interview with the author, June 23, 2011.

Afterword

1. "The Temple Mount Is a Powder Keg," *Haaretz*, October 31, 2014, http://www.haaretz.com/opinion/1.623760; Shlomo Eldar, "The Third Intifada Is Here," *Al Monitor* November 6, 2014, http://www.al-monitor.com/pulse/originals/2014/11/third-intifada-jerusalem-violence-temple-mount-religious-war.html; Rashid I. Khalidi, "Why Are Jerusalem's 300,000 Arabs Rising Up Again?" November 13, 2014, http://blogs.reuters.com/great-debate/2014/11/13/why-are-jerusalems-300000-arabs-rising-up-again/?utm_source=feedburner&utm_medium=feed&utm_campaign=Feed%3A+imeu+%28IMEU+%3A+Institute+for+Middle+East+Understanding%29; Shlomi Eldar, "Neglect, Provocation Feed East Jerusalem Unrest" *Al Monitor*, October 24, 2014, http://www.al-monitor.com/pulse/originals/2014/10/east-jerusalem-violence-discrimination-neglect-education.html; Avika Eldar, "Police Shooting of Arab Israeli Youth Could Ignite Israel," *Al Monitor*, November 10, 2014, http://www.al-monitor.com/pulse/originals/2014/11/israel-police-shot-kafr-kana-israeli-arab-or-commission.html.

2. Akiva Eldar, "Jews, Arabs Use Religion as Tool to Escalate Conflict," *Al Monitor*, November 19, 2014, http://www.al-monitor.com/pulse/originals/2014/11/jerusalem-religious-nationalistic-conflict-jews-arabs.html; "For First Time, Religion—Not Nationalism—Is Driving Palestinian Terrorism," *Haaretz*, November 19, 2014, http://www.haaretz.com/news/video/.premium-1.627336; Ari Shavit, "The Diplomatic Void Is Deadly," *Haaretz*, November 19, 2014, http://www.haaretz.com/opinion/1.627401; Ruth Margalit, "The Politics of Prayer at Temple Mount," *New Yorker*, November 5, 2014, http://www.newyorker.com/news/news-desk/furor-temple-mount; Itamar Sharon, "Jews Must Stop Temple Mount Visits, Sephardi Chief Rabbi Says," *Times of Israel*, November 7, 2014, http://www.timesofisrael.com/jews-must-stop-going-to-temple-mount-sephardic-chief-rabbi-says/?utm_source=The+Times+of+Israel+Daily+Edition&utm_campaign=2d003cd80d-2014_11_07&utm_medium=email&utm_term=0_adb46cec92-2d003cd80d-54396177; Ahmad Melhem, "After Attacks in Jerusalem, Fears Grow of Religious War," *Al Monitor*, November 18, 2014, http://www.al-monitor.com/pulse/originals/2014/11/israel-palestine-religious-war-attacks-holy-sites.html.

3. "Kerry: Israel, Jordan Agree on Steps to Reduce Jerusalem Tensions," *Times of Israel*, November 13, 2014, http://www.timesofisrael.com/kerry-israel-jordan-agreed-to-steps-to-reduce-jerusalem-tensions/#ixzz3JzLFSYcx.

4. Yossi Verter, "Despite PM's Request, Right-wing Politicians Adding Fuel to Jerusalem Fire," *Haaretz*, November 7, 2014, http://www.haaretz.com/news/diplomacy-defense/.premium-1.625051. "Why did several MKs ascend to the Temple Mount? Because it's there. And because the primaries are around the bend." Asher Schechter, "The Temple Mount Is a Powder Keg, and Arsonists Have the Upper Hand," *Haaretz*, November 14, 2104, http://www.haaretz.com/misc/writers/asher-schechter-1.304.

5. "Israeli Woman and Soldier Killed in Two Knife Attacks," BBC News, November 10, 2014, http://www.bbc.com/news/world-middle-east-29993066.

6. Uri Averny, "Blood, Wine and Gasoline," November 11, 2014, http://zope.gush-shalom.org/home/en/channels/avnery/1415975702/.

7. Jodi Rudoren and Isabel Kershner, "Israel Shaken by 5 Deaths in Synagogue Assault," *New York Times*, November 18, 2014, http://www.nytimes.com/2014/11/19/world/middleeast/killings-in-jerusalem-synagogue-complex.html; "Five Israelis Killed in Deadly Attack on Jerusalem Synagogue," *The Guardian*, November 18, 2014, http://www.theguardian.com/world/2014/nov/18/deadly-attack-in-jerusalem-synagogue; "Jerusalem Synagogue Attack Puts Israel Close to Brink," *The Guardian*, November 18, 2014, http://www.theguardian.com/world/2014/nov/18/synagogue-murders-binyamin-netanyahu-despicable-murderers; "The Conflict over Jerusalem: Murder in the Synagogue," *The Economist*, November 22, 2014, http://www.economist.com/news/middle-east-and-africa/21633850-deadly-attack-jews-prayer-raises-stakes-already-turbulent-holy; Harriet Sherwood, "Jerusalem Synagogue Attack Pushes City to New Level of Fear and Antagonism," *The Guardian*, November 18, 2014, http://www.theguardian.com/world/2014/nov/18/jerusalem-synagogue-attack-fear-antagonism; "Attack Follows Months of Rising Tension and Concern over the Risks of a New Religious Dimension to the Conflict."

8. Yishai Schwartz, "Politics Can't Explain the Israeli Synagogue Attack. Only Hatred Can," *New Republic*, November 18, 2014, http://www.newrepublic.com/article/120327/terror-attacks-ultra-orthodox-har-nof-are-self-defeating.

9. Jodi Rudoren, "In Jerusalem's 'War of Neighbors,' the Differences Are Not Negotiable," *New York Times*, November 18, 2014, http://www.nytimes.com/2014/11/19/world/middleeast/in-jerusalem-war-of-neighbors-the-differences-are-not-negotiable.html?_r=0.

10. "Hamas and Islamic Jihad Praise Jerusalem Attack," *Times of Israel*, November 18, 2014, http://www.timesofisrael.com/hamas-and-islamic-jihad-praise-jerusalem-attack/.

11. Rabbi Gideon M. Sylvester, "Israel's Barren Response to Terror," *Haaretz*, November 20, 2014, http://www.haaretz.com/jewish-world/rabbis-round-table/.premium-1.627643. "Our religious and political leaders are neither willing to separate from the Palestinians in a two-state solution nor to live together with them in dignity. Meanwhile, the death toll is rising."

12. Jodi Rudoren, "Three Arabs Are Arrested in Stabbings in Jerusalem," *New York Times*, November 24, 2014, http://www.nytimes.com/2014/11/25/world/middleeast/israeli-police-arrest-arab-suspects-in-two-jerusalem-stabbings-of-jews.html?ref=world.

13. Yossi Verter, "As Terror Escalates, Israelis and Palestinians Are Racing to the Abyss," *Haaretz*, November 18, 2014, http://www.haaretz.com/opinion/.premium-1.627122.

14. Michael Lesher, "Why Are Orthodox Rabbis Edging into Israel's Apartheid Politics?" *The Electronic Intifada*, December 5, 2014, http://electronicintifada.net/content/why-are-orthodox-rabbis-edging-israels-apartheid-politics/14078.

15. Rabbi Gideon M. Sylvester, "Israel's Barren Response to Terror," *Haaretz*, November 20, 2014, http://www.haaretz.com/jewish-world/rabbis-round-table/.premium-1.627643.

16. David Remnick, "The One-State Reality," *New Yorker*, November 17, 2014, http://www.newyorker.com/magazine/2014/11/17/one-state-reality. "Israel's conservative president speaks up for civility, and pays a price."

17. "Army Kidnaps 15 Palestinians in the Occupied West Bank," International Middle East Media Center, November 25, 2014, https://twitter.com/imemcnewstips/status/537175075963670529. "Soldiers Kidnap Twelve Palestinians in the West Bank," International Middle East Media Center, November 26, 2014, http://www.imemc.org/article/69842.

18. Saed Bannoura, "6800 Palestinians Currently Imprisoned By Israel," International Middle East Media Center, http://www.imemc.org/article/70191.

19. "Israeli Settlers Continue Their Attacks Against Palestinian Civilians in the West Bank," International Middle East Media Center, November 26, 2014; http://www.imemc.org/article/69839.

20. David Pollock, "Palestinian-Israeli Incitement Can and Should Be Curbed, Especially Now," Policy Watch 2347, The Washington Institute, December 16, 2014.

21. "UNSC Reject Resolution on Palestinian State" *Al Jazeera*, December 30, 2014, http://www.aljazeera.com/news/middleeast/2014/12/un-votes-against-palestinian-statehood-20141230212147910509.html; Jodi Rudoren, "Palestinians Set to Seek Redress in a World Court," *New York Times*, December 31, 2014, http://www.nytimes.com/2015/01/01/world/middleeast/palestinians-to-join-international-criminal-court-defying-israeli-us-warnings.html?ref=world; Amira Hass, "Abbas Asks ICC to Probe 'Israeli War Crimes' Since June 14, Palestinian source says," *Haaretz*, January 1, 2015, http://www.haaretz.com/news/diplomacy-defense/.premium-1.634986; "The Palestinians' Desperation Move," *Times* Editorial Board, *New York Times*, December 31, 2014, http://www.nytimes.com/2015/01/01/opinion/the-palestinians-desperation-move.html.

22. Associated Press, "UN Chief Says Palestine Will Join Int'l Court on April 1," *New York Times*, January 7, 2015, http://www.nytimes.com/aponline/2015/01/07/world/middleeast/ap-un-palestinians-israel-court.html?_r=0.

23. Allyn Fisher-IIan, "Israel Mulls Prosecuting Palestinian Leaders for War Crimes, Official Says," *Haaretz*, January 3, 2015, http://www.haaretz.com/news/diplomacy-defense/1.635133.

24. Netanyahu had dismissed the PA's application to the ICC out of hand on the grounds that the PA was not a state. Barak Ravid, "Netanyahu: Israel Expects ICC to Reject Palestinian request out of hand," *Haaretz*, January 1, 2015, http://www.haaretz.com/news/diplomacy-defense/.premium-1.634983.

25. Jodi Rudoren, "Tensions Mount as Israel Freezes Revenue Meant for Palestinians," *New York Times*, January 3, 2015, http://www.nytimes.com/2015/01/04/world/middleeast/tensions-mount-as-israel-freezes-revenue-meant-for-palestinians.html?ref=world&_r=0.

26. Allyn Fisher-IIan, "Israel Mulls Prosecuting Palestinian Leaders for War Crimes, Official Says," *Haaretz*, January 3, 2015, http://www.haaretz.com/news/diplomacy-defense/1.635133.

27. "Palestinian Armed Groups Killed Civilians on Both Sides in Attacks Amounting to War Crimes," https://www.amnesty.org/en/articles/news/2015/03/palestinian-armed-groups-killed-civilians-on-both-sides-in-2014-gaza-conflict/.

28. Jonathan Lis, "Netanyahu: If Reelected, I Won't Evacuate Any West Bank Settlements," *Haaretz*, January 7, 2015, http://www.haaretz.com/news/israel-election-2015/1.635696; Gidi Weitz, "Former PM Barak: Netanyahu Leading Israel to Disaster," *Haaretz*, January 8, 2015, http://www.haaretz.com/news/diplomacy-defense/.premium-1.635978; "Netanyahu Responds to Ehud Barak's Haaretz Interview: He's Still an Irresponsible Leftist," *Haaretz*, January 8, 2015, http://www.haaretz.com/news/national/1.636146.

29. Steven Erlanger "Europe Takes Stronger Measures, Albeit Symbolic, to Condemn Israeli Policies," *New York Times*, November 22, 2014, http://www.nytimes.com/2014/11/23/world/europe/europe-takes-stronger-measures-albeit-symbolic-to-condemn-israeli-policies.html?ref=world.

30. "EU Backs Recognition of Palestinian State 'In Principle,'" *Times of Israel*, December 17, 2014, http://www.timesofisrael.com/eu-backs-recognition-of-palestinian-state-in-principle/. The resolution says that the EU accepts "in principle recognition of Palestinian statehood

and the two state solution, and believes these should go hand in hand with the development of peace talks, which should be advanced."

31. Alan Cowell, "European Court Reverses Designation of Hamas as a Terrorist Organization," *New York Times*, December 17, 2014, http://www.nytimes.com/2014/12/18/world/europe/hamas-palestinian-statehood-vote-european-parliament.html?_r=0.

32. AP and Lazar Berman, "Geneva Conventions Invoke Rights of Palestinians," *Times of Israel*, December 17, 2015, http://www.timesofisrael.com/geneva-conventions-invoke-rights-of-palestinians/.

33. Yossi Verter, "Poll: Most Israelis Don't Want Netanyahu to Remain Prime Minister," *Haaretz*, December 18, 2014, http://www.haaretz.com/news/national/.premium-1.632400.

34. Isabel Kershner and Jodi Rudoren, "Netanyahu Expedites Plan for More Than 1,000 New Apartments in East Jerusalem," *New York Times*, October 27, 2014, http://www.nytimes.com/2014/10/28/world/middleeast/benjamin-netanyahu-east-jerusalem.html?mabReward=RI%3A11&action=click&pgtype=Homepage®ion=CColumn&module=Recommendation&src=rechp&WT.nav=RecEngine&_r=1. In the October 2014 Democracy Institute's Peace Index poll, to the question of why Netanyahu decided to renew the building in the territories, about two-thirds of the Jewish respondents (64 percent) said he did it to shore up his status on the right wing and among the settlers. Only a small minority (22 percent) think the decision stemmed from a real belief that renewing the construction will serve Israel's national interests. See http://www.peaceindex.org/indexMonthEng.aspx?num=285#.VHytPDHF9Cg.

35. "Why Israelis Are Buying Up Palestinian Homes in Riot-Torn East Jerusalem," *Telegraph*, November 7, 2014, http://www.telegraph.co.uk/news/worldnews/middleeast/israel/11213615/Why-Israelis-are-buying-up-Palestinian-homes-in-riot-torn-East-Jerusalem.html. "Not a single new Arab neighborhood has been built in East Jerusalem," the *Telegraph* reported, "since the Israeli takeover in 1967, in contrast to the thriving Jewish neighborhoods in the area." Jewish organizations often finance the purchase of Arab-owned properties and then rent them out exclusively to Jewish residents. The goal is part of the Judaization of East Jerusalem to prevent the division of the city in any future peace deal with the Palestinians.

36. "Ministers back bill forcing army to extend civil law to settlements," *Times of Israel*, November 9, 2014, http://www.timesofisrael.com/pm-allows-free-vote-on-civil-law-bill-for-settlements/.

37. Ben Wedeman and Susannah Cullinane, "Israel Slammed for West Bank Land Expropriation," CNN, September 2, 2014, http://www.cnn.com/2014/09/01/world/meast/mideast-israel-west-bank/.

38. Akiva Eldar, "Netanyahu's Jerusalem Construction a Stalling Strategy," *Al Monitor*, October 29, 2014, http://www.al-monitor.com/pulse/originals/2014/10/netanyahu-east-jerusalem-construction-plans-amit-segal.html#ixzz3K78WNPvn. [The units need to go through a whole series of hearings before final approval, which might be years in the making.]

39. Jonathan Weisman, "Cross Section of Democrats to Snub Netanyahu's Speech to Congress," *New York Times*, March 3, 2015, http://www.nytimes.com/2015/03/04/world/middleeast/cross-section-of-democrats-to-snub-netanyahus-speech-to-congress.html; Ruth Margalit, "Why Does Bibi Do It?," *Slate*, March 2, 2015, http://www.slate.com/articles/news_and_politics/foreigners/2015/03/netanyahu_s_speech_to_congress_why_bibi_is_antagonizing_obama_and_the_democrats.html.

40. Isabel Kershner and Majd Al Waheidinov, "Explosions at Fatah Sites in Gaza Raise Tensions With Hamas," November 7, 2014, http://www.nytimes.com/2014/11/08/world/middleeast/explosions-at-fatah-sites-in-gaza-raise-tensions-with-hamas.html?ref=world&_r=0;

"Hamas Forces Cancellation of Arafat Memorial in Gaza," *Times of Israel* November 9, 2014, http://www.timesofisrael.com/hamas-forces-cancellation-of-arafat-memorial-in-gaza/.

Ben Ariel, "Hamas Member Yahya Mousa Says Fatah Head Mahmoud Abbas Is Hurting Unity Efforts and Should Leave," *Arutz Sheva*, November 17, 2014, http://www.israelnationalnews.com/News/News.aspx/187535#.VHYT0zHF9Cg. Mousa accused Abbas of "thwarting reconciliation in favor of investment projects, security coordination with Israel and a war against political Islam." "Abbas: Only Hamas Is Responsible for the Gaza Strip," *Jerusalem Post*, November 30, 2014, http://www.jpost.com/Arab-Israeli-Conflict/Abbas-Only-Hamas-is-responsible-for-the-Gaza-Strip-383211.

Jack Khoury, Hamas Accuses PA of Giving Intel to Israel That Led to Gaza Civilians' Deaths," *Haaretz*, March 8, 2015, http://www.haaretz.com/news/middle-east/.premium-1.646997; Cynthia Milan, "Hamas Reacts to Abbas' Call for Arab Strike Against Gaza," *Al Monitor*, April 2, 2015, http://www.al-monitor.com/pulse/originals/2015/04/abbas-call-arab-strike-gaza-hamas-yemen.html.

41. "Unpaid Gaza Civil Servants Announce Ministry Strikes," Ma'an News Agency, January 17, 2015, http://www.maannews.net/eng/ViewDetails.aspx?ID=754491; "Hamas MPs Meet, Slam Abbas in Sign of Palestinian Rifts," *Jerusalem Post*, January 2015, http://www.timesofisrael.com/hamas-mps-meet-slam-abbas-in-sign-of-palestinian-rifts/; Hazem Balousha, "Hamas Unwilling to Jeopardize Palestinian Reconciliation," *Al Monitor*, February 6, 2015, http://www.al-monitor.com/pulse/originals/2015/02/hamas-fatah-unity-government-work-gaza.html.

42. Majd Al Waheidi and Jodi Rudoren, "Rival Palestinian Checkpoints in Gaza Show Cracks in Reconciliation Pact," *New York Times*, January 14, 2015, http://www.nytimes.com/2015/01/15/world/middleeast/at-gaza-border-crossing-a-symbol-of-palestinians-internal-tensions.html?ref=world&_r=0.

43. Ahmad Melham, "Palestinian Elections on Hold Until Further Notice," *Al Monitor*, October 28, 2014, http://www.al-monitor.com/pulse/originals/2014/10/palestine-presidential-parliamentary-elections-on-hold.html.

44. Adnan Abu Amer, "Israel, PA Seek to Prevent Hamas from Igniting West Bank," *Al Monitor*, December 10, 2014, http://www.al-monitor.com/pulse/originals/2014/12/west-bank-hamas-cell-israel-pa-joint-security.html.

45. Amos Harel, Jack Khoury and Reuters, "PA Holding 50 Islamic Militants, Fearing Terror Attack Will Give Election to Likud," *Haaretz*, March 20, 2015, http://www.haaretz.com/news/diplomacy-defense.

46. Daoud Kuttab, "Concern Grows Over Abbas' Autocratic Tendencies" *Al Monitor*, December 15, 2014, http://www.al-monitor.com/pulse/originals/2014/12/fatah-concerns-abbas-rule-judiciary-legislative.html; Karin Laub, "Poll: Under Abbas, Most Palestinians Say They Can't Speak Freely," *Haaretz*, December 17, 2014, http://www.haaretz.com/news/middle-east/1.632304; Amira Hass, "The Logic of Abbas the Monarch, Subcontractor of the Occupation," *Haaretz*, December 24, 2014, http://www.haaretz.com/opinion/.premium-1.633398.

47. Amos Harel, "A Weak and Desperate Hamas Tries to Rebuild," *Al Monitor*, February 9, 2015, http://www.haaretz.com/news/diplomacy-defense/.premium-1.641700. But according to other reports, Iran was financing reconstruction of the tunnels, and the IDF was aware of what Hamas was up to; "Report: Iran Financing Hamas' Military Force Reconstruction Efforts," *Haaretz*, April 5, 2015, http://www.haaretz.com/news/diplomacy-defense/1.650525; Avi Issacharoff, "Israel Turns a Blind Eye to Tunnel Construction, and the Next Gaza War," *Times of Israel*, April 5, 2015, http://www.timesofisrael.com/israel-turns-a-blind-eye-to-tunnel-construction-and-the-next-gaza-war/.

48. Adnan Abu Amer, "Hamas Reacts to Potential Egyptian Attack," *Al Monitor*, March 6, 2015, http://www.al-monitor.com/pulse/originals/2015/03/hamas-reaction-egypt-attack-gaza.html.

49. "$5.4 Billion Pledged to Rebuild Gaza," *Al Jazeera*, October 2014, http://america.aljazeera.com/articles/2014/10/12/pledge-gaza-israel.html.

50. "Middle East: UN-Backed Reconstruction Efforts Set to Kick-Off in Gaza Next Week," UN News Centre, November 20, 2014, http://www.un.org/apps/news/story.asp?NewsID=49410; "Palestinians Say Gaza Reconstruction Pledges Unfulfilled," *Times of Israel*, December 22, 2014, http://www.timesofisrael.com/palestinians-say-gaza-reconstruction-pledges-unfulfilled/. Mohammed Othman, "Gaza Relief Efforts Overrun by Corruption, Inefficiency," *Al Monitor*, October 23, 2014, http://www.al-monitor.com/pulse/originals/2014/10/palestine-aid-donors-corruption.html; "Hamas: PA Misusing Gaza Reconstruction Funds," Ma'an News Agency, January 6, 2015, http://www.maannews.net/eng/ViewDetails.aspx?ID=752045. Asmaa al-Ghoul, "Greed, Family Breakdowns Afflict Gaza Society," *Al Monitor*, December 9, 2014, http://www.al-monitor.com/pulse/originals/2014/12/gaza-society-war-repercussions-psychological-pressure.htm. Omar Shaban, "Donor Pledges Not Enough to Rehabilitate Gaza," *Al Monitor*, October 17, 2014, http://www.al-monitor.com/pulse/originals/2014/10/cairo-donor-conference-gaza-reconstruction.html. According to Shaban's analysis at least $15.5 billion are needed to properly restore Gaza's economy. The documentation submitted by the PA estimated that it needs at least $15 billion to properly restore Gaza's economy

51. Isabel Kershner, "Cost of Living Takes Center Stage in Israeli Elections," *New York Times*, December 9, 2014, http://www.nytimes.com/2014/12/10/world/middleeast/in-israeli-campaign-netanyahu-sees-vulnerability-in-soaring-living-costs.html?ref=world&_r=0; Ben Caspit, "Are Israeli Voters Worried More About Security or the Economy?" *Al Monitor*, December 9, 2014, http://www.al-monitor.com/pulse/originals/2014/12/elections-israel-security-netanyahu-syria-economy-social-gap.html.

52. Dialog Poll conducted on December 16, 2014; Yossi Verter Poll: "Most Israelis Don't Want Netanyahu to Remain Prime Minister," *Haaretz*, December 18, 2014, http://www.haaretz.com/news/national/.premium-1.632400.

53. Jodi Rudoren, "Netanyahu Says No Palestinian State If He Is Re-Elected," *New York Times*, March 16, 2015, http://www.nytimes.com/2015/03/17/world/middleeast/benjamin-netanyahu-campaign-settlement.html?hp&action=click&pgtype=Homepage&module=first-column-region®ion=top-news&WT.nav=top-news&_r=0.

54. "Netanyahu Says No Palestinian State If Re-Elected," *Al Arabiya News*, March 16, 2015, http://english.alarabiya.net/en/News/middle-east/2015/03/16/Netanyahu-Palestinian-state-will-not-be-established-if-he-retains-premiership.html.

55. Ishaan Tharoor, "On Israeli Election Day, Netanyahu Warns of Arabs Voting 'In Droves,' *Washington Post*, March 17, 2015, http://www.washingtonpost.com/blogs/worldviews/wp/2015/03/17/on-israeli-election-day-netanyahu-warns-of-arabs-voting-in-droves/.

56. See Bernard Avishai for possible electoral alliances. Bernard Avishai, "Kerry's Miscalculation on the U.N. Palestine Resolutions," *New Yorker*, December 31, 2014, http://www.newyorker.com/news/news-desk/kerrys-miscalculation-u-n-palestine-resolutions.

57. A cross section of reactions: Avi Shavit, "Disaster 2015: Israelis Must Seize the Chance to Recover Quickly," *Haaretz*, March 19, 2015, http://www.haaretz.com/opinion/.premium-1.647696; "The Struggle to Preserve Israel's Democracy Is Just Beginning," *Haaretz*, editorial, March 19, 2015, http://www.haaretz.com/opinion/1.647719. *Haaretz* columnist Zvi Barel: "Netanyahu has succeeded in overturning the principle that the state exists

for the sake of its citizens and putting in its place the Fascist belief that the citizens exist for the state." Quoted in David Shulman, "Israel: The Stark Truth," *New York Review of Books*, March 21, 2015, http://www.nybooks.com/blogs/nyrblog/2015/mar/21/israel-elections-ugly-truth/; Judith Kershner, "Abiding Rifts Within Israel Threaten to Widen with Netanyahu's Win," *New York Times*, March 20, 2015, http://www.nytimes.com/2015/03/21/world/middleeast/abiding-rifts-within-israel-threaten-to-widen-with-netanyahu-win.html?_r=1; Josef Federman, "Prime Minister Benjamin Netanyahu's Victory in Israel Elections Leaves Damage in Its Wake," *Huffington Post*, March 18, 2015, http://www.huffingtonpost.com/2015/03/18/israel-elections-benjamin-netanyahu_n_6899312.html.

58. See, for example, "Netanyahu Reveals His Duplicity, Demagoguery and Deceit," *Huffington Post*, March 17, 2015, http://www.huffingtonpost.com/alon-benmeir/; "Likud's Victory Is Israel's Defeat," http://us2.campaign-archive2.com/?u=a2e336c40140a3ad66435cef8&id=b94f0336df&e=8bfa85f29d; Jeffrey Goldberg, "PM Has Alon Ben Meir," *Huffington Post*, http://www.huffingtonpost.com/alon-benmeir/; Jeffrey Goldberg, "PM Has 'Weeks' to Prove He Supports Two-State Solution," *Times of Israel*, March 21, 2015, http://www.timesofisrael.com/jeffrey-goldberg-pm-has-weeks-to-prove-he-supports-two-state-solution/; David Shulman, "Israel: The Stark Truth," *New York Review of Books*, March 21, 2015, http://www.nybooks.com/blogs/nyrblog/2015/mar/21/israel-elections-ugly-truth/; Jeffrey Goldberg, "Israel's Dangerous Predicament," *The Atlantic*, March 20 2015 http://www.theatlantic.com/international/archive/2015/03/israels-and-netanyahus-dangerous-predicament/388315/; David Remnick, "Base Appeals," *New Yorker*, March 30, 2015, http://www.newyorker.com/magazine/2015/03/30/base-appeals; Rabbi Michael Lerner, "The Militarists and Haters Win in Israeli Elections," *Huffington Post*, March 24, 2015, http://www.huffingtonpost.com/rabbi-michael-lerner/the-militarists-and-hater_b_6892888.html.

59. "World Reacts to Israel's Choice of Netanyahu for a Fourth Term," *Haaretz*, March 18, 2015, http://www.haaretz.com/news/israel-election-2015/.premium-1.647683.

60. Sam Stein, "Obama Details His Disappointment with Netanyahu in First Post-Election Comments," *Huffington Post*, March 21, 2015, http://www.huffingtonpost.com/2015/03/21/obama-iran-deal_n_6905634.html.

61. Julie Hirschfeld Davis, "White House Antagonism Toward Netanyahu Grows," *New York Times*, March 21, 2015, http://www.nytimes.com/2015/03/21/world/middleeast/white-house-antagonism-toward-netanyahu-grows.html?hp&action=click&pgtype=Homepage&module=first-column-region®ion=top-news&WT.nav=top-news&_r=0; Jonathan Lis and Barak Ravid, "White House 'Deeply Concerned' by 'Divisive' Anti-Arab Rhetoric During Israeli Election," *Haaretz*, March 19, 2015, http://www.haaretz.com/news/israel-election-2015/.premium-1.647733; Peter Beinart, "Enraged by Netanyahu's Rhetoric, White House Officials Believe Israeli-U.S. Relations Fundamentally Changed," *Haaretz*, March 19, 2015, http://www.haaretz.com/news/diplomacy-defense/.premium-1.647859.

62. Kate Scanlon, "McCain: Obama Needs to 'Get Over' His 'Temper Tantrum' About Netanyahu's Reelection," *The Daily Signal*, March 22, 2015, http://dailysignal.com/2015/03/22/mccain-obama-needs-to-get-over-his-temper-tantrum-about-netanyahus-reelection/; Adam Edelman, "Republicans Blast Obama's Response to Netanyahu's Reelection: 'Get Over Your Temper Tantrum, Mr. President,'" *Daily News*, March 22, 2015, http://www.nydailynews.com/news/politics/republicans-blast-obama-reaction-netanyahu-win-tactics-article-1.2158730.

63. "Prime Minister Netanyahu Backtracks on Palestinian State Comments," http://www.npr.org/2015/03/19/394099697/prime-minister-netanyahu-backtracks-on-palestinian-state-comments.

64. Jodi Rudoren and Julie Hirschfeld, "Netanyahu Apologizes; White House Is Unmoved," *New York Times,* March 24, 2015, http://www.nytimes.com/2015/03/24/world/middleeast/netanyahu-apologizes-for-comments-about-israeli-arabs.html?hp&action=click&pgtype=Homepage&module=first-column-region®ion=top-news&WT.nav=top-news.

65. Christof Lehmann, "Israeli Elections Are Over: Tel Aviv Resumes Transfer of Tax Revenues to Palestinian Authority," *NSNBC International*, March 27, 2015, http://nsnbc.me/2015/03/28/israeli-elections-are-over-tel-aviv-resumes-transfer-of-tax-revenues-to-palestinian-authority/; Isabel Kershner, "Israel Releasing Impounded Palestinian Tax Revenue," *New York Times*, March 27, 2015, http://www.nytimes.com/2015/03/28/world/middleeast/israel-netanyahu-palestinians-tax-revenue.html.

66. "White House Chief of Staff: 50 Years of Israeli Occupation Must End," *Haaretz*, March 24, 2015, http://www.haaretz.com/news/diplomacy-defense/1.648465.

67. For a transcript of President Obama's interview with the *Huffington Post*, March 21, 2015, go to http://www.huffingtonpost.com/2015/03/21/obama-huffpost-interview-transcript_n_6905450.html.

68. "U.S. Senator Tells Netanyahu Congress Will Follow His Lead on Iran Sanctions," *Haaretz*, December 29, 2014, http://www.haaretz.com/news/diplomacy-defense/1.634286. "Visiting US Senator Lindsey Graham," the paper reported, "threatened to withhold US funding from the UN, and Prime Minister Benjamin Netanyahu lashed out at the Palestinian Authority, a day after a senior Palestinian official said the PA will push for a UN vote on the Palestinian statehood bid by Monday."

69. Peter Baker, "G.O.P. Support for Israel Becomes New Litmus Test," *New York Times*, March 27, 2015. The article quotes the very influential editor of the *Weekly Standard*, William Kristol, as saying, "It's remarkable. Bibi would probably win the Republican nomination if it were legal." See http://www.nytimes.com/2015/03/28/us/politics/republicans-criticize-james-baker-for-speech-on-benjamin-netanyahu.html?rref=politics&module=Ribbon&version=context®ion=Header&action=click&contentCollection=Politics&pgtype=article.

70. Haviv Rettig Gur, "The 20th Knesset—Parliament of a Splintered, Tribal Israel, *Times of Israel*, April 6, 2015, http://www.timesofisrael.com/what-the-20th-knesset-says-about-israeli-society/.

71. Gideon Levy, "Netanyahu Will Be Remembered for Speaking Israel's Truth," *Haaretz*, March 22, 2015, http://www.haaretz.com/opinion/.premium-1.648122.

72. "Mounting Pessimism About Two-State Israeli-Palestinian Solution," June 25, 2014, http://www.pewglobal.org/2014/06/25/mounting-pessimism-about-two-state-israeli-palestinian-solution/.

73. "Palestinian Public Opinion Poll No.54," December 3–6, 2104, http://www.pcpsr.org/en/node/505.

74. "Poll: ISIS Viewed Positively by 24 Percent of Palestinians," *Haaretz*, November 13, 2014, http://www.haaretz.com/news/middle-east/1.626318. *Haaretz* quotes statistics from the poll, which was conducted by the Arab Center for Research and Policy Studies in Doha, Qatar, in six Arab countries, and among the Palestinians. The poll showed that support for military action against the Islamic State was lowest among Palestinians. Asked to give an overall appraisal of ISIS, 85 percent of Arab respondents had negative or somewhat negative views. Opposition was lower among Palestinians, however, with 72 percent providing a negative or somewhat negative appraisal. Four percent of Palestinians had positive views of ISIS and another 20 percent had somewhat positive views. Only 50 percent of Saudis and 52 percent of Egyptians and Palestinians voiced support for the military campaign against ISIS; 48 percent of Egyptians and 45 percent of Palestinians, Saudis, and Tunisians opposed an operation. The survey also found that 59

percent of Arab respondents as a whole expressed support in varying degrees for the military campaign against ISIS, while 37 percent were either opposed or strongly opposed. Palestinians were least supportive of Arab participation in the coalition fighting ISIS, with 50 percent of respondents saying that they oppose the effort to "degrade and ultimately destroy" ISIS. In Egypt opposition stood at 40 percent. In contrast, 75 percent of Lebanese expressed support, the highest in any Arab country polled. Seventy percent of respondents in Saudi Arabia, which is a member of the coalition of countries fighting ISIS, also supported the move. The pollsters also asked which two countries stood to gain from the war against ISIS; 31 percent said the United States and 27 percent named Israel. Twenty-eight percent named Israel as the greatest threat to regional security; 21 percent said United States. Iran followed at 17 percent and armed Islamic groups at 13 percent. Almost three quarters (73 percent) of Arab respondents had negative or somewhat negative views of the U.S. The poll was conducted in Tunisia, Egypt, Jordan, Saudi Arabia, Lebanon, and Iraq. In addition, the poll included a sample of 600 Palestinians and a sample of 900 Syrian refugees in Lebanon, Jordan, and Turkey. See also Tom Porter, "Israeli Security Forces Arrest 'Isis Terror Cell' in West Bank," *International Business Times*, January 4, 2015, http://www.ibtimes.co.uk/israeli-security-forces-arrest-isis-terror-cell-west-bank-1481812; Jonathan D. Halevi, "Hamas Embraces the Way of the Islamic State," Jerusalem Center for Public Affairs, November 27, 2014, http://jcpa.org/article/hamas-embraces-path-of-islamic-state/. Mohammed Othman, "Gaza Salafist Leader: 'We Are Following Islamic State Ideology,'" *Al Monitor*, January 6, 2015, http://www.al-monitor.com/pulse/originals/2015/01/salafist-fighters-gaza-travel-to-syria.html; "Expressions of Support in the Gaza Strip for the Islamic State in Iraq and Al-Sham (ISIS), Which Is Affiliated with the Global Jihad," Meir Amit Intelligence and Terrorism Information Center, July 16, 2014, http://www.terrorism-info.org.il/en/article/20675; Lucy Draper, "Fledgeling Gaza ISIS Groups Operate Under Watchful Eye of Hamas," *Newsweek*, February 5, 2015, http://www.newsweek.com/fledgeling-gaza-isis-groups-operate-under-watchful-eye-hamas-304685.

75. Celine Hagbard, "PLO Decides to Suspend Security Cooperation with Israel," International Middle East Media Center, March 6, 2015, http://www.imemc.org/article/70817.

76. "Abbas Says Two-State Solution Impossible with Netanyahu," *Times of Israel*, http://www.timesofisrael.com/abbas-says-two-state-solution-impossible-with-netanyahu/.

77. Amos Harel and Gili Cohen, "Israeli Military Prepares for Possible Violent Uprising in West Bank," *Haaretz*, March 23, 2015, http://www.haaretz.com/news/diplomacy-defense/.premium-1.648419.

78. Ahmad Melhem, "The Deepening Rift Between Fatah and Hamas," *Al Monitor*, March 20, 2015, http://www.al-monitor.com/pulse/originals/2015/03/palestine-hamas-fatah-plo-accusations.html. Melhem reported that "Fatah-Hamas ties slid down a slippery slope late last week following mutual accusations of treason. This has weighed down the ties between the two movements, as well as the timid efforts to implement the stalled reconciliation deal signed in April 2014. Islamic Jihad and leftist factions attempted to prevent the collapse of reconciliation prospects."

79. Barry Petersen, "Hamas Grows with Young Teenagers Eager to Recruit," CBS News, March 20, 2015, http://www.cbsnews.com/news/hamas-grows-with-young-recruits-eager-to-fight-israelis/.

80. Shlomi Eldar, "Hamas Focuses on Rebuilding Tunnels as Gazans Suffer," *Al Monitor*, March 5, 2015, http://www.al-monitor.com/pulse/originals/2015/03/hamas-gaza-strip-tunnel-infrastructure-rebuilding.html.

81. Diaa Hadid, "Palestinian Discontent with Abbas Is Growing," *New York Times*, March 30, 2015, http://www.nytimes.com/2015/03/31/world/middleeast/among-palestinians-dis

content-with-abbas-grows.html?mabReward=R4&action=click&pgtype=Homepage®ion=CColumn&module=Recommendation&src=rechp&WT.nav=RecEngine.

82. David Kirkpatrick, "As U.S. and Iran Seek Nuclear Deal, Saudi Arabia Makes Its Own Moves," *New York Times*, March 30, 2105, http://www.nytimes.com/2015/03/31/world/middleeast/saudis-make-own-moves-as-us-and-iran-talk.html?ref=world&_r=0; Sarah Almukhtar and Karen Yourish, "Old, New and Unusual Alliances in the Middle East," *New York Times*, March 30, 2015, http://www.nytimes.com/interactive/2015/03/30/world/middleeast/middle-east-alliances-saudi-arabia-iran.html.

Bibliography

Books, Reports, Working Papers, Unpublished Materials, and Online Media

Abbas, Mahmoud. *Through Secret Channels: The Road to Oslo: Senior PLO Leader Abu Mazen's Revealing Story of the Negotiations with Israel.* Reading, UK: Garnet, 1995.

Abrahms, Max. "The 'Right of Return' Debate Revisited." Middle East Intelligence Bulletin, Washington Institute, Washington, DC, August–September 2003. http://www.washingtoninstitute.org/policy-analysis/view/the-right-of-return-debate-revisited.

Abrams, Elliott. *Tested by Zion: The Bush Administration and the Israeli-Palestinian Conflict.* New York: Cambridge University Press, 2013.

Abu, Ofir. "Nationalism, Religion, and the Breakdown of the Israeli-Palestinian Peace Process." Paper submitted to the 66th Annual Conference of the Midwest Political Science Association. Chicago: April 5, 2008. http://citation.allacademic.com//meta/p_mla_apa_research_citation/2/7/3/0/2/pages273026/p273026-32.php.

Abunimah, Ali. *One Country: A Bold Proposal to End the Israeli-Palestinian Impasse.* New York: Metropolitan Books, 2006.

Acemoglu, Daron, and James A. Robinson. *Why Nations Fail: The Origins of Power, Prosperity, and Poverty.* New York: Crown, 2012.

Achcar, Gilbert. *The Arabs and the Holocaust: The Arab-Israeli War of Narratives.* New York: Metropolitan Books, 2009.

Adalah. "New Discriminatory Laws and Bills in Israel." Adalah, Haifa, November 29, 2010.

Adalah Online. "Demolition and Eviction of Bedouin Citizens of Israel in the Naqab (Negev)—The Prawer Plan." Adalah, Haifa. http://adalah.org/eng/Articles/1589/Demolition-and-Eviction-of-Bedouin-Citizens-of-in%E2%80%94.

Adalah Online. "Discriminatory Laws in Israel." Adalah, Haifa. http://adalah.org/eng/Israeli-Discriminatory-Law-Database.

Adalah Online. "Index of Currently Pending Discriminatory Bills in the 19th Israeli Knesset (as of 24 June 2013). http://adalah.org/Public/files/Discriminatory-Laws-Database/Discriminatory-Bills-19th-Knesset-24-06-2013.pdf.

Adalah Online. "Land and Planning Rights." Adalah, Haifa. http://adalah.org/eng/category/7/Land-and-Planning-Rights/1/0/0/.

Adam, Heribert. *Peace-Making in Divided Societies: The Israel–South Africa Analogy.* Cape Town: HSRC, 2002.

Adwan, Sami, Dan Bar-On, Eyal Naveh, and Peace Research Institute in the Middle East (PRIME), eds. *Side by Side: Parallel Histories of Israel-Palestine.* New York: New Press, 2012.

Agha, Hussein. *Track-II Diplomacy: Lessons from the Middle East.* Cambridge: MIT Press, 2003.

Agha, Hussein, and Ahmad S. Khalidi. *A Framework for a Palestinian National Security Doctrine.* London: Royal Institute of International Affairs, Chatham House, 2006.

Ahmad, Feroz. *The Making of Modern Turkey.* New York: Routledge, 1993.

Alam, M. Shahid. *Israeli Exceptionalism: The Destabilizing Logic of Zionism.* New York: Palgrave Macmillan, 2009.

Albright, Madeleine. *Madam Secretary: A Memoir.* New York: Macmillan, 2003.

Al-Haq. 'Operation Cast Lead': A Statistical Analysis August 2009." Al-Haq, Ramallah, August 2009. http://www.icawc.net/fonds/Gaza-operation-Cast-Lead_statistical-analysis%20by%20Al%20Haq_August%202009.pdf.

Al-Madfai, Madiha Rashid. *Jordan, the United States, and Middle East Peace Process, 1974–1991.* Cambridge: Cambridge University Press, 1992.

Almog, Doron (Major General, res.). "Lessons of the Gaza Security Fence for the West Bank." Jerusalem Issue Brief 4, no. 12 (December 12, 2004). Jerusalem Center for Public Affairs. http://www.jcpa.org/brief/brief004-12.htm.

Al-Saadi, Yazan. "Palestinian Reconciliation: A History of Documents." *Al Akhbar*, April 28, 2014. http://english.al-akhbar.com/node/19580.

Alvanou, Maria. "Palestinian Women Suicide Bombers: The Interplaying Effects of Islam, Nationalism and Honor Culture." Working Paper 3. Strategic Research and Policy Center, National Defense College, Tel Aviv, March 2007. http://www.itstime.it/Approfondimenti/Alvanou_Palestinian_Women.pdf.

Alyan, Nisreen, Ronit Sela, and Michal Pomerantz. "Policies of Neglect in East Jerusalem: The Policies That Created 78% Poverty Rates and a Frail Job Market." Association for Civil Rights in Jerusalem, Jerusalem, May 2012. http://www.acri.org.il/en/wp-content/uploads/2012/05/The-Poverty-Policy-in-East-Jerusalem_ACRI_May-2012_ENG.pdf.

American Foreign Policy Council. *The World Almanac of Islamism*. Lanham, MD: Rowman & Littlefield, January, 2014. http://almanac.afpc.org/.

Americans for Peace Now. "Settlements 101." Washington, DC, October 2010. http://peacenow.org/settlements-101.html.

Amnesty International. *Final Report 2013: Palestinian Authority*. Amnesty International, London, May 23, 2013. http://www.amnesty.org/en/region/palestinian-authority/report-2013.

Amnesty International. *Israel/Gaza, Operation 'Cast Lead': 22 Days of Death and Destruction*. Report MDE 15/015/2009. Amnesty International, London, July 2009. http://www.amnesty.org/en/library/asset/MDE15/015/2009/en/8f299083-9a74-4853-860f-0563725e633a/mde150152009en.pdf.

Amnesty International. *Trigger-Happy: Israel's Use of Excessive Force in the West Bank*. Report MDE 15/002/2014. Amnesty International, London, February 2014. http://www.amnesty.org/en/library/asset/MDE15/002/2014/en/349188ef-e14a-418f-ac20-6c9e5c8d9f88/mde150022014en.pdf.

Ansara, Khalil. "Connectors and Dividers in the Israeli-Palestinian Conflict." Catholic Relief Services Resource Network, Baltimore, May 2012. http://resources.crs.org/wp-content/uploads/2012/05/connectors-and-dividers-in-the-israeli-palestinian-conflict.pdf.

Antonius, George. *The Arab Awakening: The Story of the Arab National Movement*. Safety Harbor, FL: Simon Publications, 2001. First published in 1939 by Simon Publications.

Arab Association for Human Rights, "2012 Israeli Jewish Public Opinion Info Sheet," October 2012. http://arabhra.files.wordpress.com/2012/11/2012-israeli-jewish-public-opinion-info-sheet.pdf.

Arab World for Research & Development. "Results of an Opinion Poll." Arab World for Research & Development, Ramallah, November 2007. http://www.awrad.org/pdfs/detailed%20result.pdf.

Arian, Asher. "Israeli Public Opinion on National Security 2002." Memorandum No. 61. Jaffee Center for Strategic Studies, Tel Aviv University, Tel Aviv, July 2002. http://d26e8pvoto2x3r.cloudfront.net/uploadimages/Import/(FILE)1190277522.pdf.

Arian, Asher. "Israeli Public Opinion on National Security 2003." Memorandum No. 67. Jaffee Center for Strategic Studies, Tel Aviv University, Tel Aviv, October 2003. http://d26e8pvoto2x3r.cloudfront.net/uploadimages/Import/(FILE)1190276735.pdf.

Ariely, Dan. *The Upside of Irrationality: The Unexpected Benefits of Defying Logic at Work and at Home*. New York: HarperCollins, 2010.

Arieli, Shaul, Roby Nathanson, Ziv Rubin, Hagar Tzameret-Kertcher. *Historical, Political and Economic Impact of Jewish Settlements in the Occupied Territories*. Tel Aviv: The Friedrich Ebert Foundation, The Macro Center for Political Economics, The Center for International Communications and Policy in Bar-Ilan University and Munchen University, July 2009. http://www.macro.org.il/lib/3218049.pdf.

Arnon, Arie, and Saeb Bamya, eds. *The Arab Peace Initiative and Israeli-Palestinian Peace: The Political Economy of a New Period*. Aix Group, March 2012. http://www.aixgroup.org/sites/default/files/publications_pdf/The%20Arab%20Peace%20Initiative%20and%20Arab-Israeli%20Peace.pdf.

Arnon, Arie, and Saeb Bamya, eds. *Economic Dimensions of a Two-State Agreement Between Israel and Palestine*. Aix Group, November 2007. http://www.aixgroup.org/sites/default/files/publications_pdf/economic_dimensions_english_website%20%281%29.pdf.

Arnon, Arie, Saeb Bamya, and Tamar Hacker. *A Framework for Permanent Agreement Concerning the Refugees: Complementary Ideas, 2010*. Aix Group, March 2010. http://www.aixgroup.org/sites/default/files/publications_pdf/Refugees%20Paper.pdf.

Aronson, Geoffrey. "A Never-Ending End to Claims." In *The Palestinian Refugee Problem: The Search for a Resolution*, edited by Rex Brynen and Roula El-Rifai, 266–84. London: Pluto Press, 2013.

Aronson, Geoffrey. "Rabin Will Have to Clarify Settlement Preferences." *Settlement Report* 4, no. 1 (January–February 1994). http://www.fmep.org/reports/archive/vol.-4/no.-1/rabin-will-have-to-clarify-settlement-preferences.

Ashrawi, Hanan. *This Side of Peace: A Personal Account.* New York: Simon & Schuster, 1995.

Astrup, Claus, and Sébastien Dessus. "Trade Options for the Palestinian Economy: Some Orders of Magnitude." Mid-East and North Africa Working Paper No. 21. World Bank, Washington DC, February 2001. http://papers.ssrn.com/sol3/papers.cfm?abstract_id=267832.

Atran, Scott. *Talking to the Enemy: Faith, Brotherhood, and the (Un)Making of Terrorists.* New York: HarperCollins, 2010.

Aumann, Moshe. "Land Ownership in Palestine, 1880–1948." Israel Academic Committee on the Middle East, Jerusalem, 1976. http://wordfromjerusalem.com/wp-content/uploads/2008/11/the-case-for-israel-appendix2.pdf.

Avishai, Bernard. *The Hebrew Republic: How Secular Democracy and Global Enterprise Will Bring Israel Peace at Last.* New York: Harcourt, 2008.

Azoulay, Ariella, and Adi Ophir. *The One-State Solution: Occupation and Democracy in Israel/Palestine.* Stanford, CA: Stanford University Press, 2013.

Baker, Ambassador Alan. *Israel's Rights as a Nation-State in International Diplomacy.* Jerusalem: Jerusalem Center for Public Affairs, 2011. http://jcpa.org/wp-content/uploads/2012/02/israels-rights-full-study.pdf.

Balaban, Oded. *Interpreting Conflict: Israeli-Palestinian Negotiations at Camp David II and Beyond.* New York: Peter Lang, 2005.

"Balfour Declaration." November 2, 1917. The Avalon Project, Lillian Goldman Law Library, Yale Law School, New Haven, CT. http://avalon.law.yale.edu/20th_century/balfour.asp.

Baramki, Gabi. *Peaceful Resistance: Building a Palestinian University Under Occupation.* London: Pluto Press, 2010.

Bar-On, Daniel, and Sami Adwan. "The Psychology of Better Dialogue Between Two Separate but Interdependent Narratives." In *Israeli and Palestinian Narratives of Conflict: History's Double Helix*, edited by Robert I. Rotberg, 205–24. Bloomington: Indiana University Press, 2006.

Bar-On, Mordechai. "Conflicting Narratives or Narratives of a Conflict: Can the Zionist and Palestinian Narratives of the 1948 War Be Bridged?" In *Israeli and Palestinian Narratives of Conflict: History's Double Helix*, edited by Robert I. Rotberg, 142–73. Bloomington: Indiana University Press, 2006.

Bar-Siman-Tov, Yaacov. *The Israeli-Palestinian Conflict: From Peace Process to Violent Confrontation, 2000–2005.* Jerusalem: Jerusalem Institute for Israeli Studies, 2006.

Bar-Siman-Tov, Yaacov, ed. *Barriers to Peace in the Israeli-Palestinian Conflict.* Study No. 406. Jerusalem: Konrad-Adenaeur-Stiftung Israel and Jerusalem Institute for Israel Studies, 2010. http://www.kas.de/wf/doc/kas_22213-1522-2-30.pdf?110316110504.

Bar-Siman-Tov, Yaacov. "Justice and Fairness as Barriers to the Resolution of the Israeli Palestinian Conflict." In *Barriers to Peace in the Israeli-Palestinian Conflict*, Study No. 406, edited by Yaacov Bar-Siman-Tov. Jerusalem: Konrad-Adenauer-Stiftung Israel and Jerusalem Institute for Israel Studies, 2010.

Bar-Tal, Daniel. *Living with the Conflict: Socio-Psychological Analysis of the Jewish Society in Israel.* Jerusalem: Carmel (Hebrew), 2007.

Bar-Tal, Daniel. *Shared Beliefs in a Society: Social Psychological Analysis.* Sage Publications: Thousand Oaks, CA, 2000.

Bar-Tal, Daniel, and Eran Halperin. "Overcoming Psychological Barriers to Peace Process: The Influence of Beliefs About Losses." In *Prosocial Motives, Emotions and Behaviors: The Better Angels of Our Nature*, edited by Mario Mikulincer and Philip R. Shaver, 431–48. Washington DC: American Psychological Association Press, 2010.

Bar-Tal, Daniel, and Eran Halperin. "Socio-Psychological Barriers to Conflict Resolution." In *Intergroup Conflicts and Their Resolution: A Social Psychological Perspective*, edited by Daniel Bar-Tal, 217–40. New York: Psychology Press, Taylor & Francis Group, 2011.

Bar-Tal, Daniel, Shiri Landman, Tamir Magal, and Nimrod Rosler. "Societal-Psychological Dynamics of Evolvement of Repertoire Supporting Peace Making: A Conceptual Framework." Paper presented at the Small Group Meeting of the European Association of Social Psychology, Jerusalem, September 7-10, 2009.

Bar-Tal, Daniel, and Neta Oren. *Ethos as an Expression of Identity: Its Changes in Transition from Conflict to Peace in the Israeli Case.* Discussion Paper No. 83. Leonard Davis Institute for International Relations, Hebrew University of Jerusalem, Jerusalem, 2000.

Bar-Tal, Daniel, and Gavriel Salomon. "Israeli-Jewish Narratives of the Israeli-Palestinian Conflict: Evolution, Contents, Functions, and Consequences." In *Israeli and Palestinian Narratives of Conflict: History's Double Helix* edited by Robert I. Rotberg, 19–46. Bloomington: Indiana University Press, 2006.

Bar-Tal, Daniel, and Izhak Schnell, eds. *The Impacts of Lasting Occupation: Enduring Challenges and Emerging Answers.* New York: Oxford University Press, 2013.

Baskin, Gershon. *The Negotiator: Freeing Gilad Schalit from Hamas.* New Milford: Toby Press, 2013.

Bavly, Dan, and As'ad Ghanem. *One State, Two Peoples: Restoring Hope for Palestinian-Israeli Peace.* Sterling, VA: Potomac Books, 2013.

Bazerman, Max H., and Margaret A. Neale. "The Role of Fairness, Considerations and Relationships in a Judgmental Perspective of Negotiation." In *Barriers to Conflict Resolution*, edited by Kenneth J. Arrow, et al., 87–106. New York: Norton, 1995.

Beilin, Yossi. "Just Peace: A Dangerous Objective." In *What Is a Just Peace?* edited by Pierre Allan and Alexis Keller, 130–48. Oxford: Oxford University Press, 2006.

Beilin, Yossi. *The Path to Geneva: The Quest for a Permanent Agreement, 1996–2004.* New York: RDV Books, 2004.

Beinart, Peter. *The Crisis of Zionism.* New York: Henry Holt, 2012.

Ben-Ami, Shlomo. *A Front Without a Rearguard: A Voyage to the Boundaries of the Peace Process.* Tel Aviv: Yedioth Ahronoth (Hebrew), 2004.

Ben-Ami, Shlomo. *Scars of War, Wounds of Peace: The Israel-Arab Tragedy.* New York: Oxford University Press, 2006.

Ben Meir, Yehuda, and Olena Bagno-Moldavsky. *Vox Populi: Trends in Israeli Public Opinion on National Security 2004–2009.* Tel Aviv: Institute for National Security Studies, November 2010. http://d26e8pvoto2x3r.cloudfront.net/uploadimages/Import/(FILE)1291193491.pdf.

Ben Meir, Yehuda, and Dafna Shaked. *The People Speak: Israeli Public Opinion on National Security 2005–2007.* Memorandum No. 90. Institute for National Security Studies, Tel Aviv, 2007. http://d26e8pvoto2x3r.cloudfront.net/uploadimages/Import/(FILE)1188302092.pdf .

Bennis, Phyllis. *Understanding the Palestinian-Israeli Conflict: A Primer.* Northampton, MA: Olive Branch Press, 2009.

Bentsur, Eytan. *Making Peace: A First-Hand Account of the Arab-Israeli Peace Process.* London: Praeger, 2001.

Benvenisti, Meron. *Sacred Landscape: The Buried History of the Holy Land Since 1948.* Berkeley: University of California Press, 2000.

Bickerton, Ian J., and Carla L. Klausner. *A Concise History of the Arab-Israeli Conflict.* 4th ed. Upper Saddle River, NJ: Prentice Hall, 2002.

Black, Eric. *Parallel Realities: A Jewish Arab History of Israel/Palestine.* Boulder, CO: Paradigm, 1992.

Bokhari, Kamran. "Salafism and Arab Democratization." *Geopolitical Weekly* (blog). Stratfor Global Intelligence, Austin, TX, October 12, 2012. http://www.stratfor.com/weekly/salafism-and-arab-democratization#ixzz2mjX4lYWa.

Boulding, Elise. *Cultures of Peace: The Hidden Side of History.* Syracuse: Syracuse University Press, 2000.

Bowker, Robert. *Palestinian Refugees: Mythology, Identity, and The Search for Peace.* Boulder, CO: Lynne Rienner, 2013.

Bowker, Robert. "The Political Management of Change in UNRWA." Palestinian Refugee ResearchNet, McGill University, Montreal, 1997. http://prrn.mcgill.ca/research/papers/bowker.htm.

Boyd, J. N., and P. G. Zimbardo. "Time Perspective, Health, and Risk Taking." In *Understanding Behavior in the Context of Time*, edited by A. Strathman and J. Jaireman, 85–108. Mahwah, NJ: Lawrence Erlbaum, 2005.

Breaking the Silence. *Our Harsh Logic: Israeli Soldiers' Testimonies from the Occupied Territories, 2000–2010.* New York: Picador, 2012.

Brenner, Michael. *A Short History of the Jews.* Princeton, NJ: Princeton University Press, 2010.

Brison, Susan. "Trauma Narratives and the Remaking of the Self." In *Acts of Memory: Cultural Recall in the Present*, edited by Mieke Bal, Jonathan Crewe, and Leo Spitzer, 39–54. Hanover, NH: University Press of New England, 1999.

Brodsky, Jenny, Assaf Sharon, Yaron King, Shmuel Be'er, and Yitschak Schnoor. "Holocaust Survivors in Israel: Population Estimates, Demographic, Health and Social Characteristics, and Needs." Report RR-553-10. Center for Research on Aging, Myers-JDC-Brookdale, Jerusalem, 2010. http://www.claimscon.org/wp-content/uploads/2014/02/553-10-Holocaust-Survivors-REP-ENG.pdf.

Bromberg, Gidon. "Will the Jordan River Keep on Flowing?" *Yale Environment 360*, September 18, 2008. http://e360.yale.edu/feature/will_the_jordan_river_keep_on_flowing/2064/.

Brooks, David, and Julie Trottier. "Confronting Water in an Israeli-Palestinian Peace Agreement." *Journal of Hydrology* 382 (January 2010): 103–14.

Brooks, David B., and Julie Trottier. *An Agreement to Share Water Between Israelis and Palestinians: The FoEME Proposal.* Revised version. Tel Aviv, Bethlehem, and Amman: EcoPeace, Friends of the Earth Middle East (FoEME), March 2012. http://aquadoc.typepad.com/files/foeme_water_agreement_final.pdf.

Brown, Michael E., Owen R. Cote, Jr., Sean M. Lynn-Jones, and Steven E. Miller, eds. *Nationalism and Ethnic Conflict.* Revised ed. Cambridge, MA: MIT Press, 2001.

Brown, Oli, and Alec Crawford. "Rising Temperatures, Rising Tensions: Climate Change and the Risk of Violent Conflict in the Middle East." International Institute for Sustainable Development, Winnipeg, Canada, 2009. http://www.iisd.org/pdf/2009/rising_temps_middle_east.pdf.

Brunton, Martin. *Colonial Land Policies in Palestine, 1917–1936.* Oxford: Oxford University Press, 2007.

Brynen, Rex. "Financing Palestinian Refugee Compensation." Paper presented at Ottawa Process Workshop on Palestinian Refugee Compensation, July 1999. Palestinian Refugee ResearchNet, McGill University, Montreal, 1999. http://prrn.mcgill.ca/research/papers/brynen_990714.htm.

Brynen, Rex. "The Past as Prelude? Negotiating the Palestinian Refugee Issue." Briefing paper prepared for Middle East Programme, Royal Institute of International Affairs, Chatham House, London, June 2008. http://www.chathamhouse.org/publications/papers/view/108831.

Brynen, Rex, and Roula El-Rifai, eds. *Palestinian Refugees: Challenges of Repatriation and Development.* New York: I. B. Tauris, 2007.

Brynen, Rex, and Roula El-Rifai, eds. *The Palestinian Refugee Problem: The Search for a Resolution.* London: Pluto Press, December 2013.

B'Tselem. "Effect of Restrictions on the Economy." B'Tselem, Jerusalem, January 1, 2011. http://www.btselem.org/freedom_of_movement/economy.

B'Tselem. "Fatalities After Operation Cast Lead, 19 January 2009–30 April 2014." B'Tselem, Jerusalem, n.d. http://www.btselem.org/statistics/fatalities/after-cast-lead/by-date-of-event.

B'Tselem. "Fatalities in the First Intifada." B'Tselem, Jerusalem, n.d. http://www.btselem.org/statistics/first_intifada_tables.

B'Tselem. "Human Rights in the Occupied Territories: 2011 Annual Report." B'Tselem, Jerusalem, March 2012. http://www.btselem.org/download/2011_annual_report_eng.pdf.

B'Tselem. "The Scope of Israeli Control in the Gaza Territory." B'Tselem, Jerusalem, last updated January 5, 2014. http://www.btselem.org/gaza_strip/gaza_status.

B'Tselem. "Statistics." B'Tselem, Jerusalem, n.d. http://www.btselem.org/statistics.

B'Tselem. "Water Crisis: Discriminatory Water Supply." B'Tselem, Jerusalem, March 10, 2014. http://www.btselem.org/water/discrimination_in_water_supply.

B'Tselem. "Water Crisis: Issues Under the Oslo Accords." B'Tselem, Jerusalem, January 1, 2011, updated April 23, 2014. http://www.btselem.org/water/oslo_accords.

Burg, Avraham. *The Holocaust Is Over: We Must Rise from Its Ashes.* New York: Palgrave Macmillan, 2008.

Butler, Judith. *Parting Ways: Jewishness and the Critique of Zionism.* New York: Columbia University Press, 2012.

Bystrov, Evgenia, and Arnon Soffer. "Israel: Demography 2013–2034: Challenges and Chances." Haifa: Chaikin Chair in Geostrategy, University of Haifa, 2013.

Bystrov, Evgenia, and Arnon Soffer. "Israel: Demography 2012–2030: On the Way to a Religious State." Haifa: Chaikin Chair in Geostrategy, University of Haifa, 2012.

Bystrov, Evgenia, and Arnon Soffer. "Israel: Demography and Destiny 2007–2020." Haifa: Chaikin Chair in Geostrategy, University of Haifa, 2008. http://web.hevra.haifa.ac.il/~ch-strategy/images/publications/pdf/demography_2007_en.pdf.

"The Cairo Agreement" ("Cairo Accord"). November 1969. Palestinian Refugee ResearchNet. http://prrn.mcgill.ca/research/papers/brynen2_09.htm.

Carrington, Karin Lofthus, and Susan Griffin, eds. *Transforming Terror: Remembering the Soul of the World.* Berkeley: University of California Press, 2011.

Carter, Jimmy. *Palestine: Peace Not Apartheid.* Reprint ed. New York: Simon & Schuster, 2007.

Cebulski, Tomasz. "Memory of the Holocaust and the Shaping of Jewish Identity in Israel." Paper presented at the Legacy of the Holocaust Conference, organized by the University of Northern Iowa and the Jagiellonian University, in Kraków, May 2007.

Challand, Benoît. *Palestinian Civil Society: Foreign Donors and the Power to Promote and Exclude.* London: Routledge, 2009.

Chartock, Roselle K., and Jack Spencer, eds. *Can It Happen Again? Chronicles of the Holocaust.* New York: Black Dog & Leventhal, 1995.

Chatham House Working Group. "The Palestinian Refugee Issue: Compensation and Implementation Mechanisms." Middle East and North Africa Summary. Chatham House, London, December 18–19, 2013.

Chomsky, Noam. *Power Systems: Conversations on Global Democratic Uprisings and the New Challenges to U.S. Empire.* New York: Metropolitan Books, 2013.

Cixius, Helene. *Manhattan: Letters from Prehistory.* New York: Fordham University Press, 2007.

Cleveland, William L. *A History of Modern Middle East.* 3rd ed. Boulder, CO: Westview, 2004.

Cohen, Erik H. *Identity and Pedagogy: Shoah Education in Israeli State Schools.* Boston: Academic Studies Press, 2013.

Cohen, Hillel. *Army of Shadows: Palestinian Collaboration with Zionism, 1917–1948.* Berkeley: University of California Press, 2008.

Cohen, Hillel. *1929: Year Zero of the Jewish-Arab Conflict.* Jerusalem: Keter Publishing House, 2013.

Cohen, Michael J. *Truman and Israel.* Berkeley: University of California Press, 1990.

Cohen, Stephen. "Intractability and the Israeli-Palestinian Conflict." In *Grasping the Nettle: Analyzing Cases of Intractable Conflict,* by Chester A. Crocker, Fen Osler Hampson, and Pamela Aall, 343–56. Washington DC: United States Institute of Peace, 2005.

Cole, Juan. *Sacred Space and Holy Wars: The Politics, Culture and History of Shi'ite Islam.* New York: I. B. Tauris, 2002.

Commission to Examine the Status of Building in Judea and Samaria. "Conclusions and Recommendations." Translation from the original Hebrew. UN Information System on Question of Palestine, New York, July 13, 2012. http://unispal.un.org/UNISPAL.NSF/0/D9D07DCF58E781C585257A3A005956A6.

Cook, Jonathan. *Israel and the Clash of Civilizations: Iraq, Iran and the Plan to Remake the Middle East.* London: Pluto Press, 2008.

Cook, Steven A. "Social Work, Violence and Palestinian Nationalism." *From the Potomac to the Euphrates* (blog). Council on Foreign Relations, Washington DC, May 8, 2014. http://blogs.cfr.org/cook/2014/05/08/social-work-violence-and-palestinian-nationalism/.

Crawford, James. *The Creation of States in International Law.* 2nd ed. Oxford: Oxford University Press, 2006.

Crocker, Chester A., Fen Osler Hampson, and Pamela Aall. *Grasping the Nettle: Analyzing Cases of Intractable Conflict.* Washington DC: United States Institute of Peace, 2005.

Crooke, Alastair. *Resistance: The Essence of the Islamist Revolution.* London: Pluto Press, 2009.

Dann, Uriel. *King Hussein and the Challenge of Arab Radicalism: Jordan, 1955–1967.* New York: Oxford University Press, 1989.

Davies, John L., and Ted Robert Gurr, eds. *Preventive Measures: Building Risk Assessment and Crisis Early Warning Systems.* New York: Rowman & Littlefield, 1998.

DellaPergola, Sergio. "Demographic Trends, National Identities and Borders in Israel and the Palestinian Territory." In *Jewish Studies at the Central European University* 7 (2009–11), edited by András Kovács and Michael L. Miller, 37–62. Budapest: Jewish Studies Project, Central European University, 2013. http://www.bjpa.org/Publications/details.cfm?PublicationID=18557.

DellaPergola, Sergio. *Jewish Demographic Policies: Population Trends and Options in Israel and in the Diaspora.* Jerusalem: Jewish People Policy Institute, 2011. http://jppi.org.il/uploads/Jewish_Demographic_Policies.pdf.

DellaPergola, Sergio. *World Jewry Beyond 2000: The Demographic Prospects.* Oxford: Oxford Center for Hebrew and Jewish Studies, 1999.

"Demography." *Ettinger Report.* http://www.theettingerreport.com/Demographic-Scare.aspx.

Deutsch, Morton. "Justice and Conflict." In *The Handbook of Conflict Resolution: Theory and Practice,* edited by Morton Deutsch and Peter T. Coleman, 41–64. San Francisco: Jossey-Bass, 2000.

"Doha Agreement on the Results of the Lebanese National Dialogue Conference, May 21, 2008." Peace Agreements Database Search, United Nations Department of Political Affairs, New York. http://peacemaker.un.org/lebanon-dohaagreement2008.

"Doha Declaration Signed Between Hamas and Fatah, February 6, 2012." *Middle East Monitor,* February 8, 2012. https://www.middleeastmonitor.com/news/middle-east/3397-full-text-of-the-doha-declaration-signed-between-hamas-and-fatah.

Dowty, Alan. *Israel/Palestine*. 3rd ed. Cambridge: Polity, 2012.

Drobles, Mattityahu. "Settlement in Judea and Samaria: Strategy, Policy, and Plans." World Zionist Federation Settlement Division. Jerusalem, September 1980. Annex to Raul Roa-Kouri, "Letter dated 19 June 1981 from the Acting Chairman of the Committee on the Exercise of the Inalienable Rights of the Palestinian People to the Secretary-General." UN Docs. A/36/341 and S/14566. June 19, 1981. http://unispal.un.org/UNISPAL.NSF/0/3E5D731750EEB69E8525696600663AD0.

Dudinski, Natasha, ed. *Religion and State in Israeli and Palestinian Society*. Conference proceedings, Jerusalem, November 22, 1995. London, Oakland, and Jerusalem: Israel/Palestine Center for Research and Information, 1996.

Duhigg, Charles. *The Power of Habit: Why We Do What We Do in Life and Business*. New York: Random House, 2012.

Edelist, Ran, and Ilan Kfir. *Ehud Barak: Fighting the Demons*. Tel Aviv: Zmora-Bitan Publishers and Miskal-Yedioth Aharonoth and Chemed Books, 2003.

Education International. *Basic Academic Freedoms and Rights Violated in Israel and Palestinian Territories*. Brussels: Education International, January 7, 2010.

Efrat, Elisha. *The West Bank and Gaza Strip: A Geography of Occupation and Disengagement*. New York: Routledge, 2006.

Eizenstat, Stuart E. *The Future of the Jews: How Global Forces Are Impacting the Jewish People, Israel, and Its Relationship with the United States*. Lanham, MD: Rowman & Littlefield, 2012.

Elazar, Daniel J. "How Religious Are Israeli Jews?" Daniel Elazar Papers Index, Jerusalem Center for Public Affairs, Jerusalem, 1993. http://www.jcpa.org/dje/articles2/howrelisr.htm.

Eldar, Shlomi. *Lehakir et Hamas* ("To Know Hamas"). Chapter 8 translated by Shlomi Eldar (Jerusalem: Keter, 2012).

Elizur, Yuval, and Lawrence Malkin. *The War Within: Israel's Ultra-Orthodox Threat to Democracy and the Nation*. New York: Overlook Duckworth, 2013.

Elon, Amos. *The Pity of It All: A Portrait of the German-Jewish Epoch 1743–1933*. New York: Picador, 2002.

Enderlin, Charles. *Shattered Dreams: The Failure of the Peace Process in the Middle East, 1995–2002*. New York: Other Press, 2003.

Esber, Rosemary M. *Under the Cover of War: The Zionist Expulsion of the Palestinians*. Alexandria, VA: Arabicus Books & Media, 2008.

Esposito, John L. *The Islamic Threat: Myth or Reality?* New York: Oxford University Press, 1992.

Esposito, John L., and John Voll. *Islam and Democracy*. New York: Oxford University Press, 1996.

Etkes, Dror, and Hagit Ofran. *Breaking the Law in the West Bank: One Violation Leads to Another: Israeli Settlements on Private Palestinian Property*. A report of Peace Now's Settlement Watch Team. Translated by Monique Goldwasser and Muayed Ghanaim. Jerusalem: Peace Now, October 2006. http://news.bbc.co.uk/2/shared/bsp/hi/pdfs/21_11_06_west_bank.pdf.

European Union Special Representative to the Middle East Peace Process. *Tāba Negotiations: The Moratinos Non-Paper* (January 2001). http://unispal.un.org/UNISPAL.NSF/0/CEA3EFD8C0AB482F85256E3700670AF8.

Farrell, Kirby. *Post-Traumatic Culture: Injury and Interpretation in the Nineties*. Baltimore: Johns Hopkins University Press, 1998.

"Fatah-Hamas Gaza Agreement." *Jerusalem Post*. http://www.jpost.com/Arab-Israeli-Conflict/Text-of-Fatah-Hamas-agreement-376350.

"Fatah-Hamas Mecca Agreement, February 2007." *Al-Akhbar*, February 2007. http://english.al-akhbar.com/sites/default/files/Mecca%20Agreement%20(Feb.%202007).pdf.

Feldman, Noah. *The Fall and Rise of the Islamic State*. Princeton, NJ: Princeton University Press, 2008.

Feldman, Stanley. "Values, Ideology, and the Structure of Political Attitudes." In *Oxford Handbook of Political Psychology*, edited by David O. Sears, Leonie L. Huddy, and Robert Jervis, 477–508. Oxford: Oxford University Press, 2003.

Finkelstein, Norman G. *Image and Reality of the Israeli-Palestine Conflict*. London: Verso, 1995.

Fischbach, Michael R. *The Peace Process and Palestinian Refugee Claims: Addressing Claims for Property Compensation and Restitution*. Washington DC: United States Institute of Peace, 2006.

Fischbach, Michael R. *Records of Dispossession: Palestinian Refugee Property and the Arab-Israeli Conflict*. New York: Columbia University Press, 2003.

Fisher, Roger, William Ury, and Bruce Patton. *Getting to Yes: Negotiating Agreements Without Giving In*. New York: Penguin Books, 1991.

Fishman, Henry, and Ephraim Lavie. *The Peace Process: Seventeen Plans in Ten Years, An Assessment of the Initiatives to Resolve the Israeli Palestinian Conflict over the Past Decade.* Tel Aviv: Peres Center for Peace and Ramallah: Palestine Center for Strategic Studies, November 2010. http://www.upsite.co.il/uploaded/files/1339_e72d9b241ada1a51328fe21fe6b9795f.pdf.

Flapan, Simha. *The Birth of Israel: Myths and Realities.* New York: Pantheon Books, 1987.

Foundation for Middle East Peace. "Israeli Settlements in the Occupied Territories: A Guide." *Settlement Report* 12, no. 7 (March 2002). http://www.fmep.org/reports/special-reports/a-guide-to-israeli-settlements-in-the-occupied-territories/israeli-settlements-in-the-occupied-territories-a-guide.

Fox, Jonathan, and Shmeul Sandler. *Religion in World Conflict.* London, New York, and Ramat Gan, Israel: Rutledge and BESA, 2007.

Freeman, Mark. *Hindsight: The Promise and Peril of Looking Backward.* Oxford: Oxford University Press, 2009.

Freimuth, Ladeene, Gidon Bromberg, Munqeth Mehyar, and Nader Al Khatheeb. "Climate Change: A New Threat to Middle East Security." Paper prepared for the United Nations Climate Change Conference, Bali, Indonesia. Tel Aviv, Bethlehem, and Amman: EcoPeace, Friends of the Earth Middle East, December 2007. http://foeme.org/uploads/publications_publ78_1.pdf.

Fried, Marc. "Grieving for a Lost Home." In *The Urban Condition: People and Policy in the Metropolis,* edited by Leonard J. Duhl and John Powell. New York: Basic Books, 1963.

Friedrich Naumann Foundation. *Localizing: Agenda 21 in Palestine.* Bethlehem: ARIJ, 2001.

Frisch, Hillel. "Has the Israeli-Palestinian Conflict Become Islamic? Fatah, Islam, and the Àl-Aqsa Martyrs' Brigade." In *Religion in World Conflict,* edited by Jonathan Fox and Shmeul Sandler, 97–111. New York: Routledge, 2006.

Fromkin, David. *A Peace to End All Peace: The Fall of the Ottoman Empire and the Creation of the Modern Middle East.* New York: Holt, 1989.

Frontline, "The Negotations." In *Shattered Dreams of Peace: The Road to Oslo* (video). PBS, June 27, 2002. http://www.pbs.org/wgbh/pages/frontline/shows/oslo/negotiations/. (The main page for the "Shattered Dreams of Peace" program can be viewed at http://www.pbs.org/wgbh/pages/frontline/shows/oslo/.)

Funk, Nathan C., and Abdul Aziz Said. *Islam and Peacemaking in the Middle East.* Boulder, CO: Lynne Rienner, 2009.

Gallup, John Luke, Jeffrey D. Sachs, and Andrew D. Mellinger. "Geography and Economic Development." CID Working Paper no. 1. National Bureau of Economic Research, Cambridge, MA, March 1999. http://www.hks.harvard.edu/var/ezp_site/storage/fckeditor/file/pdfs/centers-programs/centers/cid/publications/faculty/wp/001.pdf.

Gauthier, David. *Morals by Agreement.* Oxford: Clarendon Press, 1986.

Gellner, Ernest. *Nations and Nationalism.* Ithaca, NY: Cornell University Press, 1983.

Gilbert, Martin. *The Routledge Atlas of the Arab-Israeli Conflict.* 9th ed. New York: Routledge, 2008.

Ginossar, Yossi. "Factors That Impeded Negotiations." In *The Camp David Summit: What Went Wrong?,* edited by Simon Shamir and Bruce Maddy-Weitzman, 51–59. East Sussex, UK: Sussex Academic Press, 2005.

Gisha Legal Center for Freedom of Movement, "Gaza Snapshot 2013." In *Gaza Gateway: Facts and Analysis About the Crossings.* Gisha, Tel Aviv-Jaffa, June 2, 2013. http://gisha.org/en-blog/2013/06/02/gaza-2013-snapshot/.

Glick, Caroline B. *The Israeli Solution: A One State Plan for Peace in the Middle East.* New York: Crown Forum, 2014.

Gold, Steve. "Israeli Emigration Policy." In *Citizenship and Those Who Leave: The Politics of Emigration and Expatriation,* edited by Nancy L. Green and Francois Weil, 282–304. Chicago: University of Illinois Press, 2007.

Goldman, David P. "The Vicissitudes of Jewish Exceptionalism." Review of *On the Origins of Jewish Self-Hatred,* by Paul Reitter. *The American Interest,* February 12, 2013. http://www.the-american-interest.com/articles/2013/02/12/the-vicissitudes-of-jewish-exceptionalism/.

Goldman, Jennifer S., and Peter T. Coleman. "How Humiliation Fuels Intractable Conflicts: The Effects of Emotional Roles on Recall and Reactions to Conflictual Encounters." Work in progress, Teachers College, Columbia University, 2005. http://www.humiliationstudies.org/documents/GoldmanHumiliationIntractableConflict10March05.pdf.

Goldman, Nahum T. *The Jewish Paradox.* Jerusalem: Israel University Press, 1968.

Goodman, Hirsh. *The Anatomy of Israel's Survival.* New York: Public Affairs, 2011.

Gordon, Lewis R., T. Denean Sharpley-Whiting, and Renee T. White, eds. *Fanon: A Critical Reader.* Malden, MA: Blackwell, 1996.

Gordon, Neve. *Israel's Occupation.* Berkeley: University of California Press, 2008.

Gorenberg, Gershom. *The Accidental Empire: Israel and the Birth of the Settlements, 1967–1977.* New York: Holt, 2006.

Gorenberg, Gershom. *The Unmaking of Israel.* New York: Harper Perennial, 2012.

Gorgis, Daniel. *Saving Israel: How the Jewish People Can Win a War That May Never End.* Hoboken, NJ: John Wiley, 2009.

Gray, Jeffrey Alan. *The Psychology of Fear and Stress.* 2nd ed. Problems in the Behavioural Sciences. Cambridge: Cambridge University Press, 1987.

Great Britain and Sir Walter Sidney Shaw. *Report of the Commission on the Palestine Disturbances of August, 1929: Evidence Heard During the 1st [-47th] Sittings.* London, HM Stationery Office, 1930.

Greenfield, Tzvia. *They Are Afraid: How the Religious and Ultra-Religious Right Became the Leading Force in Israel.* Tel-Aviv: Yedioth Ahronoth (Hebrew), 2001.

Greist, John H., James W. Jefferson, and David J. Katzelnick. *Social Anxiety Disorder: A Guide.* Madison, WI: Madison Institute of Medicine, 2000.

Grinberg, Lev Luis, ed. *Contested Memory: Myth, Nationalism, and Democracy.* Beersheba, Israel: Ben-Gurion University (Hebrew), 2000.

Grinberg, Lev Luis. *Split Corporatism in Israel.* Albany, NY: State University of New York Press, 1991.

Gurr, Ted Robert. *Minorities at Risk: A Global View of Ethnopolitical Conflicts.* Washington, DC: United States Institute of Peace, 1993.

Haass, Richard N., and Martin S. Indyk, "A Time for Diplomatic Renewal." In *Restoring the Balance: A Middle East Strategy for the Next President,* a project of the Saban Center at Brookings and the Council on Foreign Relations, 1–26. Washington DC: The Brookings Institution, 2008.

Habib, Camille H. *Consociationalism and the Continuous Crisis in the Lebanese System.* Beirut: Majd, 2009.

Hadi, Hahdi Abdul, ed. *Palestinian-Israeli Impasse: Exploring Alternative Solutions to the Palestine-Israel Conflict.* Jerusalem: PASSIA, 2005.

Haider, Ali, ed. *The Equality Index of Jewish and Arab Citizens in Israel.* Jerusalem: Sikkuy Report, 2007.

"Haifa Declaration." http://reut-institute.org/en/Publication.aspx?PublicationId=1699.

"The Haifa Declaration." Mada al-Carmel: Arab Center for Applied Social Research, Haifa. http://mada-research.org/en/files/2007/09/haifaenglish.pdf.

Halperin, Eran. *On the Psychology of Inter-Group Hatred in Political Systems.* Unpublished doctoral dissertation, (Hebrew). Haifa University, Israel, 2007.

Halperin, Eran, and Daniel Bar-Tal, "Overcoming Psychological Barriers to Peace Process: The Influence of Beliefs About Losses." In *Prosocial Motives, Emotions and Behaviors: The Better Angels of Our Nature,* by Mario Mikulincer and Philip R. Shaver. Washington DC: American Psychological Association Press, 2009, 431–48. Quoted in Halperin et al., "Socio-Psychological Barriers," 2010.

Halperin, Eran, Keren Sharvit, and James J. Gross. "Emotions and Emotion Regulation in Conflicts." In *Intergroup Conflicts and Their Resolution: Social Psychological Perspective,* edited by Daniel Bar-Tal, 83–104. New York: Psychology Press, 2011.

Halperin, Eran, Neta Oren, and Daniel Bar-Tal. "Socio-Psychological Barriers to Resolving the Israeli-Palestinian Conflict: An Analysis of Jewish Israeli Society." In *Barriers to Peace in the Israeli-Palestinian Conflict,* edited by Yaacov Bar-Siman-Tov, 28–57. Jerusalem: Konrad-Adenaeur-Stiftung Israel and Jerusalem Institute for Israel Studies, 2010.

"Hamas Covenant 1988: The Covenant of the Islamic Resistance Movement," August 18, 1988. The Avalon Project, Lillian Goldman Law Library, Yale Law School, New Haven, CT. http://avalon.law.yale.edu/20th_century/hamas.asp.

Hammach, Phillip L. *Narrative and the Politics of Identity: The Cultural Psychology of Israeli and Palestinian Youth.* New York: Oxford University Press, 2011.

Hammes, Thomas X. *The Sling and the Stone: On War in the 21st Century.* Beverly MA: Zenith Press, 2006.

Harb, Imad. "Lebanon's Confessionalism: Problems and Prospects." United States Institute of Peace Briefing. United States Institute of Peace, Washington DC, March 30, 2006. http://www.usip.org/publications/lebanons-confessionalism-problems-and-prospects.

Hareuveni, Eyal. *By Hook and by Crook: Israeli Settlement Policy in the West Bank.* Edited by Yael Stein. Jerusalem: B'Tselem, 2010.

Harkabi, Yehoshafat. *The Palestinian Covenant and Its Meaning.* Jerusalem: Hotzaat Yersahalayim (Hebrew), 1971.

Harris, Lee. *The Suicide of Reason: Radical Islam's Threat to the Enlightenment.* New York: Basic Books, 2007.

Harry S. Truman Research Institute for the Advancement of Peace, et al. "Joint Israeli Palestinian Poll, June 2014." Harry S. Truman Research Institute, Konrad Adenauer Stiftung, and Palestinian Center for Policy and Survey Research, Jerusalem and Ramallah, June 2014.

Harry S. Truman Research Institute for the Advancement of Peace, et al. "Joint Israeli Palestinian Poll, December 2013." Harry S. Truman Research Institute, Konrad Adenauer Stiftung, and Palestinian Center for Policy and Survey Research, Jerusalem and Ramallah, December 2013. http://truman.huji.ac.il/.upload/Joint_press_December_2013%20(2).pdf and http://www.pcpsr.org/en/node/378.

Harry S. Truman Research Institute for the Advancement of Peace, et al. "Joint Israeli Palestinian Poll, December 2012." Harry S. Truman Research Institute, Konrad Adenauer Stiftung, Ford Foundation, and Palestinian Center for Policy and Survey Research, Jerusalem and Ramallah, December 2012. http://truman.huji.ac.il/.upload/Polls%202012.pdf and http://www.pcpsr.org/en/joint-israeli-palestinian-poll-46-december-2012.

Harry S. Truman Research Institute for the Advancement of Peace, et al. "Joint Israeli Palestinian Poll No. 46: December 2011." Harry S. Truman Research Institute, Ford Foundation, Konrad Adenauer Stiftung, and Palestinian Center for Policy and Survey Research, Jerusalem and Ramallah, December 2011. http://truman.huji.ac.il/.upload/Polls%202010%202011.pdf and http://www.pcpsr.org/en/node/392.

Hart, Alan. *Zionism: The Real Enemy of the Jews.* Vol. 1, *The False Messiah.* Atlanta: Clarity Press, 2009.

Hartberg, Martin. "Beyond Ceasefire: Ending the Blockade of Gaza." Briefing Note. Oxfam, Oxford, December 6, 2012.

Hashemi, Nader. *Islam, Secularism, and Liberal Democracy: Toward a Democratic Theory for Muslim Societies.* New York: Oxford University Press, 2009.

Hassner, Ron E. *War on Sacred Grounds.* Ithaca, NY: Cornell University Press, 2009.

Haugen, Gary A., and Victor Boutros. *The Locust Effect: Why the End of Poverty Requires the End of Violence.* New York: Oxford University Press, 2014.

Hedges, Chris. *War Is a Force That Gives Us Meaning.* New York: Public Affairs, 2002.

Hefner, Robert W. *Civil Islam: Muslims and Democratization in Indonesia.* Princeton: Princeton University Press, 2000.

Hehir, J. Bryan. "Military Intervention and National Sovereignty: Recasting the Relationship." In *Hard Choices: Moral Dilemmas in Humanitarian Intervention*, edited by Jonathan Moore, 29–54. Lanham, MD: Rowman & Littlefield, 1998.

Herzl, Theodor. *The Complete Diaries of Theodor Herzl.* Edited by Raphael Patai. New York: Herzl Press and Thomas Yoseloff, 1960.

Hever, Shir. *The Political Economy of Israel's Occupation: Repression Beyond Exploitation.* London: Pluto Press, 2010.

Hexel, Ralf, and Roby Nathanson. *All of the Above: Identity Paradoxes of Young People in Israel.* Third Youth Study of the Friedrich-Ebert-Stiftung Israel. Herzliya Pituach, Israel: Friedrich-Ebert-Stiftung Israel, 2010. http://www.fes.org.il/internal.asp?PiD=0.700&id=702.

Hicks, Donna. *Dignity: Its Essential Role in Resolving Conflict.* New Haven: Yale University Press, 2011.

Hilal, Jamil. *Where Now for Palestine? The Demise of the Two-State Solution.* New York: Zed Books, 2007.

Himadeh, Said. *Economic Organization of Palestine.* Beirut: American University of Beirut, 1938.

Hirst, David. *The Gun and the Olive Branch: The Roots of Violence in the Middle East.* London: Faber and Faber, 1977, 1984.

Hobsbawm, Eric J. *Nations and Nationalism Since 1780: Programme, Myth, Reality.* Cambridge: Cambridge University Press, 1990.

Horowitz, Adam, Lizzy Ratner, and Philip Weiss, eds. *The Goldstone Report: The Legacy of the Landmark Investigation of the Gaza Conflict.* New York: Nation Books, 2011.

Horowitz, Donald L. *Ethnic Groups in Conflict.* Berkeley: University of California Press, 1985.

Hroub, Khaled. *Hamas: A Beginner's Guide.* London: Pluto Press, 2006.

Hroub, Khaled. *Hamas: Political Thought and Practice.* Washington DC: Institute for Palestine Studies, 2000.

Huddy, L. S. Feldman, and E. Cassese. "On the Distinct Political Effects of Anxiety and Anger." In *The Dynamics of Emotion in Political Thinking and Behavior*, edited by A. Crigler, M. MacKuen, G. Marcus, and W. R. Neuman, 202–30. Chicago: Chicago University Press, 2007.

Human Rights Watch: *Under Cover of War Hamas Political Violence in Gaza*. New York: Human Rights Watch, April 2009. http://www.hrw.org/sites/default/files/reports/iopt0409web.pdf.

Human Rights Watch. *World Report 2013: Events of 2012*. New York: Human Rights Watch, 2013. http://www.hrw.org/sites/default/files/wr2013_web.pdf.

Human Rights Watch. *World Report 2012: Events of 2011*. New York: Human Rights Watch, September 2012. http://www.hrw.org/sites/default/files/reports/wr2012.pdf.

Human Rights Watch, *World Report 2009: Events of 2008*. New York: Human Rights Watch, 2009. http://www.hrw.org/sites/default/files/reports/wr2009_web.pdf.

Hughey, Michael W., ed. *New Tribalisms: The Resurgence of Race and Ethnicity*. New York: New York University Press, 1998.

Huneidi, Sahar. *A Broken Trust: Herbert Samuel, Zionism, and the Palestinians*. London: I. B. Tauris, 2001.

Hurewitz, Jacob Coleman. *The Struggle for Palestine*. 2nd ed. New York: Schocken, 1976. Originally published by Norton, in 1959.

Ignatieff, Michael. *The Lesser Evil: Political Ethics in an Age of Terror*. Princeton: Princeton University Press, 2004.

Inbar, Efraim. "The 2011 Arab Uprisings and Israel's National Security." *Middle East Security and Policy Studies* 95 (2012).

Indyk, Martin. *Innocent Abroad: An Intimate Account of American Peace Diplomacy in the Middle East*. New York: Simon & Schuster, 2009.

Institute for Middle East Understanding. "Fact Sheet: 25th Anniversary of the First Intifada." Institute for Middle East Understanding, Tustin, CA, December 6, 2012. http://imeu.net/news/article0023335.shtml.

Intergovernmental Panel on Climate Change. *Climate Change 2014: Impacts, Adaptations, and Vulnerability*. Vol. 1, *Global and Sectoral Aspects*. Edited by Christopher B. Field, Vincente R. Barros, David J. Dokken, Katherine J. Mach, Michael D. Mastrandrea, Girma Balcha, T. Eren Bilir, Monalisa Chatterjee, Kristie L. Ebi, Yuka Otsuki Estrada, Robert C. Genova, Eric S. Kissel, A. N. Levy, Sandy MacCracken, P. R. Mastrandrea, and Leslie L. White. Cambridge and New York: Cambridge University Press, April 2014.

Intergovernmental Panel on Climate Change. *Climate Change 2013: The Physical Science Basis*. Edited by Thomas F. Stocker, Dahe Qin, Gian-Kasper Plattner, Melinda M. B. Tignor, Simon K. Allen, Judith Boschung, Alexander Nauels, Yu Xia, Vincent Bex, and P. M. Midgley. Cambridge and New York: Cambridge University Press, September 2013.

Intergovernmental Panel on Climate Change. "Fifth Assessment Report (AR5)." 2014. http://www.ipcc.ch/index.htm.

International Court of Justice. "Legal Consequences of the Construction of a Wall in the Occupied Palestinian Territory." Press Release 2004/28. International Court of Justice, The Hague, July 9, 2004. http://www.icj-cij.org/docket/index.php?pr=71&code=mwp&p1=3&p2=4&p3=6&case=131&k=5a.

International Crisis Group. "Buying Time? Money, Guns and Politics in the West Bank." Middle East Report No. 142. International Crisis Group, Brussels, May 29, 2013. http://www.crisisgroup.org/en/regions/middle-east-north-africa/israel-palestine/142-buying-time-money-guns-and-politics-in-the-west-bank.aspx.

International Crisis Group. "The Emperor Has No Clothes: Palestinians and the End of the Peace Process." Middle East Report No. 122. International Crisis Group, Brussels, May 7, 2012. http://www.crisisgroup.org/en/regions/middle-east-north-africa/israel-palestine/122-the-emperor-has-no-clothes-palestinians-and-the-end-of-the-peace-process.aspx.

International Crisis Group. "Gaza: The Next Israeli-Palestinian War?" Middle East Briefing No. 30. International Crisis Group, Brussels, March 24, 2011. http://www.crisisgroup.org/en/regions/middle-east-north-africa/israel-palestine/B30-%20gaza-the-next-israeli-palestinian-war.aspx.

International Crisis Group. "Gaza and Israel: New Obstacles, New Solutions." Middle East Briefing No. 39. International Crisis Group, Brussels, July 14, 2014. http://www.crisisgroup.org/~/media/Files/Middle%20East%20North%20Africa/Israel%20Palestine/b039-gaza-and-israel-new-obstacles-new-solutions.pdf.

International Crisis Group. "Inside Gaza: The Challenge of Clans and Families." Middle East Report No. 71. International Crisis Group, Brussels, December 20, 2007. http://www.crisisgroup.org/~/

media/Files/Middle%20East%20North%20Africa/Israel%20Palestine/71_inside_gaza___the_challenge_of_clans_and_families.ashx.

International Crisis Group. "Israel and Hamas: Fire and Ceasefire in a New Middle East." Middle East Report No. 133. International Crisis Group, Brussels, November 22, 2012. http://www.crisisgroup.org/~/media/Files/Middle%20East%20North%20Africa/Israel%20Palestine/133-israel-and-hamas-fire-and-ceasefire-in-a-new-middle-east.pdf.

International Crisis Group. "Leap of Faith: Israel's National Religious and the Israeli-Palestinian Conflict." Middle East Report No. 147. International Crisis Group, Brussels, November 21, 2013. http://www.crisisgroup.org/~/media/Files/Middle%20East%20North%20Africa/Israel%20Palestine/147-leap-of-faith-israels-national-religious-and-the-israeli-palestinian-conflict.pdf.

International Crisis Group. "Light at the End of Their Tunnels? Hamas & the Arab Uprisings." Middle East Report No. 129. International Crisis Group, Brussels, August 2012.

International Crisis Group. "Squaring the Circle: Palestinian Security Reform under Occupation." Middle East Report No. 98. International Crisis Group, Brussels, September 7, 2010. http://www.crisisgroup.org/en/regions/middle-east-north-africa/israel-palestine/98-squaring-the-circle-palestinian-security-reform-under-occupation.aspx.

International Donors' Conference for the Palestinian State. "Final Statement of the Chair and Co-chairs." Paris, December 17, 2007. http://unispal.un.org/UNISPAL.NSF/0/4CB6C31B95E505B7852573B500568508#sthash.XRa7tv7g.dpuf.

International Monetary Fund. "Macroeconomic and Fiscal Framework for the West Bank and Gaza: Seventh Review of Progress." Staff Report for the Meeting of the Ad Hoc Liaison Committee. International Monetary Fund, Brussels, April 13, 2011. http://www.imf.org/external/country/WBG/RR/2011/041311.pdf.

International Monetary Fund. "Statement at the Conclusion of an IMF Mission to the West Bank and Gaza." Press Release No. 14/44. International Monetary Fund, Washington DC, February 6, 2014.

"Interview: Khalil Shikaki Discusses a New Poll on How Palestinian Refugees View the Right of Return." Narrated by Robert Siegel. *All Things Considered*. NPR, July 14, 2003. http://www.npr.org/programs/atc/transcripts/2003/jul/030714.shikaki.html.

IRIN. "Middle East: Palestinian Refugee Numbers/Whereabouts," United Nations Office for the Coordination of Humanitarian Affairs, 2010. http://www.irinnews.org/Report/89571/MIDDLE-EAST-Palestinian-refugee-numbers-whereabouts.

Isac, Jad, and Fida' Abdul-Latif. *Jerusalem & the Geopolitics of De-Palestinisation*. Jerusalem: ALECSO, 2007.

Israel Central Bureau of Statistics. "Population of Israel on the Eve of 2014: 8 Million." Media Release 357/2013. December 29, 2013. http://www1.cbs.gov.il/hodaot2013n/11_13_357e.pdf.

"Israel: Supreme Court Decision Invalidating the Law on Haredi Military Draft Postponement." Prepared by Ruth Levush. Washington DC: The Law Library, Library of Congress, March 2012. http://www.loc.gov/law/help/il-haredi-military-draft/haredi-military-draft.php.

Israel Ministry of Defense. "'Spiegel Database' of West Bank Settlements and Outposts." Translated by Yesh Din. Foundation for Middle East Peace, Washington DC, n.d. http://www.fmep.org/analysis/reference/SpiegelDatabaseEng.pdf.

Israel Ministry of Foreign Affairs. "Disputed Territories: Forgotten Facts About the West Bank and Gaza Strip." Ministry of Foreign Affairs, Jerusalem, February 1, 2003. http://mfa.gov.il/MFA/MFA-Archive/2003/Pages/DISPUTED%20TERRITORIES-%20Forgotten%20Facts%20About%20the%20We.aspx.

Israel Ministry of Foreign Affairs. "The Hamas Terror War Against Israel." Ministry of Foreign Affairs, Jerusalem, March 2011. http://www.mfa.gov.il/mfa/foreignpolicy/terrorism/palestinian/pages/missile%20fire%20from%20gaza%20on%20israeli%20civilian%20targets%20aug%202007.aspx#statistics.

Israel Ministry of Foreign Affairs. "High Court of Justice Rules on Security Fence Around Alfei Menashe." Ministry of Foreign Affairs, Jerusalem, September 15, 2005. http://www.mfa.gov.il/mfa/aboutisrael/state/law/pages/high%20court%20rules%20on%20security%20fence%20around%20alfei%20menashe%2015-sep-2005.aspx.

Israel Ministry of Foreign Affairs. "ICJ Advisory Opinion on Israel's Security Fence: Israeli Statement." Ministry of Foreign Affairs, Jerusalem, July 9, 2004. http://www.mfa.gov.il/mfa/pressroom/2004/pages/statement%20on%20icj%20advisory%20opinion%209-july-2004.aspx.

Israel Ministry of Foreign Affairs, "Initial Response to Report of the Fact Finding Mission on Gaza," Ministry of Foreign Affairs, Jerusalem, September 24, 2009. http://mfa.gov.il/mfa/foreignpolicy/terrorism/pages/initial-response-goldstone-report-24-sep-2009.aspx.

Israel Ministry of Foreign Affairs. "Israel-PLO Mutual Recognition—Letters and Speeches." Vol. 13–14: 1992–94. Ministry of Foreign Affairs, Jerusalem, September 10, 1993. http://mfa.gov.il/MFA/ForeignPolicy/MFADocuments/Yearbook9/Pages/107%20Israel-PLO%20Mutual%20Recognition-%20Letters%20and%20Spe.aspx.

Israel Ministry of Foreign Affairs. "The Madrid Framework." Ministry of Foreign Affairs, Jerusalem, January 28, 1999. http://www.mfa.gov.il/mfa/foreignpolicy/peace/guide/pages/the%20madrid%20framework.aspx.

Israel Ministry of Foreign Affairs. "Suicide and Other Bombing Attacks in Israel Since the Declaration of Principles." Ministry of Foreign Affairs, Jerusalem, n.d. http://www.mfa.gov.il/MFA/Terrorism-+Obstacle+to+Peace/Palestinian+terror+since+2000/Suicide+and+Other+Bombing+Attacks+in+Israel+Since.htm.

Israel Ministry of Foreign Affairs. "Summary of the Opinion Concerning Unauthorized Outposts." Ministry of Foreign Affairs, Jerusalem, March 10, 2005. http://unispal.un.org/UNISPAL.NSF/0/956AA60F2A7BD6A185256FC0006305F4.

Israel Ministry of Foreign Affairs. "Terrorism Deaths in Israel, 1920–1999." Ministry of Foreign Affairs, Jerusalem, January 1, 2000. http://mfa.gov.il/MFA/ForeignPolicy/Terrorism/Palestinian/Pages/Terrorism%20deaths%20in%20Israel%20-%201920-1999.aspx.

Israel Ministry of Foreign Affairs. "UN General Assembly Resolution 181 (Partition Plan) November 29, 1947." Ministry of Foreign Affairs, Jerusalem, November 29, 1947. http://www.mfa.gov.il/mfa/foreignpolicy/peace/guide/pages/un%20general%20assembly%20resolution%20181.aspx.

Israel Ministry of Foreign Affairs. "Victims of Palestinian Violence and Terrorism Since September 2000." Ministry of Foreign Affairs, Jerusalem. Last updated April 14, 2014. http://www.mfa.gov.il/mfa/foreignpolicy/terrorism/palestinian/pages/victims%20of%20palestinian%20violence%20and%20terrorism%20sinc.aspx.

Israel Ministry of Foreign Affairs. "Which Came First—Terrorism or 'Occupation'? Major Arab Terrorist Attacks Against Israelis Prior to the 1967 Six-Day War." Ministry of Foreign Affairs, Jerusalem, March 2002. http://www.mfa.gov.il/MFA/Terrorism-+Obstacle+to+Peace/Palestinian+terror+before+2000/Which+Came+First-+Terrorism+or+Occupation+-+Major.htm.

Israel National Security Project. "What They Say: The Demographic Challenge." Israel National Security Project, School of International Service, American University, Washington DC, 2013. http://www.israelnsp.org/what-they-say/status-quo-is-dangerous/israels-demographic-challen.html.

Israel Water Authority. "The Water Issues Between Israel and the Palestinians: Main Facts." Israel Water Authority, February 2012. http://www.water.gov.il/Hebrew/ProfessionalInfoAndData/2012/19-Water-Issues-between-Israel-and-Palestinians-Main-Facts.pdf.

Israeli Committee Against Housing Demolitions. "Demolishing Homes, Demolishing Peace: Political and Normative Analysis of Israel's Displacement Policy in the oPt." Israeli Committee Against House Demolitions, April 2012.

"Israeli Nationality Law, 5712-1952," April 1, 1952. Israel Law Resource Center. http://www.israellawresourcecenter.org/israellaws/fulltext/nationalitylaw.htm.

Izady, Mehrdad R. *The Kurds: A Concise Handbook.* Washington, DC: Crane Russak, 1992.

Jacoby, Tami Amanda. *Bridging the Barrier: Israeli Unilateral Disengagement.* Surrey, UK and Burlington, VT: Ashgate, March 28, 2013.

Jandt, Fred E. *Intercultural Communication: An Introduction.* Thousand Oaks, CA: Sage Publications, 1995.

Jaspal, Rusi, and Glynis M. Breakwell, eds. *Identity Process Theory: Identity, Social Action and Social Change*, 222. Cambridge: Cambridge University Press, 2014.

Jawad, Saleh Abdel. "The Arab and Palestinian Narratives of the 1948 War." In *Israeli and Palestinian Narratives of Conflict: History's Double Helix*, edited by Robert I. Rotberg, 72–114. Bloomington: Indiana University Press, 2006.

Jerusalem Institute for Israel Studies. "Table III/1: Population of Israel and Jerusalem, by Population Group, 1922–2012." In *Statistical Yearbook of Jerusalem, 2014.* Jerusalem: Jerusalem Institute for Israel Studies, 2014. http://www.jiis.org.il/.upload/yearbook2014/shnaton_C0114.pdf.

Jerusalem Institute for Israel Studies. "Table III/10: Population of Jerusalem, by Age, Religion, and Geographical Spreading, 2012." In *Statistical Yearbook of Jerusalem, 2014.* Jerusalem: Jerusalem Institute for Israel Studies, 2014. http://www.jiis.org.il/.upload/yearbook2014/shnaton_C1014.pdf.

Jerusalem Media and Communications Center. *Beg, Borrow, or Steal! Israeli Settlements in the Occupied Territories.* Jerusalem: JMCC, 1991.

Jewish Virtual Library. "Israel's Basic Laws: The Law of Return (July 5, 1950)." https://www.jewishvirtuallibrary.org/jsource/Politics/Other_Law_Law_of_Return.html.

Jewish Virtual Library. "The Official Summation of the Or Commission Report." September 2, 2003. http://www.jewishvirtuallibrary.org/jsource/Society_&_Culture/OrCommissionReport.html.

Jiryis, Sabri. *The Arabs in Israel.* New York: Monthly Review, 1976.

Johnson, Toni, and Mohammed Aly Sergie. "Islam: Governing Under Sharia." CFR Backgrounder. Council on Foreign Relations, Washington DC, July 25, 2014. http://www.cfr.org/religion/islam-governing-under-sharia/p8034.

Jones, Edward E., and Richard E. Nisbett. "The Actor and the Observer: Divergent Perceptions of the Causes of Behavior." In *Attribution: Perceiving the Causes of Behavior,* edited by Edward E. Jones, David E. Kanouse, Harold H. Kelley, Richard E. Nisbett, Stuart Valins, and Bernard Weiner, 79–94. Morristown, NJ: General Learning Press, 1972. http://isites.harvard.edu/fs/docs/icb.topic521566.files/D_jones_nisbett1971pp79-94.pdf.

Kadri, Sadakat. *Heaven and Earth: A Journey Through Shari'a Law from the Deserts of Ancient Arabia to the Streets of the Modern Muslim World.* New York: Farrar, Straus & Giroux, 2012.

Kaplan, Robert D. *The Revenge of Geography: What the Map Tells Us About Coming Conflicts and the Battle Against Fate.* New York: Random House, 2012.

Karabell, Zachary. *Peace Be Upon You: Four Centuries of Muslim, Christian, and Jewish Conflict and Cooperation.* New York: Vintage Books, 2007.

Karlin, Daniela R. "Righteous Victims: The Role of Competing Victim Identities in the Israeli Palestinian Conflict: A Social Psychological Paradigm." Dissertation for B.A., Jewish Studies, University of California at Los Angeles, 2007.

Karmi, G. "What Role for the Palestinian Diaspora After Oslo." In *Palestinian Elections and the Future of Palestine.* Washington DC: The Center for Policy Analysis on Palestine, 1996.

Karolyi, Paul T. "*Haaretz* Published Poll Exposing Jewish Discrimination Against Arabs in Israel." *Arab Human Rights Association* (blog), October 25, 2012. http://arabhra.wordpress.com/tag/dialog/.

Karsh, Efraim, ed. *Israel: The First Hundred Years.* Vol. 3, *Israeli Society and Politics Since 1948: Problems of Collective Identity.* London: Frank Cass, 2002.

Karsh, Efraim. *Palestine Betrayed.* New Haven, CT: Yale University Press, 2010.

Keissar-Sugarmen, Ayala. *A Portrait of Israeli Jews: Beliefs, Observance, and Values of Israeli Jews, 2009.* Jerusalem: Israel Democracy Institute and Avi Chai Israel Foundation, 2011. http://en.idi.org.il/media/1351622/GuttmanAviChaiReport2012_EngFinal.pdf.

Kelman, Herbert C. "Social-Psychological Dimensions of International Conflict." In *Peacemaking in International Conflict: Methods and Techniques,* edited by I. William Zartman and J. Lewis Rasmussen, 191–237. Washington DC: United States Institute of Peace Press, 1997.

Kelsay, John. *Arguing the Just War in Islam.* Cambridge, MA: Harvard University Press, 2007.

Kent, Marian, ed. *The Great Powers and the End of the Ottoman Empire.* London: Frank Cass, 1996.

Ker-Lindsay, James. *The Foreign Policy of Counter Secession: Preventing the Recognition of Contested States.* Oxford: Oxford University Press, 2012.

Khadduri, Majid. *War and Peace in the Law of Islam.* Baltimore: Johns Hopkins University Press, 1955.

Khalaf, Issa. *Arab Factionalism and Social Disintegration, 1939–1948.* Albany: State University of New York Press, 1988.

Khalaf, Samir. *Civil and Uncivil Violence in Lebanon: A History of the Internationalization of Communal Conflict.* New York: Columbia University Press, 2002.

Khalaf, Samir. *Lebanon's Predicament.* New York: Columbia University Press, 1987.

Khalidi, Rashid. *British Policy Towards Syria and Palestine, 1906–1914.* Oxford: Ithaca Press, 1980.

Khalidi, Rashid. *The Iron Cage: The Story of the Palestinian Struggle for Statehood.* Boston: Beacon Press, 2007.

Khalidi, Rashid. *Palestinian Identity: The Construction of Modern National Consciousness.* New York: Columbia University Press, 1997.

Khalidi, Rashid. *Resurrecting Empire: Western Footprints and America's Perilous Path in the Middle East.* Boston: Beacon Press, 2004.

Khalidi, Rashid. *Under Siege: PLO Decision-Making During the 1982 War.* New York: Columbia University Press, 1986.

Khalidi, Walid. *All That Remains: The Palestinian Villages Occupied and Depopulated by Israel in 1948.* Beirut: Institute for Palestine Studies, 1992.

Khalidi, Walid. *From Haven to Conquest: Reading in Zionism and the Palestine Problem Until 1948.* Beirut: Institute for Palestine Studies, 1987.

Khater, Akram Fouad. *Sources in the History of the Modern Middle East.* Boston: Houghton Mifflin, 2004.

Khatib, Ghassan. *Palestinian Politics and the Middle East Peace Process: Consensus and Competition in the Palestinian Negotiating Team.* New York: Routledge, 2010.

Khawaja, Marwan, and Åge A. Tiltnes, eds. "On the Margins: Migration and Living Conditions of Palestinian Camp Refugees in Jordan." Fafo Report 357. Fafo Institute for Applied International Studies, Oslo, 2002. http://www.fafo.no/pub/rapp/357/357.pdf.

Killelea, Steve, and Roland Schatz, eds. *Global Peace Report 2010.* Boston: InnoVatio, 2010.

Kimmerling, Baruch. *The Invention and Decline of Israeliness: State, Society and the Military.* Berkeley: University of California Press, 2001.

Kimmerling, Baruch. *Politicide: Ariel Sharon's War Against the Palestinians.* London: Verso, 2002.

Kimmerling, Baruch, and Joel S. Migdal. *Palestinians: The Making of a People.* Cambridge, MA: Harvard University Press, 1994.

Klein, Menachem. *A Possible Peace Between Israel & Palestine: An Insider's Account of the Geneva Initiative.* New York: Columbia University Press, 2007.

Klein, Menachem, Talia Sasson, Oshrat Maimon, and Tamar Luster. *Permanent Residency: A Temporary Status Set in Stone.* Jerusalem: Ir Amim, May 2012. http://www.ir-amim.org.il/sites/default/files/permanent%20residency_0.pdf.

Kloos, Julia, Niklas Gerbert, Therese Rosenfeld, and Fabrice Renald. *Climate Change, Water Conflicts and Human Security: Regional Assessment and Policy Guidelines for the Mediterranean, Middle East, and Sahel.* Report No. 10. Project on Climate Change, Hydro Conflicts and Human Security, Institute for Environment and Human Security, United Nations University, Bonn, August 2013. http://www.ehs.unu.edu/article/read/climate-change-water-conflicts-and-human-security.

Knesset. "Theodor Herzl (1860–1904): World Zionist Organization (Since Its Establishment in 1897 to the Balfour Declaration, 1917)." Knesset, Jerusalem, n.d. https://www.knesset.gov.il/vip/herzl/eng/Herz_Zion_eng.html.

Knudsen, Are, and Basem Ezbidi. "Hamas and the Quest for Palestinian Statehood." Chr. Michelsen Institute CMI Working Paper WP 2006:14. Chr. Michelsen Institute, Bergen, Norway, 2006. http://www.cmi.no/publications/publication/?4716=hamas-and-the-quest-for-palestinian-statehood.

Kock, Udo. "Between a Rock and a Hard Place: Recent Economic Developments in the Palestinian Economy." Presentation to Palestine Economic Research Institute—MAS, Ramallah. February 19, 2014. http://www.imf.org/external/country/WBG/RR/2014/021914.pdf.

Kock, Udo, Mariusz Sumlinski, and Hania Qassis. "West Bank and Gaza: Labor Market Trends, Growth and Unemployment." International Monetary Fund, Washington, DC, December 2012.

Kolbert, Elizabeth. *The Sixth Extinction: An Unnatural History.* New York: Henry Holt, 2014.

Kovács, András, and Michael L. Miller, eds. *Jewish Studies at the Central European University* 7 (2009–11). Budapest: Jewish Studies Project, Central European University, 2013.

Krämer, Gudrun. *A History of Palestine: From the Ottoman Conquest to the Founding of the State of Israel.* Princeton, NJ: Princeton University Press, 2008.

Kriesberg, Louis, Terrell A. Northrup, and Stuart J. Thorson, eds. *Intractable Conflicts and Their Transformation.* Syracuse, NY: Syracuse University Press, 1989.

Kubursi, Atif. "Palestinian Losses in 1948, Compensation Valuations and Israel's Ability to Pay." Paper submitted to Adam Smith International Ltd. but never published, McMaster University, 2008.

Kubursi, Atif A. "Palestinian Losses in 1948: Calculating Refugee Compensation." Information Brief No. 81. Center for Policy Analysis on Palestine, August 3, 2001.

Kupchan, Charles A. *How Enemies Become Friends: The Sources of Stable Peace.* Princeton, NJ: Princeton University Press, 2010.

Kupermintz, H., Y. Rosen, G. Salomon, and R. Husisi. *Perception of the Other Among Jewish and Arab Youth in Israel: 2004–2005.* Haifa: Center for Research on Peace Education, University of Haifa, 2007.

Kuriansky, Judy. *Terror in the Holy Land: Inside the Anguish of the Israeli-Palestinian Conflict.* Westport, CT: Praeger, 2006.

Kurz, Anat. "The Israel-Palestinian Political Process: Dead End Dynamics." In *Strategic Survey for Israel, 2010,* edited by Shlomo Brom and Anat Kurz, 85–97. Tel Aviv: Institute for National Security Studies, Tel Aviv University, 2010. http://d26e8pvoto2x3r.cloudfront.net/uploadimages/Import/(FILE)1283332940.pdf.

Lall, Arthur S., ed. *Multilateral Negotiations and Mediation: Instruments and Methods.* New York: Pergamon Press, 1985.

Landman, Shiri. "The Social-Psychology of Taboos: Protected Values in the Israeli-Palestinian Conflict." Paper presented at the annual meeting of the ISPP 32nd Annual Scientific Meeting, Trinity College, Dublin, July 2009.

Larson, Mary Jo. "Final Report: International Climate Change and Vulnerability Conference." University for Peace, The Hague, Netherlands, March 2007. http://www.upeace.nl/wp-content/uploads/Final-Report-Climate-Change-and-Vulnerability-Conference-2.pdf.

Lasky, Moses. *Between Truth and Repose: The World Zionist Organization, Its Agency for the State of Israel, the Means by Which It Raises Its Funds, and the Structure Through Which It Operates in the Diaspora: A Study in Organization.* San Francisco: self-published, 1956.

Laub, Zachary, and Jonathan Masters. "Islamic State in Iraq and Syria." Backgrounders. Council on Foreign Relations, New York, updated August 8, 2014. http://www.cfr.org/iraq/islamic-state-iraq-syria/p14811.

Laub, Zachary, ed. "Hamas." Backgrounders. Council on Foreign Relations, Washington DC. Last updated August 1, 2014. http://www.cfr.org/israel/hamas/p8968.

"The Law of Return Act," July 5, 1950. Jewish Virtual Library. http://www.jewishvirtuallibrary.org/jsource/Politics/Other_Law_Law_of_Return.html.

League of Arab States and United Nations Relief and Works Agency (UNRWA). "Conclusions of the Special Meeting of a Group of Supporters of UNRWA, September 26, 2013." New York: UNRWA, September 26, 2013. http://unispal.un.org/UNISPAL.NSF/0/98498B9C65D5B68F85257BF3005245C4.

Lederach, John Paul. *Building Peace: Sustainable Reconciliation in Divided Societies.* Washington DC: USIP, 1997.

Lerner, Michael. *Embracing Israel/Palestine: A Strategy to Heal and Transform the Middle East.* Berkeley: North Atlantic Books, 2012.

Lesch, Ann Mosely. *Arab Politics in Palestine, 1917–1939: The Frustration of a Nationalist Movement.* Ithaca, NY: Cornell University Press, 1979.

Lesch, Ann Mosely, and Ian S. Lustick. *Exile and Return: Predicaments of Palestinians and Jews.* Philadelphia: University of Pennsylvania Press, 2005.

Levenberg, Haim. *The Military Preparations of the Arab Community of Palestine, 1945–1948.* London: Cass, 1993.

Levitt, Mathew. *Hamas: Politics, Charity, and Terrorism in the Service of Jihad.* New Haven, CT: Yale University Press, 2006.

Levy, Edmund, et al. "Conclusions and Recommendations." In *Report on the Legal Status of Building in Judea and Samaria.* Submitted to Ministerial Settlement Committee by Commission to Examine the Status of Building in Judea and Samaria, Jerusalem, July 13, 2012. http://unispal.un.org/UNISPAL.NSF/0/D9D07DCF58E781C585257A3A005956A6.

Lewicki, Roy J., and Carolyn Weithoff. "Trust, Trust Development and Trust Repair." In *The Handbook of Conflict Resolution: Theory and Practice*, edited by Morton Deutsch, Peter T. Coleman, and Eric Marcus, 86–107. San Francisco: Jossey-Bass Publishers, 2000.

Lewis, Bernard. *The Multiple Identities of the Middle East.* New York: Schocken Books, 1998.

Lijphart, Arend. *Patterns of Democracy: Government Forms and Performance in Thirty-Six Countries.* New Haven, CT: Yale University Press, 1999.

Lindner, Evelin. *Making Enemies: Humiliation and International Conflict.* Westport, CT: Praeger Security International, 2006.

Litvak, Meir, ed. *Islam and Democracy in the Arab World* (in Hebrew). Tel Aviv: Kav Adom Hakibbutz Hameuhad, 1999.

Louis, Wm. Roger, and Robert W. Stookey, eds. *The End of the Palestine Mandate.* Austin: University of Texas Press, 1986.

Lustick, Ian S. *Arabs in the Jewish State: Israel's Control of a National Minority.* Austin: University of Texas Press, 1980.

Lustick, Ian S. "The Evolution of Gush Emunim." In *For the Land and the Lord: Jewish Fundamentalism in Israel.* Reprint ed. Washington DC: Council on Foreign Relations, 1988. http://www.sas.upenn.edu/penncip/lustick/lustick13.html.

Lustick, Ian S. *For the Land and the Lord: Jewish Fundamentalism in Israel.* New York: Council on Foreign Relations, 1988.

Ma'an Development Center. "Parallel Realities: Israeli Settlements and Palestinian Communities in the Jordan Valley." Ma'an Development Center, Ramallah: 2012. http://www.maan-ctr.org/old/pdfs/FSReport/Settlement/content.pdf.

Maier, Joseph B. "Vico's View of Jewish Exceptionalism." In *Ethnicity, Identity, and History: Essays in Memory of Werner J. Cahnman*, edited by Joseph B. Maier and Chaim Isaac Waxman, 81–92. New Brunswick, NJ: Transaction, 1983.

Maoz, Zeev. "The Pitfalls of Summit Diplomacy." In *The Camp David Summit: What Went Wrong?*, edited by Simon Shamir and Bruce Maddy-Weitzman, 203–9. Brighton, UK: Sussex Academic Press, 2005.

Marten, Kimberly. "Militia Patronage vs. the Diffusion of Professionalism: The Palestinian Authority Security Forces." Paper presented to the International Studies Association Annual Convention, San Francisco, April 3, 2013. https://barnard.edu/sites/default/files/isa_paper_2013_pasf_militias_and_diffusion.pdf.

Machover, Moshe. *Israelis and Palestinians: Conflict and Resolution*. Chicago: Haymarket Books, 2012.

Mackey, Sandra. *Mirror of the Arab World: Lebanon in Conflict*. New York: Norton, 2008.

Makdisi, Saree. *Palestine Inside Out: An Everyday Occupation*. New York: Norton, 2008.

Mamdani, Mahmood. *Good Muslim, Bad Muslim: America, the Cold War and the Roots of Terror*. Johannesburg: Jacana Media, 2004.

Mandal, Thomas. *Living with Settlers: Interviews with Yanoun Villagers*. Norwegian Church Aid and Ecumenical Accompaniment Program in Palestine and Israel, 2011.

Margalit, Avishai. *The Ethics of Memory*. 2nd ed. Cambridge, MA: Harvard University Press, 2003.

Marlow, John. *The Seat of Pilate: An Account of the Palestine Mandate*. London: Cressett, 1959.

Marlowe, John. *Rebellion in Palestine*. London: Cresset, 1946.

Marris, Peter. *Loss and Change*. New York: Pantheon Books, 1974.

Masalha, Nur. *Catastrophe Remembered: Palestine, Israel and the Internal Refugees*. New York: Zed Books, 2005.

Masalha, Nur. *Expulsion of the Palestinians: The Concept of "Transfer" in Zionist Political Thought 1882–1948*. Washington DC: Institute for Palestine Studies, 1992.

Masalha, Nur. *The Palestinian Nakba: Decolonizing History, Narrating the Subaltern, Reclaiming Memory*. London: Zed Books, April 2012.

Mathews, Weldon. *Confronting an Empire, Constructing a Nation: Arab Nationalism and Popular Politics in the Palestinian Mandate*. London: I. B. Tauris, 2006.

Mayer, Arno J. *Plowshares into Swords: From Zionism to Israel*. New York: Verso, 2008.

McCarthy, Conor. *The Cambridge Introduction to Edward Said*. Cambridge: Cambridge University Press, 2010.

McCarthy, Justin. *Death and Exile: The Ethnic Cleansing of Ottoman Muslims, 1821–1922*. Princeton, NJ: Darwin Press, 1995.

McCarthy, Justin. *The Population of Palestine: Population Statistics of the Late Ottoman Period and the Mandate*. New York: Columbia University Press, 1990.

McCullough, David. *Truman*. New York: Simon & Schuster, 2003.

McGlynn, Claire, Michalinos Zembylas, and Zvi Bekerman, eds. *Integrated Education in Conflicted Societies*. New York: Palgrave Macmillan, 2013.

McKinney, Daene C. "The Jordan River Valley Under Climate Change." Prepared for CE 397, "Transboundary Waters." Cockrell School of Engineering, Department of Civil, Architectural and Environmental Engineering, University of Texas at Austin, April 20, 2010. http://www.caee.utexas.edu/prof/mckinney/ce397/Topics/Jordan/Jordan(2010).pdf.

Meeker, Michael E. *A Nation of Empire: The Ottoman Legacy of Turkish Modernity*. Berkeley: University of California Press, 2002.

Mekonnen, Mesfin M., and Arjen Y. Hoekstra. *A Global and High-Resolution Assessment of the Green, Blue, and Grey Water Footprint of Wheat*. Value of Water, Research Report Series No. 42. Institute for Water Education, Enschede, Netherlands, April 2010. http://doc.utwente.nl/76916/1/Report42-WaterFootprintWheat.pdf.

Melaugh, Martin "Violence: Membership and Arsenals of Paramilitary Groups." In *Security Forces in the Northern Ireland Troubles*. BBC History, n.d. http://www.bbc.co.uk/history/topics/troubles_violence.

Melaugh, Martin, Fionnuala McKenna, and Brendan Lynn. "Background Information on Northern Ireland—Security and Defence." CAIN Web Service. http://cain.ulst.ac.uk/ni/security.htm.

"Middle East: Gaza Strip." *The World Factbook*. Central Intelligence Agency, June 22, 2014. https://www.cia.gov/library/publications/the-world-factbook/geos/gz.html.

Middle East Policy Council. "Is the IDF Overreacting to West Bank Abductions?" Commentary Hub, Middle East Policy Council, Washington, DC, June 19, 2014. http://www.mepc.org/articles-commentary/commentary/idf-overreacting-west-bank-abductions.

Miller, Aaron David. *The Much Too Promised Land: America's Elusive Search for Arab-Israeli Peace*. New York: Bantam Books, 2008.

Milton-Edwards, Beverley. *The Israeli-Palestinian Conflict: A People's War*. New York: Routledge, 2009.

Milton-Edwards, Beverley, and Stephan Farrell. *Hamas: The Islamic Resistance Movement*. Malden, MA: Polity, 2010.

Mirak-Weissbach, Muriel. "Who Murdered the Oslo Accords?" (from *Executive Intelligence Review*, May 21, 2004). Global Policy Forum. https://www.globalpolicy.org/component/content/article/189/38354.html.

Mirbagheri, S., and M. Farid. *War and Peace in Islam: A Critique of Islamic/ist Political Discourses*. New York: Palgrave Macmillan, 2012.

Mishal, Shaul, and Avraham Sela. *Palestinian Hamas: Vision, Violence and Coexistence*. New York: Columbia University Press, 2000.

Mlodinow, Leonard. *Subliminal: How Your Unconscious Mind Rules Your Behavior*. New York: Pantheon Books, 2012.

Mnookin, Robert. *Bargaining with the Devil: When to Negotiate, When to Fight*. New York: Simon & Schuster, 2010.

Mnookin, Robert H., and Lee Ross. "Introduction." In *Barriers to Conflict Resolution*, edited by Kenneth J. Arrow, et al., 2–24. New York: Norton, 1995.

Money-Kyrle, Roger Ernie. *Psychoanalysis and Politics: A Contribution to the Psychology of Politics and Morals*. London: Gerald Duckworth, 1951.

Morris, Benny. *The Birth of the Palestinian Refugee Problem, 1947–1949*. Cambridge: Cambridge University Press, 1987.

Morris, Benny. *Israel's Border Wars, 1949–1956: Arab Infiltration, Israeli Retaliation, and the Countdown to the Suez War*. Oxford: Oxford University Press, 1993.

Morris, Benny. *1948 and After*. Revised ed. Oxford: Oxford University Press, 1994.

Morris, Benny. *One State, Two States: Resolving the Israeli/Palestine Conflict*. New Haven, CT: Yale University Press, 2009.

Morris, Benny. "Revisiting the Palestinian Exodus of 1948." In *The War for Palestine: Rewriting the History of 1948*, edited by Eugene Rogan and Avi Shlaim. Cambridge: Cambridge University Press, 2001.

Morris, Benny. *Righteous Victims: A History of the Zionist-Arab Conflict, 1881–2001*. New York: Vintage Books, 2001.

Morris, Benny. *Road to Jerusalem: Glubb Pasha, Palestine and the Jews*. London: I. B. Tauris, 2001.

Muhareb, Mahmoud. "An Analysis of Israeli Public Opinion." Arab Center for Research and Policy Studies, Doha, Qatar, February 14, 2011. http://english.dohainstitute.org/release/67050cd8-dd9f-4ba7-9590-779e2881c869.

Muslih, Muhammad. *The Origins of Palestinian Nationalism*. New York: Columbia University Press, 1988.

Myers-JDC-Brookdale. "The Center for Research on Aging." Applied Research for Social Change, Jerusalem. http://brookdale.jdc.org.il/?CategoryID=176.

Nadler, Arie, Thomas Malloy, and Jeffrey D. Fisher, eds. *Social Psychology of Intergroup Relations*. New York: Oxford University Press, 2008.

Nadler, Arie, and Nurit Schnabel, "Instrumental and Socio-Economic Paths to Intergroup Reconciliation and Need-Based Models of Socio-Emotional Reconciliation." Paper presented at Tel Aviv University, Tel Aviv, October 2006. http://www.humiliationstudies.org/documents/NadlerIntergroupReconciliation2006.pdf.

Nadler, Arie, and D. A. Sylvan. *The Role of Victimization and Identity in the Palestinian-Israeli Conflict: Experimental and Text Analytic Perspectives*. Paper presented at the International Studies Association Meeting, Honolulu, 2005.

Nakamura, Mitsuo. "Islam and Democracy in Indonesia: Observations on the 2004 General and Presidential Elections." Occasional Publications 6. Islamic Legal Studies Program, Harvard Law School, Harvard University, Cambridge, MA, December 2005. http://www.law.harvard.edu/programs/ilsp/publications/nakamura.pdf.

Nathan, Robert, Oscar Gass, and Daniel Creamer. *Palestine: Problem and Promise, an Economic Study.* Washington DC: Public Affairs Press, 1946.

Nathanson, Roby, and Stephan Stetter, eds. *Renewing the Middle East: Climate Changes in Security and Energy and the New Challenges of EU-Israel Relations.* Tel Aviv: IEPN, 2008.

National Committee for the Heads of the Arab Local Authorities in Israel. "The Future Vision of the Palestinian Arabs in Israel." Translated by Abed Al Rahman Kelani. National Committee for the Heads of the Arab Local Authorities in Israel, Nazareth, 2006. http://adalah.org/newsletter/eng/dec06/tasawor-mostaqbali.pdf.

"National Reconciliation Document (The Prisoner's Document), June 2006." *Al Akhbar.* http://english.al-akhbar.com/sites/default/files/The%20Prisoner's%20Document%20(June%202006)_0.pdf.

Niebergall, Heike, and Norbert Wühler, "Refugee Compensation: Policy Choices and Implementation Issues." In *The Palestinian Refugee Problem: The Search for a Resolution*, edited by Rex Brynen and Roula El-Rifai. London: Pluto Press, 2013.

Niksic, Orhan, Nur Nasser Eddin, and Massimiliano Cali. *West Bank and Gaza: Area C and the Future of the Palestinian Economy.* Washington DC: World Bank Publications, 2014.

Norris, Pippa. "Stable Democracy and Good Governance in Divided Societies: Do Powersharing Institutions Work?" Faculty Research Working Paper Series, RWP05-14. Harvard University Kennedy School of Government, Cambridge, February 2005. http://papers.ssrn.com/sol3/papers.cfm?abstract_id=722626.

Norton, Augustus Richard. *Hezbollah: A Short History.* Princeton, NJ: Princeton University Press, 2007.

Noueihed, Lin, and Alex Warren. *The Battle for the Arab Spring: Revolution, Counter-Revolution and the Making of a New Era.* New Haven, CT: Yale University Press, 2012.

Nusseibeh, Sari. *What Is a Palestinian State Worth?* Cambridge, MA: Harvard University Press, 2011.

"The Nusseibeh-Ayalon Agreement," September 3, 2002. Negotiation Affairs Department, Palestine Liberation Organization. http://www.nad-plo.org/etemplate.php?id=274.

O'Brien, Conor Cruise. *The Siege: The Saga of Israel and Zionism.* New York: Simon & Schuster, 1986.

O'Donnell, Guillermo, Philippe C. Schmitter, and Laurence Whitehead. *Transitions from Authoritarian Rule.* Baltimore: Johns Hopkins University Press, 1988.

O'Malley, Padraig. *The Uncivil Wars: Ireland Today.* Boston: Houghton Mifflin,1983.

Ofran, Hagit. "The Price of Maintaining the Territories—Data from 2011–2012 Budget." Peace Now, December 26, 2010. http://peacenow.org.il/eng/content/price-maintaining-territories-data-2011-2012-budget.

Oren, Michael B. *Six Days of War: June 1967 and the Making of the Modern Middle East.* New York: Random House Ballantine, 2003.

Oren, Neta. *The Israeli Ethos of Conflict 1967–2005.* Working Paper No. 27. Institute for Conflict Analysis and Resolution, George Mason University, Fairfax, VA, 2009. http://scar.gmu.edu/wp_27_oren.pdf.

Oren, Neta. "The Israeli Ethos of the Arab-Israeli Conflict 1967–2000: The Effects of Major Events." Doctoral dissertation (Hebrew), Tel Aviv University, 2005.

Oren, Neta, and Daniel Bar-Tal. "Collective Identity and Intractable Conflict." In *Identity Process Theory: Identity, Social Action and Social Change*, edited by Rusi Jaspal and Glynis M. Breakwell, 222–52. Cambridge: Cambridge University Press, 2014.

Organisation for Economic Co-operation and Development. "General Context Indicators—Fertility." In *Society at a Glance 2011: OECD Social Indicators.* 6th ed. Paris: OECD Publishing, April 12, 2011. doi :10.1787/soc_glance-2011-7-en.

Organisation for Economic Co-operation and Development. *Supporting Statebuilding in Situations of Conflict and Fragility: Policy Guidance.* DAC Guidelines and Reference Series. Paris: OECD Publishing, February 8, 2011. doi: 10.1787/9789264074989-en.

Oslo I. "Declaration of Principles on Interim Self-Government Arrangements," September 13, 1993. The Government of the State of Israel and the P.L.O. Office of the United Nations Special Coordinator for the Middle East Peace Process. http://www.unsco.org/Documents/Key/Declaration%20of%20Principles%20on%20Interim%20Self-Government%20Arrangements.pdf.

Oslo II. "Israeli-Palestinian Interim Agreement on the West Bank and the Gaza Strip," September 28, 1995. Office of the United Nations Special Coordinator for the Middle East Peace Process. http://www.unsco.org/Documents/Key/Israeli-Palestinian%20Interim%20Agreement%20on%20the%20West%20Bank%20and%20the%20Gaza%20Strip.pdf.

Owen, Roger. *State, Power and Politics in the Making of the Modern Middle East.* 3rd ed. New York: Routledge, 2004.

Palestine International Business Forum. "Future Economic Relations Between the Palestinian and Israeli Economies." Research paper, Palestine International Business Forum, Ramallah, Tel Aviv, and Stockholm, December 2007. http://www.pibf.net/wp-content/PIBF-Report-on-Future-Economic-Relations-Dec-2007.pdf.

Palestine Liberation Organization. "The Arab Peace Initiative, Frequently Asked Questions," Negotiations Affairs Department, Palestine Liberation Organization, Ramallah, 2014. http://www.nad-plo.org/etemplate.php?id=157.

Palestine Liberation Organization. "Israeli Policies and Practices in Occupied East Jerusalem." Negotiations Affairs Department, Palestine Liberation Organization, Ramallah, May 22, 2013.

Palestine Liberation Organization. "Official Palestinian Response to the Clinton Parameters (and Letter to the International Community)." Negotiations Affairs Department, Palestine Liberation Organization, Ramallah, January 1, 2001. http://www.nad-plo.org/etemplate.php?id=98.

Palestine Papers. "Terms of Reference: Israel's Ability to Compensate Palestinian Refugees." The Palestine Papers, Al Jazeera Investigations, Al Jazeera. Last updated February 2, 2008. http://www.ajtransparency.com/en/projects/thepalestinepapers/201218231237343868.html and http://prrnblog.wordpress.com/2011/01/28/palestine-papers-continued-1-42008/.

"The Palestine Papers and the Right of Return." Christians for a Fair Witness in the Middle East, April 9, 2011. http://www.christianfairwitness.com/writings/Palestine_Papers_Right_of_return_memo.pdf.

"Palestinian Authority Opposes Hamas's Call for Intifada but Potential Triggers Include Collapse of Security Forces." *IHS Jane's Intelligence Review*, September 1, 2014. http://www.janes.com/article/42645/palestinian-authority-opposes-hamas-s-call-for-intifada-but-potential-triggers-include-collapse-of-security-forces.

Palestinian Center for Policy and Survey. "Palestinian Public Opinion Poll No. 42: 15–17 December 2011." PSR and Konrad Adenauer Stiftung, Ramallah December 2011. http://www.pcpsr.org/en/node/211.

Palestinian Center for Policy and Survey Research. "Joint Israeli Palestinian Poll No. 46: December 2011." PSR, Harry S. Truman Research Institute for the Advancement of Peace at the Hebrew University, Ford Foundation, and Konrad Adenauer Stiftung, Ramallah and Jerusalem, December 2011. http://www.pcpsr.org/en/node/392.

Palestinian Center for Policy and Survey Research. "Joint Israeli Palestinian Poll No. 48: June 2013." PSR, Harry S. Truman Research Institute for the Advancement of Peace at the Hebrew University, and Konrad Adenauer Stiftung, Ramallah and Jerusalem, June 2013. http://www.pcpsr.org/en/joint-israeli-palestinian-poll-48-june-2013.

Palestinian Center for Policy and Survey Research. "Palestinian Public Opinion Poll No. 50: 19–22 December 2013." PSR and Konrad Adenauer Stiftung, Ramallah, December 2013. http://www.pcpsr.org/en/node/189.

Palestinian Center for Policy and Survey Research. "Palestinian Public Opinion Poll No. 51: 20–22 March 2014." PSR and Konrad Adenauer Stiftung, Ramallah, March 2014. http://www.pcpsr.org/en/node/188.

Palestinian Center for Policy and Survey Research. "Polls 32–50." PSR and Konrad Adenauer Stiftung, Ramallah. http://www.pcpsr.org/en/index-psr-polls.

Palestinian Center for Policy and Survey Research. "Special Gaza War Poll: 26–30 August 2014." PSR and Konrad Adenauer Stiftung, Ramallah, September 15, 2014. http://www.pcpsr.org/en/node/492 and http://www.pcpsr.org/sites/default/files/Special%20Gaza%20War%20Poll%20english%20.pdf.

Palestinian Central Bureau of Statistics. "On the 65th Anniversary of the Nakba." Special Statistical Bulletin. Palestinian Central Bureau of Statistics, Ramallah, May 14, 2013. http://www.pcbs.gov.ps/site/512/default.aspx?tabID=512&lang=en&ItemID=788&mid=3171&wversion=Staging.

Palestinian Central Bureau of Statistics. "Per Capita GDP, GNI, GNDI, by Region for the Years 1994–2011 at Current Prices." Palestinian Central Bureau of Statistics, Ramallah. http://www.pcbs.gov.ps/Portals/_Rainbow/Documents/percapitcurrentE1994-2011.htm.

Palestinian Central Bureau of Statistics. "Performance of the Palestinian Economy, 2012." Palestinian Central Bureau of Statistics, Ramallah, May 13, 2013. http://www.pcbs.gov.ps/site/512/default.aspx?tabID=512&lang=en&ItemID=784&mid=3172&wversion=Staging.

Palestinian Central Bureau of Statistics. "Press Release on the Results of the Labour Force Survey, First Quarter (January–March 2013) Round Main Results." Palestinian Central Bureau of Statistics, Ramallah, May 16, 2013.

Palestinian Central Bureau of Statistics. "Press Release on the Results of the Labour Force Survey, Fourth Quarter (October–December 2013), Round Main Results." Palestinian Central Bureau of Statistics, Ramallah, February 12, 2014.

Palestinian Central Bureau of Statistics. "Social Survey of Jerusalem, 2010: Main Findings." Palestinian Central Bureau of Statistics, Ramallah, March 2011. http://82.213.38.42/PCBS-Metadata-en-v4.2/index.php/catalog/114/download/263.

Palestinian Centre for Human Rights. "Statistics Related to the Al Aqsa (Second) Intifada, October 2010 Update." Palestinian Centre for Human Rights, Gaza City, September 29, 2000 (last modified April 24, 2011). http://pchrgaza.org/portal/en/index.php?option=com_content&view=article&id=3044:statistics-related-to-the-al-aqsa-second-intifada-&catid=55:statistics&Itemid=29.

"Palestinian Declaration of Independence: Algiers Declaration (1988)." http://middleeast.about.com/od/documents/a/me081115f.htm.

Palestinian Media Watch. "Demonization of Jews/Israelis." Palestinian Media Watch, Jerusalem. Last modified June 15, 2014. http://www.palwatch.org/main.aspx?fi=757.

Palestinian National Authority. *The Palestinian National Development Plan 2011–13: Establishing the State, Building Our Future.* Palestinian National Authority, April 2011. http://lllp.iugaza.edu.ps/Files_Uploads/635063697861151130.pdf.

Palestinian Water Authority. *Water Supply Report, Calendar Year 2010.* Palestinian Water Authority, January 2012. http://foeme.org/uploads/Water_Report_Palestinian_Territory_Final.pdf.

"Palestinian-Israeli Interim Agreement on the West Bank and the Gaza Strip: Annex V: Protocol on Economic Relations." Paris, April 29, 1994. http://www.nad-plo.org/userfiles/file/Document/ParisPro.pdf.

Palumbo, Michael. *The Palestinian Catastrophe: The 1948 Expulsion of a People from Their Homeland.* London: Faber and Faber, 1987.

Pappé, Ilan. "The Bridging Narrative Concept." In *Israeli and Palestinian Narratives of Conflict*, edited by Robert I. Rotberg, 194–204. Bloomington: Indiana University Press, 2006.

Pappé, Ilan. *Britain and the Arab-Israeli Conflict, 1948–1951.* New York: Macmillan, 1988.

Pappé, Ilan. *The Ethnic Cleansing of Palestine.* Oxford: Oneworld, 2006.

Pappé, Ilan. "Fear, Victimhood, Self and Other: On the Road to Reconciliation." In *Across the Wall: Narratives of Israeli-Palestinian History*, edited by Ilan Pappé and Jamil Hilal, 155–76. London: I. B. Tauris, 2010. http://www.brightonpalestinecampaign.org/pdfs/Articles/Fear%20Victimhood%20Self.pdf.

Pappé, Ilan. *The Forgotten Palestinians: A History of the Palestinians in Israel.* New Haven, CT: Yale University Press, 2011.

Pappé, Ilan. *A History of Modern Palestine: One Land, Two Peoples.* Cambridge: Cambridge University Press, 2006.

Pappé, Ilan. *The Making of the Arab-Israeli Conflict 1947–1951.* New York: I. B. Tauris, 2008.

Pappé, Ilan. "The Two State Solution Died over a Decade Ago." Information Clearing House. September 15, 2013. http://www.informationclearinghouse.info/article36229.htm.

Parnell, Matthew B. "Palestinian-Americans: Construction and Maintenance of Political and Cultural Identity in Diaspora." Master's thesis, University of North Carolina, 2006. http://libres.uncg.edu/ir/uncw/f/parnellm2006-1.pdf.

"Peace Index Polls: 1994–2014." Project of Guttman Center for Surveys, Israel Democracy Institute, and Events Program in Mediation and Conflict Resolution, Tel Aviv University, Tel Aviv. http://www.peaceindex.org/indexMainEng.aspx/.

Peace Now. "Settlements and the Netanyahu Government: A Deliberate Policy of Undermining the Two-State Solution." Tel Aviv, January 20, 2013. http://peacenow.org.il/Netanyahu-summary and http://peacenow.org/images/Summary%20of%20the%204%20years%20of%20Netanyahu%20Government.pdf.

Peled, Yoav, and Nadim N. Rouhana, "Transitional Justice and the Right of Return of the Palestinian Refugees." In *Israel and the Palestinian Refugees*, edited by Eyal Benvenisti, Chaim Gans, and Sari Hanafi, 141–57. Max Planck Institute for Comparative Public Law and International Law. Berlin: Springer Berlin Heidelberg, 2007. http://link.springer.com/chapter/10.1007/978-3-540-68161-8_5.

Peleg, Ilan, and Dov Waxman. *Israel's Palestinians: The Conflict Within.* New York: Cambridge University Press, 2011.

Peres, Shimon. *Battling for Peace: A Memoir.* New York: Random House, 1995.

Peres Center for Peace and Paltrade (Palestinian Trade Center). *The Untapped Potential. Palestinian-Israeli Economic Relations: Policy Options and Recommendations.* Tel Aviv, 2006.

Perica, Vjekoslav. *Balkan Idols: Religion and Nationalism in Yugoslav States.* Oxford: Oxford University Press, 2002.

Permanent Observer Mission of the State of Palestine to the United Nations. "Palestine Liberation Organization." http://palestineun.org/about-palestine/palestine-liberation-organization/.

Peteet, Julie. *Landscape of Hope and Despair: Place and Identity in Palestinian Refugee Camps.* Philadelphia: University of Pennsylvania Press, 2005.

Peteet, Julie. "Transforming Trust: Dispossession and Empowerment Among Palestinian Refugees." In *Mistrusting Refugees,* edited by E. Valentine Daniel and John Chr. Knudsen, 168–86. Oakland, CA: University of California Press, 1996.

Pew Research Center. "As Mideast Violence Continues, a Wide Partisan Gap in Israel-Palestinian Sympathies." Pew Research Center for the People and the Press, Washington DC, July 15, 2014. http://www.people-press.org/2014/07/15/as-mideast-violence-continues-a-wide-partisan-gap-in-israel-palestinian-sympathies/.

Pew Research Global Attitudes Project, "Mounting Pessimism about Two-State Israeli-Palestinian Solution." Pew Research Center's Global Attitudes Project, Washington DC, June 25, 2014. http://www.pewglobal.org/2014/06/25/mounting-pessimism-about-two-state-israeli-palestinian-solution/.

Pew Research Global Attitudes Project. "Despite Their Wide Differences, Many Israelis and Palestinians Want Bigger Role for Obama in Resolving Conflict: Survey Report." Pew Research Center's Global Attitudes Project, Washington DC, May 9, 2013. http://www.pewglobal.org/2013/05/09/despite-their-wide-differences-many-israelis-and-palestinians-want-bigger-role-for-obama-in-resolving-conflict/.

Pollock, David. "East Jerusalem Palestinians Say UN Move Would Hurt Them: Many Prefer Israeli Citizenship." Policy Alert. Washington Institute, Washington DC: September 22, 2011. http://www.washingtoninstitute.org/policy-analysis/view/east-jerusalem-palestinians-say-un-move-would-hurt-them-many-prefer-israeli.

Pollock, David. "September 2011 Poll Shows 40 Percent of Jerusalem Arabs Prefer Israel to a Palestinian State." PolicyWatch 1867, Washington Institute, Washington, DC, November 2, 2011. http://www.washingtoninstitute.org/policy-analysis/view/poll-shows-40-percent-of-jerusalem-arabs-prefer-israel-to-a-palestinian-sta.

Porath, Yehoshua. *The Emergence of the Palestinian-Arab National Movement, 1918–1929.* London: Cass, 1974.

Porath, Yehoshua. *The Palestinian Arab National Movement: From Riots to Rebellion, 1929–1939.* London: Cass, 1977.

Prisoner's Document. *Al Akhbar.* http://english.al-akhbar.com/sites/default/files/The%20Prisoner's%20Document%20(June%202006)_0.pdf.

"Profile of the Army of Islam, a Salafist Organization Affiliated with the Global Jihad Operating in the Gaza Strip." Meir Amit Intelligence and Terrorism Information Center, Gelilot, IL, August 21, 2012. http://www.terrorism-info.org.il/en/article/20385.

Pruitt, Dean G. *Negotiation Behavior.* New York: Academic Press, 1981.

Pruitt, Dean G., and Peter J. Carnevale. *Negotiation in Social Conflict.* Buckingham, UK: Open University Press, 1993.

Qassem, Naim. *Hizbullah: The Story from Within.* London: SAQI, 2005.

Qurei, Ahmed. *Beyond Oslo, The Struggle for Palestine: Inside the Middle East Peace Process from Rabin's Death to Camp David.* New York: I. B. Tauris, 2008.

Qurei, Ahmed. *From Oslo to Jerusalem: The Palestinian Story of the Secret Negotiations.* New York: I. B. Tauris, 2006.

Ra'ad, Basem L. *Hidden Histories: Palestine and the Eastern Mediterranean.* London: Pluto Press, 2010.

Rabin, Yitzhak, and Yasser Arafat. Statements on signing of Declaration of Principles. September 10, 1993. "Israel-PLO Mutual Recognition—Letters and Speeches." Vol. 13–14: 1992–94. Israel Ministry of Foreign Affairs, Jerusalem. http://mfa.gov.il/MFA/ForeignPolicy/MFADocuments/Yearbook9/Pages/107%20Israel-PLO%20Mutual%20Recognition-%20Letters%20and%20Spe.aspx.

Rabinovich, Itamar. *The Road Not Taken: Early Arab-Israeli Negotiations.* New York: Oxford University Press, 1991.

Rabinowitz, Dan. "National Identity on the Frontier, Palestinians in the Israel Education System." In *Border Identities: Nation and State at International Frontiers,* edited by Thomas M. Wilson and Donnan Hastings, 142–61. Cambridge: Cambridge University Press, 1998.

Rabkin, Yakov M. *A Threat from Within: A Century of Jewish Opposition to Zionism.* New York: Zed Books, 2006.

Raiffa, Howard. *The Art and Science of Negotiation.* Cambridge: Harvard University Press, 1982.

Ramadan, Tariq. *Islam and the Arab Awakening.* New York: Oxford University Press, 2012.

Ramon, Amnon, ed. *The Historical Basin of Jerusalem: Problems and Possible Solutions.* Jerusalem: Jerusalem Institute for Israel Studies, 2010.

Rashid, Muhammad. *Towards a Democratic State in Palestine.* Beirut: PLO Research Center, 1970.

Ravitzky, Aviezer. *Messianism, Zionism and the Jewish Religious Radicalism.* Chicago: The University of Chicago Press, 1996.

Raz, Avi. *The Bride and the Dowry: Israel, Jordon, and the Palestinians in the Aftermath of the June 1967 War.* New Haven, CT: Yale University Press, 2012.

Reactivation of the Defence [Emergency] Regulations, Law and Administration Ordinance [Amendment] Law [1948], Article 125 of the Defence (Emergency) Regulations, Absentees Property Law, 5710-1950, which was replaced by Emergency Regulations (Absentees' Property) Law, 5709-1948 (December), Emergency Regulations (Requisition of Property) Law, 5709-1949, The Land Acquisition Law (1953), The Prescription Law, 5718-1958, The Land (Settlement of Title), Land Acquisition (Validation of Acts and Compensation) Law (1953), Ordinance (Amendment) Law, 5720-1960, The Land (Settlement of Title) Ordinance (New Version), 5729-1969, and the Land Law, 5729-1969, The Prescription Law (1958), which was amended in 1965.

Regev, H., and Amiram Oren. *The Arab Flight from the Land of Israel and the Refugee Problem.* Tel Aviv: Center for Technological Education, Ministry of Education (Hebrew), 1995.

Reinhart, Tanya. *Israel-Palestine: How to End the War of 1948.* New York: Seven Stories Press, 2002.

Reinharz, Yehuda. *Chaim Weizmann: The Making of a Statesman.* Oxford: Oxford University Press, 1993.

Reiter, Yitzhak. "'All of Palestine Is Holy Muslim Wáqf Land': A Myth and Its Roots." In *Law, Custom, and Statute in the Muslim World*, edited by Rôn Šaham, 173–97. Leiden, Netherlands: Brill, 2007.

Reiter, Yitzhak. *Options for the Administration of the Holy Places in the Old City of Jerusalem.* Jerusalem: Jerusalem Institute for Israel Studies, 2007. Available at University of Windsor, Jerusalem Old City Initiative, Commissioned Studies. http://www1.uwindsor.ca/joci/system/files/Gov-HolyPlaces-Reiter.pdf.

Reiter, Yitzhak, and Lior Lehrs. "The Sheikh Jarrah Affair: The Strategic Implications of Jewish Settlement in an Arab Neighborhood in East Jerusalem." Jerusalem: Jerusalem Institute for Israel Studies, 2010. http://jiis.org/.upload/sheikhjarrah-eng.pdf.

Reiter, Yitzhak, and Jon Seligman. "The Bone of Contention: The Political and Archaeological Aspects of Jerusalem's Sacred Compound from 1917 to the Present." In *Where Heaven and Earth Meet: Jerusalem's Sacred Esplanade*, edited by Oleg Grabar and Benjamin Z. Kedar, 231–72. Jerusalem: Yad Izhak Ben-Zvi Press and Austin: University of Texas Press, 2010.

Rekhess, Elie, and Arik Rudnisky, eds. *Arab Society in Israel: An Information Manual.* Nev Ilan, IL: Abraham Fund Initiatives, 2009.

Resource Center for Palestinian Residency and Refugee Rights. "From the 1948 Nakba to the 1967 Naksa." BADIL Occasional Bulletin No. 18. Resource Center for Palestinian Residency and Refugee Rights, Bethlehem, June 2004. http://www.badil.org/en/documents/category/51-bulletins-briefs?download=579%3Abulletin-18-from-the-1948-nakba-to-the-1967-naksa.\

Reut Institute. *The Delegitimization Challenge: Creating a Political Firewall.* Tel Aviv: Reut Institute, February 14, 2010.

Reut Institute. *Israel's Political Options Vis-à-vis the Palestinians.* Tel Aviv: Reut Institute, November 16, 2006.

Rigby, Andrew. *Palestinian Resistance and Nonviolence.* Jerusalem: PASSIA, 2010.

Rishmawi, Mervat. *The Palestinian Authority: A Critical Appraisal.* Washington DC: Center for Policy Analysis on Palestine, 1995.

Rivlin, Paul. *The Israeli Economy from the Foundation of the State Through the 21st Century.* Cambridge: Cambridge University Press, 2011.

Roberts, Sir Adam. "Just Peace: A Cause Worth Fighting For." In *What Is a Just Peace?* edited by Pierre Allan and Alexis Keller, 52–89. Oxford: Oxford University Press, 2006.

Rogan, Eugene L. "Jordan and 1948: The Persistence of an Official History." In *The War for Palestine: Rewriting the History of 1948*, edited by Eugene L. Rogan and Avi Shlaim, 104–24. Cambridge: Cambridge University Press, 2001.

Rokach, Livia. *Israel's Sacred Terrorism: A Study Based on Moshe Sharett's Personal Diary and Other Documents.* Belmont, MA: Association of Arab-American University Graduates, 1980.

Rokeach, Milton. *Beliefs, Attitudes and Values.* London: Jossey-Bass, 1972.

Rokeach, Milton. *The Nature of Human Values.* New York: Free Press, 1973.

Romirowsky, Asaf, and Alexander H. Joffe. *Religion, Politics, and the Origins of Palestine Refugee Relief.* New York: Palgrave Macmillan, 2013.

Ronit Lentin. "The Memory of Dispossession, Dispossessing Memory: Israeli Networks Remembering the Palestinian Nakba." In *Performing Global Networks*, edited by Karen Fricker and Ronit Lentin, 206–27. Newcastle: Cambridge Scholars Publishing, 2007.

Ross, Dennis. *The Missing Peace: The Inside Story of the Fight for Middle East Peace.* New York: Farrar, Straus & Giroux, 2004.

Ross, Dennis, and David Makovsky. *Myths, Illusions, and Peace: Finding a New Direction for America in the Middle East.* New York: Penguin Books, 2010.

Rotberg, Robert I., ed. *Israeli and Palestinian Narratives of Conflict: History's Double Helix.* Bloomington: Indiana University Press, 2006.

Rothchild, Alice. *Broken Promises, Broken Dreams: Stories of Jewish and Palestinian Trauma and Resilience.* London: Pluto Press, 2007.

Rothstein, Robert L., ed. *After the Peace: Resistance and Reconciliation.* Boulder, CO: Lynne Rienner, 1999.

Rouhana, Nadim. "Zionism's Encounter with the Palestinians: The Dynamics of Force, Fear, and Extremism." In *Israeli and Palestinian Narratives of Conflict: History's Double Helix*, edited by Robert I. Rotberg, 115–41. Bloomington: Indiana University Press, 2006.

Roy, Sara. *Failing Peace: Gaza and the Palestinian-Israeli Conflict.* London: Pluto Press, 2007.

Roy, Sara. *Hamas and Civil Society in Gaza: Engaging the Islamist Social Sector.* Princeton, NJ: Princeton University Press, 2011.

Rubinstein, Amnon. *From Herzl to Rabin: The Changing Image of Zionism.* New York: Holmes & Meier, 2000.

Sabbagh, Karl. *Palestine: History of a Lost Nation.* New York: Grove Press, 2006.

Sa'di, Ahmad H., and Lila Abu-Lughod, eds. *Nakba: Palestine, 1948, and the Claims of Memory.* New York: Columbia University Press, 2007.

Said, Edward W. "A Method for Thinking About Just Peace." In *What Is a Just Peace?* edited by Pierre Allan and Alexis Keller, 179–94. Oxford: Oxford University Press. 2006.

Said, Edward W. *From Oslo to Iraq and the Road Map: Essays.* New York: Vintage, 2005.

Said, Edward W. *The End of the Peace Process: Oslo and After.* New York: Pantheon, 2000.

Said, Edward W. *Peace and Its Discontents: Essays on Palestine in the Middle East Peace Process.* New York: Vintage Books, 1996.

Said, Edward W. *The Politics of Dispossession: The Struggle for Palestinian Self-Determination, 1969–1994.* New York: Pantheon Books, 1994.

Said, Edward W. *The Question of Palestine.* New York: Vintage Books, 1992.

Said, Edward W., and Christopher Hutchins, eds. *Blaming the Victims: Spurious Scholarship and the Palestinian Question.* New York: Verso, 2001.

Salibi, Kamal. *A House of Many Mansions: The History of Lebanon Reconsidered.* Berkeley: University of California Press, 1988.

Sand, Shlomo. *The Invention of the Jewish People.* New York: Verso, 2009.

Sand, Shlomo. *The Invention of the Land of Israel: From Holy Land to Homeland.* New York: Verso, 2012.

Sand, Shlomo. *When and How Was the Jewish People Invented?* Tel Aviv: Resling (Hebrew), 2008.

Sasley, Brent E., and Mira Sucharov. "Resettling the West Bank Settlers." Paper presented at the "Theory vs. Policy? Connecting Scholars and Practitioners" conference, International Studies Association Annual Convention, February 17, 2010. http://www.scribd.com/doc/79504489/Sasley-Sucharov-West-Bank-Settlers.

Savir, Uri. *The Process: 1,100 Days That Changed the Middle East.* New York: Vintage Press, 1998.

Schaeffer, Emily, Jeff Halper, and Itay Epshtain. "Israel's Policy of Demolishing Palestinian Homes Must End." Paper submitted to the UN Human Rights Council by the Israeli Committee Against House Demolitions, March 2003. http://www.icahd.org/node/478.

Scham, Paul, and Osama Abu-Irshaid. "Hamas: Ideological Rigidity and Political Flexibility." United States Institute of Peace Special Report 224, 1–22. United States Institute of Peace, Washington DC, June 2009.

Scham, Paul, Walid Salem, and Benjamin Pogrund, eds. *Shared Histories: A Palestinian Israeli Dialogue.* Walnut Creek, CA: Left Coast Press, 2005.

Schellekens, Jona, and Jon Anson, eds. *Israel's Destiny: Fertility and Morality in a Divided Society.* New Brunswick, NJ: Transaction, 2007.

Schleifer, S. Abdullah. "Izz al-Din al-Qassam: Preacher and Mujahid." In *Struggle and Survival in the Modern Middle East*, edited by Edmund Burke III, 164–78. Berkeley: University of California Press, 1993.

Schoenbaum, Michael. *The Arc: A Formal Structure for a Palestinian State*. Santa Monica, CA: Rand, 2005.

Schulze, Kirsten E. *The Arab-Israeli Conflict*. 2nd ed. London: Pearson Education, 2008.

Segev, Samuel. *Crossing the Jordan: Israel's Hard Road to Peace*. New York: St. Martin's Press, 1998.

Segev, Tom. *1949: The First Israelis*. New York: Free Press, 1986.

Segev, Tom. *One Palestine Complete: Jews and Arabs Under the Palestine Mandate*. New York: Metropolitan Books, 2000.

Segev, Tom. *The Seventh Million: The Israelis and the Holocaust*. Translated by Haim Watzman. New York: Henry Holt, 2000.

Seitz, Charmaine. "Tracking Palestinian Public Support for Armed Resistance During the Peace Process and Its Demise." Jerusalem Media and Communications Center, Jerusalem, 2011.

Senechal, Thierry. "Valuation of Palestinian 1948 Losses: A Study Based on the National Wealth of Palestine in 1948," Memorandum to Ziyod Clot, Negotiations Support Unit, July 2008, published by Al Jazeera. http://www.ajtransparency.com/en/projects/thepalestinepapers/201218231237343868.html.

Senor, Dan, and Saul Singer. *Start-up Nation: The Story of Israel's Economic Miracle*. New York: Hachette, 2011.

Shaery-Eisenlohr, Roschanack. *Shi'ite Lebanon: Transnational Religion and the Making of National Identities*. New York: Columbia University Press, 2008.

Shafir, Gershon, and Yoav Peled. *Being Israel: The Dynamics of Multiple Citizenship*. Cambridge: Cambridge University Press, 2002.

Shalev, Nir. "The Hidden Agenda: The Establishment and Expansion Plans of Ma'ale Adummim and Their Human Rights Ramification." BIMKOM/B'Tselem, Jerusalem, December 2009. www.btselem.org/download/200912-maale-adummim-eng.pdf.

Shalev, Nir. "The Ofra Settlement: An Unauthorized Outpost." B'Tselem, Jerusalem, 2008.

Shalev, Nir. "Under the Guise of Legality: Israel's Declaration of State Land in the West Bank." B'Tselem, Jerusalem, 2012.

Shalev, Nir, and Alon Cohen-Lifshitz. "The Prohibited Zone: Israeli Planning Policy in the Palestinian Villages in Area C." BIMKOM, June 2008.

Shamir, Jacob. "Public Opinion in the Israeli-Palestinian Conflict: From Geneva to Disengagement to Kadima and Hamas." Peaceworks No. 60. United States Institute of Peace, Washington DC, June 2007. http://www.usip.org/sites/default/files/PWjune2007.pdf.

Shamir, Shimon, and Bruce Maddy-Weitzman, eds. *The Camp David Summit: What Went Wrong?* Portland, UK: Sussex Academic Press, 2005.

Shapira, Anita. *Ben Gurion: Father of Modern Israel* : New Haven: Yale University Press, 2014.

Sharp, Jeremy M. "U.S. Foreign Aid to Israel." CRS Report RL33222. Congressional Research Service, Washington DC, April 11, 2014. http://www.fas.org/sgp/crs/mideast/RL33222.pdf.

Shavit, Ari. *My Promised Land: The Triumph and Tragedy of Israel*. New York: Spiegel & Grau, 2013.

Shelef, Nadav G. *Evolving Nationalism: Homeland, Identity, and Religion in Israel, 1925–2005*. Ithaca, NY: Cornell University Press, 2010.

Shenhav, Yehouda. *Beyond the Two-State Solution: A Jewish Political Essay*. Translated by Dimi Reider and Efrat Weiss. Malden, MA: Polity Press, 2012.

Sher, Gilead. *The Israel-Palestinian Peace Negotiations, 1999–2001*. New York: Routledge, 2006.

Sher, Gilead. *Just Beyond Reach: The Israeli-Palestinian Peace Negotiations 1999–2001*. Tel Aviv: Yediot Ahromot, 2001.

Sher, Gilead. "Negotiating in Times of Crisis." Paper and lecture delivered at the Wharton School, University of Pennsylvania, Philadelphia, August 19, 2003.

Shipler, David K. *Arab and Jew: Wounded Spirits in a Promised Land*. New York: Penguin Books, 2002.

Shlaim, Avi. *Collusion Across the Jordan: King Abdullah, the Zionist Movement, and the Partition of Palestine*. New York: Columbia University Press, 1988.

Shlaim, Avi. *The Iron Wall: Israel and the Arab World*. New York: Penguin Books, 2000.

Shlaim, Avi. *Israel and Palestine: Reappraisals, Revisions, Refutations*. New York: Verso, 2009.

Shoher, Obadiah. "Palestinian Problem: Anti-Jewish Racism." In *Samson Blinded: A Machiavellian Perspective on the Middle East Conflict*. Available at Lulu.com, February 2007.

Shoshan, Malkit. *Atlas of the Conflict: Israel-Palestine*. Rotterdam: 010 Publishers, 2010.

Sikkuy Online. Haifa and Jerusalem: Association for the Advancement of Civic Equality. http://www.sikkuy.org.il/?lang=en.

Simon, Uriel. "Territory and Morality from a Religious Zionist Perspective." In *Voices from Jerusalem: Jews and Christians Reflect on the Holy Land*, edited by David B. Burrell and Yehezkel Landau, 107–17. New York: Paulist Press, 1992.

Smith, Anthony D. *Myths and Memories of the Nation*. New York: Oxford University Press, 1999.

Smith, Barbara. *The Roots of Separation in Palestine: British Economic Policy, 1920–1929*. Syracuse, NY: Syracuse University Press 1993.

Smith, Lee. *The Strong Horse: Power, Politics, and the Clash of Arab Civilizations*. New York: Doubleday, 2010.

Smooha, Sammy. "Index of Arab-Jewish Relations in Israel 2003–2009." Jewish Arab Center, University of Haifa, 2010. http://soc.haifa.ac.il/~s.smooha/uploads/editor_uploads/files/IndexOfArabJewishRelations2003_2009.pdf.

Snyder, Glen Harold, and Paul Diesing. *Conflict Among Nations: Bargaining, Decision Making and System Structure*. Princeton, NJ: Princeton University Press, 1977.

Stein, Yael. "Human Rights Violations During Operation Pillar of Defense, 14–21 November 2012." B'Tselem, Jerusalem, May 2013. http://www.btselem.org/download/201305_pillar_of_defense_operation_eng.pdf.

Sternhell, Zeev. *The Founding Myths of Israel*. Princeton, NJ: Princeton University Press, 1998.

Stettner, Ilona-Margarita. "The Paris Protocol: Historical Classification." Konrad-Adenauer-Stiftung, Ramallah, December 12, 2012. http://www.kas.de/palaestinensische-gebiete/en/pages/11895/.

Stier, Oren Baruch, and K. Shawn Landers, eds. *Religion, Violence, Memory and Place*. Bloomington: Indiana University Press, 2006.

Strawson, John. *Partitioning Palestine: Legal Fundamentalism in the Palestinian-Israeli Conflict*. London: Pluto Press, 2010.

Suleiman, Michael. *U.S. Policy on Palestine from Wilson to Clinton*. Normal, IL: Association of Arab-American University Graduates, 1995.

Susser, Asher. *Israel, Jordan, and Palestine: The Two-State Imperative*. Waltham, MA: Brandeis University Press, 2011.

Swedenburg, Ted. *Memories of Revolt: The 1936–1939 Rebellion and the Palestinian National Past*. Minneapolis: University of Minnesota Press, 1995.

Swirski, Shlomo. *Israel: The Original Majority*. London: Zed Books, 1989.

Swisher, Clayton E. *The Palestine Papers: The End of the Road?* Chatham, UK: Hesperus, 2011.

Swisher, Clayton E. *The Truth About Camp David: The Untold Story About the Collapse of the Middle East Peace Process*. New York: Nation Books, 2004.

Sykes, Christopher. *Crossroads to Israel, 1917–1948*. Bloomington: Indiana University Press, 1973.

Taghdisi-Rad, Sahar. *The Political Economy of Aid in Palestine: Relief from Conflict or Development Delayed?* New York: Routledge, 2011.

Taub Center for Social Policy Studies in Israel. "Israelis Working More, Making Less." Taub Center for Social Policy Studies in Israel, Jerusalem, September 10, 2013. http://taubcenter.org.il/index.php/publications/e-bulletin/israelis-working-more-making-less/lang/en/.

Tedeschi, Richard G., Crystal L. Park, and Lawrence G. Calhoun, eds. *Posttraumatic Growth: Positive Changes in the Aftermath of Crisis*. Mahwah, NJ: Lawrence Erlbaum Associates, 1998.

Telhami, Shibley. "2010 Israeli Arab/Palestinian Public Opinion Survey." Saban Center for Middle East Policy, Brookings Institution, Washington DC, December 9, 2010. http://www.brookings.edu/~/media/research/files/reports/2010/12/09%20israel%20public%20opinion%20telhami/israeli_arab_powerpoint.

Tetlock, Philip E. "Coping with Tradeoffs: Psychological Constraints and Political Implications." In *Elements of Reason: Cognition, Choice, and the Bounds of Rationality*, edited by Arthur Lupia, Matthew D. McCubbins, Samuel L. Popkin, 239–63. Cambridge: Cambridge University Press, 1999.

Tetlock, Philip E., Randall S. Peterson, and Jennifer S. Lerner. "Revising the Value Pluralism Model: Incorporating Social Content and Context Postulates." In *Values: Eighth Annual Ontario Symposium on Personality and Social Psychology*, edited by Clive Seligman, James M. Olson, and Mark Zanna, 25–51. Mahwah, NJ: Lawrence Erlbaum Associates, 1996. http://faculty.haas.berkeley.edu/tetlock/vita/philip%20tetlock/phil%20tetlock/1994-1998/1996%20The%20Psychology%20of%20Values.pdf.

Tepe, Sultan. *Beyond Sacred and Secular: Politics of Religion in Israel and Turkey*. Stanford, CA: Stanford University Press, 2008.

Teveth, Shabtai. *Ben Gurion and the Palestinian Arabs: From Peace to War.* New York: Oxford University Press, 1985.

Thrall, Nathan. "Faith-Based Diplomacy." *Matter.* September 18, 2014. https://medium.com/matter/americas-quest-for-israeli-palestinian-peace-db27f99ad9f0.

Tibi, Bassam. *Arab Nationalism: A Critical Enquiry.* New York: St. Martin's Press, 1990.

Tilley, Victoria. *The One-State Solution: A Breakthrough for Peace in the Israeli-Palestinian Deadlock.* Ann Arbor: University of Michigan Press, 2005.

Tiltnes, Åge A., ed. *Human Capital, Economic Resources, and Living Conditions,* Fafo Report 514. Fafo Institute for Applied International Studies, Oslo, 2006. http://almashriq.hiof.no/general/300/320.political_science/327/fafo/reports/514.pdf.

Toft, Monica Duffy. *The Geography of Ethnic Violence: Identity, Interests and the Indivisibility of Territory.* Princeton, NJ: Princeton University Press, 2003.

Tolan, Sandy. The *Lemon Tree: An Arab, a Jew, and the Heart of the Middle East:* New York: Bloomsbury, 2006.

Tomeh, George J. *United Nations Resolutions on Palestine and the Arab-Israeli Conflict, I, 1947–1974.* 3rd ed. Washington, DC: Institute for Palestine Studies, 1975.

Traboulsi, Fawwaz. *A History of Modern Lebanon.* London: Pluto Press, 2007.

"Treaty of Westphalia: Peace Treaty Between the Holy Roman Emperor and the King of France and Their Respective Allies." The Avalon Project, Lillian Goldman Law Library, Yale Law School, New Haven, CT. http://avalon.law.yale.edu/17th_century/westphal.asp.

Tuastad, Dag. *The Hudna: Hamas's Concept of a Long-Term Ceasefire: A Viable Alternative to Full Peace?* PRIO Paper. Peace Research Institute Oslo, Oslo, November 2010. http://file.prio.no/Publication_files/Prio/Tuastad%20(2010)%20Hamas%20Concept%20of%20a%20Long-term%20Ceasefire%20(PRIO%20Paper).pdf.

United Nations Conciliation Commission for Palestine. "UN Final Report of the United Nations Economic Survey Mission for the Middle East: An Approach to Economic Development in the Middle East." Part 1: "Final Report and Appendices." UN Doc. A/AC.25/6/Part.1. December 28, 1949. http://domino.un.org/pdfs/AAC256Part1.pdf.

United Nations Conference on Trade and Development. "The Palestinian Economy in East Jerusalem: Enduring Annexation, Isolation and Disintegration." Geneva, May 2013. http://unctad.org/en/PublicationsLibrary/gdsapp2012d1_en.pdf.

United Nations Conference on Trade and Development. "Report on UNCTAD Assistance to the Palestinian People: Developments in the Economy of the Occupied Palestinian Territory." UN Doc. TD/B52/2. July 13, 2012. http://unctad.org/meetings/en/SessionalDocuments/tdb60d3_en.pdf.

United Nations Country Team in the Occupied Palestinian Territory. "Gaza in 2020: A Liveable Place?" Report. Jerusalem, August 2012. http://www.unrwa.org/userfiles/file/publications/gaza/Gaza%20in%202020.pdf.

United Nations Department of Public Information, "General Assembly Votes Overwhelmingly to Accord Palestine 'Non-Member Observer State' Status in United Nations." UN Doc. GA/1397. November 29, 2012. http://www.un.org/News/Press/docs/2012/ga11317.doc.htm.

United Nations Development Group. "United Nations Development Assistance Framework in the Occupied Palestine Territory: Comprehensive Analysis." Draft. UNDG, New York, November 2012. http://www.undg.org/docs/13107/oPt-UNDAF—CA-draft2.pdf.

United Nations General Assembly. "Ad Hoc Committee on the Palestinian Question: Communication from the United Kingdom Delegation to the United Nations." Letter dated August 18, 1947, from the United Kingdom Delegation to the United Nations General Assembly. UN Doc. A/AC.14/8. October 2, 1947. http://unispal.un.org/UNISPAL.NSF/0/16B8C7CC809B7E5B8525694B0071F3BD.

United Nations General Assembly. "Human Rights in Palestine and Other Occupied Arab Territories: Report of the United Nations Fact-Finding Mission on the Gaza Conflict" (Goldstone Commission Report). UN Doc. A/HRC/12/48. September 25, 2009. http://www2.ohchr.org/english/bodies/hrcouncil/docs/12session/A-HRC-12-48.pdf.

United Nations General Assembly. "Resolution 181 (II). Future Government of Palestine." UN Doc. A/RES/181(II). November 29, 1947. http://unispal.un.org/unispal.nsf/0/7F0AF2BD897689B785256C330061D253.

United Nations General Assembly. "Resolution 194 (III). Palestine—Progress Report of the United Nations Mediator." UN Doc. A/RES/194 (III). December 11, 1948. http://domino.un.org/unispal.nsf/0/c758572b78d1cd0085256bcf0077e51a?OpenDocument.

United Nations General Assembly and Security Council. "Letter dated 27 May 1994 from the Permanent Representatives of the Russian Federation and the United States of America to the United Nations Addressed to the Secretary-General. Annex: Agreement on the Gaza Strip and the Jericho Area, Cairo, 4 May 1994." UN Doc. A/49/180 and S/1994/727. June 20, 1994. http://unispal.un.org/UNISPAL.NSF/0/15AF20B2F7F41905852560A7004AB2D5.

United Nations General Assembly and Security Council, "Letter Dated 18 November 1988 from the Permanent Representative of Jordan to the United Nations Addressed to the Secretary-General." UN Docs. A/43/827 and S/20278. November 18, 1988. http://unispal.un.org/UNISPAL.NSF/0/6EB54A389E2DA6C6852560DE0070E392.

United Nations Human Rights Council. "Report of the Independent International Fact-Finding Mission to Investigate the Implications of the Israeli Settlements on the Civil, Political, Economic, Social and Cultural Rights of the Palestinian People Throughout the Occupied Palestinian Territory, Including East Jerusalem." UN Doc. A/HRC/22/63. February 7, 2013. http://www.ohchr.org/Documents/HRBodies/HRCouncil/RegularSession/Session22/A-HRC-22-63_en.pdf.

United Nations Office for the Coordination of Humanitarian Affairs Occupied Palestinian Territory. "Gaza Crisis." Last updated September 5, 2014. http://www.ochaopt.org/content.aspx?id=1010361.

United Nations Office for the Coordination of Humanitarian Affairs Occupied Palestinian Territory. "Gaza Emergency Situation Report (as of 4 September 2014, 0:800 hrs)." September 4, 2014. http://www.ochaopt.org/documents/ocha_opt_sitrep_04_09_2014.pdf.

United Nations Office for the Coordination of Humanitarian Affairs Occupied Palestinian Territory. "In the Spotlight: Area C Vulnerability Profile." Office for the Coordination of Humanitarian Affairs Occupied Palestinian Territory, Jerusalem, March 2014. http://www.ochaopt.org/documents/ocha_opt_fact_sheet_5_3_2014_En.pdf.

United Nations Office for the Coordination of Humanitarian Affairs Occupied Palestinian Territory. "Special Focus: Barrier Update." Office for the Coordination of Humanitarian Affairs Occupied Palestinian Territory, East Jerusalem, July 2011. http://www.ochaopt.org/documents/ocha_opt_barrier_update_july_2011_english.pdf.

United Nations Office of the Special Coordinator for the Middle East Peace Process. "Palestinian State-Building: A Decisive Period." Report to the Ad Hoc Liaison Committee Meeting, Brussels, April 13, 2011. http://domino.un.org/UNISPAL.NSF/0/19e5539f9124ab2085257870004d8264?OpenDocument.

United Nations Relief and Works Agency. "Food Insecurity in Palestine Remains High." Joint press release. Palestinian Central Bureau of Statistics, Food and Agricultural Organization, United Nations Relief and Works Agency for Palestine Refugees in the Near East, World Food Program, Gaza, June 3, 2014. http://www.unrwa.org/newsroom/press-releases/food-insecurity-palestine-remains-high.

United Nations Relief and Works Agency. "Gaza in 2020." UNRWA Operational Response. May 2013. http://unispal.un.org/UNISPAL.nsf/361eea1cc08301c485256cf600606959/aa1b7b90f79c031e85257b9d004de092?OpenDocument.

United Nations Relief and Works Agency. "In Figures as of 1 January 2012." Communications Office, UNRWA, Gaza, January 2012. http://www.unrwa.org/userfiles/20120317152850.pdf.

United Nations Relief and Works Agency. "Where We Work: Gaza Strip." Last modified January 1, 2014. http://www.unrwa.org/where-we-work/gaza-strip.

United Nations Relief and Works Agency, et al. "Socio-Economic and Food Security Survey, West Bank and Gaza Strip, Palestine, 2012." United Nations Relief and Works Agency, Gaza, May 2012. http://unispal.un.org/pdfs/UN-PCBS_SocEconFoodSecSurvey2012.pdf.

United Nations Security Council. Resolution 242. UN Doc. S/RES/242. November 22, 1967. http://unispal.un.org/unispal.nsf/0/7D35E1F729DF491C85256EE700686136.

United Nations Security Council. "Question of Palestine: Declaration of Independence." State of Palestine, Permanent Observer Mission to the United Nations, New York. November 18, 1988. http://www.un.int/wcm/content/site/palestine/pid/12353.

United States Department of State, Bureau of Democracy, Human Rights, and Labor. "2008 Human Rights Report: Israel and the Occupied Territories." February 25, 2009. http://www.state.gov/j/drl/rls/hrrpt/2008/nea/119117.htm.

Van Creveld, Martin. *The Culture of War.* New York: Ballantine Books, 2008.

Van Creveld, Martin. *The Land of Blood and Honey: The Rise of Modern Israel.* New York: St. Martin's Press, 2010.

Volkan, Vamik. *Blind Trust: Large Groups and Their Leaders in Times of Crisis and Terror.* Charlottesville, VA: Pitchstone, 2004.

Volkan, Vamik. *Bloodlines: From Ethnic Pride to Ethnic Terrorism.* New York: Farrar, Straus & Giroux, 1997.

Wasserstein, Bernard. *The British in Palestine: The Mandatory Government and the Arab-Jewish Conflict, 1917–1929.* 2nd ed. Oxford: Basil Blackwell, 1991.

Wasserstein, Bernard. *Divided Jerusalem: The Struggle for the Holy City.* 2nd ed. New Haven, CT: Yale University Press, 2001.

Weisburd, Dave. *Jewish Settler Violence: Deviance as Social Control.* University Park: Pennsylvania State University Press, 1989.

Weizmann, Chaim. *Trial and Error: The Autobiography of Chaim Weizmann.* Westport, CT: Greenwood, 1972.

Werrell, Caitlin E., and Francesco Femia, eds. *The Arab Spring and Climate Change: A Climate and Security Correlations Series.* Center for American Progress, and Stimson Center for Climate and Security 2013. http://cdn.americanprogress.org/wp-content/uploads/2013/02/ClimateChangeArabSpring.pdf.

West, Deborah L. *Myth & Narrative in the Israeli-Palestinian Conflict.* Cambridge: World Peace Foundation, 2003.

Wexler, Bruce, et al. "'Victims of Our Own Narratives?' Portrayal of the 'Other' in Israeli and Palestinian School Books." Study Report, February 4, 2013. http://d7hj1xx5r7f3h.cloudfront.net/Israeli-Palestinian_School_Book_Study_Report-English.pdf.

Wilkinson, Richard, and Kate Pickett. *The Spirit Level: Why Greater Equality Makes Societies Stronger.* New York: Bloomsbury Press, 2009.

Winder, R. Bayley. *The Meaning of the Disaster.* Beirut: Khayat, 1948.

Wittes, Tamara Cofman, ed. *How Israelis and Palestinians Negotiate: A Cross-Cultural Analysis of the Oslo Peace Process.* Washington, DC: United States Institute of Peace, 2005.

Wolff, Stefan. "Consociationalism, Power Sharing, and Politics at the Center." In *The International Studies Encyclopedia*, edited by Robert A. Denemark. Hoboken, NJ: Wiley Blackwell, 2010. http://www.stefanwolff.com/publications/consociationalism-power-sharing-and-politics-at-the-center.

Wolff, Stefan. "Peace by Design? Towards 'Complex Power Sharing.'" In *Consociational Theory: McGarry and O'Leary and the Northern Ireland Conflict*, edited by Rupert Taylor, 110–21. New York: Routledge, 2009.

Wolfsfeld, Gadi. *Media and the Path to Peace.* Cambridge: Cambridge University Press, 2004.

Wolfsfeld, Gadi. *The New Media and Peace Process: The Middle East and Northern Ireland.* Washington, DC: United States Institute of Peace, 2001.

World Bank. "Building the Palestinian State: Sustaining Growth, Institutions, and Service Delivery: Economic Monitoring Report to the *Ad Hoc* Liaison Committee." World Bank, Washington, DC, April 13, 2011. http://siteresources.worldbank.org/INTWESTBANKGAZA/Resources/AHLCReportApril2011.pdf.

World Bank. "Economic Monitoring Report to the *Ad Hoc* Liaison Committee." World Bank, Washington, DC, September 25, 2013. http://siteresources.worldbank.org/INTWESTBANKGAZA/Resources/AHLCreportSep2013final.pdf.

World Bank. "Fiscal Challenges and Long-Term Economic Costs: Economic Monitoring Report to the *Ad Hoc* Liaison Committee." World Bank, Washington, DC, March 19, 2013. http://siteresources.worldbank.org/INTWESTBANKGAZA/Resources/AHLCMarchfinal.pdf.

World Bank. "Fiscal Crisis Economic Prospects: The Imperative for Economic Cohesion in the Palestinian Territories: Economic Monitoring Report to the *Ad Hoc* Liaison Committee." World Bank, Washington, DC, September 23, 2012. https://siteresources.worldbank.org/INTWESTBANKGAZA/Resources/AHLCReportFinal.pdf.

World Bank. "Implementing the Palestinian Reform and Development Agenda: Economic Monitoring Report to the *Ad Hoc* Liaison Committee." World Bank, Washington, DC, May 2, 2008. http://siteresources.worldbank.org/INTWESTBANKGAZA/Resources/WorldBankAHLCMay2,08.pdf.

World Bank. "Two Years After London: Restarting Palestinian Economic Recovery: Economic Monitoring Report to the *Ad Hoc* Liaison Committee." World Bank, Washington, DC, September 24, 2007. http://siteresources.worldbank.org/INTWESTBANKGAZA/Resources/AHLCMainReportfinalSept18&cover.pdf.

World Bank. "West Bank and Gaza: Towards Economic Sustainability of a Future Palestinian State: Promoting Private Sector-Led Growth." Report No. 68037-GZ. Poverty Reduction and Economic Management Department, Middle East and North Africa Region. World Bank, Washington, DC,

April 2012. http://siteresources.worldbank.org/INTWESTBANKGAZA/Resources/GrowthStudy Engcorrected.pdf.

World Zionist Organization Online. "Mission Statement" and "About the World Zionist Organization." World Zionist Organization, Jerusalem. http://www.wzo.org.il/index.php?dir=site&page=pages&op=category&cs=3018&language=eng.

Wright, Robin. *Dreams and Shadows: The Future of the Middle East.* New York: Penguin Press, 2008.

Ya'ar, Ephraim, and Tamar Hermann. "Peace Index: August 2014." Israel Democracy Institute's Guttman Center for Surveys and Tel Aviv University's Events Program in Mediation and Conflict Resolution, Tel Aviv, August 2014. http://en.idi.org.il/about-idi/news-and-updates/august-2014-peace-index/.

Ya'ar, Ephraim, and Tamar Hermann. "Peace Index: July 2014." Israel Democracy Institute's Guttman Center for Surveys and Tel Aviv University's Events Program in Mediation and Conflict Resolution, Tel Aviv, July 2014. http://en.idi.org.il/about-idi/news-and-updates/july-2014-peace-index/.

Ya'ar, Ephraim, and Tamar Hermann. "Peace Index: August 2013." Israel Democracy Institute's Guttman Center for Surveys and Tel Aviv University's Events Program in Mediation and Conflict Resolution, Tel Aviv, August 2013. http://en.idi.org.il/media/2696449/Peace%20Index-August%202013.pdf.

Ya'ar, Ephraim, and Tamar Hermann. "Peace Index: August 2006." Tami Steinmetz Research Institute for Peace at Tel Aviv University, Tel Aviv, August 2006. http://www.peaceindex.org/indexMonth Eng.aspx?num=34&monthname=August.

Ya'ar, Ephraim, and Tamar Hermann. "Peace Index: November 2000." Tami Steinmetz Research Institute for Peace at Tel Aviv University, Tel Aviv, November 2000. http://en.idi.org.il/media/598471/peaceindex2000_11_3.pdf.

Ya'ar, Ephraim, and Tamar Hermann. "Summary: November 2000—The Peace Index, November 2000." Israel Democracy Institute's Guttman Center for Surveys and Tel Aviv University's Events Program in Mediation and Conflict Resolution, Tel Aviv, November 2000. http://www.peaceindex.org/indexMonthEng.aspx?num=127.

Yapp, Malcolm E. *The Making of the Modern Near East 1792–1923.* New York: Pearson, 1987.

Yeats, William Butler. "The Second Coming." In *Michael Robartes and the Dancer: Manuscript Materials (The Cornell Yeats)*, edited by Thomas Parkinson and Anne Brannan, 147. Ithaca: Cornell University Press, 1994. http://www.potw.org/archive/potw351.html.

Yiftachel, Oren. *Ethnocracy: Land and Identity Politics in Israel/Palestine.* Philadelphia: University of Pennsylvania Press, 2006.

Zakay, Dan. "The Impact of Time Perception Processes on Decision Making Under Time Stress." In *Time Pressure and Stress in Human Judgment and Decision Making*, edited by Ola Svenson and A. John Maule, 59–72. New York: Plenum Press, 1993.

Zakay, Dan, and Dida Fleisig. "The Time Factor as a Barrier to Resolution of the Israeli-Palestinian Conflict Barriers to Peace." In *Barriers to Peace*, edited by Yaacov Bar-Siman-Tov, 264–99. Jerusalem: Konrad-Adenaeur-Stiftung Israel and Jerusalem Institute for Israel Studies, 2010. http://www.kas.de/upload/dokumente/2011/03/barriers_to_peace/chapter7.pdf.

Zanotti, Jim. *U.S. Foreign Aid to the Palestinians.* CRS Report RS22967. U.S. Library of Congress, Congressional Research Service, January 18, 2013. http://fpc.state.gov/documents/organization/204093.pdf.

Zartman, Ira William. "Looking Forward and Looking Backward on Negotiations Theory." In *Peace Versus Justice: Negotiating Forward- and Backward-Looking Outcomes*, edited by Ira William Zartman and Victor Kremenyuk, 289–301. Lanham, MD: Rowman and Littlefield, 2005.

Zartman, Ira William. "Negotiating Forward- and Backward-Looking Outcomes." In *Peace Versus Justice: Negotiating Forward- and Backward-Looking Outcomes*, edited by Ira William Zartman and Victor Kremenyuk, 1–8. Lanham, MD: Rowman and Littlefield, 2005.

Zartman, Ira William, and Jeffrey Z. Rubin. "The Study of Power and the Practice of Negotiation." In *Power and Negotiation*, edited by Ira William Zartman and Jeffrey Z. Rubin, 3–28. Ann Arbor: University of Michigan Press, 2000.

Ze'evi Farkash, Maj.-Gen. Aharon. "Key Principles of a Demilitarized Palestinian State." In *Israel's Critical Security Requirements for Defensible Borders: The Foundation for a Viable Peace*, edited by Dan Diker, 34–49. Jerusalem: Jerusalem Center for Public Affairs, 2011. http://www.jcpa.org/text/security/farkash.pdf. and http://www.jcpa.org/text/security/fullstudy.pdf.

Zertal, Idith, and Akiva Eldar. *Lords of the Land: The War over Israel's Settlements in the Occupied Territories, 1967–2007.* New York: Nation Books, 2007.

Zogby Research Services. "ZRS Releases 2013 Israel / PalestinePoll." Washington, DC, January 30, 2014. http://www.zogbyresearchservices.com/blog/2014/1/30/israel-and-palestine-20-years-after-oslo.

Zurayq, Qustantin, and Ma'na Al-Nakba. *The Meaning of Catastrophe*. Beirut: Dar al-'Ilm lil-Malayin, 1948.

Zureik, Elia. *The Palestinians in Israel: A Study of Internal Colonialism*. London: Routledge Kegan Paul, 1979.

Articles

Abu-Manneh, Bashir. "Palestinian Actualities." *Race & Class* 54 (January–March 2013): 87–96. http://rac.sagepub.com/content/54/3/87.

Abunimah, Ali. "Palestinians on the Verge of a Majority: Population and Politics in Palestine-Israel." Palestine Center, 2008.

Abu-Sitta, Salman. "Palestine 1948: The Palestinian Town and Villages Depopulated in the al Nakba of 1948." *Palestine Land Society*, April 2008.

Achcar, Gilbert. "Assessing Holocaust Denial in Western and Arab Contexts." *Journal of Palestine Studies* 41, no. 1 (Autumn 2011): 82–95. http://www.jstor.org/stable/10.1525/jps.2011.XLI.1.82.

Adesanmi, Pius. "'Nous les Colonisés': Reflections on the Territorial Integrity of Oppression." *Social Text* 22, no. 1 (Spring 2004): 35–58. doi: 10.1215/01642472-22-1_78-35.

Ajluni, Salem. "The Palestinian Economy and the Second Intifada." *Journal of Palestine Studies* 32, no. 3 (Spring 2003): 67–73. http://www.jstor.org/stable/10.1525/jps.2003.32.3.64.

Albin, Cecilia. "Negotiating Indivisible Goods: The Case of Jerusalem." *Jerusalem Journal of International Relations* 13, no. 1 (1991): 45–76.

Alon, Ilai, and Jeanne M. Brett. "Perceptions of Time and Their Impact on Negotiations in the Arab-Speaking Islamic World." *Negotiation Journal* 23 (2007): 55–73. doi: 10.1111/j.1571-9979.2007.00127.x.

Alshaibi, Sama. "Memory Work in the Palestinian Diaspora (Personal Essay and Art)." *Frontiers: A Journal of Women Studies* 27, no. 2 (2006): 30–53. http://www.jstor.org/stable/4137421.

Antreasyan, Anais. "Gas Finds in the Eastern Mediterranean: Gaza, Israel, and Other Conflicts." *Journal of Palestine Studies* 42, no. 3 (Spring 2013): 29–47.

Arens, Omri, and Edward Kaufman. "The Potential Impact of Palestinian Nonviolent Struggle on Israel: Preliminary Lessons and Projections for the Future." *Middle East Journal* 66, no. 2 (2012): 231–52.

Astrup, Claus, and Sébastien Dessus. "Exporting Goods or Exporting Labor? Long-Term Implications for the Palestinian Economy." *Review of Middle East Economics and Finance* 3, no. 1 (2005). doi: 10.1080/14753680500063986.

Atran, Scott, and Robert Axelrod. "Reframing Sacred Values." *Negotiation Journal* 24, no. 3 (2008): 221–46. doi: 10.1111/j.1571-9979.2008.00182.x.

Atran, Scott, Robert Axelrod, and Richard Davis. "Sacred Barriers to Conflict Resolution." *Science* 317, no. 5841 (2007): 1039–40. doi: 10.2307/20037642.

Avi Sagi. "The Holocaust and the Foundation of Jewish Identity." *Azure* 42 (Autumn 2010). http://azure.org.il/include/print.php?id=552.

Avishai, Bernard, Dani Dayan, Forsan Hussein, Eva Illouz, Bassim Khoury, Erel Margalit, Danny Rubinstein, and Khalil Shikaki. "Israel and Palestine: Where to Go from Here." *Harper's* (September 2014). http://harpers.org/archive/2014/09/israel-and-palestine/.

Avishai, Margalit. "The Suicide Bombers." *New York Review of Books* 50, no 1 (January 16, 2003). http://www.nybooks.com/articles/archives/2003/jan/16/the-suicide-bombers/.

Avnery, Uri, and Ilan Pappé. "Two States or One State." CounterCurrents.org, June 11, 2007. http://www.countercurrents.org/pappe110607.htm.

Azar, Edward E. "Protracted International Conflicts: Ten Propositions." *International Interactions* 12, no. 1 (1985): 59–70. doi: 10.1080/03050628508434647.

Barnett, Jon, and W. Neil Adger. "Climate Change, Human Security and Violent Conflict." *Political Geography* 26, no 6 (August 2007): 639–655. doi: 10.1016/j.polgeo.2007.03.003. http://www.sciencedirect.com/science/article/pii/S096262980700039X.

Baron, J., and S. Leshner. "How Serious Are Expressions of Protected Values?" *Journal of Experimental Psychology: Applied* 6, no. 3 (2000): 183–94.

Baron, Jonathan, and Mark Spranca. "Protected Values." *Organizational Behavior and Human Decision Processes* 70, no. 1(1997): 1–16. doi: 10.1006/obhd.1997.2690.

Bar-Siman-Tov, Yaacov. "The Arab-Israeli Conflict: Learning Conflict Resolution." *Journal of Peace Research* 31, no. 1 (1994): 75–92. doi: 10.1177/0022343394031001007.

Bar-Tal, Daniel. "The Rocky Road Toward Peace: Beliefs on Conflict in Israeli Textbooks." *Journal of Peace Research* 35 (1998): 723–42. http://www.jstor.org/stable/425413.

Bar-Tal, Daniel. "Societal-Psychological Foundations of Intractable Conflicts." *American Behavioral Scientist* 50, no. 11 (2007). doi: 10.1177/0002764207302462.

Bar-Tal, Daniel. "Why Does Fear Override Hope in Societies Engulfed in Intractable Conflict, As It Does in the Israeli Society?" *Political Psychology* 22, no. 3 (2001). doi: 10.1111/0162-895X.00255.

Bar-Tal, Daniel, and Dikla Antebi. "Beliefs About Negative Intentions of the World: A Study of the Israeli Siege Mentality." *Political Psychology* 13, no. 4 (1992): 633–45. http://www.jstor.org/stable/3791494.

Bar-Tal, Daniel, and Eran Halperin. "The Nature of Socio-Psychological Barriers to Peaceful Conflict Resolution and Ways to Overcome Them." *Conflict & Communication Online* 12, no. 2 (2013). http://www.cco.regener-online.de/2013_2/pdf/bar-tal_halperin.pdf.

Bar-Tal, Daniel, Lily Chernyak-Hai, Noa Schori, and Ayelat Gundar. "A Sense of Self-Perceived Collective Victimhood in Intractable Conflicts." *International Red Cross Review* 91 (2007). doi: http://dx.doi.org/10.1017/S1816383109990221.

Bar-Tal, Daniel, Eran Halperin, and Neta Oren. "Socio-Psychological Barriers to Peace Making: The Case of the Israeli-Jewish Society." *Social Issues and Policy Review* 4, no. 1 (December 2010): 63–109. doi: 10.1111/j.1751-2409.2010.01018.x.

Bar-Tal, Daniel, Amiram Raviv, Alona Raviv, and Adi Dgani-Hirsh. "The Influence of the Ethos of Conflict on Israeli Jews' Interpretation of Jewish-Palestinian Encounters." *Journal of Conflict Resolution* 53 (2008): 94–118. doi:10.1177/0022002708325942.

Bar-Tal, Daniel, Keren Sharvit, Eran Halperin, and Anat Zafran. "Ethos of Conflict: The Concept and Its Measurement." *Peace and Conflict: Journal of Peace Psychology* 18, no. 1 (2012). doi: 10.1037/a0026860.

Bauman, Christopher W., and Linda J. Skitka. "Moral Disagreement and Procedural Justice: Moral Mandates as Constraints to Voice Effects." *Australian Journal of Psychology* 61, no. 1 (2009). doi: 10.1080/00049530802607647.

Bazerman, Max H., Ann Tenbrunsel, and Kimberly Wade-Benzoni. "When 'Sacred' Issues Are at Stake." *Negotiation Journal* 24, no. 1 (2008). doi: 10.1111/j.1571-9979.2007.00170.x.

Bedein, David. "On the Brink: Decline of US Trained Palestinian Security Forces." *Middle East Forum*, January 9, 2013. http://israelbehindthenews.com/on-the-brink-decline-of-us-trained-palestinian-security-forces/9263/.

Beeri-Sulitzeanu, Amnon, and Uri Gopher. "Mixed Cities and Regions: The Future Face of Israel." Abraham Fund Initiatives, 2009.

Beit-Hallahmi, Benjamin. "Some Psychosocial and Cultural Factors in the Arab-Israeli Conflict: A Review of the Literature." *Journal of Conflict Resolution* 16, no. 2 (June 1972). http://www.jstor.org/stable/173319.

Ben-Amos, Avner, and Ilana Bet-El. "Holocaust Day and Memorial Day in Israeli Schools: Ceremonies, Education and History." *Israel Studies* 4 (1999): 258–84. http://www.jstor.org/stable/30245737.

Ben-Gedalyahu, Tzvi. "Israelis Opposes Dividing Jerusalem: Poll." *Arutz Sheva*, May 31, 2011.

Ben Hagai, Ella, Phillip L. Hammack, Andrew Pilecki, and Carissa Aresta. "Shifting Away from a Monolithic Narrative on Conflict: Israelis, Palestinians, and Americans in Conversation." *Peace and Conflict: Journal of Peace Psychology* 19, no. 3 (2013). doi: 10.1037/a0033736.

Benvenisti, Eyal, and Eyal Zamir. "Private Claims to Property Rights in the Future Israeli-Palestinian Settlement." *American Journal of International Law* 89, no. 2 (April 1995): 295–340.

Berg, Carin. "Tunes of Religious Resistance? Understanding Hamas Music in a Conflict Context." *Contemporary Islam* 6 (2012). doi: 10.1007/s11562-012-0219-6.

"Bibliography of Periodical Literature." *Journal of Palestine Studies* 38, no. 2 (Winter 2009): 228–42.

Bisharat, George. Introduction to "Litigating Palestine: Can Courts Litigate Palestinian Rights?" *Hastings International and Comparative Law Review* 35 (2012): 91–98. http://repository.uchastings.edu/faculty_scholarship/40.

Bonnan-White, Jess, and Andrea Hightower, and Ameena Issa. "Of Couscous and Occupation: A Case Study of Women's Motivations to Join and Participate in Palestinian Fair Trade Cooperatives." *Agriculture and Human Values* 30, no. 3 (2013). doi: 10.1007/s10460-012-9405-7.

Bou-Zeid, Elie, and Mutasem El-Fadel. "Climate Change and Water Resources in Lebanon and the Middle East." *Journal of Water Resources Planning and Management* 128, no. 5 (2002): 343–55. http://dx.doi.org/10.1061/(ASCE)0733-9496(2002)128:5(343).

Brom, Shlomo, Giora Eiland, and Oded Eran. "Partial Agreements with the Palestinians." *Strategic Assessment* 12, no. 3 (November 2009): 67–86.

Brooks, David, Julie Trottier, and Laura Doliner. "Changing the Nature of Palestinian Transboundary Water Agreements: The Israeli-Palestinian Case." *Water International* 38, no. 6 (2013). doi: 10.1080/02508060.2013.810038.

Brown, Oli, and Alec Crawford. "Rising Temperatures, Rising Tensions: Climate Change and the Risk of Violent Conflict in the Middle East." International Institute for Sustainable Development, 2009. http://www.iisd.org/pdf/2009/rising_temps_middle_east.pdf.

Burdman, Daphne. "Education, Indoctrination, and Incitement: Palestinian Children on Their Way to Martyrdom." *Terrorism and Political Violence* 15 (2003). doi: 10.1080/09546550312331292977.

Burtonwood, Neil. "Holocaust Memorial Day in Schools: Context, Process and Content: A Review of Research into Holocaust Education." *Educational Research* 44 (2002). doi: 10.1080/00131880110107360.

Byman, Daniel. "How to Handle Hamas: The Perils of Ignoring Gaza's Leadership." *Foreign Affairs* 89, no. 5 (2010): 45–62.

Canetti-Nisim, Daphna, Gal Ariely, and Eran Halperin. "Life, Pocketbook, or Culture: The Role of Perceived Security Threats in Promoting Exclusionist Political Attitudes Toward Minorities in Israel." *Political Research Quarterly* 61, no. 1 (2008). doi: 10.1177/1065912907307289.

Challinor, Andy, Elizabeth Watson, David B. Lobell, Stuart Mark Howden, D. R. Smith, and Netra Chhetri. "A Meta-analysis of Crop Yield Under Climate Change and Adaptation." *Nature Climate Change* 4 (2014): 287–91. doi: 10.1038/nclimate2153.

Childers, Erskine. "The Other Exodus." *Spectator*, no. 6933 (May 1961): 671–75.

Cohen, Hillel. "Land, Memory, and Identity: The Palestinian Internal Refugees in Israel." *Refuge* 21 (February 2003): 6–13. http://pi.library.yorku.ca/ojs/index.php/refuge/article/viewFile/21285/19956.

Comair, Georges F., Prabhas Gupta, Chris Ingenloff, Gihe Shen, and Daene C. McKinney. "Water Resources Management in the Jordan River Basis." *Water and Environmental Journal* 27, no. 4 (December 2013). doi: 10.1111/j.1747-6593.2012.00368.x.

Dajani, Omar. "Surviving Opportunities." United States Institute of Peace, September 15, 2003.

Dalal, Marwan, "Scars of Displacement." Review of *Catastrophe Remembered: Palestine, Israel, and the Internal Refugees*, by Nur Masalha. *Journal of Palestine Studies* 36, no. 4 (Summer 2007): 108–9.

Dane, Felix, and Jorg Knocha. "The Evacuation of Migron: Israeli Settlement Practices in the West Bank and East Jerusalem." Konrad-Adenauer-Stiftung, March 29, 2012.

DeDreu, Carsten K. W. "Time Pressure and Closing of the Mind in Negotiations." *Organizational Behavior and Human Decision Processes* 91, no. 2 (2003): 280–95. doi: 10.1016/S0749-5978(03)00022-0.

DellaPergola, Sergio. "Actual, Intended, and Appropriate Family Size Among Jews in Israel." *Contemporary Jewry* 29 (2009): 127–52.

DellaPergola, Sergio. "Israel's Existential Predicament: Population, Territory, and Identity." *Current History.* 109, no. 731 (December 2010): 383–89. http://www.bjpa.org/Publications/details.cfm?PublicationID=13561.

DellaPergola, Sergio. "World Jewish Population, 2010." *Current Jewish Population Reports.* Association for the Social Scientific Study of Jewry (ASSJ), Jewish Federations of North America, North American Jewish Data Bank, New York: November 2010. http://www.bjpa.org/Publications/details.cfm?PublicationID=8075.

"Documents and Source Material." *Journal of Palestine Studies* 33, no. 4 (2004): 172–86.

Druckman, Daniel. "Determinants of Compromising Behavior in Negotiation: A Meta-Analysis." *Journal of Conflict Resolution* 38 (1994): 507–56.

Eagle, Gillian, and Debra Kaminer. "Continuous Traumatic Stress: Expanding the Lexicon of Traumatic Stress." *Peace and Conflict: Journal of Peace Psychology* 19, no. 2 (May 2013). doi: 10.1037/a0032485.

Elmusa, Sharif S., and Mahmud El-Jaafari. "Power and Trade: The Israeli-Palestinian Economic Protocol." *Journal of Palestine Studies* 24, no. 2 (Winter 1995): 14–32.

El Shakry, Omnia. "Remembrance of Things Present, Longing for Things Future." *American Anthropologist* 106, no. 1 (March 2004): 152–53.

Esposito, Michelle K. "Quarterly Update on Conflict and Diplomacy." *Journal of Palestine Studies* 40, no. 4 (2011): 127–65.

Falah, Ghazi. "The 1949 Israeli-Palestinian War and Its Aftermath: The Transformation and De-Signification of Palestine's Cultural Landscape." *Annals of the Association of American Geographers* 86, no. 2 (June 1995): 256–85.

Falk, Richard. "The Goldstone Report Without Goldstone." Review of *The Goldstone Report: The Legacy of the Landmark Investigation of the Gaza Conflict*, edited by Adam Horowitz, Lizzy Ratner, and Philip Weiss. *Journal of Palestine Studies* 41, no. 1 (Autumn 2011): 96–111. http://www.jstor.org/stable/10.1525/jps.2011.XLI.1.96.

Fattah, Khaled, and K. M. Fierke. "A Clash of Emotions: The Politics of Humiliation and Political Violence in the Middle East." *European Journal of International Relations* 15, no. 1 (2009): 67–93. doi: doi: 10.1177/1354066108100053.

Faye, Michael L., John W. McArthur, Jeffrey D. Sachs, and Thomas Snow. "The Challenges Facing Landlocked Developing Countries." *Journal of Human Development* 5, no. 1 (2004). doi: 10.1080/14649880310001660201.

Fayyad, Salam. "Palestine: Ending the Occupation, Establishing the State." Palestinian National Authority, 2009.

Feige, Michael. "Introduction: Rethinking Israeli Identity and Memory," *Israeli Studies* 7, no. 22 (Summer 2002): v–xiv. http://www.jstor.org/stable/30245583.

Feldman, Ilana. "Home as a Refrain: Remembering and Living Displacement in Gaza." *History and Memory* 18, no. 2, *Special Issue: Home and Beyond: Sites of Palestinian Memory* (Fall–Winter 2006): 10–47.

Fischhendler, Itay, and David Katz. "The Impact of Uncertainties on Cooperation over Transboundary Water: The Case of Israeli-Palestinian Negotiations." *Geoforum* 50 (December 2013). doi: 10.1016/j.geoforum.2013.09.005.

Fiske, Alan Paige, and Philip E. Tetlock. "Taboo Tradeoffs: Reactions to Transactions That Transgress the Spheres of Justice." *Political Psychology*, 18, no. 2 (1997): 255–97. http://www.jstor.org/stable/3791770.

Flaherty, Michael G., and Michelle D. Meer. "How Time Flies: Age, Memory, and Temporal Compression." *Sociological Quarterly* 35, no. 4 (1994): 705–21.

Fox, Jonathan. "Towards a Dynamic Theory of Ethno-Religious Conflict." *Nations and Nationalism* 5 (1999): 431–63. doi: 10.1111/j.1354-5078.1999.00431.x

Frankish, Tarryn, and Jill Bradbury. "Telling Stories for the Next Generation: Trauma and Nostalgia." *Peace and Conflict: Journal of Peace Psychology* 18, no. 3, *Special Issue: Of Narratives and Nostalgia* (August 2012). doi: 10.1037/a0029070.

Friedland, Roger. "Religious Nationalism and the Problem of Collective Representation." *Annual Review of Sociology*, 27, no. 1 (2001): 125–52. http://www.jstor.org/stable/2678617.

Friedman, Adina. "Unraveling the Right of Return." *Refuge* 21, no. 2 (2003): 62–69. http://pi.library.yorku.ca/ojs/index.php/refuge/article/view/21291.

Friling, Tuvia, and Moshe Tlamin. "The New Historians and the Failure of Rescue Operations During the Holocaust." *Israel Studies* 8, no. 3, *Israel and the Holocaust* (Fall 2003): 25–64.

Frisch, Hillel, and Shmuel Sandler. "Religion, State, and the International System in the Israeli-Palestinian Conflict." *International Political Science Review* 25, no. 1, *Religion and Politics* (January 2004): 77–96. http://www.jstor.org/stable/1601623.

Gallup, John Luke, Jeffrey D. Sachs, and Andres Mellinger. *International Regional Science Review* 22, no. 2 (1999). doi: 10.1177/016001799761012334.

Ganz, C. "The Palestinian Refugees and the Right of Return: Theoretical Perspectives." *Theoretical Inquiries in Law* 5, no. 2 (2004), 269–314.

Gayer, C., S. Landman, E. Halperin, and D. Bar-Tal. "Overcoming Psychological Barriers to Peaceful Conflict Resolution: The Role of Arguments About Losses." *Journal of Conflict Resolution* 53 (2009): 951–75.

Gilboa, E. "Mass Communication and Diplomacy: A Theoretical Framework." *Communication Theory* 10, no. 3 (2000): 275–309.

Ginges, Jeremy, and Scott Atran. "Humiliation and the Inertia Effect: Implications for Understanding Violence and Compromise in Intractable Intergroup Conflicts." *Journal of Cognition and Culture* 8 (2008). doi: 10.1163/156853708X358182.

Ginges, Jeremy, Scott Atran, Douglas Medin, and Khalil Shikabi. "Sacred Bounds on Rational Resolution of Violent Political Conflict." *Proceedings of the National Academy of Sciences of the United States of America* 104, no. 18 (2007): 7357–60. doi:10.1073/pnas.0701768104.

Gino, Francesca, and Don A. Moore. "Why Negotiators Should Reveal Their Deadlines." *Negotiation and Conflict Management Research* 1, no. 1 (2008): 77–96. doi: 10.1111/j.1750-4716.2007.00005.x.

Goddard, Stacie E. "Uncommon Ground: Indivisible Territory and the Politics of Legitimacy." *International Organization* 60 (2006): 35–68. doi: http://dx.doi.org/10.1017/S0020818306060024.

Golan-Agnon, Daphna. "Separate But Not Equal: Discrimination Against Palestinian Arab Students in Israel." *American Behavioral Scientist* 49 (April 2006). doi: 10.1177/0002764205284719.

Goldman, Jennifer S., and Peter T. Coleman. "How Humiliation Fuels Intractable Conflict: The Effects of Emotional Roles on Recall and Reactions to Conflictual Encounters." Columbia University, 2005.

Goodman, Yehuda C., and Nissim Mizrachi. "The Holocaust Does Not Belong to European Jews Alone." *American Ethnologist* 35, no. 1 (2008): 95–114.

Gottreich, Emily. "Historicizing the Concept of Arab Jews in the Maghreb." *Jewish Quarterly Review* 98 (2008): 433–51. http://muse.jhu.edu/journals/jqr/summary/v098/98.4.gottreich.html.

Gresh, Alain. "Reflections on the Meaning of Palestine." *Journal of Palestine Studies* 41, no. 1 (2011): 67–81.

Haidar, Aziz, and Elia Zureik. "The Palestinians Seen Through the Israeli Cultural Paradigm." *Journal of Palestine Studies* 16 (Spring 1987): 68–86.

Halabi, Zeina. "Exclusion and Identity in Lebanon's Palestinian Refugee Camps: A Story of Sustained Conflict." *Environment and Urbanization* 16, no. 39 (2004). doi: 10.1177/095624780401600221.

Halaby, Raouf. "Deir Yassin Massacre Remembered." *Counterpunch*, April 9, 2013. http://www.counterpunch.org/2013/04/09/deir-yassin-massacre-remembered/.

Halevy, Ephraim. "Israel's Hamas Portfolio." *Israel Journal of Foreign Affairs* 2, no. 3 (2008): 41–47. http://www.israelcfr.com/documents/issue6_hamas.pdf.

Hall, Brian J., Stevan E. Hobfoll, Daphna Canetti-Nisim, Robert Johnson, Patrick Palmieri, and Sandro Galea. "Exploring the Association Between Posttraumatic Growth and PTSD: A National Study of Jews and Arabs During the 2006 Israeli-Hezbollah War." *Journal of Nervous and Mental Disease* 198, no. 3 (March 2010): 180–86. doi: 10.1097/NMD.0b013e3181d1411b.

Halperin, Eran. "Emotional Barriers to Peace: Emotions and Public Opinion of Jewish Israelis About the Peace Process in the Middle East." *Peace and Conflict: Journal of Peace Psychology* 17, no. 1 (2011): 22–45. doi: 10.1080/10781919.2010.487862.

Halperin, Eran. "Group-Based Hatred in Intractable Conflict in Israel." *Journal of Conflict Resolution* 52, no. 5 (2008). doi:10.1177/0022002708314665.

Halperin, Eran, Daphna Canetti-Nisim, and Sivan Hirsch-Hoefler. "The Central Role of Group-Based Hatred as an Emotional Antecedent of Political Intolerance: The Central Role of Group-Based Hatred." *Political Psychology* 30, no. 1 (2009). doi: 10.1111/j.1467-9221.2008.00682.x.

Halperin, Eran, and James J. Gross. "Intergroup Anger in Intractable Conflict: Long-Term Sentiments Predict Anger Responses During the Gaza War." *Group Processes and Intergroup Relations* 14 (2010): 477–88. doi: 10.1177/1368430210377459.

Hamama-Raz, Yaira, Zahava Solomon, Assaf Cohen, and Avital Laufer. "PTSD Symptoms, Forgiveness, and Revenge Among Israeli Palestinian and Jewish Adolescents." *Journal of Traumatic Stress* 21 (December 2008). doi: 10.1002/jts.20376.

Hamdan, Usama. "Interview: Hamas 'Foreign Minister' Usama Haman Talks About National Reconciliation, Arafat, Reform, and Hamas's Presence in Lebanon." *Journal of Palestine Studies* 11, no. 3 (2011): 59–73.

Hanafi, Sari. "Palestinian Refugee Camps in Lebanon as a Space of Exception." *REVUE Asylon(s)* 5 (September 2008): n.p. http://www.reseau-terra.eu/article798.html.

Hanafi, Sari, Jad Chaaban, and Karin Seyfert. "Social Exclusion of Palestinian Refugees in Lebanon: Reflections on the Mechanisms That Cement Their Persistent Poverty." *Refugee Survey Quarterly* 31 (2012). doi: 10.1093/rsq/hdr018.

Hanauer, L. S. "The Path to Redemption: Fundamentalist Judaism, Territory, and Jewish Settler Violence in the West Bank." *Studies in Conflict and Terrorism* 18, (1995): 245–70.

Hanieh, Akram. "The Camp David Papers." *Journal of Palestine Studies* 30, no. 2 (2011): 75–97. http://www.jstor.org/stable/10.1525/jps.2001.30.2.75.

Hanieh, Akram. "Special Document: The Camp David Papers." *Journal of Palestine Studies* 30, no. 2 (Winter 2001): 75–97. http://www.palestine-studies.org/sites/default/files/jps-articles/2759.pdf.

Hassner, R. "To Halve and to Hold: Conflicts over Sacred Space and the Problem of Indivisibility." *Security Studies* 12, no. 4 (2003): 11–33.

Hasso, Frances. "Modernity and Gender in Arab Accounts of the 1948 and 1967 Defeats." *International Journal of Middle East Studies* 32, no. 4 (November 2000). doi: http://dx.doi.org/.

Hatemi, Peter K., Rose McDermott, Lindon J. Eaves, Kenneth S. Kendler, and Michael C. Neale. "Fear as a Disposition and an Emotional State: A Genetic and Environmental Approach to Out-Group Political Preferences." *American Journal of Political Science* 57 (2013). doi: 10.1111/ajps.12016.

Hehir, J. Bryan. "Expanding Military Force: Promise or Peril?" *Social Research* 62, no. 1 (Spring 1995): 41–51. http://www.jstor.org/stable/40971075.

Hehir, J. Bryan. "Intervention: From Theories to Cases." *Ethics & International Affairs* 9, no. 1 (1995). doi: 10.1111/j.1747-7093.1995.tb00168.x.

Hehir, J. Bryan. "Just War Theory in a Post-Cold War World." *Journal of Religious Ethics* 20, no. 2 (Fall 1992): 237–57. http://www.jstor.org/stable/40015155.

Heiberg, Marianne, and Geir Øvensen, et al. *Palestinian Society in Gaza, West Bank and Arab Jerusalem: A Survey of Living Conditions.* Fafo Report 151 Oslo: Fafo Institute for Applied International Studies, 1993. http://almashriq.hiof.no/general/300/320/327/fafo/reports/FAFO151/index.html.

Henderson, M. D., Y. Trope, and P. J. Carnevalle. "Negotiation from a Near and Distant Time Perspective." *Journal of Personality and Social Psychology* 91, no. 40 (2006): 712–29.

Hilal, Leila. "Implementing a Negotiated Settlement on the Palestinian Refugee Question: The International Dimensions." Programme Paper, Middle East and North America Programme, Regional Approaches to the Middle East Peace Process. Paper. London: Royal Institute of International Affairs, Chatham House, January 2012. http://www.chathamhouse.org/publications/papers/view/181745.

Hoekstra, Arjen Y., and Mesfin M. Mekonnen. "The Water Footprint of Humanity." Edited by Peter H. Gleick. *Proceedings of the National Academy of Sciences of the United States of America* 109, no. 9 (February 28, 2012). doi: 10.1073/pnas.1109936109. http://www.pnas.org/content/109/9/3232.full.

Holt, Maria. "Palestinian Women, Violence and the Peace Process." *Development in Practice* 13, no. 2/3 (2003). doi: 10.1080/09614520302948.

Hovdenak, Are. "Trading Refugees for Land and Symbols: The Palestinian Negotiation Strategy in the Oslo Process." *International Peace Research* 22 (2009). doi: 10.1093/jrs/fen039.

Jubeh, Nazmi. "The Palestinian Refugee Problem and the Final Status Negotiations." *Palestine-Israel Journal* 9, no. 2 (2002): 5–11.

Judt, Tony. "Israel: The Alternative." *New York Review of Books*, 50, no. 16, October 23, 2003. http://www.nybooks.com/articles/archives/2003/oct/23/israel-the-alternative/?insrc=toc.

Kagan, Michael. "Restitution as a Remedy for Refugee Property Claims in the Israeli-Palestinian Conflict." *Florida Journal of International Law* 19, no. 2 (2007): 421–89. http://scholars.law.unlv.edu/facpub/628/.

Karim, Nasr Abdul, Khalid Farraj, and Salim Tamari. "The Palestinian Economy and Future Prospects: Interview with Mohammad Mustafa, Head of the Palestine Investment Fund." *Journal of Palestine Studies* 39, no. 3 (2010): 40–51. http://www.jstor.org/stable/10.1525/jps.2010.XXXIX.3.40.

Kanafani, Marwan, and Elizabeth Schiffrin. "From Massacre to Militia: The Case Against Palestinian Disarmament in Lebanon." *Washington Report on Middle East Affairs* 25, no. 2 (2006): 38–40. http://www.wrmea.org/wrmea-archives/281-washington-report-archives-2006-2010/march-2006/11117-from-massacre-to-militia-the-case-against-palestinian-disarmament-in-lebanon.html.

Karniol, R., and M. Ross. "The Motivational Impact of Temporal Focus: Thinking About the Future and the Past." *Annual Review of Psychology* 47 (1996): 593–620.

Karsh, Efraim Nakbat. "Haifa: Collapse and Dispersion of a Major Palestinian Community." *Middle Eastern Studies* 37 (October 2001): 25–70. http://www.jstor.org/stable/4284196.

Kelman, Herbert C. "Building Trust Among Enemies: The Central Challenge for International Conflict Resolution." *International Journal of Intercultural Relations* 29, no. 6 (2005). doi: 10.1016/j.ijintrel.2005.07.011.

Kelman, Herbert C. "An Interactional Approach to Conflict Resolution and Its Application to Israeli-Palestinian Relations." *International Interactions* 6, no. 2 (1979). doi: 10.1080/03050627908434527.

Kelman, Herbert C. "The Political Psychology of the Israeli-Palestinian Conflict: How Can We Overcome the Barriers to a Negotiated Solution?" *Political Psychology* 8, no. 3 (1987): 347–63. http://www.jstor.org/stable/3791039.

Kenion, Herb. "Palestine Wins Historic Upgrade at the UN." *Jerusalem Post*, November 30, 2012.

Kessler, Joshua L. "The Goldstone Report: Politicization of the Law of Armed Conflict and Those Left Behind." *Military Law Review* 209 (Fall 2011): 69–121.

Khalidi, Ahmed Samih. "Why Can't the Palestinians Recognize the *Jewish* State?" *Palestine Studies* 40, no. 4 (2011): 78–81.

Khalidi, Rashid. "Toward a Clear Palestinian Strategy." *Journal of Palestine Studies* 31, no. 4 (2002): 5–12.

Khalidi, Walid. "Plan Dalet: The Zionist Master Plan for the Conquest of Palestine." *Middle East Forum* 37, no. 9 (November 1961): 22–28.

Khalidi, Walid. "Revisiting the UNGA Partition Resolution." *Journal of Palestine Studies* 27, no. 1 (1997): 5–21. http://www.jstor.org/stable/2537806.

Klar, Y., N. Schori-Eyal, and Y. Klar. "The 'Never Again' State of Israel: The Emergence of the Holocaust as a Core Feature of Israeli Identity and Its Four Incongruent Voices." *Journal of Social Issues* 69, no. 1 (2013): 125–43.

Klar, Yechiel, Dan Zakay, and Keren Sharvit. "If I Don't Get Blown Up . . . : Realism in Face of Terrorism in an Israeli Nationwide Sample." *Risk, Decision and Policy* 7 (2002): 203–19. doi: http://dx.doi.org/10.1017/S1357530902000625.

Klein, Menachem. "The Origins of Intifada II and Rescuing Peace for Israelis and Palestinians." Lecture at the Foundation for Middle East Peace, Washington, DC, October 2, 2002. http://www.miftah.org/display.cfm?DocId=1813&CategoryId=5.

Klingman, Avigodor, and Ezra Wiesner. "Analysis of Israeli Children's Fears: A Comparison of Religious and Secular Communities." *International Journal of Social Psychiatry* 29 (1983). doi: 10.1177/002076408302900406.

Krebs, Ronald R. "Israel's Bunker Mentality: How the Occupation Is Destroying the Nation." *Foreign Affairs* 90, no. 6 (2011): 10–18.

Kressel, Neil J. "The Denial of Muslim Anti-Semitism." *Journal for the Study of Antisemitism* 2 (2010): 259–70. http://www.jsantisemitism.org/pdf/jsa_2-2.pdf.

Krieger, Zvika. "Welcome to 'Fortress Gaza,' Home of the Newly Radicalized Hamas." *The Atlantic* (September 25, 2012). http://www.theatlantic.com/international/archive/2012/09/welcome-to-fortress-gaza.

Kuperwasser, Yosef, and Shalom Lipner. "The Problem Is Palestinian Rejectionism." *Foreign Affairs* 90, no. 6 (2011): 2–9.

Kuzar, Ron. "The Term Return in the Palestinian Discourse on the Right of Return." *Discourse & Society* 19, no. 5 (2008). doi: 10.1177/0957926508092246.

Lahoud, Lamia. "Arafat Laments Delays to Peace Talks." *Jerusalem Post*, February 1, 2000.

Lahoud, Lamia. "PA Finds Huge Hamas Explosives Cache in Hebron." *Jewish Post*, December 12, 1999.

Landes, Richard. "Edward Said and the Culture of Honour and Shame: Orientalism and Our Misperceptions of the Arab-Israeli Conflict." *Israel Affairs* 13, no. 4 (2007). doi: 10.1080/13537120701445315.

Lavi, Iris, Daphna Canetti, Keren Sharvit, Daniel Bar-Tal, and Stevan E. Hobfoll. "Protected by Ethos in a Protracted Conflict? A Comparative Study Among Israelis and Palestinians in the West Bank, Gaza, and East Jerusalem." *Journal of Conflict Resolution*, 58, no. 1 (2014): 68–92. doi: 10.1177/0022002712459711.

Lehrs, Lior. "Egyptian Plague or Spring of Youth? The Israeli Discourse Regarding the Arab Spring." Mitvim, Ramat Gan, Israel, January 2013. http://www.mitvim.org.il/en/israel-and-the-arab-spring.

Lerner, Jennifer S., and Philip E. Tetlock. "Accounting for the Effects of Accountability." *Psychological Bulletin* 125, no. 2 (1999): 255–75. http://scholar.harvard.edu/files/jenniferlerner/files/lerner_and_tetlock_1999_pb_paper.pdf.

Lesch, Ann M. "Palestinians in Kuwait." *Journal of Palestine Studies* 20, no. 4 (Summer 1991): 42–54. http://www.jstor.org/stable/2537434.

Lewis, Bernard. "The Revolt of Islam." *New Yorker* (November 19, 2001). http://www.newyorker.com/magazine/2001/11/19/the-revolt-of-islam.

Lipson, Charles. "American Support for Israel: History, Sources, Limits." *Israel Affairs* 2, no. 3–4 (1996). doi: 10.1080/13537129608719397.

Litvak, Meir, and Esther Webman. "Perceptions of the Holocaust in Palestinian Public Discourse." *Israeli Studies* 8, no. 3 (fall 2003): 123–40. http://muse.jhu.edu/journals/is/summary/v008/8.3litvak.html.

Lustick, Ian S. "Negotiating the Truth: The Holocaust, Lehavdil, and Al-Nakba." *Journal of International Affairs* 60, no. 1 (Fall/Winter 2006): 51–77.

Makovsky, David. "Imagining the Border: Options for Resolving the Israeli-Palestinian Territorial Issue." Washington Institute for Near East Policy, *Strategic Reports* 6 (January 2011).

Makovsky, David. "Obama and Netanyahu: Divergence and Convergence." Washington Institute for Near East Policy, *Policy Notes* 5 (June 2011). http://www.washingtoninstitute.org/policy-analysis/view/obama-and-netanyahu-divergence-and-convergence.

Malley, Robert, and Hussein Agha. "The Palestinian-Israeli Camp David Negotiations and Beyond: Camp David: Tragedy of Errors." *Journal of Palestine Studies* 31, no. 1 (Autumn 2001): 62–74. http://www.jstor.org/stable/10.1525/jps.2001.31.1.62.

Mallison, William T., Jr. "The Legal Problems Concerning the Juridical Status and Political Activities of the Zionist Organization / Jewish Agency: A Study in International and United States Law." *William & Mary Law Review* 9, no. 3 (1967–68): 554–629. http://scholarship.law.wm.edu/wmlr/vol9/iss3/3/.

Manna, Adel. "The Palestinian Nakba and Its Continuous Repercussions." *Israel Studies* 18, no. 2 (Summer 2013): 86–99.

Mansour, Camille. "The Palestinian-Israeli Peace Negotiations: An Overview and Assessment." *Journal of Palestine Studies* 87 (Spring 1993): 5–31.

Mansour, Camille. "Toward a New Palestinian Negotiation Paradigm." *Journal of Palestine Studies* 11, no. 3 (2011): 38–58.

Maoz, Ifat. "Coexistence Is in the Eye of the Beholder: Evaluating Intergroup Encounter Interventions Between Jews and Arabs in Israel." *Journal of Social Issues* 60, no. 2 (2004): 437–52.

Maoz, Ifat, and Clark McCauley. "Threat, Dehumanization, and Support for Retaliatory Aggressive Policies in Asymmetric Conflict." *Journal of Conflict Resolution* 52, no. 1 (2008). doi: 10.1177/0022002707308597.

Maoz, Ifat, and Clark McCauley. "Threat Perceptions and Feelings as Predictors of Jewish-Israeli Support for Compromise with Palestinians." *Journal for Peace Research* 46, no. 4 (2009). doi: 10.1177/0022343309334613.

Margalit, Avishai. "The Suicide Bombers." *New York Review of Books*, January 16, 2003.

Mason, Michael. "Climate Change, Securitization, and the Israeli-Palestinian Conflict." *Geographical Journal* 179, no. 4 (December 2013). doi: 10.1111/geoj.12007.

Massad, Joseph. "Palestinians and Jewish History: Recognition or Submission?" *Journal of Palestine Studies* 30, no. 1 (Autumn 2000): 52–67.

McGarry, John and Brendan O'Leary. "Consociational Theory, Northern Ireland's Conflict, and Its Agreement, Part 1: What Consociationalists Can Learn from Northern Ireland." *Government and Opposition* 41, no. 1 (Winter 2006): 4–63. doi: 10.1111/j.1477-7053.2006.00170.x.

McGarry, John and Brendan O'Leary, "Consociational Theory, Northern Ireland's Conflict, and Its Agreement, Part 2: What Critics of Consociationalism Can Learn from Northern Ireland." *Government and Opposition* 41, no. 2 (Spring 2006): 249–77. doi: 10.1111/j.1477-7053.2006.00178.x.

McMahon, Robert, and Jonathan Masters. "Palestinian Statehood at the UN." Council on Foreign Relations, November, 30 2012. http://www.cfr.org/palestine/palestinian-statehood-un/p25954?cid=rss-fullfeed-palestinian_statehood_at_the_u-092712.

Mearsheimer, John, and Steve Walt. "The Israel Lobby and U.S. Foreign Policy." Faculty Working Paper RWP06-011, John F. Kennedy School of Government, Harvard University, Cambridge, MA, March 2006. A shorter version appeared in the *London Review of Books* 28, no. 6 (March 23, 2006). https://research.hks.harvard.edu/publications/workingpapers/citation.aspx?PubId=3670.

Meidan-Shani, Pini. "An Israeli View: Still a Viable Concept for the West Bank." *Bitter Lemons*, July 9, 2007.

Meneley, Anne. "Discourses of Distinction in Contemporary Palestinian Extra-Virgin Olive Oil Production." *Food and Foodways* 22, no. 1–2 (2014). doi: 10.1080/07409710.2014.892738.

Miller, Aaron David. "Israel's Demographic Destiny." *Foreign Policy*, March 13, 2013. http://www.foreignpolicy.com/articles/2013/03/13/israels_demographic_destiny_palestine.

Miller, Aaron David. "The Peace Processor." *Foreign Policy*, February 15, 2013. http://www.foreignpolicy.com/articles/2013/02/05/The_Peace_Processor_Palestine_Saeb_Erekat.

Miller, Elhanan. "The Intractable Issue: Palestinian Refugees and the Israeli-Palestinian Peace Process." *ICSR*, 2012.

Mitchell, George. "How We Got Here." *Boston Globe*, September 7, 2014. www.bostonglobe.com/opinion/2014/09/ . . . /story.html.

Mitchell, George. "Israeli-Palestinian Peace Is Needed Now." *Boston Globe*, September 8 2014. www.bostonglobe.com/opinion/2014/09/ . . . /story.html.

Mitchell, George. "US the Only Power That Can Push for Peace." *Boston Globe*. www.bostonglobe.com/opinion/ . . . /story.html.

Mnookin, Robert H., E. Eiran, and S. Mitter. "Barriers to Progress at the Negotiation Table: Internal Conflicts Among Israeli and Among Palestinians." *Nevada Law Journal* 6 (2005–06): 299–366.

Molina, Oscar, and Martin Rhodes. "Corporatism: The Past, Present, and Future of a Concept." *Annual Review of Political Science* 5, no. 1 (2002). doi. 0.1146/annurev.polisci.5.112701.184858.

Montelli, Jessica. "Human Rights in the Occupied Territories." B'Tselem, Jerusalem, 2011.

Moore, Dahlia, and Salem Aweiss. "Hatred of 'Others' Among Jewish, Arab, and Palestinian Students in Israel." *Analysis of Social Issues and Public Policy* 2, no. 1 (2002). doi: 10.1111/j.1530-2415.2002.00035.x.

Morris, Benny. "The Historiography of Deir Yassin." *Journal of Israeli History* 24, no. 1 (2005). doi: 10.1080/13531040500040305.

Morris, Benny, and Ehud Barak. "Camp David and After, Continued." *New York Review of Books*, June 27, 2002.

Mullen, E. E., and L. J. Skitka. "Exploring the Psychological Underpinnings of the Moral Mandate Effect: Motivated Reasoning, Identification, or Affect?" *Journal of Personality and Social Psychology* 90 (2006): 629–43.

Munayyer, Yousef. "When Settlers Attack." Palestine Center, Washington, DC, 2012.

Mundlak, Guy. "Addressing the Legitimacy Gap in the Israeli Corporatist Revival." *British Journal of Industrial Relations* 47, no. 4 (December 2009). doi: 10.1111/j.1467-8543.2009.00754.x.

Myers, David N. "Is There Still a 'Jerusalem School'? Reflections on the State of Jewish Historical Scholarship in Israel." *Jewish History* 23, no. 4 (December 2009): 389–406. doi: http://dx.doi.org/10.1007/s10835-009-9094-y.

Nassar, Maha. "Palestinian Citizens of Israel and the Discourse of the Right of Return, 1948–59." *Palestine Studies* 40, no. 4 (2011): 45–60.

Nofal, Mamdouh, Fawaz Turki, Haidar Abdel Shafi, Inea Bushnaq, Yezid Sayigh, Shafiq al-Hout, Salma Khadra Jayyusi, and Musa Budeiri. "Reflections on Al-Nakba." *Journal of Palestine Studies* 28, no. 1 (Autumn 1998): 5–35. http://www.jstor.org/stable/2538053.

Ofer, Dalia. "The Past That Does Not Pass: Israelis and Holocaust Memory." *Israel Studies* 14, no. 1 (2009). doi: 10.1353/is.0.0023.

Ofer, Pinhas. "The Commission on the Palestine Disturbances of August 1929: Appointment, Terms of Reference, Procedure and Report." *Middle Eastern Studies* 21, no. 3 (1985). doi: 10.1080/00263208508700633.

Okhuysen, Gerardo A., Adam D. Galinski, and T. A. Uptigrove. "Saving the Worst for the Last: The Effects of Time Horizon on the Efficiency of Negotiating Benefits and Burdens." *Organizational Behavior and Human Decision Processes* 91 (2003): 269–79. doi: 10.1016/S0749-5978(03)00023-2.

Or, Theodor. "A Year to the State Investigative Commission on the October, 2000 Events." Konrad Adenaeur Program for Jewish-Arab Cooperation, Moshe Dayan Center for Middle Eastern and African Studies, Tel Aviv University, 2004. http://www.orwatch.org/doc-en/OrEng.pdf.

Orbach, Israel. "Terror Suicide: How Is It Possible?" *Archives of Suicide Research* 8 (2004): 115–30. doi: 10.1080/13811104902343787.

Pace, Jacob. "Ethnic Cleansing 101: The Case of Lifta Village." *Electronic Intifada*, March 2, 2005. http://www.electronicintifada.net/content/ethnic-cleansing-101-case-lifta-village/5493.

Pearce, Susanna. "Religious Rage: A Quantitative Analysis of the Intensity of Religious Conflicts." *Terrorism and Political Violence* 17, no. 3 (2005): 333–52. doi: 10.1080/09546550590929237.

Pechter, Adam, and David Pollack. "The Palestinians of East Jerusalem: What Do They Really Want?" Briefing, Council on Foreign Relations, Washington, DC, January 12, 2011. http://www.pechterpolls.com/wp-content/uploads/2011/01/Final-PMEP-E-Jerusalem-Briefing-for-CFR-Jan-122.pdf.

Peled, Yoav, and Nadim Rouhana. "Transitional Justice and the Right of Return of the Palestinian Refugees." *Theoretical Inquiries in Law* 5, no. 2 (2004): 317–32.

Perez, Nahshon. "Israel's Law of Return: A Qualified Justification." *Modern Judaism* 31 (February 2011). doi: 10.1093/mj/kjq032.

Peri, Yoram. "Israel at 62." *Wilson Quarterly* 34, no. 2 (Summer 2010): 56–61.

Perliger, Arie, and Ami Pedahzer. "Coping with Suicide Attacks: Lessons from Israel." *Public Money & Management* 26 (November 2006): 281–86. http://papers.ssrn.com/sol3/papers.cfm?abstract_id=937083.

Pitcher, Linda M. "'The Divine Impatience': Ritual, Narrative, and Symbolization in the Practice of Martyrdom in Palestine." *Medical Anthropology Quarterly* 12, no. 1 (1998): 8–30.

Post, Jerrold M. "Collective Identity: Hatred Bred in the Bone." *Foreign Policy Agenda* 12, no. 5 (2007). doi: 10.1111/j.1467-9221.2005.00434.x.

Pressman, Jeremy. "Visions in Collision: What Happened at Camp David and Taba." *International Security* 28, no. 2 (2003): 5–43. http://belfercenter.ksg.harvard.edu/publication/322/visions_in_collision.html.

Reiter, Yitzhak. "Family Waqf Entitlements in British Palestine (1917–1948)." *Islamic Law and Society* 2, no. 2 (1995). doi: 10.1163/1568519952599385.

Rempel, Terry. "Who Are Palestinian Refugees?" *Forced Migration Review* 26 (2006). http://www.fmreview.org/FMRpdfs/FMR26/FMR2602.pdf.

Ritov, Ilana, and Jonathan Baron. "Protected Values and Omission Bias." *Organizational Behavior and Human Decision Processes* 79, no. 2 (1999): 79–94. doi: 10.1006/obhd.1999.2839.

Rosenfeld, Gavriel David. "A Flawed Prophecy? Zakhor, the Memory Boom, and the Holocaust." *Jewish Quarterly Review* 97, no. 4 (2007). doi: 10.1353/jqr.2007.0063.

Rothenberg, Celia E. "Proximity and Distance: Palestinian Women's Social Lives in Diaspora." *Diaspora: A Journal of Transnational Studies* 8, no. 1 (1999). doi: 10.1353/dsp.1999.0019.

Rowland, Robert C., and David A. Frank. "Mythic Rhetoric and Rectification in the Israeli-Palestinian Conflict." *Communication Studies* 62, no. 1 (2011). doi: 10.1080/10510974.2011.532428.

Roy, Sara. "Living with the Holocaust: The Journey of a Child of Holocaust Survivors." *Journal of Palestine Studies* 32, no. 1 (Autumn 2002): 5–12. http://www.jstor.org/stable/10.1525/jps.2002.32.1.5.

Saban, Ilan. "Appropriate Representation of Minorities: Canada's Two Types Structure and the Arab-Palestinian Minority in Israel." *Penn State International Law Review* 24, no. 3 (Winter 2006): 563–94.

Saban, Ilan. "Citizenship and Its Erosion: Transfer of Populated Territory and Oath of Allegiance in the Prism of Israeli Constitutional Law." *Law & Ethics of Human Rights* 2, no. 2 (2008): 2–32. http://papers.ssrn.com/sol3/papers.cfm?abstract_id=1762664.

Saban, Ilan. "Minority Rights in Deeply Divided Societies: A Framework for Analysis and the Case of the Arab-Palestinian Minority in Israel." *New York University Journal of International Law and Politics* 36, no. 4 (2004): 885–1003. http://papers.ssrn.com/sol3/papers.cfm?abstract_id=903518.

Saban, Ilan. "Theorizing and Tracing the Legal Dimensions of a Control Framework: Law and the Arab-Palestinian Minority in Israel's First Three Decades (1948–1978)." *Emory International Law Review* 25, no. 1 (2011): 299–378. http://papers.ssrn.com/sol3/papers.cfm?abstract_id=1962518.

Saban, Ilan, and Muhammad Amara. "The Status of Arabic in Israel: Reflections on the Power of Law to Produce Social Change." *Israel Law Review* 36, no. 2 (Summer 2002): 5–39. http://papers.ssrn.com/sol3/papers.cfm?abstract_id=903625.

Sa'di, Ahmad H. "Catastrophe, Memory and Identity: Al-Nakbah as a Component of Identity," *Israel Studies* 7, no. 2 (Summer 2002): 175–200. http://muse.jhu.edu/login?auth=0&type=summary&url=/journals/israel_studies/v007/7.2saadi.html.

Sadot, Uri. "Israel's Demographic Time Bomb Is a Dud." *Foreign Policy*. December 18, 2013. http://www.foreignpolicy.com/articles/2013/12/18/israel_s_demographic_time_bomb_is_a_dud_israel_arab_two_state_solution.

Saideman, Lewis. "Do Palestinian Refugees Have a Right of Return to Israel: An Examination of the Scope of and Limitations on the Right of Return." *Virginia Journal of International Law* 44 (2003): 829–78.

Sayigh, Rosemary. "Dis/Solving the 'Refugee Problem.'" In *MER 207: Who Paid the Price? 50 Years of Israel* 28 (Summer 1998): 19–23. http://www.merip.org/mer/mer207/dissolving-refugee-problem.

Sayigh, Rosemary. "The Palestinian Identity Among Camp Residents." *Journal of Palestine Studies* 6, no. 3 (Spring 1977): 3–22. http://www.jstor.org/stable/2535577.

Scham, Paul, Benjamin Pogrund, and As'ad Ghanem. "Introduction to Shared Narratives: A Palestinian-Israeli Dialogue." *Israel Studies* 18, no. 2 (Summer 2013): 1–10. doi: 10.1353/is.2013.0021.

Schleifer, S. Abdullah. "The Life and Thought of 'Izz-id-Din al-Qassam." *Islamic Quarterly* 22, no. 2 (1979): 61–81.

Shaath, Nabeel. "High Level Palestinian Manpower." *Journal of Palestine Studies* 1, no. 2 (Winter 1972): 80–95. http://www.jstor.org/stable/2535957.

Shalhoub-Kevorkian, Nadera and Suhad Dasher-Nashif. "Femicide and Colonization: Between the Politics of Exclusion and the Culture of Control." *Violence Against Women* 19, no. 3 (March 2013): 295–315. doi: 10.1177/1077801213485548.

Shamai, Michal. "Life Narratives of Adults Who Experienced War During Childhood: The Case of the Attack and Bombing of Kibbutz Mishmar-Haemek in 1948." *Traumatology* 18 (2012). doi:10.1177/1534765611426790.

Shamir, Jacob, and Khalil Shikaki. "Determinants of Reconciliation and Compromise Among Israelis and Palestinians." *Journal of Peace Research* 39, no. 2 (2002). doi: 10.1177/0022343302039002003.

Sharon, Assaf. "Failure in Gaza." *New York Review of Books* 61, no. 14 (September 25, 2014). http://www.nybooks.com/articles/archives/2014/sep/25/failure-gaza/.

Shawahin, Lamise, and Ayşe Çiftçi. "Counseling and Mental Health Care in Palestine." *Journal of Counseling and Development* 90 (June 2012). doi: 10.1002/j.1556-6676.2012.00048.x.

Shechter, Hava, and Gavriel Salomon. "Does Vicarious Experience of Suffering Affect Empathy for an Adversary? The Effects of Israelis' Visits to Auschwitz on Their Empathy for Palestinians." *Journal of Peace Education* 2, no. 2 (2005). doi: 10.1080/17400200500173535.

Shehadeh, Raja. "In Pursuit of my Ottoman Uncle: Reimaging the Middle East Region as One." *Journal of Palestine Studies* 40, no. 4 (2011): 82–93. http://www.jstor.org/stable/10.1525/jps.2011.XL.4.82.

Shemesh, Moshe. "The Palestinian Society in the Wake of the 1948 War: From Social Fragmentation to Consolidation." *Israeli Studies* 9, no. 1 (Spring 2004): 86–100.

Shiblak, Abbas. "Residency Status and Civil Rights of Palestinian Refugees in Arab Countries." *Journal of Palestine Studies* 25, no. 3 (Spring 1996): 36–45. http://www.jstor.org/stable/2538257.

Shulman, David. "Gaza: The Murderous Melodrama." *New York Review of Books*, November 20, 2014.

Skitka, Linda J., and Elizabeth Mullen. "Understanding Judgments of Fairness in a Real-World Political Context: A Test of the Value Protection Model of Justice Reasoning." *Personality and Social Psychology Bulletin* 28, no. 2 (2002): 1419–29. doi: 10.1177/014616702236873.

Slone, Michelle. "The Nazareth Riots: Arab and Jewish Israeli Adolescents Pay a Different Psychological Price for Participation." *Journal of Conflict Resolution* 47, no. 6 (December 2003): 817–36. http://www.jstor.org/stable/3176262.

Smith, Anthony D. "The Ethnic Sources of Nationalism." *Survival* 35, no. 1 (1993): 48–62. doi: 10.1080/00396339308442673.

Smith, Charles D. "Review of *Shared Histories: A Palestinian-Israeli Dialogue* by Paul Scham, Walid Salem, and Benjamin Pogrund." *Middle East Journal* 59, no. 4 (Autumn 2005): 668–70. http://www.jstor.org/stable/4330191.

Smith, Pamela Ann. "The Palestinian Diaspora, 1948–1985." *Journal of Palestine Studies* 15, no. 3 (Spring 1986): 90–108. http://www.jstor.org/stable/2536751.

Snir, Reuven. "My Adherence to the Creed of Moses Has Not Diminished My Love for Muhammad's Nation: The Emergence and Demise of Iraqi Jewish Literary Modern Culture." *Jewish Quarterly Review* 98 (Winter 2008): 62–87. http://muse.jhu.edu/journals/jqr/summary/v098/98.1snir.html.

Sorek, Tamir. "Cautious Commemoration: Localism, Communalism, and Nationalism in Palestinian Memorial Monuments in Israel." *Comparative Studies in Society and History* 50, no. 2 (2008): 337–68.

Sowers, Jeannie, Avner Vengosh, and Erika Weinthal. "Climate Change, Water Resources, and the Politics of Adaptation in the Middle East and North Africa." *Climatic Change* 104, no. 3–4 (April 2010): 599–627. doi: 10.1007/s10584-010-9835-4.

"Special Document File: The Annapolis Conference." *Journal of Palestine Studies* 37, no. 3 (Spring 2008): 74–92. http://www.jstor.org/stable/10.1525/jps.2008.37.3.74.

"Special Document File: Barack Obama and the Arab-Israeli Conflict." *Journal of Palestine Studies* 38, no. 2 (2009): 64–75.

"Special Document File: Charter of the Islamic Resistance Movement (Hamas) of Palestine." Translated by Muhammad Maqdsi. *Journal of Palestine Studies* 22, no. 4 (Summer 1993): 122–34. http://www.palestine-studies.org/sites/default/files/jps-articles/1734.pdf.

"Special Document File: The Madrid Peace Conference." *Journal of Palestine Studies* 21, no. 2 (Winter 1992): 117–49. http://www.jstor.org/stable/2537235.

"Special Document File: The Palestine Papers: Chronicling the U.S. Abandonment of the Road Map." *Journal of Palestine Studies* 40, no. 3 (spring 2011): 84–114. http://www.jstor.org/stable/10.1525/jps.2011.XL.3.84.

"Special Document File: The Taba Negotiations (January 2001)." *Journal of Palestine Studies* 31, no. 3 (Spring 2002): 79–89. http://www.palestine-studies.org/sites/default/files/jps-articles/4407.pdf.

Spoerl, Joseph S. "Islamic Antisemitism in the Arab-Israeli Conflict." *Journal for the Study of Antisemitism* 4, no. 2 (2012): 595–612. http://www.jsantisemitism.org/images/journals/jsa_4-2.pdf.

Stein, Howard F. "The Holocaust, the Uncanny and the Jewish Sense of History." *Political Psychology* 5 (1984): 5–35. http://www.jstor.org/stable/3790829.

Steinmetz, George. "The Sociology of Empires, Colonies, and Postcolonialism." *Annual Review of Sociology* 40 (July 2014): 77–103. doi: 10.1146/annurev-soc-071913-043131.

Stevens, Garth, Gillian Eagle, Debra Kaminer, and Craig Higson-Smith. "Continuous Traumatic Stress: Conceptual Conversations in Contexts of Global Conflict, Violence and Trauma." *Peace and Conflict: Journal of Peace Psychology* 19, no. 2 (May 2013). doi: 10.1037/a0032484.

Suleiman, Haitam, and Robert Home. "'God Is an Absentee, Too': The Treatment of Waqf (Islamic Trust) Land in Israel/Palestine." *Journal of Legal Pluralism and Unofficial Law* 41, no. 59 (2009). doi: 10.1080/07329113.2009.10756629.

Sultan, Suhail Sami. "Enhancing the Competitiveness of Palestinian SMEs Through Clustering." *EuroMed Journal of Business* 9, no. 2 (2014): 164–74. doi: dx.doi.org/10.1108/EMJB-03-2012-0004.

Susskind, Lawrance, Hillel Levine, Gideon Aran, Schlomo Kaniel, Yair Sheleg, and Moshe Halbertal. "Religious and Ideological Dimensions of the Israeli Settlements Issue: Reframing the Narrative?" *Negotiation Journal* 21, no. 2 (2005): 177–91. doi: 10.1111/j.1571-9979.2005.00056.x.

Svensson, Isak. "Fighting with Faith: Religion and Conflict in Civil Wars." *Journal of Conflict Resolution* 51, no. 6 (2007): 930–49. http://www.jstor.org/stable/27638586.

Telhami, Shibley, and S. Kull. "Israeli and Palestinian Public Opinion on Negotiating a Final Status Peace Agreement." Saban Center for Middle East Policy, Brookings Institution, Washington, DC, December 6, 2013.

Telhami, Shibley, and Steven Kull. "Israeli Public Opinion after November 2012 Gaza War." Saban Center for Middle East Policy, Brookings Institution, Washington, DC, November 30, 2012.

Tetlock, Philip E. "Thinking the Unthinkable: Sacred Values and Taboo Cognitions." *Trends in Cognitive Science* 7 (2003): 320–24.

Tetlock, Philip E., Orie V. Kristel, S. Beth Elson, Melanie C. Green, and Jennifer C. Lerner. "The Psychology of the Unthinkable: Taboo Tradeoffs, Forbidden Base-Rates, and Heretical Counterfactuals. *Journal of Personality and Social Psychology* 78, no. 5 (2000): 853–70. doi: 10.1037/0022-3514.78.5.853.

Thabet, Abouzeid A., Ahmed Abu Tawahina, Eyad El Sarraj, and Panos Vostanis. "Exposure to War Trauma and PTSD Among Parents and Children in the Gaza Strip." *European Child & Adolescent Psychiatry* 17, no. 4 (March 2008). doi: 10.1007/s00787-007-0653-9.

Thórisdóttir, Hulda, and John T. Jost. "Motivated Closed-Mindedness Mediates the Effect of Threat on Political Conservatism." *Political Psychology* 32, no. 5 (2011). doi: 10.1111/j.1467-9221.2011.00840.x.

Thrall, Nathan. "Israel & the US: The Delusions of Our Diplomacy." *New York Review of Books* 61, no. 16, (October 9, 2014). http://www.nybooks.com/articles/archives/2014/oct/09/israel-us-delusions-our-diplomacy/.

Usher, Graham. "Letter from the UN: The Palestinian Bid for Membership." *Journal of Palestine Studies* 41, no. 1 (2011): 57–66.

Veracini, Lorenzo. "The Other Shift: Settler Colonialism, Israel, and the Occupation." *Journal of Palestine Studies* 42, no. 2 (Winter 2013): 26–42. doi: http://www.jstor.org/stable/10.1525/jps.2013.42.2.26.

Vojko Strahovnik, "Beyond the Culture of Fear: Fear and Responsibility," in *From Culture of Fear to Society of Trust*, Janez Juhant, Bojan Zalec eds., LIT Verlag Münster (December 28, 2013), 93.

Wåhlin, Lars. "Inheritance of Land in the Jordanian Hill Country." *British Journal of Middle Eastern Studies* 21, no. 1 (1994). doi: 10.1080/13530199408705592.

Wakim, Wakim. "The 'Internally Displaced': Seeking Return Within One's Own Land." *Journal of Palestine Studies* 31, no. 1 (autumn 2001): 32–38. http://www.jstor.org/stable/10.1525/jps.2001.31.1.32.

Welchman, Lynn. "The Bedouin Judge, the Mufti, and the Chief Islamic Justice: Competing Legal Regimes in the Occupies Palestinian Territories." *Journal of Palestine Studies* 38, no. 2 (2009): 6–23.

Wicken, Stephen. "Views of the Holocaust in Arab Media and Public Discourse." *Yale Journal of International Affairs* 1 (2005): 103–15. http://www.yale.edu/yjia/articles/Vol_1_Iss_2_Spring2006/wicken217.pdf.

Wohlgelernter, Maurice. "Jew and Arab: Two of the Same Source But *Not* Two of the Same Kind: A Review Essay." *Modern Judaism* 28, no. 3 (2008): 327–36. http://mj.oxfordjournals.org/content/28/3/327.full.

Wolf, Aaron T. "Shared Waters: Conflict and Cooperation." *Annual Review of Environment and Resources* 32, no. 3 (2007), doi: 10.1146/annurev.energy.32.041006.101434.

Wolfsfeld, G., Y. Alimi, and W. Kailani. "News Media and Peace Building in Asymmetrical Conflicts: The Flow of News Between Jordon and Israel." *Political Studies* 56, no. 2 (2008): 374–87.

Worchel, Stephen. "Culture's Role in Conflict and Conflict Management: Some Suggestions, Many Questions." *International Journal of Intercultural Relations* 29, no. 6 (2005). doi.org/10.1016/j.ijintrel.2005.08.011.

Yablonka, Hanna. "The Development of Holocaust Consciousness in Israel: The Nuremberg, Kapos, Kastner and Eichmann Trials." *Israel Studies* 8, no. 3 (2003). doi. 10.1353/is.2004.0011.

Zimbardo, Philip G., and John N. Boyd. "Putting Time in Perspective: A Valid Reliable Individual-Difference Metric." *Journal of Personality and Social Psychology* 77, no. 6 (1999): 1271–88. http://www.thetimeparadox.com/wp-content/uploads/2012/09/1999PuttingTimeinPerspective.pdf.

Zimmerman, Bennett and Sergio DellaPergola. "What Is the True Demographic Picture in the West Bank and Gaza? A Presentation and a Critique." *Jerusalem Issue Brief* 4, no. 19 (March 2005): n.p. http://www.jcpa.org/brief/brief004-19.htm.

Zreik, Raef. "Why the *Jewish* State Now." *Journal of Palestine Studies* 40, no. 3 (2011): 23–37. http://www.jstor.org/stable/10.1525/jps.2011.XL.3.23.

Primary Source Documents

Many important treaties, conventions, agreements, and other primary source materials discussed in this book can be viewed on the Web. Here is a listing.

Agreement Between Fatah and Hamas (Fatah-Hamas Doha Agreement), February 7, 2012. http://peacemaker.un.org/opt-agreementfatahhamas2011.
"Balfour Declaration." http://avalon.law.yale.edu/20th_century/balfour.asp.
"Cairo Accord." http://prrn.mcgill.ca/research/papers/brynen2_09.htm.
"Declaration of Independence." UN Docs. A/43/827 and S/20278. November 11, 1988. http://www.un.int/wcm/content/site/palestine/cache/offonce/pid/12353.
Declaration of Principles on Interim Self-Government Arrangements (Oslo I), Israel and the Palestine Liberation Organization, September 13, 1993. http://avalon.law.yale.edu/20th_century/isrplo.asp.
"Full Text of the Doha Declaration Signed Between Hamas and Fatah." *Middle East Monitor*, February 8, 2012. https://www.middleeastmonitor.com/news/middle-east/3397-full-text-of-the-doha-declaration-signed-between-hamas-and-fatah.
"Geneva Accord." http://www.geneva-accord.org/mainmenu/english.
The Law of Return Act (1950); The Israeli Nationality Act (1952). Israel Ministry of Foreign Affairs Archives. www. mfa.gov.il.
"Treaty of Westphalia." http://avalon.law.yale.edu/17th_century/westphal.asp.
United States Department of State, Office of the Historian. "The Madrid Conference, 1991." Last modified October 31, 2013. https://history.state.gov/milestones/1989-1992/madrid-conference.

Frequently Consulted Web Sites

Adalah, Legal Center for Minority Rights in Israel: http://adalah.org/eng/.
Al-Monitor: http://www.al-monitor.com/pulse/home.html.
Association for Civil Rights in Israel: http://www.acri.org.il/en/.
Baker Institute: http://bakerinstitute.net/.
BitterLemons: www.bitterlemons.net/.
B'Tselem, Israeli Information Center for Human Rights in the Occupied Territories: http://www.btselem.org/.
Chatham House: http://www.chathamhouse.org/.
Congressional Monitor: http://www.congressionalmonitor/.
Foreign Policy: http://www.foreignpolicy.com/.
Haaretz: http://www.haaretz.com/.
Israeli Democracy Institute: http://en.idi.org.il/tools-and-data/guttman-center-for-surveys/about-the-guttman-center/.
Jerusalem Post: www.jpost.com/.
McGill University: http://mcgill.ca/activities/index.htm.
Mondoweiss: http://mondoweiss.net/.
The National Interest: http://nationalinterest.org/.
Oxford Review Group: http://www.oxfordresearchgroup.org.uk/.
Palestinian Center for Policy and Survey Research (PCPSR): www.pcpsr.org/.
The Palestinian Review: http://www.palestinereview.com/.
Palestinian Strategy Study Group: http://www.palestinestrategygroup.ps/.
ProCon: http://israelipalestinian.procon.org/.
The Times of Israel: http://www.timesofisrael.com/.
United States Institute of Peace (USIP): http://www.usip.org/.
Van Leer Institute of Jerusalem: http://www.vanleer.org.il/en/advanced-studies.

Interviewees

Ziad Abu Amr Former member of the PLC; deputy prime minister of the Palestinian Authority.

Said Abu Jalala Director General for Environmental Quality and water expert, Palestinian Authority-Gaza.

Mukhaimer Abu Saada Professor of political science at Al-Azhar University in Gaza City.

Ali Abu Shahla Gaza businessman; vice chairman of Al-Aqsa University's board of trustees; member of the *Palestine Israel Journal* editorial board.

Ziad Abu Zayyad Former member of the PLC; former minister of state in the Palestinian Authority; deputy chairman of the Political Committee of the Euro-Med Parliament; member of the post-Oslo negotiating team that concluded the Gaza-Jericho Agreement (1994).

Elon Adar Professor of Geography and Hydrology, Ben-Gurion University; director of the Zuckerberg Institute for Water Research-ZIWR.

Azzam Ahmed Head of the Palestinian delegation in talks with Brael to end the 2014 Gaza War; lead Fatah negotiator in Fatah-Hamas reconciliation talks; member of the Fatah Central Committee; senior member of the PLO; deputy prime minister and minister of state in the national unity government (2007).

Samih Al-Abed PLO mapping expert; former deputy minister of planning; member of negotiating team at Camp David, Taba, and Annapolis talks.

Emad Alami Hamas member of the PLC.

Ismail al-Ashqar Senior Hamas member; key figure in the Fatah-Hamas reconciliation talks; member of the PLC.

Ilai Alon Professor of Islamic studies at Tel Aviv University; member of the Israeli delegation for negotiations with Syria.

Pinhas Alpert Climatologist, Tel Aviv University Department of Geophysics TAU-WeRC (Weather Research Center).

Hanan Ashrawi PLO spokesperson at Madrid 1991; member of the PLO Executive Committee; former minister of education in the Palestinian Authority; founder of MIFTAH, a pro-democracy NGO.

Tamar Asraf Resident of the Eli settlement; spokesperson for Binyamin Regional Council, which oversees forty-two settlements.

Shaddad Atili Former minister and head of the Palestinian Water Authority.

Mohammad Awad Former deputy prime minister in Gaza's Hamas government (2011); previously foreign minister and secretary-general of the government in Gaza City.

Gady Baliansky Ehud Barak's press secretary (1999–2001); director general of the Geneva Initiative.

Salah al-Bardaweel Member of the Palestinian delegation in talks with Israel to end the 2014 Gaza War; senior Hamas spokesperson; member of the PLC.

Mustafa Barghouti Key figure in Fatah-Hamas reconciliation talks; general secretary of the Palestine National Initiative (PNI); member of the PLC; member of the PLO Central Council; minister of information in the Palestinian unity government (2007).

Gershon Baskin Founding cochairman of the Israel/Palestine Center for Research and Information (IPCRI); columnist for the *Jerusalem Post*; back channel for the release of Gilad Shalit.

Tal Becker Senior policy adviser to Tzipi Livni during the Annapolis proceedings; participant in negotiations since (1991) Madrid; research fellow at the Shalom Hartman Institute.

Yossi Beilin Minister (in several posts) in the governments of Yitzhak Rabin, Shimon Peres, and Ehud Barak; prime architect of the Oslo Framework Agreement; senior negotiator at Camp David and Taba; coauthor of the Beilin–Abu Mazen Understandings; coinitiator of the talks leading to the Geneva Accord (2003).

Shlomo Ben-Ami Head of Israel's delegation to the Madrid Peace Conference (1991); Israeli foreign minister under Ehud Barak; leader of Israel's negotiating teams at Camp David (2000) and Taba (2001); cofounder and vice president of the Toledo International Center for Peace.

Meron Benvenisti Former deputy mayor of Jerusalem; administrator of East Jerusalem; former chief planning officer of East Jerusalem.

Suhad Bishara Specialist in land and planning rights at Adalah (Legal Center for Arab Minority Rights in Israel).

Gidon Bromberg Israeli director of Friends of the Earth Middle East (FoEME), a regional organization of Jordanian, Palestinian, and Israeli environmentalists who promote sustainable development and advance peace efforts in the Middle East.

Moty Cristal Founder and CEO of NEST Consulting; one of Israel's leading negotiation experts; served in various official capacities on Israeli teams negotiating with Jordan and the Palestinians.

Robert Danin Eni Enrico Mattei Senior Fellow for Middle East and Africa Studies at the Council on Foreign Relations; writer at *Middle East Matters*.

Mohammad Darawshe Co-executive director of the Abraham Fund Initiatives.

Dani Dayan Yesher Council foreign envoy; former head of the Yesha Council; strong advocate for settlements.

Udi Dekel Retired brigadier general in the IDF; head of Israel's negotiating team during the Annapolis peace process (2007–08).

Sergio DellaPergola Professor of population studies at Hebrew University's Avraham Harman Institute of Contemporary Jewry; holder of the Shlomo Argov Chair in Israel-Diaspora Relations.

Giora Eiland Retired major general in the IDF; participant in the Camp David negotiations; former Israeli national security adviser; senior research associate at the Institute of National Security Studies.

Saleh Elayan Top aide to Ahmed Qurei ("Abu Ala") since Madrid (1991); secretary of the Palestinian Cabinet of Ministers.

Akiva Eldar Israeli columnist for Almonitor.com; author; chief political columnist and editorial writer for the Israeli daily newspaper *Haaretz*.

Rebhi El-Sheikh Deputy chairman, Palestinian Water Authority-Gaza.

Oded Eran Head of Israel's negotiating team with the Palestinians (1999–2000); former director of Institute for National Security Studies; former ambassador to Jordan.

Saeb Erekat Chief Palestinian negotiator involved in all negotiations, including those at Camp David (2000), Taba (2001), Annapolis (2007–08), and the 2013–14 talks.

Dror Etkes Former director of Peace Now's Settlements Watch Project; head of the Land Advocacy Project of Yesh Din, a group working against violation of Palestinians' rights by settlers.

Salam Fayyad Former prime minister of the Palestinian Authority (2007–13); former Palestinian minister of finance.

Rabbi Avi Geisser Resident of the Ofra settlement in Jerusalem; chairman of the Council for Religious National Education in Israel.

As'ad Ghanem Professor at Haifa University's School of Political Sciences and head of its government department; codirector of Sikkuy, the Association for the Advancement of Equal Opportunity (between the Jewish and Arab citizens of Israel).

Avi Gil Former director general of Israel's Ministry of Foreign Affairs; closely involved in negotiations that led to Oslo I and peace treaty with Jordan; senior fellow at the Jewish People's Policy Institute (JPPI); close adviser to President Shimon Peres.

Gidi Grinstein Participant in the Camp David and Taba talks; founder and president of the Reut Institute.

Ashraf Mustafa Guma Sole Fatah representative in Gaza after 2007.

Shlomo Gur Deputy director of the Claims Committee; former director general of the Israeli Ministry of Justice; in the 1990s was the right-hand man of Yossi Beilin and subsequently second in command at the Israeli Embassy in Washington, DC.

Mahdi Abdul Hadi Founder and director of the Palestinian Academic Society for the Study of International Affairs (PASSIA).

Ali Haider Codirector of Sikkuy; publisher of the annual Equality Index.

Aziz Haider Professor of sociology at Hebrew University's Truman Institute for Peace and the Van Leer Institute in Jerusalem.

Ghazi Hamad Former deputy foreign minister of the Hamas government.

Akram Haniyeh Political adviser to Yasir Arafat and Mahmoud Abbas; member of the Palestinian negotiating team at Camp David (2000) and Annapolis (2007–08); founder and editor of *Al-Ayyam* newspaper in Ramallah.

Tamar Hermann Academic director of the Israel Democracy Institute's Guttmann Center for Surveys; coauthor of the institute's monthly Peace Index.

Michael Herzog Retired brigadier general in the IDF; participant in most of Israel's negotiations with the Palestinians, Jordanians, and Syrians, including the Wye Plantation summit (1998), Camp David summit (2000), Taba negotiations (2001), Annapolis talks (2007–08), and the 2013–14 talks.

Jamil Hilal Sociologist at Birzeit University; senior research fellow at Muwatin, the Palestinian Institution for the Study of Democracy.

Anat Hoffman Executive director of the Israel Religious Action Center, the legal and advocacy arm of the Reform Movement in Israel; former member of the Jerusalem City Council.

Hiba Husseini Legal adviser in peace process negotiations between the Palestinians and Israelis; member of the Palestinian team during the Stockholm Track talks.

Yousif Ibrahim Palestinian National Authority Environmental Quality Authority (EQA)-Gaza.

Martin Indyk Vice president and director of the Foreign Policy Program, Brookings Institution; returned to Brookings after serving as the U.S. Special Envoy for Israeli-Palestinian 2013–14 talks; former U.S. ambassador to Israel.

Hassan Jabareen Founder and director general of Adalah.

Oussama Kanaan Former IMF mission chief in Jerusalem; former mission chief for the West Bank and Gaza and for Syria.

Issa Kassissieh Palestine's ambassador to the Holy See since 2013; former deputy head of the PLO's Negotiations Affairs Department; former director of the International Relations Department at the Orient House in Jerusalem.

Ghassan Khatib Vice president, Birzeit University; former director of the Palestinian Authority Government Media Center (2009–12); founder and director of the Jerusalem Media and Communication Center; member of the Palestinian delegation for the Madrid Peace Conference in 1991.

Lior Lehrs Researcher at the Jerusalem Institute for Israel Studies (JIIS); as of this writing a doctoral student in international relations at Hebrew University.

Alon Liel International relations researcher; former director general of the Israeli Foreign Ministry; ambassador to South Africa; chargé d'affaires in Turkey.

Amnon Lipkin-Shahak (deceased) Former chief of the General Staff, IDF; minister of transportation and tourism; head of the Israeli military team in negotiations on the Gaza-Jericho Agreement (1994); member of Israeli negotiating team, Camp David (2000); participated in Taba (2001) and the Geneva Initiative talks (2003).

Oren Magnezy Founder and chairman of the Laurus Consulting Group; served as Prime Minister Ariel Sharon's adviser.

David Makovsky Member of the team of U.S. Middle East Peace Envoy Martin Indyk as strategist and senior adviser; Ziegler Distinguished Fellow and director at the Washington Institute.

Hani Maseri General director of the Palestinian Ministry of Information's Department of Publication and Media Organizations Affairs; head of the BADIL Resource Center for Palestinian Residency and Refugee Rights.

Pini Meidan-Shani Foreign policy adviser to Prime Minister and Minister of Defense Ehud Barak; member of Israel's negotiating team at Camp David (2000).

Dan Meridor President of the Israel Council on Foreign Relations; member of the Israeli negotiating team at Camp David (2002); former deputy prime minister.

Aaron David Miller Vice president for New Initiatives, Wilson Center; historian; analyst; negotiator; former adviser to Republican and Democratic secretaries of state on Arab-Israeli negotiations.

George Mitchell Former Special Envoy for Middle East Peace under President Barack Obama; Special Envoy for Northern Ireland under President Bill Clinton; head of Sharmel-Sheikh Fact Finding Commitee; former senate majority leader.

Yahya Musa High-ranking member of the PLC in Gaza.

Saleh al-Naami Freelance journalist writing for *Asharq Al-Awsat* (as its correspondent in Gaza), *Al-Ahram Weekly*, and Al Jazeera.

Saro Nakashian CEO and general director of the Palestine Education for Employment (PEFE); senior management and marketing analyst with Birzeit University's Center for Continuing Education (CCE).

Karim Nashashibi Former head of the International Monetary Fund in the West Bank and Gaza; former adviser to Prime Minister Salam Fayyad.

Roby Nathanson General director at the Macro Center for Political Economics; former head of the Administration for Economic and Social Research at the Prime Minister's Office.

Sari Nusseibeh Former president of Al-Quds University since 1995.

Hagit Ofran Director of the Settlement Watch project of the Israeli Peace Now movement.

Jacob Perry Former head of Shin Bet; emissary between Yitzhak Rabin and Yasir Arafat after Oslo.

Ron Pundak (deceased) Key player in Oslo II (1995); drafter of the Beilin–Abu Mazen Understandings (1995), a blueprint for an FSA; former president of the Peres Center for Peace.

Ahmed Qurei ("Abu Ala") Head of the Palestinian team in the secret Oslo talks with Israel leading to the DOP (Oslo I); leader of the Palestinian team in the Paris Protocol talks; key member of the PLO negotiating team at Camp David (2000); participant in the Taba talks; key negotiator during the Annapolis talks (2007–08).

Firas Raad Health policy expert at the Office of the Quartet Representative (OQR), which works with the Palestinian Authority, the government of Israel, and international organizations and NGOs to help build the institutions and economy for a future Palestinian state.

Jibril Rajoub Deputy secretary of the Fatah Central Committee; head of the Supreme Council for Sport and Youth Affairs; chairman of the Palestinian Football Association; chairman of the Palestine Olympic Committee; former member of the Fatah Revolutionary Council; former national security adviser to Yasir Arafat; former head of the West Bank Preventive Security Forces.

Zafrir Rinat Israeli journalist and writer.

Sara Roy Senior research scholar at the Center for Middle Eastern Studies at Harvard University, focusing on the economy of Gaza and more recently on the Palestinian Islamic movement and Hamas.

Ilan Saban Member of the law faculty at the University of Haifa.

Sabri Saidam Adviser to Mahmoud Abbas on telecommunications, information technology, and technical education; deputy secretary general of Fatah's Revolutionary Council; former minister of telecom and information technology.

Dr. Eyad el-Sarraj (deceased) Palestinian psychiatrist; founder of the Gaza Community Mental Health Program in 1990; close adviser to Hamas and Fatah in Gaza.

Uri Savir Negotiated the DOP in secret with Abu Ala; member of the Israeli team that negotiated the peace treaty with Jordan; head of the Israeli team that negotiated with Syria; president of the Peres Center for Peace.

Otniel Schneller Former Kadima member of Knesset; former secretary general of the Yesha Council.

Nabil Sha'ath Commissioner of Foreign Relation with Fatah and senior PLO Palestinian Authority negotiator; former minister of foreign affairs; de facto Palestinian foreign minister; participant in the Madrid talks (1991); head of the Palestinian negotiation team leading to the Oslo Accords (1993–95); member of the Palestinian negotiating team at Camp David (2000), Taba (2001), and Annapolis (2007–08).

Uri Shamir Professor emeritus of the Technion-Israel Institute of Technology Faculty of Civil and Environmental Engineering; part of the 1994 delegation on water negotiations with Jordan.

Gilead Sher Colonel (res.), former brigade commander, and deputy division commander in the IDF; chief of staff and policy coordinator for Israel's Prime Minister Ehud Barak; cochief negotiator from 1999 to 2001 at Camp David (2000) and Taba (2001); founding cochairman of Blue-White Future.

Khalil Shikaki Professor of political science; director of the Palestinian Center for Policy and Survey Research (PSR); coauthor of the annual report of the Arab Democracy Index.

Muhammad Shtayyeh Member of the team negotiating the terms of Palestinian participation at the Madrid talks (1991); involved in all interim agreements and final status negotiations; participant in 2013–14 talks until January 2014; senior adviser to Mahmoud Abbas; head of PECDAR (Palestinian Economic Council for Research and Development).

Hazem Shunnar Deputy minister in the Ministry of the National Economy.

Hilel Shuval International environmental engineering and water resources expert; visiting professor at the International Academy of the Environment in Geneva.

Mazen Sinokrot Palestinian businessman; founder of Sinokrot International Group; founder and chairman of the first East Jerusalem–based holding company, Al-Quds Holding; former minister of national economy.

Ephraim Sneh Brigadier general (ret.) in the IDF; former governor of the West Bank; worked clandestinely on behalf of Yitzhak Rabin with the PLO to establish a channel that would bypass the Oslo talks.

Arnon Soffer Among the founders of Haifa University; holder of the Reuven Chaikin Chair in Geostrategy; geographic specialist and demographer; longtime lecturer at the IDF's top defense college, where he heads the National Defense College Research Center.

Ramzi Suleiman Psychology professor and behavioral scientist, Department of Psychology, University of Haifa.

Naser Tahboub Former deputy minister of national economy, Palestine.

Ahmad Tibi Leader of the Arab Movement for Change; member of Knesset since 1999 and currently its deputy speaker.

Danny Tirza Colonel (res.) in the IDF; in charge of regional strategic planning and the formulation of Israel's security positions in negotiations with the Palestinians; Israel's mapper; chief architect of the separation barrier's routing.

Mary Totry Sociologist at the University of Haifa's International School.

Pinchas Wallerstein Among the founders and early leaders of Gush Emunim; former director general of the Yesha Council; former mayor of the Binyamin Regional Council (1979–2008).

Dov Weisglass Senior adviser to Ariel Sharon; one of the invitiators of the Gaza disengagement plan.

Ahmed Yaqubi Water resources technical adviser to the Palestinian Water Authority.

Danny Yatom Former director of Mossad; former Commanding General of the Central Command; military secretary to prime ministers Yitzhak Rabin and Shimon Peres; chief of staff and security adviser to Prime Minister Ehud Barak; key negotiator at Camp David (2000).

Ahmed Yousef Senior adviser to former Gaza Hamas Prime Minister Ismail Haniyeh.

Sawsan Zaher Director of the Social, Economic, and Cultural Rights Unit of Adalah.

Mahmoud al-Zahar Cofounder of Hamas in 1987; former foreign minister in the Hamas government.

Husam Zomlot Senior Fatah official; adviser to Nabil Sha'ath.

Appendix

*Non-Paper, 8 September 2006

Hamas and Israel: Peaceful Coexistence Document

Since the capture of Gilad Shalit, the two parties have defined their main objectives regarding his release as follows:

Israel: His release in the quickest possible timeframe, at the lowest possible cost, in terms of the number of prisoners to be released.

Hamas: The ability and aspiration to maintain an effective government is more important than the number of prisoners to be released.

The parties reserve the option to deal with release of Shalit either in a broader context or separately, as detailed below.

Hamas presents two alternatives:

1. A separate track (just the release of Shalit [S.E.]) in which the number of prisoners to be released will be approximately one thousand.
2. When this (the release of prisoners) is done within the larger context of the strategic approach (as presented below), the number of prisoners will "not be in the hundreds."

The prime minister of Israel's decision as relayed to Hamas (over the past months [S.E.]) was to advance the second option.

The Strategic Approach

Hamas proposes a two-tiered dialogue as follows:

1. Discussions surrounding a bundle of steps to be taken. A ceasefire and steps to stabilize Gaza, which will respond to the main areas of concern of both parties and serve to build up trust in advance of longer-term processes.

*Non-papers are designed to stimulate discussion on a particular issue and do not represent the official position of the institution or country that drafted them. Non-papers have no official status but can be very useful in starting debates on particularly sensitive issues, allowing decision makers to talk about issues they would find it politically difficult to take a firm line on. They can also be used to test the water on subjects without obliging countries to take a stand, thus avoiding potential diplomatic rows.

2. The decision to enter into a broader dialogue about the long-term vision of peaceful coexistence, which will be advanced by a third party.
3. These two aforementioned tiers will proceed simultaneously, since Hamas's readiness to make progress in the first tier is derived from Israel's willingness to make progress on the second tier.

The First Tier: Understandings Intended to Stabilize Gaza

As presented to you on 25 June 2006 (the day that the foreign envoy sent the list of understandings formulated by the Political Bureau in Damascus, and which arrived in Israel one day after the abduction of Shalit [S.E.]), below is a detailed account of Hamas's policy, effective immediately:

1. On a predetermined date, Israel will cease firing on Gaza and put an end to the assassinations. Hamas will halt all hostile activity by its forces (in June 2006 Israel refused to implement the aforementioned points in the West Bank). [Parentheses in the original.]
2. Twenty days after this, Hamas will ensure a comprehensive ceasefire by all its armed forces.
3. This channel of communication (Mashal, the envoy, Diskin, Olmert [S.E.]) will be the primary and highest channel. Only it will be authorized to decide on and approve any other, alternative channel, or alternately, the inclusion of another mediator in the process.

The Next Step: Stage C

Hamas will publicly express its commitment to cease all armed activity from Gaza. Israel will commit itself to the transfer of tax revenues, and Israel will release prisoners (Note: This clause was included in the package before the abduction of Shalit). [Parentheses in the original, S.E.] Both parties will make an effort to ensure that the border crossings are secure and kept open.

The Shalit Deal

Hamas will provide a guarantee of the health and well-being of Gilad Shalit (Done). [Parentheses in the original.] This refers to a public statement made by Khaled Mashal at the request of Yuval Diskin that Hamas commits itself to ensuring the health and well-being of Gilad Shalit, in accordance with Islamic law [S.E.].

1. Hamas will stop all firing at Israeli targets. Hamas will release Shalit, and Israel will release prisoners. Israel will release the detainees who are members of the Palestinian parliament (In response to the abduction, Israel arrested Hamas's members of parliament in the West Bank [S.E.]), as well as the other prisoners and it will release the tax revenues.

2. Hamas has accepted the proposal subject to several points of clarification. It has fulfilled its first obligation [ensuring the well-being of Gilad Shalit, S.E.]) and presented a series of questions for clarification that have yet to be answered [the questions that were relayed to Yuval Diskin over the preceding months were not included in the document].

Hamas's Strategic Vision

As presented on 25 May 2006. [Ideas for a ceasefire were presented in June.]

Proposal for Strategic Dialogue Within the Long-Term Framework of Peaceful Coexistence

This dialogue will take place through a third party. Negotiations through a third party could lead to an incremental process of implementation that could be binding for twenty-five years.

Hamas's vision, and as such, the agenda for this dialogue includes a framework for coexistence for a period of twenty-five years, marked by nonviolence and a commitment from the start of the process that it will lead to the establishment of a Palestinian state through negotiations over borders (to be based on the pre-1967 demarcation line), as well as agreements concerning tariffs, trade, etc.

It is agreed to postpone the most contentious issues, including refugees and the final status of Jerusalem, to a later date, with the expectation that until the matter is resolved, Palestinians will enjoy a separate status in certain neighborhoods of Jerusalem. Hamas is prepared to make the difficult decisions derived from this on condition that Israel is similarly prepared to do so.

The Next Step

Upon presenting our strategic approach several months ago and fulfilling our prior commitments in the Shalit package several weeks ago, Hamas is now waiting for an Israeli response regarding the two options proposed: Is Israel prepared to proceed with the strategic package, or to limit their involvement to the proposed solution to the abduction of Gilad Shalit? In this document Hamas also proposed that upon the completion of the strategic stage, the end of the armed conflict would be declared. He could only extend the offer to armed conflict not the end of conflict because issues relating to Waqf land etc. were involved.

Index